Transforming Children's Mathematics Education
International Perspectives

Edited by
Leslie P. Steffe
University of Georgia

Terry Wood
Purdue University

LAWRENCE ERLBAUM ASSOCIATES, PUBLISHERS
1990   Hillsdale, New Jersey   Hove and London

Copyright © 1990 by Lawrence Erlbaum Associates, Inc.
All rights reserved. No part of this book may be reproduced in any form, by photostat, microform, retrieval system, or any other means, without the prior written permission of the publisher.

Lawrence Erlbaum Associates, Inc., Publishers
365 Broadway
Hillsdale, New Jersey 07642

Library of Congress Cataloging-in-Publication Data

Transforming children's mathematics education : international
  perspectives / edited by Leslie P. Steffe, Terry Wood.
    p. cm.
  Includes bibliographical references.
  ISBN 0-8058-0604-0. — ISBN 0-8058-0605-9 (pbk.)
  1. Mathematics—Study and teaching (Elementary) I. Steffe,
Leslie P. II. Wood, Terry Lee, 1942–
QA11.T77 1990
372.7—dc20   90-30922
                                                                  CIP

10 9 8 7 6 5 4 3 2 1

To Christine and Robert, perhaps the beginning of an answer to your perplexing question, "How did you let schools get this way, anyway?" And posthumously, to Charles Smock, for helping us to understand a way in which to see how schools might be.

Contents

Preface		xi
Part 1: Overview		**1**
1.1.	Action Group A1: Early Childhood Years *Leslie P. Steffe*	3
Part 2: Epistemological Chapters		**17**
2.1.	Learning: The Interactive Recreation of Knowledge *Hermine Sinclair*	19
2.2.	Environment and Communication *Ernst von Glasersfeld*	30
Part 3: Knowledge and Learning Elaboration Chapters		**39**
3.1.	Knowledge and Learning in Mathematics *Jarkko Leino*	41
3.2.	Constructing Knowledge from Interactions *Robert W. Lawler*	47
3.3.	Constructivism, Phenomenology, and the Origin of Arithmetic Skills *Ference Marton and Dagmar Neuman*	62

Discussion Chapters: Learning 76

EDITORS' NOTE 76

3.4. Children Learning Mathematics 78
Brenda Denvir

3.5. Playing Games and Learning Mathematics 84
Janet Ainley

3.6. Young Children's Concept of Measure 92
Patricia F. Campbell

3.7. Some Aspects of Learning Geometry 100
Kiyoshi Yokochi

Discussion Chapters: Knowledge 106

3.8. Mathematical Knowledge of Young Learners 107
Grayson H. Wheatley and Harriet Bebout

3.9. Possibility, Necessity, Contradiction, and Probability: Implications for Mathematics Education 112
Catherine T. Fosnot

3.10. Kindergartners' Knowledge of the Preconcepts of Number 125
Jacques C. Bergeron and Nicolas Herscovics

3.11. Knowledge of the Numeration System Among Pre-Schoolers 135
Terezinha Nunes Carraher and Analucia Dias Schliemann

3.12. An Analysis of First-Grade Children's Writing Number Sentences in Solving Word Problems 142
Junichi Ishida

3.13. Young Children's Thinking Strategies and Levels of Capacity to Process Mathematical Information 156
Gillian Boulton-Lewis

3.14. Analysis of Young Children's Spatial Constructions 161
Grayson Wheatley and Paul Cobb

3.15.	Children's Competence in Forming Combinations *Lyn English*	174
3.16.	How Natural Is Fraction Knowledge? *M. A. Clements and G. Del Campo*	181

Part 4: Communication Elaboration Chapters — 189

4.1.	Communication in Early Childhood *F. Lowenthal*	191
4.2.	Multiple Perspectives *Paul Cobb*	200
4.3.	Conceptual Splatter in Peer Dialogues in Selected Japanese and U.S. First-Grade Mathematics Classes *Jack Easley and Harold Taylor*	216

Discussion Chapters: Actual Communication — 227

4.4.	Communication in the Mathematics Classroom *Max Stephens*	228
4.5.	Interactive Communication: Constraints and Possibilities *Bob Wright*	235
4.6.	The Development of Collaborative Dialogue Within Small Group Interactions *Terry Wood and Erna Yackel*	244
4.7.	Connecting Inventions with Conventions *Magdalene Lampert*	253
4.8.	Actual Communication in the Mathematical Classroom *Nobuhiko Nohda*	266
4.9.	Fostering Mathematical Communication: Helping Teachers Help Students *Julian Weissglass, Judith Mumme, and Barbara Cronin*	272

Discussion Chapters: Possible Communication — 282

4.10	Reconstructing Constructivism *George M. A. Stanic*	283

4.11.	The Nature of Communication in Early Childhood in the Contexts of Home and School *Joan Bliss*	294
4.12.	Learning Situations and Experiential Domains Relevant to Early Childhood Mathematics Education *Maria G. Bartolini Bussi*	304

Part 5: Environment Elaboration Chapters 313

5.1.	Early Childhood Mathematics and the Environment *Romanus Ogbonna Ohuche*	315
5.2.	Children's Mathematics/Mathematics for Children *Thomas E. Kieren*	323
5.3.	What Could Teacher Education Be Like for Prospective Teachers of Early Childhood Mathematics—with Particular Reference to the Environment *Leone Burton*	334

Discussion Chapters: Mathematics Curriculum 345

5.4.	Curriculum and Constructivism in Early Childhood Mathematics: Sources of Tension and Possible Resolutions *Neil A. Pateman and David C. Johnson*	346
5.5.	Mathematical Learning Beyond the Activity *Helen Pengelly*	357
5.6.	Notes on Early Mathematical Experiences *Minoru Sumio*	377
5.7.	The Role of the Teacher in Early Childhood Mathematics *Helen Mansfield*	383
5.8.	Mathematics Curriculum Design: A Constructivist's Perspective *Leslie P. Steffe*	389

Discussion Chapters: Teacher Education 399

5.9.	Constructivism and Teacher Education for Teachers of Early Childhood Mathematics *Nick James and Robert Underhill*	400

5.10.	Preparing Early Childhood Teachers for Constructive Mathematical Environments *Larry L. Hatfield*	407
5.11.	Improving Prospective Early Childhood Teachers' Content Knowledge and Attitudes Toward Mathematics *Dina Tirosh*	415
5.12.	Some Problems with Problem Solving: A Brazilian Teacher-Perspective *Beatriz S. D'Ambrosio*	424
5.13.	Teaching of Mathematics Using Comparison and Examination of Children's Mathematical Thinking *Shigeo Yoshikawa*	430
5.14.	Action Research for Professional Development: Informing Teachers and Researchers *Noelene Reeves*	436

Part 6: Conclusion Survey Chapter 449

6.1.	Cultural Perspectives on Success in Early Childhood Mathematics *Bob Perry*	451

References	465
Author Index	485
Subject Index	491

Preface

On each fourth year, an International Congress on Mathematical Education (ICME) is held under the auspices of The International Commission on Mathematical Instruction. The sixth ICME[1] was held in Budapest, Hungary from July 27–August 3, 1988 and was hosted by The János Bolyai Mathematical Society. The International Program Committee (IPC) for ICME-6, chaired by Professor Á. Császár, established seven Action Groups, seven Theme Groups, eleven Topic Areas, and five Plenary Presentations as their organizational pattern. Each Action Group and each Theme Group comprised a subconference within ICME-6 and each was given four 1½-hour time-slots on the program. An International Panel and a Hungarian Coordinator was appointed for each Group to plan its work.

In September of 1985, I received a letter from Professor Császár inviting me to be Chief Organizer for Action Group A1: Early Childhood Years (Ages 4–8) and a member of its International Panel. Little did I then realize that my acceptance of this invitation would lead to 5 years of intensive activity culminating in the publication of this book. I wish to thank the other members of the International Panel: Jarkko Leino (Finland), Francis D. Lowenthal (Belgium), R. Ogbonna Ohuche (Nigeria), and Bob Perry (Australia) for their book chapters as well as for their substantial organizational assistance. Their chapters played a most important role in the Action Group and represent the conceptual leadership expected of an International Panel.

The charge given to the International Panel, as outlined in Professor Császár's

---

[1]Hirst, A. & K. (Eds.). (1989). Proceedings of the Sixth International Congress on Mathematical Education. Budapest: Janos Bolyai Mathematical Society.

letter, was to encourage wide international participation and active discussion in the Action Group meetings. We were also asked to organize a conceptual framework for the work of the Action Group and to provide a survey lecture that would be offered to all congress participants. In response to these charges, Bob Perry was appointed by the IPC to give the survey lecture and his paper is included as the last chapter of this book. We also established as the general goal to identify the issues, problems, and opportunities presented by constructivism for mathematics education in early childhood and to make recommendations for the work in this area over the next 4 years—until ICME-7. We offer this book as partial achievement of our general goal.

After more than 2 years of organizational work, the Action Group met as a whole in its first meeting at Budapest. Five papers were presented at this first meeting: two epistemological papers (chaps. 2.1, 2.2) and three elaboration papers (chaps. 3.1, 4.1, 5.1). The intention was to initiate the process of identifying issues, problems, and opportunities presented by constructivism for mathematics education in early childhood to the participants in the Action Group. The Action Group was then broken into three subgroups in its second meeting: **Knowledge and Learning, Communication,** and **Environment** and two additional elaboration papers were summarized in each of these three subgroups (chaps. 3.2 & 3.3, 4.2 & 4.3, 5.2 & 5.3), followed by a general discussion.

Each of the three subgroups were then divided into two discussion groups and each discussion group met as an intact group in the two final meetings of the Action Group. A chairperson, an abstracter, and a recorder were appointed for each discussion group. The chairpersons had the overall responsibility for the general direction of their discussion groups and each abstracter-recorder pair had the responsibility to write a paper after ICME-6 based on the papers presented in the first two meetings, on invited discussion papers distributed during the second meeting, and on the actual discussion that transpired during the meeting as a whole (chaps. 3.4, 3.8, 4.4, 4.10, 5.4, 5.9).

The members of the International Panel viewed the activities of the Action Group as an experiment in constructivism. Our first experimental manipulation was to send the eleven papers presented during the first two meetings to the registered participants of the Action Group during late May or early June of 1988 for their perusal. The members of the International Panel felt that to hold deep and penetrating discussions over four different meeting times, the discussants needed the opportunity prior to ICME to read and to reflect on the contents of what we hoped were an outstanding set of papers. They needed time to examine the assumptions of constructivism and to contrast them with their own epistemological assumptions as well as to examine the nine elaboration papers and to identify how mathematics education in early childhood might be transformed in a constructivist framework.

The International Panel also invited authors to write the discussion papers mentioned above for each one of the six discussion groups. We wanted to guarantee the existence of each discussion group at Budapest, but that was not our main goal. Our main goal was to select paper writers internationally who were active in early childhood mathematics education without regard to their epistemological predispositions. The papers were viewed as samples of ongoing work in the field that we felt would significantly contribute to the discussions and to the achievement of our general goal. The distribution of the discussion papers along with a request that they be read by the discussants constituted our second experimental manipulation. Of course, the authors of the discussion papers were registered participants and our two experimental manipulations were focused on but not limited to them. Our intention was to encourage diversity and substance so the discussants would engage in reasoned debate concerning fundamental issues and problems facing us in early childhood mathematics education in an international context. Our hope was that the conflicts that might arise during the discussions both within and among the discussants would be at least partially worked out.

We requested that the discussion papers be completed before January 1, 1988—well before the other papers were distributed. We experienced operational difficulties that arose from the attempts made by the International Panel to provide pre-ICME reviews of the discussion papers. Our procedures did serve a purpose because several of the discussion papers were rewritten prior to ICME. But in retrospect, the review and publication of the proceedings of the Action Group should have been a part of our charge by the IPC and we should have been more explicit than we were concerning our review and publication procedures. As an International Panel, we had to build our own review and publication program and I am the first to admit that it was much less than perfect. For example, I deeply regret that several discussion papers do not appear in this book. Had we as an International Panel been able to be more explicit about our review and publication program, our expectations would have been clearer to the reviewers, to the paper writers, to the participants, and to ourselves.

There is no substitute for being at Budapest and participating in the work of the Action Group. But, because that experience was limited to participating in specific discussion groups, this book is first and foremost for the participants of Action Group A1 as they carry on with their work. However, the necessity to transform early childhood mathematics education internationally should make it of interest to anyone else who might be interested in that enterprise. It does represent the hard work, the understanding, and the time of many people and the resources of many institutions. In particular, the Department of Mathematics Education at the University of Georgia made a substantial amount of operating expenses and supplies, travel money, and released time available to me as I executed my responsibilities as Chief Organizer. The Department also released time for Ms. Valerie Kilpatrick and Ms. Louise Seagraves to spend long hours at their word processors typing correspondence and manuscripts. They deserve special tribute as does Ms. Lois Harmstad for her technical editorial work.

Dr. Tibor Nemetz, Secretary of the International Program Committee and of the Hungarian Organizing Committee, was my only contact person prior to and during ICME-6. Without our correspondence, it would have been impossible for me as Chief Organizer to carry out my work. For a long while his mostly handwritten letters were the only threads that connected me to ICME-6, and upon arriving in Budapest he provided invaluable organizational assistance.

Finally, Dr. Terry Wood deserves a lions share of the credit for seeing this book through to completion. We both wish to express our gratitude to the people at Lawrence Erlbaum Associates for publishing this book and for their competent work during the publication process.

Leslie P. Steffe, Chief Organizer
Action Group A1: Early Childhood Years
ICME-6

Part 1
Overview

Chapter
1.1

Action Group A1:
Early Childhood Years

Leslie P. Steffe
University of Georgia, USA

"Action Group A1: Early Childhood Years" was one of the action groups of the Sixth International Congress on Mathematical Education (ICME-6) held in Budapest, Hungary, from July 27 to August 3, 1988. The general goal of the action group was to identify the issues, problems, and opportunities presented by a constructivist's perspective for mathematics education in early childhood and to make recommendations for the work in this area over the next 4 years—until ICME-7. The action group was in itself an experiment in which the participants, some representing a constructivist perspective, were brought together in an effort to provide an international forum for accomplishing this general goal.

The revolutionary aspect of constructivism lies in the assertion that "knowledge cannot and need not be 'true' in the sense that it matches ontological reality, it only has to be 'viable' in the sense that it fits within the experiential constraints that limit the (human's) possibilities of acting and thinking" (von Glasersfeld, 1989, p. 162). Accepting mathematical knowledge as being viable rather than true has far-reaching consequences for mathematics education in early childhood. For example, the belief that mathematics is the way it is rather than the way human beings make it to be has permeated mathematics education at all levels and has served as the basis for the assumption that there is a perceived tradition of school mathematics that students must come to know in the way intended by society. Changing this traditionally held assumption opens up new possibilities for reform in mathematics education. Some of the possibilities for reform were presented in a framework prepared by an international panel where knowledge and learning, communication, and environment were adopted as key organizing concepts. Mathematical experience was embedded in the discussions of these three organizing concepts and served as a basis for the deliberation of how children and their teachers come to know mathematics. Although progress for reform was made at ICME-6, nearly all of the effort to isolate these possibilities and carry them to fruition remains to be accomplished. It is in this spirit that the work of "Action Group Al: Early Childhood Years" is presented.

CONCEPTUAL FRAMEWORK

The conceptual framework was developed by the International Panel with the intention of involving the participants of the action group in deep, penetrating, and sustained discussions of various aspects of early childhood mathematics education.

Two epistemological chapters clarify the underlying concepts, knowledge, learning, communication, and environment. H. Sinclair's chapter (2.1) discusses knowledge and learning and E. von Glasersfeld's chapter (2.2) is on communication and environment. Three members of the International Panel then elaborated the meaning of the epistemological concepts for early childhood mathematics education. J. Leino (chap. 3.1) extends the concepts of knowledge and learning; F. Lowenthal (chap. 4.1), communication, and R. Ohuche (chap. 5.1), environment. The intention of these chapters is to initiate the process of identifying issues, problems, and opportunities presented by a constructivist perspective for early childhood mathematics education.

Two additional chapters elaborate on each of the initial epistemological concepts; R. Lawler (chap. 3.2) and F. Marton and D. Neuman (chap. 3.3) for knowledge and learning; P. Cobb (chap. 4.2) and J. Easley and H. Taylor (chap. 4.3) for communication; and T. Kieren (chap. 5.2) and L. Burton (chap. 5.3) for environment.

These chapters then provided the conceptual framework from which the discussion groups were developed to further identify the issues, problems, and opportunities for mathematics education. *Knowledge and learning* were partitioned into knowledge, E. De Corte (Belgium), chair; and learning, G. Bell (Australia) chair. *Communication* was divided into Possible Mathematical Communication, J. Confrey (USA), chair; and Actual Mathematical Communication, G. Booker (Australia), chair. The former focused on mathematical communication that might occur in the classroom provided the conditions were favorable and the latter emphasized mathematical communication that does exist in ongoing classrooms. *Environment* was partitioned into Mathematical Curriculum, E. Dubinsky (USA), chair; and Teacher Education, J. Lochhead (USA), chair.

Several discussion chapters were prepared for each of the six subgroups, which formed the basis for the ensuing dialogue of each subgroup. All participants were encouraged to partake in and contribute to the discussion. The intention of the discussion was to further solidify the issues within a more specific view and to make recommendations for early childhood mathematics education.

An abstracter–recorder pair was established for each of the six subgroups and each pair presented a report detailing the isolated issues, problems, opportunities, and recommendations. The abstracter–recorder pairs were as follows: George Stanic (chap. 4.10) and Lynn Outhred, Possible Mathematical Communication; Max Stephens (chap. 4.4) and Howard Johnson, Actual Mathematical Communication; Neil Pateman and David C. Johnson (chap. 5.4), Curriculum; Nick James and Robert Underhill (chap. 5.9), Teacher Education; Grayson Wheatley and Harriet Bebout (chap. 3.8), Knowledge; and Brenda Denvir (chap. 3.4) and Charleen DeRidder, Learning. Each abstracter–recorder pair wrote a chapter after ICME-6 based on their experiences in the working groups and their chapters are included as an overview of each of the sections containing the discussion chapters. Finally, the International Program Committee of ICME-6 selected Bob Perry (chap. 6.1), a member of the International Panel, to write and present a survey chapter.

KNOWLEDGE AND LEARNING

From a constructivist perspective, children's mathematical knowledge is viewed as coordinated schemes of action and operation that are functioning reliably and effectively—what Sinclair (1987b) referred to as instruments of problem solving. The general question concerning knowledge that was posed for the work of the action group was: "What schemes (or coordinated schemes) of action and operation can be inferred from the language and actions of children?" The scope of this general question is indicated by the following questions:

1. How does the counting scheme develop in young children, and how does it relate to the development of numerical concepts and operations, including addition, subtraction, multiplication, and division?
2. What mathematical procedures do children use, including the ability to recognize and check counting and other arithmetical errors?
3. How can we characterize the thinking strategies used by children?
4. What constitutes logical thinking of children and how does this differ from mathematical thinking?
5. What constitutes spatial and geometrical knowledge of children?
6. What constitutes measurement knowledge of children and how does it relate to questions 1 through 5?
7. What is the role of technology in the development of children's mathematical knowledge?

Knowledge, Learning, and Social Interaction

The mathematical knowledge children can construct in early childhood and how children's learning might be fostered was investigated with reference to the previous questions. Although mathematical learning can be viewed as consisting in the adaptations children make in their functioning schemes to neutralize perturbations that can arise in one of several ways, H. Sinclair (chap. 2.1) emphasizes that learning occurs as a result of the interaction between societal presentation and endogenous processes of abstraction. "The difficulty of studying learning—and teaching—lies, in my view, in the fact that it demands the study of the processes by which children come to know in a short time basic principles (in mathematics, but also in other scientific disciplines) that took humanity thousands of years to construct." Lawler (chap. 3.2) presents an example of learning not as socially directed but as "a compensating adaptation to the deprivation of social interaction." The example consisted of a child who imitated her older sister by saying, "knock-knock," and expecting an adult (her father) to complete the joke by saying, "who's there?" The adult then deliberately changed his role by saying, "knock-knock," to which the child had no response, being unable to switch her role to fit the change in the social interaction. This created a perturbation that the child resolved by re-enacting (by herself), the two complementary roles of the past social interactions. Using this and other examples involving numerical and geometrical contexts, Lawler elucidates possible relations between social experience and personal construction of knowledge.

F. Marton and D. Neuman (chap. 3.3) emphasize the importance of mathematical experience that occurs as a result of children's interaction with their mathematical reality. They believe that the child does not consciously reflect on how to solve a problem. He or she just explores the quantitative relations inherent in it, and suddenly something stands out as a figure against a background giving the child an intuition of how it could be solved. This description of the construction of quantitative relations by children is congenial with the notion of *bricolage* as explained by Lawler; "The core idea is looseness of commitment to specific goals, with the consequence that materials and competencies developed for one purpose are transferable to the satisfaction of alternative objectives."

J. Leino (chap. 3.1) also sees mathematical learning in part as occurring in, or as a result of, social interaction. The "learning process in school is not just a knower-known relationship, a pupil with a mathematical problem, but . . . a mediated learning experience, a pupil studying with his or her teacher and peers." However, mathematical learning cannot be said to be caused by social interaction and we should not expect it to be predictable in the sense that what a child does learn in a given situation is what an adult expects the child to learn, as Leino explains, "Even though the concrete mathematical situation is simple there are always many logical ways to comprehend it. That is why pupils many times form a construct that is not the one the teacher desired or expected, and why textbooks attempt to present extremely reduced and simplified models. [T]heir value is, to my mind, highly exaggerated."

Discussion of Knowledge and Learning

Two discussion groups were devoted to identifying the issues, problems, and opportunities presented by constructivism in the area of mathematical knowledge and its learning. Not surprisingly, the first issue that emerged was, "Is there a body of mathematical knowledge all students should learn?" This issue has deep roots in the practice of mathematics education world-wide and is intimately connected with the assumption that there is a standard school mathematics that students must come to know in the way intended by society.

Several specific issues were also identified during the course of the discussion. Such issues as how to identify when learning has occurred, what tasks and constraints and forms of presentation might encourage learning, what schemes children bring to the situation that they might use in mathematical learning, and what conceptual tools are available to make sense of children's informal knowledge were included in those identified. Some participants felt that learning cannot be readily measured using paper and pencil tasks, and alternative strategies for assessing children's learning is a continuing need. Finally, it was recognized that although constructivists may view learning as consisting in adaptation and mathematical knowledge as a result of organizing experience, school mathematics is all too often viewed as a set of algorithms and rules.

COMMUNICATION

In any communication between two human beings, signals can be transmitted between the communicators, but not the intended or received meanings. This is why social interaction cannot cause learning to occur as intended by a transmitter of signals. On the receivers side, the transmitted signals have to be interpreted, establishing received meanings. Although the received meanings might be viable in so far as there is no necessity to modify them in further experiential encounters, this would not mean they match the intended meanings. There may be future experiential encounters where the received meanings are modified. From the constructivist point of view, meanings are conceptual structures (Steffe, Cobb, & von Glasersfeld, 1988; von Glasersfeld, 1987) that serve in the interpretation and organization of experience and are subject to being changed and modified by the very experience they organize. Within this general understanding of communication, the following two questions were posed for the work of the action group: (a) "What does mathematics teaching consist of in early childhood and what forms could it take?" and (b) "How can children's informal, spontaneous thinking be combined (or linked) with teaching practice?" Because interpretation depends on the particular context in which a communication occurs—the social setting, the problem situation, the goals and intentions of the communicators, the language used by the communicators, and so forth—the following focal points were suggested:

1. The mathematical knowledge and beliefs of teachers, both actual and possible.
    a. How might teachers of mathematics in early childhood view mathematics and its meaning?
    b. How might teachers of mathematics in early childhood view children's mathematics—their mathematical knowledge and its elaborations as a result of the social interactions of the children with each other and with their teacher?
    c. How might teachers of mathematics in early childhood foster the independence of children when doing mathematics, their generative power, their ability to reflect on their own problem-solving attempts, their abstractions from their own mathematical activity, and the role of play and emotions in their mathematical activity?
2. The nature and forms of mathematics teaching.
    a. How might teachers use their knowledge to foster the mathematical knowledge of children in mathematical communications?
    b. What features of children's language and actions are indicative of certain elements of knowledge the teacher might focus on?
    c. What decisions might teachers make about what children could or should do?
    d. What problematic or interactive situations might teachers use to encourage children's mathematical learning?

Elaboration of Conceptual and Contextual Diversity

E. von Glasersfeld (chap. 2.2) developed the idea "that language is not a means of transporting conceptual structures from teacher to student, but rather a means of interacting that allows the teacher here and there to constrain and thus to guide the cognitive construction of the student. This guidance, as good teachers have known all along, necessarily remains tentative and cannot even approach absolute determination." J. Easley and H. Taylor (chap. 4.3), working as teachers of first-grade mathematics classes in the United States, demonstrated the conceptual diversity among children pointed to by E. von Glasersfeld and the "unreasonableness of the common assumption that teachers, aiming each lesson for a particular conceptual goal for all pupils, would expect nearly all of the pupils to succeed and understand the same concepts." Through their teaching experiences, they observed the relative ease with which children appear to communicate novel mathematical ideas with their peers compared to communicating with their teachers. For them, the interesting question is "to explain how young children are able to form and apply so many mathematical ideas to these problems that they have not been explicitly taught, ideas that one might think have a history of development in scholarly traditions that go back hundreds if not thousands of years." Their examples sharply illustrate the necessity of interpreting the myriad of verbal and nonverbal signals children send to establish possible meanings of the children's mathematical language and actions. As P. Cobb (chap. 4.2) puts it, "The trick is to imagine a world in which children's activity does make sense."

As essential as these interpretative activities are for the teacher, they offer only a partial account of mathematical communication. P. Cobb forcefully argues for multiple perspectives including experiential, psychological, sociological, and anthropological. The advantage of assuming multiple perspectives is illustrated by F. Lowenthal's (chap. 4.1) nonverbal communication devices. Emphasizing the experiential and psychological contexts, he reports working successfully with children who, in verbally oriented normal school contexts, could be said to be at risk. These children were called "problem children" and were all at least 2 years behind in their studies relative to normative standards. F. Lowenthal describes how, after 18 months of using NVCD's, the children were no longer behind in mathematics. These considerations highlight the necessity for reform in mathematics education that emphasizes contextual as well as conceptual diversity.

Discussion of Communication

In the three sessions devoted to discussing mathematical communication, one issue that emerged was the contrast between traditional pedagogic discourse in schools and discourse outside of schools. Some participants felt that improvements in the former might emerge if the latter was analyzed from the point of view of its participants, especially from the point of view of children. There seemed to be agreement among the participants that children are not given much of a chance to express their ways and means of operating in school and that teachers need to involve children in interactive (nonverbal as well as verbal) mathematical communication.

Several specific issues also emerged. How the social norms of the school influence the fabric of interactive mathematical communication in classrooms became a major issue because the participants in a mathematics classroom must engage in open and honest mathematical exchanges. Teacher's beliefs about their role, the student's role, and the nature of mathematics in traditional classrooms are such that discussions about mathematics are almost nonexistent. In settings where negotiation of meaning occurs, the teachers view their role as that of a facilitator in helping children to understand mathematics. As facilitators, teachers coordinate their knowledge of mathematics with their knowledge of the processes children use to solve problems. In so doing, they draw on their understanding of children's processes to probe their solutions and to offer suggestions that serve to create learning environments in which problems are debated and resolved. Their knowledge of mathematics provides a framework from which to guide children's experiences.

ENVIRONMENT

An individual establishes an environment by using available conceptual operations. It is nothing more than the result of an assimilation, "the integration of new objects or situations or events into previous schemes" (Piaget, 1980c, p. 164). The result of an assimilation of a particular situation is an experience of the situation and this experience constitutes an environment in the here and now. So, a mathematical environment is relative to a particular situation or event and to the individual's available mathematical schemes. In constructivism, situations do not come ready-made. "The problem situations themselves are seen, articulated, and approached differently by the diverse cognizing subjects" (von Glasersfeld, chap. 2.2).

Our understanding of mathematical environments include those cases where acting individuals use their mathematical schemes in assimilation of re-presentations of sensory experience as well as sensory experience itself (visual, auditory, kinesthetic, tactual, or some combination of these). One person cannot create a mathematical environment for another person; people create their own mathematical environments. A teacher can, however, conceive of possible mathematical environments for children based on their observations of children's actual environments. An observer's interpretation of an observed individual's mathematical environment is itself a mathematical environment. The two individuals might see different things in what to a third person is the same mathematical situation because these two mathematical environments are relative to the assimilatory schemes of the individuals.

Given these notions concerning environment, the following two questions were posed for the work of the action group: (a) "How can we conceive of mathematical environments for children?" and (b) "How can teachers influence mathematical environments of children to facilitate their construction of mathematical knowledge?" Although the first question might seem to be already answered, Sinclair (chap. 2.1) shatters any such illusion: "Unfortunately, it appears to be extremely difficult to define 'mathematical contexts,' especially with reference to young children. Given the very general basis for the construction of logico-mathematical operations . . . almost any situation that can be commented on, asked about, indicated as desirable, etc., can lead to actions, utterances, gestures, or other communicative acts that have something to do with logic or mathematics." H. Sinclair's observation has to serve as a counter-point for those mathematics educators who would use only a particular collection of tasks as constituting what children should encounter in school mathematics.

The two questions, especially the second one, do imply reciprocal relations of children with their external reality. When children use their mathematical schemes successfully in a given situation, the schemes are viable with respect to that situation. It might be possible that certain elements of the situation apparent to an observer are unintentionally disregarded by the children and could be seen only if the children modified their schemes. These elements are candidates for mathematics learning if certain constraints can be established in the children's environment that the children want to overcome and that might lead them to modify their ways and means of operating. If successful, the modifications would permit children to see the situation from a new perspective—the children would reorganize a given environment. Given that an environment as we perceive it is our invention (von Foerster, 1984), two issues were identified for the work of the action group.

1. The nature of mathematical curriculum in early childhood.
   a. What might "mathematics curriculum" mean?
      I. How does the mathematical knowledge of children and teachers relate to mathematics curriculum?
      II. How does mathematics learning and teaching relate to mathematics curriculum?
   b. What do we mean by "possible mathematical environments" and how do they relate to curriculum?
   c. How can a teacher establish a possible mathematical environment to facilitate the children's construction of some part of their mathematical knowledge?
2. The nature of curriculum in early childhood teacher education.
   a. What is the nature and object of communication in the teacher education classroom concerning:
      I. Mathematics?
      II. Teaching mathematics in early childhood classes?
      III. Children's mathematical knowledge and learning?
      IV. Available technology adapted to early childhood?
   b. What are the products of such communication from the point of view of:
      I. The preservice teacher?
      II. The mathematics educators?
   c. What methods and technology could we use to help preservice teachers of early childhood learn with respect to question 1?

Elaboration of Curriculum as a Post Hoc Activity

If the conceptual schemes constituting mathematical knowledge cannot be conveyed or transported from one person to another by words of the language, then according to von Glasersfeld (chap. 2.2), the task of education becomes one of "inferring models of the students' conceptual constructs and then generating hypotheses as to how the students could be given the opportunity to modify their structures so that they lead to mathematical actions that might be considered compatible with the instructor's expectations and goals." Although von Glasersfeld's comment identifies what has to be done, it leaves mathematics educators with the job of learning how to do it. Toward this end, T. Kieren (chap. 5.2) identifies a view of mathematics that seems to be essential. "One such view of mathematics . . . is to see mathematics as the personal building of patterns involving distinguishing, modifying, and using patterns and forming patterns on patterns and patterns of patterns. Such a view of mathematics sees it as interactive with the rest of a knower's life . . . and is clearly historical in a personal sense. . . . Finally, it is a personally active view of mathematics." Within this view of mathematics, Kieren isolated several features of a facilitating mathematical environment in which a young child is to be an active abstracter and language user in building personal mathematics. He calls the features "categories of awareness"—multifaceted knowledge (Lawler's bricolage); complementarities of understanding (form and substance); mathematical variations and complementarities (e.g., fraction as quantity and ratio); development (Easley & Taylor's conceptual diversity); and potential for pattern and pattern growth.

Another exciting possibility for reform in mathematics education resides in the transformation of what is taken as mathematics curricula in teacher education. L. Burton (chap. 5.3) challenges several beliefs about early childhood mathematics teacher education. She identifies these beliefs as the simplicity belief (e.g., because mathematics becomes more complicated throughout schooling, its learning must develop from simple to complex), the belief in enjoyment (e.g., focusing on making books more brightly colored rather than focusing on meeting mathematical challenges), the belief in 'reality' (e.g., objective mathematical or physical reality), and the empty vessel belief (e.g., X knows something that Y must learn. It is X's job to fill Y up with the knowledge and skills). After developing several consequences of holding these beliefs, she concludes

> Whereas a syllabus is a list of desirable knowledge/skills, the achieved curriculum is demonstrated by the pupils' engagement and resultant understandings. A teacher is in no position to dictate that output in advance. So, defining a curriculum for each individual is a post hoc task for the teacher. The teacher does this by closely observing and listening to children as they engage in the challenges provided and discuss their actions. Central to this style of teaching/learning is social interaction, control, and personal interpretation within a group.

R. O. Ohuche (chap. 5.1), provides a valuable insight into the nature of social interaction in mathematical learning and development in Third world situations. "Open-ended inquiry is a nonstarter in societies where children are not usually encouraged to ask questions of adults or other children. There are indeed investigations in Third World situations, which have tended to point out that individualized instruction may not be as prize-worthy in the Third World as it is in the Industrialized countries of the Western world." Based on R. O. Ohuche's observation, it seems critical to investigate the nature and role of social interaction across different cultures to more fully understand its relation to mathematics learning and development. Ohuche also provides an interpretation of "intended curriculum," "implemented curriculum," and "attained curriculum," all of which have interpretations in curriculum theory based on traditional theories of knowledge. His interpretations provide serious challenges to more traditional interpretations and point to the necessity for a reformulation of curriculum theory within constructivism. For example, in the case of intended curriculum, Ohuche comments that

> this is usually a national, regional, or local prescription of content, objectives, and suggested activities and materials. Yet, in the constructionist view the children are expected to learn through their personal constructions. Thus, some have considered it healthier to view the intended curriculum from the perspective of setting the criteria to be used in selecting the concepts and processes that may form the basis of the activities of the learner.

This is a much more difficult task and cannot be accomplished in the absence of actual teaching and learning. As pointed out by both Cobb and Ohuche, it is contextual and we should not expect to be able to prescribe a universal curriculum.

Discussion of Curriculum and Teacher Education

The choice of mathematical content and its nature that might be appropriate for early childhood was debated at length in the working group devoted to mathematics curriculum in early childhood. Taking the environments of children as one basis for their construction of mathematical concepts and operations was advocated because the belief that children do construct their mathematical concepts and operations outside as well as inside of schooling makes everything about early childhood mathematics curricula problematic. The notion of created curricula—those mathematical environments created in the context of ongoing living and learning—is essential in a constructivist framework. Created curricula are not a priori and can be only anticipated—not prescribed. They are compatible but not identical with a child-centered approach to curriculum that was advocated by M. Sumio in which mathematics, science, and language would be drawn out of everyday situations. They are compatible also with the relatively free forms of early childhood mathematics curriculum in most English and some Australian schools. However, they were not compatible with the mathematics curriculum in countries where there is a "top-down" approach or where mathematics textbooks functionally determine the curriculum.

Abstracted curricula, on the other hand, are models created as a result of participation in ongoing mathematics teaching and learning and contain a specification of (a) mathematical concepts and operations of the involved students and itineraries of their construction including time estimates, (b) possible learning periods of the concepts and operations along with the goals and intentions of the teacher within these learning periods, (c) problem situations that can serve in the establishment and modification of mathematical learning environments by students in the learning periods, (d) critical decisions that can be made in posing the problem situations to students, and (e) sample interactive communication that can be encouraged among the participants within the learning periods.

Several recommendations emerged from the working group devoted to mathematics teacher education. According to the argument, because teacher education students bring their own experience in the learning and teaching of mathematics to higher education, these personal experiences should be a starting point for their further explorations in mathematics education. This was taken as a crucial feature of the learning environments they establish in their teacher education courses.

An issue that arose concerned that the nature, quality, and extent of the mathematical knowledge teachers need in order to function independently in the context of ongoing teaching and learning. This was identified as a critical issue that is currently receiving little or no attention in the mathematics education community world-wide and it is recommended that work be undertaken in attempts to provide insight into the issue.

FINAL COMMENTS

The issues, problems, and opportunities presented by constructivism for mathematics education in early childhood offer hope that the mathematical education of children can be continually improved in the future. Although there might be some sense of deja vu when trying to improve children's mathematical experiences using constructivist' principles, the principles encourage us to decenter and try to see the children's experiences from the children's point of view. The deceptively simple insight that the mathematical experiences of children are inaccessible to us and that we can only establish a consensual domain of experience is enough to initiate reforms in how we adults practice mathematics education. When coupled with the revolutionary aspect of constructivism, we begin to more fully appreciate how limited our educational practices are when children's mathematical realities are essentially ignored.

If children's mathematical knowledge is accepted as being legitimate mathematics, not mathematical misconceptions, then adults have the exciting challenge to learn it. This challenge is accentuated if we realize that children's mathematics can be an active, dynamically changing mathematics that is used by children in adaptations in their environments. When viewed in this way, understanding how the adults who are responsible for children's mathematics education might facilitate those adaptations becomes equally challenging. This calls for reform in at least the constitutive characteristics of mathematics curricula and mathematics teaching. But the most important reforms are perhaps those that occur in our own knowledge and beliefs concerning the nature of mathematics, children's learning, and educational processes.

ACKNOWLEDGMENTS

Appreciation is extended to George Stanic, Ernst von Glasersfeld, and Robert Lawler for their comments on earlier drafts of this chapter. We especially thank Paul Cobb, Terry Wood, and the abstracters (Brenda Denvir, Nick James, Neil Pateman, George Stanic, Max Stephens, and Grayson Wheatley) for their written documentation of the discussions that transpired during ICME-6. Portions of this chapter have appeared in the proceedings of ICME-6.

Part 2
Epistemological Chapters

Chapter
2.1

Learning: The Interactive Recreation of Knowledge

Hermine Sinclair
University of Geneva, SWITZERLAND

Although it is often necessary to start off by giving definitions of some of the terms that will be used in a chapter, this is not an easy matter. Most theoretical definitions of terms such as *knowledge, social interaction,* and *learning* are based on epistemological presuppositions, and the title of this chapter is no exception. Thus, trying to make my presuppositions clear, I first describe the constructivist (mainly Piagetian) conception of knowledge. In a second part, I discuss personal (and then wider societal) interaction within the constructivist framework, and in the last part I reflect on the learning of mathematics in very young children from the constructivist, interactive perspective. My remarks on this point are necessarily both personal and psychological (because I am not a teacher), as well as sketchy. As Steffe remarked, though learning is at the heart of our business in mathematics education, few attempts have been made to study learning, primarily because it is so very difficult. The difficulty of studying learning—and teaching—lies, in my view, in the fact that it demands the study of the processes by which children come to know in a short time basic principles (in mathematics, but also in other scientific disciplines) that took humanity thousands of years to construct. This view of learning constitutes the main leitmotiv of this chapter.

KNOWLEDGE

From a constructivist's point of view, the essential way of knowing the real world is not directly through our senses, but first and foremost through our material and/or mental actions. In this context, action has to be understood as all activity by which we bring about a change in the world around us or by which we change our own situation in relation to the world. In other words, it is activity that changes the knower-known relationship. From babies who laboriously push two objects together or who attract their mothers' attention by crying, to scientists who invent new ways of making elementary particles react, to the children or adults who try to convince their friends of their opinions, new knowledge is constructed from the changes or transformations the subject introduces in the knower-known relationship.

The source of these changes in the knower-known relationship is to be sought in the biological processes of adaptation whereby organisms transform the exterior world to fit into their organic or cognitive systems (assimilation) and transform these systems to fit with their experiences of the external world (accommodation). If adaptation, in this sense, is the source of the progress of knowledge, what are its mechanisms? Once again, it is a biological postulate that led Piaget to propose a very general mechanism, that of equilibration. All living organisms adapt to their environment and therefore tend towards an equilibrium between assimilation and accommodation. Human beings go beyond just the adaptation to an external environment. They transform it profoundly and construct evermore powerful cognitive systems, which create ever wider problem spaces, and ever further possibilities and necessities for equilibration.

Disequilibria are internal states, and arise for different reasons. Sometimes separate, limited systems of reasoning lead to different possible answers for one and the same problem and the subject becomes aware of this discrepancy. For example, in the well-known experiment of conservation in which an amount of play-dough under goes various changes of shape, young children know perfectly well that nothing was added or taken away (and will say so, when asked). They also, at a certain level, know that one can reshape the play-dough as it was before, but the fact that the transformed play-dough now is longer (or shorter, or fatter . . .) than the standard shape, which was not transformed, cannot be conciliated with the already existing inferential system that leads to the knowledge that nothing added and nothing taken away means the same amount. At other times a limited system cannot be applied to a new situation, and especially, it cannot serve to answer "why?" questions.

In other words, at all levels subjects construct "theories" (in action or thought) to make sense of their experiences and as long as these theories work, subjects will abide by them. Human beings tend to push their ideas as far as they will go and actively seek novel experiences, so they will partly conserve and partly transform their ideas when their experience widens, and new questions arise for which the theory is not adequate. This process has no predestined end—because the relation between knower and known is indissociable, there is no way to test acquired knowledge against an absolute reality.

As Piaget (1980b), who saw himself as a realist of a rather special kind, expressed it, "With every step forward in knowledge that brings the subject

2.1. THE INTERACTIVE RECREATION OF KNOWLEDGE   21

nearer to his object, the latter retreats . . . so that the successive models elaborated by the subject are no more than approximations that despite improvements can never reach . . . the object itself, which continues to possess unknown properties. . ." (pp. 221–222). This does not mean that the knowing subjects are forever living in a world of their own making; but it does mean that they can never gain absolute knowledge of reality as it is.

The fundamental constructivist view thus postulates changes in the relation between subject and object; and the movement towards better, though never perfect, knowledge of the object has as its concomitant another movement whereby subjects obtain better knowledge of their own actions or thought processes. There may not be perfect synchronicity, but sooner or later every new conquest of the world of objects will lead subjects to restructure their action or operations system, just as new deductions and inferences derived from the internal system will lead to new interrogations of reality.

These movements towards ever more viable knowledge lead to different kinds of knowledge. On the one hand, the subjects' reflections on their own coordinations of action leads to logico-mathematical knowledge. On the other hand, reflection on the properties of objects and the changes actions produce leads to the natural sciences, such as physics and chemistry. These different types of knowledge are not symmetrical. Knowledge of the world of objects cannot be constructed in the absence of some kind of logico-mathematical framework, whereas logic and mathematics can become pure, in the sense of being free from particular contents. Clearly, this confers a special status on logic and mathematics inside the edifice of human knowledge in general. However, this does not mean that logico-mathematical knowledge should be seen as a type of knowledge totally divorced from other types. To quote Piaget (1970a):

> Objects are only known via the thought of the subject, but the subject only knows himself via his adaptation to the object. The world of objects is only known to man via his logic and mathematics which are products of his own thought, but man can only understand how he constructed mathematics and logic by studying himself, i.e., through his psychological and biological functioning in the universe of reality. (p. 145)

This passage can be read as a warning against a certain "reification" of objects-of-thought. For an infant, a block is something you can push or put on top of something else or that makes a noise when you throw it, but it is also something that is not soft, not good-to-eat, not something you can put another object into. So, say, weight as an object of thought is no more or no less than the sum of the different operations the subject can perform when dealing with weight. Similarly, number as an object-of-thought is what one can do with numbers. Thus there is not one single "concept of number" but an unending series of such concepts. It remains true, however, that weight as an object of thought demands, on the one hand, abstraction of the properties of objects, and therefore observation and experimentation (Piaget's empirical abstraction), and, on the other hand, abstraction of one's own action and reasoning coordinations (Piaget's reflective abstraction). Number, as an object of thought, only demands the latter type of abstraction—in fact, the totality of logic and mathematics is based on this type of abstraction. To construct a concept of weight, several properties of objects have to be dissociated (e.g., volume, density, mass, weight itself) and organized into a system. The experimentation and organization are based on reflective abstraction, but the object's properties are what is studied, and the object's behavior in interaction with other objects (water, air, etc.) has to be observed. By contrast, at a certain level of development, for number the properties of the objects do not intervene, only the subject's organizing activities (with the minor proviso that the objects do not evaporate or melt into one another).

SOCIAL INTERACTION, SOCIETY, AND LEARNING

So far, the construction of knowledge would seem to be an almost totally endogenous process, especially as regards logico-mathematical knowledge. However, science is essentially a social enterprise, and society and social interaction in general are an essential factor in the constructivist view of knowledge.

First, there is the epistemological necessity of having a way to judge the quality of the knowledge that is acquired. There is no direct way of checking the correctness or the truth of our knowledge against reality itself, but only of judging what von Glasersfeld (1983a) called its "goodness of fit with experience, their *viability* as a means for the solving the problems," (p. 51), thus knowledge can only be considered "objective" (in contrast with subjective belief) when "it has been checked (and not simply accepted) by other scientists" (Piaget, 1965, p. 87).

In addition, there are psychological reasons for considering social interaction as essential for knowledge. Human beings do not only interact with objects and natural phenomena such as snow and flowers, but also, and in a sense primarily, with other human beings. Though Piaget referred only sporadically, and always only very theoretically, to the necessity and importance of this type of interaction, its contribution to the fundamental reflective processes is becoming clearer, especially through studies of peer-interaction among young children (Sinclair, 1987a; Stambak et al., 1983). Even very simple reciprocal imitation (one child pushing a stick through a ball of cottonwool, another doing the same, and then going on to push the ball of cottonwool up and down the stick, and the first one imitating this further action) offers both partners an occasion to see their own actions from the outside and from the inside, as it were. This may facilitate reflection on the action as an object of thought.

Furthermore, it is clear that society in general, with its accumulation of knowledge, intervenes in the individual processes of the construction of knowledge. If not, then every generation would start all over again and we would still all be at the level of cave-dwellers. Children do not interact with "pure objects, only defined by their physical properties" (Piaget & Garcia, 1983, p. 274), instead they interact with objects that have been made by their society (dolls, blocks, spoons) and that are presented to them in a context where these objects (as well as natural objects such as flowers and pebbles) have certain meanings. As the children grow older, their direct experience with objects becomes more and more subordinated to "the system of meanings the social milieu confers on the objects" (Piaget & Garcia, 1983, p. 295). Construction of knowledge therefore is, on the one hand, a result of very general processes, such as abstraction and equilibration, and, on the other hand, of the way objects are presented to the subject with their societal meanings. Society, concluded Piaget and Garcia, can modify the latter, but not the former. And, we may add, this is where learning in the sense of children integrating the knowledge of their society in their time comes into the picture. Adults in general, and teachers in particular, present children with real objects or with objects of thought in a way that makes it possible for them to rediscover or reinvent what it took their society a long time to elaborate. When Piaget, in his writings on education, asserted that "to understand is to invent or to discover," the inventions or discoveries may be new to the child, but seen from the adult's point of view, they are recreations. Our children do not have to invent the wheel—they can begin to conceptualize the intricate properties of wheels as they exist in our society. Toddlers can, and do, compare the movement of a toy car with wheels to that of a toy car that has lost one or more of its wheels. Similarly, our written numerical system is presented to our children as an object of thought. They certainly have to reconstruct it (partly endogenously and partly socially), but that is not the same as having to invent it.

Some Piagetian studies have shown the influence of subtle changes in the way objects are presented. For example, when the transformation of a ball of modeling clay into a sausagelike roll is not done in a continuous rolling action, but by taking bits of clay from one side and sticking them onto the other, children who in the traditional situation give nonconservation answers now are convinced that the amount has not changed. Inhelder, Blanchet, Sinclair, & Piaget (1975) explained this "understanding" (which is stable in the sense that afterwards the traditional mode of transformation also leads to conservation answers) as described. The taking away of bits of clay on one side centers the child's attention on the fact that first the amount becomes less, and then, when the bits are added to the other end, the amount becomes more, whereas the displaced bits remain the same. Compensation then becomes "evident," whereas in the traditional mode children focus on what to them is a "positive" aspect of the transformation—the clay is now "longer." The difficulty of taking into account both negative and positive effects of an action or thought process have often been stressed by Piaget and are particularly spectacular in numerical problems: for example, the difficulty children encounter (until 7 or beyond) when from two equal collections of chips (A and B) one chip is taken away from A and added to B and they are asked which one has more and how many more. Collection B, of course, but the children affirm that B now has one more chip than A. When the experimental situation is made more complex, difficulties persist until the age of 10 or beyond (Piaget, 1974).

In this situation, too, one can suppose that the general law (taking n chips from A to add them to B makes B have $2n$ more than A) can be constructed much earlier if the presentation of the experimental situation were changed. There must be many different ways in which the presentation of objects of thought can foster even such endogenous processes as reflective abstraction. Not all of them have to do with conflict and compensation. In other cases, the subject's cognitive system is trying to find new problems (just as all action schemes tend to be applied to more and more objects and situations) and society in the large sense, or the family, or the school, can present a hungry mind with new problems. On this point, constructivist theory rejoins Vygotsky's ideas concerning a "zone of proximal development" and the role of society and school. Constructivist psychology contributes to the study of learning mainly through the elucidation of the basic processes of knowledge acquisition. Except for the example just quoted, and Inhelder and associates (1974) studies on learning, Piagetian studies were not designed to discover in what kind of situations (either in or out of school) certain structures and procedures of action and thought are built up. The subtle, but powerful interaction between the societal presentation of objects that allows a great number of children nowadays to master scientific concepts only geniuses could construct in the past cries out for detailed study.

FOSTERING THE GROWTH OF KNOWLEDGE: TEACHING AND LEARNING

The study of learning in the sense discussed earlier (the interaction between societal presentation and endogenous processes of abstraction) seems to be particularly difficult in the field of logico-mathematical knowledge. Experimentation (suggested or demonstrated) that can lead to empirical abstraction is not adequate in most cases because there are no properties of real objects to be discovered. Piaget's maxim of "discovery" and "invention" on the part of the child makes me think that he would have agreed with Bacon (Johnston, 1974) who said the following about what he called "the delivery of knowledges":

> For as knowledges are now delivered, there is a kind of contract of error between the deliverer and the receiver. For he that delivereth knowledge, desireth to deliver it in such form as may be best believed, and not as may be best examined; and he that receiveth knowledge, desireth rather present satisfaction, than expectant inqui-

ry; and so rather not to doubt, than not to err. . . . But knowledge that is delivered as a thread to be spun on, ought to be delivered and intimated, if it were possible, in the same method wherein it was invented. . . . But . . . no man knoweth how he came to the knowledge which he hath obtained. But yet nevertheless . . . a man may revisit and descend unto the foundation of his knowledge and consent; and so transplant it into another, as it grew on his own mind. For it is in knowledges as it is in plants: if you mean to use the plant, it is no matter for the roots; but if you mean to remove it to grow, then it is more assured to rest upon roots than slips: so the delivery of knowledges (as it is now used) is as of fair bodies of trees without the roots; good for the carpenter, but not for the planter. But if you will have sciences grow, it is less matter for the shaft of body of the tree, so you look well to the taking up of the roots. Of which kind of delivery the method of the mathematics, in that subject, hath some shadow: but generally I see it neither put in use nor put in inquisition, and therefore note it for deficient. (pp. 134–135)

Bacon may well have been too sanguine as regards the methods of mathematics teaching, but his view of the delivery of knowledge as fostering its growth certainly fits the constructivist framework. Yet it is difficult for adults to "descend unto the foundations of their knowledge." This is, of course, the point where Piaget insists on studies with young children, because introspection mostly gives a distorted picture.

As adults, we have absorbed, unconsciously in the main, the meanings our society and culture attaches to objects and actions; when presenting them to children we continue to be influenced by these meanings. Just as in science in general, such meanings and values (and even fashions) can both favor and hinder progress; the child's growth of knowledge is influenced in either a positive or negative way by socially determined meanings.

It seems clear that, as Steffe suggests, one of the ways to investigate learning is to study how children and the adults they are in contact with communicate in situations with a mathematical content (verbal, but also nonverbal communication). Apart from the general necessity of personal interaction at all levels, which I have already referred to, there are still several types of "mathematically oriented" communication to be distinguished.

Unfortunately, it appears to be extremely difficult to define "mathematical contexts," especially with reference to young children. Given the very general basis for the construction of logico-mathematical operations, (i.e., reflective abstraction from action-scheme-coordinations) almost any situation that can be commented on, asked about, indicated as desirable can lead to actions, utterances, gestures, or other communicative acts that have something to do with logic and mathematics. I limit my remarks to communication that concerns quantifying and ordering, but I realize that in doing so I may miss other important points. Gestural and postural communication about such topics has not been studied, though gestures such as opening one's arms wide (*big, bigger*—curiously enough I do not think I have seen this gesture in children to mean *many*), and repeated shaking movements with shoulders or legs or feet (*again, more of the same*) are frequent from a very early age onwards.

As regards verbal communication, there is an overabundance of utterance types that concern quantifying or ordering. In languages such as English, articles (*the, a*); absence of articles ("dogs are animals"); plurals of nouns; collectives; many expressions such as all, each, every, some, more, less; comparative and superlative forms; verbs such as *begin, finish,* and *follow;* conjunctions; adverbials (*often, rarely*); even the noun form, etc, can all express quantification or order. All natural languages have long lists of such terms and morpho-syntactic devices. It is difficult for children (and adults) because these expressions have multiple meanings in natural language that do not directly correspond to the meanings logicians and mathematicians attach to them (Freeman & Stedmon, 1986).

Though some of these expressions are part of the earliest holophrastic utterances produced by babies, ideas of the quantity are present even before. Babies who scream for the adult to put back the toys that they have thrown out of their play-pen, especially when they start screaming while they are still busy throwing the last two or three over the bars, is, in my view "communicating" about quantity. The same babies will point towards the correct cup when they are nesting cups and the adult hands them one that is several sizes too small—now they are communicating about order and size. In this sense, there is communication about quantity and order already before the end of the first year of life, and my guess would be that there is quite a lot of it. Certainly, *more, encore, all gone, fini, aplu, alle-alle* are frequently produced by children before the age of two in all languages for which we have early acquisition data. Other, such as English *each*, French *chaque, chacun* appear much later. Comparatives and superlatives appear in nonimitative use between four and six, and are especially interesting when the forms deviate from adult usage e.g., "mine is openest," "there's more less" (for: even less). The precise meaning children attach to these expressions is, however, difficult to determine, even in the case of self-constructed deviant forms (Kaper, 1985).

In addition to these general quantifying and ordering terms, all languages have spoken numerals, used for many different purposes. These spoken numerals often retain traces of older nondecimal systems and contain many forms that are opaque in comparison with the transparent decimal place-value system in use in the same societies. Some research suggests that the children's task in mastering the number system is easier when their language is Korean, Chinese, or Japanese, in which numbers are expressed with straightforward regularity (13 = ten-three, 30 = three-tens, and 33 = three-tens-three).

Bergeron and Herscovics (1987) brought to light a hitherto unobserved difficulty children have with the verbal expression of fractions. Both in English and in French most fraction-words are the same as ordinals: a fifth, sixth, seventh,

2.1. THE INTERACTIVE RECREATION OF KNOWLEDGE 27

and so forth. English has only two unambiguous terms, for the fractions $\frac{1}{2}$ (one half) and $\frac{1}{4}$ (a quarter). Bergeron observed that the use of the ambiguous fraction-terms creates a "cognitive obstacle" for children in the third grade, though they (and also their younger comrades) "find ways to express their quantification of the part-whole relationship using expressions such as 'one of n parts' " (p. 364).

I am afraid that all too often natural language usage of terms for number and measurement, as well as the wording of the so-called story-problems creates cognitive obstacles on the mathematical track of our children (De Corte & Verschaffel, 1987; Sinclair, 1987b). More experimental studies on this point are necessary, as well as observational studies of discussions among adults and children of situations with mathematical content, and detailed observations of classroom interaction.

In passing, I would like to lodge a protest against the use of linguistic terms such as semantics and syntax in mathematics. Though, of course, it is one of the properties of natural languages that words can always be given new meanings, these new meanings have to be made clear, and I have not really seen a definition of syntax and semantics in mathematics. More importantly, I think that the use of these words creates false analogies: it leads nonmathematicians to think of numbers as words and of equations as sentences. But numbers are the product of the operations of the system (which would be called syntactic, I suppose): $2 = 1 + 1$; $3 = (1 + 1) + 1$, and so forth, and words are not. *Pot* and *top* are words with different meanings; they are composed of three identical phonemes and their composition has nothing to do with the syntactic rules of English. Similarly, although *pot* is included in *spot*, these two words do not have the same relationship as 2 and 3, though 2 may be considered to be included in 3. A sentence such as "the dog and the cat are hungry" and the equation $1 + 1 = 2$ are only very superficially alike; to call the latter a sentence is once again totally misleading. Misleading not so much for the children (who at the age of 6 or 7 in any case have very little idea of either the general or the linguist's meaning of the word *sentence*) as for the adults who are teaching them.

It would thus seem that the verbal presentation of objects of thought that makes it possible for children to master in a short time the knowledge created by many generations of thinkers often makes the growth of knowledge more difficult than necessary, perhaps especially in mathematics. In his rare writings on education, Piaget (1970c) referred several times to the "paradox" of mathematics. Mathematics is entirely built up from the coordinations of action-schemes and from the ensuing coherent, deductive modes of reasoning, thus how is it possible that only a minority of schoolchildren "do well" in mathematics? All of them prove to be capable of coherent reasoning in their daily lives, and many of them succeed in other school subjects. All of them succeed in Piagetian concrete operational tasks (though, of course, not at exactly the same ages). What are the reasons for the particular difficulties of mathematics, and, more generally, of scientific disciplines for which mathematics is an indispensable tool? Speculating on this problem, Piaget proposed several reasons, and particularly insisted on two of them.

First, children are all too rarely encouraged to think about a problem in logical terms (relations, implications, proportions, etc.) before trying to deal with the strictly numerical or metrical aspects. Such logical thinking would lead them to judgments such as "X must be more than Y" or "the difference between X and Y must be about the same as that between Y and Z." These are mental operations for the solving of problems; and, I would like to add, the procedural skills become "meaningful" not when linked to figurative images of accumulated apples or cars in motion, but to coherent patterns of reasoning.

The second reason that Piaget proposed for the specific difficulties of mathematics learning is the premature introduction of the written mathematical symbol system. Indeed, this conventional system of notation looks natural and necessary to adults, but it is based on profound concepts such as place-value and zero as a number. We can no longer descend into our own minds and remember how we came to understand these concepts, but several researchers have pointed out their difficulty—even children who appear to have mastered procedures based on these concepts do not really understand them (inversely, some children who have not mastered the skill do understand the concepts).

Though adults cannot remember how the mathematical concepts embodied in our number system became clear to them, this does not mean that they did not *learn* them. According to Piaget (1972), "When one thinks of the many centuries it took to arrive at our mathematics, it would be absurd to think that without the guidance (of teachers and parents) the child could arrive at a clear formulation of the central questions on his own" (p. 21).

At this point it may be appropriate to reemphasize Piaget's proposed approach to problems of interaction between society with its accumulated store of knowledge and a cognitive development with its own constructive mechanisms (i.e., research that combines educational and psychological aspects). Such research has certainly gained in importance since Piaget wrote his recommendations for the 1948 and 1972 UNESCO publications, though it is both difficult and costly. Longitudinal research is particularly costly, but it is also highly revealing (Bergeron, Herscovies, & Bergeron, 1987b; Kamii & De Clark, 1985; Steffe, Cobb, & von Glasersfeld, 1988).

It is important to emphasize that in naturalistic, observational studies very young children (from 1 to 3 years old) constantly show their spontaneous interest in mathematical actions. They make one-to-one correspondences, they align objects, they balance and fit objects into others, they compare lengths of string and pull balls of cottonwool into little bits and put them together again. When they play in a group, they show one another their discoveries and take up each other's ideas (Verba, Stambak, & Sinclair, 1982). Somehow or other, I think that schools fail to capitalize on this interest and knowledge, as they also seem to ignore the quite extensive knowledge children between three and six have of numerals they see in an urban environment (such as numbers on houses, on packaged goods, in elevators, or on speed-limit signs, Sinclair & Sinclair, 1986). The almost exclusive focus on numbers as cardinalities found in many schools leaves aside children's extensive and sound knowledge of ordinalities, of equal parts of a whole, of unquantified proportions, and induces the idea that school arithmetic has nothing to do with all they know already, but is something quite new—"for learning to count with your pencil and doing your sums" as one child expressed it. Though there is nothing intrinsically wrong with this aim, it bypasses what from the constructivist point of view is essential—the continuity by which new knowledge grows from already existing knowledge, and it obscures the all-important link between mathematics and coherent, inferential thinking as it takes place, often unconsciously, in everyday life.

Chapter 2.2

Environment and Communication

Ernst von Glasersfeld
Institute for Behavioral Research, University of Georgia, Scientific Reasoning Research Institute, University of Massachusetts, USA

In this chapter I clarify some of the epistemological considerations, concerning the concepts of *environment* and *communication*, that arise from the radical constructivist approach to the problems of knowing. Radical constructivism is, indeed, a theory of knowing, and it is radical because it differs radically from traditional theories of knowledge. It would seem appropriate, therefore, to preface the discussion of the two key concepts with a few preliminary remarks about *constructivism*, a term that has recently become quite fashionable and, consequently, is frequently being used in ways that do not seem compatible with the approach I intend to discuss here.

Good teachers and perceptive cognitive psychologists have always been aware of the fact that what we call knowledge does not enter the uninitiated head in large, complex wholes but must be built up from components that, all too often, have to be very small, elementary pieces. In Plato's Theaetetus, Socrates gives an exemplary demonstration of how such a build-up can be guided by an experienced practitioner. Thus, there is nothing new about the notion that students (or other cognitively developing organisms) have to construct such knowledge by some form of reflection on experiences provided by a teacher's discourse, a textbook, or their own living.

In his Latin treatise on epistemology of 1710, the Neapolitan philosopher Giambattista Vico (1858) formulated this notion of cognitive construction as explicitly as one might wish; and others—among them Kant (1911), Vaihinger (1913), Simmel (1895), Baldwin (1906–1911) and Piaget (1967)—have taken cognitive construction for granted. If academic psychologists and educational researchers have now come round to adopting this notion and call themselves "constructivist," it may be a sign of individual enlightenment, but, as far as their awareness of the epistemological underpinnings is concerned, it may also be misleading. Actually, Vico went a large step further in his theory of knowledge. He deliberately and explicitly renounced the traditional contention that knowledge should reflect the world in an "objective" ontological way and declared that human reason could (and should) contemplate and govern the world of human experience and not the world as God might have made it. What I have called "radical constructivism" then builds on Vico's insight and adds the perspective that instrumentalists ever since Mersenne (Popkin, 1979) have taken, namely that knowledge cannot aim at "truth" in the traditional sense but instead concerns the construction of paths of action and thinking that an unfathomable "reality" leaves open for us to tread. The test of knowledge, therefore, is not whether or not it accurately matches the world as it might be "in itself"—a match that, as the skeptics have reiterated, we could never check out—but whether or not it *fits* the pursuit of our goals, which are always goals within the confines of our own experiential world.

From the perspective of radical constructivism, the commonsense notion of environment, which underlines most scientific thinking, is untenable. This commonsense notion arises quite naturally when the child coordinates experiences from different sensory modalities and, insofar as these coordinated experiences turn out to be repeatable, "externalizes" them in the form of more or less permanent objects. Piaget (1937) called this a "Copernican revolution," which culminates with the child beginning to think of itself as "a thing among other things" in a stable universe. As the child continues and enriches the construction, this external world, then, becomes much more plausible and solid when the use of language seems to corroborate many of the sensory experiences the individual has externalized. Indeed, the objective "reality" of the sensory objects one has talked about with other experiencing subjects becomes so strong a conviction that it can lead philosophers to speak of "referents" as though these items existed independently in the "outside world" before an individual experience of them had been associated with the appropriate word. Hence, the concepts of environment and communication are intimately interconnected. However, because the externalization that generates the sphere of experience that we ordinarily call environment must have begun and proceeded to a certain level of complexity before anything like communication can take place, they will be discussed in that order.

THE CONCEPT OF ENVIRONMENT

The French poet Henri Michaux once remarked that when he woke up in the morning he felt like an amoeba groping to establish its own boundaries. This is a powerful metaphorical description of what every cognizing subject must go through before it can come to consider itself as a discrete body among other physical items in a more or less permanent world. As I suggested earlier, it is a *conceptual* process because, on the one hand, it depends on creating associations between sensory experiences (rather than on the individual experiences themselves) and, on the other, more importantly, it depends on the ability to perceive the repetition of experiences.

From a realist point of view, repetition seems to be no problem. If things are there, prior and independent of the perceiver, all one has to do to repeat, say, a visual experience, is look at something twice. In fact, realists are usually quick to flip the problem around and to declare that because we can have the same experience more than once, it is clear that the thing we experience must be there.

From the constructivist point of view, however, the first question is how do we come to know that an experience we are having now is the same that we had a moment ago? Looked at closely, there are hardly ever two experiences such that we could not find a difference between them. Yet, to give an example, in spite of the fact that the sun has set and my visual experience of the glass of wine in front of me has a different color now, compared to a moment ago, and in spite of the fact that, because I have emptied the glass and moved it closer to the bottle, it looks smaller now and has no wine in it, I have no qualms in considering it the identical glass that I saw a moment ago. In other words, there are always differences that I consciously or unconsciously disregard in order to establish the permanence of an individual identity. This disregarding differences is an essential component of the process of *assimilation,* the process that enables us to externalize experiential items.

It is most important to the present discussion to note that assimilation is an activity on our part, an activity that we have to carry out in order to establish an externalized object's individual identity and permanence. We may carry it out habitually or even "instinctively," but there is no external or logical necessity to do so. Rather, it is part of our conceptual construction of the experiential environment, and all we can infer from it about the real world is that it allows us to successfully assimilate a variety of objects sufficiently often so that it becomes useful to act as though they belonged to an objective external environment. And if something works for us with a certain reliability, we tend to think that we have discovered the workings of the real world.

The impression of an object's independent *objective existence* is greatly enhanced, once we have pooled our experiential field with "others," that is, organisms to whom we attribute much the same properties and capabilities we believe to possess ourselves. Take for example a perfectly ordinary situation. A child approaches a hot stove, reaches out, and then recoils in a way that we, who happen to observe it, interpret as indicating pain. Almost inevitably we will feel confirmed in the belief that the stove is actually there and that it is hot in an objective sense. The child, we might say, is gaining knowledge of the environment—once burned, twice shy.

We totally disregard, whenever we make such inferences, that the stove and everything else that we consider to be around the child is not an objective

2.2. ENVIRONMENT AND COMMUNICATION

environment but merely that part of our own perceptual field that we have separated from the child on whom we are focusing our attention at the moment. We conceive of the child in that environment in the same way as we consider, for example, the drawing of a flower the figure that interests us while we disregard as ground the sheet of paper on which it has been drawn. In that second case, it is quite clear that both the figure and its ground are parts of our own experience. In the case of the child getting burned, however, we disregard that everything we observe is under all circumstances part of our experience and, disregarding that it is we who have externalized it, we tend to think that what we have categorized as the child's environment has an existence that is independent of us because the child reacts to it in a way that we consider similar to the way we ourselves would react.

This does not mean that to a radical constructivist it makes no sense to speak of environment. But from the constructivist perspective organism/environment, figure/ground, subject/object, and a host of other dichotomies of the kind are categorizations that cognizing agents impose on their experience and neither of the two mutually dependent terms can ever be less subjective than the other. The contemporary foundation of the theory of subjective environments was laid over 50 years ago by the biologist Jakob von Uexküll, (1933), who showed that what an organism experiences as environment necessarily depends on the organism's ways and means of perceiving and acting.

For educational research and education, this way of thinking has certain consequences. In both disciplines, one constructs general as well as specific models of students. Although realists tend to think that their models should, and to some extent do, reflect the students as they really are, constructivists must remain aware of the fact that models cannot reflect anything but the model builders' own conceptual constructs that they have externalized and kept constant by a continual process of assimilation and accommodation. Opponents of radical constructivism are prone to interpret such statements as manifestations of solipsism, as though the constructivist approach denied a world beyond one's experiential coordinations and categorizations. In doing so, they misinterpret the role of *accommodation*. The constructivist is fully aware of the fact that an organism's conceptual constructions are not fancy-free. On the contrary, the process of constructing is constantly curbed and held in check by the constraints it runs into. It is crucial to note that, from this perspective, accommodation (i.e., a change of the model) takes place, not because a conceptual structure or model has proven false, but because it no longer serves the chosen goal. Conversely, a conceptual structure or model cannot be considered true in an ontological sense, when it continues to work satisfactorily—it can only be said to have so far maintained its viability.

The task of education, then, can no longer be seen as a task of conveying ready-made pieces of knowledge to students, nor, in mathematics education, of opening their eyes to an absolute mathematical reality that pervades the objective environment like a crystalline structure independent of any mathematician's mental operations. Instead, it becomes a task of first inferring models of the students' conceptual constructs and then generating hypotheses as to how the students could be given the opportunity to modify their structures so that they lead to mathematical actions that might be considered compatible with the instructor's expectations and goals.

It is in this sense that the term *environment* gains importance in the constructivist approach. It is an environment that teachers develop by creating what they consider constraints that are likely to guide the student to propitious accommodations. It should never be, as it unfortunately often is, an environment based on the assumption that what is obvious to the mathematical initiate will be obvious to the novice as well.

THE CONCEPT OF COMMUNICATION

In its early stages, the technical theory of communication (Cherry, 1966) has developed a diagrammatic schema that explicitly mapped the process as it appears to an outside observer. Consequently, success or failure of a communication event was determined on the basis of the observable behavior of a sender and a receiver. This schema was highly successful in the work of communication engineers. As it happened, it was also immediately applicable to the behaviorist approach to teaching and learning. There, the teacher's task was reduced to providing a set of stimuli and reinforcements that were intended to condition the student to "emit" behavioral responses considered appropriate by the teacher. In the case of subject matter that has to be learned by heart, the model and the method based on it have worked very well. There is no room in the behaviorist approach for what is ordinarily called understanding, so it is not surprising that this method rarely produces it.

In contrast, the constructivist approach to education is predominantly interested in the student's conceptual structures and operations, and focuses on behavioral manifestations only insofar as they serve the teacher or researcher to infer the student's understanding. Consequently, the original model of communication must be considerably expanded in the area of the sender and, more important still, in the area of the receiver.

Claude Shannon's work on communication (1948) was revolutionary in part because it established incontrovertibly that the physical signals that pass between communicators—for instance the sounds of speech or the visual patterns of print in linguistic communication—do not carry what is ordinarily considered meaning. Instead, they carry instructions to select particular meanings from a list, which, together with the list of convened signals, constitutes the communication code. If the two lists of the code are not available to a receiver before the linguistic interaction take place, the signals are meaningless for that receiver.

To give a simple example, if you ask at the information counter at an airport at what time the plane from Boston is scheduled to arrive, and you get the answer "2:45 P.M.," the string of acoustic signals that constitutes that utterance could have no meaning for you unless you already have the conceptual schema in your head (as part of the present-day English code) that divides the day into twice 12 hours and each hour into 60 minutes. If, however, as a competent speaker of English, you are aware of that schema, the received signals enable you to select one particular point of the 1,440 possible points that the conventional temporal schema contains.

If it is the case that such conceptual schemas—and indeed concepts in general—cannot be conveyed or transported from one to the other by words of the language, this raises the question of how language users acquire them. The only viable answer seems to be that they must abstract them from their own experience. The process of language development in children, in fact, illustrates this very well. Although it is often said that normal children acquire their language without noticeable effort, a closer examination shows that the process involved is not as simple as it seems. If you want your infant to learn the word *cup,* you will go through a routine that parents have used from time immemorial. You will point to, then probably pick up and move, an object that satisfies your definition of *cup,* and at the same time you will repeatedly utter the word. It is likely that mothers and fathers do this intuitively, that is, without a well-formulated theoretical basis. They do it because it usually works. The reason why it works is not too difficult to find. There are at least three essential steps the child has to make. The first consists of focusing attention on some specific sensory signals in the manifold of sensory signals that, at every moment, are available. The parent's pointing provides an approximate and usually quite ambiguous direction for this act. The second step consists of isolating and coordinating a group of these sensory signals to form a more or less unitary item or thing. By moving the cup, the parent greatly aids this process because this action accentuates the relevant figure as opposed to the parts of the visual field that is to form the ground. The third step, then, is to associate the isolated visual pattern with the auditory experience produced by the parent's utterances of the word *cup.* Again, the child must first isolate the sensory signals that constitute this auditory experience from the background consisting of the manifold auditory signals that are available at the moment, and the parent's repetition of the word obviously enhances the process of isolating the auditory pattern as well as its association with the unitary visual item.

If this sequence of steps provides an adequate analysis of the initial acquisition of the meaning of the word *cup,* it is clear that the child's meaning of that word is made up exclusively of elements that the child abstracts from his or her own experiences. Indeed, anyone who has methodically watched children acquire the use of new words will have noticed that what they isolate as meanings from their experience is often only partially compatible with the meanings the adult speakers of the language take for granted. Thus the child's concept of cup often for quite some time includes the activity of drinking (and sometimes even the specific activity of drinking milk) before the continual linguistic and social interaction with other speakers of the language provides occasions for the accommodations necessary to adapt the child's concept of cup to the uses of the word in contexts as divergent as the hubs of automobiles and the races of yachts. In fact, the process of accommodation and refinement of the meaning of words and linguistic expressions continues for each of us throughout our lives and no matter how long we have spoken the language, there will still be occasions when we realize that we have been using a word in a way that turns out to be idiosyncratic in some particular respect.

Once we have come to see this essential and inescapable subjectivity of linguistic meaning, we can no longer maintain the preconceived notion that words convey ideas or knowledge and that the listener who apparently "understands" what we say must necessarily have conceptual structures identical with ours. Instead, we come to realize that understanding is always a matter of fit rather than match. Put in the simplest way, to understand what someone has said or written means to have built up a conceptual structure that, in the given context, appears to be compatible with the structure the speaker had in mind. This compatibility, as a rule, manifests itself in no other way than that the receiver says and does nothing that contravenes the speaker's expectations.

From this perspective, there is an inherent and inescapable indeterminacy in linguistic communication. Among proficient speakers of a language, the individual idiosyncrasies of conceptual construction rarely surface when the topics of communication are everyday objects and events. When a conversation turns to predominantly abstract matters, however, it usually does not take long before conceptual discrepancies become noticeable and generate perturbations in the interaction. At that point, the difficulties often become insurmountable if the participants believe that their meanings of the words they have used are fixed entities in an objective world outside the speakers. If, however, the participants take something like the constructivist view and begin by assuming that a speaker's meanings cannot be anything but subjective constructs, a productive accommodation and adaptation can mostly be reached.

For this reason, I believe that the constructivist orientation can be of great benefit to the teacher. Being aware of the inherent subjectivity in the interpretation of pieces of language, the teacher will be aware also of the fact that, no matter how their instructions are formulated, they are always subject to more than one reasonable interpretation. In other words, when a student reacts in a way that is not at all the way the teacher desired or expected, this in no way indicates that the student has committed a logical error. On the contrary, the response may make very good sense to the student, simply because the concepts with which the student views the situation are discrepant from those that seem "obvious" to the teacher. In that case it is of little avail to tell students that they are wrong. Instead, it will in most instances be far more productive for the teacher to try to infer the student's current conceptual structures, no matter how illogical they may seem from an adult perspective. It is only when the teacher has some inkling of "where the student is" that ways can be found to guide the student to make an accommodation so that the student's mathematical responses might be considered more compatible with the teacher's expectations and goals.

CONCLUSION

The constructivist analysis of the two concepts discussed here goes against the traditional ideas of realists, be they naive or sophisticated, materialist or metaphysical. It treats both our knowledge of the environment and of the items to which our linguistic expressions refer as subjective constructs of the cognizing agent. This is frequently but quite erroneously interpreted as a denial of a mind-independent, ontological reality, but even the most radical form of constructivism does not deny that kind of independent reality. Constructivism merely asserts that it is not accessible to rational knowledge because it manifests itself only through the constraints that make some of our ways of acting and thinking unsuccessful; and, from the subject's perspective, any such constraint is experienced (and therefore knowable) only as the break-down of an action or thought.

The tentative suggestions constructivism might make to educational researchers and educators will not contain much that would be new to teachers who have been consistently successful in the past. The novelty resides in the fact that the constructivist's perspective provides a theoretical foundation for practices that hitherto were the outcome of intuition rather than of a deliberate, explicit program—and this new theoretical foundation is largely incompatible with the traditional dogma of the educational establishment.

At the base of the constructivist theory of knowing is first the idea that knowledge is not an iconic representation of an external environment or world, but rather a mapping of ways of acting and thinking that are viable to the acting subject in attaining experiential goals. Second is the idea that this kind of knowledge is the result of an individual subject's constructive activity, not a commodity that somehow resides outside the knower and can be conveyed or instilled by diligent perception or linguistic communication. Third, is the idea that language is not a means of transporting conceptual structures from teacher to student, but rather a means of interacting that allows the teacher here and there to constrain and thus to guide the cognitive construction of the student. This guidance, as good teachers have known all along, necessarily remains tentative and cannot even approach absolute determination. From the constructivist point of view, this must be so, not only because there is always more than one solution to a problem, but because the problem situations themselves are seen, articulated, and approached differently by the diverse cognizing subjects.

The solution of a problem will provide satisfaction (and thus increase motivation) only if it leads to the attainment of a goal chosen by the acting subject which is the most obvious corollary of this theoretical position. From this it follows that an individual's incentive to do mathematics and to get involved in the abstract operations of mathematics can only develop in an acting subject, one who has discovered the incomparable satisfaction of solving a problem chosen by oneself according to rules and criteria appropriated as one's own.

Part 3

Knowledge and Learning: Elaboration Chapters

Chapter 3.1

Knowledge and Learning in Mathematics

Jarkko Leino
University of Tampere, FINLAND

Even though it has been a long time since I went to school, I can still remember my mathematics teacher's support, "Say it in your own words." She wanted me to express my personal constructs about the mathematical topic being discussed. She was not interested in whether I could repeat the exact words of the textbook but, instead, how I had understood the matter. She was an example of what it is to be good mathematics teacher and a practical constructivist.

I have interpreted it as my role as an elaborator of the epistemological chapters by Sinclair (2.1) and von Glasersfeld (2.2) to tell in my own words and constructs how I have experienced their content and what I consider to be their importance for mathematics education. Of course, my point of view is about mathematical knowledge and learning in the early school years. My presumption is the existing and increasing world of mathematics constructed by human beings, a part of which teachers have reconstructed as their own mathematical knowledge. The pupils, with their own experiences and constructs, try to come to know mathematical concepts, operations, structures, and ideas as tools for organizing their physical, social, and mental world. The only efficient way a pupil has of learning mathematics is to meaningfully reconstruct the basic concepts of mathematics. Teachers can provide pupils with relevant contexts for mathematizing, act like a mathematician, introduce names and other terms, and help the pupils' learning processes, but they cannot give the pupils ready-made concepts of mathematics. There are also inefficient ways to learn mathematical information that seem to be easy, attractive, and quick—just to remember the names and correct responses to formalized stimuli or to do the same operations that the teacher has shown. Very soon these mechanical accesses into mathematics usually become boring to teachers as well as pupils.

I start with mathematics knowledge as subject matter, and then continue to the point of view of the knowing person, and finally deal with the process of learning mathematics in school settings.

MATHEMATICAL KNOWLEDGE

Mathematics has originally been developed for practical purposes in the fields of *mathematike tekhne* (literally to learn art) or *geometria* (to measure land). Its concepts refer to the properties and relations of objects, basically of the real world. Some concepts, such as point, line, whole number, and order, are suggested directly by material or physical objects. Beyond the elementary concepts, mathematics has been filled with rather nonperceivable concepts, such as negative or complex numbers, functions, equations, and matrices. The essential feature of mathematics is abstraction and it can be developed and studied without reference to physical subjects. However, if mathematics is to be powerful, it must embrace in one abstract concept the essential features of all the physical manifestations of that concept (Kline, 1985). The basic concepts and axioms, and the deductions from the axioms, form the mathematical structures. We must also remember the symbolism of mathematics if we try to describe mathematics in essence.

I am not going to tackle the eternal question if mathematical truth is discovered or invented. For pupils such mathematical truths as $12 - 5 = 7$ or half of 12 marks is 6 marks are discovered (and understood) or remembered. I am convinced that the value of mathematics and its position in curriculum lies in the use of mathematics throughout society. Mathematics can be considered as possible models to deduce consequences that can be checked against experiences. In and behind these models are the mathematical structures "constructed by humanity" as Sinclair (chap. 2.1) expresses it. I would like to emphasize mathematics, pure or applied, is a human activity in which the ultimate criterion is its workability.

Of course, the bulk of mathematical knowledge is huge and so are the problems of mathematical education too. The mathematical structures in the forms they have been developed and condensed by mathematicians are not accessible to pupils. Mathematical information cannot be assimilated in abstract forms. It must be meaningfully constructed by pupils, piece by piece, on the basis of earlier experiences and conceptions that are both basically contextual in nature and work as their criteria of meaningfulness and truth. We are now within the concepts of constructivism.

LEARNING MATHEMATICS

Let us recall the common situation teachers are in when they start mathematics teaching. They have some 20 pupils with individual experiences and preliminary mathematical skills and concepts. One objective of the curriculum is to teach arithmetical skills; for example, addition of whole numbers smaller than 20, like we have in the Finnish curriculum for the fall term of first graders (age 6–7 years). What does this objective mean and what can teachers do?

The whole numbers 0–20 form a subset of N, which in turn has been dealt with by mathematicians. Can teachers use this kind of knowledge (successors, operations, commutativity, associativity, etc.) as a guide to the world of mathematics? Well, this kind of mathematics gives them general ideas of modern mathematical thinking, but it is very far from the needs teachers have when confronting pupils. If teachers know (some studies have shown it, e.g., Keranto, 1978) that almost all of their pupils can already count up to seven or eight and find sums of small numbers (like two and five make seven), is it time to start to write numerals? Or is it better to open the textbook and look at the iconic models of number sets?

The questions are difficult and most teachers do not even try to answer them. So they usually open the textbook, trusting that the authors have penetrated these questions, and start working with the iconic models and written symbols of the textbook. Of course, the authors of modern textbooks are more experienced than ordinary teachers and have tried to follow the ideas offered by the theories of child development. However, the textbook is always a compromise of many different demands and traditions. For instance, the long psychological tradition of associationism is still quite dominant (at least in Finland). Mathematics is divided into small and easy steps in order to smooth the learning process of pupils and to avoid situations that may lead to failure and frustrations. Working with textbooks is an easy way to organize teaching, and it also gives the teacher opportunities to help the less advanced pupils. The results are not necessarily bad—sooner or later most of the pupils learn to count, add, subtract, and many other skills appreciated in school. But some 15% of the students, who leave the comprehensive school after 9 years, do not know even elementary arithmetical skills, and many years earlier mathematics has become a difficult and boring subject for them. In the beginning of their schooling they have learned that school-arithmetic has nothing to do with all they know already, but is something quite new "for learning to count with your pencil and doing your sums" as Sinclair (chap. 2.1) expresses it.

Constructivism emphasizes the continuity of learning—new knowledge grows from what already exists. The tasks of mathematical education are not "seen as a task of conveying ready-made pieces of knowledge to students," nor "of opening their eyes to an absolute mathematical reality" as von Glasersfeld (chap. 2.2) says. Mathematical concepts are to be constructed by individual pupils on the basis of their conceptions and earlier knowledge through the different ways of acting and thinking in mathematical situations. The mathematical concepts are not contained in the materials or objects themselves, but refer to them. In the construction process many properties of the objects have to be disregarded by the learner. Cognitive conflicts are thought to be necessary—they challenge pupils through creation of disequilibrium.

Even though the concrete mathematical situation is simple, there are always many logical ways to comprehend it. That is why pupils many times form a construct that is not the one the teacher desired or expected, and why textbooks attempt to present extremely reduced and simplified models. These textbook models may be quite unambiguous, but they are also quite abstract and separated from the real world. They do not substitute concrete objects and realistic situations, and their value is, to my mind, highly exaggerated.

Mathematizing concrete situations is necessary though they may sometimes also mislead pupils. In order to acquire mathematical knowledge (e.g., find a structure $5 = 4 + 1 = 3 + 2$), pupils have to meet the same pattern (same number, length, area, shape, mass, weight, volume) in different contexts, act with objects through suitable strategies, transform the constitutions, and so forth. Numbers, counting, and arithmetical operations are first of all a means to organize phenomena where *quantities* play part (Freudenthal, 1983). The importance of measuring continuous quantities in natural situations as a starting point for mathematics cannot be underestimated. These kinds of natural situations in our environment have been well described by Freudenthal. Mathematics has a tendency to cut the bonds with reality but this is not innate in the pupil's mind. Pupils have to construct it on their own and when they have really done this, they have reached another level of concept attainment. Knowledge springs from actions performed on the objects, not the objects themselves.

As I mentioned earlier, pupils can count at least up to seven when they enter school at the age of 6 to 7 years. This does not mean, however, that they all have already adopted the number concept in the same way. There are qualitatively different number conceptions and different levels, as is exemplified in the work of Neuman (1987). There are many different aspects of number, of which cardinality and ordinality are most commonly studied. Counting may refer to reciting a number sequence, a process of connecting numerals with the set that is counted out, or interpreting the result as a number of the counted set. "Number" as an object of thought is what one can do with numbers (Sinclair, Chap. 2.1). For some pupils, in the beginning of school, number may only be a word or name that may have a successor if it is a small number. They need a great deal of experience of acting with objects (within the framework of goals presented by a teacher) to reach counting and structuring levels of number, and not to remain at the level of conceiving number only as a symbol. That is the main reason that I have criticized working only or mostly with textbooks in early mathematics teaching. Of course, to weaken the dominant position of textbooks demands new practical ideas and theoretical approaches. Constructivism is an alternative theoretical approach, and as an example of practical applications I would like to refer to the experiment planned and implemented by Neuman (1987).

CONSEQUENCES FOR TEACHING-LEARNING PROCESS

All experienced teachers know and many studies have made it evident that pupils do not make mistakes in mathematical tasks at random, but operate in terms of the meaning they hold at a given time. It is not easy for the teacher to detect the wrong rules pupils have followed or inefficient strategies used; it is difficult even for the specialized investigators. Correct answers can, of course, be attained by means of wrong rules or inefficient strategies and the logic behind incorrect answers is often difficult to unravel. If teachers want to guide the learning processes of their pupils, they have to know what the pupils think about the topic of concern. The only way this can be achieved is through communication.

Earlier conceptions and strategies contain the seed for more developed conceptual structures, but it is easy to regress too. A teacher has to know how to get his pupils to appreciate and use higher-level thinking. There are numerous examples even of adults who still have very primitive number conceptions of computing strategies (we can only imagine what they have done during their lessons and what kind of attitudes about mathematics they convey to their own children). In order to develop mathematics teaching, it is necessary to emphasize the importance of knowing how a pupil has interpreted the mathematical situation or task—how the pupil has interpreted the goal of the problem; for example, the relation between the task and procedure that has been selected, how the pupil has implemented the procedural work with all its components, and how the pupil has understood the larger context of the task, which may include a cue for checking the sensibility of the answer. The learning process in school is not just a knower-known relationship, a pupil with a mathematical problem, but, in terms of Feuerstein (1980), a mediated learning experience, a pupil studying with his or her teacher and peers.

Constructivism has been efficiently applied in research, for instance in formulating specific conceptual models of the way children construct number concepts and operations (e.g., Steffe, von Glasersfeld, Richards, & Cobb, 1983). We also know very well Piaget's numerous and comprehensive studies that have been used as a basis for education. However, as practical educators we also know how very difficult it is to apply these theories in school settings in order to advance pupils' learning. Most textbooks that have been written according to Piaget's ideas did not satisfy Piaget himself. Even in the field of elementary mathematics teaching, where the most detailed results have been reached and theories developed, we have to confess that much more research is needed. Consider the following quotation that is in line with constructivism from the dissertation by Neuman (1987), who studied the origins of arithmetic skills.

> The constructivist theory stops at the point where the present investigation has put a question-mark. What are the thinking strategies in which abstract counters should be encouraged? Are there thinking strategies, which find their natural expression in so-called "known number facts?" How is it otherwise possible to learn these "facts"? (p. 57)

Because of the lack of relevant theories, constructivism may often be regarded by educational practitioners, as well as researchers, only as a general framework, an approach, a paradigm, or a meta-theory. The research that has been done so far can give a model of the levels of the child's mathematical development in some areas, but applying it in educational settings needs a lot of additional ideas and experimentation.

Piaget and many other constructivists have been interested in the child's psycho-epistemological development, not especially individual differences that are very important in all education. The phenomenographic research done by Ference Marton and his coworkers has shown that individuals have several qualitatively different conceptions of the important concepts that have been studied. There may also be qualitatively different developmental routes even within the same cultural environment.

Within the general framework of constructivism we can also understand and predict how a pupil typically orientates to the situation or task at present. The pupils' cognitive skills (the way they focus their attention, narrow the selection of problem category using the identified parts, compare the similarities and differences of the problem with their earlier knowledge, and select the appropriate solution) can give their teacher valuable information from which to guide the learning processes. These skills are never taught in school, singly or in conjunction with the content (Letteri, 1986). For instance, the part-whole relationship is a crucial concept for the child to adapt number concepts as well many other mathematical concepts, but do we know how, for example, to improve the child's focusing and analytical skills?

Chapter
3.2

Constructing Knowledge from Interactions

Robert W. Lawler
Purdue University, USA

> ". . . Human beings do not only interact with objects and natural phenomena . . . but also, and in a sense primarily, with other human beings. . . ."
> —H. Sinclair (chap. 2.1)

Sinclair focuses our attention on the profound issue of how interaction and self-construction relate to one another. In presenting an approach to this issue that I have found productive, I begin with a few general observations and then go on to some detailed stories of development, drawn from very detailed and meticulously analyzed corpora (in Lawler, 1985, 1986).[1] My preferred descriptions, through which I bring such general issues down to concrete cases suitable for examination, are functionalist in orientation and ultimately computational in technique. Let me illustrate the role of control knowledge in developing behavior with a simple example before going on to consider two complex examples of mathematical learning, involving integrating disparate varieties of mathematical knowledge.

LEARNING TO CONTROL INTERACTIVE PROTOCOLS

The Articulation of Complementary Roles

At the age of 2, my daughter Peggy imitated the other members of her family. She began to imitate the knock-knock jokes of her sister Miriam (8 at the time), this way:

---

[1]Central arguments bearing on the importance of the case method may be found in Lewin (1935) and in Langer (1967).

Peggy: Knock-knock.
Bob: Who's there?
Peggy: (Broad laughter).

That first night, Peggy plied her "joke" upon me time and again. Eventually, for variety, I said "Knock-knock," but she did not reply. I tried many times. Even though she sensed something was expected of her, she did not reply. I would say she could not. Early the next morning I heard Peggy talking to herself in her crib:

Peggy: Knock-knock.
Peggy: Who's there?
Peggy: (Laughter).

At breakfast, Peggy's first words were "Knock-knock," and I responded appropriately, saying:

Bob: Knock-knock.
Peggy: Who's there?
Peggy: (Laughter).

That same afternoon, Miriam confirmed my observation, "Dad, Peggy can say 'Who's there.'" I consider this a simple, lucid example of processes in the articulation of complementary roles.

Elements of the Example

A learner with a relatively inferior comprehension is engaged socially with more comprehending people—in this case focused around what is literally a script for a joke's telling. During the engagement, social demands push at the boundaries of comprehension of the person with the undeveloped perspective. The learner attaches to herself uncomprehended routines of engagement (in both the theatrical and programming senses). The process may be friendly or not so—but it is more aptly and generally described by that wide-ranging class of intimate relationships that characterizes the interactions of a small society, the home. This first type of process I call *homely* ("home-like") *binding*.

The second type of process, *lonely discovery,* occurs when the learner is deprived of social engagement—left to her own devices—and uses those devices to re-enact the uncomprehended experiences, compensating for the solitude by simulating the role of the other actor. This simulation of the other actors imposes a real demand for the distinction between roles and their relations lacking in the initial engagement. My name for this pervasive and repeated sequence of homely binding and lonely discovery is *the articulation of complementary roles.* In such

3.2. CONSTRUCTING KNOWLEDGE FROM INTERACTIONS

cases, the relation between social experience and personal construction requires more integrated discriminations for controlling or directing multirole enactment of interactive protocols than are required for acting in them. These incidents provide a succinct example of how the articulation of complementary roles creates new control structures in the mind.[2]

This empirical material and its interpretation create a puzzle for instruction. Learning occurred not because it was socially directed but as a compensating adaptation to the deprivation of social interaction. Fantasy rescued the child from loneliness; the more complex requirements of interaction with one agent simulating another as well as acting out her own role required the construction by the individual of skills of sufficient generality and lability that they could function effectively in other domains of life. How one should represent such knowledge and its changes is a complex question, one for which these observations by themselves provide insufficient guidance to permit a resolution.

INTEGRATING RELATED KNOWLEDGE STRUCTURES

An Introduction to Paper Sums

This story is about a child learning to do additions whose unit sums crossed a decade boundary. In this specific sense, it relates to "carrying." (In the development of the particular child, it also was crucial to her later learning to do vertical form sums in the hindu-arabic notation.) At the beginning of the study, Miriam then *6:0* (6 years, 0 months) was unable to add 10 plus 20 on paper in the vertical form. When I asked her the question "How much is 10 plus 20?", Miriam answered with confidence, "30." Her response to the first sum presented in (a) was quite different. "I don't know . . . 1,200?" (After this confusion, vertical lines were used frequently to emphasize column alignment.):

at 6:0		at 6:9
1 0	|3|2|4|	2 2 8 5 7
+2 0	+|2|1|2|	+4 7 3 4 5
1200	|5|0|9|	7 0 2 0 2
(a)	(b)	(c)

Despite instruction that she should not "read" the individual digits but should add within the columns and assemble a result from the columnar sums, for (b)

---

[2]One cannot argue coercively that this single incident must have been the sole generator of such a change. If, however, particular experiences are the foundation for cognitive development, then someone among them must have been the first. This experience clearly exhibits a set of characteristics that seem essential to the process.

Miriam summed the addends to "509" [2 + 1 + 4 + 2 = 9]. She received instruction for solving problems such as (c) by a procedure I call *order-free adding*—based on the very simple idea that it doesn't matter in what order one sums column digits so long as any column interaction is accounted for subsequently. After preliminary instruction, the typical problem presented was two multidigit addends in the vertical form. Her typical solution began with writing down from left to right the column sums of well-known results. Next, Miriam would return to the omitted subproblems and calculate them with her fingers. When this first pass solution produced multidigit sums in a column—a formal illegality, as I informed her—Miriam had to confront the interaction of columns. I instructed her to cross off the 10s digit of such a sum and add it as a 1 to the next left column, that is, to "carry the one." With less than 2 hours of such instruction, Miriam succeeded at solving sums with two addends of up to 10 digits; but she realized no significant gain because the procedures were subject first to confusion and then to forgetting.

An Analysis: Rules That Don't Make Sense

Why were Miriam's initial skills with paper sums vulnerable? Consider the following three representative solutions:

	2	3
|3|8|	|3|8|	|3|8|
+|3|4|	+|3|4|	+|3|4|
|6|12|	|8|1|	|9|9|
(a)	(b)	(c)

The first (a) shows no integration of columnar sums; the second (b) shows a confusion over which digit to "put down" and which to "carry" (with an implicit rulelike slogan behind the action). If you don't already understand the meaning of the rule "put down the N and carry the one," why should you prefer that to a comparable rule, "put down the 1 and carry the N" [as in (b)]? Miriam was confusable in the sense that she chose, with no regularity and no apparent reason, to apply both these rules. Although frequently instructed in the former rule, she did not remember it. The rulelike formulation made no direct contact with her underlying microview structures. Without support from "below," the rule could not be remembered. *Microview* is a term I use to specify a particular species of schema, one whose principal component is a collection of pattern-matching procedures and whose functions are executed by a cascade of activation when a pattern is adequately matched. Microviews are postulated to embody very local knowledge and to compete with one another in a race to solve problems as they interpret them. For example, a verbal query, "How much is 25 plus 10?" could be solved by counting from 25 on fingers or in terms of U.S. coin equivalences.

3.2. CONSTRUCTING KNOWLEDGE FROM INTERACTIONS

The specific character of solutions emerging as behavior provides evidence about which structure among those known to exist won the race in a given instance. At the time of this incident, Miriam's arithmetic competence is describable as embodied in a *Count view* (based on mastery of one-to-one correspondence), a *Money view* (based on coin relationships), and a *Decadal view* (based on manipulation of numbers as multiples of 10; this unusual knowledge derived from her particular experiences with computer-based materials at the MIT Logo project). These three microviews form a cluster, related as components of her mental calculation repertoire. See Lawler (1985) for more data and analyses.

Miriam eliminated her confusion by inventing a carrying procedure that made sense to her, shown in (c). "Reduction to nines" satisfied the formal constraint that each column could have only a single digit in the result by reducing to a 9 any multidigit column sum and "carrying" the "excess" to the next left column. (38 plus 34 became 99 through 12 reducing to a 9 with a 3 carried.) Miriam's invention of this nonstandard procedure (at 6:3:6), I take as weighty evidence characterizing her understanding of numbers and addition in the vertical form. (The latter we discuss shortly.) About numbers we may conclude she saw the digits as representing things that ought to be conserved, as did the numbers of the Count microview. The achievement of columnar sums by finger counting or by recall of well-known results further substantiates the relation of paper sums to numbers of the Count view. Let us declare, then, that these experiences led to the development the *Paper-sums* microview, a cognitive structure that is a direct descendent of the Count view.

Miriam did not understand "carrying" as being at all related to place value. The numbers within the vertical columns did not relate to those of any other column in a comprehensible way. Despite my initial criticism of "reduction to nines"—by asking if she were surprised that all her answers had so many nines in them—Miriam was strongly committed to this method of carrying. For Miriam, at this time, vertical form addition had nothing to do with the Money or Decadal sums she achieved through mental calculation. "Right" or "wrong" was a judgment applicable to a calculation only in the terms of the microview wherein it was going forward. I conclude then that the Paper-sums microview shows a line of descent from Miriam's counting knowledge, diverging with respect to those other microviews involving mental calculation.

Finally, what made sense to Miriam completely dominated what she was told. Why is it that the rule she was given didn't make sense? How can we recapture a sense of what that must have seemed like? To her, a number represented a collection of things with a name: "12" was a name by which reference could be made to a collection of 12 things. Digit strings may have seemed to her as words do to us, things that cannot be decomposed without destroying their signification. If you divide the word *goat* into "go" and "at," you have two other words not sensibly related to the vanished goat. Similarly, from our common perspective, if you do not see the '1' as a '10' when you decompose a '12' into a '1' and

'2,' you lose '9.' Unless you appreciate the structured representation, the decomposition of 12 can make no more sense than cutting up a word. What appears as forgetting in Miriam's case is an interference from established processes; what makes sense in terms of ancestral cognitive structures dominates what is inculcated as an extrinsic rule. (I don't claim to offer a theory of forgetting. Competition from sensible ideas of long dependability is a very good reason, however, for forgetting what one is told but can not comprehend.)

The Carrying Breakthrough

The "carrying problem" was not restricted to Paper sums and in fact began its resolution through integrating the microviews of mental calculation. Although she could add double-digit numbers that involved no decade boundary crossing, like 55 plus 22, Miriam's Decadal view functions failed with sums only slightly different, such as 55 plus 26. Sums of this latter sort initially produced results with illegal number names, that is, $55 + 26 = 70:11$ ("seventy-eleven"). In playing her favorite computer game, however, precision was not required. Miriam's typical "fix" for such a calculation problem was to drop one of the unit digits from the problem and conclude that $55 + 26 = 76$ was an adequate solution. She could, of course, cross decade boundaries by counting, but for a long time this Count view knowledge was not used in conjunction with her Decadal view knowledge. Miriam's resolution of one species of carrying problem became evident to me in her spontaneous presentation of a problem and its solution (at 6:3:23). She picked up some of her brother's second-grade homework and brought it to me:

> Miriam: Dad, 28 plus 48 is 76, right?
> Bob: How did you figure that out?
> Miriam: Well, 20 and 40 are like 2 and 4. That 6 is like 60. We take the 8, 68 (then counting on her fingers) 69, 70, 71, 72, 73, 74, 75, 76.

Here was clear evidence that Miriam had solved one carrying problem by relating her Decadal and Count microviews. When and how did that integration occur?

Integrating Disparate Microviews

We were on vacation at the time. I felt Miriam had been working too hard at the laboratory and was determined that she should have a rest from our experiments. I was curious, however, about the representation development of her finger counting and raised the question one day at lunch (at 6:3:16):

> Bob: Miriam, do you remember when you used to count on your fingers all the time? How would you do a sum like 7 plus 2?

3.2. CONSTRUCTING KNOWLEDGE FROM INTERACTIONS

Miriam: Nine.
Bob: I know you know the answer—but can you tell me how you used to figure it out, before you knew?
Miriam: (Counting up on fingers) 7, 8, 9.
Bob: Think back even further, to long ago, to last year.
Miriam: (Miriam counted to nine with both addends on her fingers—leaving the middle finger of her right hand depressed.) But I don't do that any more. Why don't you give me a harder problem?
Bob: Thirty seven plus twelve.
Miriam: (With a shocked look on her face) That's 49.

Something about this problem and result surprised Miriam. I recorded this situation and her reaction in the corpus; I did not appreciate it as especially significant at that time. My current interpretation focusses on this specific incident as a moment of insight.

Characterizing the Insight

Precisely what was it that Miriam saw? In the Decadal view, the problem "37 plus 12" would be solved thus, "30 plus 10 is 40; 7 plus 2 is 9; 49"—a perfect result. Miriam had recently become able to decompose numbers such as "12" into a "10" and a "2." This marked a refinement of the Count view perspective. If we imagine the calculation "37 plus 12" proceeding in the Count microview— with the modified perspective able to "see the 10 in the 12"—Miriam would say "37 [the first number of the Count view's perspective] plus 10 is 47 [then counting up on her fingers the second addend residuum], 48, 49"—also a perfect answer. We are not surprised that the Count view answer is the same as that of the Decadal view, but I believe the concurrence surprised Miriam. One can say that Miriam experienced an insight (to which her "shocked look" testifies) based on the surprising confluence of results from apparently disparate microviews. Insight is the appropriate common word for the situation, and I continue to use it where no confusion is likely. Its range of meanings is too broad for technical use, so I introduce a new term, the *elevation of control,* as the technical name for the learning process exemplified here. The elevation of control names the creation of a control element that subordinates previously independent microviews, in the sense of permitting their controlled invocation; some experiences of insight are the experienced correlates of control elevation.

The character of control elevation is revealed in the example. The numbers involved were of the right magnitude to engage Miriam's Decadal microview. Also, she had just been finger counting (a Count view function). If both microviews were actively calculating results and simultaneously achieving identical solutions, the surprising confluence of results—where none should have been expected—could spark a significant cognitive event: the changing of a nonrelation into a relation, which is the quintessential alteration required for the creation of new structure.

The sense of surprise attending the elevation of control is a direct consequence of a common result being found where none was expected. The competition of microviews, which usually leads to the dominance of one and the suppression of others, also presents the possibility of cooperation replacing competition. So we see, in the outcome, Decadal beginning a calculation and Count completing it. This conclusion, howevermuch based on a rich interpretation, is an empirical observation. Where we expected development in response to incrementally more challenging problems, we found something quite different: cognitive reorganization from the redundant solution of simple problems.

The elevation of control, a minimal change that could account for the integration of microviews witnessed by Miriam's behavior, would be the addition of a control element permitting the serial invocation of the Decadal view and then the Count view. Let us declare at this moment of insight the formation of a new microview, the *Serial view*.[3] Although the Serial view is achieved as a minimal change of structure, its integration of subordinated microviews permits a significantly enhanced calculation performance, one so striking as to support the observation that a new functional level of calculation emerged from the new organization. This is especially evident where knowledge is articulated by proof. Consider this example (at 6:5:24).

> Miriam and Robby, himself no slouch at calculation, were making a clay by mixing flour, salt, and water. They mixed the material, kneaded it, and folded it over. Robby kept count of his foldings. With 95 plies, the material was thick. He folded again, "96," then cutting the pile in half, flopped the second on top of the first and said, "Now I've got 96 plus 96." Miriam interjected, "That's 192." Robby was astounded, couldn't believe her result, and called to his mother to find if Miriam could possibly be right. Miriam responded first, "Robby, we know 90 plus 90 is 180. Six makes 186. [then counting on her fingers] 187, 188, 189, 190, 191, 192."

---

[3]One wants to avoid the creation of something from nothing. See in this connection the discussion of "relational conversion" in Lawler (1985, chap. 7). In Lawler (1979), I advanced the same argument, first that the boundaries between microviews are defined by networks of "must-not-confound" links that function to suppress confusion between competing, related microviews; in addition, that the conversion of these repressive links, established by experience, to more explicit relational links, generates new control structure at moments of insight. The creation of inhibiting relations between microviews to suppress confusion does the real work of structural creation. The relational conversion, in which an inhibiting relation is turned into one of richer semantic content, permits the smooth transformation in functional capability to another behavior over what otherwise would appear to be an unbridgeable gap.

3.2. CONSTRUCTING KNOWLEDGE FROM INTERACTIONS 55

We can see the Decadal well-known-result (90 plus 90) as a basis for this calculation and its relation to her counting knowledge. Both these points support the argument that Miriam's new knowledge was specifically of controlling preexisting microviews. Robby was astounded—and we too should try to preserve a sense of astonishment in order to remain sensitive to how small a structural change permits the emergence of a new level of performance.

INTEGRATING KNOWLEDGE FROM DIVERSE SENSORY MODES

Early papers of the MIT Logo project claimed that design-producing procedures written in Logo would be more comprehensible to children because one could simulate the drawing agent (the light turtle on the video display) by moving through space with her or his own body. For many children, this was not obvious. The light turtle lived in a vertical world, they in a horizontal one. Miriam played in a variety of "turtle navigation" games that led to her familiarity with a set of angle values and useful relations (90 plus 90 equals 180). She also spent considerable time playing with design-generating procedures, such as the well-known Logo polyspiral procedure:

> to polyspi : side : angle : change
> forward : side
> right : angle
> polyspi (: side + : change) : angle : change
> end

Miriam enjoyed making designs, coloring them, and sharing them with her friends. She became familiar with specific values of angles that would make her favorite designs; but these "angle" values bore no apparent relationship to her other experiences. During the core 6 months of the Intimate Study, Miriam did not give evidence of understanding how angles and movements of turtle navigation related to angles and designs produced by repetition in the video context. She could use repetition, but there was no evidence she understood it as she so obviously did in this later incident:

> Turtle on the Bed (6 : 11 : 15)
> As I work at my bedroom desk, Miriam offered to sit in my lap, but I turned her down. She moped a little, then crawled onto my bed and began to move and spin in a most distracting fashion. "What are you doing? You're driving me batty!" I complained. Requesting a pen and a 3 × 5 card, Miriam drew on it a right rectangular polygonal spiral to show what she was doing in her "crawling on the bed game." Her verbal explanation was that she was "making one of those maze things."

Whence came this connectedness in her knowledge of serial physical action to pattern? My best answer is as follows.

Cuisenaire Rods and Polyspiral Mazes

When one day the children pestered me to play with some Cuisenaire rods I had brought home from the lab, I agreed on condition that we begin with a project of my choosing. My proposal was this: after they sorted the rods by color (and thus by length as well), I would begin to make something; their problem was to describe both what I was making and my procedure. I began to construct a square maze of Cuisenaire rods. After I placed four rods, I asked the children what I was making. Robby answered immediately, "A swirl, a maze." Miriam chimed in with his answer. At that point, I asked Robby to hold off on his answers until I discussed my questions thoroughly with Miriam. Having placed eight rods, I asked the children if they could describe my procedure. Miriam could not, at first, but when I focussed her attention on the length of each piece, she remarked: "You're growing it bigger and bigger." Upon questioning, she noted the increment was "one." After Robby added rods of length 9 and 10, Miriam justified his action by arguing, "It goes in order . . . littlest to biggest," and finally described my rod selection rule as "every time you put a rod in, it should be one bigger than the last one." Miriam understood well the incrementing of length, but she showed considerable difficulty with the role of turning in the angles in my rods maze.

When I set down the 11-length (the orange and white pair of rods), I did not orient it perpendicularly to the previous length. Miriam declared the arrangement incorrect but had trouble specifying precisely what was wrong. When she rearranged the rods to place them correctly, she simply interchanged the location of the orange (10 cm) and white rods (1 cm). From this action, I infer Miriam considered the placement incorrect because two rods of the same color were adjacent to each other—but not because the one rod was colinear with the preceding one. Here I asked Robby to explain what I should have done:

Robby: You should go a right 90. It could be orange, right 90, white orange.
Bob: And what should I do after the next orange?
Robby: You probably could do an orange and red.
Bob: (Placing the new rods colinear with those preceding)
Robby: Hold it! You should do a right again.
Bob: Oh. Miriam. What should I do next?
Miriam: A right 90, green and orange.
Bob: Next?
Miriam: A right 90, purple and orange.

3.2. CONSTRUCTING KNOWLEDGE FROM INTERACTIONS 57

This is the point at which Miriam brought together in a comprehensible relation the steps and result of a maze generating procedure.

Several aspects stand out. Miriam received extensive guidance. Moreover, Miriam worked with a familiar objective, familiar objects, and applied familiar operations. (This experience was clearly important for Miriam, specifically in establishing this sort of knowledge as very personally owned: in later years, whenever offered Cuisenaire rods to play with, constructing a polyspiral maze surfaced regularly as her objective of choice.) These experiences of the rods-maze and turtle on the bed appear to have integrated and thus culminated the development of Miriam's knowledge about iteration. The preceding incident about addition focused on microviews with much in common. The turtle on the bed incident presents a concrete linking experience as a possible basis for interconnection between essentially remote clusters of microviews. *Essentially remote* refers here to Turtle Navigation's being related primarily to walking and computer design's being related primarily to seeing, thus being descended from different sensorimotor subsystems, that is, locomotive and visual.

The central issue of human cognitive organization is how disparate and long-developing structures become linked in communication to form a partially coherent mind—such as we experience personally and witness in others. The framework used here discriminates among the major components of the sensorimotor system and their cognitive descendents, even while assuming the preeminence of that system as the basis of mind. Imagine the entire sensorimotor system of the body as made up of a few large, related, but distinct subsystems, each characterized by the special states and motions of the major body parts, thus:

Body Parts	**S-M Subsystem**	**Major Operations**
Trunk	Somatic	Being here
Legs	Locomotive	Moving from here to there
Head-eyes	Capital/visual	Looking at that there
Arms-hands	Manipulative	Changing that there
Tongue/ears	Linguistics	Saying/hearing whatever

Much of the activity of early infancy specifically involves developing coordinations between these five major sensorimotor subsystems. Such a fundamental organization in the development of coordinated systems might be assumed to ramify through all descendent cognitive structures developed from interacting with the experiences of later life.

The *rods-maze* microview closed the unbridgeable gap between turtle geometry Navigation microviews and the Design cluster by playing a mediating role. The *local* character, the task-specific binding of Miriam's learning in the rods-maze incident, implies that it was not developed analogically (i.e., from her turtle geometry experiences) but *de novo* from more primitive components of the sensorimotor system. If descended directly from the coordinating scheme that results in hand-eye coordination, the rods-maze microview was effective as mediator for two reasons, which can be brought forward in the following comparison expressing the activity of the primary agents in these microviews:

Locomotive	**Mediating**	**Visual**
I move from	You (hand) move	That(thing) goes
here to there	from here to there	from here to there
Body as agent	**Hand** as remote agent	**Eye** as active agent

The primary difference between the active programs of the human locomotive and visual subsystems is the level of aggregation significant for their functioning. The body lurches forward, step by step. The eye recognizes an image as an entity by circulating repeatedly in the pattern of a closed loop, a "feature ring," which defines that object in memory. The *feature ring* is a complex recognition procedure, which represents the saccades of eye focus and the possibility of recognizing features. Its primitive elements can be described as similar to the movements of the locomotive system, going forward and turning right.[4] Because of years of developed hand-eye coordination, the eye can recognize the pattern that emerges from what the hand does, whereas it cannot recognize so simply (if at all) the pattern that emerges from the path of body movement through the plane. The rods-maze experience was able to function meditatively between descendents of the locomotive and visual subsystems because the hand, as the familiar agent for manipulating remote objects (say little toy dolls some of whom may be thought of as self or other), can make the bridge between an action of movement which a body might make and one which can be coordinated with visual results.

The Channelled Description Conjecture

The body-parts mind proposal serves the function here of separating groups of cognitive structures on a large scale. Some cognitive structures are descended from ancestors in the locomotive subsystem and others from ancestors in the visual subsystem. If there is body-based disparateness, what leads to subsequent integration? The progressive organization of disparate structures and subsystems proceeds from the needs of the individual as a complete being. The achievement of an individual's goals requires the cooperation of disparate cognitive structures and subsystems of such structures, for example, crawling to get some desired object requires the use of arms, legs, and vision. Focusing as it does on the

---

[4]See chap. 5 in Lawler (1985) or Noton and Stark (1971).

descent of cognitive structures from ancestors in the motor subsystems, the body-parts mind proposal definitely favors the activity of the subject in the creation of cognitive structures over the impression of sensations on the mind. In this specific sense, the proposal is fundamentally compatible with Piagetian constructivism.

Even if the mind is a network of information structures comprised of the same types of elements, one need not conclude that it is uniform. Microviews are shaped both by their specific descent from body-defined subsystems and their interconnection possibilities in terms of those subsystems. The connections between late-developed cognitive structures mirror and are guided by the interconnection possibilities of the sensorimotor system first explored and described in the motor programs developed during the sensorimotor period of infancy. This idea, which I name the *channelled description conjecture,* is not a hypothesis posed for experimental confirmation; rather, it is a ground of explanation found useful in making sense of knowledge Miriam developed or failed to develop during her many encounters with geometry during the Intimate Study.

The Power of Ideas and Cognitive Structure

The question of what constrains the possibility of some ideas being powerful and others not so is the crux of the channelled description conjecture. Concrete embodiments of ideas are personally owned because they are not remote from the shaping structures of the soma itself. Experiences such as those of the rods-maze are powerful precisely because they provide the links between late developed structures and the coordinating schemata (the primary integrations of the sensorimotor subsystems achieved during the sensorimotor period). They are important because they link the concrete structures of body knowledge to the more abstract descriptions of external things that blossom in maturity as the cognitive network of the mind.

In strong form, the channelled description conjecture proposes that only those concrete embodiments of ideas linking together descendents of disparate sensorimotor subsystems can be powerful; it claims that such models are the correlate in concrete thought of the correspondence schemata of the sensorimotor period and that the developing coherence of the individual's cognitive structure depends on them. Furthermore, such microviews provide the bases of construction of the more extended cognitive nets of developed minds, functioning as the ancient cities, the geographic capitals of personal importance. In contrast with a goal-oriented attempt to link feelings and thoughts—as on a basis of disparate need systems proposed in ethology, or with a Freudian focus on the conflict between competing, even conflicting homunculi in the mind—the channelled description conjecture proposes a third model of basically disparate structure: the mind is not uniform because the body, the effector agent of the sensorimotor system, is not uniform. This view is better characterized by a pun of Wallace Stevens, "my anima likes its animal," than by either the needs or conflicts of the other mentioned alternatives.

The role assigned to coordinating schemata bears on von Glasersfeld's observation (chap. 2.2) of their role in the naive assumption of the reality of external things. In his view, the correspondence of schemata in diverse modalities leads to the unwarranted inference that we can know about external things themselves. In my view, the later descendents of these coordinating schemata are primary mediators in the construction of cognitive coherence. If the assumption of the knowability of external things is an illusion (as we have all believed since Kant), it is a very strong weakness, one perhaps partly explicable by the coherence creating function that I ascribe to multimodal correspondences.[5]

WHERE DO OUR ENDS BEGIN?

> What makes men happy is loving to do what they have to do.
> This is a principle upon which society is not founded. . . . Helvetius (De L'espirit)

How do we begin to think about the challenge of fitting society's goals to those of learners? How can we instruct while respecting the self-constructive character of mind? Here is a view of the development of goals I derived years ago from Levi-Strauss (1966) and François Jacob (1977), as an extension of the notion of bricolage.

Claude Levi-Strauss (1966) described the concrete thought of not-yet-civilized people as *bricolage,* the activity of the *bricoleur*—a sort of jack-of-all-trades, or more precisely, a committed do-it-yourself man. The core idea is looseness of commitment to specific goals, with the consequence that materials and competencies developed for one purpose are transferable to the satisfaction of alternative objectives:

> The bricoleur is adept at performing a large number of diverse tasks; but, unlike the engineer, he does not subordinate each of them to the availability of raw materials and tools conceived and procured for the purpose of the project. His universe of instruments is closed and the rules of his game are always to make do with "whatever is at hand." . . . in the continual reconstruction from the same materials, it is always earlier ends which are called upon to play the part of means. . . . The bricoleur may not ever complete his purpose but he always puts something of himself into it. (pp. 17, 21)

One can appreciate the opposition of planning (the epitome of goal-directed behavior) and the opportunism of bricolage. Of course, the two are not discontinuous; all activities can be seen as a mixture of the polar tendencies represented

---

[5]For an attempt to apply such ideas directly to educational issues, see Lawler (1989) in press.

here. In addition, the relationship is not directional: there is no reason to suppose that planning is a more nearly perfect form of bricolage. One could easily view planning as a highly specialized technique for solving critical problems whose solutions demand scarce resources.

Bricolage and Cognition

Students of anatomy have named the adaptiveness of structure to alternative purposes *functional lability*. Such functional lability is the essential characteristic of the bricoleur's use of his tools and materials, so bricolage can serve as a metaphor for the relation of a person to the contents and processes of his mind. This emphasizes the character of the processes in terms of human action and can guide us in exploring how a coherent mind could rise out of the disparateness of specific experience. What are the practical advantages of discussing human activity as bricolage in contrast to goal-driven planning?

1. Bricolage presents a human model for the development of objectives; it is a more natural, thus a more fit description of everyday activity than planning.

2. It is more nearly compatible with a view of the mind as a process controlled by contention of multiple objectives for resources than is planning.

3. The most important advantage is a new vision of the process of learning. Bricolage can provide us with an image for the process of the mind under self-construction in these specific respects:

   a. if the resources of the individual's mind are viewed as being like the tools and materials of the bricoleur, one can appreciate immediately how they constrain our undertaking and accomplishing any activity.
   b. not only constraint comes from this set of limited resources; also comes creativity, the production of new things—perhaps not exactly suited to the situation but of genuine novelty.
   c. the mind, if seen as self-constructed through bricolage, presents a clear image of the uniqueness of every person:
      - each will have developed his own history of conceptions and appreciations of situations through which to make sense of the world.
      - each will have his personal "bag of tricks," knowledge and procedures useful in his past.
      - each will have his own set of different, alternative objectives to take up as chance puts the means at his disposal.

If viewed as claims, such statements are not easy to prove. However, they provide a framework for investigating learning that could be valuable by not demeaning human nature through assuming it is more simple than we know to be the case.

Chapter 3.3

Constructivism, Phenomenology, and the Origin of Arithmetic Skills

Ference Marton
Dagmar Neuman
University of Gothenburg, SWEDEN

The aim of this chapter is to point to an important difference between Piagetian constructivism and phenomenological perspectives on learning, and to exemplify this difference in relation to the origin of arithmetic skills. As our point of departure we use Hermine Sinclair's (chap. 2.1) and Ernst von Glasersfeld's (chap. 2.2) discussion of constructivism in relation to early mathematics education.

We begin with a brief reflection on the core meaning of constructivism. Sinclair declares that she uses the term *constructivism* in the sense of "Piagetian constructivism." She explains that constructivism regards individuals' mental or material actions as the main source of their knowledge. This contrasts with the empiricist notion that knowledge originates from "outer reality" through our senses impinging on our minds.

Von Glasersfeld locates constructivism in a wider intellectual context (of rationalism) and refers to the early 18th-century philosopher Giambattista Vico as its chief inspirer. Von Glasersfeld uses the term *radical constructivism* to describe the view that our knowledge is always confined to the world of human experience and that it cannot be judged against the criterion of how well it matches the world as it is; at best our knowledge will fit our activities and our goals. According to von Glasersfeld, not even the most radical form of constructivism denies the existence of a reality independent of human experience. But this "real" reality is out of our reach; it is not available for rational knowledge.

Von Glasersfeld's emphasis on the world-as-experienced as the realm of human thought comes close to phenomenology's locating the foundation of human knowledge in human experience (i.e., Bolton, 1987). In a very fundamental sense, constructivism and phenomenology share the questioning of a

3.3. THE ORIGIN OF ARITHMETIC SKILLS 63

taken-for-granted view of the nature of knowledge as a more or less accurate representation of external reality. There are, however, important differences between these two schools of thought. The difference we wish to elaborate briefly here concerns the fact that although according to constructivism, knowledge is constructed through the individual's material or mental actions; according to phenomenology knowledge is constituted through the internal relation between the knower (subject) and the known (object).

Esoteric as this distinction may seem, it has important implications for how we consider the origin of arithmetic skills. In constructivism, knowledge is a property of the individual. In phenomenology, knowledge reflects both the individual who knows and the world the individual knows about. One of the basic principles of phenomenology purports that all mental acts are directed towards something, something beyond themselves. To think, for instance, is always to think about something, and to perceive is always to perceive something. The individual's experience of the world is a relation between the individual and the world. Thus, there are not two separate entities (individual and world) plus a relation between them; the world-as-experienced is the subject of exploration. The world we know, experience, and think about must necessarily be a world known, experienced, and thought about. This leads to the conclusion that we cannot think of what a world in itself, a world not thought about, would be like. And a known, experienced, thought-about world presupposes a knowing, experiencing, thinking subject. Likewise, the acts of knowing, experiencing, thinking, presuppose a world to know, experience, and think about. It is, however, not a world only inside our heads, it is a world "out there." There is an important educational corollary of this position. Although the world can be experienced in different ways, we can argue that a particular way of experiencing it (or understanding it) is better (in the sense of being deeper, or more efficient, or the like) than another, and therefore that the particular way is educationally desirable.

The claim that there is no independently constituted reality, or that there is no absolute knowledge of transcendental nature, means simply that we cannot produce a finite description of anything. Phenomena are infinitely inexhaustible, as far as possible descriptions of them are concerned. Some modes of experience are shared by a culturally or professionally defined group of people, others of all human beings, yet others of all mammals, and so on. But we can never claim that there are no other ways of seeing a phenomenon than the ones that we know of. In this sense, the world of human beings includes the human beings themselves. An experience always takes someone to do the experiencing and something to be experienced; the experience comprises a relation between them. This is why this school of thought can be called *constitutionalism*.

We now try to link this general line of reasoning to mathematics education. We employ the Piagetian distinction that appears in Sinclair's chapter between empirical and reflective abstraction. The former refers to the abstraction of "the properties of objects" and the latter to the abstraction of "one's own action and reasoning coordination." Logic and mathematics are said to be based on the second kind of abstraction, and we can also think of it as being a higher, second order abstraction in comparison with the first kind of abstraction. Sinclair gives two examples: she argues that "weight" as an object of thought needs both kinds of abstraction, whereas "number" as an object of thought only needs the second kind. Now a phenomenologist might object that thinking about numbers reflects aspects of the world experienced and of the act of experiencing it. Numbers are thus human-world relations. The difference between a constructivist and a phenomenological view can be illustrated by referring to different interpretations of what it takes to develop elementary arithmetic skills.

A PHENOMENOGRAPHIC APPROACH TO RESEARCH

The investigation from which we extract some examples to illuminate this difference sought the origin of arithmetic skills in children's mastery of the numbers 1–10 (in the sense of their grasp of all possible relations between and within these numbers). Difficulties with basic "number facts" have been shown to be the most striking difference between children with mathematics difficulties and those without (Eriksson & Neuman, 1981; Russell & Ginsburg, 1984). We prefer to talk about basic concepts rather than number facts, because we emphasize how children see (or conceptualize) numbers and number relations instead of asking what facts they may be able to retrieve from their long-term memories. This perspective is very much in accordance with the basic tenets of the research approach called *phenomenography* (Marton, 1981) that has been developed in our research group in Gothenburg.

Phenomenography originates from the observation that whatever phenomena people encounter, there seems to be a limited number of qualitatively different ways in which those phenomena are seen, experienced, or conceptualized. The aim of this research is to reveal and describe differing conceptions and differing understandings of the various phenomena in the world around us. Moreover, it is assumed that our way of conceptualizing a certain phenomenon is the most fundamental aspect of our knowledge about and our skills related to that phenomenon.

Although Piagetian constructivism has a clear psychological orientation, the phenomenological framework—to which phenomenography clearly belongs—is more easily reconcilable with didactic considerations. The emphasis in constructivism is on material or mental actions. Phenomenology, however, takes the unity of action and that which is acted on as its point of departure. From this latter stance, descriptions of different ways of dealing with a phenomenon, in relation to the particular competency we aim to develop in an educational setting, follow naturally. The differences can be seen, with regard to a particular competency, as increasingly functional human-world relations.

In the study we draw on here (Neuman, 1987), 103 7-year-old school starters were interviewed about problems involving the number range 1–10. For example:

1. If your teacher has only 2 pencils in her box and there are 9 children wanting to make drawings, how many pencils does she have to get? (2 + __ = 9)
2. If you have only 3 crowns and you want to buy a comic for 7 crowns, how many more crowns do you need? (3 + __ = 7)
3. If your teacher has only 4 pencils in her box and there are 10 children wanting to make drawings, how many more pencils does she have to get? (4 + __ = 10)

If it was not possible to observe overt counting strategies, the children were asked how they had thought out their answers. According to the idea, it might be possible to find strategies that these as yet untaught school starters had spontaneously begun to use that were teachable and would result in the acquisition of the "ten basic concepts."

It was found that the children used four distinctly different strategies to solve these problems correctly. In the two most frequent ways of dealing with the problems, children carried out an analyzing (or structuring), rather than a counting, procedure. The children analyzed a concrete or a visualized number, which was grouped in such a way that it was possible to subitize (i.e., its numerosity could be immediately perceived). In their analysis, they could detect new ways in which the parts could be related to each other or to the whole. The third category was found to be related to the first one and it seemed to be aimed at minimizing the role of counting. The fourth kind of strategy was very rare. In this case, the children relied on a counting procedure. In the present context, this strategy is used to demonstrate differing interpretations originating from a constructivist and a phenomenological (or rather, phenomenographic) perspective.

The First Strategy: Using Finger Numbers

The most efficient and most common way of handling the three problems was to analyze a "finger number" in order to see if it was possible directly to subitize the sum, or in subtraction tasks, the unknown part of the whole. The ways in which the children used this strategy depended on whether they knew these finger numbers or not. If they did not know them, they first had to create them by giving names to each of their fingers.

Amanda, in the middle of solving a problem, described how her fingers insisted on taking part in solving it. Having failed to answer some of the questions, she suddenly said, "Let's see . . . I'll count on my fingers . . . they want me to . . ." (Neuman, 1987, p. 147). This girl did not even know that she had 10 fingers when the fingers "wanted her to use them"; she had to count them first. Still, in the last question she solved, she had already begun to understand how to use them.

Susie solved question 2 in the following way. After giving names to her seven fingers—"1, 2, 3, 4, 5, 6, 7"—starting with the left little finger and ending with the forefinger of the right hand, she said, "There . . . (watching her finger number) . . . now we can start." Having created the finger number, she could begin the process of analysis.

Susie, who neither knew the finger number for 9 nor that for 7, solved question 1 by first creating the finger number for 9. She then solved the problem in the following way:

S: She had to go and get 7 pencils.
I: So, first you counted 9 fingers . . . what did you do after that?
S: First I sort of counted 5 . . . Then I put up 2 . . . Then I put up two more . . . Then I put them down (the last 2 of the 9 fingers) and counted them again like this . . . (counts the 7 fingers on her lips) (Newman, 1987, p. 188).

Susie seemed to understand that if the known part is as small as 2, the other part cannot be subitized. However, as she watched her finger number, she discovered how to solve the problem. She discovered that it was possible to group this part into a subitizable "5 plus something" pattern. Therefore, without consciously knowing why (i.e., without consciously thinking out a way in which the problem could be solved), she "sort of counted 5," (the whole hand) and so put up 2 more fingers, up to the 2 fingers in the known part, which thus became the last fingers in the finger number. Finally, Susie took away the last 2 fingers from the 9, or "put them down," as she said. Thus, she solved a missing addend problem, which is usually experienced as additive (Carpenter & Moser, 1984) by a "take away" strategy. This concrete action has the potential to become the thinking strategy that Resnick (1983) called "choice."

Susie's finger number is similar to the ancient Roman numeral for 9, which was a picture of the hand and 4 fingers, VIIII. Just as this number has to be divided up in the parts VII/II if the V-symbol is not to be split up, Susie's fingers were divided up in order not to split up the hand. The "undivided five" creates a restriction that forces Susie and other children experiencing the "hand" as something that ought to remain undivided to create the idea that missing addends could be solved through a take away strategy.

She had to give names to her fingers in order to know where the finger numbers ended. However, when the finger numbers are known, children can solve the problem in the way Gail did. She just glanced at her fingers and answered "7" to the question "2 + __ = 9." She had given names to all her fingers and illustrated for the interviewer that the ring finger on her right hand was "9" and the forefinger was "7." It was enough for her to look briefly at her concrete row of finger numbers. She had no need to list the sequence of counting words that were the numbers of the fingers in the way Susie did. However, Gail also solved this missing addend task by taking away two instead of adding seven to the two in the known part.

Children soon learn to use an imaginary row of finger numbers in the same way that they use a concrete one. Niklas illustrates how problems can then be solved. Niklas answered the question, "4 + __ = 10," in the following way:

N: Six.
I: She has to fetch 6 . . . how did you know that?
N: How many children did you say . . . ?
I: I said that she had 10 children and 4 pencils.
N: Yes, because you should put 1 to 4 (illustrates to begin with how his fingers form 6 + 4 = 10, but changes this combination into 5 + 5 = 10 through unitizing the thumb of the second hand with the 4 fingers on that hand) and a 5 here (the thumb of the first hand is added to the second hand; thus the finger number 4 | 6 = 10 is formed).
I: ??? (The interviewer neither understands what Niklas says, nor what he does, so she asks again.) Show me . . . you put your fingers . . .
N: There are four like this . . . (the four fingers on his second hand).
I: Yes . . . and then . . . ?
N: Then I take 6 (the thumb on his second hand) . . . I mean then I take one there . . . (Neuman, 1987, p. 195).

Niklas is illustrating how he is able to change his known finger number 5 | 5 = 10 into either 6 | 4 = 10 or into 4 | 6 = 10 in his mind by moving his thumbs between his two hands. He illustrates how his separate fingers have become names (the thumbs, for example, being called "5" and "6"), but also that the finger group 5 + 1 can be called "6" and that the thumb called "6" could also be called "1." His finger numbers are simultaneously ordinal and cardinal, just like Susie's and Gail's. The "5-finger" is the last in the finger group "the hand," the "6-finger" in the group "the hand plus 1," and so forth.

The Second Strategy: Using Doubles

In this case, the whole number is analyzed in order to see if it can be divided up into two similar parts; that is, in order to see if "doubles" can be used. The children using this strategy could, for example, solve question 2 by saying "four," and explaining the question, "How did you get that straight away?" "Because 3 and 3 are 6 . . . That's how I knew. . . ." They could also use doubles in the same way that Niklas did, thus solving question 3 by saying "6" and explaining, "Because if it's 5 and 5 and 6 is 1 more . . . if we take away 1 to 4 . . . that makes 5 . . . 5 . . . (or) 1 from that 6 . . . that makes 5 . . . 5 . . . and that makes 10 . . ." (Neuman, 1987, pp. 203–204).

The Third Strategy: Putting Biggest First

A strategy was observed in which the children counted using neither fingers nor any other concrete material. It was a similar strategy to Resnick's "min" (Resnick, 1983), but it was used for counting forward in addition and in subtraction, both when the pupils counted all and when they counted on. However, practically all the children who employed this strategy either used finger numbers in a concrete or imagined way in order to solve other questions. Alternatively, they used more abstract kinds of strategies where neither finger numbers nor counting were used.

The "counting" these children performed might very well have been an enumeration of "finger names" reflecting the child's thinking about finger numbers. Of course, all children who "thought with their hands" did not tell the interviewer about it. Some children began very early to "think with their hands"—sometimes before they had begun to use concrete finger numbers. That might be because (as one boy explained it), "It's easier to think with your hands than to fold your fingers," after having said that he "thought with his hands." It is indeed rather difficult to fold the little finger, or the hand excepting the little finger.

Why did the children not need any concrete material when they used this strategy? Because they had discovered the same idea that Susie and Gail demonstrated they had found through "the undivided hand": the largest part of the number should be placed first (i.e., its first counting word, or "finger name" should be "one"). To solve question 1, they counted "1, 2, 3, 4, 5, 6, 7, . . . 8, 9 . . . 7 missing." These children realized that 9 comprises two parts, the smallest of which is 2. They intuitively understood that if you begin by enumerating the units in the other, larger part, you reach a stage where you can anticipate when there are only 2 units left. If you pause at this stage in counting, the number word said before the pause tells you what the larger part is. When they solved subtraction tasks of the kind "10 − 7 = __ ," these children counted in exactly the same way: "1, 2, 3, 4, 5, 6, 7, [pause] . . . 8, 9, 10 . . . 3 left," or just "7 [pause] . . . 8, 9, 10 . . . 3 left."

None of the pupils, however, used this counting strategy for counting backwards (e.g., in questions 1 and 2). When they thought backwards, they simply said, like Emelie said in solving question 2, "I thought, if there's 3 pens, then I take 3 away from 7 . . ." The same seemingly abstract way of thinking sometimes occurred in tasks of the kind, "If you have 10 kronor and drop 7, how many are left?" were solved. John, after having answered, "3," explained that he had thought, "10 minus 3." Other children answered that they knew that 7 plus 3 made 10.

How abstract is this kind of thinking, performed as it is by 7-year-old school starters? This question cannot be answered, but an abstract mode of thinking surely does not develop overnight. According to one hypothesis, the finger numbers or doubles first used in a concrete and later in a concrete operational way, together with the strategies in which they are used, eventually become "known number relations," or "concepts of number." As Werner (1973) pointed out, "There is an organic transition from the level of concrete optical number groups to that of purely abstract number. The concrete number groups become stripped of their picture-like properties . . . [There exists a remote] 'number schema' underlying the abstract arithmetical operation" (p. 297).

HOW QUANTITATIVE ASPECTS INHERENT IN THE PROBLEM APPEAR

Studying the ways in which the children dealt with these problems enabled us to observe how certain meanings were constituted (i.e., how certain quantitative aspects inherent in the problems became visible to the children).

When Susie tried to *work out* how many units there were in the unknown part in question 1 "2 + __ = 9," her fingers suddenly revealed their "fiveness," making it possible for her to perceive the larger part by subitizing and to discover the more functional idea that a missing addend could be solved by a take-away strategy. In Niklas' case, the hands illustrated that the thumb could be moved from one hand to the other, so that "5 + 5" became transformed into "6 + 4." And in Amanda's case, as we have seen, her fingers just "wanted to be counted." We can also imagine how the pairs and doubles first revealed themselves for the children who now use them for problem solving, for example, in dice-patterns, in the "2 + 2" legs of animals, or in the two hands. Sometimes, then, children do not consciously reflect on how to solve the problem. They simply explore the quantitative relations inherent in it, and suddenly something stands out as a figure against a background, giving them an intuition of how it might be solved.

Thus, we would argue that children's problem-solving strategies are actually formed when the quantitative relations in the problem become visible to them. That means, we assert, that certain qualities in the unordered world, the world which in some way "asks to be ordered," actually help children to create the required order. Moreover, we maintain that the skills for solving quantitative problems are not counting skills, but rather "seeing" skills. They are *analytic* skills. The children in our study apparently analyzed known numbers (e.g., doubles and finger numbers—real or imagined). In this analyzing procedure, the doubles or finger numbers revealed important qualities to the children. For example, they showed that the left hand ought to be undivided in order to subitize the large part and that it was possible to transform the groups constituted by these doubles or fingers in different ways into new part-whole relations.

The observation that conceptions of phenomena in the world are often arrived at unconsciously has important implications for teaching. If we assume that children themselves construct the knowledge that, for the moment, they feel they need, the role of the teacher cannot be much more than to wait for this moment and then to help them through answering questions, posing new ones, making different kinds of concrete elaborations, and so forth. If, on the other hand, we assume that aspects of the world the children analyze are integral parts of the problem-solving process, it becomes important for the teacher to arrange the kinds of situations where a problem becomes interesting, and also to arrange it in such a way that pupils can become aware of how it could be solved.

However, it is not sufficient to know about the strategies children use and about how they are developed in order to arrange an effective learning environment. It is also important for the researcher to follow what children do with the strategies they use. That is to say, it is important to study whether the strategies have the potential to be transformed into abstract thinking about numbers, or alternatively whether they inhibit a child's ability to create number concepts.

The Fourth Strategy: Double Counting

The school starter interviews provided little evidence of the use of "double counting" in addition and subtraction problems. This strategy, however, was commonly used by the children in a pilot study carried out before the main investigation started (Eriksson & Neuman, 1981, c.f. Neuman, 1987, p. 33). Fifty-nine children from grades 1 through 6 were interviewed, 31 of whom were receiving special education lessons regularly because of their mathematics difficulties. In this study, a most obvious and interesting difference between pupils with specific mathematics difficulties and their classmates was the fact that the former group of children could use practically no problem-solving strategies other than double counting. This group had found no method for handling the added or subtracted number if it was greater than the subitizing range (i.e., the range for number units that we can perceive immediately, usually up to 3). They tried to "hear" its size through enumerating the number words corresponding to the units in it. If the number of words was still not perceptible, they had to count them by keeping track in some way.

These children did not usually double count in the way double counting often is described (i.e., as counting number words with number words: "Three is 1, 4 is 2 . . . ," etc.). Instead, they counted the number words in the added or subtracted term on their fingers. One finger was raised for each word enumerated. In the task 9 − 6, for example, the pupil would raise one finger for each of 8, 7, 6, 5, 4, 3 and recognize that raising the 6th finger meant that counting should stop.

The double counting strategy seemed to be an effective barrier to developing mental calculation and estimation skills. Although children were observed using their fingers both for creating finger numbers and for double counting, the fingers were used in quite different ways in these two strategies. In double counting, the fingers did not replace the words in the way they did when the children used them as finger numbers. In addition, when fingers were used for double counting the parts could not be subitized within the whole, because only the added or subtracted part, and not the whole, was created by the fingers. Furthermore, in double counting, the fingers were used in order to count the words, which were enumerated during an extended period of time. Used as part-part-whole patterns in finger numbers, however, the parts as well as the whole were immediately grasped (without any enumeration of words during an extended period of time) as soon as all the finger numbers were known. Finally, children who used finger numbers quickly discovered the strategy which Resnick (1983) called "choice," because the restriction of the undivided hand forced them to solve a task of the kind presented in question 1 through taking away 2 fingers. Other important differences between the fingers used for double counting and the use of them for creating finger numbers in the latter case include:

- finger numbers were only used for problems within the number range 1–10;
- the use of finger numbers was difficult to observe because the children soon began to use them in the way Gail did, without enumerating the names of the fingers and without touching any fingers, and also in the way Niklas did, just by "thinking with his hands."

The children with mathematics difficulties did not discover the idea of choice, nor develop any further arithmetic skills. For example, they did not learn the multiplication tables, nor did they learn how to carry out division. When these pupils got multiplication tasks to solve, they proceeded as follows. They calculated 7 × 8 (for example) by saying 8 . . . 16 . . . 17, 18, 19, and so on, raising a finger for each word enumerated. However, they soon lost track of the number of times they had enumerated the eight words they counted each time on their fingers. In order to solve a problem like this, they would need to be able to "triple count" in some way.

Even in the highest grades in the compulsory school, such pupils found it necessary to resort to double counting, even when solving simple subtraction and missing addend tasks within the number range 1–10. Their difficulty had less to do with the size of the whole number than with the size of the added or subtracted part; if the first word was not "one," the last word enumerated in a counting procedure did not give the answer. This reflects, of course, our earlier-mentioned finding that children with mathematics difficulties often lack mastery of the numbers 1–10.

"Mastery of the numbers 1–10" refers to a grasp of all the relations between and within those numbers. Hence we prefer the expression "basic concepts" to "basic number facts." When a child can divide up the first 10 positive numbers into two parts, each of these building blocks in the decimal system has become a concept.

How then do children become possessors of number concepts where the 10 numbers constituting our decimal system instantly can be conceived of as divided up into two parts? The answer is that two qualities inherent in the finger numbers together give children the possibility immediately to see them so, first in a concrete way, later in a visualized—or rather "body-anchored"—and finally just in a "known" or "felt" way. These two qualities are (a) the "undivided hand" and (b) the easiness with which the thumbs (and actually also the thumb and the forefinger) can be moved in between the two hands. The 10 "basic concepts" may be thought of in many different ways. For example, 8 can be thought of as $2 \mid 6$, $4 \mid 4$, $3 \mid 5$, and so forth, and also as a part of all greater numbers. As the numbers 2 and 6 are also concepts, 8 thought of as $2 \mid 6$ could further be thought of as $1 \mid 1 \mid 3 \mid 3$ or $2 \mid 2 \mid 3 \mid 1$, and so on. The part-part-whole combinations can be transformed into new ones through adding units to, or subtracting them from, part and whole simultaneously (e.g., $3 \mid 3 = 6 \rightarrow 3 \mid 4 = 7$), or by moving a unit from one part to another (e.g., $3 \mid 3 = 6 \rightarrow 2 \mid 4 = 6$).

All the numbers from 1 to 10 become a tight network of relations within and between numbers when the "10 basic concepts" have been formed. As operations with greater numbers are only variants of operations with the first ten numbers—or operations when they are divided up at the 10-, 100-, 1,000-, and so forth, borders—the path to good arithmetic skills lies open when the 10 basic concepts have been acquired. But if these concepts are not acquired, counting becomes the only way of doing addition, subtraction, and multiplication. The sole exception occurs in the rare cases where the use of doubles is appropriate.

The pupils with mathematics difficulties had not acquired the 10 basic concepts, so they could not solve different kinds of problems (within and outside the number range 1–10) using economical analyzing strategies. Children who had learned the 10 concepts could analyze the quantitative relations inherent in the problem in order to see whether it was possible to reduce the task to one involving a multiple of 10. For example, "$82 - 7 = 75$, because if you first take 2 away from 7 (and 82 simultaneously), you get $80 - 5$, which equals 75." Unlike the use of doubles, the strategy of dividing up the number at the "10 border" has a generality that makes it useful in all kinds of problem solving. It is congruent with the decimal system, as is the use of two hands in the process by which the 10 basic concepts are created.

A CONSTRUCTIVIST ACCOUNT OF DOUBLE COUNTING

Steffe, von Glasersfeld, Richards, and Cobb (1983) described, within a constructivist framework, five increasingly sophisticated types of unit items that children create when they count. The fifth and most advanced of these counting types is supposed to illustrate reflective abstraction (Sinclair, chap. 2.1). One of several criteria set up by Steffe and associates for inferring that a child has reached this level is the ability to count counting words: "We infer this final accomplishment when the child spontaneously uses 'double counting' . . . for example, if the problem is 'to count on seven from nine' and the child says, '9 . . . 10 is 1, 11 is 2, 12 is 3 . . . 16 is—sixteen" (p. 43).

There is an apparent inconsistency between Steffe and colleagues' reference to double counting as a concrete manifestation of the most advanced counting type, and Eriksson and Neuman's (1981) observation of double counting as the dominant strategy used by children with mathematics difficulties. If, however, we take into account the Piagetian approach described by Sinclair, we can understand that the most important aim of constructivist research is to discover how more complex forms of thinking develop. A child who is able to reflect on the counting words, which have been created as "unit items" replacing more concrete "unit items," carries out a quite complicated cognitive operation, an operation indicating that the child has become a "counter of abstract unit items," that is, a child who has reached the level where "reflective abstractions" become possible. As Cobb (1986a, p. 142) explained, the child can "anticipate the conceptual result of activities that could be carried out" or "has the ability to reflect on potential activity." Double counting is not the only measure of whether a child has become an "abstract counter." The child must also be to "count on." This means that the word *seven* stands for a collection of unitary items. The children must know that if, for example, the seven marbles denoted by the word *seven* were to be counted, each of them would be associated with a specific numeral. We agree with the conclusions of constructivist researchers, these qualities in children's ways of solving problems point to their ability to carry out quite demanding cognitive operations (i.e., they show that their ways of thinking have become a somewhat more abstract quality).

However, if the aim of the research is to identify ways of grasping part-part-whole relations between the 10 basic numbers in the least cognitively demanding way (i.e., in such an way that these numbers can easily be divided up in order directly to perceive part-part-whole relations within larger numbers), then double counting can be seen to be an uneconomical strategy. It is a barrier to the development of abstract thinking of number. This does not mean, of course, that children who use double counting as their one and only strategy have less cognitive capacity than those who have found other strategies. It simply means that they have not discovered a way of conceiving part-part-whole number relations with the potentiality later to develop into abstract thinking of numbers.

CONCLUSIONS

Our aim in this chapter has been to demonstrate how Piagetian constructivist and phenomenological perspectives, despite their similarities, lead to quite different interpretations of the origin of arithmetic skills. It is critical to note that constructivism focuses on the learner's material or mental actions as the source of knowledge, whereas phenomenology focuses on the constitution of knowledge through the learner's experience of the world. Piagetian constructivism sees knowledge as something created by the individual. Phenomenology looks at knowledge as a relation between the subject (the individual) and the object (the world). We have tried to show that experiences of quantitative aspects of the world from which arithmetic skills develop describe both the act of experiencing and the phenomenon experienced. For instance, the "fiveness" of the fingers on one hand exists both in the act of experiencing the fiveness and in the fingers on the hand whose fiveness is experienced.

The differential emphasis of constructivism and phenomenology is also reflected in the different "knowledge interests" they may best serve. Although Piagetian, and in this case also radical constructivism, may provide us with an explanation of how increasingly complex mental acts are arrived at, empirically oriented phenomenology (here represented by the phenomenographic research approach) seems to lend itself more readily to educational aims. Its focus is on increasingly functional relations between individual and a specific phenomenon. The point of reference for the description is the particular competence that children are supposed to arrive at, rather than their general intellectual development. The differing interpretations that derive from the two perspectives were illustrated by looking at how the double counting strategy used for solving simple arithmetic problems is considered within the two frameworks.

These differences between the constructivist and the phenomenological perspectives should not blind us to the fact that they have some important things in common. Both deny empiricist notions of taken-for-granted knowledge, independent of and external to human beings, for example. We have also suggested that constructivism and phenomenology are complementary to each other in several respects. To explore these complementarities further would seem well worthwhile.

ACKNOWLEDGMENTS

Amadeo Giorgi of the Saybrook Institute, San Francisco, and one of the editors of this book, Leslie P. Steffe, have given extremely valuable comments on an earlier version of this chapter.

Paul Ramsden, University of Melbourne, has made the most heroic and competent efforts to bring this chapter into a reasonably comprehensible form.

The final version of the chapter was written while Ference Marton was a visiting professor at the Centre for the Study of Higher Education, University of Melbourne.

The research reported here was financed by the Swedish National Board of Education and the Tercentenary Fund of the Bank of Sweden.

Discussion Chapters: Learning

EDITORS' NOTE

As a preliminary note, we would like to provide the reader with additional background information about the origin of the discussion chapters and the role of the abstracter-recorder pairs in these discussion groups. The International Panel that planned the work of the action group made the epistemological chapters available to all of the authors who wrote elaboration chapters prior to their preparation. However, the epistemological chapters were sent to the authors of the discussion chapters after their work had been submitted, as a part of a general mailing to all of the registered participants of the action group in June 1988. The intention of the International Panel was to solicit discussion chapters that were a sample of their ongoing work in early childhood mathematics education without regard to the particular epistemological commitments of the investigators. This diversity was sought in an effort to maximize the possibility that all participants in the action group would reflect on their own world views and make their assumptions concerning knowledge, learning, communication, and environment as explicit as possible. Through intensive social interaction in an international context, the hope was that each discussion group would create a learning environment in which cognitive conflict would emerge among the discussants and the steps taken toward its resolution would begin to create a consensual domain of experience.

Each abstracter-recorder pair was responsible for preparing a written record of these discussions, and we present their analyses as the opening chapter of each set of discussion chapters to establish a context for those that follow. Each abstracter-recorder pair established their own ways of working together, which explains the difference in the authorship style. As such, Charlene DeRidder offered an independent analysis of the discussion group on learning, and some of her most salient points are included. Although her comments were intended for the discussion group on learning, they are applicable to the five other groups as well.

The issue "Is there a body of mathematical knowledge all students should learn?" emerged because it has deep roots in the practice of mathematics education world-wide. This issue pervaded all of the discussion groups because it is intimately connected with the assumption that there is a perceived tradition of school mathematics that all students must come to know in the way intended by society. In addition, several issues specific to the discussion group on learning were identified, such as how to identify when learning has occurred, what tasks and constraints and forms of presentation might encourage learning, what schemes children bring to the setting that they might use in mathematical learning, and how we know when to facilitate the child's move to a level of higher cognition. These issues illustrate that the constructivist approach to mathematical knowledge and its learning is a growing source of perturbation in the field of mathematics education and the modifications and reorganizations engendered by this perturbation is a fertile area of investigation.

Chapter 3.4

Children Learning Mathematics

Brenda Denvir
University of London, UNITED KINGDOM

The question, "What do we mean by mathematical learning?" which lies at the heart of any discussion of mathematical learning, was not explicitly mentioned in the Learning Discussion Group. The answer depends on what we mean by "doing mathematics" and is culturally dependent, with different times and places yielding a variety of norms; recitation of Euclid, practical use of sextant, bookkeeping, and computer modelling of statistical functions. "Doing mathematics" in a late 20th-century technological society has involved a shift from earlier emphases on the rote learning of standard procedures. This is rooted in several interconnected phenomena. First, there is a need to be able to handle the new technology. In addition, the rapidly changing nature of novel systems requires flexibility and adaptability in workers and consumers. Moreover, developments in epistemology over the last half-century call into question the effectiveness of purely procedural learning. In the multicultural arena afforded by ICME-6, we quickly become alert to cultural differences. Two examples serve to indicate the huge potential variations in perceptions of "learning mathematics" in the contemporary world.

- In some subcultures children have unrestricted access to microcomputers and calculators at school and at home and computers are used in most parental occupations. Whereas in other subcultures neither pupils, parents, or teachers use or ever expect to use such devices.
- Many eastern cultures place a fundamental importance on the community, while most western societies emphasize the individual. Constructivism, with its central notion of individuals as agents in their own learning fits more easily with the latter that with the former.

It is interesting to reflect on possible meanings that we might ascribe to this second example in which one theory of learning appears to serve better in some cultures than in others. Does it mean that children in different cultures learn differently? Does it mean that the ways of describing how children learn differ from one culture to another? Or is it a complex combination of factors: what is believed about children's learning and what is regarded as authoritative influence how children learn, because these beliefs influence the way children are taught and, in a wider sense, the overall environment in which mathematics, learning, and pedagogy are perceived? Different cultures have different understandings of what is meant by doing, learning, and teaching mathematics and will, consequently, pursue different research programs. These variations provide potentially rich arenas for future investigations into the learning of mathematics. The view that I present must, necessarily, be informed by my participation in British culture.

A constructivist view of what is meant by learning mathematics is, in Steffe's words, the "accommodation of schemas" in which existing mental schemas are modified in, or as a result of, their use. This language is, of course, metaphorical. We have no access to these schemas, but infer changes in cognition from changes that are observed in the behavior of the learner. The notion of "scheme" is useful. It allows us to discuss what we experience, namely that learning is difficult to recognize because so much of teaching produces certain changes in behavior without apparent "internal" change, that is change in the "scheme."

There is a growing corpus of empirical research findings that support a radical constructivist model of learning. These focus on the strategies used by children. The implications of the recognition that children use strategies that they have not been taught is far-reaching and has initiated cognitive shifts for many mathematics educators. Recognition of this phenomenon is culture-dependent. It will not be found where children are not free to invent their own strategies and it is unlikely to be found where teachers or researchers do not already regard children as agents in their own learning.

In the constructivist paradigm, the strategies that children have available are taken as evidence of their "schemes." Increasing abstraction in the strategies is taken to indicate accommodation of the scheme, which is learning. In addition, invariance in the order of acquisition of strategies across children is taken as evidence of developmental progression in learning. As a by-product of this research, numerous tasks have been devised and posed with specific constraints (e.g., Ainly) so that they will give insight into children's understanding. The prospect of more work of this nature, of the cataloging and ordering of strategies to generate a complex psychological mapping of the development of mathematical concepts clearly challenges and excites researchers. Moreover, the devised tasks are potentially valuable in teaching and learning. Valuable work might well be carried out in observing children's responses within a rich and varied classroom learning environment, as well as within the clinical interview. In addition to gathering information about children's understanding, the demands that the tasks make on the children may be carefully analyzed in order to select those that relate to children's current understanding and thus maximize the learning potential.

Some of the questions, then, that were being addressed in the discussion group related to *assessment* and *progression:*

1. What is the child's understanding? How might we infer children's mathematical understanding?
2. What are the most likely developments in the child's understanding?

The research programs generated by these questions involve longitudinal studies collecting detailed observations of children's responses to carefully defined tasks. A number of mathematical areas were specifically mentioned in future research plans and these included spatial thinking, measurement, money, continuation of the work on number, and the relationship between money and number.

Although these questions relate to areas of mathematical understanding in which comparatively little research has been undertaken, they fall within both a constructivist framework and the existing research paradigms. However, new perspectives and new issues were raised that may require new paradigms. Several concerns fall into this category. First, the importance of children and engagement with the learning activities. This is frequently dismissed as a "side issue," a necessary condition of learning but in the less important affective domain than the cognitive domain and not, therefore, worthy of deeper exploration. Similarly, the effect of new technology within the learning environment may yield deeper insights about the nature of thinking and knowledge, possibly more for its catalytic than its utilitarian function. Although these points were made without reference to a theoretical model of learning, Marton and Neuman (chap. 3.3) present a different view, rooted in a constitutionalism and, more, in what Marton terms "phenomenography."

Marton and Neuman do not focus on progression, but instead examine children's "perceptual capabilities," that is ways of "seeing" a particular phenomenon. They link particular perceptions of phenomena with the ability to effect an economical solution. Their examples of "finger numbers" indicate how solutions to some number problems are self-evident to children who are able to represent them in a particular manner. I find exciting the notion of examining children's perceptual capabilities and how they represent specific situations for themselves. In turn, the way that individuals perceive particular phenomena is a function of their intention in relation to that phenomenon. This idea of intention as crucial to thinking is similar to Murphy's (1988) notion of purpose in science education. The importance of this factor in the teaching and learning of mathematics is almost universally unrecognized. The teacher or educator who has a notion of the mathematics to be learned has a very different intention from that of the learner. Whereas the teacher's intention is for the child to learn the mathematics, children will either be task focused when their intention is related to solution or exploration of the task, or be behaviorally focused when their intention is to please the teacher, get a good mark, or avoid recrimination. Attention is given to the need for engagement in order to stimulate mathematical thinking, but rarely, if ever, to the implications of the difference in perspective and intention between the child and the teacher.

Teachers, who have already grasped the concepts that they aim to teach, see the learning tasks as examples or embodiments of the concepts and thus as a coherent part of a learning progression. They are likely to believe this even if they, themselves, do not perceive the progression. Asked, for example, to describe what is being studied, the teacher is likely to name a mathematical topic such as subtraction or volume. In contrast, children remain in the dark about what, in the teacher's view, is the true meaning of the activities. Because they do not already have the concept, they see the task not as an example of that concept, but as an end in itself, arbitrarily selected by the teacher and not, in general, located in their own world of purpose and meaning. Asked what they are doing, they are more likely to blame a particular attribute or feature of the task than its mathematical classification. Many of the elements of the task itself will evoke different meanings for children and the teacher and also for different children. In the children's perception of the task, two possible types of intention may be distinguished. One is related to the problem and the other to the method of solution. Presence of the first type of intention is crucial. Unless the children have a problem (whether or not it is the one that the teacher intended), they cannot attempt a solution and are likely to adopt a behavioral intention. For children who do perceive a problem, a range of possibilities for a solution exists, from the intentional use of a known strategy to exploratory tactics in which the "perceptual capabilities" described by Marton & Neuman may suggest a solution.

This notion of intention or purpose seriously calls into question our ability to assess children's mathematical thinking, for they are not, in general, playing the mathematical game that we would like to suppose. First we must grasp their intention, use that to determine what their understanding of the task is and only then consider what this might reveal about their grasp of mathematical abstractions.

In my view, although the phenomenographic position is not capable of providing a complete model of children's learning of mathematics, it does offer valuable insights that are in addition to the radical constructivist analysis. Just as mathematics is not about either developing abstract ways of thinking or about functional strategies, but about both, so an appreciation of number is not about either double counting or a perceptual grasp of number bond but involves both of these. Perhaps it is our urge to simplify and our failure to value the multifaceted nature of learning activities and of mathematical concepts that ultimately impoverishes children's mathematical thinking.

The "fragility" of children's scientific knowledge that Murphy (1988) described also pervades children's learning of mathematics. For example, we find children who appear to "understand" area when asked to calculate the area of a rectangle whose sides can be measured in whole centimeters and who can compare two surfaces by eye when they have a purpose in that action, but who, in every other context, behave as if there were no such word or concept. In contrast to this "fragility," Murphy emphasizes the need for "robust" knowledge. Two essential types of "rich links" seem necessary for the construction of robust knowledge. The first type is beautifully exemplified in the chapters of Lawler (chap. 3.2) and Sinclair (chap. 2.1) and relates to both perceiving the same phenomena in different ways and recognizing similar features in different phenomena. There is an element of both of these in Lawler's "intimate study" and the "surprising confluence of results where none was expected" experienced by Miriam. Both, too, are potentially present in Sinclair's notion of "actions seen from the inside and the outside" and the notion of "complementary roles." In the question of the missing addend word problems investigated by Neuman (1987), it may well be true that the most efficient strategy lies in "seeing" the "finger numbers" and the most abstract in double counting, but the most robust mathematical knowledge must surely arise from the awareness of both these possibilities and the connection between them. Marton and Neuman (chap. 3.3) describe the children whose only strategy was double counting. It would be of interest to discover if there are also children who only have "finger numbers" and what implications this has for their handling of number.

The second type of rich linking that appears important for constructing robust mathematical knowledge lies at a more global level. It involves the connections that need to be established in the learners' minds between their own worlds of meaning and purpose, the learning tasks that the teachers devise or select and the knowledge that is created because it is used in performing tasks. There is a need for these links to become explicit to the learners and for them not only to develop a capability, but also to know what capabilities they possess and their potential uses.

A number of future directions commend themselves as a result of the Budapest discussions. First, more work needs to be carried out in uncovering children's worlds and their perceptions of these worlds. Marton's proposals for continued investigation of children's perceptual capabilities are most attractive and seem to necessitate careful collaboration between psychologists and mathematics educators. However, an adequate exploration will require a broad-based empathy with children and their worlds of meaning rather than a narrow concentration of what is seen as "mathematical." Again, it is important to consider the pedagogical implications of Marton and Neuman's work in that the constructivist stance suggests that effective learning is unlikely to be achieved simply by "telling" children what is the "best way of seeing." In addition, considerable work needs to be done in devising rich learning activities. The recognition of different purposes or intentions on the part of children and their teachers suggests that we need to develop greater skill in planning engaging and meaningful tasks that do not merely "demonstrate" a mathematical concept to children who already "have" it, leaving others in the dark. Challenging tasks are needed that provoke children to make refinements of their mental and physical actions and are also capable of stimulating their perceptual capabilities. Such work relies on understanding children's perceptions of their own worlds and also on a careful analysis of the mathematics that we would like children to know. The specific mathematical areas mentioned in Budapest, money and measurement, and the difficult topic of spatial thinking will provide particular insights about children's learning in which children's perceptions and task design might well be incorporated. Finally, I am struck by the "levels" at which one might characterize variations in mathematical thinking. At the "micro-level" of individual psychology and personal style, the work of investigating children's strategies continues, and I hope the work on children's perceptions will expand. However there are two other levels of interest: the "macro-level" of the culture and the "mini-level" of the curriculum. Careful cross-cultural collaboration in comparing performance across tasks could shed valuable light on variations in learning. The interpretation of differences would require thoughtful comparisons of the culture, its assumptions, and the context of schooling. Curricular effects might well be addressed through documentation of the opportunities that new technology presents to children, the effects of these, and also what this tells us about the potential of children whether or not they have access to the new technology.

In considering cross-cultural differences and the different notions that arise within the variety of views of teaching and learning, I am struck by the analogy that may be drawn between what children do when they are learning mathematics and what researchers do in developing models of children learning mathematics. Both are enriched by making connections between different perspectives. As in the paintings of Picasso, the ability to retain the integrity of separate perspectives yet hold them creatively together is full of potential for a greater depth of meaning and communication.

Chapter
3.5

Playing Games and Learning Mathematics

Janet Ainley
University of Warwick, UNITED KINGDOM

This chapter is based on work with the Primary Mathematics Project, led by Professor Richard Skemp at Warwick University. It focuses on one aspect of the project; the inclusion of games in a mathematics curriculum for young children. An attempted rationale for the use of games for fostering mathematical learning is followed by more detailed accounts of the mathematical processes that children use, and how these may be encouraged through games. Finally, games are considered as a means of assessing children's learning, and understanding their thinking strategies.

WHY PLAY GAMES IN MATHEMATICS?

Although there are many articles in mathematics education journals about games, most of these are concerned with descriptions of particular games, and few authors attempt to address the issue of why games should be included in the mathematics curriculum. Paul Ernest (1986) reviewed some research into the use of games and uses the results of this to construct an argument for effectiveness of games as a vehicle for teaching mathematics. Ernest claimed that "games teach mathematics effectively" in four ways; by providing reinforcement and practice of skills, providing motivation, helping the acquisition and development of concepts, and developing problem-solving strategies.

The first two of these seem unequivocal: games can provide motivation for many children, and within a game, routine calculations are often repeated many times. Considerable facility with numbers can be acquired in this way, as most darts players demonstrate. In describing some studies of the effects of including games in the mathematics curriculum, Ernest (1986) claimed, "It is quite likely that this success is related to the positive effect of games on motivation and attitudes reported in some of the studies" (p. 4).

Although it is undeniable that games can provide motivation, focusing heavily on this feature may in the long term have detrimental effects on children's attitudes to mathematics. Games are often offered as a reward for those who have finished their work; the hidden messages are clearly that real mathematics cannot be fun, and that games are not difficult work. Incidentally, as a result, those pupils who least need extra motivation get most of it, and those who need the most get the least.

The second two claims (that games help the acquisition and development of concepts and develop problem-solving strategies) seem less well founded. Ernest supported them by referring to research involving particular games designed to force awareness of specific concepts or the use of certain strategies. Many games that have an ostensible mathematical content do not contain either of these features, and so it would be misleading to make these claims for all mathematical games. Ernest acknowledged this in his closing statement.

> The evidence strongly suggests that if games are to contribute to the effective teaching of mathematics they must be fully incorporated into the mathematics curriculum. During the teaching of a specific topic, or directed at a particular objective, games should be
>
> 1. selected on the basis of the desired objectives
> 2. incorporated into the teaching programme.
>
> Used in this way mathematical games have a vital part to play in aiding pupils' achievement and success in mathematics. (p. 5)

Ernest wrote, at several points, in terms of games teaching mathematics, which is misleading; at most, games can help children to learn mathematics. This is not simply a linguistic quibble. If teachers use games in the hope that the games will teach their pupils particular pieces of mathematics they will be sadly disappointed. Children will certainly learn from playing games, but what they learn will vary enormously, just as what children learn when working from a textbook varies. A well-designed game may create a good environment for learning some mathematics, but it will not ensure that the children learn the mathematics, and more important it will not replace the teacher. The teacher's role in stimulating learning during the playing of a game and monitoring the learning that is going on is vital. Having said this, games can have a useful role in encouraging children to work independently of their teacher in some respects, and this point is expanded later.

In the Primary Mathematics Project, games are selected, and indeed designed, on the basis of desired objectives and incorporated into the teaching program, but the rationale for doing this is based largely on two aspects of games not considered by Ernest. Skemp (1979) used the term *intelligent learning*, as opposed to rote or memory learning, to denote learning based on relational understanding. Because rote learning may initially produce the best results (i.e., red ticks and adult approval) for the minimum effort, many children rely on trying to learn mathematics "off by heart." Playing mathematical games discourages rote learning, because a player never knows in advance what the situation will be when she takes her turn. Even if there is no random element, such as the throw of a die or the turn of a card, in the game the moves made by other players create a wide variety of situations, and it would be impossible to rote learn the best move for each situation that may occur. Children who learn some of their mathematics by playing games will soon experience the benefits of intelligent learning and relational understanding.

Reading, writing, and mathematics form a large part of the curriculum for children in the early years of schooling. When children learn to read, they can begin straight away to use reading in the same way, and for the same purposes, as adults do; they can read for pleasure, to get information and so forth, and there is a wide range of children's books and comics designed so that they can do just that. The same is true to some extent of writing. Children write for their own pleasure, to communicate with others, to label their possessions, and so forth. When children learn mathematics, however, there is very little that they can do with it, except to complete exercises set by someone else. Certainly most children will have a few everyday contexts in which they may use some mathematics (spending pocket money, compiling football league tables, making models), but these are fairly few and far between, and in general the mathematical content is at a low level. Some children will investigate bits of mathematics simply for the pleasure of doing it, but there is very little that compares to comics. Many commercial mathematics schemes attempt to bring some realism into the curriculum by including everyday problems that mathematics can help to solve, such as carpeting a room or paving the area round a swimming pool, but in general these are problems from an adult's, not from a child's world.

Games are one way of providing the mathematical equivalent of children's books and comics. In a game there is a context for using some mathematics that you have learned, and that context is real for children because they can engage with it and the outcome matters to them. This has very little to do with the reality of everyday life. Some games may model everyday situations, but the appeal of adventure games such as Dungeons and Dragons indicates that fantasy games can be equally engaging.

In adult life perhaps the most common use of mathematics is for making predictions. The predictions may range from the apparently trivial (if I buy those new shoes, I won't have enough money left to pay the phone bill; if I leave at 2:15 P.M. I'll have enough time to go to the bank before I catch the train) to very detailed technical calculations used by engineers and scientists. What they have

3.5. PLAYING GAMES AND LEARNING MATHEMATICS

in common is that people are using some mathematical knowledge to help them predict the outcome of events. Getting the prediction wrong may have more or less serious consequences, depending on the context, but that is exactly what makes getting such predictions right satisfying. It gives you control over your environment. However, because wrong predictions about things that matter will inevitably have some unwelcome consequences, children are rarely given genuine opportunities to use their mathematics in this way. In a mathematical game, many situations will occur when it is clearly a valuable strategy to make predictions (based on mathematical knowledge) about the result of a particular move. Getting the prediction right gives the same feeling of satisfaction and control, but making a wrong prediction may mean that you lose the game. What hangs on the accuracy of your prediction is important, but not dangerous.

WHAT MATHEMATICAL PROCESSES DO CHILDREN USE IN GAMES?

The games included in the Primary Mathematics Project were almost all specially designed, because few existing games could be found that provided contexts for children to use particular mathematical skills. Also many apparently mathematical games, in which a winning move depends on getting a piece of mathematics right, depend on rules or rewards unconnected with the mathematics. For example, "if you throw a 6, you get another turn," "if you get three sum right, you can add a brick to your wall." Although mathematics is the central feature of these games, some external arbitrator is needed to judge whether each move is right or wrong; there is nothing in the structure of the game to enable players to check if they are right, or to help them correct a mistake. In contrast to this, the project games aim to have rules that reflect the underlying mathematics. When children play these games, they reinforce and enrich their understanding of mathematical content and skills, and also naturally use mathematical processes. The rest of this section illustrates this use of processes with reference to a particular game, which is described briefly later, although the issues raised are based on similarities in the behavior of children playing a wide variety of games (see example in Fig. 1).

Predicting and Testing

In *Crossing*, players need to make decisions at several different points. In order to decide whether or not to move a particular counter, the player must be able to work out where it will land, because landing on a shaded square means returning to the start. It may be necessary to make three such calculations in order to choose the best move for a particular throw of the die. Initially, young children will physically move the counter, and count out the move, to see where it will

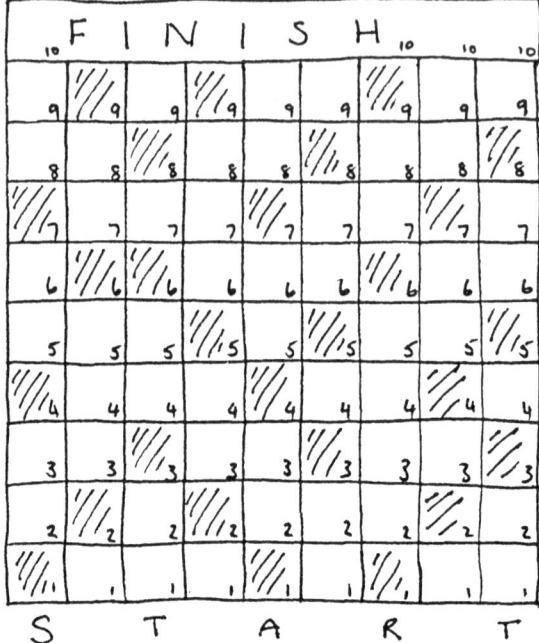

FIG. 1. Crossing. This game is for 2 or 3 players. It uses the board illustrated. Each player has 3 counters, and chooses three 'lanes' on the board in which they are to move. A 1–6 die is used.

The object of the game is to move all 3 of your counters to the finish. When a player throws the die, she may move any of her counters forward by that number of squares. The shaded squares are 'no parking' zones; if a counter lands on one of these at the end of a move, the counter must be returned to the start. The exact number must be thrown for each counter to land on finish.

land. Adding the simple rule that once a counter is touched it must be moved, transforms *Crossing* and other board games into games of prediction. Equivalent rules may be devised to have the same effect on card games, or other games that use concrete apparatus. In purely oral games, a player may be committed to standing by the first thing he or she says.

Another point at which children often make spontaneous use of predicting is when their counters get close to the finish. There is a rule that they must throw the exact number to land on the finish (i.e., row 10), children with counters on rows 7, 8, or 9 begin to say things like, "I need a 2 to finish," "I want to throw a 1." The focus of their attention moves from predicting the effect of a throw that has been made, to predicting the best throw for a particular situation. These predictions are, of course, tested when the desired throw is made, and the counter is moved. But they are often also tested in a more abstract way, by reference to number facts: "I need a 2 because 8 and 2 make 10." Incidentally, this change of focus also begins to undermine the deeply held conviction that throwing large numbers is best, and a 6 is best of all.

Conjecturing

Games like *Crossing* in which players must make predictions also encourage conjecturing: fixing on an idea to work with, and seeing how far it will work. Within a game it is easy to change to a different strategy if the first is unproductive. In most games it is only possible to make partial conjectures about the effects of any one move, because the situation for your next move is unknown. Your opponent's move may have an effect on your position, or there may be a random element, such as the throw of a die or the turn of a card. In other classroom situations, children are often unwilling to try out ideas unless they are sure that they are correct, and so do not naturally make conjectures. They may associate changing a conjecture with admitting to making a mistake. Within a game conjecturing is both natural and safe; games may provide opportunities to talk explicitly about the process of conjecturing.

Generalizing

It is not feasible to rote learn the best moves for all possible situations in a game; thus it is natural to begin to devise generalized strategies for playing a particular game. In *Crossing* there is no obvious strategy that is likely to improve your chances of winning, but some children try out different possibilities. One group of 6-year-olds decided that a good strategy might be to try to get one counter to the finish before moving any of the others. This lead one of them to make another kind of generalization. Two of children threw 4 on their first turn, and the third, Claire, threw 3. When one of the others threw 6 on the next turn, and got one counter home, Claire turned to the researcher and asked, "Is there a 7 on that die?" Claire seemed to have moved away from focusing on the numbers that were actually thrown, to looking for number combinations to 10 to get home in two moves.

In other games in the project, which have rules that reflect a mathematical structure, these strategies may be in the form of mathematical generalizations. For example, there are several card games based on rummy, which use cards with numbers on them. In these, players often develop general strategies about cards that are good to keep, and those you should always discard. In *Halves and Doubles Rummy* the larger odd numbers are of no use, and should be discarded, but low even numbers are always worth keeping, because they may be used as either halves or doubles. In *Multiples Rummy*, prime numbers (or "nasty numbers," as one group called them) always end up in the discard pile.

Checking and Justifying

Within the traditional classroom situation, there is little incentive for children to check their own work if they know that ultimately their work will be marked by their teacher. Typically teachers encourage children to check their own results, but young children find this difficult to do, and can often see little point in doing it. In the context of a game, there is a clear purpose for checking your own conjectures; once a move has been made, it cannot be undone and may have unwelcome consequences. In board games like *Crossing*, the "if you touch it you must move it" rule mentioned earlier, introduces a situation in which a teacher may want to talk explicitly about the value of checking, and discuss ways in which checking might be done.

Cheating is something that children feel strongly about, so there is also a strong incentive for players to check each other's mathematics, challenging moves that they think break the rules. If this aspect of playing games is encouraged, games can provide a meaningful context for discussion about mathematics, where clear communication and being able to justify your thinking to another player have a real purpose. However, this will not be the case if the players need to turn to the teacher for a decision about who is correct. It is important that the game contain an element enabling players to check; for example, by counting out a move on the board or using concrete apparatus. This will have the double advantage of encouraging children to have confidence in their own thinking and facilitating independent working that frees the teacher to spend time watching and listening.

WHAT CAN TEACHERS LEARN FROM GAMES?

Many of the teachers who have used the materials produced by the Primary Mathematics Project have been enthusiastic about the children's reactions to the activities, and also about what they as teachers have gained from using them. Working with the project materials means that the classroom must be organized so that the children are in small groups, and the teacher is able to give her attention to one group at a time. Teachers at one school called this "quality time," and soon came to feel that the value of these sessions outweighed the hard work involved in organizing the classroom to make them possible.

Undisturbed time with a small group means that new concepts can be introduced effectively, and the chance to observe the groups closely enables the teacher to assess children's progress and understanding. The difficulty of making judgments about children's understanding from the results of written, and even oral tests is well researched. In contrast to this, when children are playing games their thinking is much more transparent. Their actions reveal much about their thinking strategies. Observing a group playing *Crossing*, it becomes clear which children are using counting on to predict the effect of a particular move. Even if the rules prohibit moving the counter, fingers and eyes move. As one visitor to the project remarked, "It's as though their little brains are there on the table." In the context of playing a game, it is easy and natural for a teacher to question children about their thinking (Why did you chose that move?, Could you have played a different card?) without the potentially intimidating atmosphere of a more obvious assessment.

Chapter 3.6

Young Children's Concept of Measure

Patricia F. Campbell
University of Maryland, USA

The conceptualization of number is an integral component of mathematical learning in early childhood. However, as noted by Vergnaud (1987), the concept of number can be interrelated with the concept of measure. Number in its most general form is quantity. What distinguishes number from sequencing, as in rote counting, is a unit of measure distinct from a lexical item. When a child assigns a number to a collection of discontinuous items via counting, the units that the child perceives are the individual items in the collection. For a set of discrete items, children learn to determine quantity by the number of unit entities, regardless of their size or relative position. Although young children may differ in terms of the type of unit they are capable of counting (Steffe, von Glasersfeld, Richards, & Cobb, 1983), it has been proposed that in the discrete domain the processes of comparing and transforming, of incrementing and decrementing units, have a major influence on the development of numerical abstraction (Cooper, 1984; Sinclair, 1987b; Starkey & Gelman, 1982). But in addition to discrete counting, measuring may also serve as a precursor to early systems of reasoning (Sinclair, 1987b). Furthermore, the process of measuring can occur at differing conceptual levels.

In the most general case of measurement, quantity is a function of both the number and size of the units; in addition, different units may be utilized when determining the measure of a fixed quantity. If the size of a unit of measure is changed, then the number of units associated with an invariant quantity is also changed. Davydov (1982) noted this when he characterized a quantity as not having "numerical determinacy" until a unit of measurement had been identified. In the context of continuous quantity, across tasks, the young child may experience a varying unit being assigned to a fixed, invariant amount yielding a varying number. These two variations do not occur in isolation from each other. Although it may not be conceptualized by the child, the number of units is always in inverse proportion to the size of the unit being used. Moreover, the traditional evaluation for measuring a fixed continuous quantity with a particular unit assesses whether the child maintains the invariance of the size of the unit as it is iterated, while encompassing the totality of the dimension to be measured. Therefore, within a measuring task, the young child must contend with maintaining, positioning, and counting identical units while, across measuring tasks, which may or may not involve the same quantity, the identity of the unit may be inconsistent. Thus the effect of unit transformation in a continuous domain is very complex.

A CONCEPT OF MEASUREMENT

Piaget (Piaget, Inhelder, & Szeminska, 1960) defined measurement as follows: "To measure is to take out of a whole one element, taken as a unit, and to transpose this unit on the remainder of a whole: measurement is therefore a synthesis of subdivision and change of position" (p. 3). Although young children do not possess a sophisticated flexibility in defining and iterating arbitrary units of measure, and only gradually come to appreciate the quantitative power of part-whole relationships, even preschool children are able to construct sharing procedures that reflect their understanding of quantitative invariance. In that sense, young children do display an informal knowledge of measure.

A recent study by Miller (1984) reveals much about young children's interpretation of measure in varying domains. Miller assumed that spontaneous measurement procedures would be most likely to occur in sharing contexts because a sharing task requires a subsequent assessment of equivalent quantity. Children aged 3, 5, 7, and 9 years were presented with materials that represented a "pretend snack" that had been equally apportioned among three, four, or five place settings: namely, containers of counters ("candies"), strips of clay ("spaghetti"), clay square regions ("fudge"), and glasses of colored water ("kool-aid"). The children were then presented with stuffed turtles, always one less turtle than the number of place settings, and were told that one turtle was unable to attend the party. The children were asked to help the turtles by dividing the extra portion because the turtles did not know how to do so fairly—although the turtles would recognize if one of them received more than the other. Supporting devices such as rulers, measuring cups, and paper strips were also made available and identified as possibly useful implements for the task.

Only one child allocated the "candies" without concern for number; the dominant strategy, even among the 9-year-olds, was distributive counting (i.e., "One for you and one for you. And one . . ."). The prevalent use of one strategy across age groups was also noted in the case of measuring volume. Although

25% of the 3-year-old children simply poured a seemingly arbitrary amount of the colored water into each of the turtles' glasses, the dominant strategy was a repeating sequence of pouring some water and then visually comparing the level of the fluid across the glasses.

The task of sharing clay strips and clay regions required the creation of equivalent units, a demand that was avoided in the dominant strategies exhibited for sharing in the context of candy and colored water. The common strategy for the 3-year-olds was to divide the strip of "spaghetti" by cutting it into pieces of arbitrary length, taking care to distribute the same number of pieces to each turtle. In those cases where too few pieces had been cut, prohibiting an equal distribution, the children simply retrieved a piece from each of the turtles who had not received a "fair share," cut that piece in two, and gave both of the resulting pieces back to the same turtle. Thus the dominance of equality of number over equality of size in the reasoning of these preschool children was clear. The older children realized that there was one more strip than there were turtles and attempted to cut the extra strip into fractional pieces, approximating equal size by either estimating size or by folding. One size estimation strategy for the 7-year-olds was to cut an arbitrary piece and then use it as a template for cutting subsequent pieces, thus creating a unit. Another strategy for estimating size was to use the dominant unit marking on a ruler as a guide for cutting. However, these strategies did not always yield fractional pieces that could be equally distributed. Extra pieces would subsequently be subdivided again until eventually equal distribution was possible. Thus the 7-year-olds were attempting to reconcile equality of size and equality of number as they shared. Only within the 9-year-old sample was the ruler used in the conventional fashion: measure the total length of the strip, estimate an appropriate fractional length, and then cut pieces of that length. The strategies for estimating area were similar to those for estimating length. The youngest children cut the square into a number of pieces for equal distribution according to numerosity, whereas the older children attempted to define and use a unit of a constant size.

The children in this study had intuitive strategies for sharing that demonstrated knowledge of some role for equality within measurement. In the context of length and area, the older children's strategies included the criteria of creating and interpreting not just units, but equivalent units. Each of the children in this study constructed and systematically applied procedures for measuring an invariance although, perhaps due in part to the requisite cognitive demands involved in the creation of equivalent units, it was not always the quantitative invariance that an adult would measure.

INTERPRETATION OF A UNIT OF MEASURE

The reasoning about measuring that children construct entails learning about what kind of transformations alter quantity, that is learning what characteristics of number, length, area, or volume are relevant when determining how much of some substance is present (Miller, 1984). A child may know that there has been alteration of a display along a quantifiable dimension or a child may recognize an observable difference between two displays in terms of some dimension. Reasoning about these alterations or differences and interpreting their relevance within a particular domain of measure is intricate. Examining how children define units of measure or interpret measure when they encounter differing units and/or differing perceptual cues is one way to study children's construction of measurement knowledge.

In a study by Carpenter (1975), first- and second-grade children were administered classical liquid conservation tasks as well as liquid measurement tasks. The measurement tasks that presented correct numeric cues were significantly easier than those tasks that presented correct perceptual cues. Thus this study indicated that young children can understand measurement as a relationship between increased quantity and increased unit numerosity, but that there is difficulty in interpreting the effect of different units of measure.

With instruction, first-grade children learn the following regarding length measurement: the lengths of two or more objects may be compared indirectly; the length of a path is the sum of the lengths of the individual segments composing the path; and, given a fixed unit size, different lengths may be compared or ordered by examining their respective number of units. However, the inverse relationship between the size and number of units remains as a complex construct for young children (e.g., Hiebert, 1981).

Concern regarding kindergarten children's understanding of a unit of measure led Gal'perin and Georgiev (1969) to develop a curriculum that differentiated between the concept of a unit of measure and number. Assessment within their curriculum revealed impressive gains indicating that young children can be taught to interpret differing units of measure, although, in this particular reference, the exact nature of that interpretation as constructed by the children is not clear. The nature of children's conceptualization of a unit of measure is a critical issue. For example, Carpenter and Lewis (1976) maintained that young children recognize that there is a compensating relation between the number of units and unit size prior to a realization that "equal quantities are still equal even though they have measured a different number of units" (p. 57).

In each of the studies noted, units of measure were provided for the children to interpret. Although their study was not designed to assess children's construction of a unit of linear measurement, Newman and Berger's (1984) estimation task involved that facility. Kindergarten, first- and third-grade children were asked to name the numeric position of a point along a vertical line segment when only the endpoints of the line segment were numerically labeled (as 1 and 23). No marks indicating subdivisions of the segment were provided. Overall the children's accuracy improved with age, but more interesting was the age by position interaction. When the position of the target point was in the range that was classified as small, there was no significant difference in accuracy between the three age groups. At these positions, the older children's task advantage due to strategic skill in selecting the direction and starting point of a count sequence was minimized. At the small target positions, facility in defining the size of an appropriate unit of measurement and in counting a consistent iteration of that unit was key. Within these constraints, all of the sampled children were equally accurate. Thus this study offers evidence that young children can define, iterate, and count a constant unit of linear measure within supportive contexts.

LOGO AS A SUPPORTIVE SETTING FOR MEASUREMENT

Logo is an interactive programming language that has both a list processing and a graphics component. Within the graphics component of Logo, a child can direct the movements of a small triangular cursor along the quantitative dimensions of distance and direction while controlling the state of the cursor and its trail in terms of visibility and color. Logo provides an arena in which young children may manipulate units of varying size, define and create their own units, maintain unit size, estimate distance or rotation, and create length rather than endpoint representations through either iterative or numeric distance commands. Logo also permits the child to control unit size and number transformations without the distracting processing and dexterity demands associated with measuring instruments and physical quantity. Thus, it was hypothesized that Logo could provide a controlled setting that encouraged development of children's schemes for linear measure, while permitting examination of children's understanding of the measure of distance, of a unit of measure, and of the inverse relationship between unit size and number.

For this study, 26 kindergarten and 23 first-grade children of diverse ethnicities received guided Logo instruction over a 6-month period. The first-grade children received Turtle Graphics instruction in small groups of 12 children in weekly 1-hour sessions in a microcomputer laboratory (six machines). Logo instruction for the kindergarten children was presented to groups of 6 children during 15- to 20-minute sessions, approximately five sessions every 2 weeks. The kindergarten children utilized a version of Instant Logo that required the RETURN key to be struck after each single keystroke; iterative revision without screen erasure was also possible. Following each session, the Logo instructors recorded the number of minutes of individualized Logo exploration or keyboard time made available for each child. Instructional time spent in movement activities or directed Logo learning away from the keyboards was not recorded.

The children's understanding of distance in terms of a unit of measure and their conceptualization of the inverse relationship between the number of units and unit size were assessed by an estimation of distance task, administered after 2, 4, and 6 hours of individual Logo keyboard time. This computerized task presented a referent step size (unit) in the top, left-hand corner of a monitor screen, a target, and a triangular cursor. The children were asked to determine the number of referent steps (units) required to send the triangular cursor to the target. The cursor moved in response to the numeric keystroke(s) entered by the child; Logo commands were not required. Assistance was provided if the child indicated a number, but did not know the appropriate numeric digits. This task varied both the size of the unit (5, 10, or 20 turtle steps), the distance to the target (long or short), and the orientation of the distance path (horizontal, vertical, or oblique).

Across grade levels the children increased the magnitude of their first estimates as the lengths of the distances to be estimated increased. This provides further evidence that young children may construct measure as an ordered scheme relating quantity and unit numerosity as if they are applying a magnitude principle: Traversing longer distances requires more units, and therefore a larger number, than traversing shorter distances. The overall tendency was to underestimate when using the 10-step unit size, with the kindergarten children estimating distances with significantly smaller numbers than the first-grade children. For the kindergarten children, a critical construct was their characterization of "large" numbers. At Time 1, 58% of the kindergarteners relied solely on numbers less than or equal to 10, with estimates of 9 or 10 reserved for very long lines. Over the duration of the study, the kindergarten children's first estimates steadily increased; at the last administration of the task there was no significant difference in the size of the estimates between the two age groups when using the 10-step unit.

When required to use the halved unit size (5 turtle steps), the first estimates of the children were numerically larger than their estimates for those same distances with the doubled unit size (20 turtle steps), but their mean estimates increased by a factor of 1.86, not by a factor of 4. The children's estimates imply their understanding that a distance traversed with a smaller unit requires a greater number of units than that same distance traversed with a larger unit. However, the children consistently underestimated the strength of the inverse relationship between unit size and numeracy of units. Interpreting the effect of unit size was more problematic for the kindergarteners as their mean first estimates with the halved unit size was only 1.55 times their mean first estimates with the doubled unit size, as compared to a factor of 2.29 for the first graders in the Logo group.

The effects found for the accuracy data (that is the ratio of the child's first estimate of distance to the actual length of the line) mirror those found in the analysis of the first estimate data. The first graders were significantly more accurate than the kindergarteners. Over time, with the 10-step unit, the mean accuracy of the kindergarteners improved (.56, .67, .75 respectively), whereas the first graders tended to maintain a relatively high mean level of accuracy at each assessment period (.84, .88, .82). Accuracy scores reflected significantly different patterns of change across distance over time with the 10-step unit. Although the accuracy of the kindergarten children's estimates improved over time for both long (.50, .70, .74) and short (.62, .64, .76) distances, their improvement in estimating long lines was most marked between Time 1 and Time 2, as opposed to strong short line estimation improvement between Time 2 and Time 3. The first graders maintained a high level of accuracy when estimating the shorter distances (.87, .91, .90), but their accuracy in estimating the longer lines fell between Time 2 and 3 (.80, .85, .75). Analysis of the data indicated that this drop in mean estimates was due to overcompensation for the overestimates entered during Time 2. It is hypothesized that these children were beginning to eliminate very large numbers from their pool of reasonable estimates, reflecting a refinement in their concept of large numbers and their beginning grasp of extreme number-distance relations.

Unit size had a significant impact on accuracy. Again different accuracy patterns were noted. With the 20-step unit size, the children overestimated length, with this tendency being most pronounced for the first graders (mean overestimation: grade K, 3%; grade 1, 8%). With the 5-step unit size, accuracy dropped precipitously as the children underestimated the actual length (mean accuracy: grade K, .41; grade 1, .61). Over time the mean accuracy of the estimates using the halved and doubled unit size improved, but not significantly. The accuracy of the kindergartener's numeric adjustments for changing unit size was erratic, influenced by the limits of their concept of number. By the completion of the study, the first graders were beginning to accurately use their inventory of large numbers as numeric estimates. The kindergarteners were never able to adjust their estimates sufficiently to compensate for the reduction in unit size. When they entered numeric estimates using the 5-step unit size, they repeatedly seemed surprised that such a small distance had been traversed. Nevertheless, each of the children's construction of length measure permitted numerical adjustment in the desired direction to accommodate changing unit size.

In order to further assess the children's understanding of the inverse relationship between unit size and number of units, the children's numeric length estimates using the halved and doubled unit sizes were compared to their estimates of those same lines using the original unit size. Two ratios of estimated lengths were computed for paired items (original : double unit sizes and halved : original unit sizes). Optimally, these ratios were 2 : 1. The children underestimated the strength of the inverse relationship. At the completion of the study the estimates of the first graders reflected a significantly more accurate mean ratio than that of the kindergarteners (1.63 : 1 VS. 1.31 : 1). This assymetry between performance with the unit sizes suggests that these children may have been using perceptual/spatial strategies rather than numeric strategies to solve these problems. If the children were interpreting the task as one of physically iterating a given unit and mentally representing this iteration, then smaller units are more difficult because a great many more iterations need to be performed with smaller units.

CHILDREN'S CONSTRUCTION OF MEASURE

Given an environment that facilitates manipulation of units while supporting maintainance of unit size, young children may construct a measure scheme that they can apply to differing distances, even under the condition of varying unit sizes. This proficiency may involve learning three kinds of knowledge. First, lengths of different magnitudes can be ordered. The children in this supportive Logo environment were able to construct this ordering even though the individual lengths to be estimated appeared separately and in random order. In addition, number is a system for ordering quantity. Young children can understand that, in the domain of measure, the number associated with a distance can change, depending on the size of the unit that is being iterated. Further study is needed to determine if, as concluded by Carpenter and Lewis (1976), when young children numerically adjust for changing unit size they fail to conserve quantity. Furthermore, for a given unit size, progressively larger numbers are assigned to progressively larger quantities. The children were not always accurate in their estimates and a very small unit size may have required facility with an associated range of larger numbers beyond the scope of the children's existing number sense. Nevertheless, given a long-term experience with Logo, these children were able to form correspondences that preserved order relations in terms of both number and length. Readers are cautioned to refrain from generalizing these results to other settings; however, this study indicates that under supportive conditions, young children can construct measure.

ACKNOWLEDGMENTS

Portions of the research reported herein were supported by a grant from the National Institute of Mental Health, No. MSMA 1 RO3 MH423435-01. Any opinions findings and conclusions are those of the author and do not necessarily reflect the position or policy of the National Institute of Mental Health.

Chapter 3.7

Some Aspects of Learning Geometry

Kiyoshi Yokochi
Tokai University, JAPAN

Japan is in the midst of an information-oriented society, which affects mathematics education at kindergarten and elementary school. In the following paragraphs, I explain the state of things in these days, on "knowledge and learning" in particular, centering around geometry.

EDUCATIONAL STATE IN JAPAN AND THE MEANINGS OF KNOWLEDGE AND LEARNING

At present, in Japan, there are a great many "Juku" throughout the country. "Juku" in Japanese is the private cramming school with the objective of reinforcing children's scholastic abilities and preparing them for the entrance examinations of upper schools. The teaching materials at Juku mainly aim at preparing children for entrance examinations. Therefore the materials consist of the calculation of numbers, problems stated in sentences, and difficult problems solved only by specific methods. In other words, the materials consist of mechanical or stereotyped problems, and do not include enjoying mathematics, applying mathematics to children's daily life, and creating a certain mathematics. In the meantime, our society traditionally attaches importance to one's academic career. The type of occupation, which children will be able to find in future, is considerably controlled by their academic career. Therefore the parents are enthusiastic about the education for their children and many parents begin to make their children go to Juku even in the lower grades of elementary school.

3.7. SOME ASPECTS OF LEARNING GEOMETRY IN JAPAN 101

According to the nationwide survey by the Ministry of Education in 1985, 6.2% of the first-grade children (age 6–7) and 10.1% of the second-grade children (age 7–8) go to Juku (Ministry of Education, 1986). In both big cities and their outskirts, the percentage is much higher. For example, at Yamashiro Elementary School (in Kofu city) in June 1988, 14.1% of 185 first-grade and 24.0% of 175 second-grade children go to Juku. And 73.1% of first-grade and 78.6% of second-grade children attending Juku learn mathematics about 2 days per week.

In addition, a number of children, who do not go to Juku, do exercises at home using the workbooks published by famous educational enterprises. For example, the research of 31 second-grade children on those things at Honcho Elementary School (in Tokyo), in June 1988, showed the following: six of them (19.4%) go to Juku and 19 of them (61.3%) do exercises using workbooks at home. It is natural that this practice would also spread to kindergarten children. Some parents begin the special education of their children even as early as age 4.

On the other hand, Japanese elementary school teachers are eager to teach their children. Elementary schools practice education under the course of study determined by the Ministry of Education. According to the course of study, multiplication tables are located in second grade. The second-grade teachers emphasize it so earnestly in order that all the children in the class may understand and use it. If some children do not know their tables, the teachers try to cram the tables into those children by applying all the methods in their hand. Teachers do not think that these children should be left to learn the tables in an upper grade.

In the educational state previously described, the meanings of knowledge and learning—as Japanese teachers and parents interpret it—are considerably different from the meaning interpreted in other countries. In short, those meanings are the following:

Knowledge: mathematical terms; mathematical rules; how to use the terms and rules for calculations or problems stated in sentences; how to solve the problems in the text, workbooks, or Juku; and so on.

Learning: understanding knowledge within the limits of text, workbooks or Juku; memorizing knowledge; training for using the knowledge quickly and accurately; and so on.

In my view, these meanings are not good for children. We need to develop better meanings. However, even in that case, we need to keep in mind parents' concerns about the education of their children. Consequently, I propose the following alternate meanings:

Knowledge: mathematical concepts and rules, which are found by children only through their activities in the real world. The knowledge is reconstructed by themselves repeatedly, depending on their accumulated activities.

Learning: children's activities through which they find knowledge and reconstruct the knowledge for the upper one.

As you see from the Japanese educational state mentioned earlier, the children's activities for learning are realized under teachers' or parents' suggestions as well as by themselves. Needless to say, those activities ought to be pleasant and meaningful for children. Next, I give some concrete examples of the latter meanings of knowledge and learning, using geometry in particular.

Many experiments have been carried out at kindergartens belonging to the Japanese Association of Kindergarten Teachers.

SOLIDS MADE WITH CLAY

Children in early ages have passion for making solids with clay. Through these activities they grasp knowledge about solids. What are the stages of their knowledge? Consider, for example, the case of a gourd. Several experiments showed the following stages (see Fig. 1.):

1. Age 3–4: Two separated parts (balls) are connected. In other words, "from parts to a whole."
2. Age 4–5: The whole has two main parts. In other words, "from a whole to parts."
3. Age 5–6: They appreciate smooth curved solids. In other words, "finding virtue."
4. Age 6–7: They grasp the solid in space and the sun's light. In other words, "integrated grasp." (Yokochi, 1985)

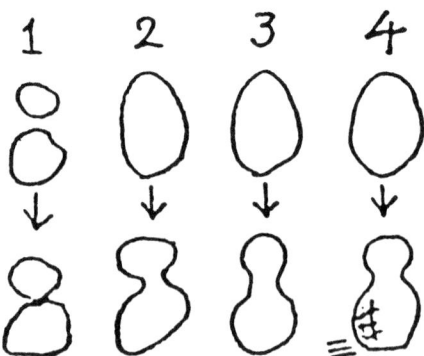

FIG. 1. Stages in making clay gourds.

3.7. SOME ASPECTS OF LEARNING GEOMETRY IN JAPAN

Some examples of children's activities for learning which were practiced at several kindergartens include:

1. For the second stage: Making pigs or cows with clay after a tour of farms. First, children make a body of outward appearance and then they pull a leg, tail, breast, and so on out of the body.
2. For the third stage: Making an opera singer, with clay. Children make it in its full expressions. (Yokochi, 1984)

DIRECTION AND RELATION OF THINGS IN SPACE

At early ages children have a passion for drawing pictures. Through this type of activity, they grasp the concept of the direction of solids in space. For example, consider the exercise of drawing a picture of persons working sideways in the field. Several experiments showed the following stages of knowledge:

1. Age 3-4: In the picture, the persons are in fullface and the things related with the persons are standing in a row with the persons. In other words, "children speak to each person and each thing, directly—subjective space."
2. Age 4-5: In the pictures, some persons are sideways. The things related with the persons are connected with them. In other words, "children begin to set persons and the things in objective space—beginning of objective space."
3. Age 5-6: In the picture, the persons are sideways. The relation of the persons and the things are drawn so as to express their real relations. In other words, "the persons and the things are set in objective space."
4. Age 6-7: The persons and things are drawn with their surroundings. In other words, "the whole of persons and things is a part of extensive space. (Yokochi, 1978, 1983)

The following are some examples of children's activities for learning, which are practiced at several kindergartens.

1. For the second stage: After an athletic meeting, drawing picture of the meeting. While calling up in their mind their directions and the relation between them and the sporting equipment at the meeting, they draw the picture.
2. For the third stage: Making a sketch of flowers arranged in a vase. Considering the direction of each flower and its position collectively, children draw the picture. (Yokochi, 1985)

DEVELOPMENT OF SOLIDS

The three-year-old children can cut paper with scissors and have a passion for making solids with paper. Through these activities, they grasp the knowledge of constructing solids. For example, consider the case of the box that is made through the development. Several experiments showed the following stages of knowledge (see Fig. 2.):

1. Age 3–4: Children cannot dissolve the box into five rectangles, and they see the box as one continuous plane. In other words, "un-specialization between solid and plane."
2. Age 4–5: Children dissolve the box into five rectangles. However they cannot grasp the rule of connection among them. In other words, "dissolving a solid into parts."
3. Age 5–6: Children grasp the rule of connection among 5 rectangles. In other words, "grasping the development."
4. Age 6–7: Children grasp the rule on the construction of development. In other words, "grasping the rule of constructing development." (Yokochi, 1985, 1976)

The following are some examples of children's activities for learning the previously presented knowledge:

1. For the second stage: Making a table and a chair by parts. First, children make parts of a table and a chair with paper. Then they assemble the parts into a table and a chair.
2. For the third stage: Making a car. First children draw the development on the paper. Then they make the car with the development. (Yokochi, 1979; 1985)

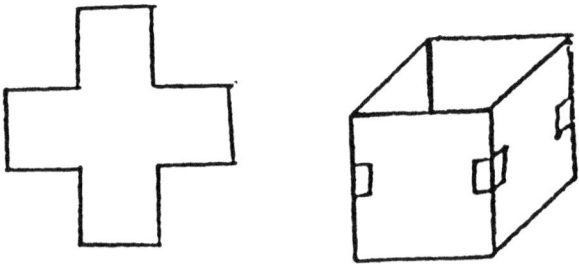

FIG. 2. Stages in children's understanding of solids.

SOME COMMENTS

In addition, I would like to indicate some points concerning geometry education for early childhood years. It is needless to say, technical terms and rules explained explicitly are the important elements of the knowledge. However, to grasp those elements as words is not necessarily a means to grasp the knowledge. The matter of great account is that children can freely use the meaning of those elements in their daily activities. In addition, geometry education for early childhood years does not consist of terms and rules. Similarly, it does not consist of questions on terms and rules. It consists of children's activities, in which those terms and rules are used. In this point, the education for early childhood years is different from that for upper grade children. Finally, geometry education for early childhood years is executed in cooperation with other subjects like drawing.

Discussion Chapters: Knowledge

Chapter 3.8

Mathematical Knowledge of Young Learners

Grayson H. Wheatley
Florida State University, USA

Harriet Bebout
University of Cincinnati, USA

In mathematics education discussions, two contrasting views of mathematical knowledge can be identified. On the one hand, mathematics is viewed as a codified body of knowledge to be transmitted to students. In this view, issues related to what mathematics knowledge all children should know arise. Most educational systems in every culture operate from this perspective. There is a drive for students to become proficient with complex procedures at an early age, particularly in oriental cultures.

On the other hand, mathematical knowledge viewed from a constructivist perspective is a learner's activity, what Sinclair (1987b) called "instruments of problem solving." Mathematics is considered to be the activity of constructing relationships and patterns—it is, for an individual, that coordinated set of schemes and actions that are functioning reliably and effectively (Steffe, chap. 5.8). Thus mathematics does not exist independent of a learner. Rather than considering mathematical knowledge as concepts, principles, and procedures, we can think of mathematics as the activity of constructing relationships and generating algorithms.

If constructing knowledge is a personal activity, it is important that children have rich experiences on which to reflect. Carrying out a procedure shown by an adult for adding 37 and 49 is not an experience rich in potential for mathematical reflection. However, determining the number of coins in a bank after 37 coins and then 49 coins have been inserted, where the individual believes they may decide how to proceed, leads to giving meaning and to the development of a viable procedure.

Viewing knowledge as action, one of a learner's activities is the construction of objects. Numbers are not "out there" in the visual world but must be made by the knower. Activity becomes transformed into an object when an individual can "run through" a self-generated action in thought, produce a result and take the result as given. Frequently we take these objects constructed by the learner as existing prior to the learner's activity of construction and, in fact, as common to all persons. Thus as we communicate with others and find they refer to the same "object" we have constructed, we slip into thinking of knowledge as a set of objects existing independent of learners. It is quite natural to talk about a parallelogram as a disembodied mathematical object and to speak to others about our parallelogram. We can talk meaningfully with others about parallelograms if they have constructed it as one of their objects. Our constructions will vary, so it will be necessary to negotiate the meanings we give to our objects of thought.

The setting in which learning takes place, as well as the context established by the learner, is crucially important. A child reasoning meaningfully does not think of 3 plus 4 in the abstract but thinks of three things and four things forming a collection that has numerosity. Clements and Del Campo (chap. 3.16) and Hunting & Sharpley (1988) provide evidence that children in nonWestern cultures often have different ways of thinking about numbers and numerical relationships. For example, in Aboriginal Australian and Papua New Guinean cultures, children do not give the same meanings to fractions as children in Western cultures. When the informal language of the cultures was used, children did much better on a variety of mathematics tasks. Although not operating from a constructivist perspective, Boulton-Lewis (Chap. 3.13) concludes that aboriginal Australian children were capable of reasoning using their natural language concepts at similar levels to other Australian children even though they consistently score lower on mathematics tasks phrased in Western language. These studies support the constructivist position that mathematics is the activity of constructing relationships because when one uses ideas that are meaningful from past experience, they are able to "knowledge."

Although this chapter focuses on mathematical knowledge, it is impossible to separate knowledge from learning and environments. Viewing mathematics knowledge as a learner activity rather than an independent body of knowns leads to quite different educational considerations. Rather than identifying the set of skills to be put in children's heads, attention shifts to establishing learning environments conducive to children constructing their mathematics. There is a social dimension of knowledge, so this learning environment necessarily includes children talking about mathematics with each other. Such learning environments would provide opportunities for children to share their ideas with peers, both in small groups and within the society of the classroom.

EMERGING THEMES OF THE DISCUSSION GROUP

In the knowledge discussion group, general agreement was reached that most early number research has been conducted with middle-class children in urban and suburban areas of developed nations. A call was made for more attention to the mathematics of children in nonWestern cultures. A study of the mathematical knowledge of children living in nondeveloped nations has potential for deepening our understanding of mathematics knowledge in general and may serve as a basis for designing appropriate learning activities.

Within each culture there are certain activities that are particularly meaningful to members of that society. For the nomadic Penans of Borneo it would be geometric patterns reflected in the rattan woven mats. For aboringial Australians it might be family relationships (Boulton-Lewis, chap. 3.13). Counting money is a meaningful activity for children in some societies. Such cultural amplifiers have the potential of being facilitative in mathematics learning and should be identified and utilized. For example, Carraher and Schliemann (chap. 3.11) looked at 5- to 7-year-old children's knowledge of money and early numeration/place value systems. A familiar setting such as money greatly enhanced the children's understanding of numeration and place value systems. It could be argued that learning is contextual. Although we may create abstract objects, they flow from contextualized experiences.

Imagery plays an important role in mathematical activity. Mathematical reasoning frequently has a dynamic character. When a person says, "I see a relationship between 6 + 4 and 5 + 5," the "seeing" is a not a perceptual but a cognitive act (Johnson, 1987). The relationship is abstract and thus cannot be seen in the visual sense. However, we argue that what is seen is a self-constructed image of the relationship. Perhaps the individual sees the 6 as broken up into 5 and 1 and the 1 "moved" with the 4 to make 5. There is a dynamic transformation on images constructed in thinking about this task. Similarly, imagery plays a central role in tangramlike tasks in which the child must anticipate a rotation of a piece to fit in a constructed space (see Wheatley & Cobb, chap. 3.14). Kosslyn (1983) suggested four aspects of the visualization activity: image construction, representation, transformation of an image, and maintaining the image. This reference frame appears potentially useful in building explanations of children's mathematical actions.

It was agreed that attention should be given to social dimensions of classroom learning. Whereas on the one hand knowledge is not disembodied and found in books, knowledge does not develop for an individual in isolation from others. Students are not lonely voyagers but learn from interaction with children and others. As Gergen (1982, p. 270) stated, "Knowledge is not something people possess in their heads, but rather something people do together." Ideas are authenticated for each individual as a class or group develops a consensus through negotiation of meanings. The viability of mathematical knowledge is determined through interactions and the knowledge development is very much a function of the social setting within which the individual exists.

Metacognition was mentioned, but the group could not agree on its use and value for children at this age. Although it is recognized that advances in mathematical knowledge result from reflecting on experience and action, the term *metacognition* may suggest a false dichotomy between thinking about the problem and thinking about thinking. As children build up knowledge in a constructivist environment, they naturally reflect on what they are doing even though this activity is not always at the conscious level. The term metacognition has been useful to persons operating in other paradigms but may be less useful to constructivists.

During the discussion, DeCorte suggested a framework for future research on young children's knowledge. The two-dimensional design included types of knowledge (domain specific, metacognitive) and types of research (descriptive, interventions including methods and technology).

SUMMARIES OF PAPERS PRESENTED

Fosnot (chap. 3.9) explains children's actions in balancing a block on a fulcrum as a constructive process characterized by necessity, possibilities, contradictions, new possibilities, and new necessities. Similar reasoning was observed by studying children's probabilistic knowledge using the rolling of a die. Three explanatory schemes described by Piaget were taken as mechanisms; presentative, procedural, and operational. Learners construct new logical necessities to explain their experience and resolve the contradictions. The dialectical constructs of necessity and possibility have potential as tools in making sense of children's actions in a broad range of mathematical activity.

Bergeron and Herscovics (chap. 3.10) study kindergarten children's knowledge of preconcepts of number. They focus on the notion of plurality and the notion of position in an ordered set. They conclude that children living in a Western urban setting, come to school already having constructed extensive knowledge about numbers but that much of their thinking is influenced by visual perception. They identify four levels of prenumber understanding, (a) intuitive understanding, (b) procedural understanding, (c) logico-mathematics understanding, and (d) formalization of previous knowledge.

English (chap. 3.15) demonstrates that children ages 4–9 can construct efficient algorithmic procedures for solving combinatoric problems. The combinatorial tasks involved dressing toy bears in three different colored shirts and shorts. As discussed by Carraher and Schliemann (chap. 3.11), as well as Boulton-Lewis (chap. 3.13), using familiar objects facilitated thinking. She identifies a hierarchy of solution paths from random selection to efficient patterning. Her findings support Bergeron and Herscovics's contention that young children have constructed ways of sense making beyond what is assumed in convention instruction.

Through historical analysis and interviews with children, Clements and Del Campo (chap. 3.16) show that some societies have not developed fraction concepts or notations. Children's intuitions about fractions as influenced by culture and language often are not related in the child's mind with school imposed

3.8. MATHEMATICAL KNOWLEDGE OF YOUNG LEARNERS   111

fraction notation and procedures. They show that children ages 3–5 have constructed concepts of fraction (sharing) and that appropriate school mathematics activities can assist children to construct meaning for fraction symbols, operations, and relationships.

Ishida (chap. 3.12) studies first-grade children's writing of number sentences for different types of addition and subtraction word problems. Ishida found that the semantic structure of addition and subtraction problems had an effect on children's number sentence forms and identified three levels of performance on children's preinstructional missing addend number sentences. Children at the highest level reorganized the sentence structure and wrote correct canonical sentence forms. Children at the middle level effectively represented the sentence structure and wrote incorrect noncanonical sentence forms. Children at the lowest level did not exhibit evidence of sentence structure understanding.

Boulton Lewis (chap. 3.13) examines children's knowledge of transitive reasoning. She found that urban aboriginal children's performance on the tasks was the same as nonaboriginal children in familiar settings (family was used) but lower on school tasks. However, aboriginal and nonaboriginal children did not differ on logical tasks, so aboriginal children should be able to perform as well as nonaboriginal children with appropriate learning experiences.

Carraher and Schliemann (chap. 3.11) looked at pre-schoolers' knowledge of the number system as evidenced by their language and actions with coins of different denominations. They found that children had difficulty coordinating units of different rank, ones, fives, and tens. From this investigation Carraher and Schliemann identified a developmental progression of number system knowledge that ranged from counting units of one only, counting fives or tens, to counting mixed values. They also found that the generation of number labels did not appear to be sufficient for understanding underlying number system principles and that, conversely, the understanding of number system principles did not always result in the accurate generation of number labels. They suggest that money items with their robust ties to children's informal experiences were useful in teaching place value concepts.

Wheatley and Cobb (chap. 3.14) identified spatial constructions in an imagery task with 6 and 7 year-old children. The model they developed to explain the children's actions considered the following constructive acts: task construal, image constructions, structuring unfilled space, judgment of size, mental rotations, and comparisons of represented images to shapes in the visual field. A set of competence levels were developed which characterized the children's actions. The analysis carries implications for early school experiences and contributes to our understanding of young children's spatial world.

Chapter 3.9

Possibility, Necessity, Contradiction, and Probability: Implications for Mathematics Education

Catherine T. Fosnot
Southern Connecticut State University, USA

Just prior to his death, Piaget was engaged in a study of the relationship between possibility and necessity. This work, originally published in French in two volumes (1981 and 1983), has recently been translated into English (1987a,b) and provides epistemologists with a rich description of the development of the notion of possibilities and the effect of the generation of possibilities on the construction of operational thought. Three types of schemes are distinguished: (a) presentative schemes involving simultaneous characteristics of objects; (b) procedural schemes or means applied toward a goal; and (c) operational schemes that "constitute a synthesis of the two previous ones; they are procedural in that they are performed in real time, but the atemporal structure of the combinatorial laws regulating operations has the characteristic of a higher order presentative scheme" (Piaget, 1987a). Through a study of 23 tasks, Piaget documents the increasing differentiation and reintegration of these three schemes, or cognitive systems. He concluded:

> Initially any object or substance in a presentative scheme will first appear to subjects not only as what they are, but also as being that way of necessity, excluding the possibility of variation or change. However, once a possibility gets actualized through the application of procedural schemes, a new presentative scheme is created, thence the complementarity of the two systems. To conceive of new possibilities, it is not enough to think of procedures oriented toward a particular goal, one also needs to compensate for that actual or virtual perturbation that is the resistance of reality to explanation when it is conceived as pseudonecessary. (Piaget, 1987a, pp. 5,6)

In the second volume he continued, "The constant alternation of closures (necessity) with new openings (possibilities) is likewise an essential characteristic of the integrated process that we are talking about. In short, necessitations and the formation of possibilities direct the whole process of structuring" (Piaget, 1987b, pp. 142).

Two studies are reported in this chapter that show evidence of an interplay between the notion of possibilities and the construction of necessity. The first study consists of a microanalysis of the development of the understanding of balance; the second delineates the development of the concept of probability. Although the second study is perhaps of more interest to mathematics educators, both are presented in order to give a fuller view of the whole process of structuring.

THE DEVELOPMENT
OF THE UNDERSTANDING OF BALANCE

Rationale

The developing notion of balance has been studied before by various researchers. For example, Karmiloff-Smith & Inhelder (1974) gave children (ages 3–7) symmetrical, asymmetrical, and blocks with hidden weights to balance on a fulcrum. The youngest children's actions were found to be representative of their egocentric schemes. They just "plunked" each block on the fulcrum, with no lateral shifts across the fulcrum to find the balance point. Their compensations, when blocks did not balance, consisted of claiming that the block was an impossible block to balance or of pushing harder on the block above the point of contact with the fulcrum. Children began to both explore the properties of the blocks and try different positions on the fulcrum because these actions obviously did not produce success. Reflection on these actions brought about a focus on the procedures that worked (lateral shifts) and eventually the construction of a theory about balance that was assumed to work for all blocks. The first theory constructed, according to Karmiloff-Smith and Inhelder, was a "center" theory (find the middle of the block and it will balance). This theory was overgeneralized across all blocks regardless of whether or not the block was asymmetrically weighted. In testing out their theories, children met with conflict. Eventually, through conflict resolution, more stable theories of balance in relation to weight were constructed.

Siegler (1978) criticized the Karmiloff-Smith and Inhelder study on both conceptual and methodological grounds and proposed instead a methodology based on the assumption that children's problem-solving strategies are rule-governed and progress from less sophisticated to more sophisticated levels with age. He created balance problem sets that yielded sharply different patterns of correct answers and errors depending on what rule was being used. His data, organized into a decision tree model, showed four rules. A rule 1 child considered only the numbers of weights on each side of the fulcrum. For a child using rule 2, a difference in weight was conclusive, but if weight was equal on the two sides, then the distance dimension was also considered. A rule 3 child considered both weight and distance in all cases; however, in a situation in which one side had greater weight and the other had greater distance, the child just "muddled through" or guessed. Rule 4, in contrast, solved all problems and was demonstrative of the torque concept.

Although Siegler's work provides consistent empirical validation of the four rule-governed behaviors he proposed, there is an obvious conceptual problem. Because he used a decision tree model, a convergent design resulted. Only certain possibilities could appear: weight, distance, "muddling through," or weight and distance. And, young children who did not understand weight were therefore considered to exhibit random, nonrule-governed behavior.

To determine whether the behaviors Siegler observed are really a function of the natural development of the principles of balance, or simply a function of the task and design used, a more open-ended task is needed with a microanalysis of the possibilities and necessities engendered by subjects. Observing the strategies children use as they attempt to balance blocks on a fulcrum rather than simply coding balance or fall responses in a tree model fashion, allows the researcher to gain insights into the variables the child is testing.

Materials

Various visually symmetrical, visually asymmetrical, and asymmetrically weighted blocks (adapted and modified from those used by Karmiloff-Smith & Inhelder) were given to children to balance on a fulcrum (See Fig. 1).

Subjects

One hundred twenty-eight children between the ages of 4 and 8 years were tested and videotaped as they attempted each block.

Measures

Strategy Scale

After observing the procedural schemes used by subjects and the possibilities they tried as they attempted to balance the blocks, a strategy scale was developed encompassing five levels. Youngest children (Level 1) simply approached the task egocentrically. Wherever they placed it, they expected it to balance. No

3.9. IMPLICATIONS FOR MATHEMATICS EDUCATION

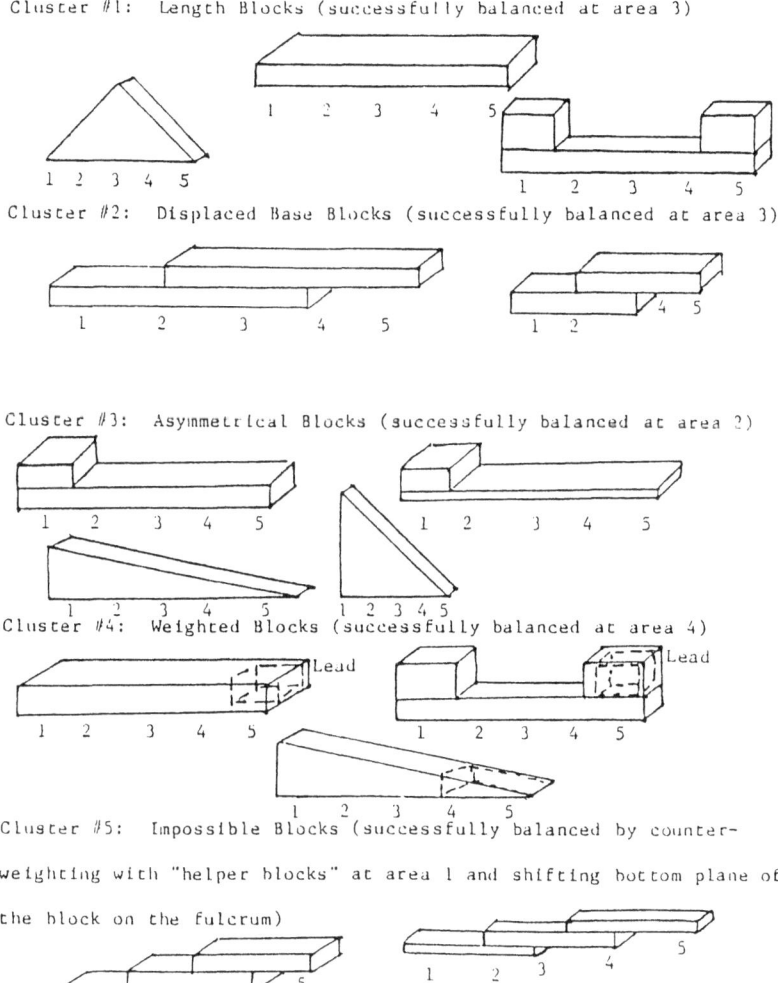

FIG. 1. Clusters 1–5 (Drawn to a 1:6 scale).

lateral shifts across the fulcrum were used. Level 2 children were distinctly different. They shifted the block as though they were looking for a midpoint of the bottom base of the block, or a midpoint of the shifts. Level 3 children, in contrast, searched for a midpoint of the whole block, a visual center. Level 4 subjects took into consideration the volume of the object and tested out the possibility that the volume had to be bisected; whereas Level 5 subjects tested the variable of weight.

Cluster Score

The blocks were classified into five clusters by the physical principle (necessity or pseudonecessity) they tapped. For example, Cluster 1 was expected to be successfully balanced by subjects who believed in the necessity of placing the midpoint of the bottom plane of the block on the fulcrum. Cluster 2 and Cluster 1, together, were expected to be successfully balanced by subjects believing that the visual midpoint of the whole block was the correct balance point. Subjects who held the belief that volume had to be bisected were expected to be successful with Clusters 1–3; whereas, Clusters 4 and 5 demanded an understanding of the need to bisect weight.

Results

The Spearman correlation coefficient was derived ($r = .63$, $p = .001$) between age and strategy level and bonferroni t tests held between levels. Mean ages of levels, respectively were: 55, 66, 76, 83, 90 months.

A Guttman scalogram analysis was performed to test the hypothesis that a difficulty order existed from one to five and that subjects passing Cluster 2 had also passed Cluster 1; subjects passing Cluster 3 had also passed Clusters 1 and 2, and so forth. The coefficient of reproducibility was .95 with a coefficient of scalability of .80 (See Fig. 2). This scale was assumed to be assessing the progressive construction of necessity because passing a cluster demanded making inferences about how the blocks in each cluster were similar, albeit perceptually different, and then believing strongly enough in the necessity of the possibility of balance to struggle with each block until balance was achieved.

Discussion

Of primary interest is the relationship of the scales to each other (See Fig. 3). A change in strategy did not necessarily reflect a change in understanding. Subjects were willing to test out new procedures and possibilities in an attempt to achieve

CLUSTERS	I	II	III	IV	V	VI
5	0	0	0	1	0	2
4	0	0	0	3	9	2
3	0	0	0	7	9	2
2	0	11	20	11	9	2
1	0	20	20	11	9	2

GUTTMAN LEVELS

FIG. 2. Guttman scalogram showing number of subjects passing each cluster at each level.

3.9. IMPLICATIONS FOR MATHEMATICS EDUCATION

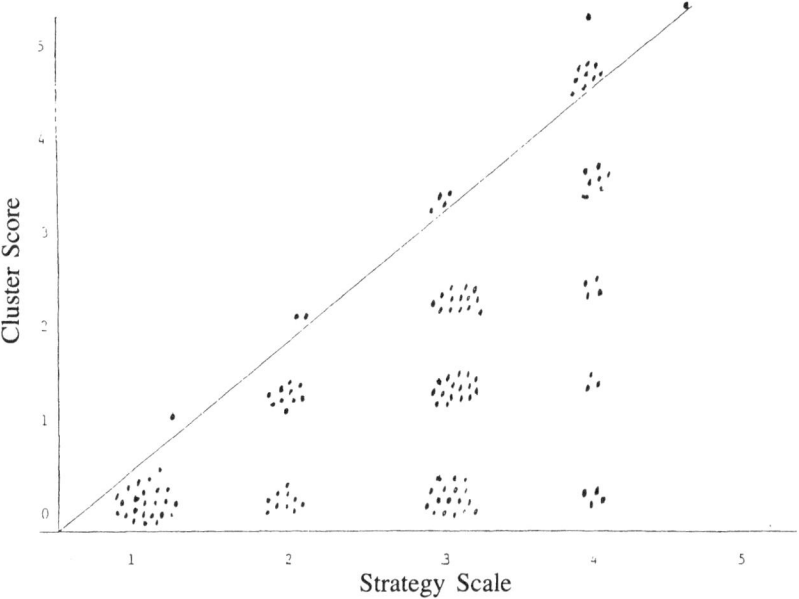

FIG. 3. Scattergram showing relationship between strategies and passing clusters.

balance, yet they did not struggle with each block (to achieve balance) until they believed (with a logical necessity) that it could be balanced. As they experimented with new possibilities, they, at times, successfully balanced blocks. These successes served as perturbations to earlier theories. In fact, reflecting on these possibilities seemed to be what enabled learners to give up erroneous theories for those more advanced. For example, youngest children began the task with an egocentric orientation: they simply plunked the block on the fulcrum with the apparent belief that wherever they put it, it should balance. No differentiation existed between the presentative, procedural, or operational schemes. If the block did not balance, they simply pushed harder or discarded the block as an "impossible one." No shifts with the block across the fulcrum occurred. Eventually, however, the possibility of a new procedural scheme was tried. Subjects began to shift the blocks that brought about success, erratic success but sufficing to make earlier egocentric schemes insufficient. The trying out of new procedural schemes seemed to eventually bring about a structural change in cognition. Subjects constructed a compensation of "when I shift the block to the right, I lose something on the left." This compensation, entailing a "reversibility of action" brought about the first real theory, the new necessity of bisecting the linear plane of the bottom of the block. This operational scheme in turn effected the presentative schemes. Subjects were observed even measuring with their fingers across the base of the blocks to find the "exact midpoint." Although this "linear center" theory worked for Cluster 1, it did not work for the other clusters. As new possibilities were tried, the "linear center theory" was modified by a more encompassing "visual center theory." Thus a new presentative scheme appeared, the simultaneous consideration of two sides of the whole block, rather than a bisection of the base. This constructive process continued producing new possibilities, new perturbations, and new necessities (Fosnot, Forman, Edwards, & Goldhaber, 1988).

Implications

This work is important because it details the endogenous, constructive process of learning. The new "necessities" or theories constructed by the learner are not a result of the passive processing of exogenous information, but instead are representative of progressive "equilibrations" from the interplay between the subject's presentative, procedural, and operational schemes. As the generation of new possibilities provides an "opening," the need for "closure" brings about the construction of new necessities directing, in Piaget's words, "the whole process of structuring."

THE DEVELOPMENT OF PROBABILITY

Probability demands a different type of mathematical necessity than the necessity resulting from actions on objects. It must be inferred from the attributes of the object, rather than deduced from the results of actions on the object. Although Piaget and Inhelder (1975) documented the structural changes in children's thinking about chance and probability, the newer work on possibility and necessity suggests that a closer look may be beneficial. Towards that aim, case studies are being collected documenting the changing ideas learners have about probability, but with a specific eye towards delineating the generation of possibilities, the resulting perturbations, and the construction of necessities. Two early childhood case studies and a discussion follow.

Brian

Brian, age 5:4, was presented with a regular cubed, six-sided die having the following faces: 0, 1, 2, 3, 4, 5. When asked what possibilities might happen if the die were to be rolled, he responded, "1." The experimenter asked if there were any other possibilities. He responded, "3." With each query of, "Any others?" he responded with a different number from the die. The numbers, however, seemed to represent arbitrary, discrete possibilities rather than a closed set of possibilities from the faces, given that only one number was reported at a time. It was as if Brian was interpreting the question of possibilities as, "What

3.9. IMPLICATIONS FOR MATHEMATICS EDUCATION 119

number will appear when thrown?" rather than, "What set of possibilities exist given this die?" This was confirmed later when Brian began rolling the die and was asked to predict what number would turn up. After several predictions and rolls of 0, 3, 5, and 5, Brian was asked whether he thought there was a "best guess" or whether it did not matter what number was guessed. At first he responded that it did not matter. He then changed his mind and predicted 7 (7 was not on the die). The experimenter responded, "You think 7 is the best guess. Why?" Brian answered, "I just know. I'm sick of 5s." What seemed apparent from this first session was that Brian's presentative scheme (what he noticed about the die), his notion of possibilities, and his notion of necessity were all undifferentiated. Anything could happen, the task was simply a guessing game of numbers he liked and wanted to appear.

In the second session, Brian was presented with a cubed, six-sided die having the following faces: 6, 7, 7, 8, 8, 9. He was asked to look at the die and think about what numbers might come up. "Seven," he quickly responded. Then, with surprise, . . . "Oh, there's two 7s!" The experimenter affirmed, "There's two 7s," then added, "Anything else that might come up?" Brian responded with 9, 6, and 8, but only giving one number at a time to the experimenter's repeated query of "anything else?" He did not notice that two 8s appeared on the die and his exploration of the die was nonsystematic. He rolled it and reported, "Nine!" The experimenter suggested he try to guess what number might appear before he rolled the die. He replied with a guess of 1, then looked puzzled, "Hmmm," he said, "there is no 1." "Oh, so could a 1 come up?" the experimenter asked. "No," Brian replied, "cuz it's not there." This instance appeared to be evidence of a beginning modification to his earlier egocentric scheme. Brian's presentative schemes were beginning to take into account what was not on the die, and thus served as a perturbation to his earlier scheme of "anything that I want could happen." This new possibility that a group of numbers, limited by what appeared on the die, began to be differentiated from his notion of necessity. In other words, the possibility existed, but the logical necessity of the limit by the object was not constructed. This differentiation became obvious in the next session.

The session began with Brian being presented with a round die, a small ball with numbers 1-6 painted on the surface. Although the ball was weighted to eventually stop it from rolling, the weight moved about freely inside the die giving each number an equal chance of appearing on a roll. When asked what numbers might appear, Brian immediately reported a set of numbers: 5, 6, 4, 1, 3, 6. His exploration had not been systematic, 2 was omitted and 6 was repeated twice. However, for the first time, Brian offered a series of numbers from the die as a set of possibilities. When asked to predict what would turn up when rolled, Brian predicted 6, but rolled a 3. He then predicted 1 ("cuz, it's the first number"), but rolled a 5. The experimenter asked, "Do you think there is a best guess? Or, do you think it doesn't matter?" At this point Brian demonstrated that the logical necessity of the object's limit was not solid. He responded, "There's a best guess, 7." The experimenter replied, "You think 7 is the best guess? Why?"

"Cuz, it's the luckiest number!" he answered with assuredness, even though 7 did not appear on the die.

The experimenter began the next session with the die from session two. "Let's make a picture together," she offered. "You tell me the numbers on the die and I'll put a check by them." Brian reported 6, 7, 8, and 9 and declared that there were two 7s and two 8s. His exploration this time was systematic; his presentative scheme seemed to be to acknowledge each face. The experimenter used graph paper and in bar graph style colored in one square each for the 6 and 9, and two each for the 7 and 8. On a separate sheet she wrote 6, 7, 8, 9 to use to record the actual rolls. Brian rolled. "Eight," he reported. The experimenter colored in a square above the number 8. Brian rolled again. Eight appeared again and was recorded. "What do you think will happen this time?" the experimenter asked. "Eight, cuz there's two of them." "Oh, you think that makes a difference?" the experimenter probed. "Yes," Brian replied with certainty. "There's two 7s," the experimenter pointed out. "I know," Brian replied. "But you still think it will be an 8?" queried the experimenter. "Yes. It came up two times before," Brian responded. The experimenter now realized Brian had not meant two 8s on the die, but instead was referring to the two previous trials. "Oh, that's what you mean: two times before," she stated for clarification. Brian responded with a clear affirmative and rolled again. Another 8 appeared. "See," he declared, "I told you it would be three 8s." Several further rolls were tried and recorded: 6, 7, 9, 8, 6, 7, 7, 8, 9, 7. "Oh look," Brian exclaimed on the last trial, "7 is catching up to the 8!" "I wonder why," the experimenter probed. Brian did not respond but rolled two more times, getting a 9 and a 7. Brian at this point seemed clearly to have constructed the necessity of the roll being dependent on the object. He also seemed to be proposing a new possibility to explain the roll, a possibility based on the "realizable"—selected on the basis of previous results. This new possibility suggested a new presentative scheme as he began taking note of the numbers that occurred. In an attempt to engender the construction of yet another possibility, the experimenter decided to deliberately call notice to a new connection. She began, "Look what I just noticed, Brian. When we looked at the numbers on the die, there were more 7s and 8s. Then when we rolled the die, we got more 7s and 8s. I wonder why?" Brian seemed puzzled. "Cuz, there's two 8s and two 7s on the die?" Brian asked. The experimenter replied, "Does that make them come up?" Although Brian was beginning to think about a new possibility, the necessity was still lacking, evidenced by his answer. "I don't know," he replied. Brian's remaining predictions during the session were all 7s and 8s, as he explained that those numbers were the "lucky ones."

Patrick

Patrick, age 7:10, when given the cubed, six-sided die with 0–5 on the faces, began with an immediate systematic exploration. When asked what possibilities might come up if one were to roll the die, he responded with 3, 5, 8. Then quickly said, "No, there's no 8 on here." He then added, "0, 1, and 4" and concluded, "That's all the numbers on there." Although Patrick's response regarding possibilities was clearly based on the necessity of a closed set given the faces of the die, the necessity of chance was not yet apparent. When asked if he thought there was a "best guess," he said, "I don't know, maybe. Maybe it's 5. My brother is 5." The experimenter asked in response, "Oh, do you think that would make a difference?" "Maybe," Patrick replied. The die was rolled and 2 appeared. "What do you think it will be next time?" the experimenter asked. "Five," Patrick responded, but then quickly changed his mind and offered 2. "Why?" the experimenter queried. "That's my sister's age," Patrick quickly responded.

In the second session Patrick was given the stacked die with two 7s and two 8s. When asked what numbers might come up, he responded, "8, 9, 7, 6." His presentative scheme appeared to involve only the numbers on the die. No mention was made of the fact that there were two 7s and two 8s. To Patrick, frequency was irrelevant. When asked to predict what numbers would come up before each roll, Patrick repeatedly chose 8 and 7 but gave the reasons that 8 was his favorite number and his age was 7. Although he seemed to be aware of the possibility that 7 and 8 would come up more frequently, his response seemed based only on "the realizable," the necessity of chance and frequency still escaped him. When the experimenter began to graph the faces of the die and the resulting rolls, Patrick appeared interested. He explained that 7 and 8 had come up the most and that there were two 7s and two 8s on the die. But when asked why 7 and 8 kept coming up he replied, "Maybe because those are the two lucky numbers I said." The experimenter probed, "Why would they be lucky?" Patrick, in turn, explained that on the die there were two 7s and two 8s, whereas only one 6 and one 9 appeared. Yet, when asked why that would matter, Patrick didn't know. What appeared to be hindering Patrick from making use of his knowledge was the lack of the necessity of chance.

In session three, for the first time, Patrick began to speak of the notion of chance. He was presented with the round die and asked, "What can you tell me about this one?" Patrick responded, "When you drop it, it just rolls around. You don't know what side it will land on." "Do you think there is a best guess?" the experimenter queried. "No, I don't think so," Patrick declared, "because it just rolls around and you don't know what will come up. When you roll it, *it* just stops." Patrick appeared at this point to have modified his earlier egocentric scheme. His new necessity involved the realization of the autonomy of the object, and its subjectivity to chance.

During the next session, Patrick was presented with a cubed die with five 0s, and one 7. "What would your best guess be?" Patrick was asked. "Zero," he responded, "because there's more 0s than 7s." "Oh, that makes a difference?" the experimenter probed. "Yes," replied Patrick. "If you roll it, it would turn out 0." The experimenter then brought out the die with two 7s and two 8s. "What about this one?" she asked. "The 6 and 9 won't come out as much because there's more 7s and 8s," Patrick explained. "Why does that matter?" probed the experimenter. "Because you can get them in two different ways," proferred Patrick. "Oh, I see," commented the experimenter. "It has to do with the different ways you can get it?" "Maybe," Patrick responded. Now that the necessity of chance had been realized, Patrick had generated a new possibility involving frequency. He continued exploring this possibility in the next session.

Patrick was presented with a pair of dice, regular game die with faces 1–6. "What possibilities might come up?" the experimenter began. "6, 2, 3, 5, 12, 10, 5, 6, 1, 2. That's all I can think of," Patrick stated. "Let's roll and see," suggested the experimenter. Six, 5, 10, 6, and 7 were rolled. Patrick realized that 7 was not on his list of possibilities and he asked for it to be added. "Before we go on, do you want me to write down any other possibilities?" the experimenter asked of Patrick. "Yes, 4, 13, no not 13, 11, 6, and 8," Patrick replied. "Why not 13?" the experimenter probed. "Because the highest you can go is 6 + 6 = 12," explained Patrick. "Oh, I see," commented the experimenter. Patrick then rolled and recorded with the experimenter: 3, 6, 5, 6, 10, 7, 8, 4, 9, 5, 7, 8. "Let's look at what numbers are coming up a lot," the experimenter suggested. "5, 7, and 8," responded Patrick. The experimenter probed, "Why do you think there are no 1s or 2s?" "I don't know; no 12s either," commented Patrick. He rolled a 6, 9, and 7, then declared, "All big numbers, or middle numbers actually." "Why do you think the little aren't coming up much?" asked the experimenter. "I don't know. Maybe because they're little," Patrick offered. "Why would that matter?" probed the experimenter. Patrick was puzzled, then suggested a new possibility: "Because when you roll them they could only come out of one of the dice." "What do you mean?" the experimenter asked for explanation. "Like a 2 on one die. You can't get a 3 from two dice," explained Patrick. The experimenter offered a contradiction "What about a 2 and a 1?" "Oh right, but you can't get a 1 with plusses. You could get a two by 1 + 1," he exclaimed as he began to check possibilities and eliminate some. "How about the ones that came out a lot? How can you get those?" the experimenter asked. "Like 7?" asked Patrick. "Right, like 7," affirmed the experimenter. Patrick began thinking of possibilities, "3 + 4, 6 + 1, 5 + 2, 0 + 7, but there is no 0." He then eliminated 0 + 7 showing evidence of the negation of possibilities. Although Patrick systematically proposed possibilities and then negated (with a necessity) the impossible ones, the inference of more ways to more chances was not yet constructed. The lack of this necessity became obvious when Patrick was asked, "Do you think it makes a difference that there's more ways to get 7 than there are ways to get 3 . . . for a best guess?" "Yes," he responded, "because 7 is higher." The experimenter challenged, "If I pick 12 do I have a better chance than 7?" "Maybe," Patrick replied. Although Patrick understood that in general 12 had more combinations than 7, he had not yet made the connection that the dice being used produced more combinations for 7 than for 12. He still needed to deduce which combinations were not possible.

DISCUSSION

Learning

A microanalysis of the relationship between possibility, contradiction, necessity, and probability suggests that learning is a case of making endogenous constructions. Through the generation of new possibilities that ultimately serve to contradict earlier schemes, the need for closure is established. Thus, learners construct new logical necessities to explain reality and resolve the contradictions. The balance study and the case studies of Patrick and Brian are evidence (in accord with Piaget's work) that meaningful learning occurs by modifying earlier levels of understanding. The contradictions resulting in disequilibrium do not stem directly from feedback, but are the result of the self-regulatory behavior of the learners as they propose new possibilities and construct new presentative schemes.

Learning, from this perspective, becomes understood as an organic process of invention, rather than a mechanical process of accumulation. In contrast to empiricist/reductionist approaches, learning is not seen as an accumulation of facts and associations. Rather, it appears that structural leaps in cognition are made throughout development, producing qualitatively different frameworks of understanding. Although maturationists may also prescribe to such stages, they assume they just unfold with development. In contrast, a constructivist perspective holds that the child must have experiences hypothesizing and predicting, manipulating objects, posing questions and possibilities, and researching answers and solutions in order for structural change to come about. To wit, imaging, investigating, inferring, and inventing become the new basics. From this perspective, the teacher cannot ensure children get knowledge by dispensing it; a child centered curriculum and instructional mode is mandated. The child must construct knowledge; the teacher needs to be a creative mediator in this process.

Knowledge

A microanalysis of the development of probability demonstrates that the concept is constructed through a series of structural changes. At first no differentiation exists between what the subject wants to happen and the limit of the object. The possible and necessary are interwoven. With the construction of the possibility of the limit of the object, a new presentative scheme based on the properties of the object occurs, eventually followed by the construction of the necessity of chance. Once chance becomes a necessity, the possibility of frequency as a factor is considered and tested bringing about a beginning notion of probability.

Von Glasersfeld (1987), among others, pointed out that knowledge itself needs to be understood as simply past constructed necessities by humans in the process of searching for closure. The research described in this chapter supports such a position. It appears we may never "know" the world in a "true" sense, separate from ourselves and our experiences, but only through our present logical framework that transforms, organizes, and interprets our perceptions. Furthermore, this logic is constructed and evolves through development as we interact with our environment and try to make sense of our experiences. In essence, cognitive development appears to come about through the same process as biological development—self-regulation or adaptation.

Perhaps the most we can hope for in our search for knowledge is a differentiation between the possibilities, contradictions, and necessities with a posted road sign along the way reading, "the road to knowledge is always under construction." From this perspective, math educators, as we study the evolving concepts of number and space in the young child, are simply observing fellow travelers.

Chapter
3.10

Kindergartners' Knowledge of the Preconcepts of Number

Jacques C. Bergeron
Université de Montréal, CANADA

Nicolas Herscovics
Concordia University, CANADA

In their introduction of the conceptual framework for this action group, the organizers point out a common misconception regarding mathematics: that mathematical objects somehow exist independently of human experience. Of course, without being a mathematician, one can be aware of the existence of a body of knowledge accumulated by mankind over the years, a body of knowledge that can be found in books, in journals, and in the exchanges of the many different communities of mathematicians. In this sense, mathematics does exist independently of one's personal experience. But this view does not lead anywhere when pedagogical concerns are at stake, when questions of learning and discovery are involved. And yet, much too often, mathematics is taught in a formal way, with little regard for the cognitive processes involved in the construction or reconstruction of mathematical knowledge by the individual learner. Quite frequently, mathematics is introduced as if mathematical objects had come about suddenly, their existence occurring in some kind of spontaneous creation seemingly unrelated to the learner's environment.

Even when elementary concepts such as natural numbers are involved, the separation of the mathematical object and the environment that has produced it will often prevent many adults from appreciating the very sophisticated constructions that children need to undertake in order integrate these into a global conceptual scheme. This is easily seen when adults and even teachers are asked, "What does it mean to understand number?" This chapter deals with this question by suggesting a model directly relating the construction of the number concept to two preliminary physical concepts, the notions of plurality and the notion of position in an ordered set (Bergeron & Herscovics, 1988; Herscovics & Bergeron, 1988a,b). Such a "physical" approach is important to teachers, because it provides them with a much richer choice of problems and activities to use in creating thought provoking and exciting learning situations for the initial acquisition of the number concept.

INFORMAL NUMERICAL KNOWLEDGE

Nowadays, for many children living in a Western urban community, their environment can provide them with many numerical experiences, and by the time they reach primary school, their knowledge about numbers is fairly extensive. Many television programs are addressed to them, and parents buy them books that they read together. If older brothers and sisters are around, the younger ones will want to imitate them, and many of the games they will play (cards, dominos, snakes and ladders, etc.) use numbers. These are but some of the situations in which they have the opportunity to use their numerical knowledge. However, most of the purely numerical activities used in first grade are limited to straightforward enumeration of discrete sets of objects. Very quickly, they move on to their first formal introduction to arithmetic operations by starting to work with addition. As a consequence, we find that right from the beginning, many children view mathematics essentially as a set of rules and procedures that they have to learn, and this often results in school mathematics being dissociated from the informal mathematics they use to solve problems (Ginsburg, 1977).

Activities dealing with various forms of enumeration are too often lacking in the early years, problems requiring different enumeration strategies are not presented very often, children are seldom asked to think about questions dealing with different numerical procedures, and rarely does the teacher try to exploit situations that can create some interesting cognitive conflicts in the child's conception of number. Yet, research has shown that for the first 3 years of primary school, different forms of enumeration remain extremely important in the solution of addition and subtraction problems (Bergeron, Herscovics, & Moser, 1986; Carpenter & Moser, 1984). Several major investigations have brought to light the complexity of the child's construction of the number concept. Everyone is familiar with Piaget's famous experiment on the so-called "conservation of number" in which a child has to decide whether or not two rows of objects have the same quantity after one of the rows has been elongated (Piaget & Szeminska, 1941/1967). Less well-known is Piaget's collaborators' work on the conservation of *quotity,* that is, the child's ability to maintain the numerical label associated with the elongated row, after having enumerated the other row (Greco & Morf, 1962). More recently, Fuson and her associates (Fuson, Richards & Briars, 1982) related the elaboration of counting procedures with the acquisition of the number word sequence. Gelman and Gallistel (1978) described in great detail the various errors that occur in children's enumeration procedures, and Steffe and his collaborators (Steffe, von Glasersfeld, Richards, & Cobb, 1983) related counting procedures with the construction of units.

One has to wonder why, with all this available information about the child's numerical development, so little of it is reflected in the classroom. A likely explanation is found in the teachers' inability to assess and integrate research results, for they seem to lack an overview of the pupils' construction of fundamental mathematical concepts (Bergeron & Herscovics, 1985). In order to provide a framework in which the construction of mathematical schemes can be perceived more globally, we have developed models of understanding particularly well-suited for describing the construction of the number concept and other fundamental conceptual schemes related to the physical world (Herscovics & Bergeron, 1983; 1988a). The latest model of understanding we have used is a two-tiered model; the first tier describes the *understanding of preliminary physical concepts*, and the second tier identifies the *understanding of the emerging mathematical concept*. The understanding of preliminary physical concepts involves three levels of understanding: intuitive understanding, procedural understanding of logico-physical procedures (procedures applied to objects in the physical world), and logico-physical abstraction. The understanding of the emerging mathematical concept can be described in terms of three components of understanding: procedural understanding of logico-mathematical procedures (applied to explicit mathematical objects and transformations), logico-mathematical abstraction, and the formalization of previously acquired knowledge. The remainder of this chapter describes in detail our investigations of the kindergartners' knowledge of the preconcepts of number.

THE UNDERSTANDING OF PRELIMINARY PHYSICAL CONCEPTS

If one looks at natural numbers in terms of their uses, one must take into account both their *cardinal* function, which enables us to measure the quantity of objects in a discrete set (Vergnaud, 1979), and their *ordinal* function, which enables us to determine the rank of an object in an ordered set. But well before children have any knowledge of number, they can distinguish between one and several objects. At stake here is the physical notion of *plurality*. In this sense, number in its cardinal function can be viewed as a measure of plurality. Similarly, children are aware of the *position* of an object in an ordered set, even without being able to determine its rank numerically. Hence, in its ordinal sense, number as a rank can be viewed as a measure of position in an ordered set. Thus the concepts of plurality and position in an ordered set are fundamental complementary schemes on which the notion of number can be built. This distinction leads to a finer discrimination between number, which is a mathematical construct, and plurality and position, which are physical constructs. These can be considered as preconcepts of the number scheme and, as such, pertain to the understanding of preliminary physical concepts.

We have investigated the kindergartners' understanding of these physical notions by interviewing 30 children aged between 5:3 and 6:3 (average age 5:9) in four different schools of the Montreal area.

UNDERSTANDING THE NOTION OF PLURALITY

In our analysis of the notion of plurality, we have found three distinct levels corresponding to different components of the children's understanding of this concept. At a first level, that of *intuitive understanding,* children can decide about plurality by simple visual estimation in the comparison of two sets. By comparing a set of 25 cubes with another set of 7 cubes and using a purely visual estimation, all 30 children interviewed were able to distinguish between more and less, and nearly all ($n = 29$) between many and few or little. But visual estimation proved somewhat more difficult in deciding if a randomly disposed set of 8 cubes had as many cubes as another equivalent set. This was evidenced by the fact that only 19 of the 30 children succeeded in this task. However, further questioning indicated that they did have a way of making sure—by counting the sets. Thus the problem here was one of misunderstanding the question asked because it did not convey to them the fact that it was a problem of estimation.

At a somewhat more sophisticated level, that of *procedural understanding,* nearly all the children in our sample were able to use concrete procedures based on one-to-one correspondences to generate rows of cubes with, respectively, the same as ($n = 30$), more than ($n = 29$), and fewer than ($n = 28$) a given row of 8 cubes. Surprisingly, 7 of our pupils (23.3%) could not generate a row that had one more cube than the interviewer's row.

But it is at the level of *logico-physical abstraction,* that is, in terms of the child's perception of the invariance of plurality of a set subjected to some figural transformations, that we have obtained the most interesting results. The first test we designed dealt with the invariance of plurality with respect to the visual perception of the elements of a set. The interviewer presented the pupil with a row of 11 chips glued to a large cardboard, then covered up three of the chips:

FIG. 1. Hidden-items task.

When asked, "Do you think that there are more chips than before, less chips than before, or the same amount as before, on the large white cardboard?" all but two of the children stated without any hesitation that there were fewer than before. Asked to justify their answers, most of them, those who could verbalize their thinking, indicated that it was because a part was hidden. Their answers did not change at all when three middle chips were hidden in front of them. When two distinct rows were presented and three chips in one of the rows were hidden, only one child believed that the plurality had not changed. We thought that these results were due to a possible misunderstanding of the question, children believing that our hiding meant they should ignore the hidden chips. Thus, the tasks were repeated by asking the child to insert the cardboard with the chips into a partially opaque plastic bag, the opaque part hiding three chips. The question

TABLE 1
Percents of Children Understanding Plurality Across Three Levels

Intuitive Understanding	Succeeded	Percent Succeeded
Visual estimation of "more"	30	100
Visual estimation of "less"	30	100
Visual estimation of "many"	30	100
Visual estimation of "few"	29	96.7
Visual understanding of "as many as"	19	63.3
Procedural understanding		
Can use a one-to-one correspondence to:		
generate a set with "as many" cubes	30	100
generate a set with "more" cubes	29	96.7
generate a set with "less" cubes	28	93.3
generate a set with "one more" cube	23	76.7
Abstraction		
Invariance of plurality with respect to:		
perspective (rotation of a plate with cubes)	22	73.3
displacement within same space (in a plate)	21	70.0
contraction of randomly disposed set	19	63.3
stretching a single row of cubes	18	60.0
dispersion of randomly disposed set	17	56.7
stretching a row in the presence of another one (Piaget's task)	12	40.0
Visual perception of the objects		
when inserted in partially opaque plastic bag		
one single row	4	13.3
comparing two rows	2	6.7
when hidden by a cardboard		
one single row	2	6.7
comparing two rows	1	3.3

now became, "Do you think that in the plastic bag, there are more chips than before, fewer chips than before, or the same amount as before we put them in the plastic bag?" Results were hardly changed: four children thought the quantity was the same in the case of a single set, two children thought so in the presence of two sets. The conclusion here is quite evident that between the ages of 5 and 6, most children depend on their visual perception of the objects in their conception of plurality.

Another task was aimed at determining the child's perception of the invariance of plurality with respect to dispersion and contraction. A set of nine cubes disposed randomly before the children was spread out in front of them and each one was asked if the quantity had changed or remained the same. Thirteen of the 30 pupils (43.3%) thought that the quantity had changed with the dispersion of the cubes. A later task on the contraction of the set yielded almost the same results (36.7%). This seemed to indicate that the space occupied might be a determining factor. The next task was designed to test this conjecture. Eight cubes were disposed randomly in a paper plate and the cubes were displaced in it so that no change in the occupied space would occur. Nine children (30%) thought that the plurality had been affected thus indicating that they had not yet achieved the invariance of plurality with respect to displacement within the same space. Even when the dish of cubes was merely rotated, 8 children (26.7%) still perceived a change in plurality.

The last set of tasks on plurality dealt with its invariance in the context of an elongated row. Eleven cubes were aligned in front of the child and the row was then elongated. Twelve of the 30 pupils interviewed (40%) thought that the elongation affected the plurality. The remaining 18 (60%) were aware of this invariance. However, when they were confronted with the Piagetian test in which one of two equivalent rows was elongated, only 12 children (40%) believed that the plurality was the same in the two rows and in this sense, we could say that they conserved plurality. Table 1 summarizes the results on the understanding of plurality.

UNDERSTANDING THE NOTION
OF POSITION IN AN ORDERED SET

As was the case with the notion of plurality, we have found three distinct aspects corresponding to the children's understanding of the notion of position in an ordered set. Again, intuitive understanding was based on visual estimation and rough approximations. Within the context of an ordered set, as exemplified by eight colored toy horses running in a race, all 30 pupils were familiar with expressions related to order such as *before, after, at the same time* or *together, first* and *last*. Only two of them did not understand the word *between*. All the children who were able to handle these tasks did so purely on the basis of visual estimation.

At a more advanced level, that of procedural understanding, they were able to use one-to-one correspondences in constructing rows of toy horses subject to additional constraints involving the order-related expressions mentioned earlier. All 30 succeeded in generating an equivalent row in which their red horse had to be positioned before or together with the black horse in the interviewer's parade. Only one child did not succeed in placing his red horse after the black one in the other row.

In order to discuss the notion of position more generally, we used the idea of a parade that we thought was more adequate than that of a race, because in a parade the objects remain in their initial order. But problems remained at the level of language. Whenever we used the words *place* or *position,* children were unsure if we meant "the site of an object" or its rank. We thus decided to use the word *number* (in French *numéro*), which had been used by some children quite spontaneously. For those who did not, we clarified matters by aligning a row of different colored cars and asking the pupils to indicate the third car and then the seventh one. We then told them that the third car was the "number three" car and similarly for the seventh.

At the level of logico-physical abstraction, we first verified if children perceived the variability of position of an object in a row with respect to the quantity preceding it. Using the parade, we removed the head car and asked our pupils if the red car still had the same number as before in the parade. Initially the red car had been in sixth position. Six of them (20%) thought that the position had not changed. These results are very much the same as those obtained in the following task where the row of objects was stretched and the children were questioned on the effect this had on the rank of one of the objects. Eight of the 30 pupils (26.7%) did not perceive the invariance of position with respect to the elongation of a row.

Another task dealt with the invariance of position in a row with respect to the visual perception of its elements. A parade of toy trucks entered a "tunnel" that hid the first three trucks. When asked how this affected the position of the red truck (the fourth truck, but now the first visible truck), 16 of the 30 children (53.3%) thought that it had kept its initial rank. Nor did the answers change

FIG. 2. Two Parades of trucks crossing a river in pairs.

FIG. 3. Will the two trucks with the arrows cross the river at the same time?

(except for one child) when the parade moved on and the tunnel now hid three trucks in the middle of the row. Quite clearly, the perception of the objects does affect the perception of rank for about half the children.

The last task was designed to verify if the child could in a sense conserve the position of an object in a row. Two parades of nine identical trucks were aligned in front of a "river" and a ferry was to cross the river with two trucks at a time, one from each parade (see Figure 2).

After the children had indicated that they used the situation by crossing two

TABLE 2
Percents of Children Understanding Position Across Levels of Understanding

Intuitive Understanding	Succeeded	Percent Succeeded
Visual estimation of "before/in front of"	30	100
Visual estimation of "after/behind"	30	100
Visual estimation of "at the same time/ together with"	30	100
Visual estimation of "first/last"	30	100
Visual estimation of "between"	28	93.3
Procedural understanding		
Can use a one-to-one correspondence to generate an ordered set in which		
an object is "before" another one	30	100
an object is "after" another one	29	96.7
an object comes along "at the same time" as another one	30	100
Abstraction		
Variability of position with quantity of objects preceding it	24	80.0
Invariance of position of an object with the elongation of the row with the visual perception of	22	73.3
—first three objects	16	53.3
—middle three objects	15	50.0
"Conservation of position" (invariance with translation of one of the rows)	3	10.0

pairs of trucks, the four trucks were put back in their respective parades. An arrow was placed on one of the trucks (the seventh one) and each pupil was then asked to put another arrow on the truck on the other parade that had the same number. The two parades were displaced unevenly, one parade exceeding the other by the length of two vehicles, so that the two marked trucks were no longer next to each other.

The children were asked, "Do you think that the two trucks with the arrows will cross the river at the same time? Do you think that the two trucks still have the same number?" Only three children believed that the two marked trucks would cross the river at the same time. Nor did the others think they had the same rank. We verified again if they understood the way the crossing would occur by asking them to show us how they would proceed. All of them handled this verification task perfectly. Quite clearly, children at this age do not as yet "conserve position." But it is equally evident that they can handle many tasks dealing with position, some of them quite sophisticated, without having to use numbers. Table 2 summarizes the results on the understanding of position in an ordered set ($n = 30$).

CONCLUSIONS

The results of our investigations are quite relevant to teaching. They show that the overwhelming majority of kindergartners have informally acquired a very extensive knowledge of the preconcepts of number, far more than most teachers realize. Our results also bear out the fact that at this age level, much of the children's thinking is influenced by their visual perception. But this does not imply that one should delay many of the more challenging activities, for it is by gradually having to cope with them that children arrive at some cognitive conflict. And it is in the resolution of such conflicts that cognitive obstacles are overcome and new cognitive structures are created.

The introduction of numbers can be used to create cognitive conflicts in many of the tasks we have described dealing with the invariance of plurality and position in a row under various figural transformations. For instance, in the tasks dealing with the invariance of plurality with respect to visual perception, before the children go through the act of inserting the cardboard with the chips in the plastic bag, they could be asked if the quantity will change. This can then be contrasted with the answer they provide afterwards, when relying on their visual perception. The process can then be repeated with the introduction of counting procedures.

Another task that lends itself well for the generation of cognitive contradiction is the ferry-crossing task used in the conservation of position test. After the children have predicted that the two trucks with arrows will not cross the river at the same time, they could be asked to demonstrate how the little trucks will cross by using one pair. And following the crossing of each pair, the initial question regarding the trucks with the arrows should be raised. Inevitably, they will be surprised to find that the two marked trucks cross together. Of course, at no time should the pupils be told that they are wrong, for it is not the answer that is important here, but the children's gradual realization of the contradictions caused by their reliance on visual perception. Nor should one expect this to occur immediately, simply because the questions have been raised. The children will need time to reflect about these and must come to their own conclusions by themselves. Telling them what they should think would prove to be counterproductive. One can never learn to think for someone else.

ACKNOWLEDGMENTS

Funds for these studies were provided by the Quebec Ministry of Education, FCAC, Grant no. 2923.

Chapter 3.11

Knowledge of the Numeration System Among Pre-Schoolers

Terezinha Nunes Carraher
Analucia Dias Schliemann
Universidade Federal de Pernambuco—BRAZIL

Young children's experience with counting in pre-school is often limited to counting objects. Counting objects is a way of counting in which children learn to establish a one-to-one correspondence between number labels and objects. This way of counting does not teach children much about the number system. They learn little about additive composition (at best, they may learn that n + 1 equals the following number in the number system), they learn little about the existence of a base (whatever they learn comes from the generativity of number labels), and they probably learn little about decomposition and recomposition. However, children are exposed in their everyday activities to money. Counting money, unlike counting objects, may teach children basic properties of the number system, which can be well understood in this situation and, we claim, can be used in school to teach the decimal numeration system with significant gains to the semantic understanding of the numeration system and with good transfer to learning addition and subtraction.

In this chapter, we discuss what we consider important conceptual questions in the understanding of the number system and then relate the results of a study with Brazilian pre-schoolers on their knowledge of conceptual aspects of the numeration system before they were ever taught how to write and read numbers above 10 in school. From the psychological viewpoint (which may be distinct from the mathematical viewpoint), we consider the following aspects of knowledge of a numeration system to be essential.

First, knowledge must be generative. That means that subjects must be able to use the limited set of basic symbols (in our case, the digits 0 to 9) in a way that allows them to generate any number they may wish. Subjects who understand our numeration system are not expected to say, "I can only count up to 25 because that's how far the teacher has taught in school." Ginsburg (1977) and also Gelman and her associates (Gelman & Gallistel, 1978; Gelman, & Meek, 1986) have shown that children understand the generativity of number labels and display this knowledge in the way they count. Their counting follows an undisturbed rhythm up to $10x + 9$—for example, 39—and then the rhythm is interrupted as they search their memories for what comes after 30. Although this generativity of number labels in fact reflects the existence of a base in the system, children may not learn much about the existence of a base from counting objects.

Second, in order to understand a numeration system, children must understand the regrouping that goes on when one goes from, for example, 39 to 40. The process of assigning number labels to objects in counting does not involve anything like regrouping. Forty, even when "generated" and not memorized as part of a sequence, may be just the next label. The child may not realize that there are now 4 tens. In contrast to counting objects, counting money may help children understand this idea of regrouping because money involves relative and absolute values. Even young children may realize that two people who have four coins have different amounts of money if one has 4 ten-cent pieces and the other has 4 one-cent pieces. They may also realize that it is possible to change one ten-cent piece for the one-cent pieces without loosing any money. In order to deal with the concept of "base," the notions of relative and absolute value must be brought into the conceptual framework for counting sums.

Third, understanding a numeration system also requires that subjects understand the possibility of combining different relative values to form a single total amount. Counting 4 ten-cent pieces, counting 4 one-cent pieces, knowing that they are different totals is not enough. It is necessary for children to be able to put these two together and to know that it gives them forty-four. The process of coordinating different relative values into one total is related to the idea of decomposition: 44 can be seen as composed of (or decomposable into) 4 ten-cent pieces and 4 one-cent pieces. Resnick (1983) has termed this the additive property of the numeration system.

The fact that money creates situations in which all these aspects of a numeration system are encountered encouraged us to verify whether children could understand some properties of number systems in pre-school before they were formally taught how to write numbers. In the Brazilian school system, children are engaged in oral counting only up to 5 or 9 in pre-school. Higher values are used, still in oral counting only, in the beginning of elementary school. Number writing is limited to one-digit numbers until about the age of seven, which corresponds to the end of the first year of elementary school. School teaching therefore is restricted to situations which do not offer a good basis for learning about the numeration system. In everyday life, however, children encounter situations in which they use or count money and which engage them in activities that can help them in their understanding of the numeration system.[1]

This study investigated whether children with no previous school instruction on the number system could understand three different aspects of numeration systems: (1) the ability to distinguish between relative and absolute value; (2) the ability to sequentially count coins of the same relative value taking number of coins and total sum into account; and (3) the ability to combine token coins of different values into a single total.

SUBJECTS

The subjects were 72 Brazilian pre-schoolers from two schools, one which is attended by children from lower socio-economic groups and another which is attended by children from a higher socio-economic group. The lower socio-economic children had higher age levels, 6/7 years, while middle-class children had lower age levels, 5/6 years.

PROCEDURE

Children were initially pre-tested on their counting ability. Their performance on this initial task was not a screening procedure but rather a procedure to determine whether they would work with values greater than 10. All problems were posed to all the children afterwards in either one of two forms. For children who could count above twenty, tokens of different colors, which we told them were money from a foreign country, were assigned the values of 10 and 1. For children who could count up to only 20, the same tokens were assigned the values of 1 and 5.

Children were asked to solve three tasks with money in a fixed order due to the fact that the tasks became increasingly more complex as the interview went on: (1) a Relative Values Task; (2) a Counting Money with Some Values Task; and (3) a Counting Money with Different Values Task. A Conservation of Number Task was also given at the end but results will not be discussed here.

---

[1] Children elsewhere may learn about writing numbers at an earlier age, in which case their school learning may be on a par with their knowledge of money or even ahead of their knowledge of money, if they have little experience with money. In Brazil, many children are exposed to small sums of money in pre-school although may vary a lot from one home to another. However, what is of interest here is not only the fact that informal learning about properties of the numeration system can occur on the basis of dealing with money but that schools can actually take advantage of money, a situation which can be used for creating meanings for basic invariants of the number system.

The Relative Values Task

Children were asked to play a money game (adapted from Carraher & Schliemann, 1983) in which tokens of two different colors were to represent different values. For children who could count above 20, nine tokens of each denomination were available with the values 1 and 10; for children who could count up to only 20, four tokens of each denomination were available with the values 1 and 5. Although the children were told that they were working with foreign money, the Brazilian currency "cruzeiro" was used to refer to the values so that the tasks would not be made unnecessarily unfamiliar.

To investigate children's understanding of relative value, they were asked to judge which of two arrays of money had the higher total value. The arrays were constructed in such a way that responses based on the number of tokens were distinct from those based on the values (for example, five tokens worth ten were compared with five tokens worth one). Three items were used: (1) in which the difference in the arrays was one token, (2) in which both arrays had the same number of tokens, and (3) in which the value of the arrays was consecutive (that is, 9 singles versus one ten for children working with ones and tens and 4 singles and one five for children working with ones and fives). The first item was treated as an example. If the child answered according to the absolute number of the tokens or could not count the money in the arrays correctly, the interviewer counted the money with the child and repeated the question about which array had more money in it, adding the total sum of money to the question (for example, "Who can buy more candy, you with these coins and 4 cruzeiros total or I, with this one coin that is worth five cruzeiros?"). Only the last two items were taken into account when responses were analyzed.

Performance on this task was classified into one of the following categories: (1) does not take into account relative value when answering; (2) takes into account the relative value but is unable to justify the answer by counting the totals; and (3) takes into account the relative values of the tokens and justifies the answer by counting the totals in each array.

Counting Money with a Single Denomination

In this task, children were engaged in a store game in which the experimenter was the salesclerk and the child purchased small toys paying for them with the token money. Four trials were used in which children were asked to pay values that involved a single denomination, two requiring that children use one-cruzeiro tokens and two requiring that children use the higher-value tokens (for example, when children attempted to pay for an item that was said to cost 20 cruzeiros, they could not use one-cruzeiro tokens because they only had nine of these tokens to play with). A passing score was given to children who succeeded in both items of each denomination (counting units and counting higher values).

Counting Money with Different Denominations

The store game continued with four more trials in which children were asked by the interviewer to pay sums that required them to combine tokens of different denominations. For children working with numbers above ten, the values were 13, 26, 35, and 42. For children working with numbers smaller than twenty, the values were 8, 12, 14, and 6.

If the child did not succeed in the first trial, which was treated as an example, the experimenter reversed the roles of seller and buyer with the child, paid for the toy while counting the money out loud, and then reversed the roles again, asking the child to pay for the next three items.

RESULTS

Slightly less (47%) than half of the children could not satisfy the conditions for working with numbers above 20 and were tested with tokens with values 5 and 1. This may, in fact, be a more difficult task than the one which uses values of 10 and 1, in which less actual computation is necessary if children can count in tens; counting by fives is not practiced at this age in Brazil but counting by tens may be observed.

In the Relative Values Task, 40% of the children did not display an understanding of relative value and took into account only the number of tokens in the array when they responded. For example, two arrays with the same number of tokens were said to have the same sum of money despite the fact that the tokens in one array were worth more than the tokens in the other.

Among the children who responded on the basis of number of tokens were, surprisingly enough, 14 who could count the total value of money in the array but persisted in saying that the array with more tokens would allow one to buy more candy. For example, Simone, 6 years old, said that 4 tokens worth one cruzeiro could buy more candy than 1 token worth five. When the experimenter asked her how much money was in each array, she responded correctly. The question was posed a second time (Who can buy more candy with this money, you with these coins that add up to 4 cruzeiros or I with this coin worth 5 cruzeiros?), she insisted that the 4 cruzeiros could buy more candy. It is possible that these children misunderstood the question: "Who can buy more candy with this money?" in view of the fact that they could name the total sum. However, it is also possible that their knowledge of numbers was such that numbers are labels attached in a fixed sequence to series of objects but do not express a necessarily increasing order of the corresponding amounts—that is, numbers may not be quantifiers for these children. In this case, there is no contradiction between saying "this is four" and "that is five" and "this is more than that." We do not have enough information to distinguish in this case whether there was a misunderstanding of whether children simply did not see numbers as quantifiers.

In contrast, 60% of all children were able to take relative value into account; 15.5% could not count the values correctly (they would, for example, say "I have four and you have a lot," without being able to say how much four coins worth five cruzeiros each add up to) and the remaining 44.5% could both count the money and make correct decisions about who could buy more candy.

Performance on the Counting Money with a Single Denomination Task was analyzed by assigning a pass only to children who counted correctly on both trials of the same denomination coins. Of all children, 29% passed only the items in which they had to count units and all the remaining passed the items in which higher values had to be counted. This task turned out to be rather difficult for the children working with tokens worth five when they had to figure out the values of arrays with two and three tokens. In their case, they could not rely on counting as easily as children counting by tens did. They had to add five and five, which they did by using their fingers. However, when they had to count an array with three tokens worth five, the children who did not have a "count on" strategy had a lot of difficulty, for they ran out of fingers to count. This difficulty may account for the fact that such a large number of children (29%) could count only the arrays with units.

The task in which children were asked to compose sums of money which had to include tokens of both denominations was passed by 39% of the children. Errors in this task included mainly two types. Some children showed a "failure to shift" behavior—that is, they were unable to shift denominations in the middle of their counting. If they started out by counting in units, they treated the tokens worth ten as units despite the fact that they were reminded of the value of the tokens. If they started out by counting the tens, they went on to count units as if they were tens despite the interviewer's reminding them of the value of the token. Another type of error, which was observed only in the example trial but was corrected after the interviewer's demonstration, was a "failure to blend"—that is, children would say the totals for each denomination without putting them together in one amount (for example, "ten and three" or "three and ten" instead of "thirteen").

Of the 38 children who were able to generate number labels systematically counting beyond 20, only 22 succeeded in all three tasks—displaying the ability to distinguish absolute and relative value, to count tokens taking relative value into account, and to combine tokens of different values in order to generate particular amounts. Of the 28 children who were able to correctly combine tokens of different values, 22 had been tested with units and tens and 6 had been tested with units and fives.

A comparative analysis of the three parts of the counting money tasks—counting units only, counting tens or fives only, and counting mixed values—showed that only two children (out of 72) who passed a more difficult item had failed an easier one.

DISCUSSION

These results uncover some interesting aspects of the acquisition of basic concepts related to the understanding of the numeration system. First, only a little more than half of the children who are able to generate numbers correctly were also able to display knowledge of basic conceptual aspects of the numeration system. Generating number labels systematically does not seem to be a sufficient condition for understanding the underlying principles. That is not very surprising and many people would expect this to be case. Second, a small number of children showed a good understanding of the conceptual aspects we were probing for despite the fact that they were not able to generate number labels systematically. This is rather surprising because it indicates that knowing number labels is not a necessary condition for understanding the numeration system. Third, the development of knowledge of the numeration system displayed by pre-schoolers in this study appears to be orderly in the sense that it is possible to find sequences in this acquisition—the type of developmental finding that can be helpful to teachers when they are planning their teaching schemas for particular topics. If one knows that some things come before others, one can plan teaching in that way. Finally, the understanding of basic aspects of the numeration system we observed in this study despite the absence of previous formal training was displayed in the context of counting money—an activity which, we suggest, is a good situation for starting children in the comprehension of the properties of numeration systems. We do not know whether the children would display this same understanding if the reference to money had been removed—a question which remains to be investigated. What we do know is that mathematics teachers have developed concrete materials which are not everyday materials but rather pedagogical devices for teaching these concepts to older children and have found that many children fail to understand what the teachers want them to learn. Presently, some teachers in Brazil are working with pre-school children under the supervision of one of our associates (Monteiro de Silva) and helping these children to go from counting money to writing numbers using place value. These results have been very encouraging. Another study has also shown that writing numbers and carrying out additions and subtractions with regrouping with the support of money has durable positive effects on children's performance in addition and subtraction calculation. Although further analysis is still called for, it seems worth pursuing the idea that monetary systems embody important conceptual aspects of numeration systems and that the meanings acquired in everyday life may make money a powerful context in which to start teaching children about numeration systems.

Chapter
3.12

An Analysis of First-Grade Children's Writing Number Sentences in Solving Word Problems

Junichi Ishida
University of Tsukuba, JAPAN

Several studies (Carpenter & Moser, 1982; Ishida, 1987; Ishida & Koyasu, 1988; Tomioka, 1961) have shown that the semantic structure of word problems is an important factor affecting children's performance on word problems. Problems in the joining/separating class have an initial quantity and some direct or implied action that causes a change in the quantity. Problems in the combine class represent a static relationship involving two distinct quantities that are parts of a whole. Problems in the comparison class involve the comparison of two disjoint quantities. These problems differ in the semantic structure used to describe the problem situation.

Furthermore, when we consider children's abilities to write number sentences in solving word problems, we should be aware of the complexity of the relation between word problems and number sentences. Number sentences have two different functions; they can be used either as a mathematical representation of the semantic relations or as a mathematical notation of the arithmetic operation for finding the answer. In some types of problems, number sentences can fulfill both functions, but in other types of problems, these two aspects have to be expressed by different number sentences. Even if most children have solved the problems using informal strategies, they failed to write number sentences because they tried to combine both functions into a single number sentence (DeCorte & Verschffel, 1987).

Carpenter & Moser (1984) found that first-grade children could learn to represent a variety of problems provided they were taught to write noncanonical number sentences to represent the action in the problem, even in the case for which they were not explicitly taught the appropriate number sentence form.

3.12. NUMBER SENTENCES IN SOLVING WORD PROBLEMS 143

Japanese children do not receive instruction in writing both canonical and noncanonical number sentences when they learn to perform addition and subtraction word problems. In fact, most word problems that were given to them at the first grade can fulfill both functions. They do not need to distinguish between the two aspects; for example, they do not learn to solve join missing addend problems. In addition to this, some teachers tend to emphasize only facts and procedures and forget to stress the meaning of the number sentences. Therefore, some children have difficulty in understanding the role of number sentences that express the relationship among quantities in the problem situation.

It is interesting to observe first-grade children's responses to join missing addend problems. It is through the analysis of their errors that we can examine the effect of the instruction in writing number sentences. Children's knowledge level should be considered in our analysis of their errors. Riley, Greeno & Heller (1983) identified three basic levels of skills for solving change problems.

For change problems, children in Level 1 are limited to external representations of problem situations using physical objects. They cannot solve join missing addend problems. Children in Level 2 can keep a mental record of the role of each piece of data in the problem. This allows children in Level 2 to solve join missing addend problems. Both Level 1 and Level 2 children are limited to direct representation of problem structure. Level 3 children have a part-whole schema, and they can construct a representation of the relationships among all the pieces of information in the problem before solving it. They do not rely on directly representing the action of the problem.

According to Riley and colleagues' three levels of skills, the way the children write the number sentence for join missing addend problems might depend on their performance levels in solving word problems. Consequently, Level 2 children could write noncanonical number sentences for representing the join missing addend problems. At this time, they could be expected to be more affected by the effect of instruction in writing number sentences.

This study investigates how first-grade children's performance and error types can change with 6-months of instruction. Specifically, it explores the group difference based on the type of children's errors committed in writing number sentences for join missing addend word problems.

1. *First trimester* (from April to July). Children have learned how to write number sentences of the form $a + b = ?$ and $a - b = ?$ to represent problem situations. They have also learned how to solve number sentences in both of these forms for sums between 0 and 10. The problem situations used for instruction were join (addition), separate (subtraction), combine (addition), and compare (subtraction).

2. *Second trimester* (from September to December). Children learned how to solve combine (subtraction) problems. The emphasis was on computation involv-

ing sums between 11 to 20. Note: In Japan, the join missing addend (subtraction) situation is taught in the second grade, not in the first grade.

METHOD

Subjects

The subjects were 137 first-grade children from four elementary schools in Aichi prefecture in Japan.

Tasks

The tasks used in this study were the following six word problems.

- Join (addition): Three children were playing. Five children came. How many children are there now?
- Separate (subtraction): Hiroko and her friends had 6 apples. They ate 4 apples. How many apples do they have now?
- Combine (addition): We enjoyed fishing. I caught 3 fish. My brother caught 4 fish. How many fish did we catch altogether?
- Combine (subtraction): There are 9 flowers altogether. Some are yellow and some are white. There are 6 yellow flowers. How many white flowers are there?
- Compare (subtraction): Yoshiko bounced a ball 7 times. Akira bounced it 5 times. How many more times did Yoshiko bounce a ball than Akira?
- Join missing addend (subtraction): Four children were playing. Then some children came. Now there are 7 children. How many children came?

All problems were constructed so as to provide relatively simple examples with respect to syntax, vocabulary, sentence length, and familiarity of problem situation. The following five number triples were used: (3, 5, 8), (2, 4, 6), (3, 4, 7), (3, 6, 9), (2, 5, 7). The number triples for the problems were selected to conform to the following specification: the sum of the two lesser numbers in each triple must be less than 10.

Procedure

All children had this test three times. In September, December, and March. Each test lasted for about 20 minutes and, in each test, manipulative objects were not available.

RESULTS

Relative Difficulty

Table 1 shows the performance data for the six problems in each of the three testing periods. In this table, the percentage of correct responses is shown. Responses were coded as correct if they were correct canonical number sentences or if they were correct noncanonical number sentences and the correct numeral was written as the answer. Examples of correct and incorrect responses to the join missing addend problem are as follows.

correct responses: $7 - 4 = 3$, Ans. 3
                      $4 + 3 = 7$, Ans. 3
incorrect responses: $7 + 4 = 11$, Ans. 11
                      $4 + 3 = 7$, Ans. 7
                      $4 + 7 = 3$, Ans. 3

The join, separate, and combine (subtraction) problems were easier than the others; most children performed well on these problem types at the time of the first test in September. The combine (subtraction) and compare (subtraction) problems were of intermediate difficulty. In the first test, they were solved correctly by about 40.0%–60.0% of children only; in the second test, about

TABLE 1
Peformance Data on the Six Word Problems for the Three Tests
($N = 197$)

Problem Type	1st Test	2nd Test	3rd Test
Join	92.4%	99.3%	99.3%
(add.)	129 (4)	136 (1)	136 (1)
Separate	87.6%	96.4%	97.1%
(sub.)	120	132 (3)	133 (2)
Combine	94.2%	97.8%	99.3%
(add.)	129	134	136 (2)
Combine	49.6%	76.6%	81.8%
(sub.)	68 (12)	105 (7)	112 (4)
Compare	59.9%	81.8%	86.1%
(sub.)	82 (1)	112 (4)	118
Join missing addend	14.6%	34.3%	51.1%
(sub.)	20	47	70 (1)

Note. In each box the upper written figure corresponds to the percentage of correct responses while the lower written figure corresponds to the frequency of correct responses. The figure enclosed in parentheses shows the number of calculation errors.

80.0% of the children performed them correctly. The most difficult problem was join missing addend (subtraction). At the time of the third test, only 47.3% performed it correctly.

At the time of the first test, the compare problem was more difficult than the separate problem. At the end of first grade, the children's performance on the problems, except the join missing addend problem was good. The results show that most children could solve problems of the types they have learned during the first grade. These results corroborate those of prior research (Riley, Greeno, & Heller, 1983).

Error Analysis

The errors children made, excluding incorrect calculations, were classified as follows:

Type A: This was assigned when the number sentence used was not appropriate in spite of getting the correct answer. For example, if children wrote the number sentence as $7 + 4 = 3$ in solving the join missing addend problem, the error was marked as type A.

Type B: The number sentence used was correct, but the answer given with regard to the question was not correct. That is, they did not write the correct numeral for the answer to the question but wrote the numeral being placed on the right side of the equal sign. For example, in the case of the join missing addend, the number sentence given was $4 + 3 = 7$ but the answer given was 7 rather than 3. Most of the errors in the join missing addend problem were of this type.

Type C: This was assigned when children did not choose the correct operation. For example, in the case of the join missing addend problem, a type C response was $7 + 4 = 11$, the answer given was 11.

Type D: This was assigned when nothing was written.

Type E: This was assigned when the error cannot be classified as type A, B, C or D.

Table 2 gives the frequency of each error type on each problem for each of the three tests.

There were relatively fewer errors in the first three problems; therefore only the last three problems were examined. We performed an error analysis for the combine (subtraction), compare (subtraction), and join missing addend (subtraction) problems that the children did not perform well at the time of the first test in September.

TABLE 2
Number of Five Error Types on the Six Word Problems for the Three Tests

Problem Type	A Type			B Type			C Type			D Type			E Type		
	1st	2nd	3rd	1st	2nd	3rd	1st	2nd	3rd	1st	2nd	3rd	1st	2nd	3rd
Join (add.)	2	0	0	0	0	0	1	0	1	3	1	0	2	0	0
Separate (sub.)	5	1	0	0	0	0	5	2	2	6	2	1	1	0	1
Combine (add.)	2	2	0	1	0	0	1	0	1	4	1	0	0	0	0
Combine (sub.)	9	6	5	17	4	4	18	18	15	19	1	0	6	3	1
Compare (sub.)	13	9	4	4	0	2	20	14	13	14	2	0	4	0	0
Join missing addend (sub.)	13	17	13	32	35	25	31	30	28	31	5	0	10	3	1

Combine (Subtraction) Problem

In the first test, B, C, and D Type errors were made very often. In the second and third tests, the number of Type B and D errors considerably decreased, but the number of Type C errors did not decrease as much.

It is not surprising, in view of the time provided to learn the combine (subtraction) problem in the instruction program, that the number of the Type B errors decreased rapidly. At the time of the first test, children had not learned combine (subtraction) problems yet, so they tended to write the number sentence $4 + 3 = 7$, which was based on the semantic structure, rather than a number sentence like $7 - 4 = 3$, which was aimed at finding an answer.

Compare (Subtraction) Problem

At the time of the first test, the frequent errors were Type A, C, and D. But the number of Type B errors, was few. Although Type D errors decreased at the time of the third test, the percentage of Type C errors remained at about 10%.

Join Missing Addend (Subtraction) Problem

At the time of the first test, Type B, C, and D errors were found frequently. Both Type B and Type C errors occurred all through three test times.

Both canonical and noncanonical number sentences were found as correct responses to the join missing addend problem at the time of the first test. Eighteen of 20 responses were canonical number sentences and only 2 were noncanonical. Although 33 children wrote noncanonical number sentences for the join missing addend problem in the first test, almost all children committed Type B error. There were a few children who wrote noncanonical number sentences and got correct answers; one in the second test, and 3 in the third test.

The number of Type C errors did not decrease sharply in solving these three problems. For the combine (subtraction) problem, there were 18 Type C errors in the first test, 18 in the second test, and 15 in the third test. In the join missing addend problem, there were 31, 30, and 28 Type C errors during the first, second, and third tests respectively.

Group Differences

As previously mentioned, first-grade children in Japan do not learn to solve join missing addend (subtraction) problems. For the purpose of further investigation, the first-grade children were divided into three groups based on the type of errors they made in the join missing addend problem excluding Type E errors.

Group 1: Children who wrote a canonical number sentence including careless mistakes in computation. ($N = 18$)

3.12. NUMBER SENTENCES IN SOLVING WORD PROBLEMS 149

Eighteen of the 20 correct responses to the join missing addend problem were subtraction sentences. Children who wrote canonical number sentences for the join missing addend problem were thought to be able to reconstruct the problem situation without relying on direct representation of the action. The performance of these children would correspond to Riley and colleagues' Level 3.

Group 2: Children whose error was Type A or B. Two children who wrote non-canonical number sentences and wrote down correct answers were included in group 2. ($N = 47$)

Children with Type A errors cannot express the number sentence correctly, though they can get a correct answer using some informal strategies. They seemed to have formulated a mind set that an answer should be written on the right side of the equal sign and the operation should be chosen in accordance with the problem situation. On the other hand, children with Type B errors can express the number sentence according to the sequence of actions, but in the case of $a + ? = c$, $? = b$ the quantity they consider as the answer is not b but c. They think that the position of the answer in a number sentence is always on the right side of the equal sign.

Children in both Type A and Type B are thought to be able to construct a mental representation relying on the direct action described in the problem. But their responses seem to be influenced by the instruction previously received in writing number sentences. These children would correspond to Riley and colleagues' Level 2.

Group 3: Children whose error was Type C or D ($N = 82$)

Children in Type C seem to write the number sentence without constructing a mental representation correctly. Thus, they cannot get a correct answer. Responses of Type D children to the combine (subtraction) and compare (subtraction) were very similar to those of Type C children. These children might correspond to Riley et al.'s Level 1.

Table 3 shows the performance data for each of the three groups on six problem types: join (addition), separation (subtraction), combine (addition), combine (subtraction), compare (subtraction), and join missing addend (subtraction) problems in each of the three tests.

Tables 4, 5, and 6 show the frequency of each error type by each group for each of the testing periods.

There was little difference in the performance of three groups in the join, separate, and combine (addition) problems through the three testing periods. Although the difference in performance between Group 1 and Group 2 was found in the combine (subtraction) and compare (subtraction) problems during the first test, this difference decreased at the time of the second and third tests.

TABLE 3
Correct Percentage of the Three Groups on the Six Word Problems for the Three Tests

Problem Type	Join (add.)			Separate (sub.)			Combine (add.)			Combine (sub.)			Compare (sub.)			Join Missing Addend (sub.)		
Test time	1st	2nd	3rd	1st	2nd	3rd	1st	2nd	3rd	1st	2nd	3rd	1st	2nd	3rd	1st	2nd	3rd
Group 1	100	100	100	88.9	100	100	94.4	94.4	100	83.3	94.4	88.9	83.3	100	100	100	83.3	83.3
Group 2	97.8	100	100	95.7	97.8	100	100	100	100	48.9	80.9	91.5	68.1	87.2	93.6	4.3	38.3	57.4
Group 3	88.7	98.4	98.4	80.6	93.5	93.5	88.7	96.8	98.4	40.3	66.1	67.7	43.5	71.0	77.4	0.0	21.0	37.1

TABLE 4
Group 1's Number of Error Types on the Three Word Problems for the Three Tests (N = 18)

Problem Type		Combine (sub.)			Compare (sub.)			Join Missing Addend (sub.)		
Test time		1st	2nd	3rd	1st	2nd	3rd	1st	2nd	3rd
Correct		15(4)	17(1)	16(1)	15	17	18	18	15	15
	A	1	1	0	0	1	0	0	3	2
	B	0	0	0	0	0	0	0	0	1
Error type	C	1	0	2	2	0	0	0	0	0
	D	1	0	0	0	0	0	0	0	0
	E	0	0	0	0	0	0	0	0	0

In the combine (subtraction) and join missing addend problems, the difference between Group 2 and 3's performances was negligable at the first time, but the difference was larger at the time of the second and third tests.

For Group 1, it was easy for children to solve the combine (subtraction), compare (subtraction), and join missing addend (subtraction) problems at the time of the first test in September. Group 2's performance of the compare (subtraction) problem was better than that of Group 3, but Group 1's performance of both problems was best. Although Group 2's correct responses of the combine (subtraction) problem were few at the first test, the rates of Type C, D, and E errors were lower than Group 3's.

As for the combine (subtraction) problem, the percentage of correct answers was high in the second test. This was due to related instruction given after the first test. The number of Type B errors was fewer during the second and third tests, and those who made Type B errors during the first test wrote canonical number sentences.

TABLE 5
Group 2's Number of Error Types on the Three Word Problems for the Three Tests (N = 47)

Problem Type		Combine (sub.)			Compare (sub.)			Join Missing Addend (sub.)		
Test time		1st	2nd	3rd	1st	2nd	3rd	1st	2nd	3rd
Correct		23(2)	38(4)	43(3)	32	41(1)	44	2	18	27
	A	4	1	1	6	2	2	13	8	3
	B	13	4	1	4	1	0	32	15	12
Error type	C	2	3	1	3	2	1	0	5	5
	D	2	0	0	1	1	0	0	0	0
	E	3	0	1	1	0	0	0	1	0

TABLE 6
Group 3's Number of Error Types on the Three Word Problems
for the Three Tests ($N = 62$)

Problem Type		Combine (sub.)			Compare (sub.)			Join Missing Addend (sub.)		
		1st	2nd	3rd	1st	2nd	3rd	1st	2nd	3rd
Test time										
Correct		25(5)	41(2)	42	27(1)	44(2)	48	0	13	23(1)
	A	4	4	4	6	6	2	0	6	7
	B	3	0	2	0	0	2	0	15	9
Error type	C	13	15	12	14	11	10	31	23	22
	D	15	1	0	13	1	0	31	3	0
	E	3	1	0	2	0	0	0	0	0

Note. The figure enclosed in parentheses shows the number of calculation errors.

As for the join missing addend (subtraction) problem, some Group 2 members still had difficulty in solving it and made Type B errors until the third test. In fact, 25.5% (12/47) of responses in the third test were Type B errors.

The performance of Group 3 was worse than that of Group 1 and Group 2 in general for each of the three tests on each of the three problem types described. This result shows that there was a group difference at the time of the first test and the difference between Group 3 and the other two groups did not decrease until the time of the third test.

The reason for the group differences during the first grade year may be attributed to the fact that the number of Type C errors committed by Group 3 did not decrease remarkably. This fact holds for three problem types: combine (subtraction), compare (subtraction), and join missing addend (subtraction). (See Table 6.)

DISCUSSION

This study tried to identify error types in solving simple word problems from the viewpoint of writing number sentences. From the error analysis of the first test, four error types appeared. These were particularly notable in the errors on the join missing addend (subtraction) problem, combine (subtraction) problem, and compare (subtraction) problem. Of these three types of problems, join missing addend (subtraction) and combine (subtraction) were not taught to children at the time of the first test.

The changes of each error type during three test times are as follows:

1. There were some children who made a Type A error at the time of the first test. Regarding this type of error, its frequency in join missing addend problems

3.12. NUMBER SENTENCES IN SOLVING WORD PROBLEMS 153

did not decrease by the third test, whereas on two other types of problems, combine (subtraction) and compare (subtraction), it decreased. (See Table 2.) This fact could be documented by looking at the change of this error type in Group 3. That is, the frequency for Group 3 was 0 at the first test, 6 at the second test and 7 at the third test. Such a pattern that the frequency of Type A errors decreased in Group 2 over testing time and it increased in Group 3 was very similar to the change of frequency of Type B errors in Group 2 and 3.

2. Most Type B errors were found in the combine (subtraction) problem and the join missing addend problem. After the children were taught the combine (subtraction) during the second trimester, Type B errors considerably decreased. However, the frequency of this error type in the join missing addend problem did not decrease during the three testing periods.

Furthermore, by investigating the change in Type B errors in each of the three groups, Type B errors did not seem to continue in general during the three testing periods. The frequency of Type B errors decreased during the second test (32/47 → 15/47) for Group 2. This error type became more frequent in the second test for Group 3, but like Group 2, Group 3's Type B errors decreased in the third test in comparison with the preceding test (15/62 → 9/62).

3. The frequency of Type C errors for the two problem types combine (subtraction) and join missing addend (subtraction) did not decrease in each subsequent testing period. This fact indicates that some of the children at Grade 1 tend to continue making this type of error during the school year. In fact, 17 out of 62 children involving Group 3 who earlier made an error of Type C or D committed same type of error in the third test.

Furthermore, this error type was found across problem types. That is, at the time of the third test, 9 of 12 children who made this error type in the combine (subtraction) problem made the same error type in the join missing addend (subtraction) problem, and 8 of 10 children who made this Type C error in the compare (subtraction) problem made the same type of error in the join missing addend problem.

This suggests that three problem types are difficult for some of the first grade children to solve. The relative difficulty of these problem types may show that children making Type C errors have difficulty in constructing a mental representation of the problem situation. On the other hand, the semantic structure of the first three problems corresponds to number sentences to find the answer. That is, in these problems the semantic structure is in agreement with the desired actions.

There were both progress and remainder subgroups in Group 2 and Group 3. In Group 2, the number of Type A and B errors decreased and the number of writings of correct canonical number sentences increased through the second and third test (progress subgroup). But 9 of 12 children who made Type B errors at the third test made the same type of error at the first test (remainder subgroup). In

Group 3, a transformation of performance level was found during three test times; the first subgroup wrote a canonical number sentence in the second test. The second subgroup made Type A and B errors like Group 2 in the second test. In the third test, Type A and B errors decreased while the number of correct canonical number sentence increased. The first and second subgroup in Group 3 can be characterized as a progress group. Meanwhile the third subgroup can be characterized as remainder group because it continued to make Type C errors during the three test periods.

Type A and B could be influenced by the arithmetic instruction during the first trimester. For every word problem they had worked on during the first trimester, the form of the number sentences for finding an answer is the same as the number sentences for expressing relationships among qualities. But in solving the join missing addend problem, children must choose the subtraction for finding the answer although the situation of the problem is additive. These error types seem to arise partly due to both a mind set formulated through instruction in writing number sentences and performance level limited to direct representation of the problem.

I need to discuss this result further from the point of children's performance level. Why were children in Group 1 not influenced by the negative effect of arithmetic instruction in the first test? The difference of responses between Group 1 and Group 2 could be interpreted as follows: children included in Group 1 can reorganize structure of the problem. They can understand the alternative problem structure: (result-set) − (start set) = (change set increased). The reorganization of the semantic structure of the join missing addend problem may mean that children have a part-whole schema. However children in Group 2 understand the problem structure only to the extent that they can grasp the context of the problem situation. That is: (start set) + (change set increased) = (result set).

Children in Group 3 seem to write number sentences without understanding the semantic structure of the join missing addend problem. They probably judge whether the problem situation is additive or subtractive based on key words in the problem text. According to De Corte and Verschaffel's (1985) competent problem-solving model, these children do not seem to pass the first stage of the model; the solution process of a competent problem solver starts with the construction of a global mental representation of the problem situation. This could be explained as follows: (a) they lack the skill required to construct a mental model of the join missing addend problem, or (b) they cannot utilize the skill, although they have acquired it, like children in Groups 1 and 2.

We should notice that although the performance of Group 3 in the third test improved in comparison with the performance in the first test, the score was lower than those of the other two groups. This may be attributed to the fact that in Group 3 there were many children who continued to make Type C errors during the three testing periods. These children also seem to be influenced by the arithmetic instruction in another sense. That is, they think that number sentences have no relevance to their real life.

FINDINGS

1. The influence of the semantic structure of the join missing addend word problem appeared in children's number sentences. Moreover, the way of writing number sentences seems to depend on children's performance level.
2. Three different groups were identified from the error analysis of the join missing addend problem:
   a. Group 1 can reorganize the problem structure so they can write the canonical number sentence for finding the answer.
   b. Group 2 can understand the problem structure relying on the direct action described in the problem.
   c. Group 3 cannot understand the relationship among the three quantities in the problem.
3. There were both progress and remainder subgroups in Group 2 and Group 3. This implies that some children are influenced by the negative effect of writing number sentences in the first grade.

Chapter
3.13

Young Children's Thinking Strategies and Levels of Capacity to Process Mathematical Information

Gillian Boulton-Lewis
Brisbane College of Advanced Education, AUSTRALIA

Cognitive theorists (Case, 1985; Fischer, 1980; Halford, 1982; in preparation) have proposed, from different theoretical perspectives, that there is an upper limit to children's capacity to process information that increases with maturation and learning. It is argued that such an upper limit determines the level at which children are able to cognize mathematical and other concepts. Halford (1982; in preparation) proposed three levels of thinking that depend on children's increasing capacity to match systems of symbols to elements in the environment. Each of the levels of thinking proposed by Halford defines a class of tasks with a common degree of structural complexity. At Level 1R (relational mappings as described by Halford, in preparation) tasks are defined as ordered pairs that include binary relations and unary operators. At Level 2 (system mappings) tasks are defined as sets of ordered triples, including combinations of binary relations (as in transitive reasoning), ternary relations, and binary operations (as in e.g., addition of single-digit numbers). In this chapter the concern is with children at Levels 1R and 2 of thinking.

It is an unfortunate but well-documented finding that aboriginal–Australian children are not usually as successful in formal school learning as their nonaboriginal Australian peers (Bourke & Parkin, 1977; Seagrim & Lendon, 1980; Watts, 1976). It was known that the children tested in 1985 and 1986 (Boulton-Lewis, Neill, & Halford, 1986; 1987a) did not perform as well as nonaboriginal children on mathematical and other tests at the completion of primary school. Such differences in performance are usually attributed to differences in cognitive style (e.g., Watts, 1976), strategies (Kearins, 1976; Klich & Davidson, 1984), or environmental factors rather than to intellectual capacity.

Because both Fischer (1980) and Halford (in preparation) contend that although capacity is not the only factor influencing performance, there is a capacity threshold for each level of thinking. It was of interest to determine whether aboriginal children reach capacity thresholds at the same ages as nonaboriginal children, and then to determine the relationship between capacity and mathematical learning. Children were tested on two sets of tasks at the same levels, one of which required school mathematics and one of which did not require that knowledge. This infers that if they could succeed with the latter they should possess the capacity to succeed with the former, given sufficient motivation and experience.

THE RESEARCH PROGRAM

A preliminary study was carried out in 1985 with a sample of 20 aboriginal children (mean age 6 years) from a large rural community (about 290 km north of Brisbane) and two measures of capacity to process information. In 1986, a sample of 75 children aged 4–8 years from the same community was tested for capacity and basic mathematical concepts (Boulton-Lewis et al., 1986; 1987b). In 1987, 120 urban aboriginal and nonaboriginal children in Brisbane schools, in the same age range as the 1986 sample were tested for capacity, knowledge of basic mathematical concepts, and school learning (Boulton-Lewis, Neill, & Halford, 1988).

Culture Appropriate Tests

This research was conducted in a cross-cultural situation; thus two of the capacity tests were chosen to allow comparison of results with those obtained with large samples of nonaboriginal children elsewhere (Case, 1985; Halford, 1980). Two other capacity tests were designed to measure levels of performance on the basis of cultural knowledge. One relied on the children's knowledge of family relationships (a matter of importance to aboriginal people) and the other on familiarity with playing cards. These two tasks separately and in combination with the other two capacity tasks were significant predictors of success with length and number concepts. The Family Structure Task is described briefly as an example.

The critical feature of transitive reasoning is the ability to integrate relations. More typical examples of transitive reasoning tasks are those requiring ordering of sets of rods such as described by Halford (1984; Halford, Mayberry, & Bain, 1986). It is the integration of relations in these tasks that increases the processing load. Our main aim was to present the task so that it made use of appropriate cultural knowledge. The Family Structure Task made use of knowledge of family relationships to test binary relations and transitive reasoning in the following way. At Level 1A of the test, after a discussion of the pictures of a family, children were required merely to recall names of family members, for example:

"That's Mary. She's the mother." At Level 1R, children were required to describe family relationships, in response to questioning, in terms of a single binary relation, for example: "This is John. He calls Hope sister because they have the same mother and father/family." At Level 2, children were required to explain that, if John is the son of Mary, and Mary is the sister of Jane, then John is the nephew of Jane, and this entails integrating relations and measures of the same essential cognitive process as reasoning that if $a > b$, and $c < b$, than $a > c$.

RELATIONSHIP OF MEASURES OF CAPACITY AND MATHEMATICAL CONCEPTS

If children could perform at Level 1 or Level 2 of the Family Structure Task, it was hypothesized that they should be able to learn mathematical concepts at the same level. For example, if they were successful at Level 1A of the Family Structure Task, they should be able to learn to recognize and name (some would say subitize) sets with from two to four members without counting. If they were at Level 1R, they should be able to learn to order objects by length, or pictorial representations of sets (e.g., 3, 4, 5, 6) by pair and by pair comparisons (relying on binary relations). At Level 2 they should be able to learn operations such as addition and subtraction and to reason transitively about length and numbers as all these tasks depend on sets of ordered triples. Regression analyses confirmed that this was generally the case. The levels of success with capacity measures were significant predictors of levels of verbal knowledge, levels of basic mathematical concepts, and logical thinking. In the 1987 research, the capacity tests were also significant as predictors of basic written mathematical knowledge.

The results from these studies indicated, as we had hypothesized, that lower school achievement by aboriginal children cannot be attributed to lesser capacity to process information or to inability to cognize basic mathematical ideas. Research with large samples of nonaboriginal children (Boulton-Lewis, 1987) also showed that capacity measures were significant predictors of levels of length and number knowledge.

FUTURE DIRECTIONS

From the research described so far, we have been able to make general statements about the relationship in early childhood between measures of capacity to process information and performance on mathematical tasks at the same levels of cognitive demand. However, because we did not record the protocol generally, we have lost some data for some tasks including details of the representations and reasoning processes that children are utilizing to reach a solution. In some cases errors have been surprisingly logical or children's use of nonstandard English has obviously confused the issue. Interviewers made note of some of these occurrences. For example the interviewers were aware of the possibility that in talking about families some aboriginal children would refer to aunts as mothers but would, if asked, explain the difference between "real" and other mothers. Some children in the rural-urban setting use a nonstandard dialect of English with, for example, increasing emphasis on the word *big* to indicate greater length or quantity. Often the phrase *they tie* is used to mean equal. We also noted use of fingers, head nodding, strategies for remembering the dots on Cucui, and various trial and error procedures.

Analyses of Protocol

In order to obtain more detailed protocol descriptions, we intend to focus our research next on a small group of children in the same age range and use a few representative tasks. We will then record all talking aloud and other behaviors (such as using fingers for counting) that occur between interviewer and child. There are examples of the use of such analyses in the work of, among others, Ginsburg (1977), Carpenter and Moser (1982), and Steffe, Cobb, and von Glasersfeld (1988). Analyses of such protocol allow description of the representations and strategies used by children at different levels of cognitive capacity and ages and provide information about difficulties that occur when tasks cause an extra cognitive load. They would also provide information about children's erroneous or partly understood concepts or strategies.

Analyses of protocol from the theoretical perspective of our research should complement and perhaps explain some results of other such analyses. We could, for example, explain why some teacher-designed representations do not produce the expected learning outcomes; we could explain why children develop their own representations, such as finger use, to reduce cognitive load; and we could provide information about the possible cognitive causes of lower school achievement. Some social and motivational causes for Aboriginal children have already been proposed elsewhere (Boulton-Lewis et al., 1986).

Modified Chronometric Analyses

Siegler and Robinson (1982) proposed that children will respond differently to different numerical problems depending on their representation of numbers and their level of confidence about the particular problem as presented. If the confidence level is high, the response is fast. If not, the child will fall back to more time-consuming strategies and representations. Some use could be made of a modified version of chronometric analysis in conjunction with protocol analysis to determine whether children at each level of capacity are responding to problems immediately because they have the necessary confidence or knowledge to do so, or are taking longer because they must choose a strategy to fit with their level of confidence.

Teacher/Researcher Cooperation

It is envisaged that protocols will be obtained from clinical teaching sessions with individuals and small groups of children and by discussion with the teacher. For example, we will discuss with the teacher, at regular intervals, those mathematical tasks in the regular program that seem to be inexplicably difficult. We will then observe the teaching of such tasks or attempt to teach them ourselves. An analysis will be made of the cognitive load imposed by the concept and the concrete representations that are used, and their value and limitations will be assessed. In this way we can observe and describe children's learning in an ongoing program.

Concept Maps

Another procedure that could be useful in this research, in explaining young children's responses, is to ask older children (year 7) in the school to represent their knowledge, for example, of numbers and operations, in a series of concept maps of the kind described by Novak and Gowin (1986). By preparing concept maps children can make their knowledge of concepts and relationships explicit in a written form. Concept maps would show what kind of semantic networks older children in the same school have learned. That, in turn, could help to identify problems that are likely to be caused for younger children by language use and incorrect or partial understanding.

CONCLUSION

In summary, the method used so far in our research has been a kind of clinical interview without the recording of protocol. This has allowed general statements to be made about the relationships between capacity measures and young children's mathematical learning. If we supplement the methods in further research by recording all children's "talking aloud" and using other appropriate procedures as previously described, within our theoretical framework, it should be possible to make further statements about the representations and reasoning processes used by children at different levels of cognitive functioning and to explain their value and limitations on the basis of the cognitive loads they impose.

Chapter 3.14

Analysis of Young Children's Spatial Constructions

Grayson Wheatley
Florida State University, USA
Paul Cobb
Purdue University, USA

> *Images are just material to be informed by our intentions.*
> —Wittgenstein, as quoted in Bloor (1983)

Although much of mathematics involves analytical reasoning, it is clear from a careful reading of the literature that spatial reasoning also plays an important role in mathematical thought (Bishop, 1980; Guay & McDaniel, 1977; Hadamard, 1954; Lean & Clements, 1981; Lin, 1979; Smith, 1964; Turner, 1982). Fischbein (1987), for example, spoke of the dialectical relationship between images and concepts in mathematical reasoning. Mathematical problem solving is often a matter of reasoning analytically, constructing an image, using the image to support additional conceptual reasoning, which in turn may suggest an elaborated image. Kosslyn (1983) called it the "race between words and pictures" (p. 162). This process of building from images to analysis and analysis to images may continue through many cycles. In studying young children's mathematical worlds, an understanding of their use of imagery becomes important. Mathematics is the activity of creating relationships, many of which are based in visual imagery.

Traditionally, psychologists have accounted for performance on spatial tasks in terms of internalization. The object is out there and children are said to form a mental picture of it almost as if they had a camera in their heads (Casey, 1976). In this scenario, a spatial pattern is taken to be fully existent in a mind-independent reality. The individual is characterized as an environmentally driven system who makes a mental copy of that spatial pattern. Performance is judged by the (inferred) match with a standard determined by the researcher who acts as a self-appointed authority. Our view is more compatible with the position that an individual gives meaning and structure to a spatial pattern based on that person's experiences that are influenced by available conceptual structures, intentions, and the ongoing social interaction in which he or she is involved. We assume that an object is given meaning by individuals as members of a community. This chapter attempts to study the meaning they give to visually experienced objects.

PURPOSE AND METHODS

Kosslyn (1983) posited four distinct conceptual acts involved in imaging. They are generating an image, inspecting the image, transforming the image, and maintaining the image. Generating the image is a personal matter. Each person gives particular meaning to what he or she perceives. Individuals vary widely in their ability to construct, re-present, and transform images. Although it is impossible to investigate the images individuals construct directly, the manner in which they use images can be inferred from their overt actions in problematic situations.

The purpose of this exploratory study was to investigate young children's imagery, re-presentations, and transformations in an interview setting by analyzing their overt actions on geometric shapes. Twenty-four first- and second-grade students from two intact classes participated in the study. The school from which the children were selected draws from a diverse population representing persons of many socioeconomic levels. The children, in general, perform somewhat above the national norm on mathematics achievement tests.

Clinical interviews were conducted that probed the children's counting level, concepts of 10, dot pattern recognition, conservation of number, class inclusion, and spatial imagery. The interviews were video recorded for later analysis. This chapter focuses on one particular spatial imagery task from the interview.

The Task

Five dark blue plastic pieces (Fig. 1) were placed to one side and a card 8" × 6" showing a square was placed in front of the child (Fig. 2a). This square is referred to as the *form*. The investigator said: "I want you to use these pieces (pointing) to make this shape. I will show you something that may help. Now watch." When the child was attentive, a 8" × 6" card on which was drawn a spatial pattern (Fig. 2b) was shown for approximately 3 seconds. If at any time the child asked to see the pattern again or if it seemed as though the child was not likely to continue, the pattern was shown again. If, in the judgment of the investigator, the child was unlikely to make further progress, the card was placed on the table in front of the child in full view. It is important to note that the child has the opportunity to operate on spatial re-presentations because the pattern is not left in view unless absolutely necessary.

3.14. YOUNG CHILDREN'S SPATIAL CONSTRUCTIONS

FIG. 1. The five shapes available to the child.

RATIONALE FOR CONCEPTUAL ANALYSIS

Conceptual analysis fundamentally assumes that children's actions are always rational given their understandings and intentions. We have all seen children who, from our adult perspective, do some strange things as they attempt to solve mathematics tasks. One reaction is to wonder how the children could be so stupid or to ask what is wrong with them. This reaction, in our view, reflects the limitations of the observer rather than the child. It reflects the inability of adults to put aside their relatively sophisticated understanding of mathematics and imagine what things might be like from the child's perspective. An alternative approach is to readily admit the inadequacy of adult mathematics for understand-

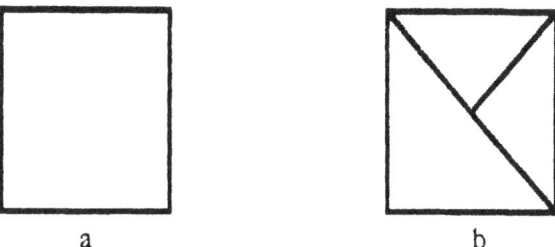

FIG. 2. The square form (a) and the pattern (b).

ing children and for planning instruction. From this perspective, children's apparently strong actions are viewed as problems for the observer to solve. The goal is to develop an understanding of children's mathematics so that their actions can be seen as rational and sensible. The focus of a conceptual analysis is therefore on children's meanings—on how they interpret and attempt to solve mathematical tasks. This type of analysis differs from a logical task analysis in that it acknowledges that much of children's knowledge is not, for them, an object of reflection and consequently does not correspond to anything the adult can see "out there."

The value of a conceptual analysis becomes apparent as soon as we use its results as a lens through which to view children's mathematical activity. We find that we understand them better, that much that had previously seemed strange or bizarre now makes sense. We also begin to develop rationally grounded expectations about what they might do in particular situations.

ACTION

Our analysis and interpretation of the interviews rests heavily on what Piaget (Piaget & Inhelder, 1956) called *action*. As Piaget stated, "All forms of spatial intuition which have been studied depend upon actions" (p. 453). We do not conceive of the pattern as being "out there" for children to capture visually and store as is in their heads, but believe that children construct through their actions an image of the pattern that may later be re-presented and transformed. "The intuition of space is not a reading or apprehension of the properties of objects but from the very beginning, an action performed on them" (p. 449). An important aspect of our analysis is our focus on children's anticipations. It is one thing to pick up a piece to see if it will fit and another to pick it up because one knows how it will fit. Fischbein (1987) called anticipations of this sort anticipatory intuitions. In focusing on these anticipations, we attempt to infer the intelligence that organizes action. For example, Jason looked at the five pieces and as he reached for a target piece, he turned his wrist to pick up the piece in such a way that when his hand was over the form, the triangle was oriented with the unfilled space. The manner in which he picked up the piece and without hesitation prepared it for placement indicated that prior to acting on the object physically, he had anticipated the result of his motor act. The children who picked up the three triangles after viewing the pattern were able to rotate their re-presentations of triangles and compare them with the plastic pieces. The act of constructing an image of the pattern as three triangles involves the act of shape construction. That is, the pattern is not viewed as a collection of lines but instead as a composite of three bounded spatial regions each of which is taken as a spatial object.

TASK CONSTRUAL

Children construed the purpose of the task in a variety of ways. At the least sophisticated level, Joleen and Johanna interpreted the task as one of covering. Joleen picked up the large triangle and placed it in the middle of the form without aligning its sides with the form. She was trying to cover the form with the piece much as we might try to cover an object with a cloth that is too small. For Ryan, who did not show evidence of constructing a re-presentable image, it was a problem-solving task. He experimented with the placement of pieces in ways unrelated to the pattern. On more than one occasion, he attempted to place the parallelogram, which was not a shape in the pattern, in a hexagonal shaped space formed by other pieces. For Anna, it was trying to place the pieces in the way they were on the pattern. However, she experienced great difficulty in doing so. It is not clear that she initially gave meaning to the pattern as three triangular regions. This is explained later. Carrie, after just one look could put the pieces in place immediately. Most of the children construed the task as placement of pieces in the form as they were in the pattern but there were notable exceptions.

IMAGE CONSTRUCTION

McGee (1979) defined one aspect of spatial ability as "the comprehension of the arrangement of elements within a visual stimulus pattern and the aptitude to remain unconfused by the changing orientations in which a spatial configuration may be presented" (p. 893). The phrase "comprehension of the arrangement of elements" implies that the shapes and relationships are contained ready-made in the "visual stimulus." It can be argued that when viewing a pattern, each of us constructs meaning for the ontological and epistemological contexts established (Feldman, 1987). "Different people, looking upon a situation, will notice different things. Our experience of seeing may depend very much on what we know about what we are looking at. And what we see is not necessarily what is there" (Lakoff, 1987, p. 129). In certain situations the drawing shown in Fig. 2b could be constructed as just lines, a company logo, $\frac{1}{2} + \frac{1}{4} + \frac{1}{4}$, or a folded napkin rather than as three triangular shapes. There are no particular meanings inherent in the pattern. The meaning a person gives to the drawing will depend on the context within which the individual operates. Although viewing the plastic pieces and square form before the pattern is shown may increase the likelihood of giving meaning to the pattern as an arrangement of space filling triangular regions, it is far from certain that the child will make the construal. As Bruner (1986) stated, "There is no seeing without looking, no hearing without listening, and both looking and listening are shaped by expectancy, stance, and intention" (p. 110).

Some students in attempting to re-present their constructed image found it no longer accessible and had nothing to guide their placement of pieces on the form. In Kosslyn's term, they were unable to maintain the image. For example, Ryan was unable to construct an image that could be re-presented. It was as if he had not viewed the pattern; he made no attempt to place pieces based on what he had "seen." After viewing the pattern, he placed two small triangles in opposite corners of the form and attempted to fit the parallelogram in the space between them. Anna, on the other hand, realized she could not construct a re-presentable image and immediately asked to view the pattern again. It was only after several looks that she was able to place one piece on the form. Immediately after viewing the pattern Shawn quickly selected the three triangles, and it was clear that he gave meaning to the pattern in terms of three triangles forming a square, but he did not construct the relative positions of the two small triangles. Carrie on the other hand, after only a brief glance at the pattern, immediately arranged the three triangles in the form of a square and moved them onto her form.

Other children, apparently attending to the global shape of the figure, constructed meaning of the pattern as just a square without component parts. Several children initially reached for the small square as their piece of choice. Some may have actually believed that the small square would fill the space. Joleen seemed surprised that the little square did not cover her form, she moved it around within the square form before finally removing it. After trying the square, Shawn said, "I thought it would fit." Anna may have constructed the pattern as just an arrangement of lines that did not define shapes.

In summary, children do not form an internal representation of external reality but gives meaning and structure to the pattern based on their context-specific cognitive resources. As Piaget and Inhelder (1956) stated, "The reconstruction of shapes rests upon an active process of putting into relation, and it therefore implies that the abstraction is based on the child's own actions and comes about through their gradual co-ordination" (p. 79).

STRUCTURING UNFILLED SPACE

After the large triangle had been put in place, several children did not construct the remaining unfilled region as a single spatial entity. For example, Anna placed two triangles as shown in Fig. 3. Her acceptance of this positioning and her

FIG. 3. Anna's positioning of a large and small triangle.

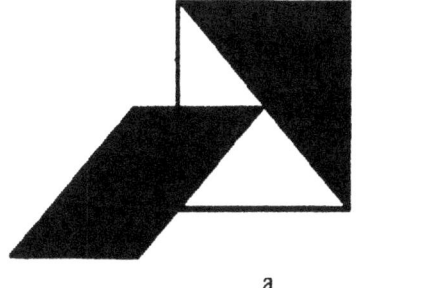 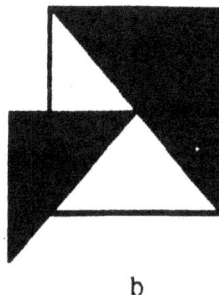

a   b

FIG. 4. Two attempts at forming a perpendicular relationship.

attempts to fit pieces into the trapezoidal region suggested she had not constructed the unfilled space as an object on which she could reflect and compare with other spatial objects. Anna was a particularly interesting case. After some struggle and several looks at the pattern, she positioned the large triangle. Then she picked up the parallelogram and moved it onto the form as shown in Fig. 4a but quickly withdrew it. She subsequently placed a small triangle as shown in Fig. 4b. These actions suggest that she had constructed a perpendicular relationship of segments as shown in Fig. 5. For her, the pattern was a relationship of line segments rather than shapes.

In the course of her solution attempt, Anna also placed the small triangle as shown in Fig. 3. She not only seemed reluctant to modify it but returned to that configuration on several occasions. Although other students contemplated this placement and quickly rejected it, Anna seemed "locked in" to it. There are three possible reasons why this configuring might have seemed plausible to Anna. First, the 45° angle of the small triangle just fits in the lower corner of the space. Second, the top edge of the small triangle is parallel to the top of the space and third, the configuration fits "nicely" within the boundaries of the form. Anna's preoccupation with this configuration again indicates that she was operating with fragmentary relationships between line segments. It seems clear, for example, that she did not construct the unfilled trapezoidal space as an object that could be compared with others.

FIG. 5. Perpendicular relationship of segments.

Jim also created the arrangement shown in Fig. 3 and tried several times to place the other small triangle in the unfilled space. He too did not construct the unfilled region as an object. In contrast Adam, looking at the arrangement in Fig. 3, picked up the other small triangle as if to place it, but did not actually put it on the form. His rejection of the placement before acting suggests that he had constructed the unfilled space as an object and compared it to the piece he was holding. This enabled him to anticipate that the small triangle would not fit before placing it on the form. Structuring unfilled space represented a significant advancement in the children's performance on spatial tasks.

Piaget (1987a) exemplified the difficulty some children have in constructing spatial objects when he analyzed their performance on a task that involved cutting a given square region to cover a congruent one. The children were asked to cut a square any way they wished and place them to cover a congruent rectangular region. Nic, age 5 years, 5 months, cut out a small square and put it on the orange region. When asked about the remaining part, she said it is not a piece, "it is nothing." She had not constructed the remaining region as a spatial object that could be compared with other pieces. In our study, Anna did not consider the covered and uncovered regions of the square as complementary. For her the uncovered part did not exist. It is like a tailor cutting shapes from a piece of cloth, the part left is scrap, whereas the shape cut out is seen as a part of a potential garment. Neither Piaget's nor our subject considered the remainder as complementary in forming the original shape. "Thus, possibility as such is not at all a state but a transition arising from a disequilibrium and characterizing reequilibration as a process, and which transforms into reality once the process is terminated" (p. 51).

Operating on Re-presented Spatial Objects

Some children were not able to use their re-presentation to select the appropriately sized shape. For example, Jason first picked up the large triangle, thinking it would fit in a particular position at the top of the form and attempted to place it in the form according to his re-presentation but found it to be too large. Rejecting the large triangle, he then picked up the small triangle and found it would fit. Jason could anticipate the position of a rotated piece but was unable to differentiate between the sizes of the small and large triangles when he compared them with the unfilled space. Apparently he was yet to construct a metric on the spatial objects re-presented. As further evidence of this interpretation, we note that when the task was first presented, he picked up the square, placed it in the form as if he expected it to cover the space. This same first move was made by other children. Shawn, for example, tried the square and said, "Oh, I thought it would work," but quickly realized his misjudgment; he was able to reflect on his mental actions.

Rotation

The ability to mentally rotate (transform) a re-presented shape greatly facilitated the children's performance on this task. The ability to pick up the large triangle and place it on the form to match the position in the pattern was accomplished by an act of mental rotation. The act of selecting the triangle was accomplished by mentally rotating a re-presentation of the piece. On several occasions, children picked up a piece and turned their hand, indicating that they anticipated the rotations necessary to position the piece in the form. Other children needed to experiment by physically rotating a piece on the form to position it. They could mentally compare their re-presentation with the plastic pieces but could not anticipate its position when rotated. For example, after he had placed two triangles as shown in Fig. 6, Shawn immediately picked up the small triangle but could not anticipate its position. It became for him a problem-solving task; how can I fit this little triangle in the remaining space? After several physical turns, he stumbled on the correct positioning.

The conceptual act of transforming an image allows the child to anticipate the result of potential physical activity. A person transforms an image for some purpose. In this task, images were transformed to make comparisons and to judge the possibility of a piece fitting in a constructed space. Some children had great difficulty transforming their images. Paivio (1971) and Piaget and Inhelder (1971) made a distinction between static and dynamic imagery. Re-presentation without a transformation would be classified as static, figurative imagery where performing a mental rotation would be dynamic and operative. Piaget and Inhelder suggested that using dynamic imagery signals a new and powerful way of making meaning. Clearly, dynamic imagery is facilitative in mathematical reasoning (Turner, 1982), whereas static imagery can be limiting (Clements, 1988).

Part-Whole Relations

Many children, after placing the large triangle in a lower left position, experienced difficulty when they attempted to place the small triangles on the form; they had not related the small and large triangles with respect to their relative positions in the square form. For example, Wesley placed the large triangle in the

FIG. 6. Shawn's positioning of a large and small triangle.

lower left corner of the form, selected the two small triangles, but could not position them. He seemed unable to anticipate the rotated position of a small triangle. In contrast, Shawn quickly placed one small triangle in position after orienting the large triangle. He had constructed the relation of the large triangle and the small triangle and was sure the third triangle would fit in the remaining space, although he had some difficulty orienting it. He had not constructed a single spatial object composed of all three triangles.

Carrie, who functioned at the highest level of the children we observed, quickly put the two small triangles together after just one look at the pattern and without hesitation moved the large triangle in position to complete the pattern. We have argued that this sophisticated performance was made possible by the application of the disembedding operation to re-present spatial objects. She constructed a fully elaborated part-whole relationship between the triangles and the square they composed. In contrast, Stephanie, at a less sophisticated level, selected the three triangles, put the large triangle in position but was unable to orient the two small triangles. She did not construct a part-whole relationship between the three triangles and the square. Similarly, Jason placed a small triangle to correspond with the pattern but had no idea how to position the others until he again looked at the pattern. On other similar tasks he also positioned one piece at a time.

Individual Differences

The children varied greatly in the way they interpreted and attempted to solve the task. Try as he did, Tim was unable to place the pieces to cover the form. He apparently could not re-present what he may have seen while viewing the pattern. He could not even do the task when the pattern was placed in front of him. He could not give meaning to the pattern in any way that would assist him in selecting pieces. Even after he had placed the three triangles directly on the pattern, he had difficulty moving them onto his form. His difficulty was one of image rather than re-presentation. Some children could put one piece in place after a single viewing of the pattern, indicating they had constructed the pattern as a collection of triangles. At the most sophisticated level, Carrie completed the task in less than 10 seconds after just one look at the pattern.

SUMMARY OF THE ELEMENTARY OPERATIONS

In the process of analyzing the video recordings, we identified a set of constructive acts discussed earlier. These acts are summarized later. In identifying the constructive acts we were guided by two principles. First, we assumed that the child's observed actions were performed for a reason that made sense to the child. Second, we posited that the child gives meaning to the pattern based on her experiences and available conceptual structures.

The elementary operations

1. The pattern is construed as a collection of spatial shapes.
2. The supplied collection of pieces is construed as a collection of shapes.
3. The relative sizes of pieces and re-presented shapes is compared.
4. The unfilled space is constructed as a spatial object.
5. Through a mental rotation, the fit of a piece with an unfilled space is anticipated.
6. A part-whole relationship between the form and the shapes that constitute it is constructed.

LEVELS

Based on an analysis of the children's actions and anticipations, five levels were identified. The classification ranged from children who gave no evidence they formed a re-presentable image to one child who placed the pieces on the form correctly in a rapid and confident manner. The elementary operations were used as a basis for the development of the distinct levels of conceptual operating and the classification of children by levels. The number of children found to be at each of the five levels is shown in Table 1.

Level One—Image of linear objects. There was no indication from their actions that they constructed an image of either the pattern or the pieces as shapes. More specifically, they constituted the plastic pieces as linear objects

TABLE 1
Classification of Children by Level
of Spatial Constuction

Level	Number of Children
1	2
2	6
3	5
4	10
5	1
Total	24

rather than as space filling objects. Two children placed the pieces around the form, not on it.

Level Two—Global covering. The child construes the pieces as shapes but does not form a re-presentable image of the pattern. The task is construed as one of covering the form but does not construct a re-presentation to guide the placement of a piece. A piece is placed on the form to cover it but the sides are not necessarily aligned with the sides of the form. For example, Joleen put a parallelogram obliquely on the form in an attempt to cover the square region with it.

Level three—Structuring an unfilled space. After putting one or more pieces on the form, the child shows evidence of constructing the unfilled space as a region. Prior to this level, a child might place two triangular pieces as shown in Fig. 3, forming a trapezoidal region to be filled and proceed to try to place pieces in the region. Other children rejected this positioning of the pieces because no pieces were available that would fill the trapezoidal space.

Level Four—Partial image construction. After the first look at the pattern, the child puts only one piece in place. The child knows which shapes are in the pattern but does not construct an image that relates the triangles to each other. Some placed the small triangles to complete the pattern by trial and error with only a few trials. Others put one piece in place, requested to see the pattern again and did not attempt to place other pieces until they looked at the pattern again. It is as if these children form the intention of noting only one piece at a time.

Level five—Relational image construction. After one view of the pattern the child proceeds with confidence to place the three triangles on the form exactly as shown in the pattern to complete the task. Such action suggests the child had formed a re-presentable image, which guided the selection and positioning of the pieces. She constructed an image of the pattern that related the component shapes to each other and to the square they form.

SUMMARY

Children's overt actions in performing a spatial task can be understood as expressions of a set of underlying constructive acts. Although we as adults conceived of the task in a particular way, children gave it their own meanings that were often incompatible with ours. The pattern shown was constructed by some children as a set of triangular regions but others gave it meaning as just a collection of lines forming a design. The most advanced children constructed the pattern as three triangular regions and also constructed the relationships of the triangles to one another and to the square they formed. Placing pieces on the form involved the act of rotation. Some children were able to mentally rotate re-presentations to anticipate fit and placement on the form. Others interpreted the pattern as a collection of triangular regions and did not construct possible relationships between these shapes. The establishment of the part-part-whole relationship seem to signal a significant advancement in the children's thinking.

As the analysis of the video recordings proceeded, it became clear that significant differences existed in the sophistication of the children's solution attempts. Using the elementary operations as a basis, five levels of performance were identified. At the highest level, the child formed the relationships between the parts and the whole after one viewing of the pattern. Other children completed the task by a step-by-step placement of pieces after repeated viewings of the pattern. At a lower level, children had constructed neither the part-whole relationship nor had they constructed the unfilled space as an object. At lower levels there was little evidence that the children had formed a re-presentable image of the pattern.

The analysis of children's spatial constructions described in this study may contribute to our understanding of how children give meaning to geometric shapes. By attempting to take the child's view, it is possible to gain insights that will enhance our understanding of children's construction of spatial and geometric relationships. It may be that spatial patterns and imagery play an equally important role in number development as well as geometry. For example, the formation of re-presentable dot pattern images may facilitate the construction of numerical relationships. With few exceptions, those children who counted abstract units and those that had constructed part-whole were at the highest two imagery levels. When we compared the children's responses on the imagery tasks with their number development classification, a strong relationship was apparent. Constructivist analyses of children's actions as they solve spatial tasks may also be useful in designing geometric and numerical learning activities that facilitate children's mathematical learning.

Activities to develop imagery should encourage the construction of abstract and dynamic imagery. Images that are excessively concrete (Clements, 1988; Paivio, 1971; Richardson, 1969) or static (Arnheim, 1969; Neisser, 1967; Piaget & Inhelder, 1971) tend to limit high levels of mathematical functioning.

ACKNOWLEDGMENTS

The research reported herein was supported by the National Science Foundation under grant No. MDR-847-0400. All opinions expressed are, of course, solely those of the authors. The authors wish to express their appreciation to Ernst von Glasersfeld and Leslie Steffe for their helpful suggestions in the preparation of this chapter.

Chapter
3.15

Children's Competence in Forming Combinations

Lyn English
Brisbane College of Advanced Education, AUSTRALIA

In this chapter, some findings from a study of young children's competence in solving novel combinatorial problems are discussed. More specifically, the following questions are examined:

1. What procedures do young children display in solving novel combinatorial tasks?
2. What is the nature of children's conceptual competence in the combinatorial domain, as inferred from their performance?

METHOD

The study in question was one of two major investigations involving a total of 115 children aged between 4 years 6 months and 9 years 10 months. Some findings from one of these investigations, in which 65 children participated, are examined. Using a clinical interview approach (Ginsburg, Kossan, Schwartz, & Swanson, 1983), each child was administered a set of five novel tasks involving the dressing of toy bears in different outfits, an outfit comprising a T-shirt and a pair of shorts. The bears were made of cardboard and were designed to stand in an upright position. The clothing items, also of cardboard, were of different colors and were backed with a piece of adhesive material to facilitate the dressing process. Each child was presented with a surplus of items, these being typically arranged as follows:

red T-shirts	blue T-shirts	yellow T-shirts
green shorts	blue shorts	pink shorts

3.15. COMPETENCE IN FORMING COMBINATIONS 175

The goal of each task was to form all possible different combinations of two items, these being selected from the sets of T-shirts and shorts provided. For four of the five tasks, the number of possible combinations was 6; for the remaining task, 9.

RESULTS

Through an analysis of the videotaped responses of each child, a number of key performance variables were identified. These included the children's *solution paths,* their *scanning actions,* and their *significant pauses* during task execution. Although it was the interaction between variables that ultimately determined the level of task success, only the solution paths are examined. The term *solution path* refers to the method of item selection in the formation of a combination. The solution paths (labelled A through F) constitute an hierarchy of increasingly sophisticated solution procedures, ranging from random item selection through to efficient patterning. These are described briefly here; a more comprehensive analysis is presented in English (1988a).

Solution Path A

Solution Path A is characterized by a random selection of items in which no item is rejected once it has been selected, even though it might be inappropriate. Children using this path do not display a procedure designed to achieve the task goal. Their sole aim is to "dress the bears."

Solution Path B

Children following this second path display a trial-and-error procedure in solving the tasks. Items are selected in a random manner; that is, there is no identifiable order in the selection process. If an item proves inappropriate, it is rejected.

Solution Path C

Children who use Solution Path C display a cyclic pattern in their selection of items, with the pattern usually evident in one type of item only (e.g., red T-shirt, blue T-shirt, green T-shirt, red T-shirt, blue T-shirt, etc.). However, although a pattern is present, it is only emerging because it is not applied consistently throughout task execution. Given these characteristics, Solution Path C may be viewed as a transitional phase in which children move away from a trial-and-error procedure towards one of an algorithmic nature designed to generate task solution (Anderson, 1985).

176 ENGLISH

Solution Path D

The emerging pattern in item selection that characterized Solution Path C is fully established in Solution Path D. As such, this path appears as the first of the algorithmic procedures. Children following Solution Path D display a consistent and complete cyclic pattern in their selection of items. Usually, the pattern is confined to one item type only, with adjustments made to the selection of the other type, for example:

> *red T-shirt*/green shorts, *blue T-shirt*/blue shorts,
> *yellow T-shirt*/pink shorts, *red T-shirt*/blue shorts,
> *blue T-shirt*/pink shorts, *yellow T-shirt*/green shorts,
> *red T-shirt*/pink shorts, *blue T-shirt*/green shorts,
> *yellow T-shirt*/blue shorts.

(The cyclic pattern is indicated by the italicized terms.)

Solution Path E

Solution Path E, the second of the algorithmic procedures, is characterized by an emerging *odometer pattern* (Scardamalia, 1977) in item selection. The cyclic pattern of Solution Path D is retained, but a new feature appears, that of a "constant" or "pivotal" item. Children are observed to repeat the selection of an item until all possible (or apparently possible) combinations have been formed with that item. Upon "exhaustion" (or apparent exhaustion) of this item, a new constant item is chosen and the process repeated. The selection of items to combine with each constant item displays a systematic cyclic pattern. For example:

> *red T-shirt*/green shorts, *red T-shirt*/blue shorts,
> *red T-shirt*/pink shorts, *blue T-shirt*/green shorts,
> *blue T-shirt*/blue shorts, *blue T-shirt*/pink shorts . . .

(Each constant item is italicized.)

The odometer pattern of Solution Path E is, however, incomplete. This can be due to the omission of a possible combination, a duplication of combinations, or a failure to recognize task completion.

Solution Path F

This final algorithmic procedure features a consistent and complete odometer pattern in item selection. Each constant item is selected in turn and all possible combinations with that item are formed. The selection of items to combine with each constant item displays a uniform cyclic pattern. A significant feature of this path is children's identification of task completion on exhaustion of all constant items. Typical comments include:

1. I know I can't dress any more bears because I've used each T-shirt with each pair of shorts.
2. There are three different T-shirts and three different shorts, so these are all the outfits I can make. (child pointing to nine different outfits)

At this point it is worth mentioning two major trends in the children's performance. First, Solution Paths B and C were favored by most children during initial task execution, with no child following Solution Path F. In addition, as children progressed on the set of tasks, a significant trend towards Solution Paths D, E, and F was observed. This was particularly evident amongst children aged 7 to 9 years. Whereas the younger children (4 to 6 years) tended to remain with the trial-and-error paths, they were still able to achieve considerable task success through their effective scanning actions. Further discussion on this point can be found in English (1988b).

ANALYSIS OF CHILDREN'S COMPETENCE IN FORMING COMBINATIONS

Underlying the present analysis of children's competence in forming combinations is the assumption that "performance structures are consequences of competence structures" (Greeno, Riley, & Gelman, 1984, p. 104). Rather than present a complete analysis of competence, attention is focused on the component of *conceptual competence,* this being inferred from the children's solution paths. Greeno and associates (1984) defined conceptual competence within the counting domain as "the implicit understanding of general principles of the domain" (p. 94). Greeno and Johnson (1985) considered *implicit understanding* to indicate the "significant functional role" principles play in "individuals' knowledge for problem solving," even though they might not "necessarily know how to state the principles or explain their significance." In accord with Gelman and Meck's (1986) stance, this chapter argues that learning in the combinatorial domain is directed by an implicit knowledge of domain-specific principles that set constraints on the nature of procedures. A number of principles have been advanced to account for children's transition from trial-and-error to algorithmic procedures (English, 1988a). The present discussion is confined to just two of these principles, namely, the *Principle of Difference* and the *Odometer Principle.*

The Principle of Difference

The Principle of Difference asserts that two or more combinations of items are different from each other if they differ in at least one item.

An implicit knowledge of the Principle of Difference is considered essential to goal attainment. Children who displayed an immature knowledge were hampered in their attempts at task solution. For example, some children were reluctant to select any item more than once, whereas others avoided any combination comprising items of the same color, (e.g., red T-shirt/red shorts). The majority of children, however, commenced the tasks with at least an elementary knowledge of the principle. These children mainly favored Solution Path B. Their "two-step" procedures, in which an item of one type is chosen independently of the other, reflected a knowledge of the relationships listed later. These relationships comprise "conjunctive concepts," which are typically the easiest for subjects to discover (Anderson, 1985).

1. If the T-shirts are different and the shorts are different, then the outfits are different.
2. If the T-shirts are the same and the shorts are different, then the outfits are different.
3. If the T-shirts are different and the shorts are the same, then the outfits are different.

With the observed improvement in solution path efficiency, it follows that many children acquired a more sophisticated knowledge of the Principle of Difference during the course of task execution. More specifically, it is posited that the foregoing conjunctive concepts were replaced by one "disjunctive" concept (Anderson, 1985) as follows: If the T-shirts are different or the shorts are different, then the outfits are different.

This enhanced knowledge is seen to contribute to children's transition from trial-and-error to algorithmic solution procedures. By focusing on items of the one type, rather than both, the amount of processing required for task solution would be reduced. By assuming that the information-processing system has a limited-capacity workspace (Klahr, 1980), it is hypothesized that a search for processing efficiency leads to the streamlining of item selection. The emergence of a pattern in children's procedures (Solution Path C) supports this hypothesis. Refinements to the pattern of item selection, evident in children's transition from Solution Path C to F, are analysed here in terms of four properties of the Odometer Principle, namely, *systematic variation, constancy, exhaustion,* and *completion.*

Systematic Variation

The property of systematic variation asserts that, within the one cycle of selection from two discrete sets of items, different combinations will be generated if items of the one type are varied systematically. This is irrespective of the second item chosen.

This property displays an inherent statement of task solution; thus it is assumed to underlie children's transition from Solution Path C to D. Given the features of these paths, it is argued that children who followed Solution Path C had an emerging knowledge of systematic variation, whereas those following Solution Path D had acquired a complete, albeit implicit, knowledge.

Children's progress from Solution Path D to E is seen to result from their attempts to further increase processing efficiency. This was apparent in children's use of a "constant" item when following Solution Path E. By holding an item of one type constant, children were able to focus their attention on varying items of the other type. It is thus assumed that, along with their knowledge of systematic variation, these children had acquired an implicit knowledge of constancy.

Constancy

The property of constancy incorporates the features of systematic variation and is defined as follows: Within the one cycle of selection from two discrete sets of items, different combinations will be generated if an item of the one type remains constant, while items of the other type vary systematically.

In addition to their knowledge of constancy, children following Solution Paths E and F displayed an implicit knowledge of one or both of the remaining odometer properties, these being exhaustion and completion.

Exhaustion

The property of exhaustion asserts that a given constant item is exhausted when it cannot generate any further combinations which are different from existing combinations.

Completion

The property of completion asserts that all possible combinations have been generated when all constant items have been exhausted.

An observed shortcoming in the actions of some children following Solution Path E was their failure to identify task conclusion. That is, they attempted to produce further unique combinations even though all constant items had been exhausted. So, it is inferred that some children following Solution Path E had an implicit knowledge of Exhaustion, but not of Completion. On the other hand, the performance of other children suggested the reverse; that is, they could identify task conclusion, but failed to exhaust all constant items.

As the procedures of Solution Path F do conform to all four odometer properties, it is assumed that children who followed this path had an implicit understanding of the Odometer Principle in its entirety. However, for several of the children, this knowledge was explicit. Not only were they able to explain their procedure when asked, but were also able to justify why they considered it to be the most efficient.

CONCLUDING POINTS

This study has demonstrated that young children have the capacity to acquire independently, an efficient algorithmic procedure for solving novel problems presented in a meaningful context. Children's conceptual competence in forming combinations has been inferred from their performance and explained in terms of an implicit knowledge of domain-specific principles. Although this knowledge plays a major role in the solution process, it is not considered to operate in isolation. Rather, its interaction with higher-order or "executive" cognitive processes (e.g., Brown, 1978) is considered to ultimately determine goal attainment. Without elaborating on this point, it will suffice to say that children's ability to carefully monitor and control their actions enabled them to achieve task success, even when their initial domain knowledge was limited.

In the light of the study findings, it is worth citing Piaget and Inhelder's (1975) comments on children's acquisition of combinatoric operations. They maintained that the combinatoric system assumes "the interaction of formal operations" and hence, is acquired from the age of 11 or 12 years. It is argued that, given a meaningful problem context, children will display greater competence than they are traditionally assigned. It follows that early mathematics programs need to capitalize on young children's cognitive competence by providing problem-solving experiences that promote the growth of independent learning and thinking.

Chapter
3.16

How Natural Is Fraction Knowledge?

M. A. Clements
G. Del Campo
Deakin University, AUSTRALIA

It is interesting to ask, "What fraction knowledge do young children bring to school?" The expression "fraction knowledge" as used here needs to be defined. For example, does an ability to share 12 identical objects equally between two people constitute fraction knowledge? In this chapter we distinguish between fraction-related knowledge (such as sharing) and fraction knowledge. A person who knows that one-half of a group of 12 objects is 6 objects will be regarded as having fraction knowledge.

Although most parents in Western cultures typically encourage their children to count ("one, two, three, . . ."), very few of them encourage their children to find "one-half," "one-quarter," or "one-third" of a whole unit. It is for this reason that it is easier to study the influence of schooling on the development of children's fraction knowledge than on the development of their knowledge about natural numbers. With the latter, it is impossible to separate the influence of schooling from that of society in general. There are many opportunities for informal natural number experiences outside the school (e.g., numbering of houses, age, calendars, money), and these outside-school experiences and what goes on in school mathematics are likely to be mutually reinforcing. However, in the case of fractions similar links are not as easily established.

We provide brief commentaries on three bodies of literature that have a bearing on the question, "How natural is fraction knowledge?" These are: (a) the history of mathematics, (b) the fraction knowledge developed by cultures outside the dominant European Western tradition, and (c) the possession and use of fraction and fraction-related concepts by preschool children, and the changes in these conceptions that occur during the early years of schooling. The place of fractions in the structure of arithmetic is also briefly considered.

FRACTIONS IN THE HISTORY OF MATHEMATICS

Although the origins of the concept of whole number are shrouded in the mists of prehistoric antiquity, the notion of a rational fraction developed relatively late and was not in general closely related to integer concepts (Boyer, 1968). It seems that Stone Age people did not need, and therefore did not construct, fraction knowledge (Struik, 1948). Boyer (1968) remarked that among what he called "primitive tribes" there seems to have been virtually no need for fractions because units of measure were chosen that were sufficiently small to obviate the necessity of using fractions. After arguing that in the prehistory period conscious formation of fraction concepts was extremely rare, Struik (1948) pointed out that anthropologists believe that specific fraction ideas were virtually unknown among early North American tribes, with only a few having vernacular words for "one-half," and even less for "one-third" or "one-quarter." He referred to a remark by G. A. Miller that the words *one-half, semis,* and *moitié* have no direct connection with the words *two, duo,* and *deux,* which seems to show that the conception of $\frac{1}{2}$ originated independently of that of integer. Boyer (1968) supported this view and pointed out that there was no orderly advance from binary to quinary to decimal fractions and that decimals were essentially the production of the modern age in mathematics.

Flegg (1983), on the other hand, claimed that the need for representing fractional parts arose in everyday life from early times. He argued that although some cultures avoided using fractions by inventing ever smaller units of mensuration, such avoidance was rare because "the fractions one-half, one-third, one-quarter, two-thirds, and three-quarters arose so often that they came to be known as natural fractions and were given special representations" (p. 75). He claimed that the widespread use and early date of these natural fractions tell us that they were the first fractions to come into everyday usage, and cited instances of their use in early Egypt, Crete, Rome, Greece, Babylon, China, and Arab countries.

Almost 5,000 years ago the Sumerians, at Ur, made extensive use of the fractions $\frac{1}{2}$, $\frac{1}{3}$, and $\frac{5}{6}$. In their society these fractions were intimately related to their everyday activities—for example, in commerce, interest rates running from 20% to $33\frac{1}{3}$% were charged (Smith, 1951). The Sumerians used a base 60 counting system, and they formalized this to include fraction concepts.

Perhaps the most celebrated extant evidence of the fraction knowledge of part of the ancient world is the inscriptions on the *Rhind Papyrus,* which derives from Egypt, about 1650 B.C. (Smith, 1951). This *Papyrus* reveals a preoccupation among Egypt's early mathematicians with unit fractions (of the form $\frac{1}{n}$), and with the fraction $\frac{2}{3}$. Except for $\frac{2}{3}$ the Egyptians thought that any fraction $\frac{m}{n}$ with m not equal to 1 (e.g., $\frac{2}{5}$) was not an elementary thing and was in some way incomplete. This led them to attempt to write each such fraction as the sum of unit fractions (or $\frac{2}{3}$). Thus, $\frac{9}{10} = \frac{1}{30} + \frac{1}{5} + \frac{2}{3}$ (Struik, 1948).

3.16. HOW NATURAL IS FRACTION KNOWLEDGE   183

The Egyptians knew that if p is a whole number, then:

$$\frac{2}{3} \cdot \frac{1}{p} = \frac{1}{2p} + \frac{1}{6p} \quad \text{and} \quad 2 \times \frac{1}{2p} = \frac{1}{p},$$

and these general results helped them to decompose $\frac{m}{n}$ fractions to the sum of unit fractions (Boyer, 1968).

It is a matter of interest that the *Rhind Papyrus* clearly demonstrates that although the Egyptians could not conceive of a fraction $\frac{m}{n}$, the modern definition for adding fractions $(\frac{m}{n} + \frac{p}{q}) = \frac{(mq + np)}{nq}$ had been established although in an indirect way. Standard histories of mathematics (e.g., Boyer, 1968; Eves, 1969; Struik, 1948) suggest that this form of fraction knowledge gradually extended throughout the Middle East, Europe, and Asia. A high-point in the history of mathematics came with the Pythagoreans in Greece, in the sixth century B.C. Not only did they analyze music using fractions, but they also were able to prove that some lengths could not be measured exactly by putting many unit lengths next to each other. This result, which is more familiarly known as the Pythagorean Theorem, had been known (more or less) in other places, for a long time, but it was the Pythagoreans who provided a brilliant logical argument, later refined by Euclid, which appeared to establish the result beyond further questioning (Dantzig, 1968; Eves, 1969; Smith, 1951).

FRACTION KNOWLEDGE AMONG INDIGENOUS GROUPS OUTSIDE WESTERN SOCIETAL SYSTEMS

James Hurford (1987) claimed that numeral systems evolve gradually in stages. There are static periods when the rules for arithmetically combining simple expressions do not change. Connecting these static periods are periods of innovation or invention when new rules are introduced. By this view, the Greeks with their insistence on a logical analysis of numbers, stood on the shoulders of the Egyptians (Gillings, 1972), and the Western European number system derives from Greek ideas.

If the use of the evolution metaphor in the last paragraph were appropriate, then it might be assumed that "modern" Western fraction concepts are at a higher, more developed stage than earlier systems used in Western countries. This would appear to be supported by our review of the literature.

There is no evidence, however, in the historical and comparative literatures, that Western fraction concepts are innate. Different groups have had common needs (e.g., food and shelter), so their fraction concepts are likely to have certain similarities; but because they faced different challenges, they have developed different fraction concepts. Such a view does not preclude the possibility of concepts having been transmitted across cultures when there has been contact between cultures. In his classic study *Number Words and Number Symbols*, Menninger (1969) provided many instances of special ways in which fractions are used in different cultures; he also gave examples of transmission across cultures (see, for instance, his discussion of how merchants in Arabia, East Africa, India, and around the Red Sea use a silent finger language to represent $\frac{1}{2}$, $\frac{1}{4}$ and $\frac{1}{8}$; pp. 213–214).

Harris (1980), in her work on the measurement concept of tribal Aborigines in Australia, reported that none of the societies that she studied had specific vernacular terms for $\frac{1}{4}$, or $\frac{1}{3}$ (although in all cases it was possible to use fraction-related concepts, such as sharing, to account for everyday situations that were regarded as important). Similarly, Lean (1988), in his comprehensive study of indigenous counting systems in Papua New Guinea (PNG), concluded that although many of the 750 PNG languages possess a word for $\frac{1}{2}$, this usually means "a part" or "a piece" and does not denote precise division into two equal portions. Only rarely are there words for $\frac{1}{4}$ or $\frac{1}{3}$. However, in actual fraction-related situations (e.g., sharing), the vernacular language is sufficient.

It seems, then, from our survey of some of the literature on fraction knowledge developed by cultures outside the dominant European Western tradition, that fraction knowledge is not naturally acquired by children of all cultures. If this is true, then the descriptions of developmental changes in fraction knowledge, such as the scheme put forward by Piaget, Inhelder, and Szeminska (1960), are relevant only within the cultural frames in which they were developed. Thus, McLellan and Dewey's (1895) statement that "the psychical process by which number is formed is from first to last essentially a process of 'fractioning'— making a whole into equal parts and remaking the whole from the parts—" (p. 138) is culture-bound and therefore dangerous if posited as universal.

As Menninger (1969) pointed out, whenever fraction ideas have appeared in traditional cultures, they have never been part of some grand generalized fraction concept, which is an artifact of Indo-European cultures, but rather, the response to local social and environmental needs. Why should Indo-European mathematical concepts be expected to develop naturally in all children?

YOUNG CHILDREN'S FRACTION KNOWLEDGE

When do children in Western cultures develop fraction concepts? Are these concepts emerging even before they commence school? Do school children link the notion of "sharing," for example, with elementary fraction concepts? Research has begun to address questions such as these.

Hunting and Sharpley (1988; in press) specifically investigated the fraction and fraction-related concepts of Australian preschool children ages 3 to 5 years. The children, in two separate studies (one involving 22 children and the other

206 children) were interviewed on a one-to-one basis and during the interviews were asked to attempt tasks involving sharing between two, three, and four dolls. In some of the tasks, formal fraction language, "half," "quarter," and "third," was used, whereas in others the less formal language of sharing was used. Some of the tasks made use of "continuous" materials (e.g., a piece of string was to be cut into two equal bits) and others involved the children in the allocation of discrete materials (e.g., 12 cracker biscuits were to be shared evenly between three dolls). Hunting and Sharpley found that the preschoolers performed much better on those tasks where informal language was used than on tasks where formal fraction terminology was used. Most of the children could share equally between two dolls, and many of them between three and four dolls; however, relatively few of them responded correctly when the word "half" was used, and hardly any demonstrated any understanding of "quarter" and "third."

Clements and Del Campo (1987) investigated the fraction and fraction-related concepts of 1,024 children in grades two through five in 45 different classes in 20 elementary schools in Melbourne. All 1,024 children attempted a wide range of pencil-and-paper fraction tasks and then 240 of them were interviewed on a one-to-one basis. During the interviews the children were asked to describe their thinking as they responded to sharing tasks that made use of informal sharing language, and to other tasks using formal fraction language ("one-half," "one-quarter," and "one-third"). One of Clements and Del Campo's conclusions was that children who can share equally are not necessarily able to give meaning to the expressions "one-half," "one-quarter," and "one-third." That is to say, the notions of "equal sharing" and "fractional quantities" are not related in their cognitive structures (Clements & Del Campo, 1987). This same conclusion was arrived at by Clements and Lean (1988), who used an expanded version of the interview schedule used by Clements and Del Campo (1987) to investigate the fraction and fraction-related concepts of 59 children in grades 4, 5, and 6 in three Papua New Guinea (PNG) Community Schools, and by Hunting (1980) in a study carried out in the United States. In Clements and Lean's (1988) PNG study, none of the interviewees had difficulty in sharing, but hardly any of them could cope with (apparently) corresponding tasks when the words *one-half, one-quarter,* and *one-third* were used by the interviewer.

MATHEMATICAL REFLECTIONS ON FRACTIONS

As we noted in our brief review of the history of fraction ideas, one of the highpoints in the history of mathematics came with the proof, by the Pythagoreans, that the length of the hypotenuse of a right-angled triangle whose other two sides were each one unit long did not correspond to a number of the form $\frac{m}{n}$, where m and n are natural numbers. This proof gave notice that in the development of number concepts, logical rigor was, ultimately, more important than intuition based on what appeared to be the demands arising from observations of reality. For although intuition had suggested that any length, for example, could have been measured exactly provided a small enough unit of length was selected, logic had shown this to be false.

The emphasis, in the Indo-European tradition of mathematics, on the need for logical consistency within any system of arithmetic meant that the development of fraction ideas was largely constrained by what was already known about whole numbers. Natural numbers could be thought of as special kinds of fractions (e.g., $3 = \frac{3}{1}$), thus the arithmetic of fractions had to contain the arithmetic of natural numbers as a special case. This logical constraint resulted in $\frac{m}{n} + \frac{p}{q}$ being defined as $\frac{(mq + np)}{nq}$, $(\frac{m}{n}) \times (\frac{p}{q})$ as $\frac{mp}{nq}$, and so on. Such definitions not only fit with observations of reality (e.g., lengths placed next to each other) but also produce a logically consistent arithmetic of rational numbers.

But because a result such as $\frac{1}{3} + \frac{1}{4}$ was more likely to be thought of as $\frac{(1+1)}{(3+4)} = \frac{2}{7}$ by young children, and because a notation such as $\frac{1}{3}$ was not easily associated in young minds with partitioning a unit into three equal sections, the arithmetic of mathematicians has never been popular with Western schoolchildren. Data from studies of how children outside the Western cultural tradition react to fraction concepts (see, for example, Clements & Lean, 1988) indicate that they are even less well received in these cultures. Thus, in schools around the world Western fraction knowledge is imposed on children.

Part of the difficulty that children experience with fractions stems from the fact that, in their minds, the definitions imposed on them are not consistent. At various times of their schooling, children are told that the fraction $\frac{1}{3}$, for instance, is concerned with each and all of the following: (a) sharing a continuous quantity between three people, (b) sharing 12 (say) discrete objects between three people, (c) dividing the number 1 by the number 3, (d) a ratio of quantities, (e) a 1 for 3 replacement operator, (f) a rational number equal to $\frac{2}{6}$, $\frac{3}{9}$, and so forth, and (g) a decimal fraction 0.333 . . . These are all fraction-related ideas, but are not necessarily easily linked with school fraction knowledge, and many of the instances are easily confused with related *ratio* concepts.

Throughout their elementary schooling, children are led to believe that the shaded part of the square in Fig. 1 represents $\frac{1}{4}$, but they are also told that the ratio of shaded to unshaded sections is 1 : 3 or $\frac{1}{3}$. They learn that $\frac{1}{3} + \frac{1}{4} = \frac{7}{12}$, yet if they "joined" the collections in Fig. 2, they might reasonably have expected the

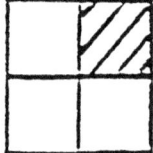

FIG. 1. $\frac{1}{4}$ or $\frac{1}{3}$?

3.16. HOW NATURAL IS FRACTION KNOWLEDGE

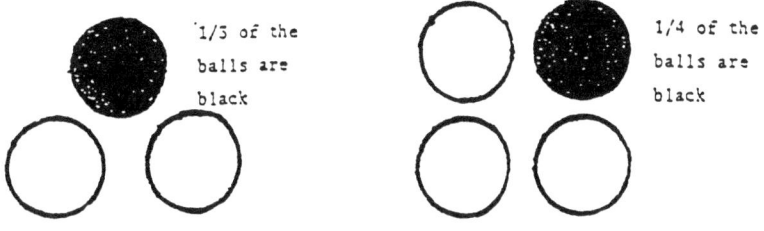

FIG. 2. $\frac{1}{3} + \frac{1}{4} = \frac{7}{12}$ or $\frac{2}{7}$?

result to be $\frac{2}{7}$. Similarly, the student who gets 1 out of 3 for an examination answer, and 1 out of 4 for another, gets 2 out of 7 altogether. The idea arising from Fig. 2 can be extended to cover continuous situations (consider, for example, what would happen if two glasses of cordial, one with one part of juice to two parts of water, and the other one part of juice to three parts of water, were combined).

It can be seen, then, that the definitions associated with fraction knowledge are not the only ones that could have been posited to achieve a logical system. Although they are not arbitrary, in the sense that they "fit" many real-to-life situations (such as the composition of lengths, time, etc), other definitions consistent with real-to-life embodiments could have been formulated. If this had happened thousands of years ago, then a very different arithmetic from what is taught in schools today might have been the result.

SOME CONCLUDING COMMENTS

From considerations of (a) the history of the development of fraction knowledge, (b) fraction ideas held by people living in non-Indo-European cultures, and (c) fraction ideas of young children, we have shown that the now universally accepted definitions of fractions and fraction operations have arisen from agreement among mathematicians, and a desire to ensure that the arithmetic of fractions is totally consistent with the arithmetic of natural numbers. Certainly, the prevailing definitions allow fraction knowledge to model some important aspects of reality, but they do not model all aspects of reality. Other definitions could have been formulated and if these other definitions had gained acceptance among mathematicians, then a radically different number system from what we have now might have been the result.

Fraction knowledge of the kind taught in Western schools certainly does not appear to be innate. Throughout the ages humans have counted by means of a large number of different numeration systems that they created; they have also measured all kinds of things by all kinds of ingenious procedures. By contrast, Western fraction concepts were a long time coming.

After summarizing research suggesting that years of tailoring experience was the best predictor of performance on tasks resembling those performed by tailors, whereas years of schooling was the best predictor for schoollike arithmetic problems, Rogoff (1981) added that "both sets of skills had restricted generalizability suggesting that school skills do not transfer more broadly than non-school skills" (p. 277). For the large majority of school children, fraction knowledge is something that is crammed into their heads in school mathematics lessons, which outside the classroom has little relevance. It is not natural, and is needed only for the purpose of studying more mathematics.

Part 4

Communication: Elaboration Chapters

Chapter 4.1

Communication in Early Childhood

F. Lowenthal
University of Mons, BELGIUM

One of the characteristics that distinguishes human beings from most animals, according to Bruner, is that they learn. Moreover, Bruner (1972) explained that human children are born immature but discover the bases of their culture through education. This education itself depends on interactions with children of the same age or, and this is more important, on interactions with older children and with adults (parents, teachers, . . .). All these interactions require some means of communication to enable young children to both explore their neighborhood and discover the regularities of their environment. These regularities must be discovered and sorted by the children who are constructing their own universe by taking into account the surrounding culture: the children will thus use the same pattern as their parents. This process requires good "communication" between the children and their elders. Bernstein, Brandeis, & Henderson (1969), Cordier (1975), and others showed that "poor communication" between young children and their closest adult models is associated with poor affective development and usually results in poor cognitive and behavioral development.

According to most researchers—and we agree—communication with young children is thus essential for their development. But these researchers do not explain what an adult should do to communicate, and certainly not what a teacher should do. They forget the children who suffer because of "poor communication" and they do not consider the possibilities offered by mathematics education to help these children. We claim that "mathematics can be a therapy" (Cordier & Lowenthal, 1973). Most researchers are so convinced that communication is important in early childhood, and indeed it is, they forget to consider whether some other, more basic element, is not at least as relevant as communication for our action group on early childhood.

In this chapter we first consider the most frequently used mode of communication—verbal language. We then examine its advantages and disadvantages. In addition, we show that any communication system must be based on a more essential element—verbal communication is based on a logic, but the link between a verbal communication and its subjacent logic is neither sufficiently explicit nor immediately obvious to make children's life really easy. This is the reason why we describe another approach that presents other advantages for deprived as well as for normal children. Finally we show that this approach, used in mathematics education, can help to solve some of the problems encountered by deprived children.

THE MOST FREQUENTLY USED MODE OF COMMUNICATION

Verbal language is a mode of communication frequently used with young children. Piaget used it for clinical observations; this mode of communication seems unavoidable for such observations that, in turn, appear to be full of interesting information. This is partially due to the wonderful flexibility of the verbal language—this mode of communication can be used during the night; as well during the day as it does not require any tool. Most important of all, words can be used to represent all possible human ideas, concepts, instructions, questions, or answers. The verbal language thus seems to be a perfect mode of communication. It can be used very easily and it offers total freedom of expression.

Nevertheless although the first element, simplicity of use, actually is favorable, the second element, super-flexibility, creates tremendous problems. In fact, young children are acquiring, or better constructing, their own language. In order to do so, they use their parents' language as a model because their own language will not be completely developed for years. As a result, the child who speaks with an adult must unavoidably use a form of language different from that used by the adult. This is not important for babies. The difference is so obvious that all adults notice it and, consciously or not, adapt their level of language to that of the infant to whom they are "speaking" (Rondal, 1983). The situation is totally different for young children who give the false impression they can use an adult language (3- to 10- or 11-year-olds). These children do not attach to all the words (or sentences) exactly the same meaning as adults do. Consequently, a child might have "understood" something the adult did not mean, and conversely the adult might "understand" something the child did not mean or fail to understand something the child has in mind.

This creates a problem that has been neglected by some psychologists when they analyzed clinical observations based on verbal interactions. It creates an even more important problem for teachers. How can a teacher be sure that the pupil has understood the concept that has been taught by means of words, or that this pupil's answer is actually an answer to the question the teacher had in mind (and not to something else the pupil has "understood")? How can teachers be sure that they understand correctly what the child meant? To make the situation worse, verbal language is full of ambiguities, sentences can be interpreted differently by two normal adults, and accent and intonation make the situation even worse. Another factor pleads against the use of the verbal language as unique mode of communication with young children: verbal language is culturally rooted and its use implies references to a cognitive background that is not always explicit and that can vary considerably from one pupil to another. This makes the task of the teacher even more difficult. We must conclude that although the verbal language sounds wonderful, it introduces in fact a communication gap that seems difficult to solve. Nevertheless, most children succeed to master it. It is thus relevant for our purpose to examine how they acquire their verbal communication system. The method they use might give us better ideas concerning the actual role of such a system and ideas concerning the techniques that might be used to favor its development.

DEVELOPMENT OF A COMMUNICATION SYSTEM IN THE CHILD

Literature concerning this topic most often focuses on the verbal kind of communication. Authors describe how the child learns to use conventional symbols—the *semantic* component of language development. On the other hand, they mention the acquisition of the rules governing the coordination and concatenation of such symbols—the *syntactic* component of language development.

According to Bruner and associates (1966), the semantic component seems independent of any logical structure. The essential word here is *association;* on the other hand, the syntactic component seems to require as prerequisite the mastery of such a logical structure. The work of Bernstein et al. (1969), Cordier (1975), and our own research (Lowenthal, 1985b) first with deprived children and later with an aphasic child seems to confirm this.

A critical study of work done by Piaget and by the neo-Piagetians and work done by Siegel (1978) show that the development of syntax depends on the mastery of logical structure. But, verbal language is the main vector of the logical structure subjacent to this verbal language. The child is thus confronted with the following situation: To master the verbal language needed to communicate, the child must first master the subjacent logical structure; and to master this structure, he should use the verbal language itself. This is a vicious circle and one can wonder whether children are able to break it. Commonly, all normal human beings have a good mastery of a verbal language. They succeeded in breaking the vicious circle! But how did they do it? How did they get a good mastery of the logical structure needed as "starter"?

The child breaks this vicious circle and acquires a first form of logic by manipulating "things" and sorting them according to given criteria or by putting them in classes created by the child for that purpose. Jakobson (1939/1964) showed that the first "things" manipulated by infants are the sounds they produce themselves. Children first learn to sort their sounds into vowels and consonants—this is their first, elementary, system of opposition. They will then use the vowel /a/ with all possible consonants. They will oppose their productions to discover or construct the rich structure constituting their basic communication system. This activity of opposing and apposing sounds such as vowels and consonants is clearly a sorting activity in existing classes, as they are perceived from the child's neighborhood, completed by a categorization activity: the creation of new subclasses within already existing classes (e.g., the distinction between /p/, /t/ and /k/ among the consonants). This double activity corresponds to the assimilation-accommodation process described by Piaget & Inhelder (1959). Later, children will manipulate everyday objects with the same purpose and sort some objects in given classes perceived from the neighborhood (e.g., the objects used to eat), but they will also categorize when they will create new subclasses by trial and error (e.g., the beakers and the cups that are subclasses of the given class, "objects used to drink"). Verbal communication has started in the meantime, but it is not yet well-organized; nevertheless, this new organization is sufficient to enable children to enrich their logical structure and this new step will help them to enrich their verbal language.

One can thus conclude that a communication system does not necessarily have verbal roots. On the contrary, a communication system seems to need logical bases to start its development for whatever occurs later and for whatever communication mode will actually be developed. This brings us closer to mathematics and thus to the importance of mathematics education in the development of a communication system. But before looking at what we might use, as mathematics educators, to favor such a development, it might be wise to try to isolate the major role of a communication system in a child's development.

HOW CAN WE FAVOR THE DEVELOPMENT OF REPRESENTATION SYSTEMS IN THE CHILD?

The first steps of the usual development of a communication system have been described in the previous paragraphs. This brief description clearly shows the importance of the mastery of logical structures as facilitators in children's construction of their communication system, their major and unavoidable tool to construct their own personal *representation* of their universe.

A communication system is needed to let young children discover the regularities of their environment, but this communication system must be based on a logical structure. The less explicit the link between a communication system and a subjacent logic, the more difficult the children's task—How can they organize their universe without clear reference to an organizing structure? As the links between verbal communication do not seem to be easily discovered by very young children, it seems reasonable to suggest that this development might be favored in children if special representation systems are presented to them. These basic representation systems must be based on the children's natural sorting and categorizing activities (e.g., Dienes, 1966), but they must avoid some of the problems of verbal language by using nonambiguous objects detached of any cultural background as basic elements of the representation system. These systems might seem to be very poor. This is irrelevant; they serve only as starters, as initiators of another richer system that would have been more difficult to acquire by the child without this initial help. But do children really need some help or is it sufficient to let them work their way through the world of usual objects?

The objects a child can manipulate are not always easy to sort: some cups are big, others small, some are red and others blue; and some cups actually look like beakers or like other objects not meant for the same use (like some "souvenirs"). It is not always obvious which criterion should be used to sort all the cups from the non-cups, because these can also be big or small, red or blue, and so forth. A little bit of logic is needed. Why can't we help children by putting a little bit of logic in the material we present to them? This is why we suggest using concrete representations of formal systems that are sufficient to perform some reasonings. We call such concrete representations *NonVerbal Communication Devices* (NVCD). These concrete representations consist of sets of tools provided with technical constraints that make some action possible and others impossible. This, in turn, suggests a logic. This kind of material offers some advantages. The objects used are the symbols, and the technical constraints presented in the material represent the deduction rules that will, or will not, be used by children.

This simple definition has numerous consequences that are all advantageous for the observer, for the child, and for the teacher.

- A NVCD is made of *concrete objects* (i.e., Dienes' Attribute blocks, Lego bricks); it can thus be used in a nearly nonverbal way to introduce problems to children and observe how they solve them. This enables the observer to avoid the problem of verbal communication used as a representation device!

- This device must also *represent* a formal system; it is thus made of many elements that are independent of any cognitive background. They are nonambiguous, and their use makes it possible to avoid the unpleasant effects of "uncontrolled pre-knowledge."

- The device is a *concrete* representation of a formal system; it is thus made of numerous little elements that can be grouped in a small number of categories. These little elements (i.e., "symbols") are easy to handle and must be used one after the other. The problem must be solved in a stepwise fashion.

- Such a device represents a formal system that is sufficient to accomplish *reasonings;* the elements that constitute the device can thus be put together in many different ways.
- Such a device is a *concrete representation* of a formal system sufficient to perform reasonings; it must thus carry one way or the other a syntax that, at the concrete level, is represented by technical constraints.
- Finally, such a device favors the *manipulation* of numerous small elements, which makes it attractive.

Generally speaking one considers that any set of objects can be used as a NVCD, provided that it is furnished with technical constraints. These constraints enable teachers to present logical problems to very young children in such a way that the teachers can be certain that their pupils have understood the question, and that they themselves will be able to observe whether the pupils are able to construct, and thus to produce a correct solution. Indeed, the solutions produced by means of such a material are built in a stepwise fashion because the device is made of numerous little elements.

CONSEQUENCES OF THE CHOICE OF SUCH A TECHNIQUE

We had the opportunity to teach mathematics to "problem children" (Cordier et al., 1975) while the classroom teacher worked with the children in the usual fashion for all the other school domains. These children had IQs slightly below average (measured using the WISC, $\bar{X} = 90$, sd = 13) and many behavioral problems. The use of the WISC enabled us to show that the verbal score was not as good as the performance score ($\bar{X}$ Verbal IQ = 86, sd = 17; $\bar{X}$ Performance IQ = 94, sd = 9). At the start of our experiment, these children were all at least 2 years behind in their studies, and this was true for all the school domains. Although these children were able to speak, their language was clearly different from normal adult language. These children's language was not logically structured. They chose to use vague pronouns instead of using the correct word and produced sentences such as, "He said that he is stupid." How many children were indicated by this sentence? Two or three or only one? This remained open to interpretation and made their teacher's life difficult.

Among other things, they systematically refused to go to school. When they were forced to attend classes, they refused to learn and do any work. We used the NVCD technique with them using a version inspired by work done by Papy and Papy (1968) and F. Papy (1970, 1971, 1972). The children started to like these lessons of mathematics and asked to have more exercises for homework. They also actively participated in a summer competition of mathematical drawings.

After 18 months of our teaching, we evaluated their scores in mathematics, in French (their mother tongue), and in all the other school domains. They were no longer behind in mathematics; without being brilliant, they had scores no longer considered to be those of retarded children. But in all the other domains, they were still at least 2 years behind. We tried to analyze this situation—it is not possible to claim that mathematics is so wonderful that scores in mathematics must be better. Our method of teaching mathematics was based on concrete representations and this enabled the children to structure more easily what was taught to them. This compensated for their very poor and nonstructured communication system, but the usual teachers did not do so in the other school domains.

We also worked with a young aphasic child (Lowenthal & Saerens, 1986) named Saïd. This child had normal development until the age of 13 months. He then had meningo-encephalitis followed by a right hemeplegia from which he nearly totally recuperated. Since the age of 13 months, the child had been unable to speak or to understand spoken words. His parents tried everything they could. Speech therapists did their best but were unsuccessful. They even tried the sign language of the deaf people (ASL was used successfully in Northern America with apes and the assumption was that this child's communication system was similar to that of an ape!). Speech therapists also tried to use the BLISS symbols (Silverman, McNaughton, & Kates, 1982), which are successfully used with some handicapped children. All this failed with Saïd. Psychologists examined the child and concluded that he was unable to perform adequately to take traditional tests. The child was thus labeled "severely mentally handicapped" and practically condemned to an education leading to nothing. When we first met this child, he was 5 years and 6 months old. He was unable to speak. He understood only five words: "yes," "no," "good," "bad," "more," and his first name, "Saïd." The five words contain only one syllable each, whereas his first name contains two syllables. It was assumed that the child understood more the intonation and the mimic of the experimenter than the words themselves (as cats and dogs do). At this stage, the child used only two symbolic gestures—one meaning "me" and the other meaning "good"; he did not try to combine them. We used classical tests with this child and he failed, probably because he did not understand the questions and lacked the required cognitive background. A neurological examination showed severe bilateral symmetrical lesions in all the cerebral zones related to "language."

We then tried a totally different approach using only NVCDs. The child immediately showed that he had some sorting competence left. It was soon obvious that some basic semantic and syntactic competences could be developed using Dienes' A-blocks. The use of the Dynamical Mazes defined by Cohors-Fresenborg (1978) and the computer language based on the pegboard (Lowenthal, 1985a) lead to further discoveries. After training based on the use of NVCDs, Saïd was able to read short sentences, to write words, and to use written words in order to define his "universe of discourse." This enabled him to communicate using gestures about objects or people he had first clearly defined. Saïd is now also able to understand spoken sentences and to answer questions that have been verbally presented with gestures. He is also able to count, to make additions and subtractions. He is certainly not a "severely mentally handicapped child," he is certainly a person who has communication problems but who seems able to cope with them.

CONCLUSIONS

A good communication system is needed by children in order to build their own representation of their environment, but one must note that every communication system is based on a subjacent logic. The links between verbal communication systems and subjacent logic are not explicit, as verbal communications are full of ambiguities and require a good pre-knowledge of the cognitive background. These verbal communication systems do not seem to be the easiest ones for a very young child. They are nevertheless essential and should not disappear. But another complementary approach might make the child's life easier. This seems to be the case with concrete representations of formal systems sufficient to perform reasonings. These representations are called NVCDs.

The use of NVCDs makes the construction of representations, and thus the development of reasonings in normal children, easier. Moreover, such constructions by-pass classical problems due to the use of the usual verbal language as a medium for communicating representations, and to the permanent recourse (voluntary or not) of the subject's cognitive background. In fact, this technique enables the teacher to observe in an objective way representations (in this case, manipulations of abstract objects) of the subject's problem-solving strategies without having to communicate anything about them in an ambiguous way.

It is even more interesting to use this technique with handicapped children, because other methods always fail because of the huge communication gap and the lack of cognitive background common to both subject and observer. NVCDs have been presented to aphasic children, mentally retarded persons, and socioculturally deprived children. In all cases the observations show that logical competences are present in them, although they do not master the classical performances associated with them—"they can do it but they cannot say it." This had not been noticed by means of other techniques, and it could not have been noticed because the basic assumption of the researchers was the absence of such problem-solving abilities. These handicapped children can thus learn to structure their universe and possibly escape at least partially from their "handicap" world. They can now, with NVCDs, solve logical problems. Teachers and psychologists can thus try to observe these children's performances in an objective way. Observations of subjects whose logic—according to all classical standards—is defective give even more relevant information concerning the way

THE natural logic works than the usual observations of well-performing normal children—usually one counter-example enriches the observer more than many examples.

ACKNOWLEDGMENTS

This chapter has been partially supported by an ANAH-Rotary grant.

Chapter
4.2

Multiple Perspectives

Paul Cobb
Purdue University, USA

> *There is only one world but this holds for each of many worlds.*
> —(Goodman, 1984, p. 278)

In recent years, an established philosophical idea, the contextuality of cognition, has come increasingly to the fore in the mathematics education research literature (e.g., Carraher & Carraher, 1987; Cobb, 1985, 1986b, 1987a; Confrey, 1987; D'Ambrosio, 1985; Schoenfeld, 1985). The development of this idea can be seen in James' (1920) notion of a mini-universe and in subsequent elaborations such as Schutz's (1962) province of finite meaning, Goodman's (1978) plurality of worlds, Shweder's (1983) divergent rationalities, and Bauersfeld's (1988) domain of subjective experience. This chapter assumes that arguments concerning the contextuality of cognition are as applicable to researchers as to mathematics students. This premise is reflected in Bruner's (1986) contention that "there are two modes of cognitive functioning, two modes of thought, each providing distinctive ways of ordering experience, of constructing reality. The two (though complementary) are irreducible to one another" (p. 11). One mode that Bruner called the logicoscientific leads to a search for universal truth conditions and "attempts to fulfill the ideal of a formal, mathematical system and explanation" (p. 12). This mode strives for predictively useful generalizations by using terminology that is claimed to be neutral, whereas imaginative application of Bruner's narrative mode leads instead to interpretive accounts of people's actions. "It deals in human or human-like intention and action" (Bruner, 1986, p. 13). Here, the focus is on developing "thick descriptions" (Geertz, 1980), on locating the particulars of experience historically in space and time, and on explicating likely connections between actions and events. Each mode "uses different techniques of presentation to project divergent assumptions about the world and different means to persuade the reader of its conclusions" (Firestone, 1987, p. 16). Each is the product of a distinct community of discourse that establishes its own implicit norms for rationally grounded debate.

This speculative chapter is written from the perspective of one who operates predominantly in the narrative or interpretive mode. I argue that even within this mode of thought, the researcher continually switches from one context to another, from one way of making sense of things to another. The three primary contexts I focus on are the experiential, cognitive, and anthropological contexts (Table 1). These contexts of sense making, it is argued, are nonintersecting domains of interpretation (Maturana, 1978). Constructs used to develop interpretations in different contexts are mutually exclusive. For example, the constructs of conceptual operation and beliefs are relevant only in the cognitive context, whereas mathematical culture is an anthropological but not a cognitive construct. The goal is to find ways of coordinating analyses developed in the various contexts. First, however, it is necessary to clarify what is meant by context.

CONTEXTS AND SETTINGS

Context, as the term is used in this chapter, is the cognizing subject's own construction and is distinguished from the situations or settings that the observer might isolate in the subject's environment. For example, the setting might be mathematics instruction in which the students have been asked to complete a set of tasks. However, the contexts within which students attempt to complete the tasks might differ radically. For some it might be a matter of trying to recall what the teacher told them they were supposed to do, whereas for others the focus could be on mathematical sense making. These students are in the same setting but act in different contexts and engage in very different forms of mathematical activity.

This example illustrates that purposes or intentions are a crucial aspect of contexts. As Wilker and Milbrath (1972) put it, "a field [or context] can only be

TABLE 1
The Experiential, Psychological, & Anthropological Contexts

	Experiential	Cognitive	Anthropological
Mathematical	Mathematico-Experiential	Mathematico-Cognitive	Mathematico-Anthropological
Social	Socio-Experiential	Socio-Cognitive	Socio-Anthropological

described by referring to the goals, purposes, and needs that are involved. The purposive factors are the prime motivating forces and provide the impetus for structuring the field" (p. 51). Similarly, Schutz (1962) contended that at each moment there are "certain possibilities of future practical or theoretical activities which shall be briefly called the 'purposes at hand.' It is this purpose at hand which defines those elements among all others contained in such a situation which are relevant for purposes" (p. 5). In the mathematics classroom, for example, if a student's conception of the general nature of mathematical activity, the self, and others is such that he or she takes for granted that the immediate purpose is to apply a prescribed procedure, then activities other than trying to remember the teacher's instructions do not arise—they are not relevant. Similarly, the experiential, cognitive, and anthropological perspectives within the narrative mode are each structured by distinct purposes.

THE EXPERIENTIAL CONTEXT

The purpose that structures the experiential context is that of attempting to infer what another's experiences might like. As we observe children doing mathematics or talking with others about mathematics, we strive to understand what their mathematical world might be like. In doing so, we assume that the children's activity is rational given their current understandings and purposes at hand. The trick is to imagine a world in which children's activity does make sense. In making these inferences, analysts can draw only on their own conceptual resources. Consequently, in attempting to understand the children's mathematics, researchers elaborate their own mathematics.

Even within the experiential context, there is a distinction to make—between potentialities and actualities (Steiner, 1987). Sinclair (chap. 2.1) speaks of potentialities when she says that

> for an infant a block is something you can push or put on top of something else or that makes a noise when you throw it, but it is also something that is not soft, not good-to-eat, not something you can put another object into. So, say weight as an object of thought is no more or no less than the sum of the different operations the subject can perform when dealing with weight. Similarly, number as an object-of-thought is what one can do with numbers. Thus there is not one single "concept of number" but an unending series of such concepts.

Sinclair's analysis of weight and number as potentialities stems from her focus on knowledge as something at hand rather than on knowledge as an object of reflection that appears to be separated from human intention and purpose. In contrast Hardy (1967) is quite explicit about his Platonist assumptions when he separates mathematical knowledge from the knower: "I believe that mathematical reality lies outside us, that our function is to discover or *observe* it, and that the theorems which we prove, and which we describe grandiloquently as our 'creations' are simply our notes of our observations" (pp. 123–124). In a similar vein, Godel (1964) claimed we "have something like a perception . . . of the objects of set theory," as witnessed by the fact that its premises "force themselves on us as being true" (p. 265). As a philosophy of mathematics, Platonism has been devastatingly critiqued, particularly by Wittgenstein (1956). Nonetheless, as a description of the subjective experience of reflecting on previously made mathematical constructions, Hardy's and Godel's accounts ring true. Once we have made a mathematical construction and have used it unproblematically, we are convinced that we have got it right—it is difficult to imagine how it could be any other way. Mathematical objects are, for all intents and purposes, practically real for the experiencing subject (Goodman, 1986).

An analysis of potentialities, guided by the metaphor of using a tool while acting in physical reality (Polanyi, 1962), attempts to analyze unreflective knowledge in action (Dreyfus & Dreyfus, 1986). Platonism, in contrast, takes objectified physical reality as its guiding metaphor (Bloor, 1976) and deals with how things seem when we reflect on previously made mathematical constructions. In my view, it is necessary to use both metaphors when accounting for students' mathematical experiences. Consider, for example, a clinical interview study that focuses on college students' construction of exponential function. The interviewer readily assumes that students' understanding of whole number arithmetic is compatible with their own for the purpose at hand and nothing occurs in the course of the interview to call this assumption into question. Both the interviewer and the student experience whole numbers as independent of their cognizing activity and, furthermore, each assumes that this understanding is shared with the other. The interview can proceed unproblematically on the basis of this Platonist assumption. It is appropriate with respect to the purposes at hand in that nothing that occurs in the course of the interview leads either the interviewer or the student to believe that there might be differences in their whole number conceptions. The assumption is part of the taken-for-granted background against which they conduct their dialogue.

The situation is entirely different when attention turns to the student's conception of exponential function. The purpose is to understand the student's meanings, realizing that they may be alien to the researcher. The researcher's purpose is to call into question his or her own taken-for-granted ways of knowing mathematics and thus penetrate beyond his or her own symbolizations and objectifications. In this case, consideration must be given to potentialities as well as actualities, to knowledge-in-action as well as to objects of knowledge. This is particularly so because students operating at the frontiers of their knowledge are in the process of making objectifications. The purpose of characterizing what Thom (1973) called the development of the existence of mathematical objects is incompatible with the metaphor of externalized physical reality. In effect, one needs a language to talk about what it might be like before one can talk as a Platonist about particular concepts.

We arrive at the conclusion that attempts to infer what students' mathematical experiences might be like involve inferences about both knowledge-in-action and objects of knowledge. It is noteworthy that the notion of mathematical knowledge assumed to be shared crept in when Platonist assumptions were discussed. This issue is addressed in more detail when the cognitive and anthropological contexts are considered. It will, in fact, be argued that a focus on students' purely mathematical experiences is overly narrow and that we should also consider their social experiences of interacting with each other and the teacher.

THE COGNITIVE CONTEXT

If we restrict ourselves temporarily to mathematical cognition, the purpose that structures the psychological context is to explain how it is that students have the mathematical experiences they are inferred to have. In other words, students' inferred mathematical worlds are the data of cognitive explanation. This is in line with Goodman's (1984) exhortation that we ask the hard but inevitable questions about the mental operations required to construct a world like that of modern physics or of everyday life. As Bruner (1986) noted, this characterization of the cognitive context is at odds with mainstream American psychology. Psychologists felt that they "had to take a stand on how the mind and its mental processes transform the physical world through operations on input. The moment one abandons the idea that 'the world' is there once and for all and immutably, and substitutes for it the idea that what we take as the world is itself no more nor less than a stipulation couched in a symbol system, then the shape of the discipline alters *radically*" (p. 105, italics added). From the cognitive perspective that Bruner, following von Glasersfeld (1984), characterized as *radical*, key constructs include scheme, conceptual operation, sensory-motor action, re-presentation, and reflective abstraction (Steffe, 1983). We note in passing that the infiltration of mathematical objects into models that purport to be cognitive in fact indicates a conflation of the experiential and cognitive contexts. The Platonist experience is something that needs to be explained by asking the hard question of how a student can have the reflective experience of an apparently mind-independent mathematical object. From the radical perspective, mathematical objects are the experiential correlates of conceptual operations. The models developed by Steffe (Steffe, von Glasersfeld, Richards, & Cobb, 1983; Steffe, Cobb, & von Glasersfeld, 1988) to account for children's early number learning illustrate this perspective. In contrast to the investigation of students' construction of exponential function, Steffe and his colleagues did not assume that whole numbers have a mind-independent existence when they investigated the mathematical worlds of first and second graders. An openness to the possibility that young children's arithmetical knowledge could be knowledge-in-action was appropriate given their purposes. Nonetheless, they necessarily had to make realist assumptions while interacting with children. Interviews and teaching sessions were conducted against the background of an assumed shared spatiotemporal reality of physical objects. The interactions proceeded unproblematically on the basis of this assumption.

The early number models developed by Steffe and, more generally, discussions of mathematical knowledge-in-action seem vague and mysterious to many in an era dominated by the computer metaphor. The difficulty arises from the fact that experience falls outside the domain of this metaphor. Computers do things, they perform, but they do not experience (Searle, 1984; Winograd & Flores, 1986). This leads to a conflict between the development of precisely specified performance models that are promulgated as the products of real science on the one hand and the belief that students learn on the basis of their experiences on the other. We have to chose between casting ourselves in the role of the hard scientist who extends a line of work directly descended from formal task analysis (Bauersfeld, 1988; Greeno, 1987) and taking students' mathematical experiences seriously. More pragmatically, it is a matter of deciding whether behavioral solution strategies or students' inferred mathematical experiences constitute the "data" to be explained. No doubt, this writer's biases are readily apparent.

The problem of coordinating experiential and cognitive analyses is not too daunting as long as we restrict ourselves to purely mathematical cognition. However, things become messier as soon as we consider the social settings such as a school classroom in which students construct mathematical knowledge. As Brousseau (1984) and Balacheff (1986) noted, a student's goal in the classroom is not to learn mathematics per se. Instead, it is to complete tasks in ways that are acceptable with respect to the classroom situation. In other words, students' mathematical activities in the classroom setting are profoundly influenced by their social cognitions. These include their beliefs about their own and the teacher's role. (It has been argued elsewhere that these two beliefs and beliefs about the general nature of mathematical activity are intimately related and constitute an evolving belief system; Cobb, Yackel, & Wood, 1989.) Students continually interpret classroom events in terms of these beliefs and thereby accept implicit obligations for their own activity and have unarticulated expectations for the activity of others (Voigt, 1985; in press). Classroom life proceeds smoothly to the extent that the teacher's and students' obligations and expectations fit or gear together.

We may conclude that students' mathematical and social cognitions are interdependent. The process of accounting for students' mathematical activity therefore involves coordinating analyses of their mathematical and social cognitions. This applies even to situations where a student works alone in the classroom and does not interact with either peers or the teacher. When students construct an implicit obligation for their own mathematical activity, the obligation becomes the overriding purpose that structures the context within which the student engages in mathematical activity. Thus, our previous discussion of the experiential context in terms of students' purely mathematical experiences was unduly restrictive. Even there, it is necessary to coordinate analyses of the mathematical and social aspects of experience. With regard to the cognitive context, typical constructs such as scheme and reflective abstraction are by themselves insufficient; sociocognitive constructs such as obligations, expectations, and beliefs are also necessary.

The process of coordinating the mathematico- and sociocognitive contexts can be clarified by reconsidering the idea of context. We typically talk of students doing mathematics in a context as though they first create and then get on with the business of acting in it. It is easy to conclude that the social context (accounted for in terms of sociocognitive constructs) influences mathematical activity (accounted for in terms of mathematicocognitive constructs) but not vice versa. As Bateson (1973) noted,

> this view . . . is likely to distract the reader—as it has distracted me—from perceiving the ecology of ideas which together constitute the small subsystem which I call "context." This heuristic error—copied like so many others from the ways of thought of the physicist and chemist—requires correction. It is important to see a particular utterance or action as part of the ecological subsystem called context not as the product or effect of what remains of the context after the piece which we want to explain has been cut away from it. (p. 338)

In other words, teachers and students modify their context as they act within their contexts. This view was well expressed by Lave, Murtaugh, and de la Rocha (1984) when they summarized their findings concerning grocery shoppers' use of arithmetic. "Neither [context] nor activity exists in realized form, except in relation with each other; this principle is general, applying to all levels of [activity-context] relations" (p. 74). "In short, activity is dialectically constituted in relation with the [context]" (p. 73). The task of coordinating the sociocognitive and the "purely mathematical" mathematicocognitive context therefore involves a continual toing-and-froing between the overarching whole and the parts that constitute it and make its existence possible. As an analogy, consider the process of reading a text. As we read along, we have unarticulated anticipations about what is to come and these influence the interpretations we give to the words and phrases we encounter (Bartlett, 1932; DiSibio, 1982; von Glasersfeld, 1983b). This corresponds to the influence of context on activity. Conversely, we modify our anticipations in the very process of interpreting particular words and phrases (Gadamer, 1986). This is analogous to the manner in which activity influences context. It is in this sense that context and activity are dialectically related.

THE ANTHROPOLOGICAL CONTEXT

The relevance of the anthropological context has been hinted at with the discussion of the social aspects of both experience and cognitive explanation. Sociocognitive analyses attempt to understand and account for classroom social life solely from the perspective of one of the participants. In contrast, the purpose that structures the anthropological context is to identify and account for aspects of a culture (or microculture) by analyzing regularities and patterns that arise as, say, a teacher and students interact during mathematics instruction. In this context, the teacher and students are viewed as members of a classroom community with its own unique microculture. As Eisenhart (1988) put it, the focus in the anthropological context is "on describing manifestations of the social order in schools and developing frameworks for understanding how students, through exposure to schools, come to learn their place in society" (p. 101). In effect, the researcher has to stand apart from the participants and look down on their interactions to identify patterns that are outside their awareness. The implicit rules or social norms that the participants appear to be following can be formulated as a first step in explaining their mutual construction of the observed patterns. However, these norms, like the patterns themselves, are entirely the observer's own making. They are derived from the researcher's experiences of observing the participants' interactions rather than from the inferred experiences of the participants as they interact with each other. This perspective might be termed the socioanthropological context. The social norms should not be thought of as objective, mind-independent entities that somehow uphold the stability of group life. According to Blumer (1969), "A gratuitous acceptance of the concepts of norms, values, social rules, and the like should not blind the social scientist to the fact that anyone of them is subtended by a process of social interaction—a process that is necessary not only for their change but equally for their retention in a fixed form" (pp. 18–19). It is easy to jump to the conclusion that members of a community internalize social norms from (the observer's characterization of) their social environment. Behavior that conforms to the norms can then be accounted for by assuming that it is driven by internalized social norms. The problem with this account is that people do not act by responding to abstract objects such as social norms that the researcher projects into their world. Instead, they act on the basis of the meaning that objects in their world have for them as they attempt to fit their activity to that of other people. Voegelin (1952) pointed out, "Human society is not merely a fact, or an event, in the external world to be studied by an observer like a natural phenomenon . . . it is as a whole a little world, a cosmion, illuminated with meaning from within by the human beings who continuously create and bear it as the mode and condition of their self-realization" (p. 27). As an example of such a little world, Schoenfeld (1987) characterized his mathematical problem-solving course as "a microcosm of mathematical culture" (p. 213). Because this and other cultural worlds are continually created by the participants, it is essential "to grasp the native's point of view" (Malinowski, 1922). This requires an analysis of the taken-for-granted interpretations, activities, and practices that give rise to the observed patterns and norms. Such an analysis coordinates the socioanthropological context with the socioexperiential and sociocognitive contexts. The purpose is to explain how the participants' ongoing interpretations of their own and each other's activity give rise to social interactions that, from the observer's perspective, appear to follow objectified social norms. In this regard, beliefs, obligations, and expectations are again key constructs that can be viewed as the sociocognitive correlates of social norms and interaction patterns.

Analyses of social norms and the corresponding obligations and expectations deal with the interpersonal relations and social roles that the teacher and students develop during mathematics instruction. As an example, I and my colleagues, Erna Yackel, Terry Wood, and Grayson Wheatley, are currently analyzing classroom life in a second-grade classroom in which instruction was compatible with constructivism. Typically, small group problem solving was followed by a teacher-orchestrated whole class discussion of the children's solutions for all areas of second-grade mathematics including arithmetical computation. Identified social norms for whole class discussions include:

- Explaining how an instructional activity that the small group completed was interpreted and solved.
- Listening and trying to make sense of explanations given by others.
- Indicating agreement, disagreement, or failure to understand the interpretations and solutions of others.
- Attempting to justify a solution and questioning alternatives in situations where a conflict between interpretations or solutions has become apparent.

Note that these norms do not deal specifically with the activity of doing mathematics—they are as applicable to a biology or reading lesson as to a mathematics lesson. This limitation of our current work is symptomatic of a larger problem in the research literature. As both Erickson (1982) and Cazden (1985) observed, ethnographic studies of classroom social life almost invariably ignore what is traditionally called academic content (e.g., mathematics). Eisenhart (1988) noted that ethnographers focus "on such things as the hidden curriculum, patterns of social interaction, or ideological conflicts in schools" (p. 100). Mathematics educators, in contrast, "are accustomed to assuming that the development of cognitive skills is central to human development, [and] that these skills appear in regular sequence regardless of context or content" (Eisenhart, 1988, p. 101). In other words, mathematics educators typically operate in the mathematico-experiential and mathematico-cognitive contexts and characterize learning in terms of individual children's conceptual developments. Ethnographers for their part operate in the socioexperiential, sociocognitive, and socioanthropological contexts and characterize learning as a process of acculturation. They are, in Goodman's language, constructing different worlds, each of which is legitimate and real. On a smaller scale, my colleagues and I are currently struggling with the issue of how to coordinate analyses of second graders' construction of mathematical knowledge with analyses of classroom social life. The root of the problem is indicated by an asymmetry in discussion of the various contexts. We talk of socioexperiential, sociocognitive, and socioanthropological contexts and of mathematicoexperiential and mathematicocognitive contexts. There is a context we are yet to construct, that which takes an anthropological stance towards mathematical knowledge. If this deficiency were addressed, mathematics educators and ethnographers could each coordinate their analyses with this context and thus develop a consensual domain in which to talk to each other more productively. (This conversation would, of course, be facilitated by mathematics educators' development of interpretivist analyses of students' mathematical activity in that anthropology is primarily an interpretivist discipline. In this regard, one can anticipate that conflicts will arise from deeply rooted beliefs if mathematics educators develop information-processing models based on the tenets of mainstream American psychology.) More pragmatically, the construction of the mathematico-anthropological context makes it possible to overcome the problem of characterizing children's construction of mathematical knowledge as a lonely voyage. For good epistemological reasons, constructivists have rejected both empiricism and Platonism as explanations of children's mathematical learning (von Glasersfeld, chap. 2.2). They have argued that children construct their individual mathematical realities by reorganizing their personal experiences in an attempt to resolve what they find problematic. Some commentators have interpreted this to mean that constructivism is a solipsistic position, that mathematics in particular and reality in general are nothing but fantasies, and that science is impossible (Kilpatrick, 1987; Vergnaud, 1987; Wheeler, 1987). It is essential that constructivists construct a new context—the mathematico-anthropological context—if they are to both avoid these interpretations of their work and develop a coherent framework within which to talk about the specifics of learning and teaching mathematics.

As a first step, it should be emphasized that learning is an interactive as well as a constructive activity (Bauersfeld, 1988; Cobb, 1986b; Cobb, Wood, & Yackel, in press; Confrey, 1987; Steffe, 1987). For example, opportunities to construct mathematical knowledge arise from attempts to resolve conflicting points of view (Perret-Clermont, 1980), attempts to reconstruct and verbalize a mathematical idea or solution (Levina, 1981), attempts to distance the self from ongoing activity in order to understand an alternative interpretation or solution (Sigel, 1981), and, more generally, attempts to construct a consensual domain within which to coordinate mathematical activity with that of others (Barnes & Todd, 1977). In short, "to understand the source and course of cognitive growth, the detailed analysis of social experience is necessary—it is the interaction that is crucial" (Sigel, 1981, p. 216).

Von Glasersfeld (Chap. 2.2) offers an example of learning in the course of social interaction when he notes "that if you want your infant to learn the word 'cup,' . . . you will point to, and then probably pick up and move an object that satisfies your definition of 'cup,' and at the same time you will repeatedly utter the word." He argues convincingly that "the child's meaning of that word is made up exclusively of elements which the child abstracts from her experience [in the course of the interaction]." This is an explanation constructed within the cognitive context in that it focuses on the meaning-making activity of one of the participants—the child. From the anthropological perspective, one can view the episode as an instance of acculturation. Cup can then be viewed as a social concept. "So if one asks the question, where is the meaning of social concepts—in the world, in the meaner's head, or in interpersonal negotiation—one is compelled to answer that it is the last of these three" (Bruner, 1986, p. 122). I want to argue that this contention is not in conflict with von Glasersfeld's analysis. Bruner and von Glasersfeld are operating in different, nonintersecting but complementary contexts. If we were to conduct an anthropological analysis of the parent-child interaction described by von Glasersfeld, we would focus on the meaning of "cup" that, from the observer's perspective, emerges in the course of the interaction. This *emergent meaning* is the meaning that the parent and child are inferred to share and makes possible the eventual smooth coordination of their activity. As is the case with social norms, emergent meanings are entirely the observer's own constructions. The notion of emergent meaning derives from Meade's (1934) analysis of social interaction. On the one hand, we have the participants' interpretations of their own and each other's actions and, on the other hand, we have the observer's analysis of their joint activity. Observers create the emergent meanings while attempting to make sense of the joint activity that they see when interpreting the interaction from the outside. This idea is closely related to Krummheuer's (1983) notion of working interim (Arbeitsinterim). A working interim is a period when the participants' interpretations of their own and each other's actions fit together and the interaction proceeds smoothly. The observer, viewing the interaction during the working interim as a joint activity, can talk about the meanings that participants appear to share. Krummheuer used the term *fit* rather than *match* to stress that although the participants believe that they understand each other, they might well be ascribing different meanings to their own and each other's actions. In other words, there may be differences in the meanings that participants think they share with the others. From the anthropological perspective, meanings are assumed to be shared (Gergen, 1985), and from the psychological perspective, they are assumed to be compatible (von Glasersfeld, 1984). In the example of the parent-child interaction described by von Glasersfeld, the task of coordinating the two perspectives involves explaining how the parent and child actively interpret each other's actions and thus mutually construct the interaction pattern from which the meaning of cup emerges for the observer. This explanation would take the form of a psychological analysis of the parent's and child's individual meaning-making activities in the course of the interaction.

Thus far, we have talked about emergent meanings in general. Within the mathematico-anthropological context, we can legitimately talk of emergent mathematical meanings. This and the related notion of institutionalized mathematical knowledge are essential if we wish to address the issue of how "children come to know in a short time basic principles . . . that took humanity many years to construct" (Sinclair, chap 2.2 in this volume) in an epistemologically sound way. It should be noted that "institutionalized knowledge" does not refer to knowledge associated with what are typically thought of as institutions in society—schools, universities, prisons, the army, or, more generally, large well-bounded organizations with clearly delineated functions. Rather, institutionalized knowledge refers to the physical and intellectual practices that are taken-for-granted by specific communities of knowers. The mathematical practices that are beyond justification in one second-grade classroom might, for example, differ in significant respects from those in another second-grade classroom. Knowledge is always institutionalized by communities of individuals who act on the basis of the interpretations they make in the course of their interactions (Blumer, 1969). The notion of a community as a collection of actively interpreting, interacting individuals can be contrasted with the everyday notion of an institution as an organization that follows its own dynamics. In the latter case, individuals are merely viewed as media for the play and expression of these dynamics. They are "cogs in the machine" who act in accord with organizational principles that "represent the application of somebody's definition of what the organization should be" (Blumer, 1969, p. 58). The activity of the individuals who constitute the organization is ignored in favor of a definition imposed on them. In contrast, I always use "institutionalized knowledge" to refer to the product of the coordinated activity of members of a community rather than to knowledge someone thinks they should have in order to carry out their predetermined roles in an organization.

The potential fruitfulness of using constructs such as emergent mathematical meanings and institutionalized mathematical knowledge does not imply that they can be taken as solid bedrock on which to anchor analyses of learning and teaching. As is the case with social norms, it is easy to subordinate individual experience to cultural knowledge by concluding that individuals internalize mind-independent cultural knowledge and that this drives their behavior. Theorists such as Comaroff (1982) and Lave (1988) proposed that the relation between the mutual construction of cultural knowledge and individual experience of the lived-in world is dialectical. In this formulation, it can be argued that cultural knowledge (including mathematics) is continually recreated through the coordinated actions of the members of a community. This is mathematics from the perspective of anthropological observer—mathematics as emergent meaning and institutionalized knowledge. The educational implications of this view of mathematics as cultural knowledge are relatively straightforward. "Induction into the culture through education, if it is to prepare the young for life as lived, should . . . partake of the spirit of a forum, of negotiation, of the recreating of meaning" (Bruner, 1986, p. 123). This is the primary anthropological reason why instruction in the classroom we observed consisted of small group problem solving followed by whole class discussions of the children's solutions for all areas of second-grade mathematics including arithmetical computation. We have already argued that this approach makes sense cognitively in that opportunities for individual children to construct mathematical knowledge arise in the course of their classroom social interactions.

The notion of emergent mathematical meanings is as applicable to the teacher and second graders as an intellectual community and to two or three children working together during small group problem solving as it is to society at large. Children can be viewed as active reorganizers of their personal mathematical experiences and as members of a community or group who actively contributes to the group's continual regeneration of the taken-for-granted ways of doing mathematics. From the anthropological perspective, these institutionalized mathematical practices have emergent meanings that constitute the consensual domain mutually constructed by members of the group. For example, as we look across video-recordings of the second-grade mathematics lessons, we (as observers) see that the practice of operating with units of 10 and of one emerged as a taken-for-granted way of doing things. It became taken-for-granted in that a point was reached after which children who engaged in this practice were rarely asked to justify their mathematical activity. It was beyond justification and had emerged as a mathematical truth for the classroom community. To be sure, when we adopted the mathematico-cognitive perspective and interviewed the children individually, it became apparent that this intellectual practice had a variety of qualitatively distinct meanings for them—their meanings were compatible rather than shared. Nonetheless, their participation in a classroom community that negotiated and institutionalized certain mathematical practices but not others profoundly influenced their individual conceptual developments. It is not just that children make their individual constructions and then check to see if they fit with those of others. Children also learn mathematics as they attempt to fit their mathematical actions to the actions of others and thus contribute to the construction of consensual domains—as they participate in the process of negotiating and institutionalizing mathematical meanings (Bauersfeld, 1980; Bishop, 1985; Voigt, in press). From this perspective, the notion of children's uncontaminated natural mathematics is a fiction. In the classroom we observed the children constructed their own nonstandard, conceptually based algorithms for adding and subtracting two-digit numbers. However, these were not natural constructions that the children made on their own. They were constrained by the nature of the instructional activities the children completed, the manipulative materials that were made available, the teacher's interventions, and the requirements that they explain and, when necessary, justify their own interpretations and solutions and attempt to understand the interpretations and solutions of others. In short, they engaged in consensually constrained mathematical activity. In an attempt to coordinate contexts, we can say that the children's and teacher's mathematical activity created the institutionalized mathematical practices that constrained their individual mathematical activity. Conversely, the institutionalized mathematical practices constrained their individual activities that give rise to the institutionalized practices. Acculturation and the institutionalization of mathematical practices are therefore a necessary aspect of children's mathematics education. Analyses that focus solely on individual children's construction of mathematical knowledge tell only half of a good story. The issue that needs to be addressed is the form that the process of mathematical acculturation should take and how it can be coordinated with what is known about mathematics learning.

COMPLEMENTARITIES

I have suggested that mathematics learning and teaching can be analyzed from six distinct vantage points or contexts. These are the mathematico-experiential, mathematico-cognitive, and mathematico-anthropological contexts and the companion socioexperiential, sociocognitive, and socioanthropological contexts. This framework of complementary though irreducible contexts was applied to the problem of truth and certainty in mathematics. The analysis involved a coordination of all three mathematical contexts. From the anthropological perspective, mathematical theorems can be seen as emergent truths that are institutionalized by the coordinated activity of members of mathematical communities. From the experiential perspective, objectivity, truth, and certainty grow out of the unquestioned belief in a shared external reality that is necessary for and is made possible by interpersonal communication. From the cognitive perspective, mathematics as the paradigm case of certainty is related to reflective abstraction from activity as the primary process by which mathematical knowledge is constructed.

Most attention in this chapter has been given to the anthropological context because (in blatantly realist language) it is the perspective most neglected by mathematics educators. We have severe difficulties if we restrict ourselves to the cognitive and experiential contexts even if our primary focus is on mathematics learning. There appear to be at least four equally unpalatable options. The first is to go with our subjective intuitions and accept Platonism as an explanatory theory despite the fact that it has been demolished by philosophical critiques. The second is to develop Mill's empiricism despite the mortal blows delivered by Frege (1960) and others. This is the approach taken by contemporary information-processing psychologists who talk of developing instructional representations. The third is the neo-Vygotskian position that might be termed *social empiricism*. As we have seen, this position posits an inexplicable internalization process as a primary learning mechanism. The fourth alternative is *radical constructivism*. This is a solipsistic position as long as we restrict ourselves solely to the cognitive context. The most inviting way out that I see is to complement cognitive constructivism with an anthropological perspective that considers that cultural knowledge (including language and mathematics) is continually regenerated and modified by the coordinated actions of members of communities. This characterization of mathematical knowledge is, of course, compatible with findings that indicate that self-evident mathematical practices differ from one community to another (Carraher & Carraher, 1987; D'Ambrosio, 1985; Saxe, 1988). Furthermore, it captures the evolving nature of mathematical knowledge revealed by historical analysis (Bloor, 1976, 1983; Grabiner, 1986; Lakatos, 1976).

This position might at first seem paradoxical; mathematical meaning can be in the world (mathematico-experiential), in the individual's head (mathematico-cognitive), and in social interaction (mathematico-anthropological). This apparent paradox is the result of one attempt to cope with an omnipresent if implicit complementary in mathematics education theorizing. As Steiner (1987) noted, the idea of "complementarily is well known . . . in mathematics education as the cause of many short-lived reform movements and "waves of fashion" that ebb and flow between the extremes of polarized positions . . . such as skill versus understanding" (p. 48). A complementarily is, then, an expression of the apparent paradox between seemingly opposite positions. Such paradoxes are not, of course, unique to mathematics education but pervade our everyday lives. We have hopes, dreams, and ambitions despite the fact that we know we will die (or, as Woody Allen put it, despite the fact that the universe will contract). Learning appears to involve a paradox. As we make progress and figure out solutions to our problems, we simultaneously construct new assimilatory mechanisms that are our own conceptual prisons. Teaching appears to involve a paradox. As Lampert (1985) put it, the dilemma of teaching "is an argument between opposing tendencies within oneself in which neither side can come out the winner. From this perspective, my job would involve maintaining the tension between . . . pushing students to achieve and providing a comfortable learning environment, between covering the curriculum and attending to individual understanding" (p. 183). Lampert goes on to illustrate that in practice it is a matter of repeatedly coping with this tension in concrete situations rather than of resolving the dilemma once and for all.

This complementary that seems endemic to mathematics education theorizing expresses the apparent paradox between mathematics as a personal, subjective construction and as mind-independent, objective truth. Accounts of students' mathematical learning typically emphasize one extreme or the other. We seem to have a choice between individual students each constructing their lonely, isolated mathematical realities or students mysteriously apprehending preconstructed mathematical knowledge in the world. As with the complementarity implicit in teaching, we cannot resolve the problem once and for all. Rather, we have to learn to cope with it in local situations by reflecting on "the underlying antagonistic relationships and mutual interactions of the two positions" (Steiner, 1987, p. 48). It is for this reason that I have discussed ways to coordinate analyses conducted in different contexts while at the same time arguing that the contexts are nonintersecting domains of interpretation. They are complementary though irreducible.

If this seems less than desirable, we can at least take heart from the observation that "hard scientists" have to cope with complementarities of their own. As Goodman (1984) comments

> The physicist flits back and forth between a world of waves and a world of particles as suits his purpose. We usually think in one world-version at a time . . . but we shift from one to the other often. When we undertake to relate different versions, we introduce multiple worlds. When that becomes awkward we drop the worlds for the time being and consider only the versions. We are monists, pluralists and nihilists not quite as the wind blows but as befits the context. (p. 278)

ACKNOWLEDGMENTS

The project discussed in this chapter is supported by the National Science Foundation under grant No. MDR 847-0400.

Chapter 4.3

Conceptual Splatter in Peer Dialogues in Selected Japanese and U.S. First-Grade Mathematics Classes

Jack Easley
University of Illinois at Urbana-Champaign, USA

Harold Taylor
Lincoln Consolidated Schools, Ypsilanti, Michigan, USA

There is a propensity for adults to form preconceptions about what is good for children, based on a rational view that there must exist a connection between what we as adults do in the way of solving problems and what children ought to do to become "like us." This logic has merit in that it attaches us to the future by keeping us culturally and intellectually relevant in the development of our society. However, it has not produced much more than schemes or methods, which at best organize and reorganize the various subjects children are confronted with in school. This view assumes that children must learn certain skills before they tackle particular problems, and they are not allowed to pursue a problem until they have mastered the particular requisite skill. The value in sometimes having a more advanced context for understanding a rationally prior system like arithmetic, and the need to reveal uses children might invent for prior systems, are usually not considered in current curriculum thinking.

Our approach to the promotion of children's thinking therefore looks irrational. It is irrational in the same sense as Galileo's pulling away from the notions of his contemporaries was irrational (during his time) or in the sense that expecting hot water to freeze more quickly than cold water would be irrational for most people today. We are trying to break our dominant rational mind set—trying to grasp a phenomenon that seems to explain teachers' resistance to allowing pupils freedom of thought. We are brainstorming, an irrational but accepted phase of scientific investigation. There can be no preconceived plan for the results of such an activity without compromising the activity itself. Teaching and learning have a similar constraint; if the teacher aims for a certain result, he is obliged to compromise the process of children's thinking. Mathematical problem solving can be seen as an expressive series of dialogues about space, shape, amount, and

4.3. CONCEPTUAL SPLATTER IN PEER DIALOGUES 217

time. Having a highly organized and superbly systematized curricula is no substitute for discovering the attributes that promote thinking and the options from which teachers have to choose. Just what these may be, remains a point of contention for researchers and teachers alike. As researchers, we think we have seen more of what the teachers see. Our method is to be sympathetic and try to avoid the pitfall of assuming a preordained logical path.

With some good fortune we have acquired transcriptions of first-grade mathematics classroom dialogues in which two teachers in Japan and ourselves teaching in the United States are trying to promote higher level thinking and cooperative thinking. In these classes, both story problems and problems about mathematical concepts have been used as challenges for the children. Perhaps the most obvious result is to demonstrate the unreasonableness of the common assumption that teachers, aiming each lesson for particular conceptual goal for all pupils, would expect nearly all of the pupils to succeed and understand the same concepts. Between the alternatives of accepting conceptual diversity (splatter) among the pupils and working for conceptual uniformity lies the hope that long-range process goals will result in conceptual power.

The relative ease with which children appear to communicate novel mathematical ideas with their peers compared to communicating with their teachers also seems important, as many of the conversations quoted later illustrate. The successful communication of a novel or unexpected idea implies, for constructivists, that it be reconstructed out of other, more familiar ideas by the recipient of the communication. If children are more familiar with each others' ideas than they are with teachers' ideas, this might imply a gap in communication.

We are deeply indebted to the teachers, the school authorities in Tokyo, Ypsilanti, and Champaign, the children, and to their parents for permission to observe, record, and transcribe more than 100 lessons from which the following excerpts were taken. Easley and his wife Elizabeth tape-recorded the first 50 mathematics lessons Watanabe sensei taught his new Japanese class of first graders. So with Elizabeth's help as translator, we can trace the day-to-day development of ideas. All these teachers saw their job as that of selecting and presenting the most challenging and relevant problems they could to their pupils and to assist them in learning communication skills needed to solve these problems, individually and in groups.

To understand the diversity of ideas a teacher is likely to encounter, what appears as an unpredictable splatter of ideas, consider the following lesson Easley conducted recently as a demonstration in a combination first- and second-grade classroom. Easley was asked to talk with the children about the experience he had in Japanese schools and to demonstrate something of the process. The class had been using Marilyn Burns groups of four problem solving, but had not used fractions in story problems before. Easley told them that the Japanese government had decided that the school should not encourage counting to add or to subtract in schools (Hatano, 1982; Easley, 1983), and he talked about different ways to add by counting. Their preferred method was to add each column separately, although they knew people who made a lot of dots and counted them.

Then, somebody wanted to know how far away Japan was, and Easley tried to remember the number of hours he had flown and to estimate how fast he flew. One boy then said that he flew to Florida, which was 900 miles away. When asked how long he flew, he said that it was hard to figure out because he flew in one plane for 1 hour, another plane for $\frac{1}{2}$ hour and a third plane for $2\frac{1}{2}$ hours. Easley wrote those times on the board vertically, without putting the fractions in a separate column. He added a plus sign and drew a line. He let the children work on it briefly and then organized them into groups of three to five to share their work. Two groups came to a consensus quickly, one for 4 hours and one for 5 hours. He allowed 2 more minutes for the other four groups who were struggling with the problem. Some groups with more than one answer split in two. The answers they had at that point included 4 hours, 11 hours, and 27 hours. The spokesperson from the group with 4 hours reported first. Then, the next group showed how, by counting the numerators of the two fractions as one, they got five. The next group had $4\frac{1}{2}$ hours. Their diagram consisted of a piece of pizza divided with 10 radial lines. Removing four of the pieces representing the 4 hours, of the first group, including all five boundary lines, there were just five boundary lines left, defining four pieces, "so four were left which made a half, therefore, the answer was four and a half."

Another group said they had 11 hours for an answer, but when they explained it at the board, they had added all the numerators and denominators to the integers getting 9 hours. There were no questions from the others as these groups presented their solutions. The next group got 8, but as they explained it, the girl "realized she had forgotten to add in one of the numerators," and so changed her answer to 9, and her group agreed with her. Another group answered 7. Their argument was that 1 and 2 were 3, and a $\frac{1}{2}$ plus a $\frac{1}{2}$ was 4. Easley asked whether, in putting together two half apples, it made a whole. "Yes," they said, "but that wasn't the same as one." With a pie diagram, divided in half twice by two perpendicular lines, another group showed that by counting the pieces, there were 4. Altogether, that made 7.

The group who had 27 for an answer were never able to show how they got it. Their diagram on the board consisted of a hexamino, changed step-by-step into a cross-shaped pentamino. Even with another member of the group to help, no explanation came forth. They were sent back to their seats, and a member of another group volunteered to help them. After a while, they came up with 5 hours by the method of the second group. By this time four or five children were asking questions of their peers and Easley was asked to name the winning answer. Taking a poll was considered fair. The poll showed nine people not voting. The boy who had made the trip announced that he was sure he was right—4 hours. Easley said he had a lot of people to convince, and the boy quickly rose and explained to the class that $2\frac{1}{2}$, plus a $\frac{1}{2}$, made 3, and 1 more made 4. Many people objected, but the time was gone, and the teacher said that they could work on it tomorrow. Easley added that this was the way mathematics was usually done in the Japanese school he had visited every day for 4 months.

Teachers instinctively "paper over" many such ideas as quickly as they can, but the strategy of treating each as an interesting idea in its own right may be a better one for building a solid foundation. Once you realize that the papered over surface is smooth but weak, and the alternative ideas about constructing mathematics are still there under the surface, waiting to break down the understanding of the next lesson, you see that the paper needs to be ripped off so that all ideas can come out where they can be evaluated.

But as a teacher, how do you explain to a visiting colleague, administrator, or parent, or even the mathematically talented student, that all this splatter is serious mathematics? Some of it we suspect may be "living," but some is constructive (Easley & Zwoyer, 1975). We've had enough time to absorb Erlwanger's Benny (1973) and other such examples as horrible evidence of what can go wrong. One serious temptation is to discard all written arithmetic in first grade (Kamii, 1984). Now we need to consider each such idea as a genuine intellectual proposal deserving every consideration before being thrown out. The other alternative is to let them remain as skeletons in the closet.

First, summarizing dialogues already quoted in the literature, there are examples in which children directly counter the expressions of their teachers' thinking. For example, for 3 days, Watanabe sensei (Easley, 1983) tried to convince his class of 39 new first graders that it was acceptable to partition three objects into two groups, with two and one objects, and five objects into groups of three and two objects. His surprise at the opposition that these partitions were unfair, was very evident, and he persisted for three lessons. After discovering that his two fellow first-grade teachers had encountered similar resistance, he, and they, abandoned all such efforts. A week later, however, no objections were raised when a subtraction table was made containing those same partitions.

Another conversation already published (Easley & Easley, 1983) illustrated another possibility that many of these dialogues show that children may drop the resistance they have raised to a teacher's point when the teacher stops actively pressing it. Here the objection was whether adding zero could be considered a case of adding, because there was no net increase. The teacher had dramatized the point with a demonstration of "pouring" into two deciliters of "orange juice" the contents of a similar but empty container. After a dramatic pouring demonstration, the resulting two deciliters of orange juice were read off and recorded. Adding a basket of nothing to a basket containing 3 apples, led to a controversial number sentence: $3 + 0 = 3$. One said there was no answer because it wasn't really adding and another said that, because zero meant nothing, zero should be the answer instead of 3. The teacher, Watanabe sensei again, was obviously fascinated by such minority opinions and did not press the majority case for 3 apples as the answer. After a few minutes of discussion, all opposition ceased. Clearly, in most of these discussions, many children enjoyed the arguments.

The following transcription illustrates that the underlying structure of the splatter of ideas lies in the difficulty of integrating the different modalities in which the children have been working. Taylor gave first graders, near the end of the school year, written story problems to work on in groups of five. Each group drew pictures of a large sheet of paper and then presented their answer in full, in a skit, to the whole class, cutting out squares of paper to use as "cookies." He found distributing 14 cookies among four children led to ideas he had not expected such as dividing 2 cookies into four equal pieces, expressing the result as a mixed number, three and two fourths, and showed a wide-spread competence in arithmetical thinking.

Sarah:	Here's our problem. A baker made 14 cookies. She gave all of them to four kids. How many cookies and pieces of cookies did each kid get? (Sarah then quizzed the class on the problem, calling on those with hands raised for their answers.)
Sarah:	How many cookies did the baker make?
Response:	Fourteen.
Sarah:	How many kids were there?
Response:	Five.
Sarah:	Nuh-uh, I'm the baker. What were we supposed to do with the 14 cookies.?
Response:	Give 'em to all the four girls.
Sarah:	What were we supposed to find out?
Response:	How many they got.
Sarah:	How many together? How many did each kid get? Let's start off with passing [out]. How many cookies do they have?
Response:	One.
Sarah:	I still have all these cookies. Maybe I can do it again. Cookie number five, (and so on for another four . . .). Now, how many does each have?
Response:	Three.
Sarah:	With four kids, I have only two left. Either two kids get four or two kids get none (meaning, presumably, she would have to add the two left to the three for only two kids).

A boy from the audience passes her a pair of scissors.

4.3. CONCEPTUAL SPLATTER IN PEER DIALOGUES

Sarah: Let's see, what if I just cut them in . . . Well I think there's 1, 2, 3, 4, left (pointing to the children), so cut these cookies into fourths, I think. For cookies number one, two slices, cut 'em again, three slices, fourths (and so on for four children). (Now she takes the last cookie.) Cut one again? Now, how many cookies?

Response: Two.

Sarah: Cut again, and how many cookies do I have?

Response: Three.

Sarah: Cut them again, and we have four. Let's pass 'em out. You get 3 cookies and $\frac{1}{4}$. (She directs each child to put the whole cookies in one hand and the fourths in the other.)

Note that she momentarily slipped into referring to each fraction of a cookie as a cookie, although it is clear from her earlier correction of audience members who made the same mistake, and her later precise specification of what each child gets that she has no illusions here. It may be part of her style of teaching to reduce conflict with the itemization modality.

Sarah: How many do they have now?

Response: Four.

Sarah: No! Three and one fourth, three and a fourth. (Cuts again.) How many cookies?

Response: Two.

Sarah: What is $\frac{1}{4}$?

Sam: When you cut a cookie into four pieces, one of those pieces is $\frac{1}{4}$. When you cut anything into four pieces . . .

Sarah: If I gave this cookie to one kid, they would get $4\frac{1}{4}$. That wouldn't be fair because everyone else would get $3\frac{1}{4}$. (She cuts). Three cookies and $\frac{2}{4}$.

Jimmy: So I have four cookies.

Sarah: No, you don't, 3 cookies and $\frac{2}{4}$ (and she itemizes each).

Several days later, when the class saw the video tape, Sarah developed her mastery of the concept of fractions further, saying that $\frac{2}{4}$ was the same as $\frac{1}{2}$ so she could have just cut each remaining cookie in half.

Sarah integrated the itemization modality, on which so many of her group and also members of the audience learn, with the abstract modality which she shares in her brief dialogue with Sam (we are indebted to Don Miller of Oakland University in Rochester, Michigan, for the idea of learning modalities).

After the next group did the same, but with 13 cookies. . . .

Sue (to Sam): There's one thing I don't understand. After you gave everyone three, you just gave out little pieces, you didn't cut up a cookie.

Sam: Well, that's because I didn't want to cut it up just then.

Jimmy: Why didn't you have numbers on the cookies?

Sam: You don't need numbers on cookies. Name one reason why you need numbers on cookies.

Sue: I know why you don't need numbers on cookies. Cookies don't have numbers on them.

Sam: I know why they don't have numbers on them. What if we had a real cookie, and that cookie was a chocolate chip cookie, and the chips were shaped as 1s and 2s, that was a first cookie and a second cookie, then what would be so special about that? Why would you need numbers? (Two or three children around Jimmy and Sue are shaking their heads and whispering.) So that's why I didn't put numbers on them.

Jimmy's question arises out of a concern for the itemization modality, which went back from this kind of problem to the class' earlier work drawing pictures for story problems, each focussing on a different operation. At least three-fourths of the children drew each item and numbered it. Jimmy had just seen two group skits based on the same operation, division. The first skit itemized the cookies and the second one did not itemize them. Sue's response appeals to reality. They are talking about real cookies that don't have numbers. Sarah used itemization in the first group's presentation to keep track of where every cookie went. Cutting up the 13th and 14th cookie was part of her itemization. Sam, unlike Sarah, did not care to keep track of which cookie was which and confidently cut up the last cookie in advance, knowing that he would arrive at just having that cut cookie left to distribute. He was eliminating an unnecessary itemization. He wants reasons for anything he does, not just precedence. He wants to know what would be special about having real cookies with numbers on them. He is in a more abstract and reflective modality than Jim and Sue, and even than Sarah.

And for the next problem with 12 cookies . . .

Sam: Well, I don't have any more cookies, so I guess each person gets three cookies.

Taylor: So when you have 12 cookies and four people it works out nicely, so there's no need to break up a cookie. Any questions?

Jimmy: I don't understand. Why didn't you have any cookies to cut up?

Sarah: (Yelling) She cut 'em up. There's 1, 2, 3, . . . (counts to 12)

4.3. CONCEPTUAL SPLATTER IN PEER DIALOGUES 223

Sam: Well, 8 + 4 is 12 and then . . .

Taylor: Do you understand? I think he's got it now. Six and six is twelve. Three and three and three and three. So twelve is an even number. It just works out well. It worked out perfectly this time. (Teachers' urge to summarize may cover over some unexplained and un-discussed problems with modalities.)

If this dialogue approach to story problems is postponed until second or third grade, where we have made a good many other video tapes not considered here, then there is a lot of dialogue spent on the algorithms themselves, as when they are simply memorized they are poorly understood and very subject to error, as Easley's demonstration lesson shows.

A first-grade class taught by Kaji sensei in Japan showed children having difficulty integrating comparison and subtraction. She followed the plan of the larger of the two sets or objects to be compared and subtract the smaller number of tiles from the larger one. She encountered some resistance to this plan in the form of children who wanted to form separate tile representations for each object or set to be compared and make a comparison between them. The subtraction model for comparison worked only for those who were happy with the subtraction idea in the context of the comparison story problems.

Kaji sensei told a "story" about five friends—one more came. Fuse kun was called on to give the number sentence. He said, "Five plus one is six," and Kaji sensei wrote it on the board. She then called up the boy who had drawn individual tiles in a shrinking, curving row for the first part. He was asked to show the number sentence with the tiles, and he began putting up a row of 1-tiles. Several people called to him to use the 5-tile. So he put a 5-tile underneath the 5 in the number sentence, a 1-tile underneath the 1, and on the other side of the number sentence, he put a 5- and 1-tile together, underneath the 6. "That's no good," Fuse kun complained, "6 and 6 are 12." But sensei said it was all right and put an equal sign between the two sets of tiles.

Fuse kun's remark, that putting 6 tiles on both sides of the number sentence is no good because they add to 12, is interesting. The equation $5 + 1 = 6$ is often represented as the action of bringing a 5-tile together with a 1-tile. Addition is already unlike subtraction because you start with two groups instead of one. To have three groups stops the action completely. If subtraction is going to be an action done to one group, then it seems more reasonable to have addition be an action done to two groups. The suggestion made earlier of having another two groups of tiles not acted on was not to place all these groups in strict relation with the numbers in the number sentence. That would result in the same static interpretation Fuse kun was objecting to, and the plus sign would sit between two groups not added. The groups acted on should move from the left side of the number sentence to the right side.

Three weeks later, Kaji sensei wrote a story problem on the board:

There were eight pencils.
Six were used. How many were left?

"Think of the number sentence!" She asked. "Is it addition or subtraction?" She drew eight pencils on the board. "I used them up," she said as she drew a loop around six of them. "How many were left over? Did it increase? Did it decrease?"

"Decrease," they said.
"What operation?" she asked.
"Subtraction," they said, and "8 − 6."
"Do it with your tiles," she said.

Miwa kun kept on separating groups of 6-tiles and 2-tiles and putting them back together. Most children, initially used 1-tiles only, but sensei asked them to use their 5-tiles. One girl complained she did not have one. Several children set up two numbers, 8 and 6, some using their 5-tile for the 8 and some using it for the 6. Sensei then asked four of the children to demonstrate at the board using the large orange magnetic tiles. Terui kun put up a 5-tile and three 1-tiles. Then he pulled down the 5 and a 1, leaving two 1-tiles at the top. "Is it all right?" he asked.

"All right!" the children said.

Uno kun went up next and put up eight 1-tiles and 5 and a 1 together, with a little space separating the two groups.

"Wrong!" several people said. While Uno kun looked hurt and sensei looked puzzled, one boy called out suddenly, "I get it!" and two others joined in.

Kaji sensei asked those who understood to explain, and a boy came up and put a minus sign in the space between the 8 and the 6 tiles. Suzuki kun put up eight 1-tiles, and moved six of them to the right. Kato went up and put an 8, made of a 5-tile and three 1-tiles, and a 5-tile with the divisions showing and a 1-tile with a minus sign between the 8 and the 6 groups of tiles. Sensei said that all of these were right, but added, "let's do it Terui kun's way." Then she reminded them to "Take 6 away, not 2 away. Kawano kun took 3 away," she continued, "and then couldn't take 2 more away without cutting the 5-tile." Kaji sensei then asked the children to check with their neighbors to see if they could do it right. They did this with the two or with the others, explaining it to themselves.

A newer tape of Kaji sensei, now teaching in a different school, showed a different kind of teacher interest and response. Kaji sensei said that she had found third-grade children interested in the shapes of regular polygons corresponding to the positive integers, and because she was trying to get her first-grade class, in their 8th week, to think about all kinds of relationships with the numbers 0–5, she used those numbers to get children to draw corresponding polygons as sequences of connected arrows. The children's polygons were not regular as she

4.3. CONCEPTUAL SPLATTER IN PEER DIALOGUES

had wished, but she was pleased by two solutions: the five-pointed star for five and a circular arrow for one, which she had earlier announced could not be closed, thinking only of straight arrows.

This suggests that children's concepts are not as rigidly constrained as adults are by subject matter boundaries. These two examples could be considered "monsters" in Lakatos' (1977) sense, as they broke traditional elementary school concepts of polygons in the pursuit of finding a relationship between numbers and polygons. If the goal of primary mathematics education is to establish rigid concepts and boundaries between subjects, then "creative mathematics" is a contradiction in terms in elementary schools. But if the goal is to establish an appreciation of mathematical thinking as a tool for solving real problems, then we need to understand the forms that creative mathematical thinking takes in primary aged children and the kinds of social situations that either promote or suppress it.

The interesting question, one that is both epistemological and pedagogical, is to explain how young children are able to form and apply so many mathematical ideas to these problems that they have not been explicitly taught, ideas that one might think have a history of development in scholarly traditions that go back hundreds if not thousands of years. Piaget and Garcia (1983) offered one explanation for the recapitulation of earlier adult concepts in the young, namely, that ideologies control their use by suppressing or releasing particular ideas, both in children and in the historical scholars, but many scholars see creation of novel ideas as necessarily the work of rare genius.

We have tried to describe conceptual splatter because we think that teachers react to it in several ways that strongly help to determine what does or does not happen to efforts to increase the amount of pupil thinking in primary mathematics classes. First of all, some teachers may be frightened by the unpredictableness of conceptual splatter because they cannot prepare for guiding it in a safe direction and because so much of it is so wrong, they do not want impressionable children hearing wild thoughts they might not think of themselves. So they may discourage any open-ended problems and try to pave the way so discussion will move in predictable channels. Children then try to "psyche out" where the teacher is leading them and become dependent on teacher hints as John Holt pointed out years ago in *How Children Fail* (1964).

In addition, some teachers may welcome the conceptual splatter but try to deal with each concept, guiding it back to the standard forms of arithmetic as gently and rationally as possible. This can work in the hands of teachers with a very flexible command of arithmetic, an attitude that mathematics is a rational subject, and confidence in their ability to think on their feet. Many primary school teachers lack one or more of these attributes, and schools lack the personnel and the economic resources to help more than a small handful of additional teachers to acquire them.

Furthermore, some teachers decide to put up the conceptual splatter and to let the children themselves deal with it, providing only general encouragement and organizational support. Presenting challenging problems and letting children work out the diversity of ideas they bring to such problems permits real and increasingly rapid progress, and teachers learn valuable mathematics in observing the process. It is not only social constructivists (from Piaget to Douglas Barnes) who have found that most children are quite capable of sorting out such matters, but also many teachers in Japan, the United States, and other countries, as well as mathematicians like Hassler Whitney who have entrusted children to work out such things with fine results.

Discussion Chapters:
Actual Communication

Chapter 4.4

Communication in the Mathematics Classroom

Max Stephens
Ministry of Education, Victoria AUSTRALIA.

The discussion group agreed on a broad definition of communication in the mathematics classroom as embracing those patterns of action, interaction, and discourse taking place between a teacher and children, and among children themselves. In preparing this commentary, I have endeavored to take account of the deliberations of the discussion group, and to place them in the context of several broader issues and questions that arose out of our deliberations. These issues and questions do need further investigation. I hope that, by including them in the report of the discussion group on actual communication, they may help to shape an agenda for research and discussion leading to the next ICME. This commentary reports on at least four issues relating to the theme of the discussion group:

1. What influences shape communication in the mathematics classroom?
2. How well does a constructivist theory of learning guide the activities of teachers in their communication with children?
3. In what ways does constructivism contribute to our understanding of communication between teachers and children?
4. In what practical ways can classroom communication be improved using a constructivist perspective?

Recorder: Howard Johnson, U.S.A.

SHAPING INFLUENCES

The discussion group emphasized that communication in the mathematics classroom is shaped by institutional and cultural factors and is further affected by the participants' beliefs about the appropriateness of their own actions and roles. It is influenced by beliefs about the nature of school mathematics and the way it is to be taught and learned. In reference to the early childhood years of schooling, the discussion group gave attention to the following factors:

- Historical traditions and constraints surrounding the early childhood phase of schooling.
- Perceived traditions of school mathematics.
- Prior experience of children at home in their learning of mathematics and their access to school and preschool programs.
- How children see themselves as learners of mathematics.
- Children's growing identification of what school mathematics is about and how they engage in it.
- Children's perceived role in relation to the teacher.
- Teachers' experiences of mathematics in their own schooling and in teacher education.
- Teachers' confidence to do mathematics and to shape their own mathematical knowledge.
- Teachers' openness to children's emergent capacities as creators and shapers of mathematical knowledge.
- Teachers' perceptions of societal and institutional expectations of their role in the classroom.
- Teachers' beliefs about appropriate patterns of work in the teaching and learning of mathematics and about what children should learn.
- How children's performance in school mathematics is assessed.

Communication in the mathematics classroom is a socially constructed phenomenon. This feature of classroom communication has been amply discussed by sociologists of education as diverse as Jean Anyon (1981), Basil Bernstein (1977), and Michael Young (1971). Constructivist theory has been slow to come to terms with these perspectives. Paul Cobb's chapter (4.2) incorporating sociological and anthropological perspectives enriches what has tended to be a limiting psychological perspective of constructivism.

Participants in the discussion group were able to draw on their firsthand experiences of early childhood education in Africa, Australia, England, Japan, Pacific Island countries, and the United States. Cultural values in some countries that encourage children to state their own point of view to a teacher may be viewed with concern in other countries where children are expected to show respect to adults and not to "speak out." Participants also recognized the considerable limitations on communication in a classroom with large numbers of children and in countries where teachers lacked proper training and access to resources.

The discussion group recognized that actual communication often reflects inequities and stereotypes of gender, race, and class. Boys, for example, may be asked more process questions and are more likely to have their responses followed through. Girls may receive praise for the neatness of their work and their ability to emulate established models of mathematics practice. Other inequities emerge when some children, because of their ethnic background, are seen as not competent in the language of instruction and as a result are unlikely to be challenged. Class inequities emerge when some children are seen as socially handicapped or deprived and as a result unlikely to succeed in school mathematics.

Several participants in the discussion group, for example Nobuhiko Nohda (chap. 4.8), argue for greater attention to cross-cultural studies of communication in mathematics classrooms. Others suggest that the model of interactive communication characterizing constructivist research of children's learning might not "sit well" with how teachers are expected to deal with children. To some extent this may be a regrettable commentary on the competence of teachers to engage in a challenging and sensitive dialogue with children, but the explanation may well lie in how teachers see their work in the classroom. Where teachers see their principal work as covering a course of instruction, which may well have been prescribed for them, or where they see their work as showing or explaining to children how to do mathematics, the models of communication valued by constructivists are likely to have little appeal.

At several times, the discussion group noted that constructivist research has been concerned primarily with the development of children's mathematical knowledge and has paid little attention to teaching. Yet the group saw an urgent need to present to classroom teachers models of communication that could be justified as more powerful ways of assisting children's mathematical development which teachers could readily incorporate into their repertoire.

HOW CAN COMMUNICATION BE GUIDED BY CONSTRUCTIVIST THEORY?

It is interesting that the discussion group on possible communication confronted the same issue. In a commentary on the work of that group George Stanic (chap. 4.10) argues that "the study of teaching and teachers must also be part of the

4.4. COMMUNICATION IN THE MATHEMATICS CLASSROOM 231

constructivist research agenda." That agenda needs to examine the following issues:

- Use of case studies to illustrate examples of interactive communication used by teachers of mathematics in early childhood classrooms.
- Documentation of possible mathematical environments where interactive communication may be encouraged.
- Supporting evidence that in ordinary classroom settings this kind of communication is successful in assisting children's mathematical development.
- The extent to which the prevailing culture of schools is hospitable to the models of communication favored by constructivist research.

The theoretical deliberations of the Action Group did not resolve these issues. It is difficult to disagree with the proposition that the teacher's role is to create a mathematical environment to facilitate children's construction of mathematical knowledge. Certainly, the Action Group received several very promising examples of what teachers might do. Chapters by Weissglass, Mumme, and Cronin (4.9) and by Lampert (4.7) were useful. However, one's acceptance of these promising models and examples depends on a practical judgment that the environments depicted in these chapters are likely to facilitate the learning of mathematics. The fact that these judgments are made within a practical framework is not intended as a criticism. The point is, a criterion for evaluating possible mathematical environments is not provided within a constructivist framework. As Sinclair (chap. 2.1) points out, "It is extremely difficult to define 'mathematical contexts' especially with reference to young children." A similar point was made by von Glasersfeld (chap. 2.2) that a mathematical environment is relative to a particular situation or event and to the individual's available mathematical schemes. I do not wish to appear too negative, but these unresolved theoretical issues do stand in the way of offering teachers theoretically sound advice. At the same time, constructivists have to take more seriously a prevailing culture of schooling where the focus is on the orderly transmission of knowledge, and on mathematics as an arbitrary set of procedures to be matched up and carried out properly.

At several points, the discussion group touched on these problems by asking when it is appropriate for a teacher to intervene in order to redirect a child's thinking. We were unable to reach agreement on this matter. Some argued that they would never do so. They would probe and question, but never redirect. Others were less sure. In hindsight, we should have been more persistent in seeking to answer this question from a constructivist perspective.

In the report of the discussion group on possible communication, George Stanic (chap. 4.10) poses a similar question, "Are children never wrong because there is good reason for what they do or say, or are they sometimes wrong but for good reasons?" This is a critical issue for teachers of mathematics, but, like our discussion on whether teachers should intervene in redirecting children's thinking, it remains unresolved. Is it appropriate for a constructivist teacher to decide that a child has stayed too long with a strategy that is able to give correct results, but is very cumbersome and time consuming? Should the teacher decide to redirect the child to a more efficient and reliable strategy? Unless the constructivist research agenda can provide a framework to help us work through these practical problems, then constructivist implications for communication in the classroom will be limited.

WHAT DOES CONSTRUCTIVISM CONTRIBUTE TO OUR UNDERSTANDING OF COMMUNICATION?

The discussion group might have pressed harder in seeking answers to these questions. They will need to be addressed in the research agenda and do not, it would be argued, detract from the illuminating power of constructivist theory. Constructivism is a radical paradigm shift in the way in which Kuhn (1970) spoke of a revolutionary change in our beliefs. Having embraced a constructivist paradigm of children's mathematical development, one can never again see communication in the classroom in quite the same way. Old models represented communication as an exchange of ideas. Through textbooks and syllabuses, teachers have been persuaded to get across certain key ideas to children in a teaching session, and they might hope to be successful in communicating definitions to most children. Success was usually judged in terms of children's ability to repeat those ideas or to replicate skills and processes. If an exchange of ideas was not successful, one looked for faults in the communicator or the receivers. Failures in communication could be attributed to a lack of clarity in presentation or not pitching it at the right level. From the receiver's end, failures could be due to inattention, laziness, or stupidity.

More gentle explanations refer to children not being ready to learn, as though they are not yet able to receive particular messages. If one sees communication as an exchange of ideas, and judges its success in terms of faithful imitation or replication, then dialogue is unlikely to be seen as an efficient or appropriate means of communicating mathematics to young children. A well-presented lesson with the teacher directing questions or demonstrating a concept with concrete learning materials would probably do a much better job.

Constructivism casts doubt on these models of communication as exchanges of ideas. Constructivist learning theory makes good teaching always problematic. Far from downgrading the role of a teacher in helping children to learn mathematics, this assumption is one that many teachers have learned to take seriously. Constructivism can help teachers to understand better what they know "in their bones." Good teachers know that their best intentions are subject to

4.4. COMMUNICATION IN THE MATHEMATICS CLASSROOM

many influences that constrain success. Good teaching is rarely episodic and is usually the result of patient work over a long period of time. Success is rarely open to prediction and requires that teachers have an intimate knowledge of their children and their subject matter.

The working group recognized the need to build stronger bridges between constructivist theory and the wisdom of teaching practice. Before our meeting in Budapest, these links may have appeared very tenuous because constructivist theory seemed to be preoccupied with an interpretive psychological model of children's mathematical development. New perspectives on constructivism did emerge for the Action Group. As discussed earlier, Paul Cobb (chap. 4.2) argues that constructivism needs to incorporate experiential, social, and anthropological perspectives. In a chapter exemplifying Cobb's position, Terry Wood and Erna Yackel (4.6) emphasize the socially constructed features of mathematical knowledge and illustrate how classroom communication between teacher and children, and between children themselves, shaped the mathematics that children learned and their appreciation of their role in creating mathematical knowledge. Francis Lowenthal (chap. 4.1) speaks from an experiential and psychological perspective and reports on a successful trial of "nonverbal communication devices" with children whose relative lack of verbal skills appeared to place them at risk in a traditional classroom setting. These chapters mark important developments in the constructivist paradigm and, through their fresh perspectives, suggest lines of action and research in classroom practice.

Further elaborations of the social and experiential perspectives are necessary to generate illustrative case studies, to describe possible mathematical environments, and to provide evidence that patterns of communication used in these contexts are successful in assisting children's mathematical development. These important theoretical developments provide a rationale and a framework for linking theory to classroom practice. In hindsight, they temper my concerns that constructivism has too many unresolved theoretical issues that stand in the way of offering sound advice to teachers.

IN WHAT PRACTICAL WAYS CAN CLASSROOM COMMUNICATION BE IMPROVED USING A CONSTRUCTIVIST PERSPECTIVE?

It is imperative that a research agenda, drawing on these new perspectives within constructivist framework, be carried out in ordinary classroom settings. Otherwise, it will lack credibility for teachers. Some teachers will, no doubt, be engaged directly in these studies, but many more can provide invaluable support through their own action-based research. In these ways, they can see possibilities for expanding the range of communication in their classrooms, while at the same time challenging prevailing models of classroom communication.

These initiatives need to encourage varied forms of communication, in the broad sense in which our working group defined it. From her long involvement in early childhood education, Helen Pengelly (chap. 5.5) argues forcefully for encouraging children to communicate mathematics in a variety of forms and in their own terms. This same argument has been made by Noelene Reeves (1986) who saw varied forms of communication as a powerful means of assisting children to understand that mathematics is about ideas (their ideas) and not just answers: "Children will intuitively use a mixture of pictures, diagrams, words, and symbols, which will reflect the level of their ability to make meaningful mathematical representation . . . they need to create this link between the reality of the experience and the abstract nature of formal recording." These varied forms of communication may have quite different purposes. One purpose is to enable children to explain what they have done. For example, explanatory writing is useful because it focuses on children's actions and mental processes that have led to a result.

Another purpose is to communicate with others. In this way, children learn that the mathematics they compose is intended to be shared, and its success will be judged on how well their ideas are communicated to other readers and listeners. It is not only through classroom discussion that children learn how other people think mathematically, but written work—when exchanged among students, displayed, or developed as part of a group project—is a powerful medium for communicating mathematical ideas and interpretations. It also serves as a reminder to us as teachers that children's thinking, when allowed individual expression, can range far beyond our preconceived limitations and expectations.

Communication can also be an imaginative exercise. This aspect of communication needs careful nurturing and support. It does not happen unless children have good models to reflect on, either from adults or other children. Making up a story or posing a problem or building up a problem when given the answer are a few ways in which we can start to challenge childrens' imagination. Children's mathematical communication should involve a balance between writing and speaking. Achieving familiarity with the formal language of mathematics remains a goal. However, if it is to have meaning for children in later years, it can only be the end result of earlier writing and speaking where there is scope for informality of expression, risk taking (including 'invented' spelling), and theorizing, which may at first appear simplistic.

CONCLUSION

In the early years of schooling, the discussion group argued strongly that the patterns of communication valued in the classroom establish a basis of knowledge, meaning, and confidence that either affirms what children can bring to and do with mathematics or steadily locates mathematics outside their range of confidence and personal competence.

Chapter 4.5

Interactive Communication: Constraints and Possibilities

Bob Wright
Northern Rivers College, AUSTRALIA

In this chapter I address the topic of communication in early childhood mathematics by describing parts of a research project I have recently completed. A theory of children's counting types (Steffe, von Glasersfeld, Richards, & Cobb, 1983) was used as a framework in conducting a teaching experiment (Cobb & Steffe, 1983) which focused on the numerical development of four children during their kindergarten year of school (Wright, 1988, 1989). The purpose of this chapter is to illustrate how the counting types theory was used in the teaching experiment and how certain constructs of that theory were manifest in the children's problem solutions. There are three features of my work that are complementary to the earlier work (cf. Cobb, 1983; Steffe, 1983; Steffe, 1984a; Steffe et al., 1983; Steffe, Cobb & von Glasersfeld, 1988). First, the children in this teaching experiment were in the kindergarten year of school, whereas in the earlier study the children were in the first and second years of school. Second, the children in this study were Australian, whereas the earlier study focused on children from the United States. Finally, this study focused on aspects of children's mathematics that were not studied in detail in the earlier study. These included activities such as counting temporal sequences of sounds and movements, and children's number word sequence development.

Substantive use of the theory of children's counting types (Steffe et al., 1983) occurred in four related aspects of the study. First, it was used in the planning of tasks of the initial interview, which provided the basis for the selection of the children. In addition, it was used to plan tasks for the teaching sessions. It also guided the conduct of the teaching sessions; that is, it informed the teaching decisions made in the "real time" of the teaching sessions. And fourth, it was used to analyze and interpret the children's mathematical behavior observed in the interactive teaching situations. This analysis and interpretation also drew on more recent theoretical expositions focusing on lexical meanings and children's accommodations in mathematical contexts (Steffe et al., 1988).

From this teaching experiment we can conclude that the theory of children's counting types (Steffe et al., 1983) remains viable for the purposes of explaining and predicting young children's mathematical behavior and therefore has an important role to play in mathematics programs for early childhood education. The theory could be applied in areas such as curriculum planning for early childhood, assessing children's knowledge, and longitudinal analyses of children's progress. Most importantly, it can inform classroom teachers about ways of interacting with children in mathematical contexts.

CONSTRUCTIVIST TEACHING EXPERIMENTS

The observational bases of constructivist teaching experiments are teaching sessions in which children solve problems while interacting with the teacher. During these teaching sessions the teacher attempts to confront the children with problematic situations designed to bring about reorganizations of the child's current mathematical thinking. The tasks are intended to be within the child's "zone of proximal development" (Vygotsky, 1935/1978). The teacher is guided by working hypotheses concerning the current status of the child's mathematical knowledge. In simple terms, this teaching approach involves first finding where the child is and then, in an open task-oriented situation, trying to bring about an advancement in the child's thinking. If the proposition that teachers must take account of the child's current knowledge is accepted, then the teaching methods of the constructivist teaching experiment seem appropriate for the classroom teacher.

The constructivist teacher assumes that mathematical knowledge cannot be handed ready-made from the teacher to the child but must necessarily be constructed by the child in experiential contexts. From this assumption it follows that, to communicate effectively, the teacher must harmonize with the child's current ways of doing mathematics. Thus, from a constructivist perspective, effective mathematical communication requires the development of a working model of the schemes currently available to the child and a working hypothesis of the child's zone of proximal development. For the constructivist teacher, advancements in the children's knowledge occur when the children modify their current ways of operating in response to a problematic situation. By way of contrast, mathematical teaching based on a belief that the teachers' mathematical knowledge can be given directly to the children does not require the teachers to know the children's current ways of operating or where the children might advance to through a reorganization of their current schemes.

Mathematical communication between a teacher and a child is exemplified in the following discussion. Jason and Ben were two of the children who participated in the teaching experiment referred to earlier. They were selected on the basis of their initial interviews that occurred in the 2nd month of their kindergarten year. Jason and Ben were taught approximately weekly from the 3rd month until the 11th month. At the beginning of the teaching experiment both children were limited to counting perceptual unit items (Steffe et al., 1983). They could count but they needed a collection of marbles, beads, and so forth in order to count.

CREATING SPATIOMOTOR PATTERNS

One kind of task frequently used in the teaching experiment involved establishing the numerosity of a partially screened collection of counters. The first time Jason could count the items of partially screened collections was during the second month of the teaching experiment. In doing so his counting resembled the counting of figural unit items described by Steffe and colleagues (1983) because he appeared to visualize the screened counters. By the end of the fifth month of the teaching experiment Jason's counting scheme had undergone a modest reorganization because when perceptual material was not available, he could now generate his own sensory material in counting. The teacher asked Jason to count a partially screened collection involving four unscreened counters and three screened counters that Jason counted prior to screening.

T: (Indicates appropriately with his two hands) In your mind put them together.

J: (Immediately begins subvocally uttering number words while sequentially making four pointing actions over the four unscreened counters. Then looks at the screen covering the three counters and, without hesitation, continues uttering number words while tracing out a spatiomotor pattern for four in the air. Then repeats the last number word aloud) 8!

When he traced a pattern for four in the air, he re-enacted counting four perceptual items. The four visible counters were arranged in a domino-four pattern and when Jason continued to count the screened counters, he apparently represented that domino-four pattern, so the traced pattern along with the counting activity "5-6-7-8" is called a spatiomotor pattern because it involves both a spatial and a motor component. For Jason, spatiomotor patterns were the source of his progress beyond being restricted to counting perceptual items. In the first 2 months of the teaching experiment the teacher had engaged Jason in activities that involved tracing spatial patterns or plane figures (triangles, squares, hexagons, etc.). It seemed likely that these earlier experiences had contributed to the development of more sophisticated countable items. The spatiomotor pattern represented progress in Jason's ways and means of operating and opened up new avenues for interactive communication with his teacher.

MONITORING COUNTING ACTIVITY

As shown earlier, Jason could now count the items of partially screened collections. At the same time, Jason consistently failed to solve tasks in which the teacher removed items from a collection that had been displayed and counted. The teacher hypothesized that Jason's counting scheme was figurative (Steffe, 1984b) and that he had the potential to construct a numerical scheme. These hypotheses informed the teacher's mathematical communication with Jason and essentially defined his zone of proximal development. Jason gave the first indication that he could unite discrete items together to make composite units in a teaching session 2 weeks later. He was presented with a task in which the teacher directed him to look away while he separated and then screened three counters from a collection of ten that Jason had already counted.

T: How many did I take away?
J: (Utters the number words subvocally while pointing with the index finger of his right hand at each of the seven counters) 1, 2, . . . 7. (Pauses for 2 seconds during which time he raises his right hand to his temple, then continues uttering number words subvocally, coordinating each utterance with a movement of his left index finger on the desk) 8, 9, 10, (pauses briefly and then repeats the utterance of the last three number words while again moving his left index finger on the desk for each number word) 8, 9, 10. (Pauses for 2 seconds) 3!

After counting the seven visible counters, Jason reorganized his counting activity. This involved extracting himself from the sensory activity of counting perceptual items. After counting "8, 9, 10," I hypothesized that Jason "united in thought the results of his previous counting activity. . . . [This involved] taking the results of a sequence of counting acts as a unit" (Steffe et al., 1983). As he continued to count to 10, Jason used his left index finger in recording counting acts. His utterances and actions served as material for making discrete experiential items that he took together as one thing. This "taking together" is indicated when he monitored counting "8," "9," "10" the second time he continued to count. This indicated that Jason was beginning to reconstitute the experiential results of counting as numbers or as composite units.

Immediately following the task described, the teacher placed twelve counters on the table and asked Jason to count them. The teacher then asked Jason to turn away and then hid two of the counters. On his first attempt to figure out how many counters had been hidden, Jason counted the 10 visible counters from one and then continued counting to 26. The following is his second attempt:

J: (Moves each counter in turn) 1, 2, . . . 10, (places his right index finger on the desk) 11—, (pauses briefly) is 1. (Pauses briefly and then makes a small hop with his finger on the desk) and 10 is two, (another hop) and 12—umm, twe—, (hops back to his left with his finger) ni—, 9 is 1, (continues making, on each count, a hop to his right with his index finger) 10 is 2, 11 is 3, 12 is 4, 13 is 5, 15 is 6, 17 is 8, (pauses briefly) 19 is—, ni—19, (pauses briefly) is 19, and 20!

This was the first occasion in the teaching experiment that Jason counted counting acts. Spontaneously monitoring his counting acts was an accommodation of his counting scheme. This accommodation occurred independently and was a permanent change as was confirmed in the next two teaching sessions. On these occasions Jason consistently kept track of up to five counting acts in continuations of counting when finding how many items had been removed from a previously displayed collection. The accommodation of monitoring served in the transformation of his counting scheme from a figurative to a numerical scheme. Because of this result, the accommodation is called *engendering* (Steffe et al., 1988).

INTERACTIVE COMMUNICATION IN THE NUMERICAL STAGE

The counting solutions discussed previously provided some of the indications that Jason's counting scheme was becoming numerical. By the seventh month of the teaching experiment there was solid indication that he had made that achievement. The kinds of tasks presented to Jason in the last 3 months of the teaching experiment included subtraction. These tasks were used to explore the range of strategies Jason might use and the kinds of accommodations he might make in subtractive situations in the context of interactive communications with his teacher. In a comparative subtraction task, the teacher placed a collection of six red counters and four yellow counters and screened each after Jason counted them. Jason's task was to figure out how many red counters would remain if each yellow counter was placed on a red counter.

Description of the Interactions

On his first attempt Jason counted from 1 to 6, and then on to 9, while making pointing actions over the screened collections. The teacher explained the task again to Jason, who then place his hands over his eyes and thought for a period of 35 seconds. The teacher then made the inference that Jason was not making progress and decided to unscreen the counters, first one collection and then the other while stating the number of counters in each collection. He did not allow

Jason to see the unscreened collections coincidentally because the intention of the teacher was to stimulate Jason's re-presentation of the counters and operations using the re-presented collections. The teacher was successful, because Jason placed his hands back over his eyes again and thought for a period of 3 seconds. He then pointed at a location above the screened collection of four counters and quickly moved his hand in a semicircular arc to a point above the other collection, and then back to the smaller collection. He repeated the over and back movement six more times, and then looked at the teacher with a smile and said, "Two." This interactive communication contained only minimal verbal exchanges and most of it was nonverbal. The teacher's action was based on his knowledge of Jason's mental operations and his intention to help Jason modify his knowledge.

Explanation of Jason's Action

Jason had consistently failed to solve tasks of this kind when the collections were hidden on previous occasions. On each previous occasion, the teacher eventually removed the screens and allowed Jason to take the items of the smaller collection one by one and place each onto an item of the larger collection. In this way Jason was able to determine how many items in the more numerous collection could not be matched with an item from the less numerous collection. On this occasion Jason re-enacted his prior actions at the level of re-presentation. Jason was not observed independently operating in this way again. However, the local modification is enough to include comparative subtraction in Jason's zone of proximal development.

CREATING AND COUNTING POINTING ACTS

Ben, like Jason, was taught approximately weekly throughout the 10 months of the teaching experiment. Early in the 9th month, Ben's counting scheme finally evolved into a figurative scheme in that he could count a hidden collection of items even when the items of the collection were separated into two hidden portions. The progress that he made was made in the context of interactive communication with his teacher. Without this interaction, it is doubtful that Ben would have made the accommodation indicated in the following protocol. The teacher displays and then screens each of two portions of a collection, one hiding five and the other four counters.

    T: 5 and 4?
    B: (Bends forward and places the left side of his face on his left arm which is on the desk. Looks along the desk toward the screens. Utters number

words coincident with making pointing acts over the screen covering the 4 counters.) 1, 2, 3, 4 (turns to the screen covering the 5 counters and continues uttering number words coincident with 2 pointing acts over the second screen), 5, 6 (sits up and then makes another pointing act at the second screen), 7.

After 30 seconds of waiting time, the session continued.

T: (Points at the screened portions in turn) 5 and 4?
B: (Bends forward until the left side of his face is on the desk. Looks along the desk toward the screens. Utters number words coincident with making pointing acts over the screen covering the 5 counters) 1, 2, 3, 4, 5 (turns to the second screen and continues uttering number words coincident with pointing acts over the second screen), 6 (pauses briefly), 7, 8, 9.

Remembering that it took 9 months for Ben to learn to count the items of a collection that were hidden in two places provides a reason to view his limitation as constraints in interactive communication. The teacher could not expect Ben to reflect on his actions for the purpose of isolating numerical relationships nor could he expect Ben to remember any but the most intuitive of the basic facts. Moreover, the teacher could not expect Ben to imagine what the results of counting might be were it to be carried out. His counting scheme was not *anticipatory*. Ben's meaning of number words consisted of the transitory *experience* of counting or its results and did not exist for him independently of actually counting. These were only some of the constraints of the teacher as he worked with Ben. He was also constrained in the type of tasks he could present. So, Ben's achievement was indeed significant for the teacher because Ben could now at least create an experiential meaning for number words when perceptual items were not in his visual field. But the teacher still experienced all of the constraints previously noted.

FAILURE TO MONITOR COUNTING

Ben's counting scheme remained figurative throughout the teaching experiment. By its conclusion he had not been observed to monitor counting and had given no indications that he had advanced beyond the figurative stage in the construction of his counting scheme. In the last teaching session with Ben, the teacher hypothesized that monitoring counting was within Ben's potential and presented activities that might have led to this modification. In one such activity, Ben was asked to count a collection partitioned into screened portions of six and five items.

B: I shall start off with the 6. (Slowly utters number words while successively pointing over the screened portion of 6) 1, 2, . . . 6. (Places the left side of his face on the desk and continues uttering and pointing as before) 7, 8, . . . 12.

T: (To encourage monitoring) 6 and 5!

B: (Looks upward and to the left, and then counts quickly and rhythmically in coordination with pointing acts directed alternately at 2 spots over the screen) 1-2, 3-4, 5-6, 7—. (Pauses and then counts the first portion again quickly and rhythmically as before but this time looks at the screen) 1-2, 3-4, 5-6. (Pauses, looks upward and to the left, and then continues) 7—. (Pauses, looks at the second screen and counts slowly while trying to feel the counters through the screen) 7, 8, . . . 15.

The way Ben counted to 6 confirms that he counted his pointing acts. However, there is no indication that he monitored his continuation of counting beyond 6. In fact, the second time he counted, counting beyond six was more primitive than the first time. This illustrates how Ben differed profoundly from Jason who was frequently observed monitoring counting during the last part of the teaching experiment.

THE ROLE OF INTERACTIVE COMMUNICATION

The previous discussions and examples underline the crucial contribution that interactive communication between teacher and child can make to advancements in the child's knowledge. This emphasis on interaction is consistent with Vygotsky's assertion that "instruction is one of the principal sources of the schoolchild's concepts and is also a powerful source in directing their evolution" (1934/1962). Distinctive features of the approach described earlier include the use of problem-oriented contexts and the teacher's adherence to a theoretical model of number learning (Steffe et al., 1983; Steffe et al., 1988). In posing problems for the child, the teacher is not only guided but constrained by the theoretical model. Furthermore, that the theoretical model was derived from intensive and longitudinal observations of children operating in similar problem-oriented contexts is a important strength of this teaching approach. The approach is in harmony with that used in a recent classroom teaching experiment (Cobb, Wood, & Yackel, in press) in that it "encourages [children] to construct solutions that they find acceptable given their current ways of knowing." Indeed, the use of interactive communications like those previously exemplified would seem to complement teacher-directed whole class activities and small group activities in developing collaborative dialogue (Cobb et al., in press).

In this chapter, a mode of communication between a teacher and a child, labelled "interactive communication," has been discussed and exemplified. The distinctive characteristics of the interactive communication discussed in this chapter are: (a) it occurs in a problem-oriented mathematical context; (b) it is informed by a constructivist learning theory that applies specifically to the mathematical content in question; (c) it is constrained by the child's zone of proximal development that the teacher has determined as a result of prior observations of the child; (d) it takes account of the utterances and actions evident in the child's current problem-solving activity; and (e) it has the purpose of bringing about qualitative advancements in the child's current mathematical knowledge. I believe that interactive communication as described should feature prominently in early childhood mathematics and agree that "one of our most important jobs as educators is to capitalize on our distinctively human ability to engage in intensive and extensive interactive communication with our students" (Steffe, 1987).

CONCLUSION

The descriptions given earlier provide insight into parts of a teaching experiment in which the theory of children's counting types (Steffe et al., 1983) was applied to study the numerical development of four children in their kindergarten year. Furthermore, these descriptions indicate how that theory and more recent theoretical formulations by Steffe and his collaborators (Steffe et al., 1988) can be used in longitudinal analyses of the mathematical development of prenumerical children. These descriptions also provide examples of interactive mathematical communications with young children and illustrate how such communications can bring about qualitative advancements in children's mathematical knowledge.

In the study described in this chapter, the theory of children's counting types (Steffe et al., 1983) guided the planning, conducting, and analyzing of teaching sessions. That theory and more recent expositions of children's arithmetical meanings and strategies (Steffe et al., 1988) can similarly guide interactive communication in early childhood mathematics. Specific constructivist theories of children's acquisition of number knowledge such as these have been developed only in the last 10 years. Nevertheless constructivists would readily acknowledge that teaching approaches that embody what they would describe as interactive mathematical communication have been around for a good deal longer. Specific constructivist theories of mathematical learning are useful to the early childhood teacher because the theories provide bases from which the teacher can develop working models of the child's current knowledge and possible advancements. In this way, the theories provide bases for and constrain the interactive communications between the teacher and the child.

Chapter
4.6

The Development of Collaborative Dialogue Within Small Group Interactions

Terry Wood
Purdue University, USA

Erna Yackel
Purdue University-Calumet, USA

Our work derives from a constructivist's view of language and thought. On the one hand, the work is influenced by Piaget's theory of equilibration, cognitive conflict, and the importance placed on peer interaction (Piaget, 1970a). And on the other, it is guided by Vygotsky's view of the importance of learning within the context of social interaction and the crucial nature of human discourse (Vygotsky, 1962). Specifically, we have conducted a research and development project that investigated the mathematical learning of second-grade children as they used instructional materials designed to be compatible with models of early number learning (Steffe, von Glasersfeld, Richards, & Cobb, 1983; Steffe, Cobb, & von Glasersfeld, 1988). Small group problem solving and whole class discussions were the primary instructional strategies for all aspects of the mathematics, including arithmetical computation. These two strategies resulted in opportunities for learning that do not occur in traditional classrooms, including those that arise from collaborative dialogue (Barnes & Todd, 1977), as well as from the resolution of conflicting points of view (Perret-Clermont, 1980).

Genuine mathematical problems can arise in the course of social interactions in small group problem solving, as well as from an individual child's attempts to complete instructional activities (Yackel, Cobb, & Wood, in press). Peer group interaction gives rise to learning opportunities by encouraging both an exchange of viewpoints and verbal elaboration. When children are committed to collaborate, they try to make sense of each other's interpretations of the situation at hand and engage in mutually supportive activity. Language plays a critical role in this process. Barnes and Todd (1977) described the value of collaborative dialogue as follows: "[Collaborative] moves are mutually supportive: by taking the trouble to elicit an opinion from someone else, or by utilizing what has been said by extending it further, the group members ascribe meaningfulness to one another's attempts to make sense of the world. This helps them to continue, however hesitantly, with the attempts to shape their own understanding by talking" (p. 36). As Barnes and Todd made clear, the value of collaboration goes beyond that of resolving conflicts that may arise when partners work to achieve consensus. Learning opportunities arise naturally in the course of dialogues characterized by a genuine commitment to communicate (Rommetveit, 1985). When children attempt to make sense of each other's problem-solving attempts, they must extend their own conceptual framework to try to construct a consensual domain with their partner. This may occur when partners arrive at the same answer via different solution methods, as well as when one child tries to explain a perceived error in another's thinking. Additionally, language can both help children reflect on their own understanding when they give explanations (Levina, 1981) and help them reconceptualize their own cognitive constructions as they attempt to make sense of their partner's explanations.

The manner in which the classroom norms were mutually constructed within the whole class discussions has been previously discussed (Cobb, Wood, & Yackel, in press; Cobb, Yackel, & Wood, 1989). In this chapter we intend to focus on the development of the norms for collaborative dialogue within the context of the small group interactions. The teacher's initial interventions in the children's conversations served to establish the expectations and obligations for their roles in the discourse that were crucial to the development of the collaborative dialogue essential for the meaningful negotiation of mathematical viewpoints and solutions.

NATURE OF DISCOURSE PROCESSES

The nature of the relationship of language to thought lies in exploring the "social-interactional features of verbal communication such as states of intersubjectivity and social reality, and patterns of dyadic communication control" (Rommetveit, 1985, pp. 183–184). The attainment of states of intersubjectivity depends on the basic dyadic discourse pattern of speaker's privilege to determine what is meant and listener's commitment to make a sense of what is being said by adopting the speaker's perspective. A symmetric pattern of communication exists only when unlimited interchangeability of dialogue roles constitute part of the conditions of the interaction. As adults, our intuitive mastery of these dialogue roles is taken for granted, but for young children these roles are still being constructed in the course of their interaction with others (Bruner, 1986; Kaye & Charney, 1980). The development of these roles is greatly aided by dyadic communication between the child and the adult in which the expectations and obligations for participation in the dialogues can be initiated and maintained by the adult. The ground work for the negotiation of meaning in discourse occurs in early mother/child interactions, which later extend to encompass teacher/child interactions that occur in the classrooms (Cazden, 1988; Mehan, 1979). By virtue of these adult/child interactions the child has an opportunity to participate in collaborative dialogues. The ability to engage in such communication indicates the success of the interaction between the children in small groups. It is in the course of these collaborative interactions that children participate in states of intersubjectivity from which genuine communication about mathematics can occur.

TEACHERS'S ROLE
IN THE MUTUAL RECONSTRUCTION OF NORMS
FOR COLLABORATIVE DIALOGUE

We have selected one pair, Karen and Craig, to illustrate how these norms of discourse were developed within the small groups. The two children were paired at midyear, well after the norms for collaborative dialogue had been established within the classroom. The teacher often reassigned pairs to accommodate changes in cognitive levels or social interactions. For us, Karen and Craig's pairing offered a contrasting case in the otherwise typical rearranging of pairs because they were initially unable to negotiate a consistently cooperative working relationship, and their interaction at times resulted in conflict, misunderstanding, and confusion. The two children presented a problematic situation within a well-established setting and thus offered an opportunity to observe how norms for collaborative dialogue were mutually constructed. The children were videotaped daily as part of the ongoing research and development project. These video-recordings together with ethnographic field notes formed the data corpus.

As the children worked in small groups, the teacher moved about the classroom observing and interacting with individual pairs of children. Her first objective was to establish with the children the obligations and expectations for collaborative dialogue necessary to make possible the meaningful discussion of mathematical solutions. In this role, the teacher exerted her authority to help establish and maintain the discourse within the pairs. It was her intention to let the children conduct the dialogue themselves, and in so doing her primary goal was to act as listener, only interjecting as a speaker in order to help the children maintain the interchangeability of their dialogue roles as they learned to engage in collaborative discourse. As such, the teacher did not attempt to model the appropriate discourse pattern, but rather her intent was to develop an interactive process by maintaining the children's roles in the dialogue. In doing this, she provided opportunities for the children to participate in dialogues in which they could express their thoughts about mathematics and simultaneously learn to engage in genuine communication. To illustrate this, we present the following episode that occurred 2 weeks after Karen and Craig were paired and begins as they were completing an activity page designed to encourage the use of thinking strategies for solving the following problems: $47 + 19 = \_\_$; $48 + 18 = \_\_$; and

4.6. THE DEVELOPMENT OF COLLABORATIVE DIALOGUE

49 + 17 = __. The teacher approaches after they have just finished the problem 47 + 19 = __ for which Karen gives the answer 66. The teacher listens to her answer and asks:

> T: Do you agree Craig? (Craig shakes his head yes as he writes down the answer.)

The teacher in her initial comments establishes for herself and the children the fact that they ought to follow the previously established classroom norms of verbalizing their solutions to problems, listening to alternative solutions offered by their partner, and attempting to reach a consensus. The episode continues as the teacher reads the next problem.

> T: Okay. Now this is 48 + 18 equals? Okay, let's take a look here.
> Karen: (Holding up her thumb, starts to count) 48, forty. . . . That's just the same!

As Karen excitedly points to 47 + 19 on the worksheet, the teacher looks at Craig waiting for him to respond, but he continues writing the answer on the sheet. She then takes his turn in the dialogue and asks Karen, "What is just the same?" By doing this, the teacher provides an appropriate response, which allows Karen to continue the dialogue, and yet also places her under the obligation of explaining what she meant.

> Karen: (Continues excitedly.) If you take 1 from the 19 and put it with the 7 . . . , (She hesitates and looks at the teacher, while Craig leans forward to look closely at the problem). And [it] makes 48 and that makes this just the same [as 48 + 18].
> T: Do you see that Craig? Do you see what she is trying to say?
> Craig: What?
> T: She is saying that 47 + 19 = 66. Do you see this? I mean you've gone through this and you two understand how you got it. Do you?
> Craig: (Shakes his head yes.)

The teacher, realizes from Craig's remark, "What," that although he leaned forward to look at the problem, he really was not listening to Karen's explanation. She tells him in a direct manner that when his partner gives a solution to a problem, it is his obligation to listen and try to understand the explanation. The teacher continues:

> T: Look at the next problem, 48 + 18 equals. She said its the same number.

Karen: Yeah, because you take 1 from the 19 and add it to the 47 and that makes. . . . (She hesitates.)
T: Forty-eight.
Karen: Forty-eight and 18 there. . . .
Craig: (Interrupts excitedly.) Oh! I know what she's tryin' to say. Take 1 from here and add it here.
T: Right!
Craig: It's got to be the same answer or you can add it here and add to here. (He points from 47 to 48 and from 18 to 19).
Karen: No. Take one from. . . . (She points to the 19.)
Craig: (Interrupts) Takes 1 from here (points to the 19) and add it here (points to the 47).
T: Exactly!

As Karen re-explains her solution method, the teacher's role becomes one of inserting only an occasional word to maintain the momentum of dialogue. As Karen is talking, Craig listens to her explanation and begins to make sense of it. His excitement is evidenced by his attempt to re-explain her solution. Karen, however, listening to his explanation, notices his error and attempts to clarify it. Craig, interrupts and then re-explains the solution indicating he does understand Karen's solution.

As the dialogue between the children became collaborative, the teacher became less of a speaker and more of a listener, thereby letting the pair maintain the dialogue with only occasional help for her. From the teacher's perspective, her role in the dialogue is in contrast to that of a traditional teacher. She does not in any way attempt to tell Craig the method Karen has used to solve the problem. Instead, her intention is to support the interactive nature of their discourse by making interventions that enable them to continue with their dialogue. Conversely, the children come to realize that it is their responsibility not only to provide explanations but to listen to the other's solutions. In this role, the teacher mutually establishes with the children the expectations and obligations necessary to conduct collaborative dialogue as they engage in mathematical activity.

STUDENT'S RECONSTRUCTION OF NORMS FOR COLLABORATIVE DIALOGUE

The methods children used to demonstrate to each other that they are willing to cooperate form an integral part of collaborative dialogue. Acts that involve using and extending another's ideas and solution attempts affirm that the children are ascribing meaning to their partner's work (Barnes & Todd, 1977), and as such

4.6. THE DEVELOPMENT OF COLLABORATIVE DIALOGUE

they support the activity of the partner. Verbal cues to listen to an upcoming explanation or remark, as well as interruptions that respond to or extend a comment, are other indicators of the intention to collaborate.

Collaborative dialogue can result in opportunities to learn not only when children give explanations, but also when they listen to their partner's explanations and attempt to develop a framework in which both their own constructions and the partner's explanations makes sense (Barnes & Todd, 1977). As they use, extend, or question each other's solution attempts, they ascribe meaning to them and thereby help to sustain the dialogue. The collaborative nature is present not only when children try to understand their partner's thinking but also when they invite their partner to consider their thinking. "Look" and "come here" are, for them, signals of invitations to consider and react to what is about to be said.

We illustrate the nature of the discourse with an episode of Karen and Craig working together to reach consensus as they solve 39 + 19 = ___. This episode simultaneously illustrates both how children extend their conceptual framework to accommodate to their partner's explanations and how they reconstruct the established norms to maintain the dialogue with assistance.

Craig: (Uses a hundreds board and starts counting at 40 on the board.) 40, 41, 42, 43, . . . , 57, 58, 59. (While counting he does not visibly keep track of his counting acts.)

Karen: Thirty-nine, 49. That's 10 (pointing to the hundreds board. She continues counting on her fingers starting at 50. She puts up one more finger with each number word utterance and stops when 9 fingers are up). 50, 51, 52, 53, 54, 55, 56, 57, 58.

In the process of trying to resolve the disagreement between their answers, each child first repeats his or her solution several times. Finally Karen figures out the possible source of Craig's error. She offers an explanation based primarily on her own solution method, but modifies it in an attempt to accommodate Craig's thinking.

Karen: You're not even counting [meaning keeping track of your counting]. Come here. I'll explain how I got my number. See you have 39 and you plus 10 more and that's 49. 50, 51, 52, 53, . . . , 58. (This time Karen counts on the hundreds board by pointing to numerals on it with her pencil. Simultaneously, she uses fingers of both hands to keep track of her counting acts. She stops when 9 fingers are up.) There's 19. So it has to be 58.

Here Karen adapts her explanation to Craig's method by using the hundreds board. In doing so she assigns significance and validity to Craig's attempt to solve the problem and thereby sustains her commitment to collaborate. Because

Craig did not understand her first explanation even though she repeated it several times, she attempts to develop a consensual domain that can encompass both her own and Craig's methods and counts on the hundreds board rather than on her fingers but keeps track (which Craig failed to do). However, she still counts the first 10 in one step, "39 and you have plus 10 and that's 49." Karen's strategy is somewhat successful. Craig watches closely as she explains and immediately initiates the following remark, "Look, okay." This remark is an invitation to Karen to continue the collaboration as they try to resolve the problem of achieving consensus.

> Craig: Look, okay. 10 plus that, 49 (pointing on the hundreds board to 39, then 49). And then, look 50, 51, (still pointing to the hundreds board) 52, . . . , 58. Fifty-ni . . . (hesitates).

For the first time in this episode, Craig creates and counts ten as a single, discrete unit of some type rather than ten separate units of one. His hesitation at 59 seems to indicate some uncertainty, suggesting that Karen's elaborated explanation has led him to reflect on his counting activity. As Craig counted, Karen kept track of his counting on her fingers. In doing so, she both exemplified the need to keep track of the counting and demonstrated a method for doing so. Unfortunately, she started at 49 rather than 50. This prompted the next verbal interchange.

> Karen: You went 11. You had to go to 10.
> Craig: Look, 50, 51, . . . (counting on the hundreds board) . . . 55. Okay! 50 (now Craig starts keep track on his fingers) 1, 2.

For the first time in the episode, Craig evidences that he understands the need to keep track of his counting acts but seems confused about how to do it. Karen takes over and once more demonstrates the solution method she has been advocating.

> Karen: 39, 49, 50 (starts keeping track on her fingers) 51, . . . , 58.

As Karen counts, Craig also keeps track of her counting, but he only puts up eight fingers. He now tries to convince Karen that his answer of 59 is correct. After repeating his original solution he then changes methods in order to produce an argument that will convince Karen. Now it is Craig who has to reconceptualize his solution to try to construct a consensual domain. The method he decides to use is to count backwards on the hundreds board from 59 in an attempt to verify his answer. As he does so, he keeps track of his counting acts. He points

4.6. THE DEVELOPMENT OF COLLABORATIVE DIALOGUE

to the numerals on the board but also records how many counting acts he has performed verbally. Again, he invites Karen's attention with "See, look...."

Craig: See, look, 1, 2, 3, 4, 5, 6, 7, 8, 9

Karen: (Interrupts and takes over the counting task from Craig.) 10 (pointing to 49), 11, 12, 13, ..., 20 (pointing to 39). Twenty! Twenty! Twenty! But this [number in the problem] is only 19. So ... 58.

By taking over the counting, Karen once again gives credibility to Craig's problem-solving attempts. A long pause then ensues, during which both children appear to be reflecting. Then Karen repeats her original explanation one more time.

Karen: 39, 49. That's 10.

Craig: (Interrupts) 49 [meaning the answer is 49].

Karen: No, its not. I'm trying to show you how I got the number. 39, 49 (pointing on the hundreds board). Then 1 (holds up one finger) 50, 51, 52, 53, ..., 58 (Karen holds up an additional finger each time she says a number's word starting at 50 and stops when she has 9 fingers up).

After further discussion, Craig counts silently on the hundreds board, erases the 59 he had written down on the activity page and says, "58, because I know why. You're counting this one up here (referring to 40)."

In this problem-solving episode both Karen and Craig had to extend the conceptualizations that gave rise to their original solutions as they strove to communicate with each other. Their sincere attempts to make sense of each other's activity are indicated by the way in which they used and extended each other's ideas and by their direct verbal invitations to one another. Through their interactions, they reconstructed the norms for collaborative discourse established within the context of small group problem solving. The teacher's early interventions in the children's discussions, which were intended to help the children develop roles and establish obligations for discourse, served to establish the smooth functioning of the collaborative dialogue necessary for the construction of consensual domains and mutually developed problem solutions.

Collaboration among children as they work in small groups on mathematics activities is intimately related to the dialogue in which they engage. The teacher serves a crucial role in helping children maintain and thus develop necessary discourse patterns for collaborative dialogue by initiating the mutual construction of norms for such dialogue. When children's interaction, as they attempt to complete mathematics activities, is characterized by collaborative dialogue the conditions for the possibilities of learning occur. Equally important, the interaction itself serves to further sustain the norms that make the collaborative dialogue possible.

ACKNOWLEDGMENTS

The research reported in this chapter was supported by the National Science Foundation under grant number MDR 874-0400.

Chapter 4.7

Connecting Inventions with Conventions

Magdalene Lampert
Michigan State University, USA

This chapter describes part of a research and development project in school mathematics teaching. It covers a series of eight lessons that occured in the fall 1987. It is about communication in a mathematics classroom and provides evidence for the argument that students can actively contribute to constructing mathematical meaning while at the same time gaining experience with the conventions that enable discourse in the discipline. The focus is on the role a classroom teacher might take in supporting the development of students' ideas and relating them to mathematical traditions.

The students who participated in this project were all of the students in the fifth-year class (11-year-olds) in a public school in a midwestern university town in the United States. They were not sorted by ability, and they represented a wide variation in both ability and socioeconomic status. All lessons were audiotaped and recorded in writing by an observer and analyzed for mathematical and pedagogical content by the teacher. The topic of instruction was a typical part of the upper primary curriculum—finding fractional parts of a population. The lesson activities included small group and whole class teacher-led discussions of problems, work on representing fractions of actual and imagined populations, and the collaborative construction of physical and numerical algorithms.

SETTING THE TONE FOR STUDENT PARTICIPATION

On the first day of school, I began to teach my fifth-grade mathematics class with some whole-group conversation about how many students were in the class, how many were new to the school that year, whether there were more boys than girls, how many had siblings in the school, and so on. The lessons that I describe here evolved out of that conversation and connected students' thinking about fractions of a population with the traditional symbols and operations associated with fractions in school lessons. As the teacher of these lessons, I deliberately acted as a mediator between students' thinking and mathematical conventions as I moderated discussions and taught students about the meaning of symbols and expressions.

The purpose of this chapter is to stand back from that role and analyze it, thus I refer to myself throughout as "the teacher" rather than using the first person to describe what I did, but the reader is cautioned against equating this post hoc analysis with a report on what I was thinking while teaching. Just as the mathematical thinking that gets recorded in deductive proofs is not the same as the mathematical thinking that goes into creating a mathematical argument, a post hoc analysis of why a set of teaching acts "makes sense" is not the same as the construction of those acts in the classroom.

THE CLASS AS A COMMUNITY OF DISCOURSE ABOUT MATHEMATICS: A PEDAGOGICAL THEORY OF CLASSROOM COMMUNICATION

There were 25 students in the class, and they were asked to propose ways to divide themselves into groups for working on math. Students commented, "Groups of five would work out evenly, but that is too many people to try to get together on something." The students agreed to form groups of four, with one larger group of five. The desks were arranged in this configuration. The arrangement of the desks provided a familiar context in which the students could think about equivalent parts of the group. The teacher then posed the problem for the class of figuring out "what part" of the group fell into different categories—girls, boys, new to the school, and so forth, and students speculated on why we could not divide the class exactly evenly into groups of four. This conversation laid the groundwork for the introduction of mathematical language, symbols, and procedures to represent fractions of the class population.

In class discussions, students were expected to give reasons publicly for their assertions—reasons that were supposed to "make sense"—to them, to the teacher, and to their peers. This routine of interaction was established assertively by the teacher as the social structure that would serve to support connections among individuals constructing mathematical meaning for themselves, the public culture of the school classroom, and the discipline of mathematics (Lampert, 1988). In adopting this approach to organizing social interaction, it was assumed that individuals actively construct meaning as they learn, and that when this is done in the classroom, it is of necessity a public and social process (Cazden, 1988). The class as a whole was considered to be a community of discourse engaged in developing a common culture of ideas about a mathematical topic (Balacheff, 1987; Brown, Collins, & Duguid, 1989). The teacher's role in the discourse community was derived from the fact that he or she is a more experienced knower of the discipline. From this perspective, the teacher takes on the social responsibility of initiating students to mathematical conventions in a way that will enable them to use these conventions as tools for developing and communicating their own thinking (Pea, 1987; Vygotsky, 1978). Gradually, the teacher effects a connection between students' ways of creating mathematical meaning and mathematics as it is practiced in the world outside the school.

The teacher's role in classroom communication, as I have construed it here, involves managing the tensions between individual learners and social conventions. Communication is established as this tension is resolved on two levels: at the level of mathematical conventions, developed in the discipline over time and used in the wider society outside the classroom in mathematical discourse, and at the level of classroom conventions, developed in the context in which students interact with one another and with their teacher and form their own community of discourse. Although individuals attach their own meaning to the language and symbols of discourse, communication in the classroom is made possible when there is some congruence among individual meanings and the shared meaning expressed in the culture in which individuals work together on academic tasks (Cazden, 1988). Individual students can and do interact with both mathematical conventions and classroom conventions. Because of her expertise in using the conventions of the discipline, the teacher is in a powerful position to shape those interactions in ways that enhance the possibility that students will attach meanings to their mathematics that are congruent with those that are accepted by other users of mathematical language and symbols (Freudenthal, 1978). Communication between the classroom and the larger community of users of mathematics is made possible by students learning to use the conventions of the discipline that they learn from the teacher. This is the theory of communication that drove the design of the lessons described here and the development of the role that the teacher took during those lessons.

ORGANIZING CLASSROOM DISCOURSE AROUND STUDENTS' MATHEMATICAL IDEAS

In the second lesson on "fractions of a population" there was a lively disagreement about how many students would be in "half" the class, with attention to the fact that dividing the class in half meant that there were two halves for which to account. The disagreements centered around whether two halves could have unequal numbers (12 and 13) and the fact that you could not have $12\frac{1}{2}$ persons in a group. Neither could you have two groups of 12 and leave someone out. This disagreement was not resolved, which tells something more about the design of the teacher's role. In the classroom as a mathematical discourse community, teachers offer vocabulary, encouragement, suggestions, and support for revisions, but they are not authorities who provide answers or procedures to be followed. The teacher's role is to model a way of knowing (mathematical) that depends for its veracity on reasoning about relationships among quantities. The source of judgment about whether an assertion is reasonable is the community of discourse, not the teacher.[1]

The mathematical task of the second lesson was to determine how many students would be in each group if the class were divided into halves, thirds, fourths, fifths, and sixths. After "unit" fractions were determined and discussed, the class was asked to consider what two-thirds of the class would be, or three-fourths. The students used several different strategies to find these fractional parts of the class and they were challenged by their peers and their teacher to defend the legitimacy of their procedures. For example, one student explained what two-sixths of the class would be as follows:

> For one-sixth, we figured out it was four *or* five. If you double four, it's eight, and if you double five, it's ten, and nine is exactly between eight and ten, so two-sixths must be nine.

Another student rebutted, referring to actual groups in the room:

> Sometimes when you put two groups together, you get eight, and sometimes you get nine, but you will *never* get ten, because there is only one group of five, and all the rest have four. So the *better* answer (for two-sixths of 25) is eight, but it *could be* nine.

Another student said

> It can't always be nine, because that would mean you would have to have 27 kids in the class.

The following representation of the students' ideas was constructed by the teacher at the blackboard while they spoke to the class. It is a notation intermediate between the student's idiosyncratic expressions of their mathematical thinking and the conventions of the discipline:

$$2/6 = 9 \quad \text{(left side)}[2] \qquad\qquad 2/6 = 9$$
$$\text{If } 2/6 = 9 \quad \text{(middle)} \quad then\ 6/6 = 27. \quad \text{But if } 2/6 = 8 \quad then\ 6/6 = 25.$$
$$2/6 = 9 \quad \text{(right side)} \qquad\qquad 2/6 = 8$$

---

[1]See Polya (1954) and Lakatos (1976) for an explication of the role of the community of discourse in determining the nature of mathematical truth.

[2]These locations refer to clusters of students' desks in the room.

HOW THE TEACHER ACTS TO CONNECT INVENTIONS WITH CONVENTIONS

The purpose of the teacher's using language and the chalkboard to supplement students' expression of mathematical arguments is to help students making the argument to express themselves to other individual members of the class. It also serves to make an individual's way of thinking about something part of the common culture of mathematics in the classroom by providing a public representation of the ideas. In every case where a student's way of representing mathematics is made public by the teacher in this manner, the student is acknowledged by the teacher and the class as the person responsible for the ideas. The teacher takes the role of representing students' arguments in a form that enables both communication among class members and the acquisition of conventional symbols and terms. In this way, conventions that are familiar to the teacher are introduced gradually in response to student assertions. The students' ostensive language for constructing mathematical relationships is restated by the teacher in terms that approach mathematical formalisms while intending to retain the meaning communicated by the student (cf. Freudenthal, 1978, p. 242).

The progress of the class toward developing public algorithms for finding fractions of discrete populations began when they were figuring out what three-eights of the class would be. Someone asserted that it would be "nine," and then explained that she had noticed on the day before that "when you wanted three-fifths, you took what one-fifth was and multiplied it by three, and the same was done for three-sixths." So she guessed you could follow that procedure for three-eights. She then supported her assertion by saying that when she checked it with a drawing, it was "right." She was grappling with the big mathematical questions that go into the creation of algorithms, rather than taking them for granted or simply doing as she was told by the teacher. The questions now on the floor for discussion were: What procedures "work," and under what conditions? How do the procedures have to be modified when the numbers don't "come out even"?

In all of the students' work on fractions of populations, no procedural rules were given by the teacher. Using the language and drawings created in the lessons by students and teacher together, the students speculated about procedures and the conditions under which they should "work."[3] The teacher's role

---

[3]The question of what constitutes "proof" that a procedure works under certain conditions in a class of 11-year-olds is a most interesting one. According to my current pedagogical thinking, what matters is that the seat of authority is not the teacher or the "answer book," but some argument that makes sense to the participants. Often their arguments refer to concrete instantiations of operations to prove that an answer is reasonable, or that a procedure is appropriate. In doing mathematics this way, they are not unlike the ancient Hindu creators of arithmetic and algebra (Kline, 1980; Stewart, 1987).

in the algorithm-generating discussions was to encourage and mediate the arguments that arose between those students who blindly applied an algorithm once it was asserted, and those who "proved" the reasonability of their answer by reference to the population. The teacher's social role in these lessons was to make the environment safe for those students who wanted to disagree with their peers and to help everyone clarify his or her position in an argument.[4] The teacher's role as a more experienced knower of the discipline was to supplement students' language, symbols, and representations with those conventionally used by practitioners of mathematics. By enacting these roles, the teacher was contributing to the possibility that classroom communication about mathematics would have some congruence with individual student's thinking and with thinking about the same ideas in the wider mathematical community.

In the course of their discussions, some students were continually unsatisfied with assertions like "$\frac{1}{2}$ of 35 dimes could be 17 or 18." They wanted to work out "which answer is more right." What they brought to this question was some learned formalities, like "you always round up," and the idea that everything in mathematics ought to be precise. Their concerns echoed old arguments in the discipline, and brought them to a high level of discussion about algorithmics.[5] The teacher and children worked together on clarifying the circumstances under which they should choose the higher number or the lower and agreeing on when they could not choose.

By the fifth day of working on fractions of a population, many students had "invented" the familiar algorithm: given a fraction written in the conventional form, divide the population by the denominator and multiply the answer to that by the numerator. Some students began to answer with some version of that algorithm when they were asked: "How did you figure it out?" They were routinely challenged to go beyond this "procedural" explanation to defend the use of these particular arithmetic tools to work out the problem. The teachers' role in this period of instruction was to maintain and value the connection between syntax and semantics. This was particularly important in the public forum of the classroom, where for reasons of efficiency some students are all too ready to "copy" a procedure that others have invented without being able to trace its development back to a meaningful source. Some students were still using drawings of one sort or another at this point to do every problem that was posed, and almost all students could produce a drawing if called on to do so to illustrate their procedures. The one exception was a student who said that what he did was first to multiply the number of the population by the numerator of the fraction

---

[4]This construction of the mathematics teacher's role follows Polya (1954, pp. 3–8), who described the "intellectual courage" required to make mathematical assertions and defend them.

[5]See for example, Kline's (1980) description of the arguments about the calculus and Stewart's (1987) discussion of the axiom of choice.

4.7. CONNECTING INVENTIONS WITH CONVENTIONS   259

and then divide by the denominator.[6] He knew his method "worked," he said, because it turned up the same answer as the methods of his classmates, but he did not know how to "draw it." The balance of the lessons in this unit were directed toward managing the tensions between wanting an efficient procedure for solving the problems that were posed and keeping the procedure connected with the actions on quantities that it was intended to represent. The purpose of maintaining this connection, from the teacher's perspective, was based on the assumption that if students used procedures that became disconnected from actions, they would be unable to monitor whether a procedure was being used appropriately.

With everyone solidly capable of finding a fractional part of a population of discrete and indivisible members (e.g., people, who cannot be divided into parts to make the groups come out evenly), the teacher introduced the problem of populations that were composed of objects that could be reasonably broken up into parts. Now students needed to further develop their strategies to figure out what to do with the left overs. Their various representations of these problems were made public by the teacher using the chalkboard and they were adopted by other members of the class to find solutions. The ways in which the "left overs" were divided up were varied. Given the problem to represent "$\frac{7}{8}$ of 36 cookies" for example, some students put four whole cookies in each "eighth" and then "cut up" the remaining four cookies, some of them cutting the leftovers into halves to get eight pieces; some cutting them into quarters to get 16 pieces and then assigning 2 of those pieces to an "eighth," and some cutting all of the leftover cookies into eight pieces and putting one piece from each leftover cookie into each "eighth" group. More and more interesting variations emerged when numbers were involved that did not have common factors. For example, students found "$\frac{2}{9}$ of 32 sheets of paper" by putting three papers into each "ninth" and then inventing ways to equally distribute the leftover five sheets. Some would divide them in half and put half a sheet into each "ninth," leaving a half-sheet of paper still to be distributed. This might be cut into nine pieces, leaving the student with the challenge of figuring out how to "name" the contents of each "ninth" and then double it to find two-ninths.[7]

---

[6]This is actually a more efficient algorithm because you only need to figure out how to cope with the "remainder" once, even though it cannot be as directly related to the physical operations one performs to find a fractional part of a population.

[7]Activities like this raise interesting questions about how one might think about the "usefulness" of school mathematics. It is, of course, true that no one would ever be confronted with the "real" problem of finding "$\frac{2}{9}$ of 32 papers". Even if they were, they would be unlikely to use these sorts of procedures to solve such a problem. The point of my posing such problems for my students was not preparing them for practical problem solving. This work was meant to pose mathematical challenges that would lead students to think about operations on objects as a basis for understanding numerical relationships.

AN ANALYSIS OF LEARNING ALGORITHMS FROM THE TEACHER'S PERSPECTIVE: THE TENSION BETWEEN EFFICIENCY AND MEANING

After several days of individual and small group work on finding fractions of different sorts of populations, many students had adopted the arithmetical routine of "divide and then multiply" that had evolved out of their work with performing operations on physical objects and drawings of objects. It was faster and easier than drawing, and relatively reliable. They were "doing mathematics" in the sense of finding an efficient strategy that could be applied in all kinds of cases without attending to the particularities of the situation. But as the teacher watched them and listened to them work in this way, it seemed as if the meaning of those operations as actions performed on objects had been lost in the transition from algorithmic drawings to calculations using numbers.

There is much to be said about how and whether the efficient use of algorithms relates to meaningful mathematical activity, both from the perspective of the historical development of mathematics as a discipline, and from the perspective of learning psychology (Nesher, 1986; Stewart, 1987). But I address this issue from a *pedagogical* perspective. My goal as a teacher was to have my students develop the ability to find a fraction of a population and to know why the procedures they were using were appropriate. I saw that goal being subverted by their having "picked up" a set of rules to follow and their following those rules without relating them to the process of finding a fraction of a population. My evidence for this was that students who had done perfectly well at solving problems using drawings or objects were now only writing numbers and symbols on their papers and the arithmetic operations they were using did not match the drawings they had made to represent their thinking about the problems.

For example, one student had written on her paper:

$$5 \overline{)11} 2 \text{ r. } 1$$

She said that what she would do next is: "Multiply by 3, and then because there are two groups, you divide the 'remainder one' in half and put half in each group. So it is six and one-half cookies." This procedure mixes some elements of familiar numerical algorithms with actions that had been performed when she was using drawings to find fractions of populations (i.e., "put half in each group"). Because she did not actually connect a drawing with what she did to the numbers, however, she confused the quotative and partitive interpretions of division. Instead of giving the "2" its appropriate meaning in relation to the problem that had been posed (i.e., two in each group) she interpreted it as "two groups," when the fraction in the problem actually means there should be five groups of cookies. In response to a request from the teacher to "Show me what all those numbers mean," she then drew on her paper:

saying that the five circles were a representation of the "5" in "5)11."

DESPAIR, AND A MATHEMATICAL ANALYSIS OF A PEDAGOGICAL PROBLEM

It is at this point that despair can overcome the good intentions of school teachers who are attempting to make mathematics meaningful for children. Had all the time we spent on representing and sense-making been wasted? Would it not be easier just to tell them how to place the numbers in relation to one another, and have them practice the procedure over and over again until it was memorized? This might get some successful performance in the short term, but it would not result in either understanding the procedure or learning what mathematics was all about. Maybe the problem was that numerical conventions had been introduced too soon. But because students come to fifth-grade with a store of accumulated knowledge from home and school and elsewhere about how to do mathematics, it would have been impossible to keep meaningless procedures out of the classroom. The problem that the teacher needed to solve was how to be responsive to the mathematical knowledge that students bring to lessons, while at the same time teaching them to monitor the appropriateness of the procedures they were inclined to use.

The following lesson was based on the analysis that the students' confusions primarily arose in connecting an interpretation of the denominator of the fraction as a divisor with the operation of dividing up the population. Because the divisor in this case is meant to indicate how many groups the population is to be divided into, and not how many are in each group, students were inclined to use the numerical algorithm to find the "answer." The physical algorithm for division that had become popular in the class (i.e., count to the number indicated by the divisor and circle, count again and circle, until you have used up the population, and then count how many groups you have circled) is an innappropriate strategy to use when the divisor tells you how many groups, and not how many are in each group.

One student had devised a physical algorithm that represented the identification of the denominator with the number of groups. If the problem to be solved were: "$\frac{1}{3}$ of 28 cookies," for example, she would make a ring to enclose the whole population, and then divide it into segments, the number of segments corresponding to the denominator. Then she would "go around" the ring, placing a tick into each segment until she used up the whole population. Another girl who said she would think about such problems by asking herself, "What can I multiply by three that will get me an answer near 28?" was also performing a similar strategy. But most students continued to be attracted to the more efficient mechanical process:

$$3 \overline{)28}^{\ 9\ r.\ 1}$$

and then to be lost when they tried to connect this operation with the process of finding fractions of a population.

The teacher's role became somewhat more didactic in response to the loss of meaning that had been observed in the students' work. Proceeding on the assumption that mathematical symbols were worthwhile for students to learn, but that they would be useful only if students understood what the conventions were meant to indicate, the teacher emphasized the association of the "bottom number" in the fraction with the "How many groups?" interpretation of division. Whether students used numbers or drawings, they were reminded that this was the question that the number in that position of the fraction was intended to answer.

To consolidate the class around this interpretation of the denominator of the fraction in the context of "population" problems, the class was assigned to: "Draw a representation to find $\frac{3}{4}$ of 17 bananas." The teacher asked several students how they decided to make four groups, and they each referred to the denominator of the fraction. They were also able to relate "circling" three groups with the numerical symbol in the numerator. They used numerical algorithms, but the teacher worded the assignment so as to push them to make the connection with a pictoral representation and to use that representation to edit their work with numbers. In this process, the numerical algorithm for division became a usable tool for finding the solution efficiently without losing the meaning of the problem.

PUBLIC CONSTRUCTION OF AN ALGORITHM AS AN ASSESSMENT OF STUDENTS' KNOWLEDGE IN THE COMMUNITY OF DISCOURSE

After two more days of individual and small group practice on teacher-assigned and student-invented "fractions of a population" problems, a whole group discussion was held for the purpose of writing a set of "directions" that someone might follow who did not know how to do this sort of problem. The task was now

4.7. CONNECTING INVENTIONS WITH CONVENTIONS 263

to communicate with the "world" outside of the community of discourse, that is, the class community that had created the procedure in their talk together about the problems. Students asserted their contributions and others students revised them. The end result was produced with little teacher input, except asking for clarification and recording on the chalkboard what was said. All but four members of the class made an active contribution to this discussion; two of the students who did not contribute had very limited English-speaking ability. The choice of a group production as an exhibit of what the students had learned was deliberate. What was being assessed was the connection between individual abilities and the public mathematical knowledge in use in the classroom community of discourse. It was a test of the extent to which students would agree on the procedures that were appropriate to follow to find a fraction of a population, and whether they had the capacity to recognize inappropriate procedures when they were proposed. (Later, individual assessments were conducted by giving students problems to work out and represent in symbols and drawings.)

The first problem that was posed for this exercise was chosen for its familiarity. After a set of directions was written for this problem, another less familiar problem was posed, and the directions were revised to fit the second problem. The first problem was: "$\frac{3}{4}$ of 10 bananas." The first student to offer a suggestion for directions said: "Make four groups." Another asserted the revision: "No. You have to say, 'Make four *equal* groups.'" The students worked together to communicate those aspects of the procedure that had heretofore been taken for granted in their conversations with one another, but for this more "public" product needed to be made explicit. After several such suggestions and revisions, what they had up on the board was:

1. Draw ten things.
2. Make four $\wedge$ groups. (What number times four equals the number *closest* to ten that is below ten?)
          equal
3. Cut the two circles in half because you need four pieces.

"What next?" asked the teacher. They said, "Count how many in each group, and times by three." After this statement was added to the list of directions on the board, the whole class went through the list, following the directions as they were written, and they were satisfied with them. After doing a few similar problems, and introducing the use of color to distinguish elements of the problems, the class then reconstructed the directions more generally as follows:

1. Draw as the green number of things.
2. Make the blue number of equal groups.
3. Cut the remainder up if you can so there is an equal piece in each group.

3. Circle the red number of groups.
4. Count how many things there are in the circle.

Although their language was not yet at the level of formal mathematical symbols, it was now considerably more removed from the ostensive language they had been using in earlier conversations with one another about their procedures. The articulation of step three was the most discussed, and also the clearest indication that the students were making a connection between the numerical algorithm and their drawings. This lesson was the denouement of the class' work together on "fractions of a population."

SUMMARY: THE TEACHER'S ROLE

In the lessons described, the teacher did the following things to connect students' mathematical inventions with the content and discourse of conventional mathematics:

- expected students to make sensible assertions;
- expected students to defend their use of conventional algorithms;
- represented students' assertions in language and drawings that would create a bridge from individual ideas to classroom communication, and on to disciplinary conventions;
- managed the social organization of the class group as a community of discourse;
- expected and supported the revision of asserted ideas;
- kept the discussion focused on the public agenda;
- directed the discussion toward assertions about general mathematical "truths" and the conditions under which they would hold;
- directed the consolidation of individual student constructions into a public construction of the class about a mathematical procedure.

The communication that developed as the teacher took on these tasks served to mediate between the individual constructions made by students to express their understanding of a mathematical operation and the symbols and numerical procedures that have developed as conventions, at least in part because they are more efficient than drawing pictures. This efficiency appeals to students, as it does to mathematicians, but careful teaching is required to avoid losing meaning as efficiency is gained.

ACKNOWLEDGMENTS

This project has been undertaken with support from the Spencer Foundation through a fellowship granted by the National Academy of Education.

Chapter 4.8

Actual Communication in the Mathematical Classroom

Nobuhiko Nohda
University of Tsukuba, JAPAN

Work with problem-solving is central at all levels of mathematics teaching. The assigned problem becomes the object of the mathematical activities, and the setting of the problem together with related actions performed by the teacher constitute the major method by which mathematics is expected to be conveyed to the learner. The notion of words as containers in which the teacher "conveys" meaning to pupils is misguided. To see this, we retrace our own steps and review how the meaning of words was acquired at the beginning of our problem-solving.

Next, the relationships between the given problems and activities of pupils in a classroom can be treated in a meaningful way only if both of these two components are investigated in their relationships to some important aspects of mathematics education. What determines the value of the problems is their experiential adequacy, their goodness of fit with experience, their viability as being constructed as solvable problems by the pupils, and the viability that they will promote the consistent organization that we call understanding (von Glasersfeld, 1987).

We cite an example of the problem-soiving activities between teacher and learners (Fig. 1). Some of the roles of the teacher at different stages of the teaching/learning process are: instructor to teach mathematical knowledge and skills (top-down); educator to help pupils in problem solving (bottom-up); and decision maker to judge whether or not teaching goes ahead. The teachers' explication of such roles is integrated with their specific actions and serves in establishing their background and context for the interactions between their pupils' actual and inner activities in connection with their subjective words.

The previous sentences illustrate the essential and relational character of communications between teacher and learners. Thus, their subjective approaches

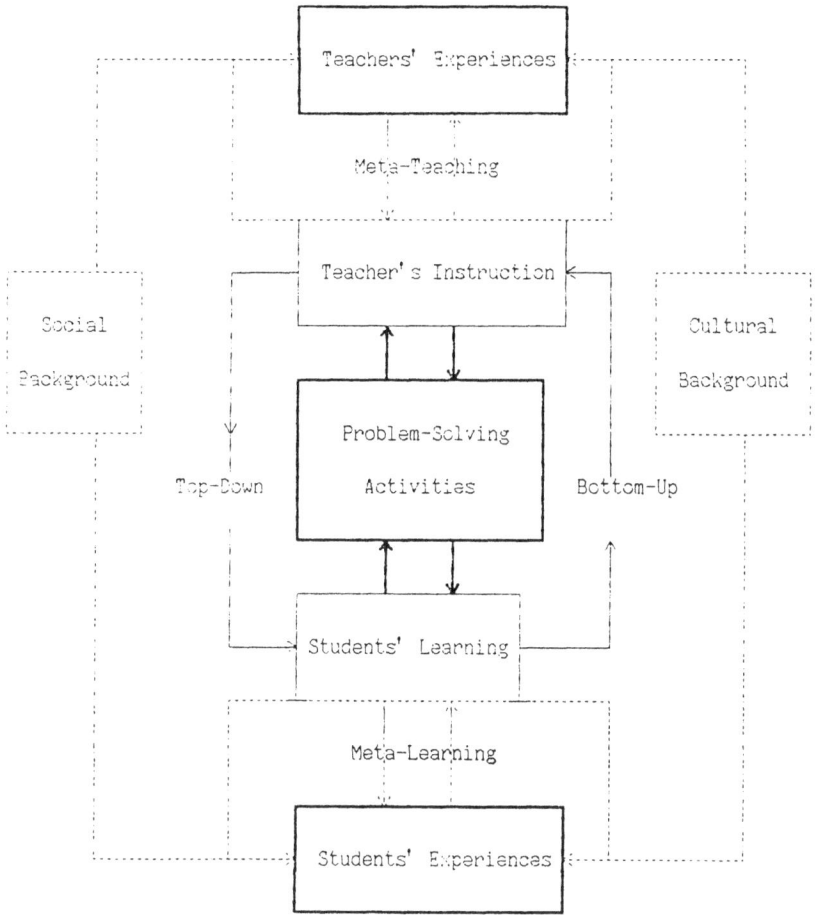

FIG. 1. Problem-solving activities.

in problem-solving do not ensure that learning matches the intended teaching. The interpreted problem is influenced by subjective factors and the presentation of the problem is conditioned by moves of the teacher. These moves are again made and interpreted respectively by the teacher and the learner. They are not mind-independent.

Accordingly, communication using problem-solving as an organizing principle in Japanese mathematics learning calls for meta-learning under the teacher's support. This communication views mathematics classroom teaching as controlling the organization and dynamics of the classroom for the purposes of sharing and developing mathematical thinking (Nohda, 1986).

The educational goal we are concerned with here is that of sharing and developing mathematical meaning. On the basis of this approach we now propose three key concepts that we use to structure our ideas and methods of teaching in the mathematics classroom.

Activity—chosen to emphasize the learner's involvement with problem solving mathematically, at least, by means of the teacher's presentation of mathematical problems;
Communication—chosen to accentuate shared meanings with goals and methods of problem-solving underlying all teaching;
Negotiation—chosen to emphasize the goal-directed interaction of problem-solving, whereby teacher and learner seek to attain their respective mathematical goals.

We analyze the problem-solving processes of early childhood in the mathematics classroom using these three key concepts.

MATHEMATICAL PROBLEM SOLVING IN LOWER ELEMENTARY SCHOOL

We use nonroutine problems or problem situations (Christiansen & Walther, 1985). These are nonroutine problems that must be solved by the pupils independently in the mathematics classroom (Nohda, 1983).

We use the problem of pattern finding. One of the dominant themes of cognitive research into problem-solving in recent years has been pattern finding. However, much of this research has been in nonmathematical contexts (Lester, 1982). For the purpose of this study, we consider the mathematical activities in the following two cases. One core is the underlying pattern in the problem, that is, the nature of the problem itself. The other is the feature of the strategies in pupils' problem-solving. The former means the structure of problem and the rule in it, and so forth. The latter is the mode of action applied in pupils' problem-solving. Therefore, in order that pupils might do better in their problem-solving, it is necessary for them to share the understandings of problems through some communications with their teachers. For pupils who fail to understand the problem or feel difficulty in solving it, the reason would be that there is no sharing of understanding or way of solving the task through the interactions between tasks and pupils under the teacher's instruction.

Survey Test

Subjects in this study were first, second, and third graders selected at random in an elementary school in Tsukuba City near Tokyo. This test was carried out in May 1986, shortly after the beginning of a new school year in Japan.

4.8. ACTUAL COMMUNICATION

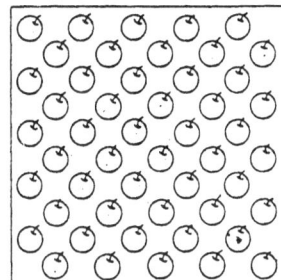

FIG. 2. Apple problem.

Survey procedures were to let the pupils read the problem themselves after the classroom teacher handed the problem to them. Then the teacher read the problem out loud for all pupils to hear and gave them 15 minutes to solve it.

Survey Problem: The Apple Problem (See Fig. 2)

1. How many apples are there in this figure? (Count the number without skipping any and without counting any apple more than once.)
2. Show different ways of counting the apples. How many different ways of counting can you think of?
3. Of all your ways of counting, mark the one you think the best.

The feature of this problem's pattern is two 5 by 5 arrays of apples (i.e., the pattern is 2 × 5 × 5 as shown in Fig. 3.)

Table 1 shows the result of the survey for item 3.

The difficulty of this problem lies in that at a first glance it appears difficult to count. For first-grade pupils, it is difficult for them to count well after arranging and regrouping the apples into composites, although it is easy for them to say the number words up to 50. For second-grade pupils, it is easy for them to count apples arranged and regrouped into pairs, groups of fives, and groups of tens,

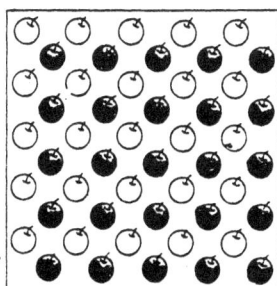

FIG. 3. Problem pattern.

TABLE 1
Result of Survey Problem

	First Grade			Second Grade			Third Grade		
	Male	Female	Total	Male	Female	Total	Male	Female	Total
A. Correct Counting									
Numbers	17	17	34	15	23	38	17	17	34
Correct	9	2	11	8	9	17	13	13	26
No response	5	7	12	2	9	11	1	0	1
B. Ways of Counting									
One by one	12(9)	10(2)	22(11)	5(4)	8(4)	13(8)	2(0)	7(7)	9(7)
Pairs			0	1(0)	2(0)	3(0)	2(2)	2(2)	4(4)
Group of five			0	1(0)	0	2(0)	9(8)	4(2)	13(10)
Group of ten			0	1(1)	2(1)	3(2)	3(3)	3(2)	6(5)
Aslant			0	4(2)	5(3)	9(5)	0	1(0)	1(0)
The others			0	1(1)	1(1)	2(2)	0	0	0

Note. ( ) in parentheses in the Table 1 are those pupils with correct answers.

and aslant. Almost all of the third-grade pupils achieved the correct answers and two-thirds of them counted after the arranging and regrouping the apples into pairs, groups of fives and tens. The first-grade pupils did not develop such mathematical patterns and many of the third-grade pupils already knew and used these patterns. Thus, we selected the second-grade pupils for our teaching experiment.

ACTUAL COMMUNICATION
THE SECOND-GRADE CLASSROOM

The second-grade class (Male = 17, Female = 18) we used in this study was composed of pupils from another elementary school in which we had carried out the previously mentioned survey test. But the results were almost the same as in the survey school in Tsukuba City. The lesson was done in June 1986.

A classroom teacher started as follows: the pupils were each given a picture of apples which was a larger picture than usual, and the teacher put the same picture of apples on the blackboard. Then, the teacher asked the pupils, "How many apples are there in this figure?" and explained some notions to them: "Counting the apples under consideration without leaving some out or counting some twice."

The pupils wrote their answers on the answer sheets for about 10 minutes after the teacher explained the problem. While the teacher was observing and looking through the pupils' activities of solving the problem in detail, he advised some

4.8. ACTUAL COMMUNICATION

pupils to count and then made them think of more ways of counting. He found out their different ways of solving as follows:

1. Almost all pupils were checking and counting apples one by one vertically or horizontally, or filling numerals in the sketch of each apple. Some pupils made errors in counting the apples in this case.

2. One-fifth of the pupils counted the apples in pairs and some pupils who counted 2, 4, 6, 8, and so on, continued to add apples until 50. Almost all of these pupils gained the correct solution. A few pupils had the results but could not calculate 2×25.

3. Four pupils who counted 5 apples together counted accurately and relatively quickly.

4. Nine pupils who counted 10 apples together counted correctly and quickly.

5. A rather small number of the pupils used a symmetry of figure as the way of aslant counting. In this case, adding numbers aslant was the key.

Chapter
4.9

Fostering Mathematical Communication: Helping Teachers Help Students

Julian Weissglass
Judith Mumme
Barbara Cronin
University of California, Santa Barbara, USA

> *I remember teaching borrowing in the second grade. It just makes me cringe when I think of it now. They didn't have to know what they were doing. It was just the mechanics, know the mechanics. This is a nine so you're going to borrow one so you make it eight. They had no idea what they were doing. It was at you own seat, do your own paper, no copying, don't talk, math was a very quiet time.*
> —reflections of a first-grade teacher

Mathematics is a way of looking at and making sense of the world. It is a beautiful, creative, and useful human endeavor that is both a way of thinking and a way of knowing. The goal of mathematics instruction is to help students develop and deepen their understandings of mathematics as well as their abilities to communicate their ideas to others. The process of communication helps students construct as well as express mathematical meanings.

This chapter addresses mathematical communication. We examine how teachers' abilities to foster young children's communication can be improved. In the course of this chapter we present our views on the reasons for promoting communication, suggest criteria for assessing communication in the classroom, and make some recommendations on how to help teachers. We do not directly address the nature of children's communication. We acknowledge that there are both qualitative and quantitative issues involved and our values have influenced our approach; however, analysis of these issues is beyond the scope of this chapter. Pimm (1987) provided a perspective on these issues.

Mathematical communication is receiving increased attention from educators. One of the five general goals for students in the *Standards for Curriculum and*

Evaluation of the National Council of Teachers of Mathematics (1989) is "learning to communicate mathematically." In a position statement on the education of young children, the U.S. National Association for the Education of Young Children (1988) suggested that "primary-aged children be provided opportunities to work in small groups on projects that provide rich content for conversation."

Communication between individuals involves the exchange of ideas, messages, feelings, or information. In the classroom communication involves children as both senders and receivers. As senders, children communicate their thoughts, feelings, understandings, or questions in several ways: (a) verbally, (b) physically (e.g., body language), (c) by manipulating objects, (d) pictorially, or (e) symbolically (using written words or mathematical symbols). As receivers, they may listen, observe, read, question, interpret, and reflect. Based on prior experiences, each individual brings personal meanings to any communication; the intended message may not necessarily be the message perceived.

REASONS FOR COMMUNICATION

We have identified five reasons for promoting *child-directed* communication about mathematics:

1. *It clarifies children's thinking.* When children talk or write about mathematics, it helps them refine and clarify their own thinking and gain a greater understanding of concepts.

2. *It empowers children as learners.* It can assist children in taking charge of their learning by increasing their access to and control of their thoughts. "Thinking about their thinking" reduces dependence on outside authorities.

3. *It reduces anxiety and alienation.* Opportunities to interact with peers and express feelings reduces the fear that many children experience in traditional classroom environments and frees the child to function more effectively.

4. *It establishes some common understandings.* Although mathematics can be done in isolation, its development as a discipline is a social process that requires communication and shared meanings. Children engaged in a dialogue about mathematics will discuss the meaning of words, learn the crucial role of definitions, and expand their thinking by articulating their ideas and listening to others.

5. *It assists the teacher in thinking about the child as learner.* The communication process can provide a glimpse of the child's reality, allowing the teacher to set up new situations for children to expand and build their mathematical understandings.

Classroom communication has traditionally been teacher-controlled, with the teacher doing most of the talking and demonstrating. However, with the goal of fostering communication, the teacher's role becomes one of setting up situations where children can take charge of their communication. Most teachers will need assistance in changing their instructional methods to reach this goal.

APPROACH WITH TEACHERS

Over the past 2 years we have been working with teachers in Project TIME (Teachers Improving Mathematics Education)—a 3-year site-based professional development project involving over 200 teachers (K–12) from 13 schools (75 teachers K–3). A crucial component of the project involves a teaching specialist (a teacher released from all classroom responsibilities) who provides the on-site support and serves as an agent for change in mathematics education. A goal of the project is to empower teachers as decision makers who determine the mathematical learning experiences appropriate for their children. The project's approach is based on the following assumptions: (a) learning is an inherent human activity, (b) each person has an immense capacity for learning, an innate eagerness to learn, and a desire to communicate this learning to others, and (c) the learning process is affected by internal feelings and external situations.

We define learning as the complex process of interpreting sensory input (received from the environment) by comparing and contrasting it to past experience and previously understood information, then evaluating, organizing, and storing it so that it is available for use in new situations. We believe that children construct their understanding through interaction with their environment and this environment includes other people. Learning situations should provide the student with the opportunity to work in small groups with concrete objects, discuss problems and solutions with classmates, and reflect on and communicate ideas.

Just as we believe children construct their understanding of mathematics, we believe that teachers construct their understanding of learning and teaching. There are several aspects of the project's approach that promotes teachers' understanding of the value of children's communication: (a) hands-on activities, (b) reflecting on activities, (c) discussion of issues, (d) classroom demonstration lessons, (e) one-to-one support from teaching specialists, and (f) support groups. Structured time is set aside for teachers to talk about themselves, their experiences, and their feelings without interruption in small groups (support groups) or pairs (dyads). This process helps teachers learn how to listen better, process ideas, and address their feelings about teaching, learning, and change. Teachers take turns listening to each other using the following guidelines: (a) equal time for each person to talk while the other listens, (b) no advice, interpretation, or analysis by the listener during or after the dyad, (c) confidentiality, and (d) no complaints about the person who is listening (Weissglass & Weissglass, 1987).

Participation in Project TIME is voluntary, however each year 90%–100% of the teachers at each site participate in 6–8 all-day seminars (including hands-on activities, processing, discussion, and planning), attend 1-hour weekly support groups, observe 5–10 demonstration lessons, and implement new ideas in their classrooms (Mumme & Weissglass, 1988).

CLASSROOM OBSERVATIONS

Because we wanted to know how the project was affecting teachers' ability to structure an environment that promotes children's mathematical communication, we observed teachers in their classrooms and later interviewed them. Nine teachers in three schools were selected for our study. At each site we asked the teaching specialist to identify one teacher who they considered to be very effective and one who had shown considerable growth during the project. We selected a third teacher randomly. Each teacher was observed twice (several months apart) and then interviewed. Permission to observe was obtained from each teacher, but they were not told that the focus was on communication.

During the observations children were observed for the following: (a) Is there communication going on? (b) In what forms? (c) What is the type of communication? (e.g., Do children ask questions of each other? Do they explain their thinking to each other?)

Teachers were observed to determine how they were fostering or hindering communication: (a) Does the activity promote communication? (b) Does the teacher allow for free exploration of materials/ideas? (c) How does the teacher pose questions? (d) How does she or he give instructions for children to interact? (e) At what point does the teacher intervene? (f) Are the children encouraged to show or write about what they've been working on? (g) How are children's feelings about math dealt with? (h) Does the teacher stress process or product?

The teacher interview consisted of the following questions: (a) In what ways do you see children communicating in your classroom? (b) What in your classroom encourages children's communication? (c) What do you see as the effects of increased communication among children? (d) When you plan a lesson, do you specifically think about children's communication? (e) Have there been any changes in children's communication since you began the project? (f) How have project activities influenced the way you consider children's communication?

To provide some examples of the kinds of communication observed and the teacher's thoughts about fostering communication, we briefly summarize the observations and interviews of two teachers. Teaching specialists were interviewed to provide an additional perspective.

CASE STUDY 1

Observation

Martha, a second-grade teacher, has 18 years teaching experience (grades 1, 3, 5, and 6). In the first observation children explore money. In a previous lesson the children examined coins and small denominations of paper money. The children became so excited that Martha made a special trip to the bank to include some larger bills ($10, $20, $50, $100) for this lesson. The children examine and talk about the money. She asks them questions such as, "How many pennies in a dime?" She calls on children for answers whether or not they have raised their hand, accepting all answers and asking probing questions. She shows them a trading game with play money. When helping out a classmate, she suggests, "Try not to tell him, see if you can help by asking him a question." Martha circulates observing, questioning, and encouraging the children to explain their thinking. "Why are you choosing that one?" "How are you making your decisions?" At the end of the lesson she asks, "Did you do very much math in this game?" She asks the children to teach their parents how to play the game at home.

During the second observation we see the first day of a long-term activity integrating science and mathematics. The children are to design puff-mobiles (cars made out of straw, straight pins, beads, and paper.) which will involve estimating and measuring distances, recording data, and graphing. Martha asks, "What is the energy for a puff-mobile?" Several children quickly respond, "You blow on it." Before they break into groups, she asks them how much time they think they need to complete their projects. Martha listens and waits patiently for the children's answers that range from 30 minutes to 1 hour.

Martha visits all the groups to observe and ask questions. In one group a child is uninvolved and she helps the group become aware of this and decide how to include the child. She does not tell them what to do or how to do it. The children are making their puff-mobiles and conversing. "Don't make the sail too big," cautions one child. "No, it needs to be big and wide to catch the wind," explains another. As the groups finish, they test out their puff-mobiles on a track and measure the distance travelled. At the end of the day Martha allows time for the children to write about their experiences and express their feelings concerning the project. The children will continue with the activity the next day.

Interview

Martha indicates that she encourages children's communication by structuring situations where they interact in cooperative groups, respond to oral and written questions, talk and write about their experiences or what they have learned, and discuss their predictions at the beginning of an activity. She tries to provide a nonthreatening environment where children feel open and safe in their communication. "We may be laughing with you, but never at you." All answers are accepted. It is important to allow wait-time for answering questions, to let one person talk at a time, to communicate that what each child has to say is important, and to include those children who have difficulty communicating verbally. The children participate in deciding which activities they will do. Each day she asks the children to think about what they did in math so they can tell their parents what they are doing in math. She has the children ask their parents to help with homework.

"Communication has always been an underlying goal of mine, but now I see my role more as a facilitator to keep it on course. I feel an inner glow when I find the children really talking to one another." Martha just recently extended her communication goals into mathematics. For example, children write about math. "In the beginning of the year when we started out, I tried to walk them through the writing process to make it more enjoyable. 'How could you explain that to someone?' 'How can you extend that sentence?' A lot of this goes back to effective questioning which is something I've always tried to do. As a result of the way I'm doing math now, I think there is more of an opportunity to 'hear their thinking.'" The children are finding it easier to express mathematical ideas. Children have become better able to write about their feelings and answer one another's questions, and their feeling of self-worth has increased. "I also have found that the children's talk about numbers is carrying over to other parts of the day. We've also done more cooperative groups as a result of Project TIME. Through these they are learning to communicate with a variety of children."

"Project TIME has allowed me to be much more enthusiastic about math and that enthusiasm carries over to the children." The project has given her the ability to use the textbook only as a resource, to think about ways she can enhance lessons, to look for activities that allow the child to explore and play, and to consider the role of communication. As a result of the support groups and dyads the teachers at her school feel more comfortable about going to one another for help.

Teaching Specialist's Comments

The teaching specialist who has been working with Martha reported significant changes in her teaching. There is much more child talk and less teacher talk. Children have greater control over their activities. The children appear to be more open and willing to share themselves.

Martha is a willing learner herself and takes many ideas back to the classroom. This did not happen immediately; the one-to-one support helped to develop the level of trust and increase her willingness to take risks in trying new ideas. She is trying to fine-tune her teaching. "Martha is now more willing and capable of looking at things from a child's point of view. I've noticed she is also more interested in how children think as a result of the project. She really tries to hear and understand what they are saying."

CASE STUDY 2

Observation

Sara, a third-grade teacher, has 23 years teaching experience (grades 2, 3, and 4). During the first observation Sara introduces pentominos (shapes formed from five squares, each square sharing at least one side with another) to the children. She begins the lesson in a large group using questions to develop the ideas, "How many ways can we attach two squares? three squares? four squares?" The children work together to explore the possibilities. They talk about their ideas and draw shapes on the blackboard. When Sara suggests they look at five squares, she gives them a couple of examples. "Don't show us," shouts one child, "we want to find them." One child asks how many solutions there are. Sara does not tell them, saying they might find more than she has on her information sheet. Sara explains they are going to have a competition between tables so it will be necessary for them to work in groups of four. Even though they were instructed to work together, many children work independently. Some children appear to be confused about what to do. Others find several arrangements, draw them on grid paper, and cut them out. Sara does little monitoring of the work. She announces that it is time to post their discoveries and calls on groups one at a time to tape their shapes on the blackboard. The level of excitement escalates. She encourages the children to compare their discoveries and talk about which shapes are the same and which are different. Sara tells them that tomorrow they can arrange them in the shape of a rectangle. This announcement sends the children who have not come up with many pentominos scrambling to find more.

During the second observation Sara brings the children together in a group to tell them that they will be working with attribute blocks. She explains that they will get to examine the blocks for awhile then play a game. She defines "attribute." She allows time for the children to ask questions. One child states, "I forgot what an attribute is." "Color, shape, and size," reiterates Sara. In small groups children begin free exploration with one box of blocks per group. As soon as the boxes are opened the conversation begins. The decision of how to divide them is left up to the children. One group of five decides to divide by colors (this excludes one child) and in another group they decide to each take five at a time, then three, and finally two at a time until all the blocks are distributed. Some children are busy constructing block faces, beds, and garages, while another group is playing a guessing game they learned from the Teaching Specialist. One child decides to write a story about her block arrangement, and others are playing a version of tiddlywinks, hockey, and bowling. Sara interrupts them to teach a game. They are to take turns adding to a train of blocks in which each block added must have a difference of one attribute. The children become immediately involved and once again the conversation flows.

Interview

Sara indicates that she encourages children's communication by setting up small group activities. Some of the activities are specifically designed to increase communication. This benefits children by helping them learn to get to know one another, listen to others, and learn to work in a group.

As a result of her involvement in Project TIME, Sara presents more opportunities for the children to talk about math, identify the mathematics in an activity, and express their feelings about activities. Small group instruction encourages communication. Some children feel more comfortable asking a peer for help, rather than going to the teacher. Children know they are free to help others in their groups, not to give the answers, but to try to convey the process.

The project has significantly changed her view of teaching. She used to feel that it was the teacher's role to "instruct" and the children's role to be silent and listen. Except when the lesson is being explained, she no longer expects the children to sit quietly. She describes feeling more a sense of cooperation with the children, like a team working together. Her awareness of the value of setting up math differently evolved through her participation in seminars, dyads, and support groups.

Teaching Specialist's Comments

The teaching specialist indicated that prior to Sara's involvement with the project her teaching consisted of children individually doing paper and pencil tasks from the book. Discussion played no role in learning mathematics. She initially resisted the idea that what could be interesting mathematically for the children would also be interesting for her and vice versa. She was resistant to incorporating new ideas. That is changing. Sara now sets up small group activities and has children keep a "learning log" where they write their feelings about math, the things they have learned, and any questions. These are significant changes for her. There is much room for growth, but many of the ideas are new to her. Time and patience will be required.

CONCLUSIONS

"Constructivism itself is a change from focusing on teaching behaviors to focusing on learning" (Simon & Schrifter, 1988). This chapter considers how teachers can change their focus in regard to children's communication. The two teachers observed represented neither the best nor the worst of the teaching practices we have observed in Project TIME. (Martha was identified as the "improved" teacher by her teaching specialist and Sara was selected randomly.) Both have made significant changes in their instructional programs and in their beliefs about children and learning—typical of the changes that other teachers in the project are making. Each teacher brought a different set of experiences and backgrounds. Each is growing at different rates in her understanding of the role of communication and in their ability to implement a constructivist philosophy.

As a result of our work, we have formulated recommendations on the nature of the activities and events that facilitate implementation of a constructivist philosophy.

1. Provide mathematical learning experiences. Teachers need to experience mathematics meaningful to themselves as learners, to communicate in the context of learning mathematics, and to discover and develop relationships using hands-on (concrete) materials. From their own education, many teachers have a misperception of mathematics as a series of rules to be memorized. With this perception, discussion of mathematics has little value. When teachers construct mathematical ideas in meaningful contexts and explore open-ended questions or interesting situations, mathematics is established as a discipline worthy of discussion. Experiences with hands-on materials help build the teacher's understanding of important mathematical ideas. This provides the foundation for creating similar activities with children who often lack the language to engage in discussions about mathematical ideas apart from concrete experiences. As one project teacher put it, "The use of manipulatives just leads to communication among the children. They do something when they're exploring; they stumble on to neat things. Anybody who does that wants to share it with somebody else."

2. Develop listening skills. How do children learn how to listen? One way is by being listened to. Another is by seeing listening modeled by others. Therefore, teachers can foster children's communication by listening carefully to them. The quality of communication depends on the quality of the receiver's attention. If teachers increase the attention they have available for children, their students' communication will improve. Dyads and support groups develop listening and observational skills, and increase teachers' attention for children. One teacher sums it up, "When teachers can communicate better, it opens up the climate for children to communicate better."

3. Empower learners. For both adults and children, communication is closely linked to having control over one's own learning. In order for learners to engage in meaningful communication, they must feel that their efforts are worthwhile, that they are in charge of what they are doing, and that they can choose what, when, and how to communicate. Most teachers' experiences as students were in environments closely controlled by others. If teachers experience the joy of being in control as a learner, they will have the motivation and the model to help them structure a learning environment that allows children to assume control of their own learning. Recipes, packages, and prescribed curriculum sequences all serve to remove the control from the teacher.

If we believe in empowering teachers, we must accept that they will grow at their own rates. Respecting teachers and acknowledging their right to construct their own understandings are essential if they are to afford children the same rights.

4. Address feelings about mathematics. The ways teachers were taught and the behavior patterns they developed for coping with feelings exert a strong pull on their teaching. They need to become aware of their own feelings about mathematics and how it was presented to them. When teachers share their experiences as learners and talk about their feelings, they are better able to deal with their own feelings about mathematics and relate to those of their students.

It is a complex and arduous task to change from traditional instructional practices. Much work remains in developing professional development activities to support our goals for communication in the classroom. One thing is clear. Many teachers held in high regard under traditional standards are far from having established an environment that fosters communication. Educators should not underestimate the enormity of the task or the commitment of time and resources that are required to implement a constructivist philosophy in the classroom. But, when adequate resources are devoted to the task, the changes are rewarding to all concerned—the teacher, the child, and the society.

Discussion Chapters:
Possible Communication

Chapter 4.10

Reconstructing Constructivism

George M. A. Stanic
University of Georgia, USA

My purposes in this chapter are to briefly summarize the lively discussion within the Possible Communication discussion group, pointing out connections with the earlier chapters when appropriate, and, even more important, to draw from those discussion issues I believe constructivist teachers and researchers, especially those interested in the communication process, should continue to address in the time between now and the next International Congress (ICME-7).

A BRIEF SUMMARY OF THE DISCUSSION IN THE POSSIBLE COMMUNICATION GROUP

The initial discussion focused on communicating with "handicapped" children, a topic arising from the chapter (4.1) by Francis Lowenthal. There was clear recognition of the need to consider alternative forms of communication for children with special needs, but concerns were also expressed about the inappropriate use of the term *handicapped* and grouping too many children (with different needs) under one label. The initial discussion lead to a broader discussion of important elements in communication. For example, we discussed the importance of teachers being aware of their preconceptions that might interfere with coming to understand how a child views particular situations, problems, or materials. We discussed the need for a teacher to establish a relationship with a child in order to encourage interaction and communication. And we emphasized

---

Recorder: Lynn Outhred, Macquarie University, Australia

the vital role of the child in the communication process in which the teacher needs to involve the child in a dialogue where there is a chance for the child to express ideas, and the teacher needs to avoid "jumping in" too quickly. Two other ideas introduced by participants had to do with the importance of allowing and encouraging children to interact with each other (Maria Bartolini Bussi, chap. 4.12; see also chap. 4.3 by Jack Easley and Harold Taylor) and of challenging traditional pedagogic discourse in schools by comparing such discourse with discourse at home (Joan Bliss, chap. 4.11).

The second discussion followed up on and extended the issues raised in the prior discussion. For example, teachers' being aware of children's cultural backgrounds was emphasized as fundamental in the communication process. We again focused on the importance of children interacting with each other and discussed the small group as a vehicle to encourage such interaction. The discussion of the importance of listening (i.e., the teacher listening) in the communication process was expanded to include the issue of when and how teachers should intervene. A final issue raised, but not adequately discussed, had to do with how our exclusive focus on the subject area of mathematics fits with young children not seeing rigid subject area boundaries in their lives outside of school.

ISSUES ABOUT COMMUNICATION THAT REQUIRE MORE ATTENTION

In my role as abstracter, I see at least four issues that could serve as the focus of further work by researchers and teachers interested in possible classroom communication about mathematics. (Left off this list is the "rigid boundaries" issue mentioned earlier, which would appear to be relevant to the entire action group and which is, I think, extremely important.) These issues are as follows:

1. What is teaching? What is communication? How are they related to each other?

2. Given that listening is a crucial element of communication, how should teachers decide when to listen, when to intervene, and how to intervene? (Are children never wrong because there are always good reasons for what they do or say, or are they sometimes wrong, but for good reasons?)

3. How does the community (e.g., the classroom community) contribute to an individual's construction of knowledge? (Are shared meanings possible?)

4. What alternative forms can communication take? (How can teachers help children who have problems with traditional "school forms" of communication?)

Issue 1: What Is Teaching? What Is Communication? How Are They Related to Each Other?

The issue of the relationship between teaching and communication lies behind all the discussions in both communication groups (actual and possible), but it was not really discussed explicitly during any of the sessions. Although communication was—along with environment and knowledge and learning—one of the three "key organizing concepts" of the action group, both of the questions presented by the organizers to guide the work of the communication group were about teachers and teaching: What does mathematics teaching consist of in early childhood and what forms could it take? How can children's informal, spontaneous thinking be combined (or linked) with teaching practice? Furthermore, both of the more specific "aspects of communication" the group was to focus on had to do fundamentally with teachers and teaching (i.e., the mathematical knowledge and beliefs of teachers, both actual and possible, and the nature and forms of mathematics teaching). Each of the seven questions posed by Steffe that were used to clarify the two aspects mentioned either teachers or teaching (e.g., How might teachers of mathematics in early childhood view mathematics and its meaning? How might teachers use their knowledge to foster the mathematical knowledge of children in mathematical communications?). I believe we need to clarify what we mean by *teaching,* what we mean by *communication,* and how teaching and communication are related to each other. It seems to me that teaching is part of the topic of communication and is simultaneously much larger than communication as a topic.

I have asked myself why the group was called *communication* if all the structure that was given focused on teaching. The intent, I think, was a worthwhile one. Characterizing the teaching act as being fundamentally an act of communicating, rather than simply talking, makes the child so much more important in the process: talking requires only one person; communicating, at least two. You can talk to a child; you have to communicate with a child. Viewing teaching as if it were a process of communication requires that teachers take the ideas and the words of children seriously, giving children opportunities for expression and reflection. Because using communication as one of the key concepts for the action group brought with it a potentially rich view of teaching, my concern about calling the group communication rather than teaching may seem unfounded or unimportant. However, I still worry about the vision of teaching in constructivism because I do not want constructivists in mathematics education to give up the teaching arena to others, allowing others (and themselves, tacitly) to define teaching in a limited way.

At times, it has appeared as though some constructivists have been reluctant to use the term *teaching,* believing perhaps that different terms are needed to capture the relationships among members of a classroom community. At other times, some constructivist researchers have explicitly expressed their intent to focus on learning rather than teaching, as though the focus on learning were both the essence of constructivism and the answer to all of the problems of working with children in school. At still other times, we have been told (as we were told during the first meeting of the action group) that the main problem with early childhood environments is that "they contain teachers" and that too often teachers feel the need "to get in there and teach." The comment was made, at least in part, in jest, and the idea behind it is related to the "listening and intervention" issue discussed later. Perhaps the intention was to push us to see the teacher from the child's point of view. But embedded in the comment is an unfortunate and impoverished view of teaching—of what teaching might be and of what it is in many classrooms. The problem with early childhood environments is not that they contain teachers, but that the conditions of most environments (i.e., classrooms) constrain teachers and limit teaching.

The brilliant work constructivist researchers have done, that members of this action group have done, certainly is testimony to the need to look more closely at children and how they learn and testimony to the fact that mathematics educators, not just educational psychologists, should be doing the looking. Furthermore, researchers certainly have every right to limit themselves to studying how children learn. But the study of teaching and teachers must also be a part of the constructivist research agenda. It is ironic that the excellent "teaching experiments" that some constructivist researchers have conducted have been used primarily to support conclusions about how children learn when they tell us as much or more about how children might be taught.

The point is not that radical constructivists have not thought about this issue but that classroom teaching has not been an essential part of constructivist research. Fortunately, a few constructivist researchers have begun to look more closely at teaching and the constraints under which teachers must work in schools and classrooms (e.g., Cobb, Wood, & Yackel, in press). The greatest strength of the chapters written by members of both the actual and the possible communication groups is rooted in that fact that many of the authors took seriously teaching as a process and teachers as people. And the greatest strength of the entire action group was that teachers were a part of the group and were there to remind everyone to take them and their profession seriously.

This interest in teachers and teaching is important because knowing about how children learn simply is not enough. The knowledge that researchers have constructed about how children learn does not lead to a one-to-one mapping from learning to teaching. Practical and ethical arguments are required in order to make the leap from learning to teaching—practical arguments when we ask how a teacher might organize a classroom of 30 children to help them construct mathematics individually and communally, and ethical arguments when we ask what we should teach these children and why we should teach one thing (or encourage one experience) rather than another. Arguments need to be made not just for a particular type of mathematical experience but, more broadly, for the role of mathematics in the entire school curriculum. In a school world where we cannot teach everything that might be known to everyone and where we must choose to teach this rather than that, choosing to teach mathematics at all, much less a particular form of mathematics, is a moral and ethical choice that mathematics educators, including constructivists, too often take for granted. That teachers have been left out of this decision-making process (where it even exists) is as much an obstacle to constructivism playing a larger role in school mathematics as anything I can think of. Constructivists certainly would argue and have argued for the empowerment of teachers, but coming to grips with how teachers might be empowered requires that we look beyond communication. Again, as important as communicating with children is, teaching comprises much more than just communication.

Even at those times when we think we have a reasoned implication for teaching from research on learning, the school as an institution and the wider society in which the school exists may not provide a supportive environment for the suggested teaching practice. We can and should work toward change in the institution of schooling and even toward change in the wider society, but that, too—that process of working toward change in school and society—should be part of our view of what teaching is all about and, therefore, part of constructivist research and theory. If we look at teaching as an act involving teacher and student, communication becomes a marvelous way to capture the essence of teaching. If, however, we look at teaching as also including the constraints teachers must overcome in order to have the opportunity to communicate with students, the essence of teaching becomes much more than communicating. After all, the notion of communicating with students is not new or unique to researchers who label themselves as constructivists. Constructivists can provide a unique view of what communication might look like in the classroom, but the suggestions will be empty if not made with a view toward other ethical and political dilemmas of teaching.

I do not mean to diminish the importance of communication in the classroom and the enlightened view of communication espoused by constructivists. It may be that the communication group had an appropriate name and focus. But nowhere in the three main areas—knowledge and learning, environment, and communication—was there a recognition of the need to look at ethical and political dilemmas of teaching, and some group should have had that responsibility. On Day 3 of the Congress, Harold Taylor, a teacher in Michigan and coauthor with Jack Easley of a chapter (4.3) for the communication group, asked that teachers be given the opportunity to fail with dignity. His need to ask that and my own response to what he said makes me think that we have not yet done enough to recognize and support teachers, and that is another reason why I am concerned about something as apparently trivial as calling the group communication rather than teaching.

Issue 2: Given That Listening Is a Crucial Element of Communication, How Should Teachers Decide When to Listen, When to Intervene, and How to Intervene? (Are Children Never Wrong Because There Are Always Good Reasons for What They Do or Say, or Are They Sometimes Wrong, but for Good Reasons?)

The first question within Issue 2 is based on the themes of listening and gentleness and reluctant intervention that came up in the discussions of both the possible communication group and the entire action group. (When I mentioned this issue during the last session with the possible communication group, some members wanted to be certain that being gentle not be misconstrued as incompatible with being challenging, even "tough" when necessary. All, however, agreed with the importance of listening and reluctant intervention.) Essentially, people in the possible communication group concluded that if teachers would just do more listening to children, much would be accomplished. Now, getting teachers to listen to children—or, perhaps more important, giving teachers the opportunity to listen to children—is no easy task, but it cannot be separated from helping people come to know when and how to jump in, to respond, to intervene as they work with children.

A related and more specific question came up as a result of a story told to the possible communication group by Jack Easley about an interaction between a teacher and a child. Essentially, the child gave a very creative reason for getting an "incorrect" answer and thereby frustrated the teacher. Among other things (including the child's motives in providing the explanation and alternative ways for the teacher to respond), we talked about the possibility of children being wrong or making a mistake: Are children never wrong because there are always good reasons for what they do or say, or are they sometimes wrong but for good reasons? An answer to this question may require that we make distinctions between different kinds of mistakes children make; furthermore, using terms like *mistake* requires that we clarify frames of reference (i.e., from whose frame of reference or what frame of reference can we label something as wrong or as a mistake). But the question of whether a child can be wrong is important because a teacher's explicit or implicit answer to it determines, to a certain extent, the form and content of classroom interactions.

Both questions within issue 2 are related to the broader question of the role of relativism in constructivism. And both questions deal with what, exactly, it means to be a constructivist mathematics teacher. In a wonderful essay that appeared in the *Harvard Educational Review,* Paul Cobb (1986c) described the distinction between empiricist-oriented constructivists and radical constructivists. Both types would claim that mathematical knowledge is "constructed actively by the child in the process of adapting to [her or] his environment" (p. 301). The main difference between the types lies in their different view of knowledge and reality. According to Cobb, empiricist constructivists, of whom he is critical, "locate knowledge in an external environment and see it existing independent of the child's cognitive activity" (p. 302). Radical constructivists, on the other hand, believe that knowledge does not exist independent of the knower and that all of "learning is a problem-solving process in which the learner attempts to overcome obstacles or contradictions that arise as he or she engages in purposeful activity" (p. 302). According to the radical constructivist, "the adult observer who 'sees' . . . knowledge 'out there' is consciously reflecting on structures that he or she has imposed on reality" (p. 302).

Cobb rejected the empiricist belief that "the instructional goal is to lead the learner to construct correct knowledge—knowledge that *corresponds* to or *matches* that located in the mind-independent reality" (p. 303). A radical constructivist would claim that "the teacher cannot lead children unerringly down a chosen developmental path. The best that can be done is to devise activities that give rise to problems for children while, at the same time, anticipating and 'looking out for' undesirable constructions" (p. 303).

It seems to me that a central question for the radical constructivist, and for the communication part of the action group, has to do with how a teacher is to decide whether a particular mathematical construction is "desirable" or "undesirable," apart from some vision of correct or valuable knowledge. Even focusing on the idea of helping a child construct knowledge that is viable or knowledge that "works" for that particular child in a particular situation, rather than on helping the child construct correct knowledge, does not overcome the problem here. We have schools, teachers, and researchers because people are not content with viability or what works in a particular situation. Teachers encourage children to move beyond what they already know. So the question of what constitutes a teacher's "end-in-view" remains, even if we admit that an end-in-view may change and that alternative ends may arise in the context of activity. Declaring that teachers should devise activities that "give rise to problems for children" begs the question of how, again apart from some vision of correct or valuable knowledge, a teacher is to decide what sorts of problems children should encounter. These questions clearly link the work of the possible communication group with that of the environment group on curriculum and the knowledge and learning groups.

My concerns are not by any means an argument for the empiricist constructivist viewpoint. They simply represent a call for more work on these questions by radical constructivists in mathematics education. In fact, my concerns are very much related to the questions the organizers asked the communication groups to focus on (e.g., How might teachers of mathematics in early childhood view mathematics and its meaning? How might teachers use their knowledge to foster the mathematical knowledge of children in mathematical communications? What decisions might teachers make about what children could or should do?).

Another perspective on this issue can be drawn from Maxine Greene's (1987) analysis of aesthetic education. The same sorts of questions arise, for example, in the teaching of literature. In explaining how she teaches a novel, Greene said: "Taking the view that a predefined meaning is not hidden in a novel, say, to be unearthed, I work to encourage students to treat their encounters with [novels] . . . as open-ended situations, occasions for them to achieve a text as meaningful without any expectation of 'inexorableness' or inevitability or total coherence at the end" (p. 8). Assuming that there may be an undesirable student text, or at least a very limited text, just as there may be an undesirable student mathematical construction, the question for teaching literature is upon what basis a teacher who believes in "the inascertainability of what any novel finally signifies" (p. 8), as Greene does, make decisions about her or his students' texts.

A partial answer comes not in Greene's discussion of literature but in her discussion of painting. "The undertaking that is aesthetic education," said Greene, "depends a great deal on the grasp of the language or symbol systems identified with each particular art form. There has to be some conceptualization of the painting *qua* painting before the perceived field opens out to the 'eye and mind' " (p. 5). According to Greene, "If we know at least enough to notice what there is to be noticed, to locate the work somewhere in what we think of as an 'artworld,' there may be . . . a transfiguration and defamiliarization of our notions of space and relationship, even as there may be a transfiguration of experience" (p. 5). She was speaking here, I think, about the set of shared meanings human beings have developed about art, about the knowledge of art that in some way allows one to see more in a painting. Greene, while emphasizing individual interpretation of works of art, also recognizes the value of the collective knowledge human beings have developed about art. It is this collective knowledge that, in a context of appreciating and encouraging individual interpretation, can be used by a teacher to guide a student's interpretation of a painting or a student's creation of his or her own text while reading a novel.

I do not see Greene's idea of "knowing at least enough to notice what there is to be noticed" (p. 5) as analogous to Cobb's description of the empiricist constructivist as one who argues that "low-level skills involved in performing basic tasks must be learned before problem solving can occur" (Cobb, 1986c, p. 302). Instead, I see Greene's respect for the collective knowledge developed by human beings as a helpful reminder to those radical constructivists, who, ironically, have enormous respect and appreciation for the experience and mathematical constructions of individual children but apparently little faith (or at least little expressed faith) in the logically organized subject matter of mathematics that reflects the collective experience of human beings. It may be true that "the adult observer who 'sees' . . . knowledge 'out there' is consciously reflecting on structures that he or she has imposed on reality," but is it not remarkable that so many human beings have imposed similar structures on reality. How, exactly, are we to conceive of the relationship between the individual and the social construction of mathematics?

John Dewey (1902/1964), the great resolver of apparent dichotomies, asked in "The Child and the Curriculum": "What, then, is the problem?" He answered that

> it is just to get rid of the prejudicial notion that there is some gap in kind (as distinct from degree) between the child's experience and the various forms of subject-matter that make up the course of study. From the side of the child, it is a question of seeing how his experience already contains within itself elements—facts and truths—of just the same sort as those entering into the formulated study; and, what is of more importance, of how it contains within itself the attitudes, the motives, and the interests which have operated in developing and organizing the subject-matter to the plane which it now occupies. From the side of the studies, it is a question of interpreting them as outgrowths of forces operating in the child's life, and of discovering the steps that intervene between the child's present experience and their richer maturity. (p. 344)

Although a constructivist would naturally be concerned about the gap-in-degree-rather-than-kind idea, given the work of Piaget and others which shows qualitative differences (i.e., differences in kind) in thinking between children and adults, Dewey's claim about similarities in experience does not deny differences in thinking. Dewey goes on in "The Child and the Curriculum" to discuss how the teacher might use her or his own knowledge of subject matter to plan and help the child reconstruct experience, and he thereby provides some insight on our question of when and how teachers should intervene as they work with children.

Whether or not mathematics has an independent existence outside of individual human beings, the issue remains as to how teachers who have come to appreciate the abstract, collective human experience, the shared meanings we call mathematics, can use what they know to help children reconstruct their experience. The way in which radical constructivists resolve this issue will determine whether constructivism will have a wide and lasting impact on school mathematics. And because there is, I think, a strong connection between the work of Dewey and Piaget, especially when we compare specific works such as "The Child and the Curriculum" and, for example, Piaget's *Genetic Epistemology* (1970a), looking more closely at the connection might help in the struggle.

Issue 3: How Does the Community (e.g., the Classroom Community) Contribute to an Individual's Construction of Knowledge? (Are Shared Meanings Possible?)

This issue follows directly from the notion of shared meanings in the previous discussion of Issue 2. The role of the community must be considered in any discussion of communication and the construction of knowledge. Maria Bartolini

Bussi (chap. 4.12) raised this issue as she described some of her own work, and it was in that context that she mentioned the concept of *shared meanings*. Because there was some disagreement over the possibility of people "sharing" meanings or knowledge, I included the question here as something to focus on in future work by constructivist researchers and teachers. Linking the idea of shared meanings with what Paul Cobb referred to as "consensual domains" may be a helpful direction to take.

Issue 4: What Alternative Forms Can Communication Take? (How Can Teachers Help Children Who Have Problems with Traditional "School Forms" of Communication?)

As I said earlier, much of the time in the possible communication group's initial session was spent on a discussion of handicapped children, brought up by Lowenthal (chap. 4.1). I have tried to broaden the issue a bit by focusing on alternative forms of communication. It is through this issue that we may see a link between Lowenthal's concerns about communicating with the handicapped child and Joan Bliss' comparison of communication in the contexts of home and school. This issue of alternative forms of communication should also push radical constructivists to continue to make connections with the work of anthropologists and sociologists who are studying the relationship between culture and cognition (e.g., Laboratory of Comparative Human Cognition, 1983; Rogoff & Lave, 1984).

Simply knowing that students learn differently and about different things in different contexts is not enough, however. The implications for schooling largely depend on our vision of the purposes of schooling. Some philosophers (e.g., Floden, Buchmann, & Schwille, 1987) have suggested that we should look at the school as a singularly unique context that provides the opportunity for "breaking with everyday experience." The implications of what we know about children's learning in alternative contexts would certainly be different for them than for people who want schooling to be more like everyday experience. The point, again, is that constructivist theory and research must explicitly deal with general questions, such as what the purpose of schooling is, as well as the specific question of how children learn mathematics.

CONCLUSION

We have a rich tradition in mathematics education of discussions about what mathematics is and why we should teach it, but it is a neglected tradition. Perhaps the greatest benefit of the constructivist movement in mathematics education is that it can help us recapture this tradition by raising questions about the form and content of school mathematics. The greatest problem in the movement, as Cobb (1986c) pointed out, is the blurred distinction between radical constructivists and others who call themselves constructivists. Constructivism is a remarkable idea in danger of becoming a slogan, just as *progressivism* became a slogan earlier in this century.

In some ways, radical constructivist researchers in mathematics education have accepted as unproblematic a general constructivist theory of knowledge and learning and have proceeded to do insightful, necessary, and valuable investigations of children learning particular concepts. The time has come, I think, for constructivists to take the theory of constructivism itself as problematic and to reconstruct it in a way that will be even more beneficial to both researchers and classroom teachers. The discussions of the possible communication group represent an important step in this difficult but necessary process of reconstructing constructivism.

ACKNOWLEDGMENTS

I gratefully acknowledge Les Steffe for his comments and questions on previous drafts of this chapter. Although his concerns led me to make important additions and changes, this acknowledgement should not be interpreted to mean that he agrees with the final version.

Chapter 4.11

The Nature of Communication in Early Childhood in the Contexts of Home and School

Joan Bliss
University of London, UNITED KINGDOM

This chapter addresses the possible forms of mathematical communication that might occur in the classroom for children between the ages of 4 and 8, and the role of play, language, and emotion in the child's learning. Rather than consider specifically mathematical communication, I focus on the nature of communication in general during this period. In order to better understand the child's situation at this time, the chapter examines the following areas:

1. The social setting of the child between ages of 4 and 8
2. Learning in early childhood
3. The nature of the home context
4. The nature of the school context
5. Collaborative learning and reading
6. Collaborative learning and mathematics

THE SOCIAL SETTING OF THE 4-TO 8-YEAR-OLD

The context in which learning takes place is very different for the child aged 4 and for the child aged 8, so it is crucial to examine first what happens socially to children during this time. One of the more important steps for any child in this age range is going to school, whether at 5 as in England, or at 6 as in many European and other countries. Quite a few children will already have participated in various forms of schooling: play school, nursery, and so forth, usually for a limited number of hours, but "going to school" at 5 or 6 is the beginning of compulsory education. Simplistically one could see the role of the home as being the major learning context prior to the age of 5 or 6, whereas with this transition this role gets shared between the two contexts, home and school. As Wells (1985) said, "they (children) move from the familiar and supportive environment of their home into the larger unknown world of school."

Teachers face the problem that some children who are active, willing learners before coming to school appear to become passive, slow, or reluctant learners in school. Why do children range in this manner? Hughes (1986) argued that if he had found beginners at school experiencing difficulties in mathematics, he would have understood what happens in school but, "Instead we have something of a paradox: young children appear to start school with more mathematical knowledge than has hitherto been thought. In that case, why should they experience such difficulty with mathematics?" (p. 36). But is this phenomenon only related to mathematics? Research in other areas both provides examples of children as competent learners and highlights that things also go wrong for them in school. Wells (1985) showed through his Bristol Language Development Project that by the age of 5, children have mastered the English language sufficiently well so to be able to cope with a wide range of linguistic situations. He stated,

> The first and perhaps the most important single finding from our study is that, with one exception, all the children that we have observed had achieved a mastery of English by the time they started school. (p. 4)
>
> This makes it more disturbing that, as soon as we observed the children in school, we found the anticipated strong relationship between family background and educational attainment. (p. 5)

These comments reflect the concerns of much of the work initiated under the American Head Start program in the early 1960s.

Other researchers have also shown that children are competent language users. MacLure and French (1981) discussed children from a wide range of social backgrounds who coped with school: "There is little in the nature of the interactional demands which will be made of them in school that they will not have become familiar with at home, at the level of conversational structure. It is possible, however, to identify areas where home and school differ, but these do not lie in the types of conversational structures as occurring in each setting" (p. 237).

So then it appears that some children experience difficulty in school not only in mathematics but also in their native language and possibly in other areas. I propose, as have others to be discussed later, that it is the nature of the context in which children learn and communicate that presents the difficulty. If so, it would seem essential to characterize both the learning that goes on prior to school and the context of home and school in order to be able to contrast and compare the differences between these two environments.

There is considerable development in the age range of 4–8 of interest. Existentially, early childhoods between the ages of 2 to 5 is a magic period because the child is liberated from the all important practical sensory-motor period into a world where the imagination has no bounds—with the 4/5-year-olds still part of the world of imagination, while their 6- and 7-year-old peers are emerging from it into the rather more serious world of school. Winnicott (1964) said of this early childhood period: "For the little child we allow a wider area than we allow for ourselves in which imagination plays a dominant role, so that playing which makes use of the world and yet retains all the intensity of the dream, is considered characteristic of the life of children."

LEARNING ABOUT THE WORLD THROUGH PLAY, LANGUAGE, AND FEELING

Play then will be taken as one of the themes through which much of learning in preschool context takes place. Piaget (1946) showed how play progresses from practical rituals before the age of 18 months or so to a rich symbolic play where assimilation dominates, because the nature of play is such that accommodation is not promoted. Piaget's work (1932) also shows how through play (e.g., game such as marbles) children develop a gradual understanding of the nature of rules. Although for the 4-year-old a rule is not seen as having a social function of regulation as a negotiated act, by the age of 7 the types of negotiation that are relevant to the creation of rules begin through forms of "incipient cooperation."

The child's world is that of the home, the garden, and of parks and commons, where he or she has walked or played with parents or peers. Through this activity children learn about space long before any formal schooling. The description of Piaget & Inhelder (1948) of the development of spatial notions reveals that from about the age of 4 and earlier children use topological notions such as those of proximity—distinguishing things that are close from those that are distant, separation, order, surrounding, and so forth, so that, for example, curvilinear forms are isolated long before rectilinear ones.

Much of children's spatial development can be seen also through their drawings, as Goodnow (1977) showed. Pointing out that "most of them (the drawings) have charm, novelty, simplicity, playfulness, and a fresh approach that is a source of pure pleasure," she also points out that "they [the drawings] may be regarded as expressions of our search for order in a complex world, as examples of communication, as indices of the types of society we live in, as signs of intellectual development, as reminder of our own lost innocence and verve" (p. 10). Bliss and Ogborn (1988) and Bliss, Ogborn, and Whitelock (in press) proposed that young children's ideas about motion originate through their actions on and experience of the physical world. That is, through play and exploration children learn a great deal about how objects move, how to stop or start them moving and also how to keep them moving. They postulate that these actions are interiorized at a very early age and become fundamental but tacit knowledge, persisting into adulthood. These studies show that such ideas are certainly present in primary school children and in secondary school children independent of age.

Parallel with play and as important in its own right is the development of language. Halliday's (1975) work with his own son, Nigel, from 9 months onwards was revolutionary because it revealed, by a study of Nigel's prototypical linguistic utterances, the manner in which a child learns how to convey meanings long before the classic two-word utterance. These meanings come into existence through interaction with significant others in the search for personal meanings. Halliday identified four functions—instrumental ("I want"), regulatory ("do as I tell you"), interactional ("me and you"), and personal ("here I come"), which characterize the child's earliest utterances. Although all are essentially concerned with social interaction, they allow the construction of language rules. Halliday showed that from 18 months Nigel developed three other functions for "pretend-play" (imaginative), for the purpose of exploring the environment (heuristic) and for communicating new information (information). In much the same manner as Halliday, but with children in early childhood, Wells (1985) provided numerous examples of the way in which children learn about how language is used for interpersonal purposes, and also how through conversation arising from activities, children also learn about the activities themselves and their organization.

Meek (1985) brought together the notions of play, language, and emotion in her essay on the language of play, paradox, and fictions. She argued (Bateson, 1973) that "without the development of these discourses in childhood, within the domain of the imaginary—of unreality, dreams and stories—children would become trapped in an endless interchange of stylized messages, a game with rigid rules, unrelieved by chance or humour." Play with words, making things up—sense and nonsense, narrative play—are all vital elements to the child's early childhood development. Referring to Vygotsky's idea that the creation of imaginary situations is not something that happens by chance "but is rather the first manifestation of the child's emancipation from situational constraints," she emphasized that play through story telling allows children to project their emotions onto imaginary situations. Thus Meek suggested that play both "generates and controls emotions so that the delineation of reality itself may depend on make-believe, on knowing that one can handle both the 'actual' and the 'made-up.' "

Meek's thinking stresses the importance of emotion and the child's affective development. This issue can be only touched on here but to neglect it would be to deny a vital aspect of the young child's existence. Winnicot's (1964) description of this period is perhaps sufficient to underline its importance. "A need of the well-developed four-year-old is to have parents with whom to identify. . . . The operative factor is the parent. . . . the two parents' inter-relationship as perceived by the child. It is this that the child takes in, and imitates or reacts against, and it is this also that the child uses in a hundred ways in the personal process of self-development" (p. 180). The move that children make from home to school will be fundamental to their complete development. Not only will it involve unfamiliar styles of learning but also and more essentially, new and different people, namely teachers. The teachers will, in turn, establish for the child new roles, different sets of expectations and very wide ranging and different social, emotional, and cognitive goals. That is, children enter a world very different from the one they have been used to, which can be both confusing and distressing to the child. Wells (1985) argued that in spite of much theorizing about this issue, there had been little systematic study of "the actual experience of children making this crucial transition apart from the studies of Bernstein (1973) and Tough (1977)," and so he set out to describe some of the "main characteristics of children's experience of talk at home and at school."

In order to better understand the home context, I propose to follow Wells' analysis because, although its focus is talk and not mathematical communication, it considers talk in terms of a conversation with an adult, and in this manner it will be possible later to compare the nature of communication between parent and child and teacher and child. As Wells (1985) wrote: "Talking with adults can be seen as providing the context in which children learn the language of their culture and simultaneously learn the way in which experience is organized within that culture" (p. 1).

Bruner (1981) also stressed the crucial nature of the role of the adult in managing communication in interactions with children in his discussion of the Language Assistance System (LAS). "The first thing to note about the role in this system is the adult's willingness to share or even hand over control to the child once he had learned to fulfill the conditions on speech. However obvious this may seem, it is a *sine qua non* of the adult's role in the system" (p. 45).

The Home Context

Wells (1985) took Halliday's view that language or talk is not a question of learning words or grammatical rules but "rather of learning to construct shared meanings as part of collaborative activities in which the words and sentences both refer to the shared situation and reflect a particular orientation to it" (p. 101). Wells characterized children's early learning as follows:

1. Children experience a reciprocal form of interaction in which meanings are negotiated and not unilaterally imposed, that is,
   - Children are treated as equal partners in conversation, for a large proportion of the time.
   - Children are encouraged to take initiatives and are helped to extend topics that they propose.

2. Much of children's learning occurs in the context of purposeful practical activity, very often jointly engaged in with an adult.

Thus the main characteristics of learning in the home context are that it is spontaneous and unplanned, arising from the activities of the participants, and focused and given meaning by the context in which it occurs. Wells argued that there are both strengths and limitations to this sort of learning. The main limitation of such learning is its sporadic and often unsystematic nature, with some areas of learning being developed while others remain rare encounters.

On the other hand, its strength comes from the child's purpose in the activity that "sustains his or her motivation to understand" and also from the context that provides "support for the new concepts to be grasped and the new connections to be made." Thus, although usually such learning is tied to specific contexts, it will be effectively learned because it is normally in function of a goal chosen by the child so that children gain confidence in their own ability both to formulate problems and to find solutions to them.

School Context

Wells, in characterizing the school context, makes it clear that there is a difference in the ratio of adults to children but he still considers that this does not justify the enormous differences summarized in Table 1. Wells commented that possibly the most striking difference in terms of defining the home and school context is the reversal between the situation at home where adults are willing to extend children's topics and the situation at school where adult utterances mainly pursue adult topics. As he says: "Compared with parents, teachers, it appears, are typically far more concerned to pursue their own topics—to follow their own

TABLE 1
Comparison of Children's Language Experience at Home
and at School: Mean Values (*Wells, 1985, p.* 160)

	Home	*School*
% of all adult-child sequences that are one-to-one	99	58*
% of sequences that are child-initiated	73	16*
% of child utterances to adult that are questions	12	3*
% of adult utterances that are questions	15	21
% of adult utterances that extend child's topic	38	14*
% of adult utterances that pursue adult topic	14	40*
% of adult questions that are 'display' questions, that is, where answer is known	20	52*

*Differences significant at 1% level (Mann-Whitney U Test).

agenda—than to accept and extend topics offered by the child." Commenting on what he considers to be effective learning at home and at school, Wells suggests that "to be most effective the relationship between teacher and learner must, at every stage of development, be collaborative. Teaching, thus seen, is not a didactic transmission of preformulated knowledge but an attempt to negotiate shared meanings and understandings" (p. 73).

Collaborative Learning and Reading Projects

Collaborative learning came to play an important role on the educational scene in an unexpected manner in research in reading. The rationale behind much of this work was to look at the problem of working-class children who performed less well than their middle-class peers when it came to reading in school. The Haringey Project, directed by Jack Tizard (Tizard, Schofeld, & Hewson, 1982), had as one of its main goals to ask the parents of children in top infant classes, essentially from disadvantaged backgrounds, to listen to their children read aloud several times a week, with materials sent home from school. Such a simple but direct method showed startling results in that, when compared with a control group, reading had improved tremendously and the improvement was sustained over time. Various other projects, such as the Coventry project, stressed the notion of cooperation between teachers and parents, and children, and confirmed the findings of the Haringey project. The Pitfield project, otherwise known as PACT (Parents and Children and Teachers), in a similar study extended their reading project to over 100 primary schools involving a large majority of parents in all schools.

The findings of the various reading projects filtered through into mathematics education when the Norman Thomas report (1985) on improving primary schools suggested "that a scheme is developed and monitored parallel to PACT in which parents are encouraged to join with teachers in helping their children to make progress in mathematics." At that time Ruth Merttens, a mathematics teacher, had started to do some work with Dorothy Hamiltin of the PACT project at her local teacher's Centre. Merttens (1987), writing about her experience of teaching mathematics prior to work with PACT said, "I was uncomfortably aware of the division between what I thought and taught as a teacher, and what I practiced and believed as a parent." By Spring 1985, Ruth Merttens was planning a new project, IMPACT, which was to mirror PACT but in mathematics education, and by September of that year the pilot project had been launched.

COLLABORATIVE LEARNING AND IMPACT

For Ruth Merttens and Jeffrey Vass, codirectors, the most general goal of IMPACT was to involve parents in a structured way in their children's learning. Merttens (1987) described the aims of the project as:

- First, because a great deal of "implicit" mathematics happens at home, although not generally recognized as such by either parents or teachers, this should provide the basis for the mathematics to be done at home. She argued that many of the formal activities of school use the same sets of skills as the informal activities of the home.
- Second, because children are required to explain at home what they have learned in schools, the project should help promote the transfer of skills learned in the context of the classroom to a new and different context: the home or street. Thus the child initiates the activity and the child acts as "the main source of instruction as to what is to be done," in this way avoiding the problem of parents who know no mathematics and feel insecure about their mathematical ability.

The project developed three kinds of materials that were to be sent home: data collecting exercises (e.g., tasks where child and parent were required to find out or collect information); "doing," making or completing activities (e.g., making a hand span and measuring things at home, completing a number spiral); games and investigations, the focus of the task being the activity or the process rather than the result itself. The results of the work at home would then feedback into school to provide a focus for classroom activity.

Contact with parents was considered essential and meetings to inform them about IMPACT were held at all hours: before school, after school, and also in the evenings. Once the project started, the flow of information from the school to home happened naturally. But the flow of information from parents back to school was problematic. Regular feedback meetings with parents, although crucial to the project, were much harder to organize. The informal meetings before or after school were vital in providing time when parents and teachers "listened" to each other and when their roles became blurred. To be sure of feedback, an idea from the PACT project, comment sheets, one for the child and one for the parent, was adopted with each filling out one of these forms for each activity each week.

Merttens, commenting on the changes in parent/teacher relations and patterns of contact, wrote: "IMPACT is operating at the boundaries of the constructed social relationship between teachers and parents. Effecting changes in these relations involves not only altering the patterns and routines by which these are regulated, but also by making a conscious effort to avoid the apartheid caused by maintaining each group's exclusivity and sense of its own complicity" (p. 103). Merttens considered that the pilot study provided some evidence to show what might or could constitute a supportive learning environment for mathematical development.

The pilot project lasted for 18 months and has resulted in the financing by the Department of Education and Science of a 3-year project that started in September 1987, based at the Polytechnic of North London. Merttens and Vass, codirectors of the project, issue annual reports. Commenting on her work on

IMPACT, Merttens said, "One of its (her work) great strengths is that the focus of attention, not only for me, but for all the teachers and parents involved, shifts from being on the teaching of maths, to being on the LEARNING of maths. I realize that after 16 years of teaching it, I am not very interested in the teaching of mathematics. But I am fantastically interested in how children—and adults—learn it. IMPACT represents a start in this vein" (p. 108).

A CAUTIONARY NOTE

Francis (1987) reviewed the research on parental involvement in hearing children read and showed that some of the results are equivocal. One such study in this area was that of Hannon (1987) with 76 children in Sheffield over a period of 3 years in which the children showed no significant improvement in their reading. Francis went on to argue that there is an important distinction to be made between practices that occur naturally at home and those that are a parental extension of school practice in the home. She showed, based on work such as that of Heath (1983) and Tizard and Hughes (1984), that natural home practices are very varied and based in everyday life contexts. In this way, "Reading may be fragmentary, but it is meaningful and interesting because it serves everyday purposes," not unlike Well's description of learning at home. As for the parental extension of school practice in the home, she argued: "It is not an implicit part of child-rearing practice, but an explicit formula for education purposes. It cannot, therefore, be taken for granted that it will productively graft onto home-based learning." Francis went on to argue that in the area of reading, at home and at school, oversimplification or lack of theory, as well as the methodology lacking a sufficient grounding in ethnography "may lead either to rejection of a possible useful activity because it fails to show conclusive outcomes on restricted measures, or alternatively too ready an acceptance of an activity without exploration of possibly more productive alternative versions."

CONCLUSIONS

Wells (1985) summed up children's experience of school as bewildering because "they suddenly find themselves expected to fit in with someone else's definition of what is interesting and to learn what someone else prescribes. It is not surprising, therefore, that some children become tongue-tied and appear much less competent than they really are" (p. 159).

However, underlying this is, I would argue, something much more profound, the problem of authority. Walden and Walkerdine (1985) showed that for older children, while following rules, both mathematical and behavioral, leads to successful task completion, challenging the rules of mathematical discourse, and thus teacher's authority, was often more important for real understanding. Wells' analysis of the home context, which showed children as successful learners because they were active participants in situations of their own choice, leads him to advocate collaborative learning. Collective learning requires that neither of the partners sees themselves as an authority but that the relationship is based on reciprocity. If, as Wells and others suggest, in the more classic classroom context it is the teacher who defines the situation, that is, what is interesting and what is to be learned, can the young child of 5 or 6 be expected to challenge this? Challenging the rules on internal discourse of mathematics may be difficult, challenging the rules of 'pedagogic discourse' (in the sense of Bernstein), particularly if one is only 5 or 6, is more or less impossible! Collaborative learning and parental involvement in learning show significant potential but still more research, particularly if they are to be considered in mathematics education.

Chapter 4.12

Learning Situations and Experiential Domains Relevant to Early Childhood Mathematics Education

Maria G. Bartolini Bussi
Università di Modena, ITALY

Since 1983, the Educational Research Group, of which I am a member, has been deeply involved in a general project for preschool teacher training, with the financial support of the Municipal Authorities of Modena. This project is ongoing, under the direction of a particular expert for each subject area (e.g., P. Guidoni for Science Education, H. Sinclair for Linguistic Education, M. Bussi for Mathematics Education), and involves each teacher of the Municipal preprimary schools (about 150 teachers or 1800 children). About 40 teachers have been attending the Mathematics Education area since 1983. This chapter aims to report the main methodological outcomes of the collective research carried on by the members of the group and the teachers of the municipal preprimary schools of Modena.

TEACHERS AND SCHOOL MATHEMATICS

At the beginning of the research project, the teachers had a very cautious (nearly suspicious) attitude toward mathematics. Almost all of them had depressing personal school experiences and little knowledge of mathematics content. They had a very rigid opinion about what constituted appropriate mathematics activities. The only activities that we were able to observe in the classrooms were acts of classification, ordering, construction of sets, and recognition of early cardinal numbers as equivalence classes of sets of concrete objects, chiefly of structured materials.

The first challenge of the research project was changing this negative attitude toward mathematics. It was immediately clear that this work would require a great deal of time.

We began to work with teachers, alternating (a) the study of mathematical content (e.g., natural numbers or measuring); (b) the review of research on learning processes (e.g., research on early number meanings); (c) the discussion of teaching method problems (e.g., the teacher's role in carrying on a collective discussion or in observing children's work); (d) the critical analysis of some particular projects for the teaching of mathematics in preprimary school; and (e) the analysis of protocols that were collected by the teachers in their own classes.

As a primary result of the research project, we have developed some firm beliefs that may be summarized as follows. First teachers and researchers are research-partners, so it is necessary to make their cooperation really equal. Their roles are different because, for instance, teachers are responsible for lesson planning and for classroom work, whereas researchers are responsible for collecting products, keeping up relations with other research groups, and fostering reflections on classroom work. In spite of that, they need a common framework with regards to the main results of international educational research either from a theoretical point of view (e.g., learning processes or observation methods) or from an applied point of view (e.g., projects or school experiences). In addition, teachers must work within the tradition of their social and school environment. This belief can affect the choices made by researchers. Finally, we have given up the idea of planning a fixed sequence of lessons or of learning situations and even of experimenting with learning situation with fixed constraints. It is not possible (and not even desirable, as to our aims) to impose on attentive and enthusiastic teachers some experimental constraints that compress their work in the classroom and forbid them to follow an unexpected hint aroused by pupil interaction. So, even if we use observation outcomes and techniques that are results of theoretical research, we reserve the right to adjust them because of the different aims we pursue. We are investigating neither the learning process nor the learning situation one by one, but their relationships within a long-term educational project.

We aim at documenting networks of learning situations that force the use of significant mathematical tools. The network is generated by connecting several working routes that have been planned and experimented with by the teachers involved in the project. Their colleagues draw their inspiration by the individual learning situation or by the whole working route but may decide to cross the network in a different way.

MATHEMATICAL TOOLS AND EXPERIENTIAL DOMAINS

As an early result of the research project, we have elicited some mathematical tools that may be grouped according to the set of underlying activities, as follows:

- Property of objects (activities: classifying, ordering, posing relationships).
- Early numbers (activities: comparing, counting, ordering, measuring, coding).
- Early measure (activities: comparing, quantifying).
- Space relationships (activities: exploring, locating objects, localizing).
- Time relationships (activities: ordering, exploring periodicity, exploring).

The list is not exhaustive and the groups are not mutually exclusive because a network of relationships may be drawn between their members.

Pupils' activity takes place in particular contexts (experiential domains); particularly, meanings related to mathematical tools are general within each experiential domain. Within the tradition of our schools, we have elicited some experiential domains which may be grouped according to the following headings:

- Ritual school activities. It is the whole of organizing activities that are carried on in the classroom daily (e.g., calling the roll, reading the calendar, preparing the snacks, setting the tables for lunch, and arranging the cots for nap).
- Summer holiday reconstruction. It is an early activity in the school year and aims at a retrospective reflection on the summer experiences (collecting and ordering some souvenirs; recalling the travel, as for length, means of transportation, travel companions, memoirs, differences between holiday and school activities).
- Traditional games. It is the activity of playing, explaining and representing games (e.g., counting out-rhymes, ring-a-ring-o'roses, cat-in-the-corner).
- Kitchen experiences. It is the activity of preparing some simple food or drink (e.g., cakes, orange juice, milk and coffee).
- Money experiences. (either with currencies or with fanciful coins).
- Watch and calendar readings. It is the activity of becoming acquainted with the traditional instruments of time measurement.
- Wood blocks constructions. It is the activity of playing, planning, and representing the results of a wood block game.

Besides, teachers resort to other more occasional experiences that may occur in school life or that are planned by the teachers.

Within every experiential domain, teachers choose a learning situation, that is, a task (or a sequence of tasks) related to the particular experience that forces children to use some particular mathematical tool and to build some particular meaning. In a second step, teachers foster the decontextualization of knowledge, forcing children to discuss altogether the tool in itself.

In the following sections of this chapter, we explain what kind of learning situations are useful to foster children's mathematical activity, by means of social interaction, that the children have with each other (peer interaction) and with a mathematically cultured teacher.

LEARNING SITUATIONS

A significant learning situation has some particular features that may be summarized as follows:

- It must fit for personal and scholastic history of the child, considering his or her prior experiences, opinions, and knowledge.
- It must fit for extrascholastic environment (e.g., family life, social context).
- It must consider the two aspects of learning experiences (Mellin-Olsen, 1987); the individual (intrapersonal) and the collective (interpersonal).
- It must be developed considering not only the past experience and knowledge, but even the future needs, utilizing the zone of proximal development (Vygotsky, 1962).
- It must provide and use various modes of representation that could help children in solving problems they would otherwise fail to solve.
- It must encourage children to reflect on their own learning, gaining experience of the power of thinking tools (Mellin-Olsen, 1987).
- It must foster the building of socially shared problem-solving strategies, in order to stress social aspects of knowledge.

In practice, teachers follow, even if not strictly, a general working outline that may be explained as follows:

A Priori Analysis

It is carried on by teachers (mostly in training workshops) and is related to the mathematical content, the difficulties documented as regards similar tasks, the necessary instruments, the possible connections, the possible problem-solving strategies, the educational goals, and the way of working (individual or collective).

Introductory Collective Discussion

As soon as a particular task has been chosen in a fixed context, teachers may begin the classroom experiments. Usually, the teacher begins with a collective discussion to introduce the problem. The discussion aims at (a) collecting the prior opinions and fostering early critical analysis of their effectiveness, (b) recollecting available information, and (c) motivating new experiences and the introduction of new words (Pontecorvo, Castiglia, & Zucchermaglio 1983). For instance, if the activity regards the use of various measurement instruments, possible questions are: "What does it mean measuring? When do your parents or you yourselves use this word?" If the teacher realizes that the pupils' common background is not sufficient, she proposes some experiences (such as playing freely for some time) in order to recollect prior experiences and to form a new basis of common ones.

Problem Situation

The teacher suggests a problem situation related to the particular experience. It may be (Brousseau, 1981):

1. A communication task: How may we represent the game or the situation?
2. An action task: Let's get morning snack ready!
3. A decision task: How shall we restore the balance? Why?
4. A formulation task: Let's try to describe exactly how to use a ruler!

The choice of the problem situation is very important, because it must (a) be interesting and involving for children, (b) be meaningful as for contents and for following development of mathematical knowledge, and (c) be open and arouse different strategies.

Activity

The activity takes place individually or collectively, according to a priori analysis. In this phase, pupils aim at solving the particular problem.

Coding

Children are always encouraged to represent the experience in another communication language, individually or collectively. The coding is used either in problem-solving phase (in order to plan future action) or after the problem-solving phase (in order to reconstruct the experience).

Individual Decoding

This phase may take place immediately after the coding or later, in order to discuss whether the representation tools are effective for reconstructing the experience in the memory. By having a situation in which the decoder is not the author, the ambiguity of some choices becomes more evident. This is an incentive to discuss all together and to look for better conventions.

Individual Tutoring

When some particular problem arises, the teacher draws out of the group a single child in order to give him/her an individual opportunity to discuss and to elicit difficulties. Peer interaction is often as effective as teacher work.

Whole Class Discussion

After the activity, either an individual or a small group one, it is necessary to put the individual experience into a social context. The teacher raises a whole class discussion in order to foster the development of verbal language and the mental reconstruction of the experience. In discussion, the construction of shared knowledge and the collection of something like a history of the group strategies occurs. The discussion may concern the effectiveness of the used mathematical tools in the given situation or the feature of a mathematical tool in itself. In the former case, children may discuss the use of counting strategies in solving a particular problem. In the latter case, children may wonder what numbers are and what the experiences are where numbers are useful. In the former case, children are exploring the within-concept network, whereas in the latter they are exploring the between-concept system (Lesh, Landau, & Hamilton 1983).

Retrospective Reflection

When a learning situation has been carried out in the classroom, the teacher's work is not yet finished. We ask teachers to collect children's verbal protocols and other products. This material permits a kind of retrospective reflection in order to discuss with colleagues in the training workshops the problems and the results of a particular learning situation.

Parents also are traditionally involved in discussions on educational choices and learning processes with meetings in the schools and with public shows or school newspapers collecting children's products. So, learning situations are developed in the school but are closely linked with the social environment of the children.

Examples

At first, I briefly describe a learning situation that takes place in a rich context-bound domain selected from the ritual school activities.

Consider the act of setting the table for a preschooler. In our classes the children are often responsible for setting the tables. This task requires them to be sure to provide dish, glass, spoon, fork, knife, and napkin for a child. One jug of water and one basket of bread are provided for every four children and so on.

Whereas these requirements remain the same, other factors vary, which make this indeed a challenging activity for the children. First, the numbers of children vary. Second, children may choose their own arrangement of seats at the small tables (they usually fit for six or eight children), according to their particular criteria (full every table, if possible friends shall sit together! do not allow a child to sit alone, and so on). The waiter on duty must put their choices in writing (at the very beginning after the action, but, later on, before laying the tables). Children may draw their arrangements or use a form that reproduces a map of the tables on the basis of a class agreement. In both cases, they must reproduce the significant numbers: the present children and the table companions for each table. Their drawings are saved to help the waiters in the following days. In fact, every day, children may choose whether to manage the situation by themselves or consult the collection of the drawings, look for the same number n of children or for $n + 1$ or for $n - 1$.

In this experience, we may recognize many mathematical experiences such as:

1. Cardinal number meaning construction.
2. Counting skills.
3. Exploring the number chain as from any number.
4. Regular and irregular pattern arrangements.
5. Time succession.

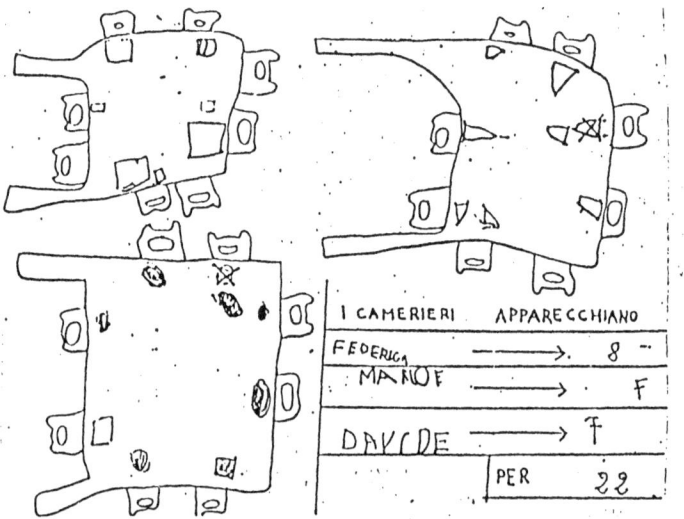

FIG. 1. In this case we have three different waiters (Federica, Mario and Davide), one for each table. The present children are 22 and their subdivision is the following: $7 + 7 + 8 = 22$

4.12. LEARNING SITUATIONS AND EXPERIENTIAL DOMAINS

6. Periodicity experiences (every day almost at the same time).
7. Space maps.

But more significant are some methodological features such as:

1. Using mathematical tools to solve a concrete problem.
2. Gaining an early knowledge of "great" numbers in their oral and written form.
3. Eliciting the criteria that have determined the choices.
4. Adapting the strategy for one's own working style and competency.
5. Planning a representation tool and assessing its effectiveness.
6. Using collective knowledge and historic records of the group in order to solve an individual task.

The previous example takes place in everyday school life and shows that even ordinary school activities may be used in a mathematics education project. Other activities may arise from experiences related to other school subjects.

For instance, within a project of science education, children were encouraged to observe and to describe some spiders and cobwebs. Then, they were asked to construct models of cobwebs (at first, big ones with cords laid on a gymnastic tool, and then small ones with cardboard support, woolen yarn, and glue). The difficulties of the children ($3\frac{1}{2}$-years-old) were not manual but conceptual, because most of them refused to fill the empty space and laid the cords and the yarns along the support sides. The same results were found in the drawings. We and the teachers discussed these results and planned a working route to explore the solid space. The steps of the route are the following:

1. Observing spiders and cobwebs.
2. Observing two-dimensional figures.
3. Filling a plane figure (what does it mean to fill a model of a dish with different materials).
4. Describing the contour of a plane figure.
5. Building a three-dimensional model of a house with cardboard.
6. Building a model of the school with occasional materials (such as boxes, cardboard tubes, pieces of wood).
7. Building a model of a house with a standard model to observe.
8. Building a model of a ship, castle, house, merry-go-round with occasional materials (small group work).
9. Drawing the built model with different points of view.

The working route has been experimented with by 4-year-old children. The results are at the disposal of all the teachers in the next workshop.

ACKNOWLEDGMENTS

The following persons who have been carrying on the research are: M. Bussi, P. Quattrocchi, P. Bandieri, P. Lancellotti. The research has been supported by the Ministero della Publica Istruzione and by the Consiglio Nazionale delle Recerche (C.N.R. grants No. 83.01358.01, 84.01953.01, 85.02615.01, 86.02112.01, 87.00960.01).

Part 5

Environment:
Elaboration Chapters

Chapter 5.1

Early Childhood Mathematics and the Environment

Romanus Ogbonna Ohuche
University of Nigeria, WEST AFRICA

My task is enormous: to elaborate on the environment with regards to mathematics learning of young children in relation to both the framework developed by the action group and two well-presented chapters by Hermine Sinclair (chap. 2.1) and Ernst von Glasersfeld (chap. 2.2).

Les Steffe (chap. 1.1) explained an environment to be the result of an assimilation. It is dependent on the particular situation or event that served in assimilation as well as on the particular conceptual operation used. An environment, then, is the individual's experience of what, from an observer's point of view, is not the individual. Sinclair (chap. 2.1) added: "All living organisms adapt to their environment and therefore tend towards an equilibrium between assimilation and accommodation. Human beings go beyond just the adaptation to an external environment. They . . . construct evermore powerful cognitive systems, which create ever wider problem spaces, and ever further possibilities and necessities for equilibration." Von Glasersfeld (chap. 2.2) elaborated: "It is an environment that teachers develop by creating what they consider constraints that are likely to guide the student to propitious accommodations. It should never be, as it unfortunately often is, an environment based on the assumption that what is obvious to the mathematical initiate will be obvious to the novice as well."

My basic approach will be to try to discuss the nature of both the early childhood mathematics curriculum and curriculum in early childhood teacher education as both relate to the environment. Indeed the position should be taken that in each case there is not just a curriculum; rather there is a progression from an intended curriculum to an attained curriculum through an implemented curriculum. At each of these levels the role of the environment would seem to be different because the variables at work are, for the most part, different. The intended curriculum is environmentally determined to the extent that different nations may prescribe different curriculum contents, and even within nations different materials and different examples may be used to interpret the prescriptions. However, for the implemented curriculum such factors as teaching agent, language, teaching technique, technology, learning environment, and evaluation are important variables, whereas for the attained curriculum the abilities, attitudes, characteristics, and interests of learners, as well as techniques of assessment are valid variables.

EARLY CHILDHOOD MATHEMATICS CURRICULUM AND THE ENVIRONMENT

The beginning point in early childhood mathematics curriculum is what I have called the *intended curriculum*. This is usually a national, regional, or local prescription of content, objectives, and suggested activities and materials. Yet, in the constructionist view, the children are expected to learn through their personal constructions. Thus, some have considered it healthier to view the intended curriculum from the perspective of setting the criteria to be used in selecting the concepts and processes that may form the basis of the activities of the learner.

Whatever is the case, it is agreed that in the years 4 to 8, number and numeration, three of the four basic operations of arithmetic (namely addition, subtraction, and multiplication), practical and descriptive geometry, and measurement are necessary contents that children may use in increasing their intuition and inquisitiveness, or, in the words of Eleanor Duckworth (1987), in "the having of wonderful ideas." Activities in the content area of number and numeration involve one-to-one correspondence, classification, counting, grouping, ordering, and experiences in parts of a whole. Among other things, such activities should enable children to move from the preoperational stage to the stage of concrete operations.

Practical and descriptive geometry at this level is expected to cover aspects of topological space, three-dimensional geometry, shapes, plane figures, and squares and other corners. Prescriptions in many countries, however, omit topological space, considered crucial experience of the young child by Piaget. Estimation is also unfortunately not prescribed by many countries at this level. What is usually expected is measurement of length, size, money, time, weight, area, and capacity. Yet, where appropriate, such measurements should be preceded by estimates.

Considerable flexibility is necessary to allow for different school environments as we move from schools that may not have enough desks for pupils to those that have mathematics laboratories and computer-assisted facilities. Yet, I am aware that because the ultimate aim of mathematical activities is abstraction, the environment factor is relatively marginal at the level of the intended curriculum.

Nevertheless, whatever curriculum guide is available, it is the teacher who has the responsibility of implementing the same in a particular classroom. What the teacher covers out of the specifications of the intended curriculum is what I have called the *implemented curriculum*. It is heavily environmentally determined because it is a function of such variables as prescribed content, the teacher, the language of instruction, teaching techniques, available educational technology, the learning environment, and the method of assessment of learning; all of which are dependent on the environment. This environmental factor was responsible for one of the major project lessons learned from the 10-year pan-African Entebbe mathematics project and the related Science Education Programme for Africa (SEPA). That lesson was that open-ended inquiry is a nonstarter in societies where children are not usually encouraged to ask questions of adults or other children. There are indeed investigations in Third World situations, which have tended to point out that individualized instruction may not be as prize-worthy in the Third World as it is in the industrialized countries of the Western world.

Consider the teacher factor. That is itself dependent on such variables as the personality, qualification, experience, attitude, interest, and values of each teacher. The hope is that these variables will interact and blend in the teachers in such a manner that they will create opportunities to enable children to have "wonderful ideas." The teacher's task is to inspire, through setting up conducive activities for meaningful investigations, creative activities. Constructivism will consider an early childhood mathematics teacher effective who will set up concrete or semiconcrete activities from the environment to enable young children to have and enjoy their "wonderful ideas" and edge naturally at their own pace toward abstract mathematical concepts and processes.

It is necessary for teachers to use materials with which children can feel naturally at home and that therefore can excite their interest and curiosity while exposing them to a great variety of mathematical activities. Although such experiences with the physical environment may be based on given contents in the implemented curriculum, the overriding objective should be to lead each child to a positive attitude towards learning and train everyone in such fundamental skills as observation, classification, computation, and measurement, as well as to increase the ability of each learner to raise questions and solve problems. The teacher has to be creative and flexible and must be willing to encourage the exploration of alternative paths of action. The teacher has to view the content of the curriculum as a vehicle that enables children to investigate their environment in order to gain some measure of understanding of the same.

Each time I write something similar to this, I get reminded of a kindergarten class of 5-year-olds in Monrovia, Liberia, about 15 years ago. The teacher came to class one day and set up two improvised butterfly nets outside her classroom because her curriculum specified butterflies. These nets ended up staying on the spot for more than 4 months and by the time they were down the children had used butterflies to count, add, subtract, classify, measure, and do other things. The class kept a record of the number of butterflies caught each day by each net. Totals of the daily catch of butterflies could thus be obtained. Then one day one of the children observed that one butterfly was not moving. It was dead. This led to tabulation of the daily loss of butterflies. Measurements of various parts were also made.

By the second week the children had their parents hunting for butterflies. In the third week one student brought a colorful caterpillar to class. The class preserved it in a jar and there were many different suggestions as to how to keep it alive. Two days later this caterpillar spun a cocoon. So, silk thread started appearing round it until the children could see only the thread. The children had to wait 2 weeks before they saw a white-winged moth come out of the silk. Then, the teacher brought another caterpillar to class. This one took 3 days to spin a cocoon and 13 more days to become a moth. Another caterpillar took 24 days to spin a cocoon. The teacher now brought two books written for young children. One was on caterpillars and the other was on butterflies. The children looked at the photographs of caterpillars going through their life cycles. The discussions that followed made each child aware that there were different types of butterflies, and they agreed that the first two caterpillars were of the same species. The children had "wonderful ideas" while learning mathematics, science, language, and other subjects.

Recently I read a lovely book by Constance Kamii. Being where I am, I suspect that many of you read the same book before me. Yet there is a fascinating summary in it that I wish to share with you at this point.

In relation to first grade she stated:

1. Number is not empirical in nature. The child constructs it through reflective abstraction from his own mental action of putting things into relationships.
2. Number concepts can be taught. While this may be bad news for educators, the good news is that number does not have to be taught, as the child constructs it from within, out of his natural ability to think.
3. Addition does not have to be taught either. The very construction of number involves the repeated addition of "1." (Kamii & DeClark, 1985, p. 25)

Continuing, the author makes the point that arithmetic cannot be taught through social transmission. Rather, the environment and social climate created by the teacher are essential for the development of logico-mathematical knowledge. The teacher's role is to create an atmosphere in which each child can reflect and reinvent numbers. Games are crucial for the achievement of this objective.

At the third level of curriculum, there is the *attained curriculum*. It is really the "it" as far as curriculum is concerned. It is the curriculum as perceived and interpreted by the learner who, in the case of early childhood mathematics, is a child. The child cannot learn what he does not want to learn and what he is not ready to learn. Again in the words of Constance Kamii, "if the child cannot construct a relationship, then all the explanation in the world will not enable him to understand the teacher's statement." What I have called the attained curriculum is dependent on such learner characteristics as achievement, aptitude, attitude, interest, and motivation, as well as on the method used in assessing what the child knows.

CURRICULUM IN EARLY CHILDHOOD TEACHER EDUCATION

It has to be taken for granted that our main objective in teaching number in early childhood is to encourage children to mathematize through reflective abstraction. This abstraction "involves the construction of relationships between/among objects." This is to be contrasted with empirical abstraction as is used, for instance, in the acquisition of length as a property when the child has to concentrate on the said property and ignore others. In either case, children have the best chance of succeeding if they are encouraged to make maximal use of the immediate environment.

Thus a teacher of young children has to be someone who can stimulate each child to make both empirical and reflective abstractions in their environments. Two conditions are necessary and sufficient. Such a teacher has to have personal confidence in relation to the subject taught, as well as to understand children in general and specific children in particular.

How should a teacher of young children be educated from a constructivist's perspective to learn mathematics, to teach mathematics to children, and to accurately assess the mathematical knowledge of children?

The beginning point of teacher effectiveness is in an understanding of the subject he or she teaches. Teachers of mathematics must also learn mathematics through the construction of logico-mathematical knowledge, which should enable them to establish relationships mentally. This is an internal experience. Thus the teachers' mathematical environment should be similar to that of the child they will teach. Reflective abstraction should be encouraged through the application of games and puzzles, and education in mathematics should include challenges in problem-solving situations. The education of teachers of mathematics at all levels, but especially those who will teach mathematics to young children, should emphasize the acquisition of competence through the exploitation of practical activities. Only then can each teacher develop enough confidence in the efficacy of practical activities.

Indeed, there should be more complementarity among the mathematicians, mathematics educators, and other educators who contribute to the education of the teacher of mathematics of young children. Teacher education should be such that foundations of education courses, mathematics content, and general mathematics teaching methods enjoy a high degree of integration. Such integration ought not be difficult if these groups of teachers (mathematicians, mathematics educators, and other educators) would adopt the techniques of teaching as their confrontation of points of view and the use of practical activities.

By implication the teacher of mathematics of young children is expected also to use confrontation of viewpoints and practical activities in teaching mathematics to them. Social interaction is a necessary condition for children to develop their natural ability to think logically, invent numbers, and solve other mathematical problems. For, according to Constance Kamii (1985) "situations in daily living and group games provide opportunities for children to think."

Indeed for sometime now I have held the view that although the ultimate goal of mathematics is abstraction, young children should approach such abstraction through concrete and semiconcrete activities rooted in their environment. Mathematical environments created for early childhood learners should include games and puzzles, especially local ones, which may be used as tools for reflective abstraction. Examples of concrete activities are the classification of concrete objects, counting pebbles, paper cutting, and shopping with play or real money. Examples of semiconcrete activities are drawing of Shongo children's networks, showing fractions on number lines, and drawing of plane figures. Claudia Zaslavsky (1973) documented some games and puzzles for Africa. The feedback from each child to himself and from other children as such activities take place encourages the development of logico-mathematical thinking.

The role of the environment in the mathematical activities in specific contexts has been treated by Gay and Cole (1967) and Ohuche (1973, 1975). Also the *African Child and His Environment* (Ohuche & Otaale, 1981) presents a documentation of classification and conservation studies as completed in Africa about 10 years ago.

It remains for me to deal briefly with the assessment of the mathematical behavior of young children. First, traditional intelligence tests fall far short of the expectations of constructivists for measures of aptitudes. In addition, in constructivism the process of learning is as important as, if not more important than, the outcome of learning. In many countries of the world the paper and pencil text/examination has become the main measure of achievement in schools and preschools. In practice such tests and examinations are summative in nature and designed to measure mostly recall of information. Constructivism would rather have techniques of assessment of young children's mathematical achievement stressing the successful completion of activities and encourage the further development of logico-mathematical thinking.

In their work with children, Piaget and his associates used three basic approaches. The first approach is the clinical interview technique. It is similar to the interviewing technique used by clinical psychologists. It encourages the children to give the interviewer an insight into their thinking while that interviewer listens, dialogues with them, and at times interjects views that may either clarify issues or appear to contradict the views of the children. The second is the observational technique. Unlike the observational techniques developed by Gessell, Piaget and his associates studied and analyzed the organization and structure of children's activities and how these are developed. Two basic tools are used: listing of children's spontaneous activities and the confrontation of individual children with tasks to solve that would enable the observer to study their reactions. The third technique has been applied successfully with older children. Here, several activities and materials play important roles in the type of understanding that prompts both the actions and verbal responses of the child.

Ideally, constructivism would expect a testing situation in which a clinical interview approach is used. This would of course be problematic in a school setting, especially if enrollment is large. Some constructivists have, therefore, tried to develop group tasks that retain fundamental elements of the clinical interview approach. Whatever the case, it is necessary to draw a distinction between traditional tests, which mostly emphasize memory, and tasks that bring out the basic structure of the child's thinking. Constructivism will apply tasks based on the immediate environment in assessing the mathematical behavior of young children.

CONCLUSION

I conclude, but not before I present briefly our Nsukka study of errors that children make in adding and subtracting numbers. Our approach was to construct tests based on the current intended national primary school mathematics curriculum and to administer them to 149 primary two pupils in the 7 to 8 age bracket, 94 primary three pupils in the 8 and 9 age bracket, 70 primary four pupils in the 9 to 10 age bracket and 74 primary five pupils in the 10 to 11 age bracket. Each class level got a test appropriate to that level. We then carried out an analysis of strategies applied by those children who indicated consistent error patterns. Results indicated nine different types of errorful procedures with a slight developmental trend. It was noted that addition and subtraction had been taught to them in terms of specific examples such as $5 + 7 = 12$ and $24 - 16 = 8$. Under such conditions they could not construct relationships and therefore failed to understand what was supposedly taught.

Thus, a mathematical environment for young children has to be viewed as a setting in which games and puzzles are available to encourage the children to develop logico-mathematical thinking. The mathematics curriculum in action for young children should be such that tasks and investigations are stressed and only teachers who are themselves educated in problem-solving and investigative approaches can meaningfully teach mathematics to children. Indeed to teach mathematics to children means to create situations that enable them to reinvent numbers and exercise their right of reflective abstraction.

Chapter 5.2

Children's Mathematics/ Mathematics for Children

Thomas E. Kieren
University of Alberta, CANADA

> *What is mathematics, that children could know it? What are children that they could know mathematics?*
> —paraphrase of McCullough, 1962

> *The task of education . . . becomes a task of first inferring models of the student's conceptual constructs and then generating hypotheses as to how students could be given the opportunity to modify their structures so that they lead to mathematical actions.*
> —von Glasersfeld, chap. 2.2

> *The movement towards better—though never perfect—knowledge of the object has as its concomitant another movement whereby subjects obtain better knowledge of their own actions or thought processes . . . the subjects reflection on their own coordinations of action leads to logico-mathematical knowledge.*
> —Sinclair, chap. 2.1

The paraphrase of McCullough (1962) sets the tone for this chapter (and indeed for the work of the entire working group). To me the questions indicate a fundamental interrelationship between mathematics as a discipline with substance, content and history, and human society in which it exists.

I see these questions orienting us to the fundamental relationship between the child as knowledge builder or grower—the child's mathematics—and the mathematics for children that she or he could know. Any mathematical environment and the environment maker must account for the human knower of mathematics and mathematics as humanly knowable. The central feature of what follows is an orientation to a set of awarenesses about the mathematical environment. This is prefaced by brief considerations of a view of mathematics itself and a view of humans as knowers that form a basis for such awareness.

MATHEMATICS

In his creative analysis of ways of mathematical thinking, Rucker (1987) borrowed from Jung the notion of an archtype and used a tetrad to show the four classical areas of mathematics. See Figure 1. If we think of mathematical environments in terms of traditional school curriculums, one could say that the curriculum was, in some way, about this tetrad. Even for young children, one could use these elements to discuss their mathematical environment. Of course number and the concomitant study of arithmetic has been and is at the heart of such environments. Even here, as noted by Freudenthal (1983), as children learn to control counting, they move toward some intuitions of the infinite. As they move from counting on schemes to part-part-whole schemes of understanding operations on whole numbers, they move toward intuitions of algebra (properties of equality and operations). And as they come to a preliminary understanding of fraction as quotient, they come to a quantitative intuition of continuous space.

Thus, this tetrad (and selected elaborations along the lines joining the four nodes) seems to represent a set of propositional truths out there to be known. Such knowing may be done by research mathematicians approaching mathematics in a classical, logical, timeless way. Or such truths may be selected, organized, and told to young children by teachers operating in a school curriculum. Yet such a view of a mathematical environment seems far from the view of von Glasersfeld (chap. 2.2) who claims that "(personal) knowledge cannot aim at truth in the traditional sense, but concerns the (personal) construction of paths of action and thinking that our unfathomable (mathematically) reality leaves open for us to tread." Nor does it seem congruent with the action coordination/reflexion knowing scheme of Sinclair (chap. 2.1) or with Maturana and Varela's (1987, p. 25) claim about human knowledge (Figure 2). It would seem that a classical view of mathematics represents a topical search for knowledge out there and that mathematics knowing for children rather than doing might be "doing what they have been told" (by hopefully benevolent adults).

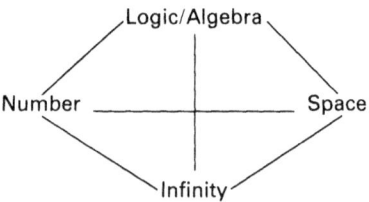

FIG. 1. An image of the classical areas of mathematics.

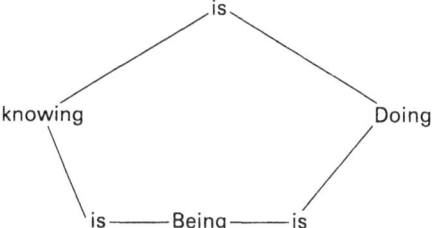

FIG. 2. The identification of knowledge and action.

A constructivist view of knowing, especially by young children, would imply a different view of mathematics. One such view of mathematics that might be more congruent is to see mathematics as the personal building of patterns involving distinguishing, modifying, and using patterns and forming patterns on patterns and patterns of patterns. Such a view of mathematics sees it as interactive with the rest of a knower's life (a source of patterns of action for reflexion) and is clearly historical in a personal sense—one's past mathematical history is a source of ways of acting and judging what one should do/know next. Finally, it is a personally active view of mathematics.

It is interesting to note that such a definition of personal mathematics is supported by current mathematical thinking. Steen (1988) saw mathematics as the seeking of patterns in number, space, science, computers, and the imagination. Furthermore, Davis and Hersh (1986) argued that under the apparent timelessness of formal mathematical propositions is their meaning, which is "bound up with application, intuition, with arrangement, with computation, with art, with mysticism—in short the whole mathematical experience" (p. 199). To them, treating mathematics as propositions dissociated with the knower is to separate mathematics from its meaning (whether this meaning be made through validating personal intuitive models or through evaluation using metamathematical arguments; Detlefsen, 1986).

Thus it would seem that for a mathematician or for a young knower, both our understanding of contemporary mathematics and our understanding of constructive knowledge building suggest a view of mathematics built on personal, historical experience of the knower.

THE YOUNG CHILD AS MATHEMATICAL KNOWER

What is the preschool or early school-age child like as a knower of such mathematics or as a maker of such patterns? It is beyond the scope of this chapter to explore this question in any depth. This is a brief discussion of the assumptions underlying later orientations to a mathematical environment of such children.

Following Maturana and Varela (1980), the young child is considered to be a composite autopoietic being—that is, the child is self-referencing and self-maintaining within a sphere of behavioral possibilities including the child's own mental activities (including mathematical ones). It is further assumed that this mental action environment is itself multifaceted, a view congruent with that of Minsky (1985).

As suggested by von Glasersfeld (chap. 2.2), promotion of growth in such a being is done through the perturbation of the sphere of behavioral possibilities. However, as Maturana and Varela (1987) argued, such perturbations (in our case of the mathematical action sphere) can be either enabling or destructive (or in fact ignored by the child) to the extent that they fit with the existing constructs held by the child. Thus building an environment for mathematical action of a child, let alone a whole class, is not a trivial activity.

There are two features of the young mathematical knower that further temper our understanding of the environment. First the child in this age range is becoming capable of abstract thought. For Maturana and Varela (1980) this means that a child can distinguish between personally held ideas and those ideas that appear driven by outside sources. Evidence for such abstraction is found in children's reactions to the following task: "When from the equal collections of chips (A and B), one (or more, N) is taken from A and added to B, children are asked which set now has more, A or B, and how many more." Sinclair (chap. 2.1) noted that children from 7 years of age can cope with this task (and even learn the $n - 2n$ generalization), whereas younger children have difficulty. It would seem that the younger children act simply on their observation/reaction to the environment, whereas the 7-year-olds act on their own idea (abstraction) of the environment. This view is congruent with Piaget (1980a) who saw a change from exogenously governed knowledge to endogenously constructed knowledge in children in the early school age range. It also related to the work of Kosslyn (1983) who saw younger children as avid visualizers.

Steffe, Cobb, and von Glasersfeld (1988) provided ideas that further clarify this distinguishing of ones own ideas (as objects for mental action). Children can run through and unitize the objects of a collection to create concepts of these objects. Re-presenting actions on such objects yields figurative items. The same mechanism allows for the creation of abstract items; that is, the figural items are unitized to create abstract items stripped of their sensory qualities. Such abstract items or ideas are in the sphere of behavior for the child and are distinguished by the child from figural or externally referenced ideas.

In forming such abstractions and building their own mathematics, children use language. Following Maturana and Varela (1980), language has an orienting function. That is, language does not carry information from speaker to listener but can serve an orienting function for the latter. In particular, language allows children to orient themselves to their own actions, particularly mental ones, thus facilitating abstraction and the use of their own patterns in the building of new patterns.

One might further speculate that young children use language in an informal manner. Adapting the ideas of Frye (1982), one might say that children use language either in the presence of their object/actions or as "put for" these object/actions. There is some indirect evidence from Steffe, Cobb, & von Glasersfeld (1988) that children also manipulate language itself in idea development; still this language appears, if independent of actions, to be an analog of such actions.

In other work (Kieren, 1988), I have characterized an ideal structure of a person's mathematical knowledge. Such knowledge was seen as an integrated structure growing from ethnomathematical knowledge (ones own mathematically related knowledge gained through everyday life experience) to intuitive mathematical knowledge (knowledge deliberately in the mathematical domain but built through a conjoint use of protomathematical thought tools—e.g., counting, dividing equally, "rationing," imagery or figural items, and the informal use of language that may well be standard mathematical language). In an ideal structure, the two informal knowledge systems would form a base for technical symbolic knowledge that derived from more formal thought actions and patterns of symbolic transformation. Finally there would be mathematical knowledge based on deductions within a set of axiomatic assumptions. Of course, one should not think of a single mathematical knowledge system for a person but many interrelated ones. Furthermore, one should not think of growth coming in four stages. These four layers only reflect various kinds of support and tools needed by the person. For young children it seems reasonable to look for mathematical environments that transcend but help them organize their own everyday phenomena in a new way (Freudenthal, 1983). Thus although school mathematical environments should, as stressed by Sinclair (chap. 2.1), allow children to use the same reflective abilities they use in everyday life (including its mathematical aspects), intuitive mathematical environments also include experience aimed at abstract objects, which are however supported by figural representations and informal language.

IMPLICATIONS FOR THE ENVIRONMENT

If a child is an active abstractor and language user in building personal mathematics—seen even for a young child as a science of patterns—what is the nature of an enabling environment for such action? What follows are several categories of awareness that a person interested in such environments should consider. Each such category is supported by a brief example taken from transcripts of mathematical conversations with 7- and 8-year-old children from research conducted by Beryl Wales (1984), and by me in 1987–1988. Because of my continuing interest in rational number knowing, most of the reported conversations revolve around the study of rational number ideas in quotient situations.

Multifaceted Knowledge

In building mathematical environments, one must be aware of the multifaceted nature of the personal, historical, growing mathematical knowledge of children. As Sinclair (chap. 2.1) points out, children do not have just one number construct, but many. This view also seems congruent with Minsky (1985), who would see a society of a person's mathematical mind and an agent that selects various constructs for use. This is illustrated in the following description of task work by children aged 7 years, 6 months to 8 years, 5 months. Three children were interviewed and observed while working on several number tasks. They had just worked on two problems with identical structure (each of which had illustrative material):

1. A farmer picked 50 eggs into a basket. He put the basket down to do other tasks. The dog came along and dumped the basket. Some eggs were broken. The farmer counted 39 eggs left. How many were broken?
2. I (the interviewer) had 10 Loonies (one dollar coins) in my pocket. I must have had a hole in my pocket because I lost some. When I got home I had 7 coins. How many were lost?

These three children (and the other 25 interviewed) all attempted to solve both problems using subtraction algorithms in the form

$$\begin{array}{r} 50 \\ -\underline{39} \end{array}$$

and all were successful at least on the second item. The children were then faced with a task that is based on the work of Comiti (1983).

> There are two bags, one with red chips and one with white chips (more than the number of red chips). Show me exactly as many white chips as red chips.

In this case there were 17 red chips and, as was the case with Comiti's children of the same age, although corresponding would have yielded the easiest solution, all three children here counted and insisted that this was the only way to do the task. They became curious as to how many more white chips there were than red chips. They counted and established that there were 22 white chips. Now they had just done tasks 1 and 2 in the manner suggested on that same day. One would have thought they would have subtracted 17 from 22. However, they found the task quite puzzling and finally one of the three, Wanda, said, "Oh, I see," and proceeded to count up from 17 to 22 making a tally on her fingers.

It is important to note that children do have, and should be enabled by our instruction to have, many constructs of the mathematical knowledge we would like them to build. Although later more sophisticated constructs might seem to displace and be "better than" earlier ones, in the ideal a child should be able to call a construct that seems to best match the needs of the situation, these needs being those of the child.

Complementarities of Understanding

One could argue that rational numbers or fractions grow out of and organize the phenomenon of sharing or dividing up. In this sense they are quantitative in nature. For the child in an everyday environment, the act of sharing is mathematically simple. If the sharable object is continuous, it means dividing up, but the concentration is on simply getting an equitable piece to all ("fair shares," which may not even be equal).

However, in a mathematical environment (an environment aimed at helping the child build constructs) the natural complementarity of form and substance of mathematical constructs becomes evident. The examples given illustrate children building new ideas (or making accommodations) one using form, the other substance.

> Hanne (age 7) was faced with the physically represented task of comparing the resulting shares when three pizzas are divided among seven persons (including Albert) and one pizza is shared among three persons (including Betty). The single question, "Who gets more (or are their shares the same)?" has been shown to be difficult even for 10- and 11-year-olds. Asking first, "How much does Albert get?" and, "How much does Betty get?" enabled 7- and 8-year-olds to work on such questions. They seemed to call up problem solving schemes from their own everyday activities.

In this case Hanne said (to two other girls), "Lets skip Albert; it's too hard." It would seem that she could not think of dividing up three objects at once in this setting and probably didn't have a practiced "seventh" action. She then said, "Betty is easy. You Y it." She then proceeded to carefully divide the "pizza" into thirds in the form of a Y on the circle image. After considerable discussion with her peers, she then looked carefully at the three-for-seven situation. She now rather quickly divided each of the three pizzas into three parts and connected each third to one of seven persons. She then divided the remaining two-thirds piece together into seven parts and announced, "Albert gets more. He gets one-third and a bite." (All of her actions had been a complete puzzle to the other two girls.)

What is critical here is that Hanne did not appear to know how to divide three among seven (and didn't seem to have "seventh" as an abstract item). She became aware of her own knowledge of "thirding," which seemed to be an abstraction for her. She now "called" this abstraction and used its *form* in the three-for-seven situation leaving her with a now dividable piece. One might say that she had for herself replaced the substance of "thirding" with its form which in this case was not a standard symbol, but a geometric sign ("Y").

It would appear that Hanne's knowledge of the form of thirding (that is its sign representation) engendered an accommodation which itself was not yet a new form but was substantially correct. Here the child uses the form of an old pattern to engender the substance of a new one.

> Robert (age 8) worked with Don and Kath in the following fraction comparison setting. Albert and one other person share three pizzas. Six persons including Betty share nine pizzas. The same quantitative and comparison questions are asked as before.

All three children immediately seized on the fact that in the first situation "half" can be used. They all agree to divide the three pizzas into halves and indicate that three such pieces go to each person.

They then turn to the nine for six situation and all try to use the "form" of halving with the nine pizzas. They simply repeat the half pattern on all nine pizzas. Then all become lost trying to assign pieces to persons, and Don and Kath give up. Robert asks for a clean sheet to try again. Now he appears to revert to the *substance* of finding the quotient. He indicates that one whole pizza should go to each of six persons. He then uses half and divides the remaining three into two parts. He assigns one of these 6 halves to each person. To confirm this reattention to the substance of finding a quotient (as opposed to the form of "half"), Robert then goes back to his previous sharing of three among two. Now he circles one whole pizza and indicates it goes to Albert and one whole to the other person. The remaining middle pizza, already halved, is shared between the two.

Thus we have illustrated that in mathematical environments, children can understand in terms of both form and substance. Mathematical constructs that are abstractions beyond everyday experience should be both formal and substantial for children. Form and substance are essential complimentarities in mathematical patterns, and mathematical environments need to take this into account.

Mathematical Variations and Complementarities

The example in the preceeding section emphasized that general knowing actions used by children in building mathematical patterns or knowledge are both formal and substantial in nature. However, mathematical environments, which are connected but that are elaborations of childrens' everyday (mathematical-logical) worlds, force children to confront variations and complementarities in mathematical patterns and concepts themselves.

For example, although a child sharing cake with friends may divide up a substance and simply assign (correspond) pieces to persons, in an intuitive figural representation of such a situation, a child is confronted with both quantity and ratio. For example, the act of cutting a cake into four parts immediately faces the child with both quantity (size of piece) and number (of pieces). When the act of dividing up, say among two persons, is done, each share itself is a quotient or quantity (½ a cake) and a ratio (two of four pieces). Children have to be faced with and come to control fractions both as quantity and ratio. They must grow to see their fraction construct as a complimentarity of these features. Mathematically, of course, this is not surprising. The axiomatic structure "governing" rationals, that of a quotient field, has as its central feature that rationals are quotients equated as ratios.

Mathematical environments for children should feature such variations and complimentries. In the realm of number, it is important that fraction constructs that should grow out of the everyday logical experience of sharing (muchness) should not be subsumed by whole number constructs (manyness) even though one can do so in adult logical terms. Because fractional numbers connect with a related but different everyday logic than that of whole numbers (as well as are elements of a different axiomatic pattern), it is important that this variation not be environmentally reduced to an extension of whole number instruction or thinking.

Development

Much has been said and written about the need in a mathematical environment to account for individual differences. For young children this is vividly so. The early school years represent a time of many well-known developmental changes affecting the ability to make various levels of mathematical abstractions.

For example, a rectangle representing a cake was (easily) "cut" into eight equal pieces (by folding) by groups of 7- and 8-year-olds. The pieces were identified with children's names. The children were then faced with the following challenge.

A	B	C	D
E	F	G	H

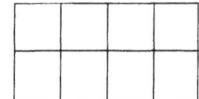

Can you cut *one piece* of the other cake which is as big as piece____and piece____put together.

There was tremendous variation in children's responses to this item, and these were dependent on which pieces were to be combined. For example, most but not all of this group ($n = 28$) of 7- and 8-year-olds could successfully cut one piece the same size as B and E together (most said they just slid B on top of E in their heads and made a cut like it). Although a few children appeared to know that any two pieces together could be matched by the same cut piece, most found the combination B and G or F and H very difficult to match with a single cut piece on the second cake.

It is not the purpose of the previous example to describe developmental differences empirically or to pose a test for such. As I used this task as part of an environment to face children with fractions as quantities, it did become clear to

Potential for Pattern of Pattern Growth

The previous section orients one to the impact of historical and developmental variations in children's responses to mathematical tasks and hence to potential "limitations" on the environment for any individual child at a particular point in time. However, if one views mathematics as the study of patterns and the person as a maker/distinguisher of such patterns, then in building the environment, one needs to be aware of the potential in young children for growth through the use of patterns of their own patterns. Because mathematics involves form and the language of a symbol system, such patterns of patterns can be substantial (and for these children concrete or figural in nature) or formal (dealing with interiorized and/or symbolic) patterns.

In working with a "cake problem" similar to one presented earlier, three 8-year-olds, Charles, Sylvia, and Shawn, took a cake cut in eighths and further subdivided (by folding) the cake into 32 equal parts. They worked on a number of cake sharing situations of their own making and seemed to enjoy using the language of eighths, sixteenths, and thirty-seconds to discuss various quantities. To end the sessions, I displayed a rectangle that was half a cake and asked, "How many thirty-seconds make a half?" All three thought for a few seconds (and likely did not count, although I can't be sure) and responded 14, 18, and 20. These were obviously very good estimates. Then Charles said, "I know it exactly." He then pointed to four thirty-seconds in clockwise order on the paper and said, "Four thirty-seconds make an eighth." Then repeating the same pointing pattern in the air, said, "And 4 eighths make a half, so four times four make 16 thirty-seconds make a half."

Thus in setting a mathematical environment, one must be aware of the limitations of the knowers but also the inherent pattern making power of knowers.

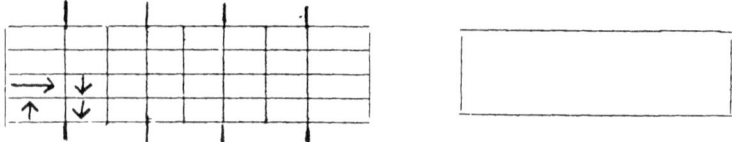

FIG. 3. Finding how many thirty-seconds make a half.

CONCLUDING REMARKS

In one of the opening quotations in this chapter, von Glasersfeld (chap. 2.2) saw the task of education (or environment setting) as inferring the current state of each student's constructs (or pattern making in an area of mathematics) and generating hypotheses as to situations (environments) that would allow students to modify these constructs toward better or richer mathematics. This means that the environment must contain both "devices" to help with such state of inferring and help students grow from their current mathematical states.

Such environments and devices should among other things take into account the five orientations already discussed:

1. Children's mathematical constructs or pattern-making capabilities are and should be multifaceted.
2. Children's mathematical actions should take into account the complementarity of form and substance.
3. Mathematics for children should help them with fundamental variations and complementarities in mathematical patterns.
4. Children's mathematics and actions are limited at any time by their development and experience.
5. Mathematics for children should allow for and develop the fantastic power of children making patterns on and of patterns.

A natural source of pattern-making material comes from everyday experience with (mathematical) patterns of number and space; thus the "topic" areas in a mathematical environment for children need not radically change. Nor do these orientations suggest that the mathematical language in the environment be reduced or eliminated. In fact, such language, informally used, gives the child pattern-making power. The original assumptions and these orientations do suggest that prematurely symbolic tasks in arithmetic or about space are likely destructive of children's mathematics and should not play a central part in mathematics for children. Mathematics for children (as developed by children themselves, teachers, curriculum builders or researchers) should account for and help further develop the children's mathematics.

ACKNOWLEDGMENTS

Some of the ideas in this chapter arose from lively discussions with Susan Pirie at the University of Warwick and Les Steffe at the University of Georgia. Partial Support for the research reported in this chapter from SERAL grant, Faculty of Education, University of Alberta.

Chapter 5.3

What Could Teacher Education Be Like for Prospective Teachers of Early Childhood Mathematics— with Particular Reference to the Environment

Leone Burton
Thames Polytechnic, UNITED KINGDOM

In preparing teachers for early childhood education, there are some deeply held beliefs that must be challenged: (a) the belief in simplicity; (b) the belief in enjoyment; (c) the belief in reality; and (d) the most powerful, the empty vessel belief. I address each of these in turn and, in the process, speak to the role of the teacher in constructing an environment that supports and develops a child's mathematical constructs.

THE SIMPLICITY BELIEF

Permeating our teaching of mathematics is an assumption that because the subject becomes more and more complex, the learning of the subject must develop from simple to difficult. So, very young children are confronted with mathematics carefully structured to acknowledge its development. Thus, for example, children will first be taught simple subtraction of one-digit numerals, followed by subtraction of two-digit numerals with decomposition, and so on. Furthermore, subtraction will be dissociated from its links with addition (and certainly from its links with division) and treated as an algorithm operating in a vacuum. I want to suggest that, for a learner, coming to terms with any one of the stages identified by a teacher might be more or less complex, depending on the current state of that child's mathematical experience. Although the mathematics might be simple, the learning task can be highly complex. At the same time, paradoxically, however, an expectation of complexity can be confronted by a child working confidently and competently at a mathematical task that has not, apparently, been encountered before in the classroom.

Confronting the simplicity myth in teacher education implies that prospective

5.3. WHAT COULD TEACHER EDUCATION BE LIKE

teachers need to be placed in situations in which they can observe and listen to small groups of children exploring the complexity underlying their mathematical observations and, at the same time, demonstrating through discussion their current state of understanding. In this way, future teachers develop the skills of closely observing and using their mathematical behaviors to inform decisions about a child's state of knowledge, skills, and processes. Teachers learn that children's learning conforms to the dictates of common sense, the common sense that is available to children whose knowledge reflects their experience. Central to a reconstruction of that knowledge is a set of experiences that challenges the current state of their understanding. That is, in von Glasersfeld's terms, the current state of knowledge must be insufficient for the pursuit of the present goal, confronting the child with the need to modify that state. Described in this way, the complexity of demands becomes apparent. There is complexity for the child because the reconstruction process will be challenging, possibly difficult, and initially resisted. There is complexity for the teacher in creating the environment most conducive to initiating and sustaining the necessary challenge. The alternative is to present children with knowledge and skills defined by adults and ease them into a use of that knowledge and those skills by modeling 'correctness'. This style of teacher behavior, frequently encountered, is predicated on the assumption referred to by von Glasersfeld that "what is obvious to the mathematical initiate will be obvious to the novice as well." Daily experience in classrooms refutes this assumption.

When working with a group of 7-year-old children who had been using apparatus to build up and break down numbers, the teacher asked the children to make some sums (sic) of their own and write them down. She asked them to start with a number smaller than 10, and the children suggested 8. She then asked for a number under 8. Children's responses included 8 - 5, 8 - 4, and 8 - 7. However, one child wrote,

$$\begin{matrix} 8 \\ 4 \end{matrix}$$

explaining that the 4 was under the 8. The same child, when asked to take away 8 from 10, rubbed out the 8. The teacher commented, "It is very easy to rush the children into working without apparatus. One must keep on using it until absolutely certain that the child understands the principle of taking away" (Ensor & Malvern, undated).

In my view, this child was attempting to deal with the situation in which she was placed by responding very literally to the words she heard because, for her, the task itself carried no meaning. Complexity, for this child, lay in attempting to interpret the meaning of instructions. There is no information about her skill in handling a task of subtraction of single-digit numerals. The teacher, on the other hand, had an agenda that assumed that the task was meaningful for all the children with whom she was working. Faced with apparently bizarre behavior, the teacher invoked belief in reality and simplicity to explain it away.

The following exchange between a 4-year-old and his teacher is recorded in Vivian Paley's *Wally's Stories:*

> "We have three 12s in this room," Wally said one day. "A round 12, a long 12, and a short 12. . . The round 12 is the boss of the clock, the long 12 is the ruler, and the short 12 is on the calendar."
> "Why is the 12 on the calendar a short 12?" I asked.
> "Me and Eddie measured it. It's really a five. It comes out five on the ruler."
> "You mean it's five inches from the edge of the calendar?"
> "Right. It's five." Wally stared thoughtfully at the clock.
> "I'm like the boss of March because my birthday is March 12. The 12 is on the top of the clock." (Paley, 1981.)

It is not too difficult to imagine a response to Wally's first statement along the lines of—but 12 cannot have a shape; it tells you how many—which would be enough to ensure that the nature of the child's thinking about numbers would remain hidden. Of course it would not be changed by such an interjection, just repressed away from adult sight and hearing. Instead, the teacher's question seeking information and elucidation makes clear that for Wally, spatial positioning is at this moment far more important than what is being positioned. In contrast, there follows a discussion, reported by Desforges and Cockburn (1987), between an experienced teacher and a 6-year-old after the child had been asked to draw something fat:

> Mrs. E: Now this was quite a good idea but I wonder who knows what it is (holding a picture up). Andrew?
> Andrew: A fat square.
> Mrs. E: It looks like a fat square, doesn't it? You can't really have fat squares if you think about it. (p. 72)

It is a fundamental shift for a person training to be a teacher, or indeed for an experienced teacher working with young children to accept what a child says as their best possible pass at making sense of their world. Furthermore, acceptance implies an intrusion on the artificialities, such as syllabus, curriculum, or test, that we invent to sustain the game of school. By accepting a child's offering, we open the door to working with that child in an area that is meaningful but problematic. This frequently is inconsistent with a previous decision what today's lesson will be about. It requires considerable confidence and understanding to abandon a plan and allow children to dictate the direction of their own questioning.

I believe that an important move towards offering children this kind of autonomy is to provide the kind of activities in the classroom that encourage personal interpretation in a group learning context. This encourages the clash and consideration of conflicting understandings rather than, as conventionally, struggling to remove ambiguities and sanitizing the mathematical thinking. With young children this usually means relying on an oral, rather than a written, introduction and expecting and encouraging a physical representation through materials. By oversimplifying and overconstructing the learning pathway, we permit only our own style of learning and we retain control of what may be learned and, often, try to retain control of how. By releasing that control, we allow children to reinterpret the task, to bring it close enough to their level of understanding in order to be able to do something with it, but also to experiment creatively if they feel so inclined. In these ways, the learning becomes a natural function of their interaction with a strange, inexplicable and wonderful world rather than an externally imposed demand lacking the logic of connection or need.

THE BELIEF IN ENJOYMENT

Trainee teachers assume, quite correctly, that miserable or unhappy children will have much greater difficulty in learning at school than those children who are enjoying what they do and are at ease in the classroom. Unfortunately, however, there is often little reflection on what is meant by enjoyment, what its qualities are particularly in the context of learning, and how these might be sustained. I suspect that in the United Kingdom this is one of the results of a low-status profession attracting entrants who frequently have not themselves experienced intellectual control and challenge. Consequently, they have not experienced the associated satisfaction and enjoyment when that challenge is dealt with. It is crucial to teacher education, therefore, that students not only have the experience of meeting mathematical challenges, but also the pedagogic discipline of analyzing the outcome of those meetings, both for their learning potential and for their classroom implications. Central to such experiences is, I believe, the process of reflection, which needs to be institutionalized within the framework of the mathematical education program.

Frequently, I am told by experienced teachers how much their classes are enjoying the latest mathematical scheme and, therefore, how much better it is than whatever it has replaced. I am sure that children do develop consumer loyalty to certain schemes, but the reason for this loyalty rarely has anything to do with learning mathematics. More often, the new books are more brightly colored than the old, have less writing on each page, feature well-designed and illustrated pages, and so on. In the United Kingdom, the recent trend has been towards individualized learning so that, instead of a whole class being issued the same book, children work through a scheme at their own pace. In the same classroom, one child can be on a book designated as more advanced while another works from a book that precedes it in the hierarchy of difficulty. Having one's own book elicits a personalized feeling although it also induces competition to finish more books. It decreases the number of opportunities for children to work together and listen and learn from one another. In addition, it is the nature of prepackaged learning that it cannot respond to the kinds of interpretative possibilities that were discussed earlier.

Trainee teachers and teachers in in-service courses are encouraged to re-think the role of the classroom scheme. One method is to place them in a situation with a group of children and a challenge. For example, Brissenden (1988) reported on an activity given to four 4-year-olds in a reception class. The children were asked to find all the combinations of red and orange Unifix cubes, which would make five cubes in a row. The following dialogue occurred:

Peter: I put that first—I've got three red and two orange.
Steven: I've got the same as you, but I've got three orange and two red.
Jodie: I've only got one red and I've got four orange.
Charlene: I've got the same as Peter.
Steven: Look, I've got all red this time so now all we need is all orange and then we've finished. (p. 124)

The activity was repeated to find the missing number stories.

Using a transcript such as the previous one as a stimulus, students can first of all attempt the activity themselves. Then, they try the activity in a classroom with a similar group of children and record all their observations. The aim is, first, to encourage them to analyze the mathematics and the mathematical thinking that was necessary to attempt the activity. Then, in addition, to convince them that children will engage with activities that are purposeful and will pursue mathematical inquiries even though there is no contributory adult. Moreover, they can be challenged to decide how to respond to the children's results, how to test their decisions about what the children understand from what they have done and what kind of activity would be appropriate as a next challenge to this group of children. Most importantly, the students have the experience themselves, and then follow it by observing the children behaving similarly. The components of the experience that are central to learning are:

1. Accessibility—an activity has to be couched in terms that make it possible for a learner to interpret its demands and embark on some action; really useful activities are equally accessible to those with widely different levels of mathematical sophistication. I have watched 9-year-old children, as well as M.Sc. level mathematics, try the Milk Crate problem: 18 bottles and placed in a 6×4 milk crate so that every row and every column has an even number of bottles in it. The children are far more inventive in developing the problem! (Burton, 1980)

2. Engagement—an activity that does not provoke enough interest to motivate learners to pursue an inquiry is hard to defend;

3. Intellectual challenge—learners respond positively to a feeling of being extended by the thinking that an activity demands of them;

4. Satisfaction that comes from surmounting the challenge. Children will say,

reflects an apparent confusion between the concreteness of the representational form that is offered to a child and the unreal mathematical relation that it is representing. A box of Cuisanaire rods or a set of Dienes Multibase Arithmetic Blocks are real objects. It is an altogether different matter what they represent for the child, if anything. Children have been observed obtaining correct solutions to number questions such as $7 + 3 =$, using Cuisenaire rods as a form of infant adding machine when they cannot explain what is happening with the numerals that the rods are presented as representing. They also can be observed exploring complex relations, say about fractional numbers, when the rods are used not as a replacement or representation of mathematical abstraction but as interesting objects with certain mathematical attributes, and where the mathematical abstractions are realities.

This notion of real world and mathematical abstract world, which for many teachers of young children is an algorithm for placing the child into a mathematically abstract context supported by some form of concrete representation, is a fundamental misconception. The reality of the world of concrete representation can be reality for a child only if it carries meaning for that child. Any abstractions that are then invoked by the child are a result of that child's construction of personal meaning out of the context. It is not a matter of holding a child using concrete apparatus until abstraction is possible, as if this were a linear procedure, but rather of always recognizing the need to slip in and out of representations in exactly the same way as particular examples are used to enhance the meaning of a generalization. (See, for example, Sinclair, chap. 2.1, and von Glasersfeld, chap. 2.2).

Furthermore, there is the reality invoked by projects such as USMES of so-called 'real mathematics', that is, children undertaking to tackle an issue in their environment, which is amenable to mathematical modeling and problem solving. The most frequently cited examples of this latter interpretation are running a school fete or sports day, reorganizing the school dinner queue, or creating a school garden.

There is, in addition, another reality that the previous interpretations ignore and that is the reality of the inner world of the child. It is, I believe, that reality that overrides others when children's reactions in the mathematics classroom are apparently bizarre or out-of-context. It is also that reality that underlies the stimulation and interest that children will show in tackling puzzles and diversions of a pure mathematical kind. When the 4-year-olds mentioned earlier were investigating the number of different combinations of red and orange rods to make five, the artificiality of the question did not intrude on the reality of their activity. Indeed, because children enjoy thinking about numerical and spatial information, their games and puzzle books are full of mathematically based activities.

Classroom reality, therefore, must accommodate to the child's inner reality, as well as provide an external environment that enables the child to build a mental bridge to the experienced world. There are two messages here for the classroom teacher. The first is to make use of activities in the mathematics classroom that enable children to control their own learning and to confront their own needs. These activities include mathematical puzzles and diversions, as well as projects using mathematical modeling. That is, their reality to the child will be as vivid whether they are 'pure' or 'applied' so long as it is within the child's choice to interpret and implement the activity. The second is to make use of the children's engagement in order to observe and learn about the child's understanding and needs.

THE EMPTY VESSEL BELIEF

The view of mathematics pervading schools and, particularly, school texts is of a codified body of knowledge and skills. Belief in the power of that codified collection is related to the mechanistic and technological society that it has partly been responsible for creating for us. Far from recognizing the ingenuity, creativity, and inventiveness displayed by people, this view reifies the knowledge and the skills. As a result, in schools children are force-fed knowledge and skills according to a timetable that is usually laid down by authorities outside the school. Innovative and creative children often become "low-attainers" in mathematics because they cannot or will not perform in the manner subscribed. Conforming children are so described because they willingly become the objects of didactic teaching styles that rely on a transmission model of learning. X knows something that Y must learn. It is X's job to fill Y up with the knowledge/skills. It is Y's job to reproduce that knowledge on demand. There is no recognition within this model that X and Y might, or might not, share the same perception of the knowledge/skill that Y's current state of knowledge/skill might be too far away from the requisite knowledge/skill to make its acquisition meaningful.

The assumption that children come to the classroom empty of all mathematical knowledge and skills other than what has previously been taught (and often empty of that too) is a denial of observable experience. Children are extremely adept at deriving, using, and transforming knowledge especially that which they encounter in situations in which they are wholeheartedly involved. For example, knowledge of the language of space travel (weightlessness, gravity, orbit, etc.) was rapidly acquired through media presentations, fictional and nonfictional, and surfaced in classrooms before teachers had considered the syllabus implications. More than once I have stumbled on serious discussions of a mathematico-philosophical nature taking place between unsupervised children such as two 8-year-olds who were discussing the nature of infinity. Rowlands (1984) drew attention to the ways in which children in control of their own activities make

> predictive propositions . . . supported by argument and tested. The process of framing such hypotheses places the child at a stage removed from direct and concrete experience. It involves not only such questions as: "What will happen

if . . . ?" which may be no more than an expression of curiosity, but also: "Which of these possible explanations is the correct one?" "How can I discover this?" Such questions are suggestive of an inquiry which is systematic and "formal" in the Piagetian sense. (p. 78)

So, far from being empty vessels, children in the classroom have as much going on in their minds as adults do and are constantly attempting to make sense of what they currently hold in the light of what is being encountered. As I have said, what they currently hold is partly a function of out-of-school experience. But, as the error literature in mathematics, or Repair Theory as outlined by Brown and van Lehn (1980), has amply demonstrated, within-school experience provides input that cannot always be relied on to be interpreted in the way in which the teacher expects. Particularly noticeable is that teachers subscribe to a belief in children's knowledge but behave as though that knowledge is either unimportant or inoperable. Whereas, examining the reasons that children give for current mathematical behavior underlines the recognition that they are attempting to package new learning into old mental constructs and that sometimes previous learning results in mis-learning. The simplest example was referred to earlier, the usual development in the teaching of subtraction; first single-digit subtraction, then double-digit subtraction and finally double-digit subtraction requiring decomposition ($9 - 4 =$, $29 - 14 =$, $24 - 19 =$). The child who has correctly dealt with examples similar to the first two but whose response to the third example, $24 - 19$, is 15 is correctly applying a piece of mis-learning, which was unplanned by the teacher and unaccounted in the previous correct response. That was that you always take the smaller numeral from the larger. This rule produces only incorrect responses in the third case. In a very real sense, the child who has 'learnt' this rule can be said to have been 'taught' it even though it was never featured in a lesson plan! In this sense, prior experience acts most powerfully to override current learning.

Two kinds of learning therefore provide data to falsify the empty vessel belief, the learning accomplished out of formal lessons and the unaccounted learning accomplished in formal lessons. Both can be accommodated by a teacher who shifts in teaching style from a transmission model to a facilitating model. Both can be most effectively used in the teacher education process as a means of establishing the need for different learning and teaching styles.

CONCLUSION

Implicit in the dismantling of the four beliefs outlined is a move towards teaching and learning in a different way. This has been emphasized in the use of particular words, some of which related to teachers' and some to pupils' behavior.

The teacher has a responsibility for setting up a classroom environment in which pupils are challenged to reconstruct their understandings and to learn from those reconstructions. Underlying this kind of environment is a view of the curriculum that is distinct from the syllabus. Whereas a syllabus is a list of desirable knowledge/skills, the achieved curriculum is demonstrated by the pupils' engagement and resultant understandings. A teacher is in no position to dictate that output in advance. So, defining the curriculum for each individual child is a post hoc task for the teacher. The teacher does this by closely observing and listening to children as they engage with the challenges provided and discuss their actions. Central to this style of teaching/learning is social interaction, control, and personal interpretation within a group. Equally important is for the teacher to interact with children intermittently and not to dominate the exchanges or the interpretations. Finally, the practice of reflection by both teacher and pupils must be institutionalized so that everyone recognizes the process whereby knowledge and skills are acquired. Instead of rushing headlong through a mathematics program, impelled to move on to the next page or next book, pupils need space to stop and consider what is new about their current state, what they still do not understand, and so on. Teachers need space to consider the surprises with which certain pupils have confronted them, other pupils mathematical needs, and the abilities, knowledge, and skills demonstrated by some pupils. Only after they have considered this information, are they in a position to make decisions about future action.

Teacher education programs need to focus on all forms of pupil material in classrooms as well as video, transcripts, writings, and tapes to engage students with the implications of providing pupil challenges and then observing and collecting data about the outcomes. Recognition of the ceiling that mathematics schemes can place on children's mathematical behavior, constraining them to perform within prescribed limits, is the first step towards liberating them to learn and use mathematics in imaginative ways. As a group of teachers participating in the Calculator Aware Number (CAN) Curriculum aspect of the Primary Initiatives in Mathematics Education Project wrote:

- Given the freedom to explore mathematics with the calculator children do things 'out of order,' because they are no longer constrained by their ability to calculate with pencil and paper.
- Much of the traditional number curriculum was based on the acquisition of pencil and paper methods for calculation. The CAN Curriculum sweeps all that aside, and replaces it with a greater emphasis on understanding number, and on carrying out number operations both mentally and with the calculator.
- We can no longer speak with confidence about what children are capable of understanding. Young children use large numbers, exhibit an understanding of place value, make use of negative numbers. All these have happened through the use of a calculator without the formal teaching of the topic.
- We are now interested in children developing process skills, such as those found in a problem solving and investigative approach to mathematics learning. (PRIME Project, 1987, p. 21)

Discussion Chapters: Mathematics Curriculum

Chapter 5.4

Curriculum and Constructivism in Early Childhood Mathematics: Sources of Tension and Possible Resolutions

Neil A. Pateman
Deakin University, AUSTRALIA

David C. Johnson
Eastern Michigan University, USA

After spending the first session in plenary and the second session as part of the subgroup entitled environment, the discussion group concerned with mathematics curriculum in early childhood education met for 1½ hours on each of the mornings of Day 6 and Day 7 of the Congress. The topics discussed included the notion of curriculum itself and how different it would need to be in a constructivist framework, the basic ideas of constructivism, the mathematical content suitable for early childhood, the problems involved in engaging teachers with curriculum reform, the political nature of curriculum reform, the place of a philosophy of mathematics and its teaching in curriculum reform, professional development of teachers, and ever-present concerns about assessment and evaluation.

The brief for the group was to establish areas of concern for those interested in developing early childhood mathematics curriculum from a constructivist perspective and to make recommendations related to those concerns as a consequence of its discussions. As a means of focusing its work, the group was expected to center on three generative questions provided by the panel that organized the action group:

1. What might "mathematical curriculum" mean? (And how is it related to the knowledge of children and teachers?)
2. What do we mean by "possible mathematical environments" and how do they relate to curriculum?
3. How can teachers establish a possible mathematical environment to facilitate the children's construction of some part of their mathematical knowledge?

5.4. SOURCES OF TENSION AND POSSIBLE RESOLUTIONS

From the outset it was apparent that group members had widely diverging backgrounds and interests. The strongest feature of the subgroup was the many differing ideas that were aired and discussed, ranging from the relatively free form of early childhood mathematics curriculum in most English and some Australian schools, to the understandable immediate professional concerns of a textbook representative and a curriculum director, both from the United States. The concerns of the textbook representative were essentially related to perspectives generated from the perceived reality that in the United States (and in many other countries, although to differing degrees) each teacher relies almost exclusively on a single textbook (usually the same textbook series within a particular school) as directly providing the mathematics curriculum for that teacher's grade. How will a constructivist outlook change what now goes by the name "textbook"? Whose responsibility is it to initiate and carry out such changes? The concerns of the curriculum director were not identical but sprang from a similar source; the reality is that teachers expect to be provided with some kind of prospective curriculum document. How will such a document look if it is to embody constructivist principles? Who should have the responsibility for writing such a document?

Some things the group tacitly agreed on in relation to mathematics in early childhood education are that mathematics is a social construction, not an externally determined body of objective knowledge; that at the early childhood level, teaching concepts by transmission is inappropriate; that at all levels the teacher's knowledge of mathematics is a critical factor as is the teacher's willingness to accept that their own knowledge will change through interaction with children; and that children's natural language is an important communicative device right from the beginning.

This chapter attempts to briefly outline the response of the group to the three framing questions asked by the organizing panel and then to document those issues that seemed of most concern to the group. These issues emerged from the exchanges that took place during the meetings of the group as its members directed their attention to the framing questions. Wherever possible we intend to focus on points of tension between the two principal ideas of interest to the members who chose to participate in this section of the action group: curriculum and constructivism.[1] Many comments made by group members were obviously influenced by presentations in the sessions of the action group prior to the meetings of this subgroup. Some attempt will be made to trace the genesis of lines of thought and issues to the earlier presentations and discussions.

---

[1] This account is our attempt to make meaning of the proceedings; the reader is interacting with their reconstruction of events. Such a reconstruction is markedly different from the actual events; we cannot help but selectively filter some of the information and to entirely lose other pieces of it. The risk that something we perceived as incidental may well have been important commentary must be taken! Such are the vagaries of human interaction in the struggle for communication.

REACTIONS OF THE GROUP FRAMED IN THE PERSPECTIVE OF THE ORGANIZING PANEL'S QUESTIONS

What Might "Mathematical Curriculum" Mean? (And How Is It to Be Related to the Knowledge Of Children and Teachers?)

In an earlier joint session of the action group, Leone Burton (chap. 5.3) makes a case for distinguishing between *syllabus* and *curriculum*. From her viewpoint a syllabus is the prospective document (prewritten, so forward-looking), whereas curriculum for her is what is apparently in place after implementation (written after the fact, as a historical document perhaps). This distinction would not be so easily accepted in the relatively new fields of curriculum theory and curriculum evaluation. In these growing fields, a syllabus is little more than a topic outline together with references to a textbook. A curriculum for most theorists in the fields mentioned is also meant to convey much more than content covered and methods used.

Following up, Steffe (chap. 5.8) makes a comment that has far-reaching implications for those wishing to attempt to develop constructivist curricula for learning mathematics. He says something to the effect that we know the effects of what we are currently doing only in retrospect; that is, after reflection on the perceived events in the classroom. He goes on to comment that we cannot separate environment, curriculum, and learning; we act together to create content, we cannot create experience for others, and we must understand that curricula are created in environmental situations. These ideas form part of the basis of his concept of the "abstracted curriculum."

With this as background from the earlier sessions, the question of the nature of curriculum was by far the most perplexing of the three major concerns for the group and the one that was most discussed. Right from the outset there was disagreement about the definition of the term *mathematical curriculum*. There is no general agreement amongst educators about the meaning of the word *curriculum*, as its appropriation is still contested in education. There are those who insist that we must take into account all the experiences a child undergoes in the course of schooling, including those coming under the heading of the *hidden curriculum*, a term meant to include unrecognized elements of the child's daily activities in and out of school hours. Many suspect that children pick up on messages unintentionally delivered by teachers, parents, and peers. Such all-encompassing definitions certainly regularize the undeniably substantial contributions of so-called extracurricular activities, but leave us with an insurmountable documentation problem.[2] In the case at hand, we are faced with the notion of defining the term *mathematical curriculum*, something perhaps doubly contentious.

---

[2]An important question to consider here is how we can either prospectively define a useful

What Do We Mean by "Possible Mathematical Environments" and How Do They Relate to Curriculum?

The possibility that a classroom could be regarded at times as a mathematical environment was novel to many members of the group. However, many indicated that their ideas of how mathematics might be developed in small children were not at all inconsistent with thinking about the provision of materials and situations as constituting an environment for stimulating and sustaining mathematical growth. This question easily merged into the next.

How Can a Teacher Establish a Possible Mathematical Environment to Facilitate the Child's Construction of Some Part of His or Her Mathematical Knowledge?

The way in which this question was framed allowed the group to focus indirectly on the idea of constructivism itself as a way of structuring how one thinks about mathematics and its teaching at a fundamental level. Part of the problem has already been discussed in the response to the first broad question. The starting point for group discussion on this question was provided by von Glasersfeld (chap. 2.2), Sinclair (chap. 2.1), and Leino (chap. 3.1), who each clearly advocate constructivism as an appropriate guiding framework for teaching mathematics to children at the early childhood level. For each of these three, the most effective environment for mathematical learning would be one planned from constructivist principles. The question of what constitutes a mathematical environment is hardly addressed!

ISSUES THAT AROSE DURING THE GROUP'S DISCUSSIONS

The Nature of Constructivism

Consider the following notions:

> You cannot convey meaning from language alone. Some processes *cannot* be directed, others can—it is the teacher's role to decide. (von Glasersfeld, chap. 2.2)
>
> Actual situations leading to specific logicomathematical knowledge are not known yet. Children must organize their own interactions into knowledge about the world. (Sinclair, chap. 2.1)

---

curriculum document or successfully document a curriculum history, with so broad a definition of curriculum as our starting point. It seems important to make every effort to make it very clear what the term *curriculum* is to mean in our context.

Von Glasersfeld makes it very clear that there are two beliefs to be set aside if one is to begin to understand how to build constructivism into a mathematics curriculum. These beliefs are (1) language transfers knowledge, and (2) our invariants must be the invariants of others. He takes the position that we can know the knowledge of others only by using our own conceptual elements and that conceptual structures cannot be transported from the head of one person to the head of another by the use of language. We must each make our own meaning, and we must each learn to monitor our own actions. This position led to much of the discussion of the nature of constructivism in later sessions.

Sinclair clearly sees the processes of coming to know and learning to learn as essentially different. Personal reorganization of one's knowledge as one struggles to make meaning is "coming to know," whereas there is a social element for the child to cope with while "learning to learn" in school situations. How will the constructivist teacher make sense of the potential differences? It is important to accept that we do not know what situations will lead to the construction of logicomathematical knowledge and to accept that some processes are not able to be directed, which makes the teacher's role much more uncertain. Of course this does not mean that it is an impossible one! It does point up the dangers of relying on mass presentation of material through a written text where pupils are expected to be at the same place in the text—a "one-paced" program.

As a consequence of these and similar comments, the group still feels in need of more guidance as to the nature of constructivism itself. For several members, the ideas of constructivism are new and need elaboration, whereas some of the members of the group feel that they have been teaching from a constructivist perspective all along.

Curriculum in a Constructivist Framework

The group heard discussion that it is inadequate to consider curriculum as a set of content objectives together with activities for reaching those objectives. The forward-looking nature of such a limited document is misleading; it fails to allow for the differences between children, nor can it articulate the social dynamics at work in any particular group at any particular time. It is far more important for the teacher to record a kind of ongoing curriculum history of a particular group (or groups) of children and to try to use these historical records in determining some perspective on where these children might go in their future mathematical work. In addition, any overall curriculum framework should contain something about the way the writer of the document thinks about mathematics and teaching mathematics. In some countries mathematics teachers are deeply involved in curriculum decisions, whereas in other countries the mathematics teacher for a class has full responsibility for all aspects of the curriculum.

Steffe's (chap. 5.8) idea of the abstracted curriculum is briefly presented as a new way of thinking about curriculum that might hold promise for the construc-

5.4. SOURCES OF TENSION AND POSSIBLE RESOLUTIONS 351

tivist teacher. In his view, created curricula are generated in the communicative interaction among classroom participants and are abstracted by those participants (including the teacher). The interaction takes place in an environment that provides a context for mathematization. Steffe insists that children's mathematics is constructed in the environment. This suggests that the resulting constructions will be both heavily context-dependent and, in part, socially determined.

Left unanswered, or rather unaddressed, is the issue of how textbooks might look in a constructivist framework. Most remarks directed toward textbooks as currently constituted are fairly negative. Many of the group members regard textbooks as unable to create anything like satisfactory mathematical environments for children because of the uniqueness of each group of children and the unavoidable fixed nature of written text. To be fair, few textbooks are used as their writers intend them to be used. Many contain excellent ideas and activities for children, but need to be interpreted and brought to life by creative teachers. A major problem seems to be that the textbooks imply that all children in a particular grade should be doing the same thing at the same time, and further that the appropriate time can be entirely predetermined without knowledge of the children in the class. It seems that these are implications drawn by most teachers. Often teachers move ahead to the next topic even though they know that many children in the class have not managed to learn the concepts just covered; their prespecified curriculum dictates a certain amount of time for some particular set of ideas and teachers feel bound to follow that time allotment no matter what. How can this behavior be reconciled with the ethical commitment a teacher would espouse to each child in the class?

The group agreed that the constructivist teacher brings an extra set of burdens to the task of curriculum development. The belief that children construct their own mathematics out of their actions and their reflections on those actions (in social settings) makes everything about early childhood mathematics curriculum problematic: content (which can hardly be rigidly prescribed in advance by the constructivist teacher), methodology (which probably needs to be idiosyncratic to children and context), and assessment (particularly difficult for those so used to competitive ratings). The constructivist teacher will need to be somewhat of an opportunist, and also an able elementary mathematician willing to continue to learn both about mathematics and children in the attempt to develop them as autonomous creators of their own mathematics. An important aspect of constructivism is the belief that children must become responsible for their own learning in the sense that they understand that their side of the educational contract is to strive to make their own meanings and to learn to negotiate those meanings with teachers and fellow students.

Now there is another side to this coin of curriculum development. Should one choose to disregard traditional ideas about curriculum and adopt the idea that the curriculum is continually created, then the advantage of being a constructivist teacher of mathematics lies in the extra opportunities for that ongoing creation during the everchanging contexts of teaching and learning. When there is tension between two forces, one way to relieve that tension is to think differently about the definition and meaning of one of the forces!

Constructivism remains relatively untried in the everyday classroom setting. For those who express skepticism concerning the viability of an approach relying on the teacher's ability to construct (and frequently reconstruct) images of the children in the class as mathematicians, the work of the group at Purdue led by Paul Cobb (chap. 4.2) is useful. An important part of Cobb's program is its response to the challenge of developing a curriculum based on constructivist principles in typical classroom settings under the constraints of the institutional expectations of a school corporation. There is little doubt that the challenge has been met with more than moderate success (Cobb, Wood, & Yackel, in press).

Educating Teachers;
The Professionalism of Teachers

Discussion of curriculum in a constructivist framework naturally turned to concerns about the issues of educating teachers and the professionalism of teachers in a constructivist context. This was prefaced by the remarks of Lochhead when asked the question, How do we get teachers to teach this way? In England teachers have accepted responsibility for curriculum development for many years, a responsibility that some of those present felt is about to be taken away from them in a political move seen as an attempt to deprofessionalize teachers. The group recommended that teachers should become adept at both clinical methods and recording the outcomes of their teaching in qualitative ways if they are to try to use constructivism in their teaching of mathematics. Several present felt that this was too great a responsibility to place on a teacher of 30 children in one classroom if that teacher is responsible for covering at least six disparate content areas each day.

Another related issue arose from Leino's (chap. 3.1) presentation. He makes it clear that the point of view of the practitioner must be respected in the development of possible environments in which it might be possible for children to engage in the construction of their own mathematical knowledge. He also maintains that mathematics can be developed without direct reference to concrete objects but that the contextual nature of children's construction of mathematical ideas is important. He adds that children cannot be expected to abstract mathematics from textbook illustrations, and then issued the caution that we may never reach simple enough theories; teachers start with their own experience, their own subjective theories of learning. It was clearly Leino's opinion that teachers would do better if they started thinking about their teaching from a constructivist perspective.

Leino signals an important aspect of the nature of teaching; it can hardly be an atheoretical pursuit. The extent to which teachers are aware of their own theory

5.4. SOURCES OF TENSION AND POSSIBLE RESOLUTIONS   353

of action (in terms of personal knowledge and beliefs) and its relationship with their own teaching practices is problematic. But without such self-awareness, it is unlikely that constructivism (or any -ism for that matter!) can powerfully influence teaching practice. Also interesting are questions about mismatches between personal theories teachers hold about teaching and their knowledge and beliefs about mathematics as each teacher strives to understand why they act as they do. The power of personal experience is of two-fold importance for constructivism; teachers must develop an explicit belief that children's mathematics is a legitimate mathematics, and also a belief in their own ability to construct a useful model of the child-as-mathematician. It should be obvious that every teacher's knowledge and beliefs are a product of experience[3] (and of course reflection on that experience), that some teachers have chosen to be more explicitly reflective than others, and that the product of reflection for any one person will be essentially idiosyncratic, even after recognizing the central role of social interaction in the construction of human knowledge.

At this time it is important to remember that there are many interpretations of constructivism; as with so many educational terms, it means different things to different people. The argument that we somehow share something called a "negotiated reality" is rejected by radical constructivists because it leads to acceptance of an accessible, ontological reality. This is not to deny the existence of such an external reality; the radical constructivist insists that such a reality is not directly accessible. Thus even after "negotiating" and "agreeing" we are each left with our own construction and cannot know the constructions of another. Rather we make indirect inferences about the usefulness of one another's constructions through the process of judging one another's actions in context as appropriate or not.

The Issue of Appropriate Content

On the issue of content deemed appropriate for early childhood, strong arguments are presented by Sumio (chap. 5.6) in favor of a child-centered approach in which mathematics, science, and language would be drawn out of everyday situations. If such an approach were to recognize that teachers come to educational situations with their own knowledge and perspectives, then this approach could certainly be adapted by those interested in pursuing constructivist views. The approach fits in that it makes prescribing content for all children of a particular age impossible; the teacher would need to seize each event and use it as

---

[3]The notion of experience needs some clarification. Clearly we mean more than the physical impressions of our environment collected through hearing, feeling, smelling, touching, and seeing. Our reading, our interpretations of the speech of others and the actions of others, must also be included, as must our emotional responses to all of these. Every attempt at making meaning of our situation; whether that situation be physical, mental, or emotional, contributes to our experience.

a possible opportunity for assessing each child's mathematical reaction. However, the concern was raised that without emphasizing the teacher's role as a creator of specific situations, there was the risk that many important mathematical contexts might never arise to involve the children and so allow appropriate construction of concepts. Thus many feel that this is not at all feasible as a solution for the teachers in their countries who need the security of recognizably familiar content neatly presented in careful sequence. (This points up a major difficulty: Can one be a constructivist mathematics teacher with little content knowledge of mathematics? It is agreed that the first requirement of a constructivist teacher of mathematics is at the very least the possession of an open attitude towards mathematics and a willingness to learn more about mathematics along with the children.)

Much of the discussion focuses on the content issue with the subsequent recommendation that much more time should be given over to the development of ideas of space and geometry that are currently neglected in favor of developing efficiency in computation. Constructivist ideas are particularly suited to such a pursuit, taking the spatial environment of the child as a natural starting point. An interesting point is made by Mansfield (chap. 5.7) in her support for the introduction of ideas of surface as an appropriate starting point rather than the traditional one-dimensional approach through open and closed curves, which leads to the concept of straightness and then the recognition of shapes based on numbers of line segments and vertices. There is a general feeling that the usual approach to geometry in the early childhood mathematics program is far too static. More emphasis should be placed on perspective, motion, and transformation. There is considerable support for starting off in the kindergarten grade with early ideas of space before the introduction to number, which is the usual starting point for almost all currently used curricula in early childhood mathematics. Furthermore, many think that it may be better to introduce number in the context of space and geometry than through traditional approaches emphasizing early symbolism.

Many favor eliminating the imposition of traditional algorithms for arithmetic operations in early childhood mathematics in favor of allowing children to construct their own units and their systems. Such an approach may lead children to develop their own algorithms. This has been encouraged in English schools for some time. There is also some discussion concerning the use of computers, particularly calculators. Most are in favor of such use, although no precise recommendations are made as to how to go about introducing these devices into classrooms and making them part of the everyday mathematics program.

A related question of abiding concern is the extent to which individual teachers should bear responsibility for the mathematics curriculum in their classrooms. If we think of curriculum as a prospective document we are bound to be disappointed; children rarely learn all those things we mean them to, and even more rarely do they learn them in the way we want.

SUMMARY OF ISSUES AND RECOMMENDATIONS

Thus, the most important issues for mathematics educators (and here the group clearly includes teachers at all levels as mathematics educators) interested in pursuing a constructivist framework are first, to determine what the term *mathematical curricula* should mean for participants involved in the development of such a framework, and second, to decide how to embody that meaning into usable curricula documents. Perhaps as well as informing the reader of possible content, such curriculum documents should convey to the reader a sense of broader purpose, some elements of the educational philosophy supporting why the documents were written in this form, and related aspects of methodology. Constructivists have the challenge of developing such curricula documents. Due to the nature of the supporting epistemology, constructivists will insist that they need to develop models of children as mathematicians before much more can be done, either in relation to choice of content or methodology. They will embed themselves deeply in the experiential side of mathematics classrooms as participants in mathematics teaching with the aim of learning what mathematics curricula might be like in early childhood education. Furthermore, they will insist that mathematics teaching and learning cannot be separated from the development of mathematics curriculum, and will give serious consideration to creating in their classrooms mathematical environments of the kind described by Kieren (chap. 5.2).

Thus the principal tension between curriculum development and constructivism that seems to run throughout can be seen as a conflict between current ways of thinking about curriculum development in early childhood mathematics and ways of thinking about that development based on constructivism. Resolving the conflict in the manner described earlier will go a long way towards shaping the form of constructivist curricula documents. An important part of that resolution will be to have curricula developers abandon their present focus on presenting content-as-product in favor of tackling the reality of the diversity of thinking that exists within each classroom. The curricula developers need to move from content-based curricula towards curricula that take the children's mathematics into account. This is not to say that content is not important, but it should not be the only concern of the curriculum developer. Recent developments in the philosophy of mathematics (e.g., Tymoczko, 1985) would indicate that mathematics is not the logically developed, objective body of knowledge independent of human activity portrayed for children by most texts. Rather, it is a consequence of social interaction like all other human knowledge. We may do children a serious disservice in presenting mathematics to them as a finished product instead of as a special way of supporting ongoing enquiry into aspects of the world.

Constructivism itself is also a source of tension between traditional curriculum practice and a constructivist-based methodology. Traditional curriculum practice focuses on the treatment of a whole class or group in relation to the content to be covered, whereas most constructivist-based research has aimed at explicating the mathematics of children as individuals or in clinical groups of two or three. We need more work on the relation between constructivism and the social context of the classroom as is being done by Cobb et al. (in press). It is explicit management of this social context that will lead to the possibility of the "mathematical environments" Steffe would like to see.

Many of the problems that will need to be overcome if constructivism is to gain ground as a legitimate way of thinking about teaching early childhood mathematics come down to two basic philosophical questions: how might children think about mathematics and what does it mean to teach mathematics? Neither question has easy answers, and it is unfortunate that there is so little opportunity in current teacher preparation programs for prospective teachers at any level to even struggle to find their own answers. It seems to be stating the obvious to suggest that teacher education will need to have a very different face if it is to prepare teachers in sufficient numbers to make any real difference to how mathematics will be taught.

Chapter 5.5

Mathematical Learning Beyond the Activity

Helen Pengelly
Waltle Park Teachers Center, SOUTH AUSTRALIA

Everyone has a set of experiences unlike those of any other, and each person's view of the world is filtered through the sieve of these experiences. Children then, like adults, will always perceive a situation from a framework that is uniquely theirs. Furthermore, any situation can be seen only in the light of individual interpretations. Therefore activities set up in a mathematics lesson can never be considered to be absolute. These experiences are merely the vehicle for thinking, and children use them to make meaning in a way that is possible at that particular stage and time in their learning.

But although there are differences in personal interpretation, pictures depicting a collective view of children can also be painted. These need not detract in any way from the unique characteristics that can be attributed to each and every child. Generalities can be formed identifying similarities in children's thinking. There is a way of thinking that is shared by all children.[1] And just as there are common elements in the way children personalize experience, there are also generalizations that can be made about how this thinking develops. In all aspects of young children's learning it is possible to use the knowledge gained from generations of children to predict the broad growth pattern of individuals. Learning to talk, walk, read, or socialize are just some instances where development follows a predetermined pattern. Mathematical learning is another.

The traditional breakdown of mathematical content into bite-sized sequenced bits is not, I believe, the reverse of the process children use to build mathematical

---

[1] This way of thinking is influenced by the different groupings by which children can be defined. Ethnic, gender and/or socioeconomic groupings, for example, will generate characteristics that depart from each other in both major and minor ways.

knowledge. Such a linear analysis defies the development of understandings about the complex networks that interlock parts of mathematics with each other. If children had access to more significant mathematics than behavioral objectives permit, would they learn about these relationships and enjoy a depth of understanding not common in school mathematics? This is the question this chapter addresses. I also explore the parallels that exist in the thinking, and in the development of thinking, amongst groups of children in one key aspect of young children's mathematical learning—the structure of the number system.

TOWARDS AN UNDERSTANDING OF THE STRUCTURE OF THE NUMBER SYSTEM

Let me set the scene. Six- and 7-year-old children were each given pop sticks, elastic bands, dice, and a tens and ones board and told: "Take from the center pile the same number of pop sticks as the number thrown on the dice. There is one rule. No more than nine sticks can stay in the ones column." The purpose of the activity was for children to understand the Base Ten nature of our number system. It was many months before they realized this goal. Throughout this long arduous process we remained convinced of three things. First, children are naturally curious human beings with an innate desire to learn. Second, the Base Ten system took centuries and the contribution of many civilizations to develop to its current degree of sophistication, and is significant mathematics. Third, the Base Ten activity—the material and rules—provided a model of the structure of the number system. At no stage did we tell children what to do. We trusted the activity would demonstrate the structure. We also believed children would process ideas that were part of their experiences with the activity. They worked with this model for many months. From the outset they were captivated by it, choosing to do it in free choice time and even raiding the cupboards at home and finding toothpicks a viable substitute for ice cream sticks.

Our patience and faith eventually paid dividends. But it was only with hindsight that we were able to make sense of the learning and see how each part in the learning sequence was significant to the growth in understanding the structure itself. The initial stages of the process showed children preoccupied with the materials and the actions required to interact with them. It was the most superficial and insignificant qualities that managed to capture their attention. As the activity became more familiar to a child, the physical actions required less deliberation, opening the way for other details to emerge. Session by session the thinking developed. A child may begin by addressing addition, and as it was mastered, the thoughts moved on to a more detailed analysis of the exchanging process and then on to the way place value effects face value. It became increasingly apparent to me that the activity could be thought about at many different levels. Gradually the layers unfolded, and with each unfolding, children

5.5. MATHEMATICAL LEARNING BEYOND THE ACTIVITY 359

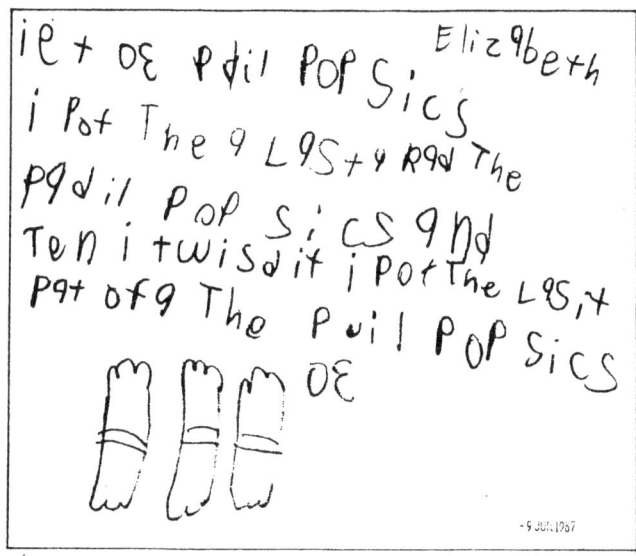

FIG. 1. Attending to the activity itself.

explored different ideas, systematically arriving at new insights. It was only when all the outercasings had laid bare the core that the relevance of the activity to the structure of the mathematics became apparent to children. I use children's recordings to describe this process in more detail. A child was not expected to record until the teacher thought that she or he had gained enough information about the game itself. For some children this took several lessons, whereas others would master it in just one or two.

Attending to the Activity

The first recordings the children did were very descriptive of the physical activity as they worked with the materials. Elizabeth was primarily concerned with her actions as her step-by-step description shows. "I put the elastic around the paddle pop sticks and then I twisted it. I put the elastic part over the paddle pop sticks" (Figure 1). The explicit descriptions of the roll of the dice, the getting of the pop sticks, the tying up with rubber bands and then placing them on the board is shown by Kristy when she recorded ". . . I threw the dice. I got 6. I put them in the 1s column. That makes 10. I put the elastic band around . . ." (Figure 2) and then a month later ". . . that makes 12. I take 10 out and exchanged them" (Figure 3). At this early stage, the rules and actions of the game were what Michael used to describe the task and emphasized his orientation toward the physical features as much as to the numbers that were being generated. ". . . score now 13, cut down to 10, got 2 (3?) left . . . I have to bundle, score now 20 . . ." (Figure 4). These

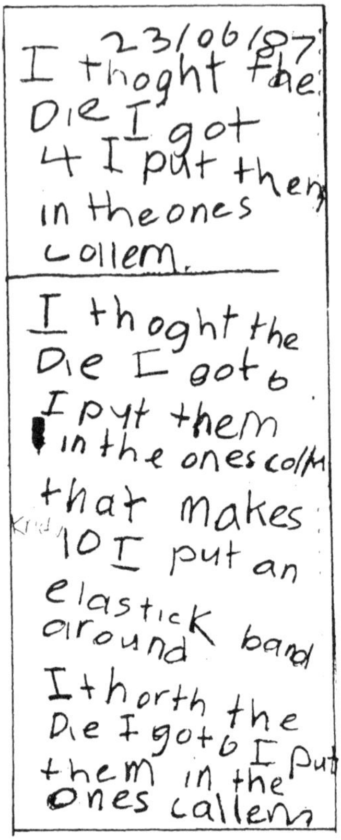

> 23/06/87
> I thoght the
> Die I got
> 4 I put them
> in the ones
> collem.
>
> I thoght the
> Die I got 6
> I pyt them
> in the ones colm
> that makes
> 10 I put an
> elastick band
> around
> I thorth the
> Die I got 6 I put
> them in the
> ones callem

FIG. 2. Describing actions.

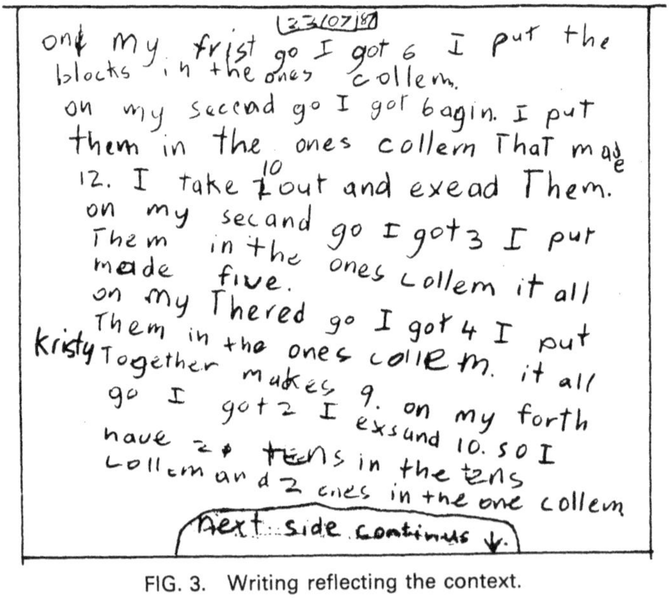

> 23/07/87
> on my frist go I got 6 I put the
> blocks in the ones collem.
> on my secend go I got 6 agin. I put
> them in the ones collem That made
> 12. I take 10 out and exead Them.
> on my secand go I got 3 I put
> Them in the ones collem it all
> made five.
> on my Thered go I got 4 I put
> Them in the ones collem. it all
> Kristy Together makes 9. on my forth
> go I got 2 I exsund 10. so I
> have 2 tens in the tens
> collem and 2 ones in the one collem
> next side continues ↓

FIG. 3. Writing reflecting the context.

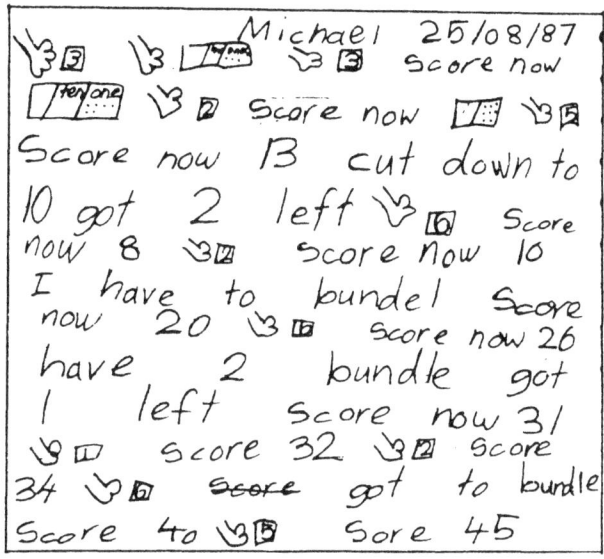

FIG. 4. Using words, pictures, and diagrams to describe actions.

children recorded thoughts that were very much bound up by issues peripheral to the Base Ten structure—the activity that modelled it.

Attending to the Numbers

As children became more familiar with the activity, they no longer needed to think so consciously about their actions and as interest in the material faded, they were challenged by the numbers thrown on the dice and the evolving total. Amanda recorded each pair of throws and the total "1,1,2 (1 + 1 = 2), 3,6,9 (3 + 6 = 9) . . ." and periodically gave the running total ". . . and end up with 11. . ." (Figure 5). By placing the numbers thrown on the die in quotation marks, Susan was able to distinguish these numbers from the total "1, 6, 4, 4, adds up to 15 . . ." (Figure 6).

Jenny kept tally of the evolving total "15 6 21 1 22 . . . (15 + 6 = 21, 21 + 1 = 22, . . .)" (Figure 7). Two weeks later she used a method to record addition facts that had proved successful before "2 + 1 = 3, 6 + 5 = 14 . . . (2 + 1 = 3 3 + (6 + 5) = 14 . . .)" (Figure 8). Although these sums were arithmetically incorrect, Jenny's thinking was not. The total, 14, was determined by adding the 3 from the previous total to the 5 and 6. Jenny was clear about the idea behind the symbols. Mathematical language evolved as a means of expressing and manipulating ideas and their relationships. At this stage Jenny was content that her symbols were a valid description of the relationships with which she was working. It seemed senseless to impose any restrictions on her thinking until she had

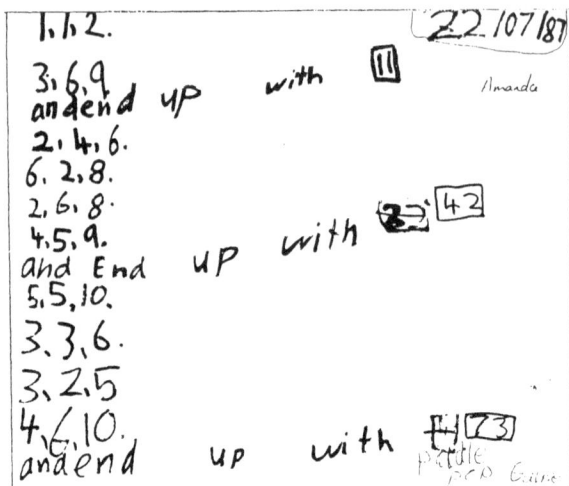

FIG. 5. Focusing on the numerical relationships.

had a chance to explore the idea more fully. Learning that the addition algorithm was unsuitable was a significant experience in itself that Jenny was able to explore at a more appropriate moment. Inventing more suitable methods to express ideas was part of this process. Children were able to explore how symbols can be used to represent experiences. The accepted tens and unit format assumes knowledge pertaining to the structure of the number system that children at this stage of their learning were yet to acquire. To try to communicate the ideas using this was likely to confuse rather than clarify their thinking.

Michael, also interested in his accumulating total, was part way through the activity when he suddenly asked, "How do you record bundling?" The third line of Fig. 9 shows his first attempt to record the exchanging process. But his interest was diverted when he found an easier and more efficient method of representing the changing total—the addition algorithm. Any thoughts of grappling with a method for recording the exchanging process was lost for the time being.

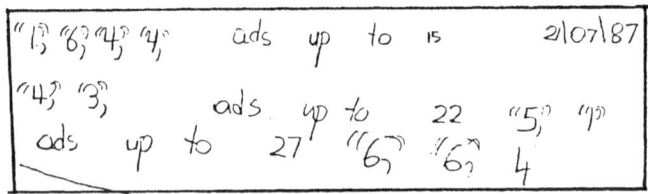

FIG. 6. Adding the numbers.

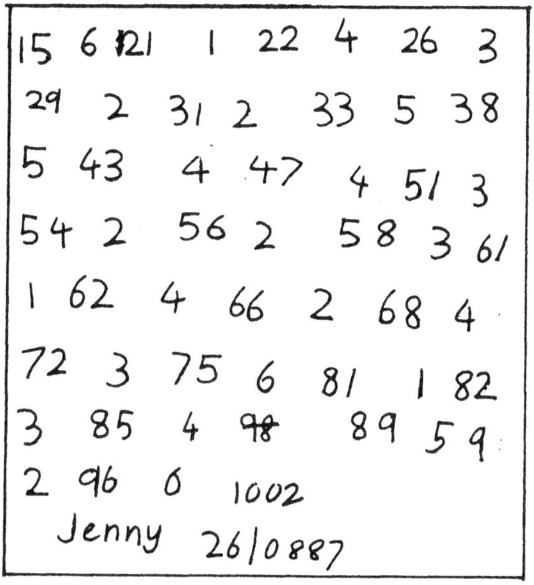

```
15  6 121  1  22  4  26  3
29  2  31  2  33  5  38
5  43  4  47  4  51  3
54  2  56  2  58  3  61
1  62  4  66  2  68  4
72  3  75  6  81  1  82
3  85  4  98  89  5  9
2  96  0  1002
Jenny  26/08/87
```

FIG. 7. Accumulating the total.

One of the reasons it was important for children to work with the same activity time and time again was so they could focus on the ideas within the model and not remain transfixed by the activity itself. At this stage of development, the children were not yet thinking about how the Base Ten system worked, but they were getting plenty of practice at adding! The ability to do algorithms was one of

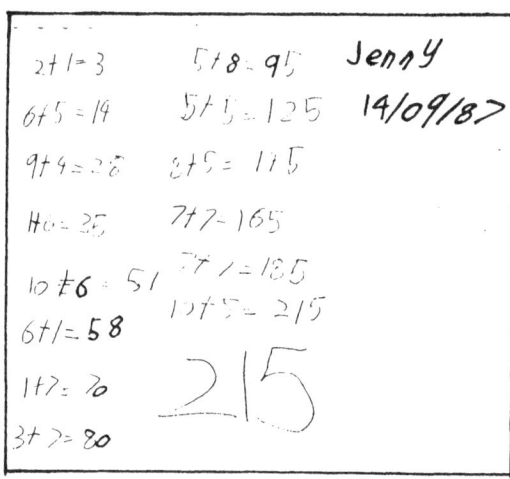

FIG. 8. Using the addition algorithm.

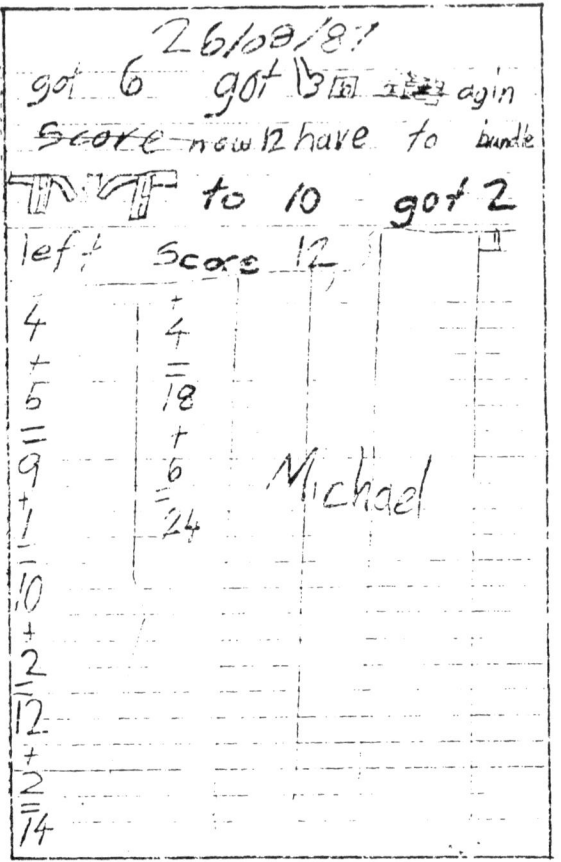

FIG. 9. Using the numbers and symbols for efficiency.

the outcomes of a much broader investigation. Although we did not focus on addition, there was certainly evidence of a great deal of repetition and practice of addition facts and processes. They were always adding the total on the dice as well as the overall total. The strategies for determining the sum of two numbers became more efficient and children developed proficiency in mental calculations and in writing "sums." By the end of the process, they all had instant recall of the basic addition facts. Although the children were yet to address Base Ten in any significant way, our faith in the process was sustained by these very demonstrable outcomes. The acquisition of facts and skills was not inhibited by an investigation of a larger "chunk of mathematics." In fact, it would seem it enhanced the learning outcomes of children. It also had an extremely positive effect on attitudes towards mathematical learning.

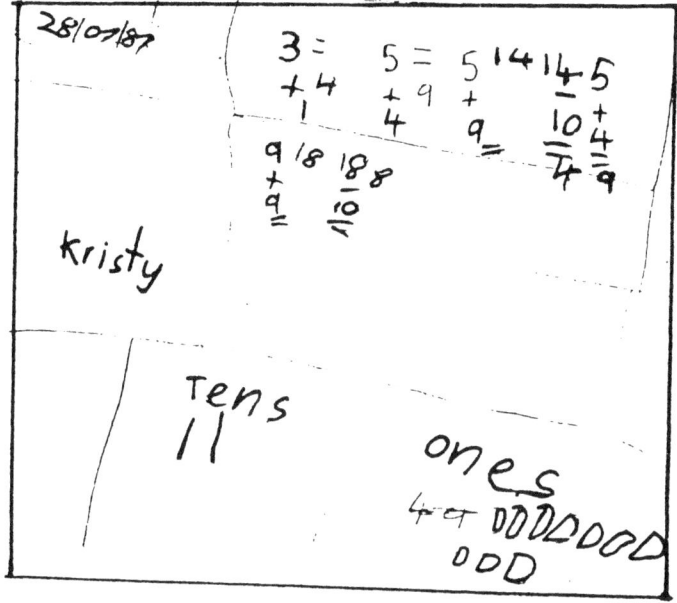

FIG. 10. Exchanging into groups of ten.

The Exchanging Process

At last! After several months working with Base Ten materials, the children started to identify the exchanging process as a significant feature. This was, after all, the purpose for setting up this activity. Once they were confident with equating ten ones to a bundle and counting by ten, Base Ten blocks were substituted for the pop sticks and bands. Kristy "3 + 1 = 4, 5 + 4 = 9, 14 − 10 = 4 . . ." (Figure 10), Adam "6 + 4 (large numerals) 10 (totals in small print) . . ." (Figure 11) and Amanda ". . . 7 + 2 = 9 9 + 3 = 12, one bundle and two 1s . . ." (Figure 12) all created a special box or column to record the groups of 10 as they accumulated. Alfina kept a tally of her throws and grouped by 10 for "easy counting" (Figure 13). Kristy made a note every time she exchanged ". . . 9 + 2 = 11, 1 bundle 10 . . ." (Figure 14) and finds the reverse no problem ". . . 90 − 1 = 89 undo bundle . . ." (Figure 15). These children needed time to attend to other aspects of the task before they were able to tackle something as fundamental to the structure as the exchanging process. The time spent exploring ideas within the task was not a waste of time. On the contrary, it created an internal framework so that children's thinking could eventually take on board information so pertinent to the Base Ten nature of the number system.

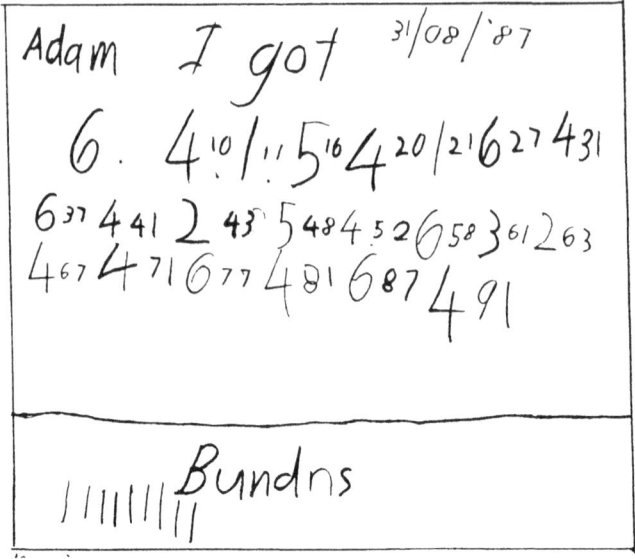

FIG. 11. Identifying groups of ten.

Michael indicated his increasing awareness of the structure by the way he organized his recording into columns. In the 1s column he wrote "5 + 9 = 14 . . ." (Fig. 16). As this is more than 10, he takes the 10 from 14 and records it in his 10s column and disregards this part of the 14 when he adds " . . . 14 + 9 = 13 . . ." (Fig. 16). His accumulating total of 10s is computed in the same way "1 + 1 = 2) . . ." (Fig. 16). When he had 10 groups of 10 in the 10s column, he decided he needed another column, 100s, to store them in. A couple of weeks later, Michael was prepared for a similar event as he had organized a 100s column before he began (Fig. 17). Although Michael had been able to transfer the initial rule into the next power of 10, his recordings were quite onerous. If he were to abstract the principles beyond the physical exchanging process, then it would be necessary to draw his attention away from it. We did this by modifying the activity.

Once children had reached this level of thinking, as indicated by Michael, we gave them "tens and ones dice." Using these dice they could generate numbers between 10 and 100. This tactic took away the busyness of previous activities, making it possible to refine the recording of the exchanging system.

Using More Conventional Formats

Eventually, children discovered they could manipulate numbers and communicate the ideas and processes by working with numerals using the same method they had once used when manipulating objects. The children began to work with

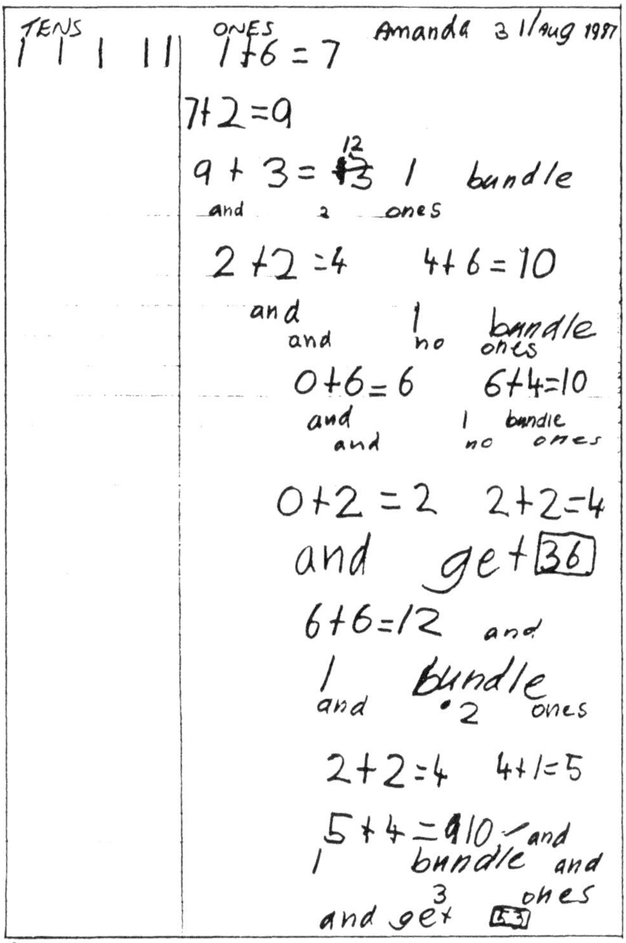

5.5. MATHEMATICAL LEARNING BEYOND THE ACTIVITY

```
TENS  | ONES
1 1 1 | 1 1 1    1+6 = 7    Amanda 31/aug 1987
               7+2 = 9
                              12
               9 + 3 = 1̶3̶    1 bundle
                 and      2   ones

               2+2 = 4      4+6 = 10
                 and           1     bundle
                  and         no     ones
               0+6 = 6      6+4 = 10
                 and           1     bundle
                  and         no     ones

               0+2 = 2      2+2 = 4
               and   get [36]
               6+6 = 12   and
               1    bundle
                and     • 2   ones
               2+2 = 4      4+1 = 5
               5+4 = 9 10  and
               1    bundle   and
                              3   ones
               and get [43]
```

FIG. 12. Recording groups of ten.

numerals within the 10s and 1s framework. Each sequence of events was included in the recording. The total in the 1s column was recorded before withdrawing the groups of 10. There has been no attempt to exchange the groups of 10 once they get beyond 100 (Figures 18, 19). Alfina demonstrates clearly her comprehension of face and place value and she says, "Five and 6 is one 10 and 1 unit. Five 10s and two 10s and the other 10 make 80, so the answer is 81" (Figure 20). She is also able to regroup without including the step in her writings. Such an understanding of the value of the numbers was obvious in all children when they reached this stage of the process.

These children were able to find sums within the framework with ease. Earlier

FIG. 13. Tallying using groups of ten.

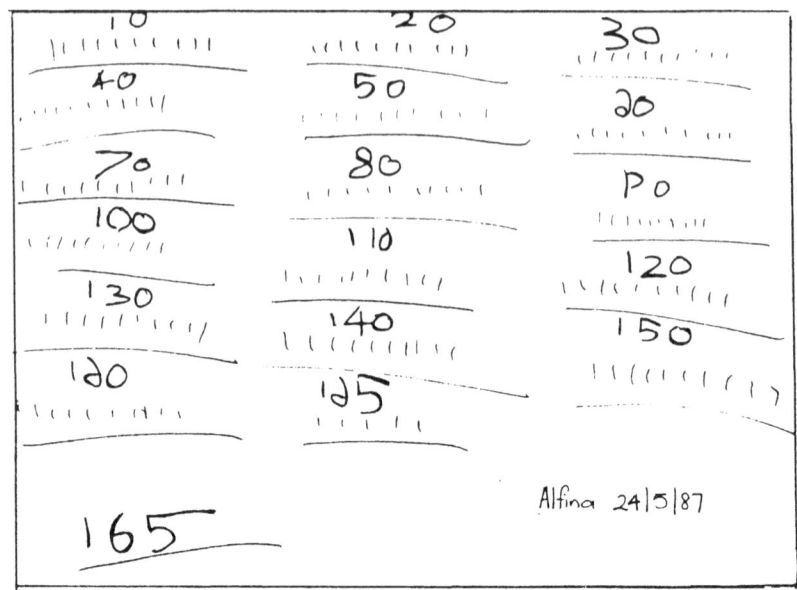

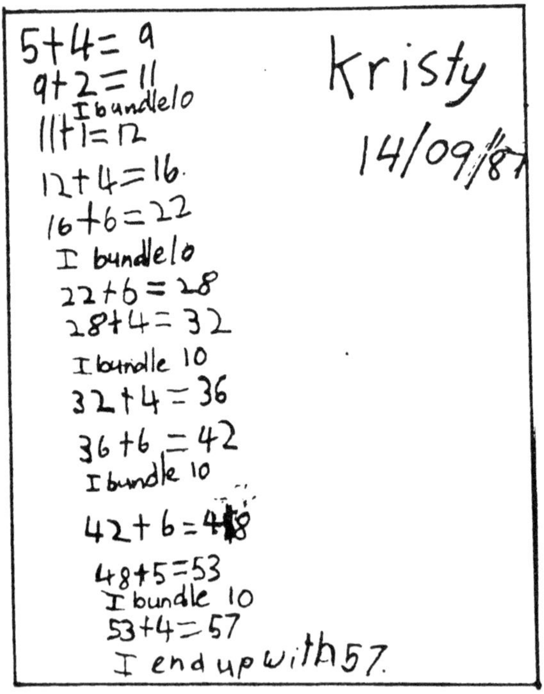

FIG. 14. Identifying the exchanging process.

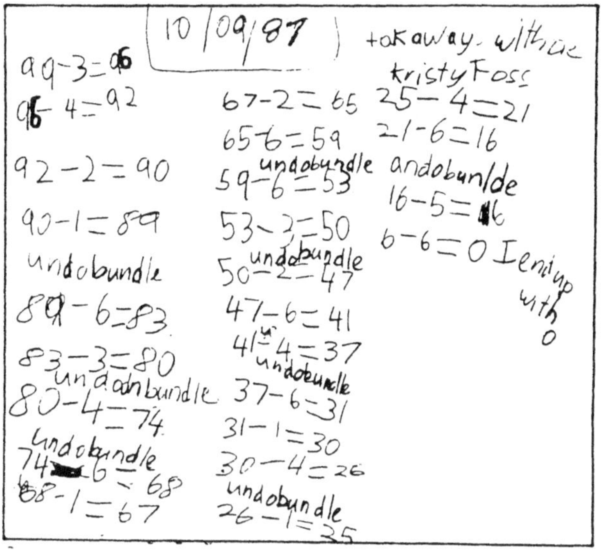

FIG. 15. Subtraction—the reverse of addition.

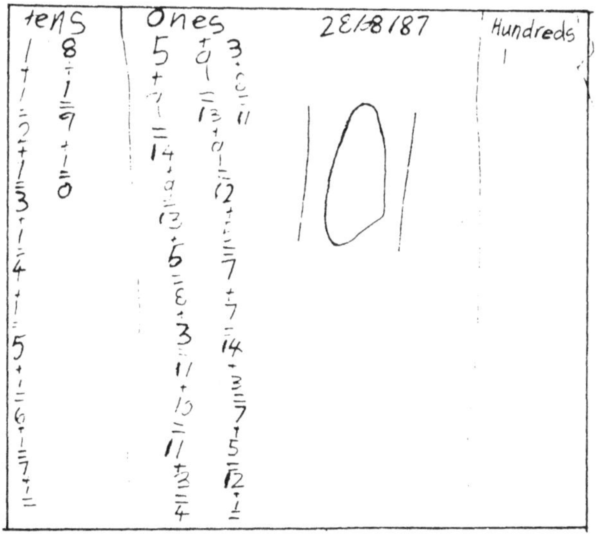

FIG. 16. Using the framework.

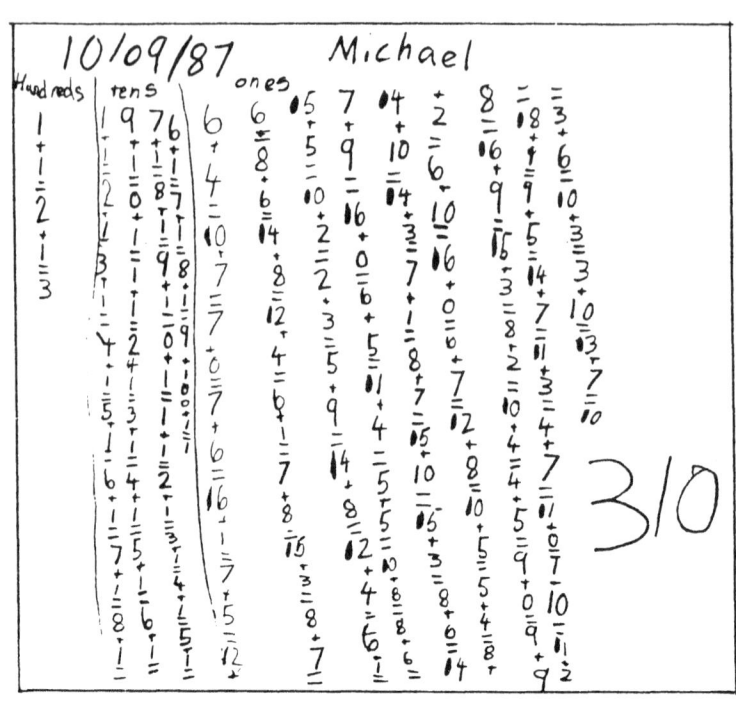

FIG. 17. Repetition and practice.

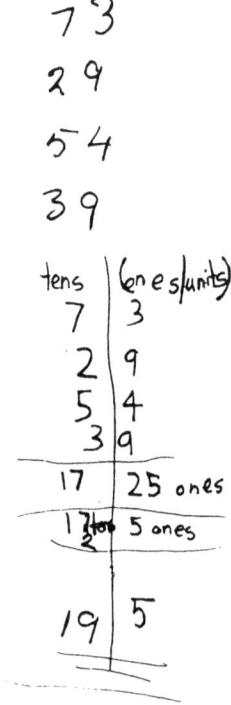

FIG. 18. Becoming conventional.

5.5. MATHEMATICAL LEARNING BEYOND THE ACTIVITY

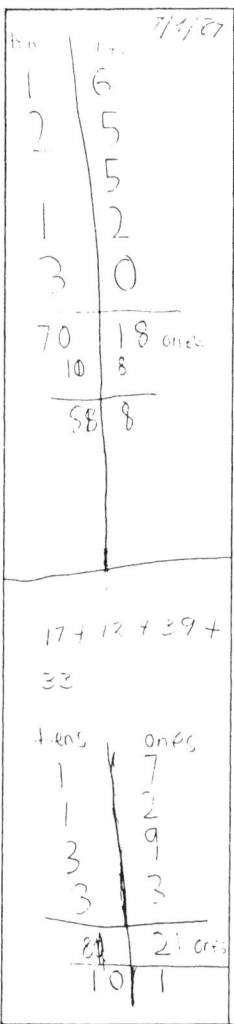

FIG. 19. Manipulating numerals.

in the process children worked below 100. To encourage this, they were told "when you get into the 90s, you have to take whatever you throw on the dice away from your total." Subtraction and decomposition were being explored simultaneously with addition.

So, from months of exploring, what had the children learned? They gained all the skills of adding, subtracting, exchanging, and decomposing. They could describe numbers in their expanded form and clearly identify face and place value. They learned effective and efficient ways to record calculations, and they were confident naming, writing, and ordering numbers up to 100. These children also had automatic response to addition and subtraction facts. In the end, these

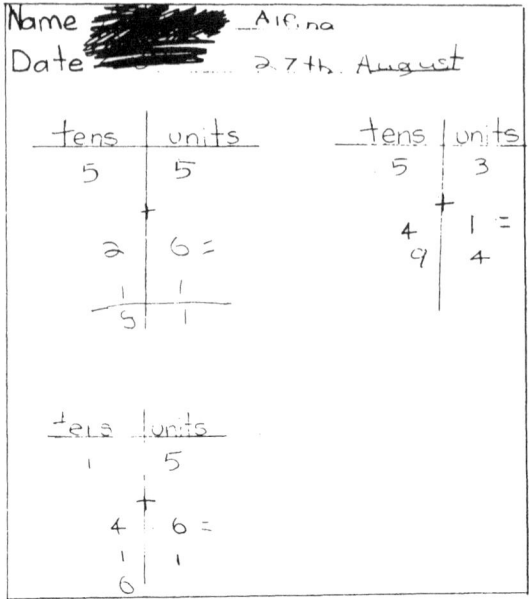

FIG. 20. Using the algorithm.

outcomes take on an appearance similar to the objectives in scope and sequence statements. It is evident that children put this information together for themselves, within the framework set by the teacher, in a distinctly different manner to the simplistic development of skills through behavioral objectives. At every stage of the process described here, children were always working with specific ideas within the context of the number system itself. Every idea was thought about as it related to other ideas and to the framework as a whole.

The difference between breaking down mathematical concepts into behavioral objectives and building mathematics in this more wholistic setting is similar to the difference between trying to find out what a flower looks like, by analysis of each petal in isolation from every other petal, and gaining an impression of a flower by watching it form and bloom. It is the shape of the petals and the way they are interwoven, together with color and fragrance, that ultimately determine the characteristics of a flower.

Extending the Rule

Kristy and Michael operated beyond the set task. They had been doing some work with patterns and realized the work they had been doing with Base Ten could prove useful. They used what they had learned about the Base Ten system to assist them in an exploration of multiplication. Unlike at the previous level,

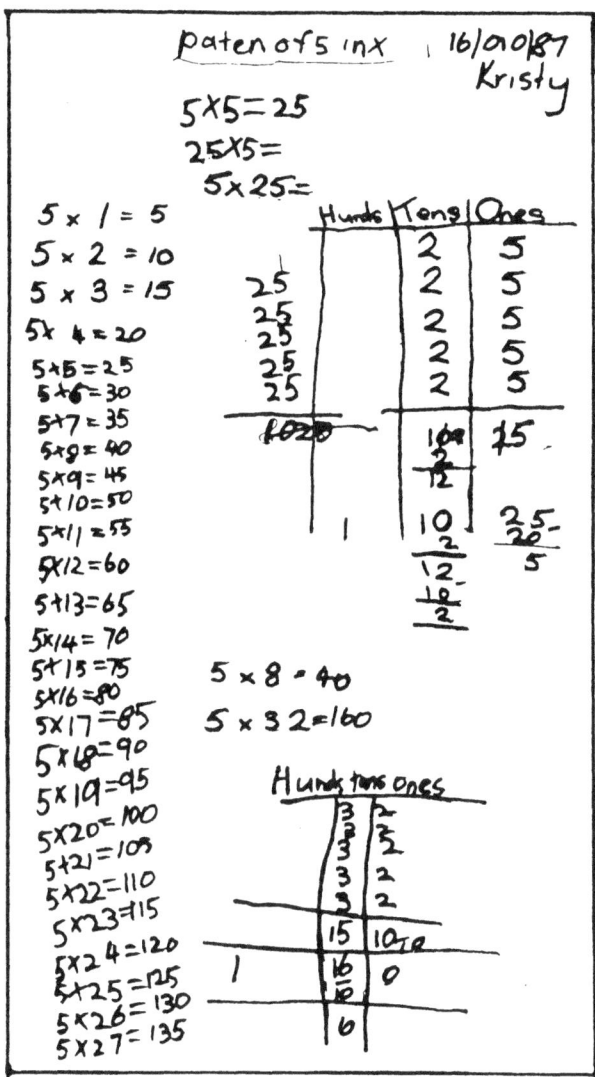

FIG. 21. Beginning to multiply.

they were no longer content to have more than 10 of a group in any of the columns. The workings indicate that they were able to use their understanding of the structure demonstrated by the model, to predict that groups of ten 10s will make 100s (Figure 21) and groups of ten 100s will make 1000s (Figure 22).

Kristy still needed to include paper workings of the exchanging process. She added the five groups of 5 in the 1s column and wrote 25. After computing "25

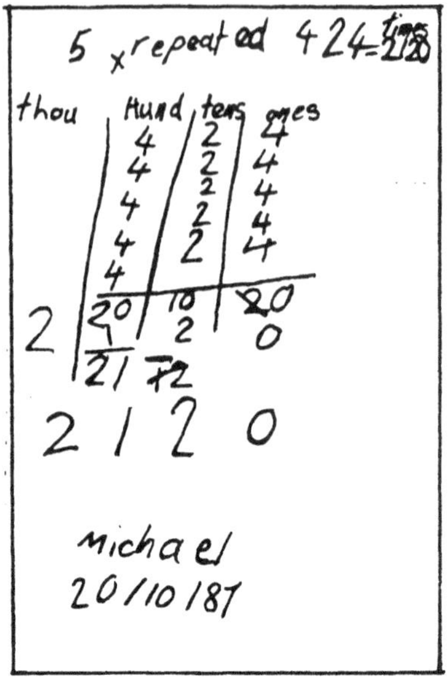

FIG. 22. Working with larger numbers.

— 20 = 5" to find out how many 1s are left from exchanging the two 10s, she then added "10 + 2 = 12" (12 tens) before taking 10 (10s) away "12 − 10 = 2" and ended up with 100, two 10s and 5 units (Figure 21). Similarly, Michael did the exchanging calculations on paper (Figure 22). Given time, these children were confident enough to discard this step by mentally computing these relationships. The children themselves were able to make decisions about the amount of detail they required at any stage in the process. We always maintained the freedom for children to explore the model in a way and at a level they chose. As these representations indicate, each child moved progressively from one idea to the next as their understanding grew.

IMPLICATION FOR CURRICULUM

The ability to transfer the principles that govern the number system was made possible because of the many weeks given to ideas within the model that were subsidiary to the structure but within the context of it. The structure of the Base Ten system was not an entity in itself, but rather a collection of all the bits that were pieced together to complete a jigsaw. All pieces eventually connected with one another because of the relationships that existed between them. Many of these relationships were at first not apparent, but these bonds grew stronger as the total picture emerged. Individual pieces remained meaningless unless viewed in the context of the total puzzle.

5.5. MATHEMATICAL LEARNING BEYOND THE ACTIVITY

When learning is more piece-meal, as it is when planned from scope and sequence statements, the likelihood of developing a wholistic perspective is reduced markedly. Take for example the Base Ten system. The objectives in a conventional mathematics curriculum describe such aspects as adding, adding with exchanging, decomposing, place value, and so forth. Teaching, and consequently learning, converges to these finite outcomes. Every specific objective is an entity in itself, distinct, but theoretically linked to other units. All too often these links fail to be realized in class programs. This leads to serious shortcomings. Objectives, defined so narrowly, produce a skill-based curriculum. In the instance just cited, these objectives do not address the structure of the system itself. But these very activities presume an understanding of the structure. Children are expected to learn how to operate within this structure even though they have no comprehension of it or, for that matter, experience with it.

It is no wonder multiplication, division, and decimals are so difficult to learn and have a habit of monopolizing the curriculum in the primary years. If children are to learn mathematics from a structural as well as a factual perspective, then we need to identify significant mathematics for children to learn that is described in much broader settings than behavioral objectives permit. The structure of the Base Ten system is one of these key mathematical ideas. The previous examples of children's work outlined a gradual transition to a greater, clearer understanding of the Base Ten system. At each stage there were profiles illustrating how individuals stamped their own impression onto an idea. But each sample was categorized into a framework according to the general idea the child had focused on. Despite surface differences in the way a child thinks about and represents an idea, there is a predictability about what ideas will be addressed and in what sequence. Beyond the differences, similarities can be found, similarities in the basic idea and in how it develops. But a class of children do not all think about the same idea at the same time. Each one has a time frame that is his or her own. So at any given time, as the dates on the included samples indicate, children "'see' different things in what to an observer is the 'same' situation." During the initial stages of an investigation, a child cannot be thought to be neglecting certain aspects of the model. Instead, these unregarded aspects should be thought of as ideas not yet accessible to the learner because they are hidden behind other ideas that are still to be explored.

Whenever a group of children were working together with the 'same' mathematics, each one's focus differed in either of two ways. Children were either thinking about the same general feature within the model, but using organizational strategies and thought processes that were not alike, or children were thinking about different ideas within the model. These ideas were hierarchical. In the beginning the structure remained undiscovered. It was only as ideas within the activity were dealt with that a child could see the structurally essential elements. The longer a child worked with the model, the more sophisticated, abstract, and generalized the deliberation and consequently the recordings became. But this can only happen if materials and activities reflect images of mathematics from a wholistic perspective.

As individual children established clarity and order at any one level, they were ready to address the substance contained within the next layer. When referring to levels, I do not wish to conjure up images of a linear relationship between stages. I prefer to think of the layers in a three-dimensional setting, similar to a rose. A rose in bud reveals nothing of its inner self, the outside petals holding tight, protecting all that is within. The petals leisurely unfold, gradually exposing beauty and fragrance until the magnificence of the flower in full bloom is realized. After the flower, the hip—the fruit of the rose—forms and then the seeds—a springboard for new life.

I liken a young child's perspective of the structure of the number system to that of a novice's view of the rose. A rose bud gives no hint of the beauty it hides, just as the Base Ten structure is concealed by the activity that models it. The bud opens and inner petals take their turn to display their color. The Base Ten activity also opens up and ideas within it are displayed for systematic investigation. Eventually, after all the petals are exposed, they drift away and the fruit of the rose remains. Similarly, once all the ideas that characterize the number system are mastered, the structure becomes apparent, incorporating all the ideas that have gone before. Such mastery is the springboard to further mathematics.

Chapter 5.6

Notes on Early Mathematical Experiences

Minoru Sumio
Bunkyo College, Tokyo, JAPAN

Between the ages of 3 and 6, children develop very rapidly, both physically and mentally. Moreover, not every child's development is the same; some develop very quickly, jumping several stages, whereas some are slow developers. The period between the ages of 3 and 6 is one of great potential for the acquisition of concepts.

Given that the rates and stages of children's development are different from one child to the other, the job of the teacher is to structure a suitable environment to enable the children to make their own way. For younger children, mathematical guidance should be made dependent on their real-life activities and experiences. One should not attempt to construct a formal mathematics curriculum separate from such activities and experiences.

Indeed, the best way to teach mathematics to younger children is perhaps to help them to see the mathematical properties that coincide with their play activities. It follows that the mathematical properties found by children will be different according to their individual experiences. It is much more important for children to discover mathematical properties for themselves than to be taught what adults consider mathematical thinking.

It is nonsense to expect that the same questions and workbooks will produce the same answers and achievements. So the good teacher does not expect uniform progress. The rate of progress will largely depend on the depth of the experiences of each child. On the question of teaching methods, it is not good to interrupt children when they are engaged in a creative process or make-believe activities, and it is equally unhelpful for the teacher to set aside a time for free play and then simply stand back. The teacher must understand what constitutes a good environment for children's mathematics and must give careful advice that incorporates acceptance of their activities and is designed to draw out their mathematical ability and enable it to develop. The teacher has a heavy responsibility for fostering children's progress.

EXAMPLE 1: UNDIFFERENTIATED CONCEPTS

On Children's Day in Japan, children make paper carps and attach them to a pole so that they blow in the wind. A kindergarten teacher was asked to make carps with groups of children. After the carps were finished, Group A cried, "Our carp is the largest." But Group B did not agree and said, "Our carp is much larger than yours." The teacher advised them to compare the size of the two carps. So the children laid the carps on top of one another and found that Group B's carp was larger than Group A's. But Group A members still continued to say, "Our carp is the largest." Finally, the teacher realized that when Group A members said their carp was the largest, what they really wanted to say was that carp was the oldest one.

The children were unable to differentiate 'old' from 'large.' In Japanese, the same word, *okii* can be used for large and old, so that, for example, we can ask children who is the largest, meaning who is the oldest. The word *large* in Japanese has a variety of meanings, such as high, long, tall, wide, heavy, and old. To enable children to differentiate between these meanings is the initial stage of mathematics.

EXAMPLE 2: JUNE. A CLASS OF 5-YEAR-OLD CHILDREN (FINAL YEAR IN KINDERGARTEN) COUNTING AND TRYING TO COUNT LABELS

Children in the class have a place to put their own things, a place to hang their hats and coats, a drawer for their belongings, and a place for their indoor shoes.

Teacher: "Today I'm going get each of you to write your own name and stick labels on your drawer, on the place where you hang your coat and the box where you put away your shoes. This is because the labels we've been using up to now have become dirty and torn, and I want to have nice new ones. Also, up to now I've written out everything, but you're all 5 now and able write your own labels. So, let's start!"

The children showed great interest in the teacher's suggestion. "What do I write on? What picture shall I draw on my label?" and so forth, each one asking something different. Teacher: "Here are the labels. How many for each of you?" Child 1: "Um . . . there's the drawer and the shoe-box" (bending his thumb and index finger as he spoke). Child 2: "And the coat-hook. So 3 labels." (There are four children in each group.) Teacher: "Right, will the leaders of each group for

5.6. NOTES ON EARLY MATHEMATICAL EXPERIENCES

today count up how many labels you each need for yourself and the other members of the group and then come and get them from me."

The children showed the following variety of thought processes.

1. One child came to the teacher to fetch four labels, distributed one each to the other members and himself, and repeated this process three times.

2. One child came to fetch three labels for Child A, three for Child B, three for Child C, and then three for himself

3. "Nine labels please," said one child. When asked how he had arrived at this number, he pointed his finger at Child D and wagged it three times, then did the same for Child E and the same for Child F. He got nine labels and distributed them, and then realized he had none for himself.

4. "Nine labels please," said another child. When he was asked how he reached nine, he explained that he counted first in twos—two, four, six—pointing at the children G, H, and I, and then again in ones—seven, eight, nine. So he got labels and distributed them, and then he too became aware that he had none for himself.

5. "You've been teaching us how to add up," said one child. Pointing at Child J and Child K, he said that three and three were six, then standing in front of Child L, he counted seven, eight, nine, then pointing to himself, he counted ten, eleven, twelve, and asked for twelve labels.

EXAMPLE 3: USING UNITS FOR MEASURING WEIGHT

This is an example to make children find that unit and number are convenient for measuring the weight of a thing. For a class of 5-year-old children, a birthday party was held once every month for the children born in that month. The mothers would come to the party and talk about when their children were born and how they brought them up. At the December party, A's mother came and talked about the time A was born. "He was just the same weight as a bag of oranges, and if I tossed him up in the air, he would be so pleased," she said. Now A was by far the largest boy in the class, so everyone was very surprised at the thought of him being tossed up in the air like a bag of oranges.

Then the class teacher suggested that all the children should each collect and try holding a bag of oranges of the same weight as they were when they were born. The next day, there was a great deal of talking among the children who had found out their weight when they were born. S said that when she was born, she weighed as much as five bags of oranges. This produced a lot of protests that this was far too heavy for a baby. Nobody paid any attention to how heavy one bag was. Instead, all the children said that S was mistaken. When the teacher inquired more closely, S produced a net bag, holding only a small number of oranges, and when the children saw it, they finally realized the difference between this bag and the bag they had imagined.

Then the teacher brought out a large 3 kg bag of oranges, containing three smaller bags weighing 1 kg each, that she had prepared. After all the children had the chance to hold the large bag, the teacher untied it and took out the smaller bags. "I wonder who weighed as much as one bag and who as much as three," she said. At this, the children said that the teacher was being unfair and that she should have said at the start how many bags were in the big bag. At this, the teacher decided to make the children think a bit more deeply. "For you children in this class, if you want to show someone how heavy you were when you were born, it's all right to use a bag of oranges like this, but if M (a popular boy who recently moved from Tokyo to Hokkaido) wanted to do this, what would he do?" she asked. Japanese oranges are not so frequent in Hokkaido as in Tokyo. The children discussed among themselves what sort of things could be found in Tokyo and Hokkaido and came up with soy sauce, milk, juice, beer, canned goods, and so forth.

Example 3 takes up the problem of the weight corresponding to one unit. The original intention of the teacher was to get the children to become physically aware, by actually holding something, of the weight of a newborn child, but the lesson then developed in an unexpected direction. The teacher used the fact that A's mother talked about one bag of oranges and S about five bags of oranges to produce a 3 kg bag containing three smaller bags and to enquire closely into why the children were so surprised that each time what happened was different from the image they had formed in their minds. Wanting to make the children aware of a generally familiar unit as a preliminary stage prior to expression in figures, the teacher also raised the problem of how to explain this to a friend who had come from a long way away.

EXAMPLE 4: MEASURING LENGTH

In the second term of the final year in kindergarten (5-year-old children), an excursion was planned to a park where steam engines would be on display. The children were motivated, and it was decided that they could bring along books and models. Interest rose rapidly and in this atmosphere the terms D-51 and C-63 started to be used. When the children realized that 'C' and 'D' were symbols for the number of driving wheels that made the train run, interest focused on these wheels. On the poster about the engines, there was the following sentence, "The size of the driving wheels that support the heavy steam engine and make it run will make everyone gasp with wonder." When the children heard this, it gave rise to a lot of questioning as to how big the wheels might be. So then the class teacher tried to get the children to develop some hypotheses with the aim of

5.6. NOTES ON EARLY MATHEMATICAL EXPERIENCES   381

measuring these against the real thing. An old car tire was placed against the blackboard and the size of a bicycle tire shown in comparison with this. Then the possibilities for the size of the engine driving wheel were narrowed down to three: (a) the size of the tire on an adult bicycle, (b) the same size as the height of the tallest pupil in the class, and (c) the same size as the teacher's height. It was impossible to imagine anything bigger than this. At the initial stage of deciding between the three possibilities, many supported (c), but when it was seen how big a circle of that radius would be, the children changed one after the other to supporting (b).

In fact, when they got to the park, they found that the actual size of the wheel was clearly bigger than any of the children, and in particular the wheel on the C-type engine measured more than 2 meters. The problem that then arose was how they would be able to reproduce this on the blackboard in the classroom. So, the teacher stood in front of the wheel with the children a little way away trying to estimate by holding up their hands the extent to which the teacher's height fell short of the height of the wheel. "No, a bit further apart" or "About this much more" were heard. Then someone said that if they had a long piece of string, it would help, but there was nothing suitable nearby, so they borrowed the Principal's belt. But the belt was too short to measure the wheel. So the next problem that arose was how to measure the difference between the length of the belt and the size of the wheel. The teacher held the belt so that it hung down from the top of the wheel and then the children tried various means of measuring the remainder. The various units tried included the hand from wrist of fingertips, the distance from elbow to fingertips, right and left hands placed alternately on the wheel, the width of a hand or the size of a shoe. "My shoes are 18 cm," said the child who tried this method, "so I can measure the distance." But almost all the children used the method of standing in front of the wheel themselves and seeing to what part of their body the end of the belt reached. But then it occurred to one of the boys, T, that if the teacher stretched out her arm, the edge of the wheel would come to a point just below her wrist. It was decided in the end that this method of measurement was the best and the point was marked with a ballpoint pen on the teacher's arm. Then the next day the children were able to reproduce the size of the wheel on the blackboard.

Example 4 shows how children used semiconcrete objects for comparison and developed their own units in a task involving measurement. The problem was not simply one of measuring the size of a driving wheel, but of reproducing the size in another location, that is, the blackboard in the children's classroom, so the need for a semiconcrete object arose. The teacher's belt served this purpose, but it was too short, so a new problem arose. In these circumstances, it would have been possible to carry out the measurement using the belt as one unit, but none of the children thought of that. Perhaps the reason they didn't think of using the belt as a unit was because they realized, by estimating with their eyes, that size of the wheel would not correspond to a multiple of the length of the belt. It is very interesting to compare the different methods of measurement that the children adopted after this. What happened was that the majority of children used part of their own body as a unit of length, finding in every case that this was shorter than the length of the belt, and in trying to measure in this way, they were using a method adopted since very ancient times.

Chapter 5.7

The Role of the Teacher in Early Childhood Mathematics

Helen Mansfield
Curtin University of Technology, WESTERN AUSTRALIA

In this chapter, I want to discuss some of the implications of a constructivist view of learning for the role of the teacher in early childhood mathematics. The constructivist view of learning sees new knowledge as modifications of current knowledge in the context of the learner's physical and mental actions and reflection on those actions. A key question in this discussion is how the teacher can help young children to construct mathematical knowledge.

THE STUDENT

The constructivist view of learning implies that the knowledge and beliefs that students bring to a given learning situation influence the meanings they construct in that situation. Different students will enter any learning situation with different knowledge and beliefs and may construct different knowledge from the newly presented situation. This means that each student's existing knowledge and beliefs about a topic must be known by the teacher and taken into account in designing an effective teaching program for that topic. Different activities may be required for different students learning the same topic, or at least different aspects of those activities may need to be emphasized. Knowledge is not the same as believing. It is possible for students to construct a meaning or process for use in school mathematics and yet to reject it for use outside the classroom because it does not fit the perceived reality of the student's outside experiences (Mansfield & Happs, 1987).

Learning implies conceptual change. Conceptual change can involve additions to the student's conceptions or alternatively a more radical restructuring of ideas. Writers in science education, such as Hewson (1981) and Posner, Strike, Hewson, and Gertzog (1982), suggested that for cognitive change to occur, students must be dissatisfied with their existing ideas, and new ideas must be intelligible, plausible, and more useful than the existing ideas in order for the student to modify those existing ideas.

It is not always easy to promote conceptual change in mathematics because students' existing ideas are often resistant to change. This may be because students' ideas are not capricious. They have an internal logic that has been tested against reality and always previously found adequate in explaining reality.

The personal characteristics of the student may contribute to the difficulty of effecting conceptual change. For example, some students are flexible when exposed to new ideas, whereas others are more resistant to change. Children who in early childhood learn to seek certainty, dislike ambiguity, and distrust new ideas may face problems when confronted by demands for change. As Head (1986) pointed out, the strength of resistance to change is dependent on the process by which existing ideas have been reached. Ideas and beliefs may have been reached either after full consideration of alternatives or by foreclosure to prevent uncertainty. In the latter case, a new idea may be resisted as it opens up the area of uncertainty once again.

Another important implication of the constructivist view of learning is that the student must be an active and reflective thinker. As Kamii argued (1981; 1985), this entails reducing adult power so that students can construct knowledge in an autonomous rather than a heteronomous way. An example of how this might be done is to respond to a student's error, such as $4 + 3 = 6$, not by correcting it but by asking the student to explain how he or she obtained the answer. In this kind of situation, students often correct themselves as they are required not only to produce an answer but also to reflect on the process by which they obtained that answer.

If teachers always provide the correct answers or tell students that they are wrong, they deprive the students of the possibility of correcting their own reasoning and accepting responsibility for their own knowledge. This encourages in students a view that knowledge is something transmitted by the teacher for which the teacher, rather than the students, has responsibility. When students depend on the teacher to supply processes and answers, they may rely on the certainty of old ideas and become resistant to change.

Some of the difficulty teachers face in promoting conceptual change may be because students are satisfied with their existing ideas, thus teachers need to provide activities that challenge those ideas. In mathematics lessons, this might perhaps be done by placing students in problem-solving situations where the correct views must be constructed and used in order for the problem to be solved. The teacher can also try to set up situations of conflict that focus the students' attention on discrepancies between existing views and perceived reality. For example, if a student says that $4 + 3 = 6$, the teacher might ask the student to find the answer to 3 + 3. If the same answer of 6 is given, students are placed in a position of conflict that they can be asked to resolve.

In order to overcome the difficulty of effecting conceptual change due to a fear of uncertainty on the part of the student, the teacher can develop a classroom climate in which students are encouraged to express newly formulated and sometimes, from the teacher's perspective, incorrect ideas. These ideas can be treated as informative and potentially useful rather than as items to be corrected. A supportive environment will help students to acquire the confidence to persevere with their attempts to reason about situations and to reflect on and communicate their reasoning.

The fostering of autonomy needs to begin in early childhood classes. Attitudes towards mathematics and towards oneself as an autonomous learner of mathematics begin in the early years. By the age of about 12, students' views of what teaching and learning should be like are firmly developed and students are resistant to efforts to make them autonomous, as the Project for Enhancing Effective Learning has shown in Australia (Baird & Mitchell, 1987). Indeed, in many junior primary school classrooms, students have already learned that the only source of correct processes and answers is the teacher. Many have come to believe that mathematics is what the teacher tells them to do in lessons labelled "mathematics." This surely is a situation that is foreign to the constructivist view of learning.

THE ROLE OF THE TEACHER

In order to provide a classroom environment that promotes autonomy and the active construction of meaning by students, the teacher must undertake many functions. One of the key tasks of the teacher is to ascertain the existing knowledge and beliefs that each student brings to each learning situation. This can perhaps best be done by talking with the students as they engage in mathematical activities and by listening to and observing them as they interact with each other and act on the materials and ideas with which they are engaged. While students interact with each other during their activities, they are exposed to differing points of view that they must attempt to coordinate. Students can be encouraged to exchange points of view and to challenge or correct each other's opinions. Essentially, then, in mathematics lessons a reasonable level of noise must be accepted.

The task may be made easier if teachers have an idea of what they expect their students to know or believe. The extensive recent research on young children's arithmetic might help to suggest ways of thinking that young children use when engaged in arithmetic tasks, as might also the research on misconceptions. There is not a corresponding corpus of research on young children's thinking on spatial tasks. Unfortunately, the research on children's arithmetic that is available does not always seem consistent. For example, Kamii and DeClark (1985) suggested that "subtraction may not be appropriate as an objective for first graders" yet Sato (1984) found with a sample of 4- to 6-year-old children in Japan that the removing aspect of subtraction is easier to understand than addition and recommended that it should be taught before addition to kindergarten children. Such research is carried out in particular cultural contexts and the findings depend on cultural factors such as the structure of the language being used, as well as the types of tasks being presented to the children. For this reason, different researchers often reach different conclusions about the same research question, making the interpretation of research findings difficult for others. Not all classroom teachers are familiar with the existing research, and researchers and teacher educators have an important role in sifting, evaluating, and communicating research findings to teachers.

Whereas an analysis of students' ideas may tell teachers what ideas students are likely to bring to the classroom, teachers also need to know where they want students to go in their construction of knowledge. Students may not construct the mathematical ways of thinking that are found useful by mathematicians because these are partly social knowledge and are not necessarily intuitively obvious. For example, when third graders are using Base Ten blocks to model subtraction, both with and without regrouping, they often remove the larger blocks first although the written algorithm we teach requires them to subtract the ones digits first. Even some college students who have years of familiarity with the algorithm subtract from the left with the Base Ten materials. This observation reinforces the view that some of the written processes we teach may not be the most appropriate because alternative written processes may record better the actions that students most commonly perform with materials.

The challenge is to encourage students to construct, through sharing and negotiation, a common mathematical meaning or process that is valid, without undermining their own abilities or distorting the mathematics. If this constructed view appears to be restricting the students' further learning, the teacher can again challenge the students' view and help them construct a new meaning that is more useful to them.

Given a range of mathematical ideas that teachers want their students to construct, they must devise teaching situations that have the potential to provide opportunities for such constructions. Most of the situations that are found in the preschool or in the junior primary classroom are not intrinsically mathematical. Sand, water, and block play are common activities in the preschool. Activities involving manipulation of small objects, counters, Unifix cubes, geometric shapes, and so on are common in most junior primary classrooms. Such activities become mathematical only when children act on these materials, reflect on their actions, and focus on these attributes or relationships that we generally regard as mathematical. For example, identifying common attributes, arranging objects in patterns, counting, describing shapes, and comparing sizes of geometric blocks would generally be regarded as mathematical activities, whereas tasting and throwing blocks would not. Conversely, of course, many activities that are not generally regarded as mathematical have the potential to involve mathematical thinking if the teacher recognizes this and promotes it. For example, if children were throwing blocks, they could observe which blocks do or do not roll on landing, leading to a discussion of round and flat surfaces.

Even when teachers recognize the potential for mathematical thinking that is present in an incidental classroom situation or a planned activity, they must have the skills that will enable them to help students use these situations to construct new mathematical knowledge. Teachers need to be able to suggest features for the student to observe or approaches for the student to try. By appropriate questioning, they may be able to help students to articulate and extend their ideas.

Although questioning is usually seen as beneficial in encouraging students to extend their thinking, questioning may sometimes undermine the student's autonomy. This can occur when the student perceives the teacher's question as a signal that the student's ideas are wrong. Students may then try to guess the response that the teacher wants rather than reflect on their own ideas. This type of student reaction seems most likely to be elicited when the teacher frequently asks students how they obtained particular answers as an indirect way of pointing out their errors. On the other hand, questions that invite students to satisfy the teacher's own genuine curiosity or to explain their reasoning to another student with a different answer seem more clearly to respect the students' efforts and to encourage reflection.

Teachers need the ability to set up situations that present conflicts between the student's existing ideas and new ideas, and they need to be aware of the student's possible resolutions of the conflicts. Sigel (1981; 1984a; 1984b) described what he calls "distancing strategies," which are procedures that can be used by teachers to help young children develop cognitively by recognizing and resolving inconsistencies between what the child expects and what actually occurs in the environment. These procedures are called "distancing strategies" because they serve to separate the child psychologically from the immediate present. That is, they invite the child to take perspectives that differ spatially or temporally from the child's immediate perspective.

Low-level distancing strategies include having the child perform actions such as labelling, describing, observing, or demonstrating. An example of a low-level strategy would be having a child describe a set of objects or observe and describe an action performed by the teacher, such as moving some objects apart. Medium-level distancing strategies include having the child describe similarities and differences and enumerate, sequence, and reproduce patterns or actions. An example of a medium-level strategy would be having a child describe the similarities amongst a group of objects and how they differ from another set from which they have been separated.

High-level distancing strategies include having the child evaluate consequences, competence, performance, or effect; and inference casual relations and their effects; and generalize, plan, and propose alternatives to resolve conflicts. An example of a high-level strategy would be asking children to say how they could find out which of two groups of objects had more in it, or how they could convince someone else who differed that they are in fact correct. The frequency with which preschool children are challenged by higher-level distancing strategies is positively related to children's performance in tasks requiring reconstructive memory and the ability to predict outcomes (Sigel, 1984a). The strategies described by Sigel suggest ways that teachers of young children can help them to advance their knowledge by perceiving and resolving discrepancies, although children's ability to do this will of course be limited by their current expectations and knowledge.

The task of teaching mathematics to young children is demanding. If teachers are ill-equipped to respond to the demands, their task in implementing a constructivist view of learning is indeed difficult. Clearly they must be able to recognize the knowledge and beliefs that individual children bring to each topic, select activities that will enable children to progress from their existing knowledge towards the desired knowledge, use skills such as questioning and distancing strategies to set up conflicts, and help children to resolve those conflicts.

On the other hand, the role of the teacher in implementing a constructivist view of learning can be very empowering. Teachers can be imaginative and innovative in selecting activities and materials for their particular group of students. They can arrange experiences, including social experiences, that will provide opportunities for students to make discoveries for themselves, rather than to memorize information provided by them. They can develop and use strategies that promote autonomous thinking in their students.

In places where teachers traditionally follow textbooks written by other people, teaching with a constructivist focus becomes difficult and restricted. In places where teachers traditionally write their own programs, guided by a syllabus and choosing from a range of curriculum materials to implement their program, teaching with a constructivist focus is much easier. The challenge for such teachers is to choose activities appropriate to their students and to develop the skills and knowledge of children's thinking in mathematical tasks that will enable them to provide an environment in which children are challenged to take responsibility for their own learning.

Although none of the teachers' tasks is particularly easy, I suggest the reward for the teachers, both in terms of a more stimulating classroom and in terms of their own and the students' increased autonomy, is well worth the effort.

Chapter
5.8

Mathematics Curriculum Design: A Constructivist's Perspective

Leslie P. Steffe
University of Georgia, USA

The current "top down" approach to mathematics curriculum in the USA is exemplified in such notions as intended and implemented curricula and in ideal, implemented, and achieved curricula, where each is viewed as an approximate subset of the one above it. The intended or ideal curriculum is of primary concern in some of the available documents proposing curriculum changes in the USA in that redistributions of mathematical content, with the inclusions of some currently missing parts and omissions of some currently used parts, have been recommended. We also have the recommendations that "standardized tests of achievement . . . should be administered at major transition points from one level of schooling to another" (A Nation at Risk, 1983) and "clear standards for achievement must be established at each grade level in order to create an institutionalized climate of expectations to which students will respond" (McKnight 1987). The top down principle of curriculum design is caught nicely in a statement made by Griffiths (1983) at ICME-4.

> In countries like the U.S.A., the problems of a mobile population and the low esteem of teaching as a job have induced the dream of a superficially simple description of a curriculum by means of an algorithm: the pupils are to pass through stages S1, S2, . . . , Sj, and when a pupil is judged to be in stage Sn at T; the algorithm moves him into stage Sn + 1 by time t + h where h depends on n. (p. 358)

Although the two factors isolated by Griffiths unquestionably contribute to the top-down principle, the principle that the mathematics curriculum exists independently of the teachers and students who use it is a more pervasive factor. This principle has been undermined by the results of the Second International Mathematics Study (SIMS, 1986). McKnight (1987) isolated teaching and learning strategies called *rote*.

> This use . . . suggests a view that learning for most teachers should be passive—teachers transmit knowledge to students who receive it and remember it mostly in the form in which it was transmitted. This might be considered as an approach of "rote teaching" and "rote learning." (p. 81)

Teachers and students clearly do not use ideal mathematics curriculum as intended. It is understandable that teachers who have studied mathematics extensively might view it as being somehow disembodied from human experience because of the dominance of structuralism and formalism (Byers, 1983). At the beginning of this century, Brouwer (1913), in his inaugural address at the University of Amsterdam, noted that in the case of formalism there is a "presupposition of a world of mathematical objects, a world independent of the thinking individual." This presupposition permeates mathematics education at all levels and is a basis for the principle that mathematics curriculum exists independently of the teachers and students who use it. Brouwer (1913) provided an alternative view, "the question of where mathematical exactness does exist, is answered differently by the two sides; the intuitionist says: in the human intellect, the formalist says: on paper."

THE FIRST FEATURE OF CURRICULUM DESIGN

Brouwer's viewpoint is compatible with the constructivist principle that "the environment as we perceive it is our invention" (von Foerster, 1984). If this principle is accepted, it legitimizes the mathematical knowledge of the other. Individuals who believe that mathematics is the way it is—having mind independent existence—rather than the way human beings make it to be might reject the necessity to reformulate the meaning of curriculum in the top-down approach. This is particularly unsettling because in my way of thinking, the mathematical knowledge of the other is taken as relative to one's own frame of reference.

The mathematical knowledge of the other, from the perspective of the observer, is established using conceptual elements belonging to the observer, so it might seem that what is being proposed is nothing but solipsism—the theory that one's own knowledge is the only thing that can be known or verified. It has been interpreted in this way by Vergnaud (1987) and by Wheeler (1987). However, von Foerster (1984) explicitly rejected solipsism: "The solipsism claim falls to pieces when besides me I invent another autonomous organism." According to von Foerster's analysis, the mathematics of the other is not only in my imagination, because if I agree, say, that there is another organism not unlike myself, I have to agree that the other organism can insist that his or her mathematical reality is the sole mathematical reality and that everything else is in his or her imagination, including my own mathematical reality. However, I cannot agree that my mathematical reality is simply a concoction of the other's imagination and so I have to accept the other's mathematical reality as distinct from my own. As observer, the only way I can know it is to make a model of it.

Viewing the mathematics of teachers and students as being of primary interest as well as the mathematical knowledge of mathematicians leads to a general change in the assumptions permeating mathematics curricula design. As valuable as mathematical recommendations for intended or ideal curriculum might be, it is counterproductive to posit an intended or ideal curriculum independently of teachers and students that can be then used by them. In a relativistic world view, various frames of reference must be taken into account, and this is my first feature of curriculum design.

I have previously separated a teacher's mathematical knowledge into three parts; the part we would attribute only to the teacher, the part we would say the teacher has in common with students, and the part we would attribute only to students (Steffe, 1985). The latter part is a model of the students' mathematical knowledge that we would say is not a part of the teacher's mathematical knowledge per se. This separation is especially crucial because it helps in understanding the relation between teachers' mathematical knowledge and that of their students. The mathematical knowledge of students as perceived by teachers is an invention of the teachers.

THE SECOND FEATURE OF CURRICULUM DESIGN

Mathematical knowledge is viewed as being constructed as a result of dynamic goal-directed mathematical activity in an environment. If an environment is an invention of the actor, it follows that an environment is established as the result of an assimilation, which is "the integration of new objects or situations and events into previous schemes" (Piaget, 1980c). The result of an assimilation of a particular situation is an experience of the situation and this experience constitutes a learning environment in the immediate here and now. So, a mathematical learning environment is the result of an assimilation, which is a relative operation, relative to the observer's mathematical situation and to the assimilator's mathematical knowledge. Viewing assimilation in this way is my second feature of curriculum design.

THE THIRD AND FOURTH FEATURES OF CURRICULUM DESIGN

A mathematical learning environment for students is the teachers' experience of what they intend for the students to assimilate. To distinguish between mathematical learning environments for and of students, I use "possible mathematical learning environments" and simply "mathematical learning environments," respectively. A mathematical learning environment is a variable experiential field whose contents are specified by a community of participants. Viewing a mathematical learning environment in this way is my third feature of curriculum design.

Possible mathematical learning environments are designed by a teacher in part with respect to students' zones of potential development (Vygotsky, 1956) and in part with respect to students' actual level of development (Sinclair, 1988). The latter is determined by the situations the students can independently solve and the former is determined by the problems the students can solve with the help of a teacher. In constructivism, a zone of potential development of a specific mathematical concept for a given student is determined by the modifications of the concept the student might make in, or as a result of, interactive communication in mathematical learning environments. It is an observer's concept.

Zones of potential development and possible mathematical learning environments depend on each other, so it is possible for a student to have differing zones of potential development with respect to the same concept. The particular modifications of a concept could diverge in one of several directions depending on the possible mathematical learning environments encountered by the student that, in turn, are dependent on particular modifications. This realization places teachers in a crucial position with respect to the mathematical development of their students. Nevertheless, the unavoidable dependence does not mean that the students' zone of potential development is wholly dependent on possible mathematical learning environments nor does it mean that the students can learn anything the teacher wants them to learn in the immediate future.

A particular modification of a mathematical concept cannot be caused by a teacher any more than nutriments can cause plants to grow. Nutriments are used by the plants for growth but they do not cause plant growth. Teachers are constrained in specifying what they place in the students' zone of potential development by what the students make from their experiences in particular mathematical learning environments. So, zones of potential development are negotiated through the interactive communication that transpires in mathematical learning environments. Viewing zones of potential development in this way is my fourth feature of curriculum design.

THE FIFTH FEATURE OF CURRICULUM DESIGN

If mathematical knowledge is viewed as being constructed as the result of goal-directed mathematical activity in a mathematical learning environment, then how it might be learned is caught by von Glasersfeld's (1987) comment that "knowledge is not passively received but actively built up by the cognizing subject." Active mathematical learning consists in the adaptations that individuals make as a result of their experiences. These adaptations can occur in a flash of insight (Wertheimer, 1959), during periods of rest and reflection (Cobb & Steffe, 1983; Hadamard, 1954; Steffe, Cobb & von Glasersfeld, 1988), or during periods of mathematical activity. Essentially, mathematical learning involves accommodation of current mathematical concepts to neutralize perturbations that can arise in one of several ways. As such, it includes what Polya (1962) meant when he stated that to have a problem means "to search consciously for some action appropriate to attain a clearly conceived, but not immediately attainable aim."

Like it or not, teachers currently are principal actors in how students establish and modify their mathematical environments. We have seen the results of not casting teachers at the left center of the mathematics education stage as intelligent human beings with the authority to make important educational decisions in the rote learning reported in SIMS. Teachers do make decisions for students to learn in this way by default and apparently do not accept responsibility for their actions. For example, they rank developing a systematic approach to solving problems and an awareness of the importance of mathematics in everyday life as the two most important goals of mathematics education (SIMS, 1986). Rote learning is not compatible with these goals.

Mathematics teachers obviously believe (McKnight, 1987) that active mathematical learning is not a part of the mathematics curriculum. The finding that decision making is dominated by the textbook (SIMS, 1986), rather than being based on the mathematical knowledge their students can actively learn is consistent with the practice of transmitting mathematics to students. The tenet that mathematical knowledge is constructed as the result of active mathematical learning is clearly being violated by mathematics education world-wide. Viewing active mathematics learning as being a part of mathematics curricula is my fifth feature of curriculum design.

THE SIXTH FEATURE OF CURRICULUM DESIGN

Taking the teacher's frame of reference as well as the student's frame of reference into account in curriculum design has far-reaching consequences. Neither is the central reference (von Foerster, 1984). In other words, a curriculum should not be student-centered any more than it should be teacher-centered, and whatever mathematics curriculum might be, it can be in part found in the mathematical learning environments of individuals.

Teachers must decenter and attempt to modify their possible mathematical learning environments in experiential contexts to fit the mathematical learning environments of their students in order to establish mathematical communication. The teachers' environment, then, includes their interpretations of their students' mathematical learning environments and their modifications of possible mathematical learning environment to fit those interpretations. Mathematics teaching consists of the interactive communication in this consensual domain of experience. Interactive communication provides an opportunity for teachers to create problematic situations through which they can engender the perturbations that drive mathematics learning. If the students are successful in neutralizing these perturbations by modifying their current knowledge, they can establish a modified environment; they can see the old environment in a new way. Viewing mathematics teaching as being a part of mathematics curricula is my sixth feature of curriculum design.

THE SEVENTH FEATURE OF CURRICULUM DESIGN

A teacher can play a crucial role in students' modifications of current mathematical learning environments as well as in their initial establishment, if there is some modicum of awareness of the mathematical operations of students. Teachers who are aware of the mathematical operations of their students could base their interactive communication on those models. Sensitive teachers might also realize that although students might seem to perform the same mathematical operations as they do, these operations might be qualitatively different from their own. There is also the case where students might be able to perform only part of the conceptual operations of which a teacher is capable. In either case, a student will inevitably establish a different mathematical learning environment from the teacher. It is all the more complicated because different students are likely to be able to perform different conceptual operations. Constructing a reality of "shared" experiences by all concerned encourages the interactive communication that serves in encouraging the reorganization of experience as well as the autonomy of its participants (Cobb, 1985).

Casting teachers and students as the principal actors in establishing and in modifying mathematical learning environments in the context of ongoing mathematical teaching and learning, changes the traditional view of teachers and students as users of the mathematics curriculum to teachers and students as creators of mathematics curricula. Viewing teachers and students in this way is my seventh feature of curriculum design.

THE EIGHTH FEATURE
OF CURRICULUM DESIGN

The generative power of children can be impressive when they are working in mathematical learning environments that are conducive to constructive activity. However, children's generative power has only begun to be charted. Mathematics teachers at all levels have an exciting choice between being participants in specifying the generative power of their students or taking what their students can learn as being already specified by an a priori curriculum. However, possible mathematical learning environments could quickly become surrogates for mathematics textbooks. It is crucial for mathematics teachers to develop the belief that they do mathematics and create mathematics curricula in the context of ongoing mathematics learning and teaching. As mathematics teachers it is crucial for them to develop the belief that they can understand the mathematics of their students and how to foster its construction.

I cannot emphasize enough that, using their own mathematical knowledge, mathematics teachers must interpret the language and actions of their students and then make decisions about possible mathematical knowledge their students might learn. The confidence to make decisions and to take the consequences of making those decisions must be a part of a viable model of teaching that will rival the classical model of transmission of knowledge. Regardless of the array of possible environments that are available to the teachers, they must understand that their decisions are involved in the creation of mathematics curricula. Taking the decisions of teachers into account is my eighth feature of curriculum design.

THE NINTH FEATURE
OF CURRICULUM DESIGN

In a curriculum framework that emphasizes created curricula rather than implemented and achieved curriculum, there is still a role for something like an ideal or intended curriculum. My alteration, however, is to change ideal curriculum to *abstracted curricula,* because an ideal is platonic and uninfluenced by experience, emotion, or personal knowledge, all of which are involved in human decision making. The plural "curricula" rather than the singular "curriculum" is used to emphasize diversity and variability rather than homogeneity and constancy in educational practice in mathematics.

Abstracted mathematics curricula are established through the process of experiential abstraction. They are models created as a result of participation in ongoing mathematics teaching and learning. These models contain (a) a specification of possible mathematical learning periods along with the goals and intentions of the teacher within these learning periods, (b) mathematical concepts and operations of the involved students within the learning periods and itineraries of construction of those concepts and operations including time estimates, (c) problem situations that can serve in the establishment and modification of mathematical learning environments by students with the learning periods, (d) critical decisions that can be made in posing the problem situations to students (Brown & Walter, 1983), and (e) sample interactive communications that can be encouraged among the participants within the learning periods. Replacing the ideal mathematics curriculum with abstracted mathematics curricula is my ninth feature of curriculum design.

THE TENTH FEATURE OF CURRICULUM DESIGN

In the case of abstracted mathematics curricula, teachers can choose from among various models, modify a certain model, generate hybrid models using parts of those available, or else freely generate their own models. Through acts of interpretation and choice, teachers can generate possible mathematical learning environments that they believe fit one or more students of a group. These choices are analogous to the negotiations that should be involved in establishing mathematical learning environments. Just as we want students to take responsibility for their own learning, we want teachers to take responsibility for their own teaching. Abstracted mathematics curricula are to mathematics teachers as possible learning environments are to mathematics students. Viewing abstracted mathematics curricula in this way is my last feature of curriculum design.

A goal structure for abstracted mathematics curricula such as the one elaborated by Treffers (1987) is needed. But this element of abstracted mathematics curricula is just as dependent on experiential fields as the latter are dependent on the former. Curriculum developers should not take their goals for mathematics education as fixed ideals that stand uninfluenced by their teaching experience. Goal structures that are established prior to teaching experience are only starting points and must undergo experiential transformations in actual teaching and learning episodes. Although curriculum developers can have an initial goal structure, what a goal structure for an abstracted mathematics curriculum eventually consists of is not simply a transformation of the initial goal structure. Hypotheses can be formulated and tested, but curriculum developers should expect to learn certain elements of mathematics teaching and learning only through experiential abstraction. The resulting curricula should be made public through communication among teachers and it is in this sense that curriculum can be considered as a sociological construct.

FINAL COMMENTS

Piaget (1964) identified experience as one crucial factor of intellectual development and this applies to curriculum developers as well as to the teachers and students who create mathematics curriculum. I cannot emphasize enough that curriculum developers who aim at learning what mathematics curricula might consist of must embed themselves in mathematics teaching and learning as well as opportunities to reflect on their experiences. How to encourage reflection and abstraction, especially one's own, can be very sensitive. Becoming aware of one's own ways and means of operating when solving educational problems and modifying those ways and means to meet certain constraints is precisely what is involved in reflection and abstraction. In fact, one of my explicit goals when immersing myself in teaching and learning situations is to become increasingly aware of my own actions as a mathematics teacher and in controlling and monitoring those actions. I believe this sense of the self teaching mathematics is crucial in developing curricula and in sustaining motivation to solve the problems that are presented in context of mathematics teaching and learning.

What goes by the name of mathematics curriculum development in radical constructivism by necessity starts with the mathematical knowledge of teachers and students and any person who purports to be a developer of curriculum must be first and foremost a mathematics teacher. We have seen the tragic results of available (textbooks) and adopted (again textbooks) curriculum in the Second International Mathematics Study. In the curriculum framework I am proposing, there are no such concepts in the same sense nor is there an ideal curriculum in the sense intended. Mathematics curriculum changes should not go by those routes. Rather, there are curriculum changes by common consent. This means, if SIMS is any indication, that teachers must construct a world view where they see themselves and their students as the primary actors in creating mathematics curricula in the context of ongoing teaching and learning.

This very fundamental understanding of what it means to be a teacher has powerful implications for curriculum developers as they strive to create abstracted mathematics curricula, because mathematics teaching and learning must serve as material in whatever experiential abstractions are made. By being embedded in ongoing mathematics teaching and learning, both as actors and participants, curriculum developers can isolate regularities in their experiential world. These patterns are the basis for forming the concepts (or models) that I have called abstracted mathematical curricula—a conceptual generalization that curriculum developers can abstract from a group of experiences for the purpose of categorizing and systematizing new experiences (von Glasersfeld & Steffe, 1987).

Finally, one of my goals as a curriculum developer is for teachers to construct a network of mathematical concepts and operations that could deepen, unify, and extend their conceptions of mathematics curricula. This network of mathematical relations is to transcend the mathematical knowledge of the students they teach but include it as a special case. The mathematics teachers must engage in mathematical explorations. Otherwise, if we continue to produce a priori curriculum where the mathematical concepts and operations are prescribed, the teachers will be encouraged only to continue avoiding the responsibility for their own learning and will quite likely remain unmotivated to become active in mathematics and mathematics curricula. It is crucial for mathematics teachers to develop a belief that they are people of mathematics because they do and teach mathematics (Steen, 1986). As people of mathematics, it is also crucial for them to develop a belief that they understand the mathematics of their students and how to foster its construction. The specifications of abstracted mathematics curricula and of possible mathematical environments are places where it becomes possible for a constructivist mathematics educator to provide insight in mathematics education.

Discussion Chapters:
Teacher Education

Chapter
5.9

Constructivism and Teacher Education for Teachers of Early Childhood Mathematics

Nick James
Open University, UNITED KINGDOM

Robert Underhill
Virginia Tech, USA

The Teacher Education Discussion Group consisted of 20 people who attended all the sessions of the action group. The following countries were represented: United States of America, Australia, United Kingdom, Finland, Japan, Brazil, Israel, Canada. Two presentations were given to the subgroup, one by Bob Perry on behalf of Ogbonna Ohuche and the other by Leone Burton. Six others were distributed as background reading to be read by all participants in the 2 days preceding Days 6 and 7, when a lively and fruitful discussion of the issues for teacher education arising out of these works occurred. Almost all of these are included in this book and reference will be made to them in this chapter where appropriate.

Five areas of concern emerged from our discussions. There was a remarkable degree of consensus in these areas that, it was felt, would provide a good focus for work over the next 4 years before ICME-7: a consensus that was all the more remarkable when you take into account the international diversity of the group. We have expressed these as areas for concern to try to ensure that readers do not see these as answers to the questions framed for this group by the International Panel. Rather they should be seen as arenas that we might need to enter in the struggle towards views on what mathematical teacher education could be like for teachers of mathematics in early childhood. This was a very interesting discussion group because the view of the environment in mathematics teacher education is where the constructivist position is least well understood.

In the interests of brevity, the questions before the group are not restated here because they are given in Les Steffe's overview of the work of the action group in Chapter 1.1.

AREA 1: CREATING ENVIRONMENTS FOR PROSPECTIVE TEACHERS

This contains the idea that teacher educators should practice what they preach and work in the same way with their students as they might hope their students would eventually work with children. Hatfield (chap. 5.10) makes this point very strongly when he says that "the teacher education environment must itself be constructive. This will require the constructivist teacher educators to engage in the kind of actions that they expect the future teacher to use."

The group also explores some of the problems that might face teacher educators taking a constructivist view of their task. The reader can get a feel for the background to our discussions by reading the chapters before the group at the time and which follow.

From Sinclair (chap. 2.1) comes the thought that children perceive teachers not as people who work alongside children in their attempts to construct meaning but rather as people who asked questions to which they already know the answers. Perry (chap. 6.1), whilst introducing Ohuche (chap. 5.1), speaks of "teacher lust" where teachers desire to have pupils see things the teacher's way thus preventing children from exploring the problems that concern them. This can often cause children to see their teachers as people who prevent them from doing sensible things.

Burton (chap. 5.3) highlights a conflict for the group when she describes four deeply held beliefs about teaching mathematics that would need to be challenged in prospective teachers. Kieren (chap. 5.2), on the other hand, provides a lovely counterpoint to Burton's thought by presenting accounts of children "building new ideas (or making accommodations)" in the very kind of environment that Burton was calling for. One account in particular stood out for us. It was the story of how Hanne (aged 7) solved the problem of finding a third of a pizza by "Y-ing it"!

Arising from these ideas, the group recognizes the enormous problem facing teacher educators. Instead of trying desperately to cover a set body of knowledge, they would need to start with their students' experiences of learning mathematics (built up mostly over the past 12 schooling years of their young lives!). They would also need to start with their students' theories of learning mathematics and then construct environments that would enable them to consider alternatives. The chapters by Hatfield (5.10), D'Ambrosio (5.12), and Tirosh (5.11), amongst others, stress the importance of finding these starting points and working from there. In entering the arena described in this area, the following question was before us all:

> What are the implications for teacher education of first finding out about the experiences and beliefs of both prospective and serving teachers and then, taking

those as the starting point, creating environments which will enable those teachers to grow towards a constructivist view of learning and teaching mathematics?

AREA 2: MAKING THE ACTIONS OF TEACHER EDUCATORS EXPLICIT

This area of concern really grows out of the first and requires teacher educators to attend not only to what was done in a particular learning situation but also to how it was done. Kieren's account of how Hanne "Y-ed the pizza" is a case in point. Here is an excellent study of what a child was doing in the process of building her mathematical ideas, but how did the teacher behave in the situation? Were there things that he did that somehow demonstrated to the children that he valued their thoughts, things that encouraged Hanne to continue exploring her ideas? Were there things that might have enabled the other two girls so to question Hanne that they too might have come to understand what she was doing? How does Leino (chap. 3.1) foster child-to-child discussion without intervening in their thinking? How can he listen-in to their discussions and yet not in any way interfere with their attempts to make meaning? If we had some feel for the answers to these questions, we might be better able to build our own idea of constructivist approaches.

By reflecting on the how of their actions and making these explicit to their students, teacher educators might enable prospective teachers to get a feel for what they, in their turn, might need to attend to when working with children in schools. Several of the background chapters for this discussion group draw specific attention to the how. Hatfield (chap. 5.10) suggests the need to investigate the attitude of teacher educators towards their students' struggle for meaning. Yoshikawa (chap. 5.13) explains how teachers (and presumably teacher educators) must be good moderators of discussion, knowing how to listen carefully and how to convey ideas to other children. Reeves (chap. 5.14) especially speaks to this area of concern. She talks of teachers "modeling language for thought," of the importance of a social dynamic in the classroom, and of teachers being aware of their part in the construction of children's mathematical thinking. In this context, the importance of identifying classroom organization and management issues that contribute to the creation and maintenance of a "conjecturing atmosphere" in mathematics classes is discussed. The need to identify the specific expectations of student/pupil behavior that teachers and teacher educators appear to hold in constructivist settings is also discussed.

Detailed case-studies that focus not only on the pupils' learning but also on the styles of teaching being used are therefore needed to throw light on these and other actions of constructivist teacher educators (and teacher's) in their classrooms. Many feel that identifying these and making them explicit would go a long way towards describing the nature and object of communications in teacher education (and school) classrooms.

AREA 3: MAKING THE TRANSITION FROM A 'TRANSMISSION-OF-KNOWLEDGE' TO A CONSTRUCTIVIST VIEW

This area of concern is very much related to the notion of culture-shock. Consider the child whose only experience of learning mathematics has been one of meticulously carrying out teacher's algorithms and learning how to provide the answers that the teacher wants. Now consider the culture-shock provided by an open question like, "Can you tell me what you've done to arrive at this item here?" Invariably this elicits guilt-ridden expressions of fear and failure like "What's wrong, what's wrong?" What will that child need to reassure him or her that there is no suggestion of right or wrongness, just a genuine attempt to enter that child's thought processes?

Transitions such as this are no less difficult for teachers, prospective or otherwise. They have to come to terms with a different set of expectations of them as teachers. In a constructivist world teachers are not required to be "fillers-of-empty vessels," as Burton (chap. 5.3) explains. Instead, they are required to participate in mathematical environments with the learners, to enter into their attempts to build new ideas in mathematics and, as Leino (chap. 3.1) says, to learn how best to help their pupils mathematize their activities. This could be very alien to most prospective teachers of mathematics.

When D'Ambrosio (chap. 5.12) speaks of the decision to implement problem-solving approaches in the state of Sao Paulo, she notes how "many of the considerations of these educational innovations were contradictory with current teaching practices" and how "the attitudes and beliefs . . . among Brazilian mathematics teachers serve as barriers in the implementation of the measures!" She also calls for a crucial change in teacher education which requires method and content classes not to work in opposition to one another. Similarly Reeves (chap. 5.14) refers to problems at the teacher education stage of implementing a constructivist view. Every department at the training institution wanted its "particular thing" done during the students' teaching practice. Students were presented with conflicting views of learning that presented enormous problems for implementing a constructivist view at the teacher education stage.

Further research is, therefore, required to inform educators (and, by implication, teachers in schools also) of what might be involved in helping students (and pupils) make the transitions described here.

AREA 4: IDENTIFYING THE PROCESSES BY WHICH STUDENTS CONSTRUCT MATHEMATICAL KNOWLEDGE IN LEARNING ENVIRONMENTS

Here a distinction was being drawn between the processes and products of learning. Hatfield (chap. 5.10) refers to the use of "problematic approaches" in teacher education. He goes on to say what the nature of a problematic approach in the construction of mathematical knowledge was, giving a very full description of how he sees the processes involved. These were not dissimilar to the problem-solving approaches already referred to by D'Ambrosio (chap. 5.12). Yoshikawa (chap. 5.13) talks about "good mathematical problems" that would encourage activity and discussion and lead to the construction of maths concepts, principles, or rules.

James, coauthor of this chapter, has developed a process model of the investigative thinking processes by which learners appear to construct their knowledge. The model (Fig. 1) involves learners exploring lots of special cases, gradually abstracting the "sameness" they perceive and expressing that generality. Also involved are processes of convincing oneself and others of the contexts within which the learners perceived generalization works.

By analogy, the model also describes the process by which prospective teachers might come to formulate their view of teaching mathematics. Suppose partic-

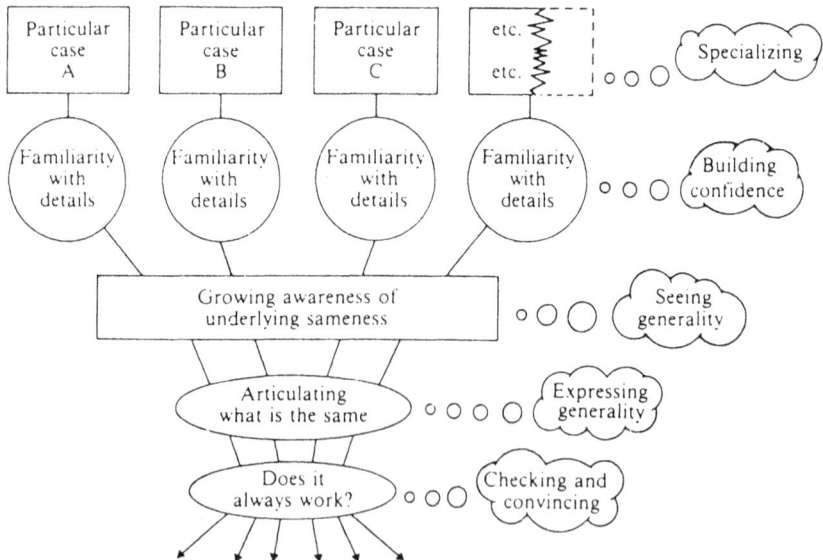

FIG. 1. A model of investigative thinking processes.

ular cases A, B, C, D, and so forth are instances in which prospective teachers are encouraged to build new ideas in mathematics for themselves during the mathematics teacher education classes they attend. It is possible to imagine that they might begin to identify certain samenesses in the constructivist teaching approaches being used, checking them out during their own teaching practices. For prospective teachers, the box marked "Does it always work?" in fact represents a life-long process of professional development, reflecting on and refining their methods of teaching—a constant construction and reconstruction of their views on teaching mathematics. Case studies focusing on the processes of constructivist thinking such as those described here might help to specify these processes more fully, thus enabling teacher educators (and teachers) to identify more readily when those thinking processes are at work in their students (or pupils).

AREA 5: CONSTRUCTING MATHEMATICAL KNOWLEDGE: A LIFE-LONG PROCESS

The notion of a life-long process of professional development emanates from some of the ideas described in the fourth area of concern. Here it was taken a stage further. As one member of the group put it: "For 12 years prospective teachers have thought and been taught one way. What chance have we for change in the ten weeks of teacher education?"

However, acceptance of the view expressed here would mean that the pressure to train prospective teachers within the time span given to teacher educators would be lifted from them. Instead the task before teacher educators becomes a question of attending, where necessary, to the problems of transition from transmission models of learning to constructivist ones and professional development becomes a process begun during the initial teacher education and continued throughout a teacher's professional life.

There are tremendous implications for the relationship between pre-service training and in-service training here. The latter would need to build positively on the former, leading to a seamless-robe view of professional development. As one member of the group said "long term efforts for change through one or two years induction would need to be operated collaboratively by universities and schools."

CLOSING REMARKS

This discussion group of the Action Group on the early childhood years happened to contain a large number of practicing classroom teachers. For a long while they listened to the teacher educators and researchers amongst us going on and on about their view of what teachers did or did not do in their classrooms as if the teachers themselves had no views of their own about children learning mathematics. Finally one of the teachers exploded: "Teacher educators and researchers need to recognize practicing classroom teachers *do* reflect on their actions and we *do* write about them. One has only to read what teachers in the PRIME project, the RAMP project and advisory teachers in England are doing. But you sometimes make us ordinary teachers feel rejected and somehow inferior when it comes to expressing our views. We don't feel that accounts of our observations are valued and respected."

In response, therefore, to this heart-felt cry from the classroom teachers amongst us, our times together in Budapest came to an end with the following recommendations being formulated by the group:

1. Forum should be set up in which the sharing of findings by practicing teachers, researchers, and teacher educators alike would be valued and respected.

2. Over the next 4 years, we should all generate write-ups of the environments we created, describing both what we did and how we did it, and these should be circulated through the previously suggested forum. The hope is that out of these we might, as a group of mathematics educators, build new constructs about ways of learning and teaching mathematics.

Chapter 5.10

Preparing Early Childhood Teachers for Constructive Mathematical Environments

Larry L. Hatfield
University of Georgia, USA

Within the mathematical environments of the young child, perhaps the most important contributing person is the child's teacher. If we wish to influence the mathematical environments of children, we must carefully consider the roles that the teacher can play in facilitating the child's construction of mathematical knowledge. That is, we who seek to prepare effective teachers must ponder how we might influence teachers in ways that allow them to engage in constructive mathematical approaches with their students. In this chapter I address the general question posed by the International Panel: What could mathematical teacher education be like for prospective teachers of mathematics in early childhood?

PAST MATHEMATICAL EXPERIENCES

It requires little argument to support the view that today the experiences in school mathematics for most children appear to be occurring from quite nonconstructivist perspectives. To most practicing teachers, the nature of their mathematics curriculum seems to be predetermined, externally prescribed (indeed, mandated), objectified, logically organized with an appropriate scope and sequence set by mathematical and curricular authorities, having fixed aims with measurable outcomes, and centered in physical textual materials. This view of curriculum is predicated on a realist conception of mathematics as external information to be transmitted or received; young children are treated as imitative organisms with only limited intellectual capacities such as perception and memory.

The effects of such experiences seem to be largely negative and limited, with many children developing thin, brittle knowledge and strong dislikes for doing what they think is mathematics. The basis for these teaching practices and beliefs seems to be tradition—teachers first experience these perspectives themselves as students in the schools and, regretfully, again in the universities. When they enter the role of teacher, they join an institutionalized tradition for perpetuating these types of experiences, a tradition that they largely accept, adopt, and maintain.

Changing World Views

Teachers can be helped to transform their traditional perspectives and beliefs about their own mathematics and about children's mathematical activity. They can come to view their mathematics curriculum as a dynamic social construction in which they and their students share opportunities and responsibilities. They can grow to acknowledge and accept the idiosyncratic necessity of knowledge construction, the significance of interpersonal relationships and social dynamics in facilitating constructive experiences, the problematical nature of communication, and the uncertain qualities of each child's mathematical growth. They can adopt roles that permit them more freedom to explore as collaborators with children the possible quantitative and spatial interpretations and meanings to be found in situations that can give rise to mathematical constructs.

They can realize that much of the standard content of the conventional, textbook-centered curriculum consists of concepts and procedures characterized in terms of adult conventions and thus is nothing more than agreements about powerful ideas that have been adopted for convenience. They can understand that when these adult conventions are simply modeled by the teacher for imitation by children, superficial meanings are likely to result as the child struggles to accommodate to imposed structures. Early childhood teachers can come to appreciate the absolute essentiality of affording children opportunities to grapple with quantitative situations in which their own reasoning is given the chance to develop. Children's inventions and formulations (though almost always different from) can usually at some point in the child's experience be related to these adult conversations if this is desirable.

To move away from this generational recycling of strict adherence to the imitation of adult mathematical conventions, prospective mathematics teachers need to shift in their world views toward more constructive perspectives and practices. A key factor in helping them undergo such an epistemological transformation is the nature of their experiences during their mathematical and professional education studies as they are preparing to become mathematics teachers.

Crisis in Identity

The challenge to mathematics teacher educators is great, for essentially the prospective teacher must be stimulated and guided toward confronting, criticizing, and in fundamental ways, refuting aspects of their own personal development in school mathematics. That is, any advocacies for more constructive views will at least implicitly suggest a critique and denial of the acquisition of one's own knowledge. Furthermore, the problematic nature of the exploration of concepts and procedures may oppose the learning style of the teacher who has felt satisfactory success in listening, watching, and imitating what is essentially "mathematics of the other." These confrontations may thereby arouse resistance and rejection, because it will seem to the teacher that what is being recommended is quite different from what one recalls about one's own "successful" school mathematical experiences.

Perhaps the resolution of this confrontation of self-identity lies in their opportunities as prospective teachers to experience university-level mathematics constructively. Through firsthand experiences in building-up new mathematical ideas and through reflection and discussion of such experiences, they might begin to sense what it could be like for children to construct mathematical ideas for themselves. Moreover, they must be encouraged to find themselves as teachers, exploring their own teaching actions in the classroom so that they develop and understand the open, problematic, child-centered style of the constructivist teacher.

CONSTRUCTIVE TEACHER PREPARATION ENVIRONMENTS

What kind of teacher education environment might facilitate the prospective early childhood teacher's development as a constructivist mathematics teacher? This must surely be problematical, but I propose a framework for characterizing important qualities of such an environment.

It appears that among the most powerful influences on beginning teachers are their perceptions and inferences about their own teachers and about their own recalled experiences as learners. Thus, the teacher education environment must itself be constructive in nature as it is experienced by the prospective teachers. The situations in which they experience their thinking about mathematics and mathematics teaching must be perceived by the teacher as constructive contexts. This will require constructivist teacher educators to engage in the kind of actions that one expects future teachers to use and to sponsor the type of activities for prompting knowledge construction that future teachers would hopefully become oriented to develop and provide for their students.

Mathematical Thinking of Teachers

For example, a serious, sincere effort should be made by the teacher educator to probe the mathematical thinking of individual teachers in order to formulate a model of each teacher's knowledge vis-à-vis "their mathematics" (i.e., the teacher educator's conjectural model of the teacher's mathematics). This may involve the conduct of clinical-type interviews with the preservice teachers, as well as observations of their mathematical activities during individual or group instruction. It seems many preservice early childhood teachers have limited, immature, mechanistic mathematical knowledge that is affected by negative emotions, such as fear, insecurity, or anger. I believe that we teacher educators must help them to identify and openly confront these conceptions and feelings if they are to overcome their own handicaps. But this needs to be done in a supportive, nurturing manner so that positive growth can result. These handicaps must be seen to be "O.K." because it may not be "their fault" but rather that they are the victims of distorted curricular aims and ineffective mathematics teaching. By witnessing the teacher educator's attempts at understanding and constructively guiding the mathematical knowledge of themselves and other classmates, they may come to adopt similar pedagogical perspectives and strategies.

What may be critical is the attitude exhibited by the teacher educator toward the struggle to understand the teacher's mathematics, to stimulate and guide the teacher toward further mathematical growth, and to engage in reflective abstraction about the teacher's mathematics. The inferences drawn by the novice teacher about the significance of this perceived attitude and of these efforts by the teacher educator could have a lasting effect on their own didactical knowledge and practice. I would assert that a constructivist attitude or predisposition in the teacher educator is needed to result in the kind of professional growth that may lead to a transformation of experiences of children in school mathematics.

Mathematical Communication

To nurture important *mathematical communication* with each teacher as well as the disposition to value such communication, the teacher educator should be willing to engage the teacher in discussions of mathematics. Through such interaction it may be possible for the novice teacher to begin to understand how a constructivist teacher might try to access and to think about a child's mathematics. It will be necessary for many mathematics teacher educators to shift away from their tendency to lecture and demonstrate "their finished mathematics" toward situations in which hesitant, insecure teachers might grow in their willingness to share their ideas. It is likely that by engaging the teachers in situations in which group problem solving and discussion can occur, they will come to trust their own role in the group dynamic, including the willingness to openly share one's mathematical strengths and weaknesses. In these groups even the most hesitant teacher must be encouraged to offer suggestions about how to proceed toward a solution to the posed mathematical problem. It may be necessary for the teacher educator to allow the group to engage the situation without intervention in order to permit the more hesitant to take risks and participate. Thus, constructivist teacher educators must first "practice what they preach" in order to stimulate each teacher to experience, and come to value, effective mathematical dialogues.

Adopting Problematic Approaches

The conduct of the teacher education courses should be to approach mathematics in a problematic style. What is the nature of a problematic approach in the construction of mathematical knowledge? Perhaps the following aspects are suggestive of important qualities to consider in adopting and implementing a problematic approach in early childhood teacher education.

1. A problematic approach presumes that a student's struggle to understand basic mathematical ideas (eg., multiplication, fraction, or variable) is itself a mathematical problem of great significance (at least to the student and to the teacher).

2. Participants would be encouraged to view their mathematical activity in relation to building-up specific items of knowledge as well as more general modes and processes involved in personal intellectual development:
- Problems to be solved are opportunities to develop one or more solution paths specific to the problem, but are also situations to become more aware of one's problem-solving capabilities and limitations.
- Concepts to be understood can be explorations of variations and constraints leading to a complex but functional cognitive scheme, but can also reveal possibly generalizable strategies for making sense of new ideas.
- Procedures to be formulated can be problematic occasions to identify, organize, test, refine, and justify the possible steps of a method for processing an entire class of tasks, but developing new procedures can lead to understandings about algorithmics as the study of how procedures are designed.
- Generalizations to be justified can be contexts for exercising one's logical reasoning.

3. It promotes an "open" quality to the mathematical situation so that the participants experience the freedom, indeed the expectation, to explore plausible alternatives, to formulate investigations, to invent nonroutine methods, and to express their own suggestions. The prospect of unexpected paths or results must always be present. In contrast to the "guided discovery" teaching method wherein a result known to the teacher determines the course of events, the problematic approach should allow, indeed encourage, unexpected directions and results.

4. A primary purpose in approaching the problematic mathematical situation is to experience the kind of thinking that is stimulated and that unfolds. This

purpose is above and beyond the apparent surface goals related to completing a task or remembering a method. Process-orientation by both teacher and student is integral to a problematic approach.

5. Within the social dynamics of the classroom, the importance of communication in order to engage in, and benefit from, a problematic approach must be emphasized. Students must be encouraged to share their thinking, because this permits other students to interact with their own ideas through the interpretations and reactions they formulate to what they hear and see. This also permits the teacher to make ongoing decisions about what to suggest or to question next in the discussion. For the constructivist teacher the open sharing of ideas through verbal interactions of students and teacher provides an important source of data for making inferences about "their mathematics" as the teacher is struggling to formulate and refine a theoretical model of the individual student.

A problematic approach is a teaching style in which the search for meaning and understanding involves both teacher and students in plausible actions directed toward making sense out of a situation. It acknowledges that the opportunity to experience and confront the situation and its resolution to a firsthand fashion is essential. Thus, while participants are striving to make discoveries and construct insights, they sensitively avoid destroying the challenge for others by prematurely revealing their own successes before others may have time to proceed. Teachers must learn to help students respect the rights of each other in "doing it their own way and at their own pace."

To me, the essential factor effecting high-quality mathematical experiences that could lead to growth as a generative thinker involves the sense of being problematic (Hatfield, 1988). Today, much attention is being focused on the adoption of problem solving as a central goal of the curriculum. But, what is sought in experiencing a deep sense of "being" problematic goes much deeper into the psyche of the teacher and students. A problematic perspective needs to pervade the sense of being in the mathematics classroom. There is no problem "out there," written on the board or stated by the teacher. The problem to be solved is "within me," and thus it is essentially the internal condition of the solver. As one becomes aware of it, accepts it, acts on it, struggles with it, nurtures it, persists, makes progress, perhaps solves it and reflects upon it, it must be clear that the problem is integral to solver—"it becomes me, and in some fundamental sense, I become it."

Reflection

A constructivist teacher education environment must be sensitive to the role of self-conscious reflectiveness (Bruner, 1973) in building-up knowledge. This aspect of mathematical experience has begun to receive greater theoretical attention (Mason, Burton, & Stacey, 1982; Thompson, 1985), but it is still largely absent from classroom teaching practices. Again, if we wish to see teachers begin to develop their competence and disposition to include this phase in the experience of their students, then within a problematic approach we teacher educators need to encourage opportunities for the teacher participants to reflect on their mathematical experiences.

In reflection one may find deeper significances and meanings that help to clarify and consolidate the abstractions under consideration. When teachers are engaged in intentional efforts to think about their experiences in order to highlight important actions and consequences, these perceptions have more potential for use on future occasions. This important mental activity can include attention to meta-knowledge issues for the teacher, such as: How do I learn? How do I know when something is correct or "true?" What is the nature of my knowledge? What might I do to help myself learn more effectively? What effects do my feelings have on my mathematical thinking? Are there particular ways of thinking that I seem to use? Can I become more intentional in my use of these modes of thought? Papert (1980) suggested that, given an environment that is rich in situations involving mathematical and scientific phenomena that can be explored playfully and constructively by children, they will naturally encounter points in their activity when they will consider epistemological questions.

Experiencing Mathematics for Children

To facilitate constructivist perspectives in preparing early childhood mathematics teachers, the teacher education environment must feature mathematical situations that can, in turn, be posed to children. That is, teachers need opportunities to experience concepts and problems that may be similar to those we would want children to construct. For example, challenges to develop one's own way of finding products or quotients can be posed in a manner analogous to what might be done with children. Or, teachers can explore ideas for paper-folding representations of fractions within a group activity emphasizing the types of conceptual questions we would hope to see children pondering. Or in an approach appropriate to young children, teachers can design and make rulers for measuring segments using their own system of units as a basis for discussing the nature of linear measure. What is sought is a reconstruction of fundamental conceptual schemes (knowledge that many of these preservice teachers may lack) in the context of professionalized experiences. Professionalized mathematical experiences include attention to the epistemological and pedagogical dimensions for teaching children. After engaging in activities during which they are confronting the mathematical meanings for themselves, attention can be focused on questions related to how children might experience these situations and how the teacher might behave in approaching these situations constructively.

Finally, I believe that a constructive teacher preparation program must involve the novice teachers in numerous directed experiences with children throughout their preservice studies. The nature of these experiences must relate to, and reinforce, the constructivist perspective. The teacher educator would, at times, function in the role of teacher with the participating children in order that the preservice teachers might witness and interpret the interactions. A central activity would find the teacher educator and the teachers collaborating in their analysis of each child's mathematical activity in order to make instructional decisions. At other times, the novice teacher would engage one or more of the children in activities in order to gain firsthand experiences in teaching.

SUMMARY

A focus on the child's construction of mathematical knowledge can serve as the fundamental perspective in designing and conducting a teacher preparation program for early childhood teachers. To help practicing teachers shift in their classroom practices toward more constructive experiences for their students, we teacher educators must engage our preservice teachers more constructively. This includes our efforts to build models of their mathematics, to nurture mathematical communication, to adopt problematic approaches, to foster self-conscious reflectiveness, to pose mathematical situations similar to what children might experience, and to incorporate routinely direct contacts with children into the teachers' studies. If we seek to improve the mathematical experiences of children, we must begin by improving the mathematical experiences of early childhood teachers.

Chapter
5.11

Improving Prospective Early Childhood Teachers' Content Knowledge and Attitudes Toward Mathematics

Dina Tirosh
Tel-Aviv University, and Kibbutz Teacher Training College, ISRAEL

Mathematics educators emphasize the basic principle that in early childhood teacher education programs, mathematics teaching must take into account students' knowledge, conceptions, and attitudes toward the subject. A second fundamental principle is the importance of constructing mathematical environments that allow learners to develop their own mathematics knowledge.

These principles have raised several questions for early childhood teacher educators. How can the prospective teacher's own conceptions and attitudes toward mathematics be used in the development of their teaching expertise? How can learning environments be structured so as to help prospective teachers deepen their understanding of mathematics? How can mathematics educators design their instruction to serve as models of sound teaching practice?

This chapter discusses several ways for enhancing the mathematics content knowledge of prospective early childhood teachers. It also suggests activities for improving their attitudes towards mathematics, in line with the two principles mentioned earlier. These activities are intended to help prospective teachers improve their ability to interpret both the mathematical language and the mathematical actions of their students, and to encourage them to take a more active role in establishing suitable goals, methods, and environments of learning.

HELPING PRESERVICE TEACHERS CHANGE THEIR CONCEPTIONS OF MATHEMATICS

Thom (1973) and Wavrik (1980) noted that any form of instruction rests on the philosophy towards the subject of those who teach it. Mathematics is often viewed as an arbitrary collection of facts, methods, and rules (Wagner & Zimmermann, 1986; Whitney, 1987). Teacher education programs should involve prospective teachers in activities that will encourage them to develop and expand their mathematical perspectives. It is essential for prospective teachers to experience mathematics as a human activity, a study of patterns and relationships, a way of thinking, an art, a language, and a tool.

One way that may help prospective teachers change their conceptions of mathematics is to use the "what if not" strategy. (Brown, 1984, Brown & Walter, 1983). This is a "problem posing" strategy that includes the following five major stages:

Stage One: Choose a starting point that could be a mathematical problem, a theorem, or a concrete material such as geoboards.

Stage Two: List some attributes of the problem, of the theorem, or of the concrete material.

Stage Three: Ask "what if not," which means what if some of the attributes were not as described in stage two, and list the alternatives.

Stage Four: Use these new alternatives as a basis for posing new problems.

Stage Five: Select some of these problems and try to analyze or answer them.

One such "What if not" activity that I have used with prospective teachers is called *rectangles*. In this activity the starting point is the problem "calculate the area of a rectangle given that the width is two meters and the length is three meters" (Brown & Walter, 1983). The prospective teachers are instructed to list the attributes of the problem. Their lists usually include attributes such as: "We are asked to calculate an area," "Two numbers are given," "The width and length are specified." In the next stage the prospective teachers ask "what if not" for these attributes and list some alternatives. Three of the alternatives that the prospective teachers almost always specify are: "Only the length is given," "Only the area is given," "The sum of the width and length is given." On the basis of these alternatives, the prospective teachers pose various problems. One possible problem is: "Do two rectangles that have the same sum of width and length have the same area?" Exploring such a problem leads to a comparison of the concepts of area and perimeter and may result in deepening and extending their understanding of these concepts.

These types of activities encourage prospective teachers to be engaged in an inquiry-based activity. They foster active involvement in the mathematical processes of inventing, abstracting, proving, and applying. Prospective teachers experience the processes of making conjectures and choosing problems to work on and thus taking responsibility for their own learning. In an essential follow-up discussion, the prospective teachers communicate about their different posed problems and the various ways they had used to solve them. This seems to help break their static, bounded image of mathematics. It also may counteract the "one right way to solve a problem" syndrome that many of them share.

"What if not" is one method for generating environments that encourage mathematical inquiries. Other activities that encourage free exploration, such as nonroutine word problems, puzzles, and practical problems also allow prospective teachers to experience the creative, dynamic, and vital nature of mathematics.

FOCUS ON PROSPECTIVE TEACHERS' ATTITUDES TOWARD MATHEMATICS

Becker (1986), Baxter (1983), Bulmahn and Young (1982), and Rees and Barr (1984) showed that many prospective teachers dislike mathematics. One reason is their feeling that they "cannot do mathematics" (Rees & Barr, 1984). Moreover, a substantial number of the prospective teachers suffer from mathematics anxiety and believe that they are doomed to failure in that field. It seems logical that a prospective teacher who succeeds in studying mathematics will have an improved attitude towards the subject. Hence, teacher education programs should create situations that provide opportunities for the learners to become aware of their own potentialities in mathematics.

Another way of attaining these results is through introducing topics such as Number Theory and Cantorian Set Theory. These topics do not require a profound mathematical background, yet they are relevant to the prospective teachers' future work. Success in studying these topics can serve to engender satisfaction and confidence, and attitudes correspondingly reduce anxiety and negative attitudes towards mathematics.

The individual teaching interview is another method for encouraging prospective teachers to change their attitudes towards mathematics and to develop a sense of responsibility for their own learning. In this interaction with the teacher-educator, the prospective teacher is given an opportunity to explore some mathematical topics in an accepting, nonevaluating atmosphere. Prospective teachers participate in deciding the content and the processes of the interviews. They choose the topic (usually one that they feel they do not quite understand) and are encouraged to reflect on their knowledge, to help diagnose their misunderstanding, and to search for ways to overcome it. A major portion of these interviews is devoted to analyzing ways of consolidating the newly learned information and to discussing metacognitive processes with which prospective teachers can monitor and control their own thinking.

An illustration of a series of individual teaching interviews with one prospective teacher is as follows. The prospective teacher was aware of her insecurity in solving simple multiplication word problems such as: "A motorcycle runs 40 miles per gallon. How far will it travel on .75 gallon?" In the first interview we decided that she should find out a number of similar problems, then describe, in as many details as possible, the thinking processes she experienced while solving each of these problems. In the second interview this assignment was used to diagnose her misunderstandings and to discuss their sources. Several ways for overcoming these misunderstandings were thought out. One of them was analyzing a number of transcribed interviews between mathematics teachers and children who had similar difficulties. She was encouraged to study the various methods that were used to help these children overcome their misunderstandings.

In a third interview, possible ways of consolidating her newly learned information were discussed. She chose to use two methods to solve similar problems: drawing a diagram to illustrate a given word problem and estimating its answer. Finally, she constructed a "written dialogue" between herself as a teacher and a student who had encountered similar difficulties.

Over the past 3 years, I have interviewed about 200 prospective teachers according to this format. Many of them commented that the interviews made them "feel better about mathematics." Some said that the interviews made them realize that they were not hopeless in mathematics and that they could overcome their misconceptions. Others noted that they had learned "a great deal about ways to keep track of their processes of thinking." One student said: "It was the first time that I was encouraged to admit that I did not understand and I was given a chance to do something about it. I felt responsible for my own learning."

Aside from the benefits to the prospective teacher, such interviews can also be fruitful for the mathematics educators. They have an opportunity to study the learners' cognitive processes and conceptions and monitor the effects of various remedial strategies.

The importance of helping prospective teachers enjoy doing mathematics is reinforced by Paul (1985), who claimed that "a person, who has not experienced success and satisfaction in working with mathematics . . . will serve as a poor role model and will thus likely increase students' negative attitudes about mathematics."

HELPING PROSPECTIVE TEACHERS DEEPEN THEIR MATHEMATICS CONTENT KNOWLEDGE

Shulman (1986a) distinguished among three categories of content knowledge: (a) subject-matter knowledge, which is "the comprehension of the subject appropriate to a content specialist in the domain"; (b) pedagogical content knowledge, which refers to "the understanding of how particular topics, principles, strategies and the like in specific subject areas are comprehended or typically misconstrued"; and (c) curricular knowledge, which is "the familiarity with the ways in which knowledge is organized and packaged for instruction in texts, programs, media, workbooks, other forms of practice, and the like."

These have crucial effects on a teacher's responses to various class situations, such as when a second-grade student claims that the minuend is always greater than the subtrahend. Teacher education should provide prospective teachers with the appropriate content knowledge for dealing with these situations.

Subject-matter Content Knowledge

From the wide-ranging issue of subject-matter content knowledge, we chose to focus on the claim that "the teacher need not only understand *that* something is so, the teacher must further understand *why* it is so" (Shulman, 1986b). This distinction between knowing only "that" and knowing both "that and why" has been widely discussed in the mathematics education literature (Hiebert, 1986; Nesher, 1987; Skemp, 1976; Vinner, 1986). Many educators emphasize the importance of leading the students toward a relational understanding of mathematical content. However, such education can be provided only by mathematics teachers who themselves have such a perspective.

Many prospective elementary school teachers have serious misunderstandings about basic mathematical concepts such as zero, multiplication, division, infinity, and the concept of proof (Graeber, Tirosh, & Glover, 1989; Greer & Mangan, 1986; Harel & Martin, 1986; Martin & Wheeler, 1987; Wheeler & Feghall, 1983). Clearly, teacher education programs should provide opportunities for overcoming misconceptions and gaining a relational understanding of mathematics.

Following is an example of a mathematical environment designed to help prospective teachers deepen their understanding of the concept of number, the number system and the arithmetic operations. The prospective teachers work in small groups. The members of each group imagine that they are natives of an isolated island, that they have no number system, and that they are beginning to construct one. They have to make decisions about the type of number system they will create.

This activity helps prospective teachers raise and answer such questions as: Is it necessary to have ten digits? Is it possible to construct a number system with more than ten digits? With only one digit? Is zero needed? What verbal number sequence will be used? What written numerals will be chosen? How could the number system be designed so that the natives would be able to communicate about quantities? What strategies can be used to add two numbers in the new number system? Is it necessary to agree on one strategy for adding numbers, or can members in the group use their own strategy? Is there one preferable strategy? What is the essence of the standard multiplication algorithm? Can the same principle be used to multiply two numbers in the new number system? Should all countries use the same number system?

These and other questions urge prospective teachers to rethink the rules, facts, and agreements in the usual number system, which they generally accepted as self-evident and unquestionable. While constructing their new number system and defining and performing arithmetic operations with it, they clarify basic facts that they must understand as early childhood teachers. Through such activity prospective teachers learn to communicate with each other about mathematics. These conversations may help them develop their ability to reflect on their own reasoning and learning processes as well as those of others.

During this activity, prospective teachers are encouraged to use mathematics methods books, mathematics education journals, and books on the history of mathematics. Reading about the development of the number system, the history of zero, nondecimal bases, and alternative computational procedures for the mathematics operations may help them widen their horizons and deepen their understanding of mathematics.

Pedagogical Content Knowledge

A major item of pedagogical content knowledge is that of "the conceptions and the preconceptions that students . . . bring with them to the learning of the most frequently taught topics and lessons" (Shulman, 1986b). Research has documented that children bring a great deal of formal and informal knowledge to almost any mathematical learning situation, which significantly influences what they learn from instruction (Carpenter & Peterson, 1988). It is vital for prospective teachers to gain a profound understanding of children's conceptions and misconceptions and of the processes by which children study mathematics, so that they can take this knowledge into consideration when designing their instruction.

Much research has focused on the mathematical knowledge of young children (Carpenter, Moser, & Romberg, 1982; Gelman & Gallistel, 1978; Ginsburg, 1983; Steffe, von Glasersfeld, Richards, & Cobb, 1983; Steinberg, 1985). Topics have included conceptions of number, stages of understanding in the acquisition of number concepts, strategies used to add and subtract, and misconceptions. Preservice teachers can gain insight into children's mathematical thinking through assigned reading of the "classic" papers on these topics and by self-initiated searches for articles dealing with specific topics. This will help them learn where to find such information. They should become familiar with the various mathematics teachers' journals and educational research journals.

Videotapes of young children in mathematical activities can also illustrate their knowledge. A prospective teacher can view children doing mathematical tasks, identify the strategies they are using, determine if these strategies lead them to give appropriate responses, describe how these children would react in related activities, and suggest activities that will help the children gain further understanding of the topic.

In simulation games, one prospective teacher can act out the part of a child holding a specific misconception, while another plays the role of a teacher who identifies the misconception and generates activities to help the child overcome the misconception. This may develop the ability to evaluate mathematical knowledge through diagnosis in individual interviews, provide feedback on the appropriateness of solution strategies as well as the correctness of responses, and identify inconsistencies in children's thinking modes.

A more direct way of studying children's thinking is by interviewing the children themselves. This helps make prospective teachers aware of (a) the qualitative differences between the thinking of adults and children, (b) the different styles of thinking among children, and (c) the rich store of informal mathematical knowledge that children possess. They will learn that "children's invented strategies . . . are frequently more efficient and more conceptually based than the mechanical procedures included in many mathematics programs" (Romberg & Carpenter, 1986). Furthermore, they will understand the importance of relating their instruction to the knowledge of their students.

Preservice early childhood teachers should know not only the characteristic conceptions of the age levels they intend to teach, but also those of students in upper classes. They should be aware that adolescents tend to attribute properties of operations with whole numbers, such as that "division always makes smaller," to all numbers (Bell, 1982; Hart, 1981; Sowder, 1986). Teacher education programs should deal with issues related to this tendency, such as: Should early childhood teachers introduce properties of whole numbers that do not apply to extended domains of numbers? Should students be encouraged to use these properties when solving story problems? How should teachers handle questions about these properties? Preservice teachers should learn to consider the consequences of such decisions not only on the immediate performance of their students, but also on the formation of a sound basis for the further study of mathematics.

Curricular Knowledge

It has been clearly documented that textbooks often determine the curriculum in elementary mathematics classes and that many teachers and prospective teachers rely heavily on one or two mathematics textbooks as a main source of planning and teaching lessons (Bush, 1986; Freeman, Kuhn, Porter, Floden, Schmidt & Schwille, 1983; Lindquist, 1984). However, research surveys and analyses of mathematics textbooks reveal that most textbook surveys and analyses of mathematics textbooks reveal that most textbooks introduce mathematics as a fragmented topic, split into cases and subcases (Fey, 1979; Suydam & Osborne, 1977). The emphasis is on computation and low-level cognitive processes, and important aspects such as estimation are often omitted. Moreover, not enough consideration is given to the knowledge that children bring with them to the learning of the mathematics topics. Therefore, teacher education programs should instruct prospective teachers in the value and use of alternative curriculum materials and in determining the appropriateness of such materials for the whole class or for individuals.

One method to accomplish these ends is to have each prospective teacher develop a section of curriculum for teaching a specific mathematical topic. This should be presented and discussed in class, with a rationale for why it was designed the way it was. A logical continuation would be to test the curriculum with a small group of children and to write an improved version based on the feedback.

There is a great variety of instructional mathematical material available, and new materials are constantly being created. Thus, teacher education programs should instruct prospective teachers about how to use resource systems. One type of rapidly developing resource is computerized database. By working with databases to find information on textbooks, courseware, videotapes, and manipulatives, prospective teachers can learn to handle curricular information and broaden their knowledge of available activities.

This will help prospective teachers learn various ways of using manipulatives, calculators, and computers with young children. It will make them aware of the capabilities and limitations of textbooks. It will also encourage them to use everyday situations to nurture their students' understanding of mathematics-related topics in early childhood programs, such as clocks and money.

FINAL COMMENTS

A major theme of this chapter is the need to assist prospective early childhood teachers in widening their perceptions and improving their attitudes toward mathematics. Of course this goal cannot be separated from the equally vital need of improving their mathematics content knowledge. We agree with Reyes (1984) who claimed that "positive attitudes are important, but positive attitudes without an adequate understanding of mathematics will not prepare students to live successfully in a technological world." Too often, however, teacher educators focus narrowly on the development of skills and knowledge while neglecting the affective domain. For the sake of both the prospective teachers and their future students, it is important to help the prospective teachers decrease their mathematics anxiety, change their mechanistic conceptions of mathematics, and raise their confidence in their ability to do mathematics.

In addition, many mathematics teachers perceive their main role as that of transmitting information that is written in mathematics textbooks to their students. This form of instruction has not yielded much success in developing the children's mathematical understanding. We hope that prospective teachers who participate in activities such as those described here will gain enough confidence in their ability to carry out responsibilities such as determining suitable goals, methods, and learning environments for their students. This approach may well motivate them to dare to create their own ways of teaching, as well as constantly trying to suit them to each of their students.

ACKNOWLEDGMENTS

I would like to thank Ruth Steinberg and Rafi Nachmias for their most helpful comments.

Chapter 5.12

Some Problems with Problem Solving: A Brazilian Teacher-Perspective

Beatriz S. D'Ambrosio
State University of Campinas, BRAZIL

The purpose of this chapter is to raise issues for discussion in the Action Group on Early Childhood Education at ICME-6. I was asked to discuss the problem of teacher education with regard to aspects of the environment that should influence the preservice and in-service programs. Although initially I intended to discuss this topic more generally, I have decided to use the problems of the Brazilian educational system to raise the issues that I consider of fundamental importance to this discussion. Thus, I begin with a description of the Brazilian scenario of early childhood education. Subsequently, issues about teacher education will be raised focusing on the reality of Brazil. With some variations, a similar scenario applies to all of Latin America. Countries with traditionally strong and universal school systems, like Argentina, Chile, and Uruguay, bear more similarities with Brazilian and other countries' private systems accessible to the upper middle classes. But by and large the scenario presented here can be considered applicable to the majority of Latin America.

THE REALITY OF THE BRAZILIAN CHILD

Brazilian society is afflicted by serious problems that directly influence the country's educational system. In general, poverty is the state of existence of a large portion of the population. The population is in continuous and unrestrained growth, which only increases the poverty levels. Disease is widespread among the poor, and lack of sanitation increases the severity of this situation. Undernourishment prevails and compromises the lives and health of the poor. Although relevant research has shown that cognitive damages resulting from infancy malnutrition can be compensated by an appropriate methodology (Assis, 1976), the cost involved in this is high. Infancy malnutrition is considered to cause damage affecting early childhood schooling. It has become clear that a good strategy for keeping children in schools is to offer a substantial meal during school hours. In fact, state authorities have been considering holding the school in session all year round, without vacation, so that children will not be deprived of their daily nutritious meal during the vacation period. This complex of problems underlies any discussion of education, including mathematical education, in Brazil and similarly, as it was observed before, all over Latin America. Within this same context, infant mortality is extremely high, and at a very young age the children who have survived take on adult responsibilities and share in the work force of the family.

Within this scenario the role of formal education, modeled on a western framework, becomes one of rewarding the privileged few and condemning the poor majority to a continuous state of poverty and suffering of inequalities (Harrison, 1982). Access to school by the rural poor is limited. When this is overcome, academic failure becomes an inescapable reality. Only 30% of the children that began primary school will finish eighth grade (Secretaria de Estado da Educacão, 1986a).

Children of the lower socioeconomic strata of the population begin their formal schooling in first grade at the age of 7. Until then these children have had no access to any type of formal education. Therefore, these children spend much of their early years on the streets or helping the parents in some type of artisanal profession or in the marketplace. In these cases they have informal training related to the professional activities of the parents. In many of these cases the activities involve a mathematical component, particularly related to elementary arithmetic involved in money transactions (Carraher, Carraher, & Schliemann, 1985). Specific examples of children's informal mathematical knowledge will be discussed later.

The problem is compounded by the high drop-out rates in the early years of schooling. Close to 50% of the children attending first grade do not get promoted to second grade (Secretaria de Estudo da Educacão, 1986b). The little schooling that these children receive becomes practically irrelevant because, according to some authors (e.g., Myrdal, 1968), at least 4 years of education are necessary to assure that the individual does not fall back into a state of illiteracy.

On the other hand, children of the middle and upper socioeconomic strata of the population have very different experiences during their early childhood years. In fact, the majority have access to some type of formal education, in particular through preschool programs.

EDUCATIONAL INNOVATIONS IN THE STATE OF SAO PAULO

Recently the state of São Paulo has taken a few measures in an attempt to deal with the complex issues of the reality of the children attending the early years in school.

One such measure taken was to combine the first and second grades in the elementary school as a single 2-year unit. The purpose was to reduce the extremely high drop-out rates in the early grades. There are no long exams or promotion from first to second grade, instead the children naturally proceed from one topic to the next according to their readiness. Since the system was adopted, frequently at the end of the first year of this sequence, a child who is able to read, write, and do arithmetic, is thus advanced to the third grade. This reveals the extreme conservatism of teachers who do not realize the other important aspects of schooling at this early age. A majority of teachers still believe that schooling is limited to the transmission of content, followed by practice and drill.

Another measure taken was the implementation of a preschool program for all children. This program (PROFIC) intends to work with the less advantaged children in an integral form, that is, involving health, nutrition, culture, and early concept development. The program intends to base all the work on children's experiences and cultural values. The intention is to redefine the school as an instrument of instruction (which it already is) and protector of the children under its responsibility (Secretaria de Estado da Educacão, 1986a).

Simultaneously, the state has also produced a new curriculum guide for the elementary and secondary schooling process. The guide is the result of reflections on the previous guide, written as a consequence of the new mathematics movement in the 1960s; the results and consequences of the implementation of the previous guide; the need for a redefinition of the curriculum in order to implement the new program of continuity between first and second grades; and the need for a program that prepares the students for real-life situations and simultaneously develops mathematical thinking skills. The guide proposes that a problem-solving approach permeate the entire schooling process, so as to develop in the students critical thinking skills, as well as mathematical creativity (Secretaria de Estado da Educacão, 1986c). Although commendable, the proposed curriculum has received much criticism, especially from the teaching community. The implementation of such a curriculum would require a change in teachers' beliefs about mathematics learning and instruction. More will be said about this in the next section, which focuses on the requirements of teacher education in order to fulfill these educational measures taken by the state of São Paulo.

Unfortunately one aspect of this last measure that is in contradiction with the previously described project (PROFIC) is the lack of consideration in the guide of the children's experience based knowledge with which they arrive in schools. As mentioned earlier, through PROFIC the child's reality is the basis of educational work. Hence their ethnomathematics, that is, "the mathematical knowledge, ideas and intuition with which children arrive at school, derived from preschool experience within their own environment" (Howson & Wilson, 1986) becomes essential in planning the mathematical curriculum for the early grades. Instead of considering this aspect of children's mathematical knowledge, the guide, as has traditionally been the case, implicitly considers that children's mathematical knowledge is acquired exclusively in school. In other words, children begin to learn mathematics when they start the schooling process.

TEACHER EDUCATION WITHIN THIS FRAMEWORK

In order for the state of Sao Paulo to successfully implement the measures taken that try to deal with a few of the numerous problems of the Brazilian educational setting, measures will also have to be taken in the teacher education (preservice and in-service) process. Many of the considerations of the educational innovations proposed are contradictory with current teaching practices and teacher beliefs about mathematics learning and even the nature of mathematics.

Many studies have raised issues about teacher attitudes and beliefs about mathematics (eg., Silva, 1987; Thompson, 1985). In summary, let us discuss a few of the attitudes and beliefs that I have identified as present among Brazilian mathematics teachers that have served as barriers in the implementation of the measures taken by the state of São Paulo.

Teacher education programs have traditionally taught future teachers how to teach mathematics to children independently of the cultural background of the children in the classroom. Consequently teachers believe that they can teach mathematics without actually understanding the children's previous experiences, which depends on an understanding of their cultural setting.

The question raised for discussion is: "How do we include this cultural component to develop consciousness and awareness of children's cultural background in the teacher education programs?" This seems to be particularly important in the early grades when there are the greatest differences in experiences, because a good part of children's later experiences will be related to school situations.

This also requires that teachers realize the fact that school mathematics is not unrelated to out-of-school mathematics or ethnomathematics. To this point, school mathematics has been taught independently from the mathematics used in real-life situations. In fact, Carraher, Carraher, and Schliemann (1985) suggested that the algorithms learned in school are rarely used in the market situations. Instead, the individuals use their informal algorithms.

Carraher, Carraher, and Schliemann (1987) provided several examples of Brazilian children's (more specifically, children from Recife) informal algorithms for elementary arithmetic. The following examples are extracted from their study and are used to illustrate algorithms acquired by children through "out of school" experiences.

> Eduardo. . . . Computation: 243–75.
> "You just give me the two hundred [He meant one hundred]. I'll give you twenty-five back. Plus the forty-three that you have, the hundred and forty-three, that's one hundred and sixty-eight." [Instead of operating on the 243, the child operated on 100, subtracted 75 and added the result to 143, which had been set aside.] (p. 91–92)
> Eva. . . . Computation: 252–57.
> "Take away fifty-two, that's two hundred, and five to take away, that's one hundred and ninety-five." [The child decomposed 252 into 200 and 52; 57 was decomposed into 52 + 5; removing both 52s, there remained another five to take away from 200.] (p. 92)

In both situations the children used oral solutions to the subtraction problems and did not attempt to use the formal algorithms learned in school. These solutions illustrate an understanding of the concepts of number and quantities as well as of the operation of subtraction, which greatly contradicts the results of their performance in school mathematics.

In this regard, the question raised for discussion is: "How do we develop in future teachers the belief that children's informal algorithms should be valued? Furthermore, that this is knowledge that has been constructed by children through their experiences and needs to serve as a basis for future learning rather than be ignored." A difficulty that will emerge from such considerations is the fact that our teachers are not prepared to be researchers or, putting it more simply, questioners. How do we prepare teachers to be able to identify children's informal algorithms so as to prepare instruction based on these?

Another important aspect that must be reconsidered is the fact that each aspect of the mathematics curriculum is considered a "stepping stone" to further mathematics. The reality of the schools in the developing countries requires that this become less true of the curriculum. Too many children are required to stay home and help the family during certain seasons of the year. Unfortunately these do not coincide with the vacation periods. Every topic covered in mathematics has many prerequisites and serves as prerequisite for many other topics; thus these children (generally from the lower strata of the population) are at great disadvantage in school. Furthermore, in a reality with the high drop-out rates of these countries, it is unrealistic to teach mathematics within this perspective.

Hence the following question is posed for discussion: "How could each day of mathematics instruction in the school life of a child be valuable in itself, rather than simply preparing the child for future learning of mathematics?"

One possibility of dealing with this question may be the problem-solving approach to mathematics instruction. Where problem solving is not viewed as a topic to be covered or a skill to be developed at the end of a chapter, but rather as the methodology used to approach all topics in the mathematics curriculum.

5.12. SOME PROBLEMS WITH PROBLEM SOLVING 429

The biggest problem with respect to the implementation of such an approach to the teaching of mathematics is the teachers' understanding of what is mathematics. As long as they believe that school mathematics is the teaching of the proficient use of algorithms, new approaches to the teaching of mathematics will not become part of schooling. Hence, the change must begin in the teacher education programs. Furthermore, teachers must experience this new methodology in their own learning of mathematics. Mathematics methods classes proposing new methodology are working in opposition to mathematics content classes that remain very traditional, reinforcing teachers' beliefs about the learning of mathematics as a reproduction of algorithmic knowledge. A crucial step in teacher education programs would be the coherence, or at least the cooperation, of both content classes and methods classes in the preparation of the effective teacher. If we believe that experience is a strong component in the learning process, then we must realize that the prospective teachers are also learning from their experiences, which are not limited to their methods classes.

Summarizing, teacher's awareness of children's ethnomathematics, self-contained curricular units, and coherence of contents and methods in teacher education seem to be basic issues to be raised in discussions on directions for teacher education programs for early childhood mathematics learning and instruction.

Chapter 5.13

Teaching of Mathematics Using Comparison and Examination of Children's Mathematical Thinking

Shigeo Yoshikawa
Joetsu University of Education, Niigata, JAPAN

The purpose of this chapter is to discuss teacher training for elementary school mathematics. Special emphasis is placed on the ways in which this training takes into account the ways in which children construct mathematics through their own activities. It focuses on the methods of teaching elementary school mathematics to children ages 6 to 8 (grades 1 to 3).

Japanese elementary school teachers are trained and licensed to teach every school subject. In particular, preservice teachers study mathematics education and formal mathematics, including algebra and calculus. As part of their training, they study the goals of mathematics education, and how teaching materials and teaching methods can be used to accomplish those objectives. In the teacher education classroom, two points should be emphasized:

1. There are many differences between formal mathematics and school mathematics. The contents of school mathematics should be constructed by children through their activities.

2. Elementary school teachers must be able to teach mathematics to the entire classroom, as well as to small groups of students and to individual students. The teacher must also be able to help children compare and/or examine their ideas that emerge as a result of their classroom problem-solving activities.

SOME CHARACTERISTICS OF ELEMENTARY SCHOOL MATHEMATICS

Many of the preservice teachers who have studied formal mathematics in high school and at the university tend to have a relatively limited view of mathematics. For example, some students see mathematics as a deductive, logical system, and think that studying mathematics means reading the textbooks and remembering what is written in them. Other students think that mathematics has nothing to do with the real world. Some students are attracted by the use of symbols and say that mathematics cannot be communicated without symbols.

These narrow and fixed views of mathematics do more harm than good in teaching elementary school mathematics. Those who are going to teach mathematics to children should take a flexible attitude toward mathematics, especially toward elementary school mathematics.

In this regard, there are many ways in which the study of formal mathematics can be helpful to preservice teachers. It helps them appreciate mathematical ideas, to understand the background of the birth of mathematical concepts, and to consider the educational significance of mathematics. It remains, however, the responsibility of mathematics educators to make certain that preservice teachers are aware of many differences between formal mathematics and elementary school mathematics.

Freudenthal (1973) divided mathematics into two types, based on the problem-solving activities involved. They are "ready-made mathematics" and "acted-out mathematics." Mathematics teachers in schools should avoid just giving students "ready-made mathematics." They should make certain that students construct mathematics through their activities.

Kotou (1978) listed the differences between elementary mathematics and formal mathematics as follows:

Elementary Mathematics	*Formal Mathematics*
Intuitive	Discursive
Inductive, analogical	Deductive
Local	Global
Personal	Formal
Semantic	Syntactic

The word *constructive* might be added to the column of elementary mathematics in this table. In high schools and universities, teachers often lecture students in mathematics. The students listen and try to understand. This type of teaching is not acceptable in elementary school classrooms. If the teacher simply gives complete, ready-made mathematics to children, they have difficulty understanding why they have to learn it, and what kind of value it has.

Teaching "constructive" mathematics, however, helps children develop the ability to think mathematically, which is a prime objective of mathematics education in Japan. Mathematical thinking contains two types of ideas: (a) ideas involved in the materials of mathematics and (b) ideas involved in the method of mathematics.

CLASSROOM TEACHING USING COMPARISON AND EXAMINATION

Generally, there are about 40 children per class in Japanese elementary schools, and classes often exceed 40 in urban schools. The entire class is taught using the same materials at the same time. The teacher explains the material, gives directions, and asks the students questions. There may be discussions between the teacher and the students, or among the students. This teaching style, called "teaching to the whole," is widespread in Japan.

There are advantages and disadvantages of "teaching to the whole." On the one hand, teachers can present the same material impartially to all the children and teach more efficiently and systematically. On the other hand, teachers have difficulty responding to individual learning abilities when teaching many children at the same time.

Construction of Mathematics Using Comparison and Examination

We should also teach children either in small groups or individually to help them construct mathematics, and to help improve their ability to think mathematically.

One way to do this is to compare and examine their thinking and ideas. At the beginning of the class, the children are given some mathematical problems to solve and, when appropriate, materials with which to work. They work individually or in a group to solve the problems. When they have finished, the teacher helps them examine and compare their solutions, the ways in which they were reached, and the ideas generated by their work.

All of the children participate in these activities, so they can all take part in the discussion and construct mathematics as they change or adjust their original ideas.

Here are two examples of this teaching method:

Measurement of Length (Age 7, Grade 2)

The purpose of this exercise is to introduce the concept of units of length. Children have already learned about direct comparison of lengths and about indirect comparison of length, using suitable mediums.

In the classroom every child is given a toy car that runs for some distance (powered by a rubber band). The children are divided into groups and race their toys against the other children in their group. The winner in a group is the child whose toy runs for the longest distance. The length is measured using a suitable unit chosen by the group, such as a book, a pencil, and so forth. The names of the winners are published after the competition.

Then the teacher asks the question, "Who is the winner in our class?" The children give their opinions and ideas. They argue with each other and start to

TABLE 1
An Example of Published Winners

Group	Winner	Length
A	Tarou	Five pencil lengths
B	Hanako	Four book lengths, and a little
C	Jirou	Six pencil case lengths

examine their activities. One child says: "A pencil case is longer than a pencil, so I think the length of Jirou's is longer than the length of Tarou's." Another child says: "I cannot compare Hanako's with Jirou's because I don't know which is longer, a book or a pencil case." As a result of such discussion, children begin to notice that they should have selected the same unit to measure length before the competition.

Division of Integers (Age 8, Grade 3)

The purpose of this exercise is to help children understand the principle and procedure involved in the division of integers. The children have memorized the multiplication table through 9×9.

Children can easily answer a problem like $12 \div 4$, because they remember $3 \times 4 = 12$. However, when the teacher poses a problem like $72 \div 4$, children have difficulty answering it. The teacher gives some time for children to seek the correct answer and emphasizes that they are allowed to use arbitrary materials or methods. Later, children discuss their ideas:

- Idea 1. Using estimation: Since $80 \div 4 = 20$, the answer to $72 \div 4$ is a bit smaller than 20. When I calculated 18×4, I found that the answer was 72.
- Idea 2. Using manipulative activity: I manipulated 72 marbles. Dividing them into four, I counted the number of marbles. The answer is 18.
- Idea 3. Using addition: When I added 4 repeatedly, 18 times, I got 72.
- Idea 4. Using multiplication: Because I know that $4 \times 9 = 36$, I calculated $36 + 36 = 72$. So, $9 + 9$, which is 18, is the answer.
- Idea 5. Using multiplication: First, I calculated $4 \times 10 = 40$, then I calculated $72 - 40 = 32$. Because I know $4 \times 8 = 32$, the answer is $10 + 8 = 18$.

The teacher and the children compare and examine these ideas. It is important for the teacher as well as the children to recognize the value involved in each idea. The discussion of the children using comparison and examination should be well-monitored by the teacher in order to produce good mathematical thinking. In the discussion, the following opinions should be emphasized:

- Idea 1 is a convenient method. We can easily find a number that is near to the correct answer.

- Idea 2 and Idea 3 take too much time and we might make mistakes in computation.
- Idea 4 is not usually available.
- Idea 5 could be used in every division problem.

Through discussion, children can construct the principle and the procedure involved in division of integers by expanding Idea 5.

The Role of the Teacher in Classroom Teaching

The classroom teacher plays an important part in helping children construct mathematics using comparison and examination. To be effective, the teacher must be able to pose good mathematical problems or problematic situations. A good mathematical problem includes mathematical materials that encourage activities through which the children will construct mathematical conceptions, principles, or rules. The materials for these activities must be relevant to mathematics. A good mathematical problem must stimulate children to attempt it. Some may not solve it completely, but children must try it or they will have difficulty participating in the discussion. A good problem will also allow various mathematical ideas to emerge. If the children have many ideas, the teacher can make the classroom discussion far more vivid and interesting.

The teacher should also be a good moderator of discussions. In order to be a good moderator, the teacher should first listen carefully to what each child says, should praise and appreciate the child's ideas, and should convey the ideas to the other children. Sometimes it is necessary for the teacher to restate the ideas in simpler form. The teacher should arrange children's ideas in order, or divide them into groups; should identify similar ideas that have the same meaning mathematically; and should help children build ideas by expanding or combining the ideas produced by others. If an essential idea that is needed to construct mathematics is not produced by the children, the teacher should present it to them. And sometimes teachers might play the devil's advocate for the sake of argument. That is to say, they might oppose an idea with which they do not necessarily disagree, in order to show its meaning or validity.

Capabilities of the Good Mathematics Teacher

Mathematics teachers should have certain skills for the teaching mentioned. Mathematics educators should help preservice teachers develop the following capabilities:

1. The ability to anticipate the direction of children's activities in the classroom. They should understand the typical child's thinking well enough to predict how he or she is likely to react to specific teacher assignments.

It is difficult for pre-service teachers to understand children's activities without the experience of visits to classrooms in elementary schools where they can observe children in action. This can be supplemented in the university classroom by having one student play the role of the teacher and the other students play the role of the children.

2. The ability to think mathematically. Teachers should be able to appreciate mathematical thinking and be able to grasp mathematical meaning quickly. They need to know how the ideas in elementary school mathematics grow in high school and beyond. They must be able to select or write good mathematical problems.

In order to get such a mathematical power, it is necessary to study formal mathematics. However, that alone is not sufficient. Teachers must be able to reconstruct the contents of elementary school mathematics from the standpoint of the children who will have to construct it for themselves.

Chapter 5.14

Action Research for Professional Development: Informing Teachers and Researchers

Noelene Reeves
Ministry of Education, WESTERN AUSTRALIA

Australia has recently completed a 3-year national project focusing on literacy and numeracy at the early childhood level. Funded through the Commonwealth Schools Commission, the project entitled Basic Learning in Primary Schools (BLIPS) aimed to raise levels of attainment, particularly of target groups of children, through professional development programs and research projects.

It became very apparent at the commencement of the BLIPS program that early childhood mathematics education did not have readily available research and professional literature to support mathematics education initiatives in the classroom. It was also apparent that mathematics lacked the interest and commitment from teachers in Australia that language and literacy education generally generates. Australian early childhood mathematics educators had to ask, "Why?" Whatever was happening nationally and internationally at the research and curriculum development level was not filtering through the classroom teachers. Comparing the state of play, it was agreed that early childhood teachers think of themselves as language teachers; they read language journals and many are members of PETA (professional associations). Whereas for mathematics, we do not have a long history of research on how children learn mathematics, unlike the language area where there have been clear, widely agreed on learning principles (Report, National BLIPS Mathematics Conference, 1987, p. 1). BLIPS mathematics programs set out to:

1. Establish principles of children learning mathematics.
2. Create links between language learning and mathematics education.
3. Restore teacher confidence in personal mathematical ability.

4. Focus on the mathematical learning of girls, other cultural and language groups, and socially disadvantaged groups.
5. Involve parents.

ACTION RESEARCH

The topic of this chapter is to elaborate on one particular feature of the professional development program that has made a significant difference in the quality of language and mathematics education in Australia: that of action research by teachers in their own classrooms over a period of time.

An essential component of the BLIPS early Literacy Inservice Course on language and literacy learning was the concept of "spaces learning" and "classroom action research" by the participants. Time to observe and monitor children and time to discuss with peers and reflect on the outcomes was built into the course structure. The evidence from their own classrooms and the learning that came from sharing experiences proved to be the greatest change agent in the teachers' understanding of reading and writing development and classroom practice.

A similar approach has been adopted by a number of mathematics education projects around Australia with exciting outcomes. Teachers participating in the programs have been required to try a particular activity or set up a particular situation to observe and collect children's responses. These responses are then discussed by the teachers at the next session of the course and collated and acted on in a number of ways, not the least by researchers in early childhood mathematics education. The benefits have been considerable:

1. Teachers have become better informed about the nature of mathematics and the mathematics curriculum.
2. Teachers have become more aware of children's thinking and mathematical development.
3. Teachers are beginning to articulate principles of learning mathematics and mathematical language/literacy.
4. Researchers have a great deal more evidence to call on about children learning mathematics than could ever be appreciated using more traditional methods of research.

To illustrate what is emerging about teacher development and child development in mathematics education from action research, I have selected three areas: (a) problem solving and strategies, (b) pattern and representations, and (c) classification and language. I have also restricted myself to evidence from Western Australia because I am most familiar with the programs there, but I must point out that there is a great diversity of endeavor around Australia and that action research from many other Australian States has informed and influenced the Western Australian directions.

In all the Western Australian action research tasks, the basic principles are (a) an appropriate context; (b) materials and activity; (c) talk before, during, and after the activity; and (d) children's own recording/representation.

PROBLEM SOLVING

Given a problem, how do children think about it, set about solving it, represent it? Teachers generally agreed that previously they rarely gave children problems that allowed for creative solutions. The 'problems' were more likely to be exercises in procedures to assist them master skills or acquire basic information.

The Staircase Problem

The Mathematics in the Early Years (MITEY) participants were asked to find out how young children would sum consecutive numbers. First, the teachers had to contextualize the problem for their children. For example, a teacher of 5-year-olds asked how many pieces of fruit the caterpillar in the book *The Very Hungry Caterpillar* ate? They made a class picture, cutting and pasting the fruit on the picture over Monday to Friday, talking about the number of pieces each time. The 6-year-olds either built a staircase of Unifix blocks and were asked to work out how many blocks they had used or made spot cards 1–10 and summed the spots. The 7-year-olds read the *Twelve Days of Christmas* or a counting book of farm animals and the teachers asked for totals. Teachers used a large range of materials, situations, or literature to contextualize the problem to suit their own particular children.

The teachers reported the following strategies and representations. The younger children attempted to count the concrete materials, usually not very successfully as they lost their way! But one 5-year-old totalled the fruit just by looking and mentally counting. Another said, "15, because I remembered it was 10 yesterday." He had been keeping a mental tally over the 5 days. These children were preprimary children (noncompulsory, half-day attendance).

By Year One (5–6-year-olds), children were making individual pictorial representations of the problem. The majority were not organizing it very well but were using counting, tallying, and addition strategies to ascertain the total. Dots and strokes in groups, triangular representations, and numerical symbols were evident.

By Year Two (6–7-year-olds), most children tried to add and used formal representations but there were some interesting exceptions. A 6-year-old invented for herself a pairing strategy to make 10s, and another summed in a pyramid fashion. One 7-year-old conceived the staircase on a grid of 100 squares to give 50 and 10 half-squares!

The teachers were able to discuss the range of strategies and representations and to marvel at the thinking skills of such young children. They were also able to see the many children they thought were coping adequately were not able to organize information and were relying on teacher direction and memory to get by. Teachers then talked about problem solving in new ways; as learning process skills, as developing organizational strategies, as thinking creatively about number and spatial relationships, and as being a "window on the mind." They became highly competent at recognizing the potential of classroom contexts for mathematical problem solving.

The Mouse and Cheese Problems

Having read Rosemary Well's *Noisy Nora* (1978) for language/literacy development, the children in Year Two at Swanview Primary School (6–7-year-olds) made some mice in craft. Then their teacher, Mrs. Cindy Gower, set a problem.

> If you had 9 tails, 13 ears, 12 eyes and 15 legs, how many mice could you make?

Most children worked it out. Some went and got material and physically re-enacted the task. The majority drew the mice. The teacher recorded their oral responses. Chris made up his mind how many mice he wanted to make and found there were not enough parts. Luke stopped after the first statement and several children thought a three-legged mouse close enough. The most perceptive of the children dealt with each piece of information in turn as their representations show in Fig. 1.

Luke:	Nine of course, 9 tails, 9 mice.
Chris:	I made 7 and I've got 27 legs. I needed more legs.
Matthew:	Six because there were 12 eyes.
Lance:	Four mice because I ran out of legs.
Lucas:	Three because they've got everything they need.
Anita:	There are only 3 because they've got all 4 legs equals 12 and that leaves 3 over.

Scott, a recent arrival, said, "I didn't understand what you were talking about." *Noisy Nora* and her family provided another problem.

> If they had 16 pieces of cheese and Father Mouse had to have 2 pieces more than Mother, Nora and her sister, whilst baby brother had 1 piece less (which seemed very fair to the children), how many pieces would they get?

FIG. 1. The mouse problem.

FIG. 2. The cheese problem.

The children drew the family of mice and took 16 cubes and manipulated them until the result met the criteria. (See Fig. 2.) This teacher created similar problems around many classroom situations and the children showed considerable development in dealing with information systematically when problem solving, including Scott who no longer thinks such requests strange.

PATTERNS

What do young children think a pattern is? How soon can they recognize and use information about patterns in their thinking? At the beginning of this topic, the teachers were very unsure themselves about pattern in mathematics. The idea of looking at patterning beyond some simple arrangements of shapes or number

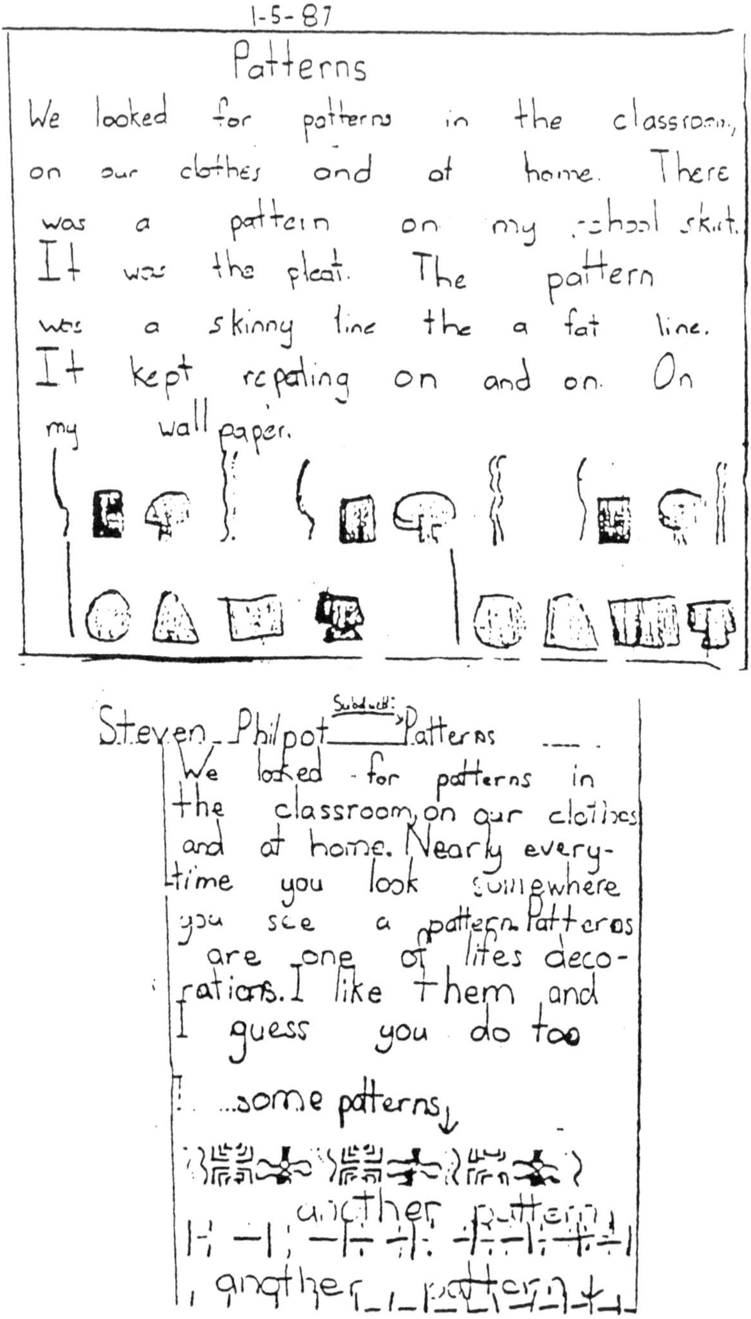

1-5-87

Patterns

We looked for patterns in the classroom, on our clothes and at home. There was a pattern on my school skirt. It was the pleat. The pattern was a skinny line the a fat line. It kept repeating on and on. On my wall paper.

Steven Philpot — Subject: Patterns

We looked for patterns in the classroom, on our clothes and at home. Nearly everytime you look somewhere you see a pattern. Patterns are one of lifes decorations. I like them and I guess you do too

...some patterns↓

another pattern

another pattern

FIG. 3. Children's patterns.

representations brought furrows to the brow. The action research in this area has been exciting and rewarding. The word pattern was quite familiar to young children but the teachers soon discovered that the notion of pattern involving repetition was not well understood. As long as the representation was colorful and not too realistic it was a pattern. Children recognized that fabric and wallpaper had patterns but for the reasons stated, not because of any mathematical relevance.

Teachers in South Australia working with Helen Pengelly had already been developing teaching strategies for generating and interpreting number patterns through a wide range of media and materials they had captured in photographs. These photographs set Western Australian teachers thinking about the underlying mathematical principles and they were anxious to watch their own children exploring similar ideas and others suggested by the MITEY course writers.

Pattern making with materials and through music and movement led children to recognize pattern in the environment and then the ability to extend patterns for problem solving. The children's descriptions and representations provide insights into their growing perceptions fostered by their teachers. (See Fig. 3.)

Mrs. Kath Moore gave her Year One (5–6-year-olds) at Floreat Primary School an activity that required the children to discover how many triangles were needed to make a boat. (See Fig. 4.) Together they talked about the five triangles needed for one boat and then progressed to how many for two and then three boats. The following day they discussed the worksheet again, and then they were asked to work out how many triangles they would need to make ten boats. Some of the strategies the children used are shown in their reproduced representations. Others used blocks and counters in groups of five and several said, "I did it in my head." (See Fig. 5.)

Following the action research, teachers reported that their enhanced apprecia-

FIG. 4. Triangles in a sailboat.

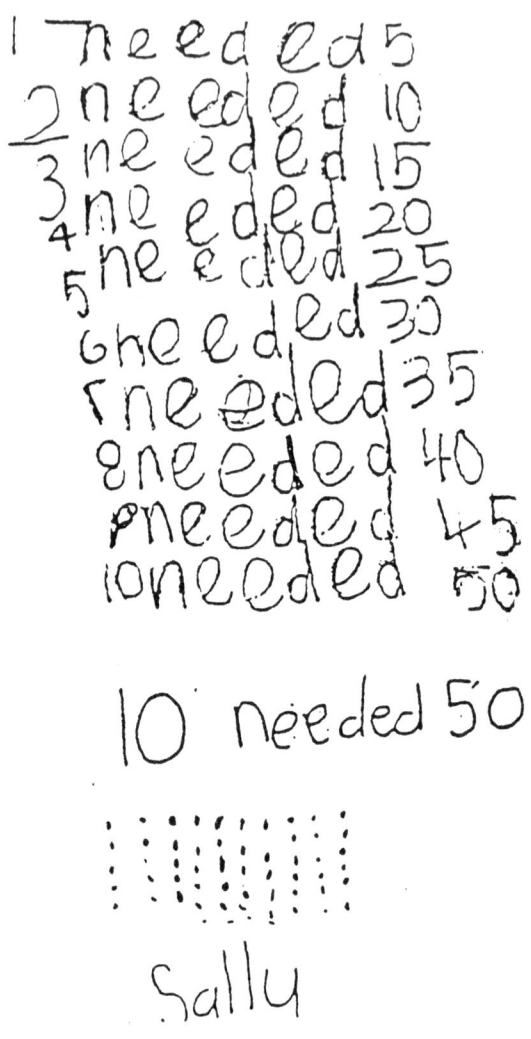

FIG. 5. Children's strategies for finding the number of triangles needed to make sailboats.

1 5 2 +10
⋮
3 +15
4 + 20
5+25
6 + 30   50
7 + 35
8+40 the ancu was ↑

1 5   7 35
2 10. 8 40
3 15 9 45
      10 50
4 20
5 25   50
6 30   the ast is

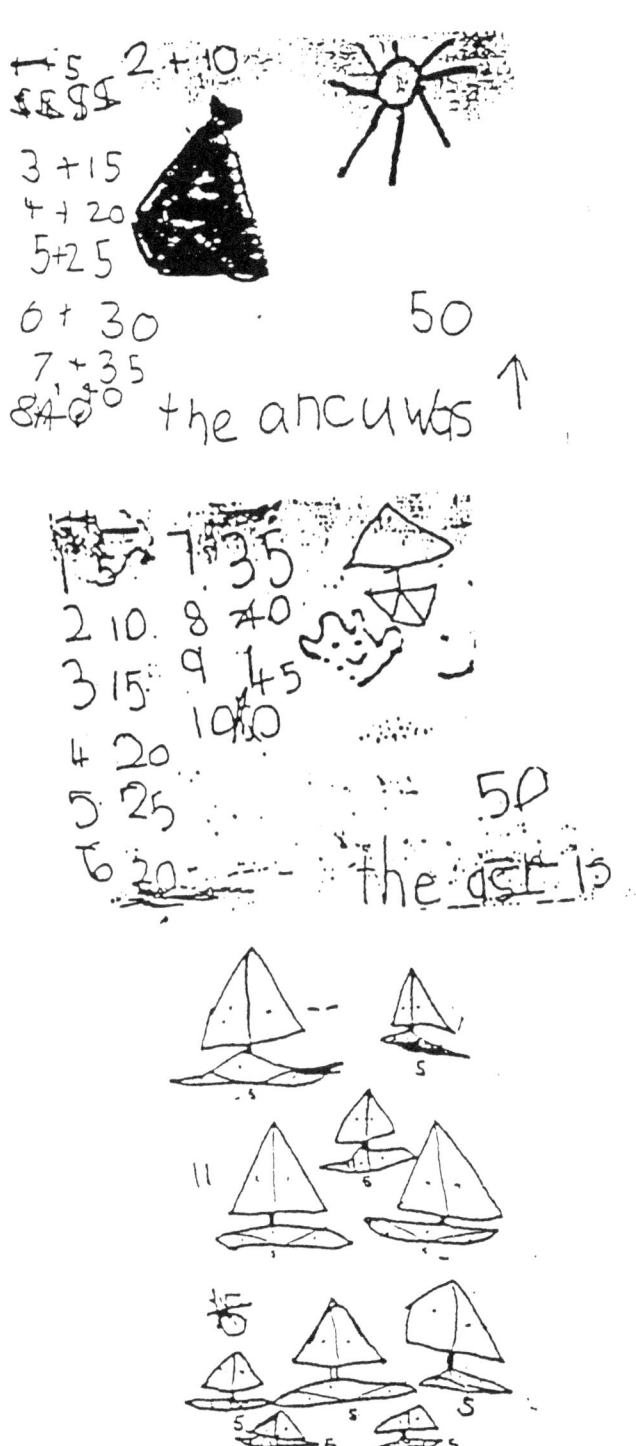

tion of pattern for operations, ordering, prediction, and problem solving had turned a neglected area of the mathematics curriculum into a foundation study in the early years of school.

CLASSIFICATION

The creation of sets and subsets depends on recognizing or determining common attributes. How do young children think and talk about classification tasks? Do young children have the necessary language abilities to match the mathematical concepts we are trying to develop?

As an additional MITEY project, early childhood education (ECE) teachers in six Perth metropolitan schools and one in a center for language delayed children undertook action research for a research team in a pilot study for a Project of National Significance on Language and Mathematics. Without the action research, the social dimensions of the role of language in mathematics learning would be difficult to appreciate. At the same time, the professional development of the participating teachers became evident as the project proceeded. The teachers, researchers, and speech pathology students from Curtin University became partners in watching children do and talk mathematics in the classroom and the clinic. It was professional development for all concerned.

In the action research, the teachers took the same topic and developed it over time. From simple classification tasks to more complex tasks using diagrams and grids in the mathematics lesson and across the curriculum, teachers watched, listened, and documented children's strategies, language use, and verbal reasoning. Speech students analyzed transcripts of individual case studies, and researchers attempted to pull it all together into a framework.

As a result of the action research, teachers have highlighted the social dynamics of the classroom as a determinant of individual children's thinking. Children are swayed by the reasoning of a group leader and accepting of that point of view whether valid or not. This tendency appears stronger as children get older. Faced with disagreement, a 5-year-old is more likely to demonstrate independence of thought than a 7-year-old. A competent 7-year-old, however, confident of performing classification tasks to personal satisfaction, says little, apparently internalizing speech rather than choosing to explain.

From observations, the participating teachers discussed at length the importance of modelling in the mathematics classroom. Modelling language such as adjectives and adverbs for classification is an obvious need. But the need to model language for thinking; to talk through a task; to provide reflective language, metalanguage, language for if/then, or for a hypothesis is proving to be an even greater need for young children. Modelling thinking might be the greatest need of all. The idea of modelling process is not new, for example, when teaching formal representation, but it is usually presented as procedure rather than thinking. Modelling the way an author thinks through the composition of a written text is the way process writing is taught in numerous ECE classrooms in Australia. Modelling the way a mathematician thinks through a problem rather than the test mentality so common at present could be the future of ECE mathematics education.

The teachers in the project are now very conscious of their own part in the construction of mathematical thinking in individuals. From being conscious of peer group dynamics, they started to analyze the way they interacted with groups, their use of language in conversation, the amount of language that was management versus teaching, and the kind and quality of language they modelled for the children. They talked about scaffolding, the deliberate situational and language propositions they used to bring about thoughtful responses from children, to extend or create new possibilities for logic or language development.

The result of the study is another story, but the action research component has informed teachers and researchers alike about the language needs of mathematics education that include the social discourse as well as the personal competencies of individuals.

CONCLUSION

The experience of teacher educators involved in the BLIPS mathematics education programs would confirm that teachers themselves are responsible for their successful professional development. The environment that fosters a valued contribution from the learner, that expects active participation, and that establishes a network of peer support would appear useful. But an environment that empowers teachers to learn from children through action research informs not only teachers, but the field of mathematics education itself.

ACKNOWLEDGMENTS

To Kath Moore, Cindy Gower, Sue Retallack, Sue Horoch and all the other teachers who have participated in the inservice programs, my thanks for the evidence from their action research and their insights in discussion.

To my fellow researchers Jean Rice, Bruce Shortland-Jones, Anne Zubrick, and the research team from Curtis University, my thanks for their work and scholarship.

Part 6

Conclusion: Survey Chapter

Chapter 6.1

Cultural Perspectives on Success in Early Childhood Mathematics

Bob Perry
MacArthur Institute of Higher Education, AUSTRALIA

I wish to commence by thanking the organizers of ICME-6 for the honor that they have bestowed on me in inviting me to write this chapter. It is a daunting task to be asked to survey early childhood mathematics education around the world, and when no other guidelines are given, it gives me an opportunity to choose a particular aspect of great interest, at least of great interest to this writer. Consequently, I have chosen to discuss cultural perspectives on success in early childhood mathematics. I have selected this topic because I feel that we need to consider what we mean by success and in particular how that success is shown by young children.

Let me introduce these issues by relating a story. It occurred during some research that I was carrying out with young children and deals with a 6-year-old boy named Joshua. Joshua and I were looking at a solution to a number of different problems and we ended up with this one.

> I'm going to have a party, and at this party I plan to invite two friends. I have already bought the lollies for the party and in the packet there are sixteen lollies. The question that I set Joshua was, "How many lollies would each of us get?"

After a great deal of mental arithmetic, counting on his fingers, counting by twos and by threes and fours and fives and sixes and so on, Joshua declared that there was no answer, that the problem was impossible, and that he had done it every way imaginable. I even invited him to use some counters. So he counted out by twos until he had sixteen counters in front of him. He then proceeded to share these into three collections, one for each of the party goers. Of course, there was one left over. I asked him what he might do with that one and his answers were quite intriguing.

Joshua: Well you could share out the lollies before all the friends came and have the extra one yourself, or you could give the extra one to your mother.
Perry: Yes, are there other things you could do?
Joshua: Yes, you could cut it into two pieces and give each of your friends half each.
Perry: Right, but anything else you could do?
Joshua: (After some thought): Yeah, you could cut it into quarters and you could each have a quarter.
Perry: Would that use all of the lollies?
Joshua: Yes, well, really not quarters, no, they're sort of halfway between a half and a quarter.

Joshua's response would suggest that even though he had no formal education in the workings of fractions he seemed to have quite a clear notion of what a fraction is and even some idea of how you might order fractions. This distinction between formal and informal notions of early childhood mathematics education forms one of the bases for this presentation.

PLAN OF PRESENTATION

In the rest of this chapter, I plan to consider the notion of success as applied to early childhood mathematics. This notion of success has many dimensions and its investigation in the context of young children is fraught with difficulty. Much of a young child's learning is informal in the sense that it is being developed without the aid of teachers and a school setting. There is generally little pressure of time or achievement and consequently little need to measure success in any of the traditional forms.

Many people would argue that, in fact, traditional formal schooling hampers children's success in mathematics education. However in this chapter, I do not want to deny the importance of the teacher in developing children to a successful level in early childhood mathematics. Rather, I wish to consider cultural perspectives of success by focusing on issues such as who or what determines a successful level; is the level of success real to the children; and what can we as mathematics educators do to ensure that each child develops in a manner which is relevant, enjoyable, and challenging.

Obviously, early childhood mathematics education has as one of its aims to develop in young children the ability to succeed in mathematics. Of course, this success is developed in the context of the society and the culture in which the children find themselves. I hope that you will take the ideas I offer during this chapter and place then into your own context. I challenge you to think about what success means to you and to the children you teach, and I challenge you to think about how you might go about developing success in those children. I do not promise answers to these questions. (My students often complain I will not give answers to the questions asked in class. It is not so much that I will not give them, it is often that I do not know the answers. My response to the students is, "If I did know the answers, why would I ask the questions?") So here are my questions.

1. What does early childhood mathematics education look like?
2. What is meant by success in early childhood mathematics education?
3. Who determines success in early childhood mathematics education?
4. Is early childhood mathematics education real to the children?
5. What is the role of language in early childhood mathematics education?
6. What is the role of technology in early childhood mathematics education?

Finally, I would like to give a couple of examples of valuable approaches to research in early childhood mathematics education and suggest a few likely avenues for future work.

What Does Early Children Mathematics Education Look Like?

The brief of Action Group 1 at this Congress is to consider the mathematics of children aged approximately 4 to 8 years. In many countries, this age range limitation results in our considering children before they attend their first formal schooling, but for most, it represents a short period before a child's formal schooling begins as well as 2 or 3 years of this formal schooling. This period of a child's life is critical in forming a foundation for future learning, not only in terms of content and approach but also in terms of the learner's attitude to mathematics and to learning.

In his presentation to the Early Childhood Action Group at ICME-5 in Adelaide (reported in Carss, 1986), George Eshiwani made the distinction between formal and informal education. Basically, the distinction he was making relates to education in some sort of "institution" such as a preschool, day-care center, or school versus education outside these institutions in places such as the home, the street, market places, farms, villages, and so on. Another distinction that can be made is that Ershiwani's "formal" education usually involves a trained adult "teacher" while "informal" education only rarely does. In spite of this lack of a trained teacher (or, perhaps, because of it), the children learn a great deal of mathematics through the informal mode. I do not need to go into details here as we are all well aware of them. However, it is pertinent to note general characteristics of the approach to learning shown by children in this informal period. First, children learn as individuals through their play and activity; they do not learn by acting like passive sponges (I am reminded of the contradiction that seems to be perpetrated in the title of Maria Montessori's classic *The Absorbent Mind*, 1967). Second, in this play and activity, children act on real materials— materials that are relevant to their context. Third, there is access and use, by the children, of the children's own language. Strange symbols and language are not imposed on them as they learn (or even before they do). It is, generally, the children who decide when they have played enough, learned enough or used up enough time, and it is the children who decide what activities might be undertaken.

Such an approach to children's learning can be contrasted with the formal settings identified earlier. Even before children enter schooling, they are confronted with approaches that are quite different to the informal approaches they have experienced. I am reminded of one preschool I visited in Africa last year. The total enrollment was 350 children aged between 4 and 6 years. There were seven classes, each with two teachers. Both the size of the preschool and the size of the classes would be unheard of in Australia, but the most striking feature was the formality of the teaching. The 4-year-olds I observed were very busy sticking shapes to a page to make patterns, the 5-year-olds were modelling shapes in clay while the 6-year-olds were working in their workbooks, on "simple" addition examples. The fact that everyone in each of these classes was doing the same as everyone else seemed to defeat the idea of individualization that most preschools, in Australia at least, hold dear. Let me say, however, that the children in the African preschool seemed quite happy with their lot even though it was obviously quite different from the approach they would take to their learning outside the preschool.

Further insights into approaches to learning can be gleaned from governmental statements on preschool education. For example:

> The preschool year aims at preparing children for normal school routine. There is no actual teaching, but children get used to playing and cooperating with other children and thus gradually become acclimatized to school. (Danish Ministry of Education, 1984, p. 11)

> For children between the ages of three and six years, nursery schools are operated, both as a complement to education in the family and as a means to ensure a good start in formal education. (Austrian Ministry of Education, Arts and Sports, 1986, p. 16).

> Most Swiss children can attend 'nursery' before entering '*primary school*'. . . . Such schools are usually attended by children between the ages of 4 and 6. . . . Provision is often made to start reading and even mathematics in the top classes of these nursery schools. (Egger, n.d., pp. 2–3).

The notion of preschools as a preparation for school is widespread and many systems of schooling treat the preschool as, de facto, an extra year of school on

6.1. CULTURAL PERSPECTIVES   455

which later learning can be built. On the other hand, many children, particularly in developing countries, do not attend preschools and must cope with the formality of schooling ab initio.

Several other features arise from these governmental statements. The notion that "there is no actual teaching" in a preschool certainly begs the question "What is teaching?" while the provision to start 'even mathematics' emphasizes the point made in the following:

> What is remarkable is the little influence that mathematics in culture has on school mathematics curriculum. . . . We might note, for example, that teachers of language assume that the students have some outside experience of language and try to build on it. However, teachers of mathematics usually assume that students know little or nothing about numbers and measurement before coming to school and everything has to be learned in the school. (Nebres, 1987, p. 15).

Early childhood mathematics education has informal and formal aspects, both of which need to be considered carefully. The approaches used in the formal settings often do not match the children's natural approaches. It would seem that, particularly in the early childhood years, a more appropriate match could be made.

What is Meant by Success in Early Childhood Mathematics Education?

The word *success* is an emotive term that, in education, conjures up notions of objectives, assessment, and evaluation and, very strongly *failure*. The Macquarie Dictionary defines success, inter alia, as:

1. The favorable or prosperous termination of attempts or endeavors.
2. The gaining of wealth, position or the like. (Macquaraie Library, 1982, p. 1723)

The first of these definitions considers success as the favorable completion of actions. Of course, the word *favorable* has different meanings, too. In our context, it has to do with the attainment of certain objectives dealing with mathematical learning. These may be content or affective objectives and may be determined either by the learner or by a group of adults who may or may not know the learner. This analysis brings out yet another difference between the informal and formal mathematics education of young children. In the informal education, the objectives for learning are usually set by the learner and, if announced at all, are usually announced in terms of the child's own actions ("I am going to climb that tree," "I will make some cakes," "I am having fun"). For the most part, success is also measured by the learner although there may be some feedback from other people. On the other hand, formal education progressively removes the setting of objectives from the learner to the teacher and, often, states these objectives as a response to teacher action ("As a result of the activities and materials provided, the child will. . ."). Responsibility for measuring a child's success becomes the province of the teacher who provides feedback to the children in terms of achievement of the objectives.

The second dictionary definition is most pertinent to success in mathematics, even at the early childhood level. One has only to listen to parents skite about the number to which their child can count or the shapes that are known (that is, can be named) to realize that one of the key objectives for children's learning is prestige for parents. Within classrooms, too, position and esteem are linked to success at a variety of tasks, some of which may be mathematical. There is no doubt that, at least in cultures reflecting a Western tradition, success in mathematics, as measured from the objectives set by the cultures, can give the learner a position far beyond that reflecting the true worth of the achievement.

Often, one of the consequences of striving for success in education is the discovery of failure. In some countries this is pronounced and I think of places such as the USA where standardized testing is often the norm. The results of such testing will highlight some successes but will also identify many "failures." The affective learning derived from this identification can be devastating.

Who Determines Success in Early Childhood Mathematics Education?

The answer to this question is the same as the answer to the question "Who determines the objectives for learning in early childhood mathematics education?" And the answers to both questions really require a detailed review of the development of mathematics in a cultural sense.

In *The Shape of School Mathematics in the 1990's,* Nebres (1987) traced the influence of culture on the shape of school mathematics. He made the point that school mathematics "was shaped in a *particular historical and cultural context: the Western Europe of the industrial revolution.*" He goes on to argue that this "canonical curriculum was simply *transplanted to developing countries*" and resulted in "a very special place for mathematics in the curriculum and a remarkable uniformity of content in mathematics curricula all over the world." It is with this uniform content of mathematics curricula that most early childhood mathematics educators are familiar in their own learning and it is therefore not surprising that it is this same uniform content that is being implemented at the early childhood level today.

Many eminent mathematics educators have argued that this is not the way things should be. D'Ambrosio (1986), in his address to ICME-5, defined very clearly the notion of cultural diversity and its influence on curriculum design for mathematics education.

I bring to the picture an extra dimension of much more complex nature, that is, cultural diversity. The same place, same instant, but different cultural background make the situation entirely different. If you have in a classroom at a certain moment, a child from a family of working parents, or a child from a family of professional father and a non-working mother, things are completely different. Not to mention when you have different ethnic backgrounds, which happens so often in both developed and developing countries. The big challenge I see in education in rapidly changing societies is how to bring this cultural diversity into curriculum design. (pp. 4–5)

Of course, this "cultural diversity" not only affects what the learners bring to the particular learning task at hand but also determines what is considered to be success in this learning. There is a need to recognize the cultural context in which this determination takes place.

There is growing concern that evaluation procedures have been based upon factors which are internal to the disciplines and to the school systems both at the local classroom and at the national and international levels, without taking into account cultural components. On the other hand, assessment and evaluation procedures that do not take into account sociocultural influences on teaching and learning may strongly bias both the assessment procedures used and the interpretation of the findings obtained. (Reported in Carss, 1986, p. 241)

My own country, Australia, provides many examples of cultural diversity and its impact on children's mathematics education. In many schools in Sydney, there are children from over 40 different countries. Such diversity has many advantages, but does bring with it real challenges. One of the major cultural groups within Australian society is the Aboriginal people who settled in Australia some 40,000 years ago. A mere 200 years ago, to this year, their country was taken from them by western Europeans, namely the British. Of course, along with the British came the canonical mathematics curriculum including its canonical approach to learning. In recent years Aboriginal educators have been working towards establishing the notion of an Aboriginal "pedagogy" in our schools, based on their own traditional ways of learning. While it is obviously an oversimplification to dichotomise pedagogies into Aboriginal and non-Aboriginal, such a division does serve to highlight several keypoints. Table 1 compares two general groups of pedagogies.

For me, the most striking feature of this table is the similarity between it and the generalities made earlier regarding Eshiwani's formal and informal learning. It is too long a bow to draw to conclude that all Lister is considering is this same distinction, as children's informal learning strategies are obviously affected by the formal strategies learned by them from their cultural environments. However, it can be suggested that a wholehearted continuation of such informal methods

TABLE 1
Two General Groups of Pedagogies

Non-aboriginal	Aboriginal
Much non-Aboriginal learning is formal, i.e., conducted as follows:	Most Aboriginal learning in Australia is "informal", i.e, conducted as follows:
in specific educational institutions—buildings	without specifically arranged educational institutions and buildings
by trained teachers who have specific office of 'teacher'	by various relatives
with the content having little immediate application to everyday life and survival	with content having immediate relevance to, and arising out of everyday life and survival
largely through verbal instruction and explanation	largely through non-verbal means—learning by doing, little explanation
often imparted in compact highly organized courses which take comparatively little time	in most cases it is time consuming, most skills being learned over many years
often learning a highly conscious process	often learning not a highly conscious process
expected to learn by themselves—individual	learn in groups cooperative from older, wiser people
learn for the future	learn for the present

Note. From "A National Journal for Teachers of Aboriginies" by H. Lister, 1987, *The Aboriginal Child at School, 15*(1), p. 5. Copyright 1987. Reprinted by permission.

into formal schooling would be of benefit to Aboriginal children in Australia, in particular, and to many other groups of young children as well.

The determination of success in early childhood mathematics education is clearly affected by the culture in which this success is measured. Often, the values of this culture are not in complete accord with the general values of society in which the culture exists and this can lead to some conflict. For example, Blair (1986) made the following comparison of "excellence" in schooling as seen by the overall Australian society and Aboriginal people.

1. *Overall Society.* "The excellent child at school then successfully proceeds from grade to grade, performs well academically, is called upon by people in authority to perform tasks for them. This child conforms to the rules, accepts the teacher's answers as 'gospel,' never questions the classroom milieu, and competes, striving to be the best in the school or class."

2. *Aboriginal People.* "The Aboriginal excellence may be defined in terms of equality of community and group acceptance. The measures of this excellence may be:

Aboriginal community acceptance
Action or practical implementation
Group sharing and willingness to participate.

The excellence in Aboriginal society is therefore not individually based, it is not competitive. The measures of excellence are few. The criteria are set by the whole. Performance is not measured during a pregnant pause or during a moment of triumph. It revolves around a person's place in that community. It revolves around a person's family."

Of course, this potential conflict appears in most countries throughout the world, particularly in those developing countries with a colonial background.

Is Early Childhood Mathematics Education "Real" to Children?

The question of the reality of young children's mathematical education as opposed to its relevance is one that has not received a great deal of attention. D'Ambrosio (1986) introduced his "reality—individual—action—reality" cyclical model to help him argue for the development of "ethnomathematics." He takes "action" as the basis of the cycle, making the point that he sees "action as a modifier of reality, which is continually changing." In early childhood mathematics education, the importance of the children's own actions has long been understood. It is through these actions that children are able to bring their own reality to the mathematics which they learn.

Of course, action is dependent on having something or someone to act on and young children's mathematical education will be much more real to them if the "raw materials" on which they act are part of their reality. These materials might be ideas already developed or they might be concrete manipulatives or they might be mathematical symbols. In any case, they need to have been fully assimilated into the children's reality. This implies that any materials used by children to help develop mathematical ideas must have a firm place in the children's realities before they are used to introduce new abstractions. Hence, materials that are not natural to the children require a lot of introductory "free investigation" before they can be satisfactorily used as learning materials for mathematical abstractions. Base Ten blocks that have great appeal as a learning material, to people who understand Base Ten numeration, are often used by children, supposedly learning about the numeration system, as no more than abstract pseudo-symbols. Of course, materials must also be "real" to the mathematics that is being learned. For example, it is often popular to use decimal money (such as dollars and cents) to illustrate numeration ideas. For some children, this can be quite confusing because of the weak model for grouping in tens given by the material.

There is a great need for mathematics educators to look at the lives of children within the context of their societies and to identify both the mathematics used and the methods and materials used to learn this mathematics. One attempt to do this at the early childhood level was reported by Pereira (1987) to the 1987 Southeast Asian Conference on Mathematical Education. On the other hand, some of the misconceptions that may arise from working inside a real but restrictive contextual framework are outlined by van den Brink (1984). The work of Donaldson, reported in Hughes (1987), on embedded and disembedded thinking further emphasizes the need for real contexts in which children can experience their new mathematical learnings.

Making early childhood mathematics real to the children learning it is obviously one of our aims. One well-tried way of doing this is to allow children themselves to "suggest" the content to be taught, through the problems which they bring to the class situation. This obviously requires a great deal of perceptiveness and resourcefulness on the teacher's part but can provide an atmosphere in which the children feel they can do some real work.

What is the Role of Language in Early Childhood Mathematics Education?

Clearly, language is a very important factor in the ways in which mathematics is learned by young children. A great deal of research has been carried out on role of language. The importance of this role is further emphasized by the fact that an entire topic area has been given over to it at this Congress.

At the early childhood level, a child's natural language is one vehicle by which mathematical development and understanding can be gauged. It is a stimulus for activity and learning, and it is a medium through which this learning is carried out. However, the child's natural language is often inadequate to meet such demands.

First, the natural language of the young child can be such that its development does not allow the child to adequately describe actions on materials or ideas. In such a case, the child either has to make up a description with at least some meaning to the learner or else learn a new word, supplied by a teacher, at the same time as the new action is being assimilated. Neither of these is disastrous, but teachers need to be aware of the need to develop natural language in its mathematical dimension as well as in other facets.

In addition, the age-old problem of mathematical symbolism and its introduction needs to be continually broached. There are indications in some countries that the introduction of written mathematical symbols is being delayed somewhat, hopefully until the children have had sufficient experience with the idea being symbolized to understand them. However, in countries exposing a Western tradition imposed on an underlying indigenous culture, there appears to be an overbearing belief that one has to get children writing symbols as early as possible. To be sure, written responses are easier to manage in a large class than oral responses, but are they the appropriate response to ask of the children?

Moreover, it is possible that the natural language of some learners simply does not have words to describe some of the mathematical ideas being introduced or does not have words which distinguish between mathematically different ideas. For example, in some languages the words *circle* and *sphere* are denoted by the same word (in much the same way as a young child might call them both *round*). This may lead to some confusion between the children and the teacher.

Furthermore, teachers need to develop skills in adapting their own language to a level that will allow explanations to be made to children while still maintaining the precision needed to clarify the concept. They also need to develop skills that enable them to listen to, monitor, and understand children's language while the children are involved in mathematics.

Of course, all of the issues concerning language that I have listed are complicated and confused when one moves into a bilingual situation. The topic area on language and mathematics at ICME-5 in 1984 reported on many of the difficulties of learning mathematics in English when English was the learner's second language. A more extensive description of some important work with children in Nigeria is contained in Watson (1987), who found qualitative and quantitative differences between the number learning of monolingual Yoruba, monolingual English, and bilingual English-Yoruba children. In many countries, particularly in Africa, there is a changeover between the child's indigenous language and the "colonial" language during the first few years of school. This not only causes confusion for the children but also great concern for many of the teachers who have not developed sufficient competence in the "colonial" language to use it fluently. Many of the decisions about which language is used as the language of instruction are taken at a political rather than educational level. Early childhood educators need to be sure that their voices are heard when these decisions are made.

Finally, in this section, I would like to raise some issues about textbooks. The role of the textbook is intimately related to the way in which language is used in mathematics learning because the text requires certain language abilities of the children using them. If someone from another planet landed in an early childhood mathematics lesson in almost any developed country in the world, the first object it would see would be the text! I thought, maybe 10 years ago, that I could foresee the demise of children's textbooks but they are still here—bigger, brighter, glossier, and more expensive. Many of them now have teachers' guides that wax lyrical about activity approaches, talking about mathematics, concrete materials, and problem solving. These teachers' guides are the basis of the programs, usually, and in many cases—I would suggest, the best examples—they are all that is needed to develop a sound mathematics program. Mathematics educators in general, and early childhood mathematics educators, in particular, should work towards providing teachers with the confidence to gradually remove texts from their classrooms and develop programs that are meaningful to their own children. Textbook publishers and the governments of developing countries should try to resist the temptation to "take the easy way out" by declining deals that result in foreign texts being used in situations for which they were not designed. Once again, the money would be better spent on the development of competent teachers or, at least, adaptations of appropriate programs.

What is the Role of Technology in Early Childhood Mathematics Education?

There have been many waves of technology pass through the waters of early childhood mathematics education. When I was first becoming interested in how young children developed mathematical ideas, the "in" technology was Cuisenaire rods. Now, there was a technological wonder! What amazing things you could do with those! I remember standing in awe as children found the cubes of numbers by stacking rods together. Little did I, or the children, realize that the skills they were learning, while spectacular, were not particularly relevant to their lives or their future mathematics. Nevertheless, there was a whole generation of school children who learned that five was always colored yellow and that two was always red and that if you put them together, you got black! No wonder we have so many abstract artists in our world!

The technology available in our world today is simply stunning in terms of its potential impact on our lives. In some countries, the very fabric of business, commerce, engineering, communication—in fact, almost every corner of human life—has been affected. Yes, even in early childhood settings, the ubiquitous computer is showing its value, both as a learning tool and as an aid in administration. There can be no doubt that computers have the potential to change the way in which mathematics is learned at the early childhood level. (Of course, computers have a much wider application than this narrow focus, but I do not at the moment.)

The work of Seymour Papert and his LOGOphiles has already had a major impact on mathematics learning and will continue to do so for a long time. Martin Hughes (1987) linked LOGO to number work with young children with much success. Campbell and Fein (1986) explored many of the general issues associated with microcomputers and young children, most of which impinge on mathematical learning. This is also true of the recent publication by Porter (1988) who looked at computer use in schools. The obvious conclusion to reach from the insurmountable amount of literature concerning the introduction of computers into mathematics classrooms at the early childhood level is that we are all faced with a technology of great potential that many children will be using in their informal learning. It is up to us to grapple with ways that will allow the exploitation of the full potential of the technology in our own early childhood settings. Of course, computer technology is expensive, even with the realization that costs are decreasing as demand increases. Those of us who have worked or are working in other than rich, technologically advanced countries know that it will be quite some time before early childhood educators will have to come to grips with a computer in the classroom. Hopefully, we will be able to learn from some of the mistakes made by educators in the countries that are further advanced down this track.

One form of technology relevant to early childhood mathematics education but that does not enjoy the high profile of the computer is the calculator. I believe that the calculator has a power to liberate mathematics education that is akin to that of the computer but for much less cost. At the early childhood level, calculators can be used to introduce vast tracts of number work in a way that is much less tedious than some traditional methodologies. Early introduction of calculators to young children can help build up a confidence that will allow the sensible use of the calculator in later years.

The introduction of calculators at an early level into the mathematics education programs of developing countries or with educationally disadvantaged groups of children within developed countries can help bridge the gap and allow a more equitable base from which children can launch their future mathematics learning. Research on ways in which calculators can benefit the early mathematics education of young children has tended to be swamped by that dealing with computers with the result that the potential of the technology has never been fully realized. Nevertheless, there is sufficient solid evidence for us to be confident that our continued efforts with calculators and young children will ultimately benefit the children and help bring them success in their mathematics learning.

In a chapter of this type, it is very difficult to cover the highlights of the topic for each and every part of the world. No doubt, I have omitted or glossed over many issues that are very important to many of you. I do not apologize for this but simply emphasize that this is a personal chapter. However, I do want to mention two recent publications that, to me, indicate the extent and direction of a lot of research in early childhood mathematics education as we move toward the 1990s. Let me again emphasize that my choice of these two examples is not a snub at all the other excellent work that has been done and is being done—at no stage did I ever see this chapter as being a review of the literature in the field. Rather, it is a clear indication of my belief that the only valid route to success for our children in mathematics learning is for the adults involved to have an intimate knowledge of what thinking and processing is going on in the children's minds.

The first publication is *Construction of Arithmetical Meanings and Strategies* by Steffe, Cobb, and von Glasersfeld (1988). The studies reported use a constructivist "teaching experiment" methodology to investigate ways in which young children develop numerical meaning and facility. The work uses and extends the theory of counting types which is detailed by Steffe, von Glasersfeld, Richards, and Cobb (1983). The work of Action Group 1 is based on constructivist principles. Although the constructivist approach has a number of critics, it would seem to me to be one that should be investigated to its fullest. No doubt this will occur in the Action Group.

The second publication is *The Origins of Arithmetic Skills—A Phenomenographic Approach* by Neuman (1987). This delightful book describes an extensive investigation of the development of arithmetical concepts in school starters. One of the key features of the investigation is the "phenomenographic" approach in which "the children's own strategies, and the conceptions of these strategies were thought to express, formed categories of description" (Neuman, 1987, p. 5). Again, I am sure, Neuman's work will be extensively canvassed during this Congress.

These are two examples of research that can only increase our knowledge of children's learning of early mathematical ideas and, hence, leads us to construct more successful methods for encouraging this learning. I know that there are many other such examples—the program for Action Group 1 is ample testimony for this.

CONCLUSION

In this chapter, I have considered the notion of success in early childhood mathematics education—success for the children learning, success for adults teaching and researching, and success for the educational systems providing facilities, finances, and organizations. Such notions of success are clearly related to the cultural milieu in which they are being measured. I have tried to give a broadly based commentary on some of the issues that I see as important from my own, culturally biased, perspective. In doing so, I wish to challenge the readers' thinking on what might be done in their own situations.

At the systematic level those countries that have established early childhood mathematics education programs show no real movements towards major structural change in what they are doing. To be sure, minor refinements of both approach and extent are constantly being made but there does seem to be an air of stability. Hopefully, those countries for whom early childhood education is a new field will learn from the earlier experience of others and move to this stability of structure quickly. Once the system is established, there will be resources to refine the programs offered.

I believe that the key to success in early childhood mathematics education for children, teachers, and educational authorities is to realize that successful learning results when the objectives for learning of all three groups are in accord and when teachers know what is going on inside the children's heads and from what background it has derived. This is not something that is being said for the first time, but it is something that must be emphasized.

The challenge for early childhood mathematics educators throughout the world is to find out and use what their children already have in their heads. Dagmar Neuman (1987) summarized this challenge beautifully when she wrote, "If teachers knew about, and used, children's own ways of learning maths, the teaching of maths, by adults would end up in the learning of maths by children" (p. 5).

References

Anderson, J. R. (1985). *Cognitive psychology and its implications* (2nd Ed.). New York: W. H. Freeman.
Anyon, J. (1981). Social class and school knowledge. *Curriculum Inquiry II, 1,* 3–42.
Arnheim, R. (1969). *Visual thinking.* Berkeley, CA: University of California Press.
Assis, O. M. (1976). *A solicitação do meio e a construção das estruturas lógicas elementares nas crianças.* Unpublished doctoral dissertation, Universidade Estadual de Campinas, Campinas.
Austrian Federal Ministry of Education, Arts and Sports. (1986). *Austria: Organization of education 1984–86.* Vienna: Bundesministerium fur Unterricht, Kunst und Sport.
Baird, J. R., & Mitchell, I. J. (Eds.). (1987). *Improving the quality of teaching and learning: An Australian case study—the Peel project.* Melbourne, Victoria: Monash University.
Balacheff, N. (1986). Cognitive versus situational analysis of problem-solving behavior. *For the Learning of Mathematics, 6* (3), 10–12.
Balacheff, N. (1987). Processus de preuve et situations de validation. Educational Studies in Mathematics, 18, 147–176.
Baldwin, J. M. (1906–1911). *Thought and things or genetic logic.* New York: Macmillan.
Barnes, B. (1982). *T. S. Kuhn and social science.* New York: Columbia University Press.
Barnes, D., & Todd, F. (1977). *Communicating and learning in small groups.* London: Routledge & Kegan Paul.
Bartlett, F. C. (1932). *Remembering: A study in experimental and social psychology.* Cambridge: Cambridge University Press.
Bateson, G. (1973). *Steps to an ecology of mind.* London: Paladin.
Bauersfeld, H. (1980). Hidden dimensions in the so-called reality of a mathematics classroom. *Educational Studies in Mathematics, 11,* 23–41.
Bauersfeld, H. (1988). Interaction, construction, and knowledge: Alternative perspectives for mathematics education. In T. Cooney & D. Grouws (Eds.), *Effective mathematics teaching* (pp. 27–46). Reston, VA: National Council of Teachers of Mathematics.
Baxter, J. (1983). Status and trends in mathematics teacher education. In M. Zweng, T. Green, J. Kilpatrick, H. Pollak, & M. Suydam (Eds.), *Proceedings of the Fourth International Congress on Mathematics Education* (pp. 90–92). Berkeley, CA: Birkhauser.

Becker, J. R. (1986). Mathematics attitudes of elementary education majors. *Arithmetic Teacher, 33* (5), 50–51.
Bell, A. (1982). Diagnosing students' misconceptions. *Australian Mathematics Teacher, 38*, 6–10.
Bennett, N., Desforges, C., Cockburn, A., & Wilkinson, B. (1984). *The quality of pupil learning experiences.* Hillsdale, NJ: Lawrence Erlbaum Associates.
Bergeron, A., Herscovics, N., & Bergeron, J. C. (1987). Kindergartener's knowledge of numbers: A longitudinal case study. In J. Bergeron, N. Herscovics, & C. Kieran (Eds.), *Proceedings of the Eleventh International Conference on the Psychology of Mathematics Education* (Vol. 2, pp. 352–360). Montreal: PME.
Bergeron, J. C., & Herscovics, N. (1985). Bringing research to the teacher through the analysis of concepts. In T. Romberg (Ed.), *Using research in the professional life of mathematics teachers: Proceedings of One of the Fifth International Congress on Mathematical Education Subgroups on the Professional Life of Teachers* (pp. 114–123). Madison: University of Wisconsin.
Bergeron, J. C., & Herscovics, N. (1987). Unit fractions of a continuous whole. In J. Bergeron, N. Herscovics, & C. Kieran (Eds.), *Proceedings of the Eleventh International Conference on the Psychology of Mathematics Education* (Vol. 2, pp. 357–365). Montreal: PME.
Bergeron, J. C., & Herscovics, N. (1988). The kindergarteners' understanding of discrete quantity. In A. Borbas (Ed.), *Proceedings of the Twelfth International Conference on the Psychology of Mathematics Education* (pp. 162–169). Veszprém, Hungary: PME.
Bergeron, J. C., Herscovics, N., & Moser, J. (1986). Long term evolution of students' conceptions: An example from addition and subtraction. In M. Carss (Ed.), *Proceedings of the Fifth International Congress on Mathematical Education* (pp. 275–277). Boston: Birkhäuser.
Bernstein, B. (1973). *Class, codes and control II: Applied studies towards a sociology of language.* London: Routledge & Kegan Paul.
Bernstein, B. (1977). *Class, codes and control III: Towards a theory of educational transmissions.* London: Routledge & Kegan Paul.
Bernstein, B., Brandeis, B., & Henderson, D. (1969). Speech of lower-class children. *Developmental Medicine and Child Neurology, II*, 113–116.
Bernstein, R. J. (1983). *Beyond objectivism and relativism: Science, hermeneutics, and praxis.* Philadelphia: University of Pennsylvania Press.
Bishop, A. (1980). Spatial ability and mathematics education: A review. *Educational Studies in Mathematics, 11*, 257–269.
Bishop, A. (1985). The social construction of meaning—a significant development for mathematics education? *For the Learning of Mathematics, 5* (1), 24–28.
Blair, N. (1986). *Aboriginal "excellence" in schooling.* Paper presented at the 1986 South Pacific Association for Teacher Education Conference. Hobart, Tasmania.
Bliss, J., & Ogborn, J. (1988). A model of common sense ideas in dynamics. In P. J. Black & A. Lucas (Eds.), *Children's informal ideas.* London: Croom Helm.
Bliss, J., Ogborn, J., & Whitelock, D. (in press). Secondary pupil's common sense theories of motion. *International Journal of Science Education.*
Bloor, D. (1976). *Knowledge and social imagery.* London: Routledge & Kegan Paul.
Bloor, D. (1983). *Wittgenstein: A social theory of knowledge.* New York: Columbia University Press.
Blumer, H. (1969). *Symbolic interactionism: Perspectives and method.* Englewood Cliffs, NJ: Prentice-Hall.
Bolton, N. (1987). The programme of phenomenology. In A. Costall & A. Still (Eds.), *Cognitive psychology in question* (pp. 234–254). Brighton: Harvester.
Boulton-Lewis, G. M. (1987). Recent cognitive theories applied to sequential length measuring knowledge in young children. *British Journal of Education Psychology, 57*, 330–342.
Boulton-Lewis, G. M., Neill, H., & Halford, G. S. (1986). Information processing and scholastic achievements in Aboriginal Australian children in south-east Queensland. *The Aboriginal Child at School, 14* (5), 42–55.

Boulton-Lewis, G. M., Neill, H., & Halford, G. S. (1987a). *Research into educational potential of Aboriginal children in south-east Queensland*. Report to the Australian Institute of Aboriginal Studies. Canberra, Australia.

Boulton-Lewis, G. M., Neill, H., & Halford, G. S. (1987b). Information processing and mathematical knowledge in Aboriginal Australian children in south-east Queensland. *Australian Aboriginal Studies, 2*, 63–65.

Boulton-Lewis, G. M., Neill, H., & Halford, G. S. (1988). *Educational potential and mathematical achievement in urban Aboriginal children in south-east Queensland*. Report to the Australian Institute of Aboriginal Studies, Canberra, Australia.

Bourke, S. F., & Parkin, B. (1977). The performance of Aboriginal students. In S. F. Bourke & J. P. Keeves (Eds.), *The mastery of literacy and numeracy* (pp. 131–155). Melbourne: Australian Council of Educational Research.

Boyer, C. B. (1968). *A history of mathematics*. New York: Wiley.

Brissenden, T. (1988). *Talking about mathematics*. Oxford: Basil Blackwell.

Brousseau, G. (1981). Problemes de didactique des décimaux. *Recherches en Didactique des Mathématique, 2* (1), 37–127.

Brousseau, G. (1984). The crucial role of the didactical contract in the analysis and construction of situations in teaching and learning mathematics. In H. G. Steiner (Ed.), *Theory of mathematics education* (pp. 110–119). Occasional paper 54. Bielefeld: IDM.

Brouwer, L. E. J. (1913). Intuitionism and formalism. *Bulletin of the American Mathematical Society, 20*, 81–96.

Brown, A. (1978). Knowing when, where, and how to remember: A problem of metacognition. In R. Glaser (Ed.), *Advances in instructional psychology* (Vol. 1, pp. 77–165). Hillsdale, NJ: Lawrence Erlbaum Associates.

Brown, J. S., Collins, A., & Duguid, P. (1989). Situated cognition and the culture of learning. *Educational Researcher, 18* (1), 32–42.

Brown, J. S., & Van Lehn, K. (1980). Repair theory: A generative theory of bugs in procedural skills. *Cognitive Science, 4*, 379–426.

Brown, S. I. (1984). The logic of problem generation: From morality and solving to deposing and rebellion. *For the Learning of Mathematics, 4* (1), 9–20.

Brown, S. I., & Walter, M. I. (1983). *The art of problem posing*. Philadelphia: Franklin Institute Press.

Bruner, J. S. (1972). Nature and uses of immaturity. *American Psychologist, 27*, (8), 687–708.

Bruner, J. S. (1973). *The relevance of education*. New York: Norton.

Bruner, J. S. (1981). The pragmatics of acquisition. In W. Deutsch (Ed.), *The child's construction of language* (pp. 39–55). London: Academic Press.

Bruner, J. S. (1986). *Actual minds, possible worlds*. Cambridge, MA: Harvard University Press.

Bruner, J. S., & Haste, H. (Eds.). (1987). *Making sense: The child's construction of the world*. London: Methuen.

Bruner, J. S., Olver, R. R., & Greenfield, P. M. (1966). *Studies in cognitive growth*. New York: Wiley.

Bulmahn, B., & Young, D. M. (1982). On the transmission of mathematics anxiety. *Arithmetic Teacher, 30* (3), 55–56.

Burton, L. (1980). Problems and puzzles. *For the Learning of Mathematics, 1* (2), 20–22.

Bush, W. S. (1986). Preservice teachers' sources of decisions in teaching secondary mathematics. *Journal for Research in Mathematics Education, 17* (1), 21–30.

Byers, B. (1983). Beyond structure: Some thoughts on the nature of mathematics. In J. C. Bergeron & N. Herscovics (Eds.), *Proceedings of the Fifth Annual Meeting of the Psychology of Mathematics Education—North America* (pp. 31–40). Montreal: Canada.

Campbell, P., & Fein, G. (Eds.). (1986). *Young children and micro computers*. Englewood Cliffs, NJ: Prentice-Hall.

Carpenter, T. P. (1975). Measurement of concepts of first- and second-grade students. *Journal for Research in Mathematics Education, 6*, 3–13.
Carpenter, T. P., & Lewis, R. (1976). The development of the concept of a standard unit of measure in young children. *Journal for Research in Mathematics Education, 7*, 53–58.
Carpenter, T. P., & Moser, J. M. (1982). The development of addition and subtraction problem solving skills. In T. P. Carpenter, J. M. Moser, & T. A. Romberg (Eds.), *Addition and subtraction: A cognitive perspective* (pp. 9–21). Hillsdale, NJ: Lawrence Erlbaum Associates.
Carpenter, T. P., & Moser, J. M. (1984). The acquisition of addition and subtraction concepts in grades one through three. *Journal for Research in Mathematics Education, 15* (3), 179–202.
Carpenter, T. P., & Peterson, P. I. (Eds.). (1988). Learning mathematics from instruction. *Educational Psychologist, 63* (2), 77–202.
Carpenter, T. P., Moser, J. M., & Romberg, T. A. (Eds.). (1982). *Addition and subtraction: A cognitive perspective*. Hillsdale, NJ: Lawrence Erlbaum Associates.
Carraher, T. N., & Carraher, D. W. (1987). *Mathematics as personal and social activity*. Paper presented at the International Conference on Success or Failure? The Child's Development at School, Poitiers, France.
Carraher, T. N., Carraher, D. W., & Schliemann, A. D. (1985). Mathematics in the streets and in schools. *British Journal of Developmental Psychology, 3*, 21–29.
Carraher, T. N., Carraher, D. W., & Schliemann, A. D. (1987). Written and oral mathematics. *Journal for Research in Mathematics Education, 18*, 83–97.
Carraher, T. N., & Schliemann, A. D. (1983). Fracasso escolar, uma questão social. *Cadernas de Pesquisa, 45*, 3–19.
Carss, M. (Ed.). (1986). *Proceedings of the Fifth International Congress on Mathematical Education*. Boston: Birkhäuser.
Case, R. (1985). *Intellectual development: Birth to adulthood*. New York: Academic Press.
Casey, E. S. (1976). *Imaging: A phenomenological study*. Bloomington, IN: Indiana University Press.
Cazden, C. (1985). Classroom discourse. In M. C. Wittrock (Ed.), *The handbook of research on teaching* (3rd ed., pp. 432–463). New York: Macmillan.
Cazden, C. (1988). *Classroom discourse: The language of teaching and learning*. New York: Heineman.
Cherry, C. (1966). *On human communication* (2nd ed.). Cambridge, MA: MIT Press.
Christiansen, B., & Walther, G. (1985). Task and activity. In B. Christiansen, A. G. Howson, & M. Otte (Eds.), *Perspectives on mathematics education* (pp. 243–304). Dordrecht: Reidel.
Clements, K. (1988). *Visualization is not always helpful*. Paper presented at the Sixth International Congress on Mathematics Education, Budapest, Hungary.
Clements, M. A., & Del Campo, G. (1987). Fractional understanding of fractions: Variations in children's understanding of fractional concepts, across embodiment. In J. D. Novak (Ed.), *Proceedings of the Second International Seminar on Misconceptions and Educational Strategies in Science and Mathematics* (Vol. 3, pp. 98–110). Ithaca, NY: Cornell University.
Clements, M. A., & Lean, G. A. (1988). Discrete fraction concepts and cognitive structure. In A. Borbâs (Ed.), *Proceedings of the Twelfth International Conference on the Psychology of Mathematics Education* (Vol. 1, pp. 215–222). Veszprem, Hungary: PME.
Cobb, P. (1983). *Children's strategies for finding sums and differences*. Unpublished doctoral dissertation, University of Georgia, Athens.
Cobb, P. (1985). Two children's anticipations, beliefs, and motivations. *Educational Studies in Mathematics, 16*, 111–126.
Cobb, P. (1986a). An investigation into the sensory-motor and conceptual origin of the basic addition facts. In L. Burton & C. Hoyles (Eds.), *Proceedings of the Tenth International Conference on the Psychology of Mathematics Education* (pp. 141–146). London: University of London Institute of Education.
Cobb, P. (1986b). Contexts, goals, beliefs, and learning mathematics. *For the Learning of Mathematics, 6* (2), 2–9.

Cobb, P. (1986c). Making mathematics: Children's learning and the constructivist tradition. *Harvard Educational Review, 56,* 301–306.
Cobb, P. (1987a). An investigation of young children's academic arithmetic contexts. *Educational Studies in Mathematics, 18,* 109–124.
Cobb, P. (1987b). Information-processing psychology and mathematics education—A constructivist perspective. *Journal of Mathematical Behavior, 6,* 3–40.
Cobb, P., & Steffe, L. (1983). The constructivist researcher as teacher and model builder. *Journal for Research in Mathematics Education, 14,* 83–94.
Cobb, P., Wood, T., & Yackel, E. (in press). A constructivist approach to second grade mathematics. In E. von Glasersfeld (Ed.), *Constructivism in Mathematics education.* Dordrecht: Reidel.
Cobb, P., Yackel, E., & Wood, T. (1989). Young children's emotional acts while engaged in mathematical problem solving. In D. B. McLeod & V. M. Adams (Eds.), *Affect and mathematical problem solving: A new perspective* (pp. 117–148). New York: Springer-Verlag.
Cohors-Fresenborg, E. (1978). Learning problem solving by developing automata networks. *Revue de Phonétique Appliquée, 46–47,* 93–99.
Cole, M. (1971). *The cultural context of learning and thinking.* London: Methuen.
Comaroff, J. L. (1982). Dialectical systems, history and anthropology: Units of study and questions of theory. *Journal of South Africa Studies, 8* (2), 143–172.
Comiti, C. (1983). Evolution du statut et du rôle du comptage au cours de l'année de l'enseignement obligatorie en France. In M. Zweng, T. Green, J. Kilpatrick, H. Pollak, & M. Suydam (Eds.), *Proceedings of the Fourth International Congress on Mathematical Education* (p. 504). Boston: Birkhäuser.
Commonwealth Schools Commission. (1987). *Multiplying Chances (for all).* National BLIPS Mathematics Conference, Canberra, Western Australia.
Confrey, J. (1987, July). *The current state of constructivist thought in mathematics education.* Paper presented at the annual meeting of the International Conference on the Psychology of Mathematics Education, Montreal.
Cooper, R. G. (1984). Early number development: Discovering number space with addition and subtraction. In C. Sophian (Ed.), *Origins of Cognitive Skills* (pp. 157–192). Hillsdale, NJ: Lawrence Erlbaum Associates.
Cordier, J. (1975). *Une anthropologie de l'inadaptation—La dynamique de l'exclusion sociale.* Bruxelles: Editions de l'Universite de Bruxelles.
Cordier, J., & Lowenthal, F. (1973). Can new maths help disturbed children? *The Lanceta,* 383–384.
Cordier, J., Lowenthal, F., & Heraux, C. (1975). Enseignement de la mathématique et exercice de verbalisation chez les enfants caractériels. *Enfance, 1,* 111–124.
D'Ambrosio, U. (1985). Ethnomathematics and its place in the history and pedagogy of mathematics. *For the Learning of Mathematics, 5,* (1), 44–48.
D'Ambrosio, U. (1986). Socio-cultural bases for mathematical education. In M. Carss (Ed.), *Proceedings of the Fifth International Congress on Mathematical Education.* Boston: Birkhäuser.
Danish Ministry of Education, (1984). *Education in Denmark.* Copenhagen: Ministry of Education.
Dantzig, T. (1968). *Number: The language of science.* London: George Allen & Unwin.
Davis, P. J., & Hersh, P. (1986). *Descartes dream.* Boston: Harcourt Brace & Jovanovich.
Davydov, V. V. (1982). The psychological characteristics of the formation of elementary mathematical operations in children. In T. P. Carpenter, J. M. Moser, & T. A. Romberg (Eds.), *Addition and subtraction: A cognitive perspective* (pp. 157–238). Hillsdale, NJ: Lawrence Erlbaum Associates.
De Corte, E., & Verschaffel, L. (1985). Beginning first graders' initial representation of arithmetic word problems. *Journal of Mathematical Behavior, 4,* 3–21.
De Corte, E., & Verschaffel, L. (1987). The effects of semantic and non-semantic factors on young children's solutions of elementary addition and subtraction word problems. In J. Bergeron, N. Herscovics, & C. Kieran (Eds.), *Proceedings of the Eleventh International Conference on the Psychology of Mathematics Education,* (Vol. 2, pp. 375–381). Montreal: PME.

Desforges, C., & Cockburn, A. (1987). *Understanding the mathematics teacher.* Lewes: Falmer Press.
Detlefsen, M. (1986). *Hilbert's program: An essay on mathematical instrumentalism.* Dordrecht: Reidel.
Dewey, J. (1964). The child and the curriculum. In R. D. Archambault (Ed.), *John Dewey on education,* (pp. 339–358). Chicago: University of Chicago Press.
Dienes, Z. P. (1966). *Construction des mathématiques.* Paris: Presses Universitaires de France.
DiSibio, M. (1982). Memory for connected discourse: A constructivist view. *Review of Educational Research, 52,* 149–174.
Dreyfus, H. L., & Dreyfus, S. E. (1986). *Mind over machine.* New York: Free Press.
Duckworth, E. (1987). *"The having of wonderful ideas": And other essays on teaching and learning.* New York: Teachers College Press.
Easley, J. (1983). A Japanese approach to arithmetic. *For the Learning of Mathematics, 3* (3), 8–14.
Easley, J., & Easley, E. (1983). What's there to talk about in arithmetic? *Problem Solving, 5,* 3, 1, 2.
Easley, J., & Zwoyer, R. (1975). Teaching by listening. *Contemporary Education, 1,* 2.
Egger, E. (n.d.). *Swiss schools.* Zurich: Pro Helvetia.
Eisenhart, M. A. (1988). The ethnographic research tradition and mathematics education research. *Journal for Research in Mathematics Education, 19,* 99–114.
English, L. D. (1988a). *Young children's competence in solving novel combinatorial problems.* Unpublished doctoral dissertation, University of Queensland, Australia.
English, L. D. (1988b). *Young children as independent learners.* Paper presented at the Seminar on Intelligence, Melbourne, Australia.
Ensor, B., & Malvern, D. (undated). *Children talking mathematics.* (Research report). Reading University and Bershire LEA Mathematics/Language Project.
Erickson, F. (1982). Taught cognitive learning in its immediate environment: A neglected topic in the anthropology of education. *Anthropology and Education Quarterly, 13,* 149–180.
Ericksson, R., & Neuman, D. (1981). *Räknesvaga elevers matematikundervisning under de sex första skolaren.* [Mathematics teaching for children weak in maths during their first six school years]. Unpublished manuscript, University of Goteborg, Department of Education, Goteborg.
Erlwanger, S. (1973). Benny's conception of rules and answers in IPI mathematics. *The Journal of Children's Mathematical Behavior, 1* (2), 157–283.
Ernest, P. (1986). Games: A rationale for their use in the teaching of mathematics in school. *Mathematics in Schools, 15* (1), 2–5.
Eves, H. (1969). *An introduction to the history of mathematics* (3rd ed.). New York: Holt, Rinehart & Winston.
Feldman, C. F. (1987). Thought from language: The linguistic construction of cognitive representations. In J. Bruner & H. Haste (Eds.), *Making sense: The child's construction of the world* (pp. 131–162), London: Methuen.
Feuerstein, R. (1980). *Instrument enrichment.* Maryland: Baltimore University Press.
Fey, J. (1979). Mathematics teaching today: Perspectives from three national surveys. *Arithmetic Teacher, 27* (7), 10–16.
Fischbein, E. (1987). *Intuition in science and mathematics.* Dordrecht: Reidel.
Fischer, K. W. (1980). A theory of cognitive development: The control and construction of hierarchies of skills. *Psychological Review, 87* (6), 477–531.
Firestone, W. A. (1987). Meaning in method: The rhetoric of quantitative and qualitative research. *Educational Researcher, 16* (7), 16–21.
Flegg, G. (1983). *Numbers, their history and meaning.* New York: Schocken Books.
Floden, R. E., Buchmann, M., & Schwille, J. R. (1987). Breaking with everyday experience. *Teachers College Record, 88,* 485–506.
Fosnot, C. T., Forman, G. E., Edwards, C. P., & Goldhaber, J. (1988). The development of an understanding of balance and the effect of training via stop-action video. *Journal of Applied Developmental Psychology, 9* (1), 1–26.

REFERENCES 471

Francis, H. (1987). Hearing beginning readers read: Problems of relating practice to theory in interpretation and evaluation. *British Educational Research Journal, 13* (3), 215–225.
Freeman, D., Kuhn, T., Porter, A., Floden, R., Schmidt, W., & Schwille, J. (1983). Do textbooks and tests define a national curriculum in elementary school mathematics? *Elementary School Journal, 83,* 501–513.
Freeman, N. H., & Stedmon, J. A. (1986). How children deal with natural language quantification. In I. Kurcz, G. W. Shugar, & J. H. Danks (Eds.), *Knowledge and language.* Dordrecht: Reidel.
Frege, G. (1960). *The foundations of arithmetic.* New York: Harper & Row.
Freudenthal, H. (1973). *Mathematics as an educational task.* Dordrecht: Reidel.
Freudenthal, H. (1978). *Weeding and sowing: Preface to a science of mathematical education.* Dordrecht: Reidel.
Freudenthal, H. (1983). *Didactical phenomenology of mathematical structures.* Dordrecht: Reidel.
Frye, N. (1982). *The great code.* Toronto: Academic Press.
Fuson, K. C., Richards, J., & Briars, D. J. (1982). The acquisition and elaboration of the number word sequence. In C. J. Brainerd (Ed.), Progress in cognitive development (Vol. 1), *Children's logical and mathematical cognition* (pp. 33–92). New York: Springer-Verlag.
Gadamer, H. G. (1986). *Truth and method.* New York: Crossroad.
Gal'perin, P. Y., & Georgiev, L. S. (1969). The formation of elementary mathematics notions. In J. Kilpatrick & I. Wirszup (Eds.), *Soviet studies in the psychology of learning and teaching mathematics* (Vol. 1, pp. 189–216). Stanford, CA: School Mathematics Study Group.
Gay, J., & Cole, M. (1967). *The new mathematics and an old culture: A study of learning among the Rpelle of Liberia.* New York: Holt, Rinehart & Winston.
Geertz, C. (1980). Blurred genres: The refiguration of social thought. *American Scholar, 49,* 165–179.
Gelman, R., & Gallistel, C. R. (1978). *The child's understanding of number.* Cambridge, MA: Harvard University Press.
Gelman, R., & Meck, E. (1986). The notion of principle: The case of counting. In J. Hiebert (Ed.), *Conceptual and procedural knowledge: The case of mathematics* (pp. 29–57). Hillsdale, NJ: Lawrence Erlbaum Associates.
Gergen, K. J. (1982). *Toward a transformation in social knowledge.* New York: Springer-Verlag.
Gergen, K. J. (1985). The social constructionist movement in modern psychology. *American Psychologist, 40,* 266–275.
Gillings, R. J. (1972). *Mathematics in the time of the Pharaohs.* Cambridge, MA: MIT Press.
Ginsburg, H. P. (1977). *Children's arithmetic.* New York: Van Nostrand.
Ginsburg, H. P. (Ed.). (1983). *The development of mathematical thinking.* New York: Academic Press.
Ginsburg, H. P., Kossan, N. E., Schwartz, R., & Swanson, D. (1983). Protocol methods in research on mathematical thinking. In H. P. Ginsburg (Ed.), *The development of mathematical thinking* (pp. 8–46). New York: Academic Press.
Godel, K. (1964). What is Cantor's continuum problem? In P. Benacerraf & H. Putnam (Eds.), *Philosophy of mathematics: Selected readings* (pp. 258–273). Englewood, NJ: Prentice-Hall.
Goodman, N. (1978). *Ways of world making.* Hassocks, Sussex: Harvester Press.
Goodman, N. (1984). *Of mind and other matters.* Cambridge, MA: Harvard University Press.
Goodman, N. (1986). Mathematics as an objective science. In T. Tymoczko (Ed.), *New directions in the philosophy of mathematics* (pp. 79–94). Boston: Birkhäuser.
Goodnow, J. (1977). *Children's drawing.* London: Fontana.
Grabiner, J. V. (1986). Is mathematical truth time-dependent? In T. Tymoczko (Ed.), *New directions in the philosophy of mathematics* (pp. 201–213). Boston: Birkhauser.
Graeber, A., Tirosh, D., & Glover, R. (1989). Preservice teachers' misconceptions in solving verbal problems in multiplication and division. *Journal for Research Mathematics Education, 20* (1), 95–102.
Greco, P., & Morf, A. (1962). Structures numériques elémentaires (Vol. XIII), *Etudes d'épistémologie génétique.* Paris: Presses Universitaires de France.

Greene, M. (1987, April). *The conceived and the imagined: An aesthetic educator's viewing of mathematics*. Paper presented at the annual meeting of the American Educational Research Association, Washington, D.C.

Greeno, J. G. (1987). Instructional representations based on research about understanding. In A. H. Schoenfeld (Ed.), *Cognitive science and mathematics education* (pp. 61–88). Hillsdale, NJ: Lawrence Erlbaum Associates.

Greeno, J. G., & Johnson, W. (1985). *Competence for solving and understanding problems*. Pennsylvania: University of Pittsburgh, LRDC.

Greeno, J. G., Riley, M. S., & Gelman, R. (1984). Conceptual competence in children's counting. *Cognitive Psychology, 16*, 94–143.

Greer, B., & Mangan, C. (1986). Choice of operation: From 10-year-olds to student teachers. In L. Burton & C. Hoyles (Eds.), *Proceedings of the Tenth International Conference on the Psychology of Mathematics Education* (pp. 25–30). London: University of London Institute of Education.

Griffiths, H. B. (1983). Success and failures of mathematics curricula in the past two decades. In M. Zweng, T. Green, J. Kilpatrick, H. Pollak, & M. Suydam (Eds.), *Proceedings of the Fourth International Congress on Mathematical Education* (pp. 358–362). Boston: Birkhäuser.

Guay, R. B., & McDaniel, E. D. (1977). The relationship between mathematics achievement and spatial abilities among elementary school children. *Journal for Research in Mathematics Education, 7*, 211–215.

Hadamard, J. S. (1954). *The psychology of invention in the mathematical field*. New York: Dover Publications.

Halford, G. S. (1980). A learning set approach to multiple classification: Evidence for a theory of cognitive levels. *International Journal of Behavioral Development, 3*, 409–422.

Halford, G. S. (1982). *The development of thought*. Hillsdale, NJ: Lawrence Erlbaum Associates.

Halford, G. S. (1984). Can young children integrate premises in transitivity and serial order tasks? *Cognitive Psychology, 16*, 65–93.

Halford, G. S. (in preparation). *Children's understanding: The development of mental models*. Hillsdale, NJ: Lawrence Erlbaum Associates.

Halford, G. S., Mayberry, M. T., & Bain, J. D. (1986). Capacity reasoning: A dual-task approach. *Child Development, 57*, 616–627.

Halliday, M. A. K. (1975). *Learning how to mean*. London: Edward Arnold.

Hannon, P. (1987). A study of the effects of parental involvement in the teaching of reading on children's reading test performance. *British Journal of Education Psychology, 57*, 56–72.

Hardy, G. (1967). *A mathematician's apology*. Cambridge: Cambridge University Press.

Harel, G., & Martin, G. (1986). The concept of proof held by preservice elementary teachers: Aspects of induction and deduction. In L. Burton & C. Hoyles (Eds.), *Proceedings of the Tenth International Conference on the Psychology of Mathematics Education* (pp. 386–391). London: University of London, Institute of Education.

Harris, P. (1980). *Measurement in tribal Aboriginal communities*. Darwin: Northern Territory Department of Education.

Harrison, P. (1982). *Inside the Third World* (2nd ed.). New York: Penguin.

Hart, K. (Ed.). (1981). *Children's understanding of mathematics: 11–16*. London: Murray.

Hatano, G. (1982). Learning to add and subtract: A Japanese perspective. In T. P. Carpenter, J. M. Moser, T. A. Romberg (Eds.), *Addition and subtraction: A developmental perspective* (pp. 211–223). Hillsdale, NJ: Lawrence Erlbaum Associates.

Hatfield, L. (1988, February). *Enhancing school mathematical experience through constructive computing activity*. Paper presented at the meeting on Epistemological Foundations of Mathematical Experience, Athens, GA.

Head, J. (1986). Research into "alternative frameworks": Promise and problems. *Research in Science and Technological Education, 4* (2), 203–211.

Heath, S. B. (1983). *Ways with words*. London: Cambridge University Press.

Herscovics, N., & Bergeron, J. C. (1983). Models of understanding. *Zentralblatt für didaktik der mathematik, 83* (2), 75–83.

Herscovics, N., & Bergeron, J. C. (1988a). An extended model of understanding. In M. Behr, C. Lacampagne, & M. M. Wheeler (Eds.), *Proceedings of the Tenth Annual Meeting of the Psychology of Mathematics Education—North America* (pp. 15–22). De Kalb: Northern Illinois University.

Herscovics, N., & Bergeron, J. C. (1988b). The kindergarteners' understanding of the notion of rank. In A. Borbes (Ed.), *Proceedings of the Twelfth International Conference on the Psychology of Mathematics Education* (pp. 385–392). Veszprém, Hungary: PME.

Hewson, P. (1981). A conceptual change approach to learning science. *European Journal of Science Education, 3,* 383–396.

Hiebert, J. (1981). Cognitive development and learning linear measurement. *Journal for Research in Mathematics Education, 12,* 197–211.

Hiebert, J. (1986). *Procedural and conceptual knowledge: The case of mathematics.* Hillsdale, NJ: Lawrence Erlbaum Associates.

Hodgkin, L. (1976). Politics and physical science. *Radical Science Journal, 4,* 13–18.

Holt, J. (1964). *How children fail.* New York: Dell.

Howson, G., & Wilson, B. (Eds.). (1986). *School mathematics in the 1990's.* Cambridge: Cambridge University Press.

Hughes, M. (1986). *Children and number.* Oxford: Basil Blackwell.

Hughes, M. (1987). *Children and number difficulties in learning mathematics.* Oxford: Basil Blackwell.

Hunting, R. P. (1980). *The role of discrete quantity partition knowledge in the child's construction of fractional number.* Unpublished doctoral dissertation, University of Georgia, Athens.

Hunting, R. P., & Sharpley, C. F. (1988). Fraction knowledge in pre-school children. *Journal for Research in Mathematics Education, 19* (2), 175–180.

Hunting, R. P., & Sharpley, C. F. (in press). Pre-schoolers' cognitions of fractional units. *British Journal of Educational Psychology.*

Hurford, J. (1987). *Language and number.* Oxford: Basil Blackwell.

Inhelder, B., Blanchet, A., Sinclair, A., & Piaget, J. (1975). Relations entre les conservations d'ensembles d'éléments discrets et celles de quantités continues. *Année Psychologique, 75,* 23–60.

Inhelder, B., Sinclair, H., & Bovet, M. (1974). *Apprentissage et structures cognitives.* Paris: Presses Universitaires de France.

Ishida, T. (1987). On relative difficulties of addition and subtraction word problems. *Bulletin of WJASMNE: Research in mathematics education, 13,* 1–7.

Ishida, J., & Koyasu, M. (1988). The effect of problem structure upon choosing operations and making up stories in word arithmetic problems. *Science Education, 12* (1), 14–21.

Jacob, F. (1977). Evaluation and tinkering. *Science, 196,* 1161–1166.

Jakobson, R. (1939/1964). Les lois phoniques du langage enfantin et leur place dans la phonologie générale. In N. S. Troubetzkoy (Ed.), *Principes de phonologie.* Paris: Klincksieck.

James, W. (1920). *A pluralistic universe.* New York: Longmans.

Johnson, M. (1987). *The body in the mind.* Chicago: University of Chicago Press.

Johnston, A. (Ed.). (1974). *The advancement of learning and New Atlantis/Francis Bacon.* Oxford: Claredon Press.

Kamii, C. (1981). Piaget for principals. *Principal, 60* (5), 12–17.

Kamii, C. (1984). Children's ideas about written number. *Topics in Learning and Learning Disabilities, 1* (3), 47–59.

Kamii, C. (1985, February). *Can there be excellence in education without knowledge of child development?* Paper presented at the annual meeting of the Chicago Association for the Education of Young Children, Chicago.

Kamii, C., & De Clark, G. (1985). *Young children re-invent arithmetic*. New York: Teachers College Press.
Kant, I. (1911). *Kritik der reinen Vernunft* (2. Auflage, 1787). Akademieausgabe, Berlin: Georg Reimer.
Kaper, W. (1985). *Child language*. Holland: Foris, Dordrecht.
Karmiloff-Smith, A., & Inhelder, B. (1974). If you want to get ahead, get a theory. *Cognition, 3,* 195–222.
Kaye, K., & Charney, R. (1980). How mothers maintain "dialogue" with two-year olds. In O. Olson (Ed.), *The social foundations of language and thought: Essays in honor of Jerome S. Bruner* (pp. 103–121). New York: Norton.
Kearins, J. (1976). Skills of desert Aboriginal children. In G. E. Kearney & D. W. McElwain (Eds.), *Aboriginal cognition: Retrospect and prospect* (pp. 199–212). Atlantic Highlands, NJ: Humanities Press.
Keranto, T. (1978). *Child's developmental level of number concept at pre-school age* (Report No. 1). Helsinki: University of Tampere, Institute of Teacher Education.
Kieren, T. E. (1988). Personal knowledge of rational numbers: Its intuitive and formal development. In J. Hiebert & M. Behr (Eds.), *Research agenda project: Research in middle school number learning* (pp. 162–181). Reston, VA: NCTM.
Kilpatrick, J. (1987). What constructivism might be in mathematics education. In J. C. Bergeron, N. Herscovics, & C. Kieran (Eds.), *Proceedings of the Eleventh International Conference on the Psychology of Mathematics Education* (pp. 2–27). Montreal: PME.
Kitcher, P. (1986). Mathematical change and scientific change. In T. Tymoczko (Ed.), *New directions in the philosophy of mathematics* (pp. 215–241). Boston: Birkhäuser.
Klahr, D. (1980). Information-processing models of intellectual development. In R. H. Kluwe & H. Spada (Eds.), *Developmental models of thinking* (pp. 127–162). New York: Academic Press.
Klich, L. Z., & Davidson, G. R. (1984). Toward a recognition of Australian Aboriginal competence in cognitive functions. In J. R. Kirby (Ed.), *Cognitive strategies and educational performance* (pp. 155–202). London: Academic Press.
Kline, M. (1972). *Mathematics in western culture*. New York: Penguin.
Kline, M. (1980). *Mathematics, the loss of certainty*. Oxford: Oxford University Press.
Kline, M. (1985). *Mathematics and the search for knowledge*. New York: Oxford University Press.
Kosslyn, S. (1983). *Ghosts in the mind's machine*. New York: Norton.
Kotou, S. (1978). *Algebraic expressions*. Tokyo: Kaneko Shobo.
Krummheuer, G. (1983). Das Arbeitsinterim im Mathematikunterricht. In H. Bauersfeld, H. Bussman, G. Krummheuer, J. H. Lorenz, & J. Voight (Eds.), *Lernen und Lehren von Mathematik* (pp. 57–106). Köln: Aulis Verlag Deubner & Cokg.
Kuhn, T. S. (1970). *The structure of scientific revolutions* (2nd ed.). Chicago: University of Chicago Press.
Laboratory of Comparative Human Cognition. (1983). Culture and cognitive development. In P. H. Mussen & W. Kessen (Eds.), *Handbook of child psychology* (4th ed., Vol. 1). *History, theory, and methods* (pp. 295–356). New York: Wiley.
Lakatos, I. (1976). *Proofs and refutations*. Cambridge: Cambridge University Press.
Lakoff, G. (1987). *Women, fire and other dangerous things*. Chicago: The University of Chicago Press.
Lampert, M. L. (1985). How do teachers manage to teach? Perspectives on the problems of practice. *Harvard Educational Review, 55,* 178–194.
Lampert, M. L. (1988). The teacher's role in reinventing the meaning of mathematical knowing in the classroom. In M. Behr, C. Lacampagne, & M. M. Wheeler (Eds.), *Proceedings of the Tenth Annual Meeting of the Psychology of Mathematics Education—North America* (pp. 433–480). DeKalb, IL: Northern Illinois University.

Langer, S. (1967). *Mind: An essay on feeling*. Baltimore: Johns Hopkins University Press.
Lave, J. (1988). *Cognition in practice: Mind, mathematics and culture in everyday life*. Cambridge: Cambridge University Press.
Lave, J., Murtaugh, M., & de la Rocha, O. (1984). The dialectic of arithmetic in grocery shopping. In B. Rogoff & J. Lave (Eds.), *Everyday cognition: Its development in social context* (pp. 67–94). Cambridge, MA: Harvard University Press.
Lawler, R. W. (1979). *One child's learning*. Unpublished doctoral dissertation, MIT, Cambridge.
Lawler, R. W. (1985). *Computer experience and cognitive development*. New York: Wiley.
Lawler, R. (1986). *Cognition and computers: Studies in learning*. New York: Halsted Press.
Lawler, R. W. (1989). Shared models: The cognitive equivalent of a lingua franca. *Artificial Intelligence and Society, 3*, 3–27.
Lawler, R. W. (in press). Thinkable models. *Journal of Mathematical Behavior*.
Lean, G. A. (1988). *Counting systems of Papua New Guinea*. Lae: Papua New Guinea University of Technology.
Lean, G. A., & Clements, M. (1981). Spatial ability, visual imagery, and mathematical performance. *Educational Studies in Mathematics, 12*, 267–299.
Lesh, R., Landau, M., & Hamilton, E. (1983). Conceptual models and applied mathematical problem solving. In R. Lesh & M. Landau (Eds.), *Acquisition of mathematics concepts and processes* (pp. 263–343). New York: Academic Press.
Lester, F. K. (1982). Building bridges between psychological and mathematics educational research on problem solving. In F. K. Lester (Ed.), *Mathematical problem solving: Issues in research* (pp. 51–85). Philadelphia: Franklin Institute Press.
Letteri, C. (1987). Mathematics as a cognitive science. In P. Kupari (Ed.), *Mathematics Education Research in Finland. Yearbook 1986* (pp. 1–8). Finland: University of Jyvaskyla, Institute of Educational Research.
Levina, R. E. (1981). L. S. Vygotsky's ideas about the planning function of speech in children. In J. V. Wertsch (Ed.), *The concept of activity in Soviet psychology* (pp. 279–299). Armont, NY: Sharpe.
Levi-Strauss, C. (1966). *The savage mind*. Chicago: University of Chicago Press.
Lewin, K. (1935). The conflict between Galilean and Aristotelian modes of thought in contemporary psychology (D. K. Adams & K. E. Zener, trans.). In *A dynamic theory of psychology: Selected papers of Kurt Lewin* (pp. 1–42). New York: McGraw-Hill.
Lin, C. (1979). Imagery in mathematical thinking and learning. *International Journal of Mathematics Education in Science and Technology, 10*, 107–110.
Lindquist, M. M. (1984). The elementary school mathematics curriculum: Issues for today. *Elementary School Journal, 84* (5), 595–608.
Lister, H. (1987). A national Journal for teachers of Aborigines, *The Aboriginal Child at School, 15* (1), 3–16.
Lowenthal, F. (1985a). Pegboard as basis for programmation—in 5- and 6-year olds. In L. Streefland (Ed.), *Proceedings of the Ninth International Conference for the Psychology of Mathematics Education* (Vol. 1, pp. 47–52). Noordwijkerhout: PME.
Lowenthal, F. (1985b). Non-verbal communication devices in language acquisition. *Revue de Phonetique Appliquée*. 73–75, 155–166.
Lowenthal, F. (1987). Représentation concrète de systèmes formels et structuration d'une communication. *Revue de Phonétique Appliquée, 82–84*, 231–245.
Lowenthal, F. (1988). Non-verbal communication devices in language acquisition. *Revue de Phonétique Appliquée*, 73–75, 155–156.
Lowenthal, F., & Saerens, J. (1986). Evolution of an aphasic child after the introduction of NVCDS. In F. Lowenthal & F. Vandamme (Eds.), *Pragmatics and education* (pp. 301–330). New York: Plenum.

MacLure, M., & French, P. (1981). A comparison of talk at home and at school. In G. Wells (Ed.), *Learning through interaction*. (pp. 205-239). London: Cambridge University Press.
Macquarie Library (1982). *The Macquarie dictionary*. Sydney: Macquarie Library.
Malinowski, B. (1922). *Argonauts of the western Pacific: An account of native enterprise and adventure in the archipelagoes of Melanesian New Guinea*. New York: Dutton.
Mansfield, H. M., & Happs, J. C. (1987, July). *Students' understanding of parallel lines: Some implications for teaching*. Paper presented at the Second International Seminar on Misconceptions and Educational Strategies in Science and Mathematics, Ithaca, Cornell University.
Martin, G., & Wheeler, M. M. (1987). Infinity concepts among preservice elementary school teachers. In J. Bergeron, N. Herscovics, & C. Kieran (Eds.), *Proceedings of the Eleventh International Conference on the Psychology of Mathematics Education* (Vol. 3, pp. 362-368). Montreal: PME.
Marton, F. (1981). Phenomenology: Describing conceptions of the world around us. *Instructional Science, 10*, 177-200.
Mason, J., Burton, L., & Stacey, K. (1982). *Thinking mathematically*. London: Addison-Wesley.
Maturana, H. (1978). Biology of language: The epistemology of reality. In G. A. Miller & E. Lennenberg (Eds.), *Psychology and biology of language and thought: Essays in honor of Eric Lennenberg* (pp. 27-63). New York: Academic Press.
Maturana, H., & Varela, F. J. (1980). *Autopoiesis and cognition*. Dordrecht: Reidel.
Maturana, H., & Varela, F. J. (1987). *The tree of knowledge*. Boston: The New Science Library Shambhalu.
McCullough, W. (1962). *Embodiments of mind*. Cambridge, MA: MIT Press.
McGee, M. (1979). Human spatial abilities: Psychometric studies and environmental, genetic, hormonal, and neurological influences. *Psychological Bulletin, 86* (5), 889-917.
McKnight, C. (1987). *The under achieving curriculum*. Champaigne: Stripes Publishing.
McLellan, J. A., & Dewey, J. (1895). *The psychology of number*. New York: Appleton-Century-Crofts.
Meade, G. H. (1934). *Mind, self, and society*. Chicago: University of Chicago Press.
Meek, M. (1985). Play and paradoxes: Some consideration of imagination and language. In G. Wells and J. Nicholls (Eds.), *Language and learning: An interactional perspective* (pp. 41-57). London: Falmer Press.
Mehan, H. (1979). *Learning lessons: Social organization in the classroom*. Cambridge, MA: Harvard University Press.
Mellin-Olsen, S. (1987). *The politics of mathematics education*. Dordrecht: Reidel.
Menninger, K. (1969). *Number words and number symbols—A cultural history of numbers*. Cambridge, MA: MIT Press.
Merttens, R. (1987). *IMPACT—The story of a project*. Unpublished master's thesis, King's College London, London, England.
Miller, K. (1984). Child as the measurer of all things: Measurement procedures and the development of quantitative concepts. In C. Sophian (Ed.), *Origins of cognitive skills* (pp. 193-228). Hillsdale, NJ: Lawrence Erlbaum Associates.
Ministry of Education (1986). Survey of children's learning activities outside schools. *Monbu Jiho, 4*, 87.
Minsky, M. (1985). *Society of the mind*. New York: Viking.
Montessori, M. (1967). *The absorbent mind*. New York: Holt, Rinehart & Winston.
Mumme, J., & Weissglass, J. (1988, July). *Improving mathematics education through site based change: Preliminary report*. Paper presented at the Sixth International Congress on Mathematics Education, Budapest, Hungary.
Murphy, P. F. (1988). Insights into pupils' responses to practical investigations from the A. P. U. *Physics Education, 23* (6), 330-336.

Myrdal, G. (1968). *The Asian drama: An inquiry into the poverty of nations* (Vol. 3). New York: Twentieth Century Fund.
National Association for the Education of Young Children. (1988). *Appropriate education in the primary grades.* Washington, D.C.: NAEYC.
National BLIPS Mathematics Conference. (1987). *Multiplying Chances (For All).* Canberra, Western Australia.
National Commission on Excellence in Education. (1983). *A nation at risk.* Washington, D.C.: Government Printing Office.
National Council of Teachers of Mathematics. (1989). *Curriculum and evaluation standards for school mathematics.* Reston, VA: NCTM.
Nebres, B. (1987). The shape of school mathematics in the 1990's: A report on the ICMI study on school mathematics in the 1990's. In O. Sit-Tui (Ed.), *Proceedings of fourth Southeast conference on mathematical education* (pp. 14–21). Singapore: Institute of Education.
Neisser, U. (1967). *Cognitive psychology.* New York: Appleton-Century-Crofts.
Nesher, P. (1986). Are mathematical understanding and algorithmic performance related? *For the Learning of Mathematics, 6* (3), 2–9.
Neuman, D. (1987). *The origin of arithmetic skills: A phenomenographic approach.* Goteborg: Acta Universitatis Gothoburgensis.
Newman, R. S., & Berger, C. F. (1984). Children's numerical estimation: Flexibility in the use of counting. *Journal of Educational Psychology, 76,* 55–64.
Nohda, N. (1983). *A study of "open-approach" strategy in school mathematics teaching.* Tokyo: Toyokan.
Nohda, N. (1986). *Open-mind of children in arithmetic teaching.* Tokyo: Kobonshoen Publishing.
Noton, S., & Stark, R. (1971). Eye movements and visual perception. *Scientific American, 224,* 6, 34–43.
Novak, J. D., & Gowin, D. B. (1986). *Learning to learn.* Cambridge: Cambridge University Press.
Ohuche, R. O. (1973). Geometry, estimation and measurement in traditional Sierra Leone. In *Education in developing countries of the Commonwealth* (pp. 329–338). London: Commonwealth Secretariat.
Ohuche, R. O. (1975). The uses of real numbers in traditional Sierra Leone. *West African Journal of Education, 19* (2), 329–338.
Ohuche, R. O. & Otaale, B. (Eds.) (1981). *The African child and his environment.* Oxford: Pergamon Press.
Paivio, A. (1971). *Imagery and verbal processing.* New York: Holt, Rinehart & Winston.
Paley, V. G. (1981). *Wally's Stories.* Cambridge, MA: Harvard University Press.
Papert, S. (1980). *Mind storms: Children, computers, powerful ideas.* New York: Basic Books.
Papy, F. (1970). *Les enfants et la mathématique,* (Vol. 1). Bruxelles: Didier.
Papy, F. (1971). *Les enfants et la mathématique,* (Vol. 2). Bruxelles: Didier.
Papy, F. (1972). *Les enfants et la mathématique,* (Vol. 3). Bruxelles: Didier.
Papy, F., & Papy, G. (1968). *L'enfant et les graphes.* Bruxelles: Didier.
Paul, C. A. (1985). Some cautions on short-term solutions. *Mathematics Teacher, 78,* 82–84.
Pea, R. D. (1987). Cognitive technologies for mathematics education. In A. H. Schoenfeld (Ed.), *Cognitive science and mathematics education.* (pp. 89–122). Hillsdale, NJ: Lawrence Erlbaum Associates.
Pereira, R. (1987). The strategies of teaching early primary mathematics, especially in rural areas. In O. Sit-Tui (Ed.), *Proceedings of fourth Southeast conference on mathematical education* (pp. 105–110). Singapore: Institute of Education.
Perret-Clermont, A. N. (1980). *Social interaction and cognitive development in children.* New York: Academic Press.
Piaget, J. (1932). *Le jugement morale chez l'enfant* (The moral judgment of the child). Paris: Alcan.

Piaget, J. (1937). *La construction du réel chez l'enfant* (The construction of reality in the child). Neuchâtel: Delachaux et Niestlé.
Piaget, J. (1946). La formation du symbole chez l'enfant. (The formation of symbols in the child). Neuchâtel: Delachaux & Niestlé.
Piaget, J. (1964). Learning and development. In R. E. Ripple & V. N. Rockcastle (Eds.), *Piaget rediscovered: Report of the conference on cognitive studies and curriculum development* (pp. 7–20). Ithaca: Cornell University Press.
Piaget, J. (1965). *Insights and illusions of philosophy*. Paris: Presses Universitaires de France.
Piaget, J. (1967). *Biologie et connaissance*. Paris: Gallimard.
Piaget, J. (1970a). *Genetic epistemology*. New York: Columbia University Press.
Piaget, J. (1970b). *Psychologie et épistémologie*. Paris: Denoël Editions.
Piaget, J. (1970c). *Science of education and the psychology of the child*. New York: Viking.
Piaget, J. (1972). *Où va l'éducation?* Paris: UNESCO.
Piaget, J. (1974). *Recherches sur la contradiction* (Vol. 2) Paris: Presses Universitaires de France.
Piaget, J. (1980a). *Adaptation and intelligence: Organic selection and phenocopy*. Chicago: University of Chicago Press.
Piaget, J. (1980b). *Les formas élémentaires de la dialectique*. Paris: Gallimard.
Piaget, J. (1980c). Schemes of action and language learning. In M. Piattelli-Palmarini (Ed.), *Language and learning: The debate between Jean Piaget and Noam Chomsky* (pp. 163–167). Cambridge, MA: Harvard University Press.
Piaget, J. (1987a). *Possibility and necessity: Volume I. The role of possibility in cognitive development*. Minneapolis: University of Minnesota Press.
Piaget, J. (1987b). *Possibility and necessity: Volume II. The role of necessity in cognitive development*. Minneapolis: University of Minnesota Press.
Piaget, J., & Garcia, R. (1983). *Psychogenèse et histoire des sciences*. Paris: Flammarion.
Piaget, J., & Inhelder, B. (1948). *La représentation de l'espace chez l'enfant*. Paris: Presses Universitaires de France.
Piaget, J., & Inhelder, B. (1956). *The child's conception of space*. London: Routledge & Kegan Paul.
Piaget, J., & Inhelder, B. (1959). *La genèse des structures logigues élémentaires: Classifications et sériations*. Neuchâtel: Delachaux et Niestlé.
Piaget, J., & Inhelder, B. (1971). *Mental imagery in the child*. New York: Basic Books.
Piaget, J., & Inhelder, B. (1975). *The origin of the idea of chance in children*. New York: Norton.
Piaget, J., Inhelder, B., & Szeminska, A. (1960). *The child's conception of geometry*. New York: Basic Books.
Piaget, J., & Szeminska, A. (1941/1967). La genèse du nombre chez l'enfant. Neuchâtel: Delachaux et Niestlé.
Pimm, D. (1987). *Speaking mathematically: Communication in mathematics classrooms*. London: Routledge & Kegan Paul.
Polanyi, M. (1962). *Personal knowledge*. Chicago: University of Chicago Press.
Polya, G. (1954). *Induction and analogy in mathematics*. Princeton: Princeton University Press.
Polya, G. (1962). *Mathematical discovery: On understanding, learning, and teaching problem solving*. New York: Wiley.
Pontecorvo, C., Castiglia, D., & Zucchermaglio, C. (1983). Discorso e ragionamento scientifico nelle discussioni in classe. *Scuola e città, 34* (10), 447–462.
Popkin, R. H. (1979). *The history of skepticism from Erasmus to Spinoza*. Berkeley, CA: University of California Press.
Porter, R. (1988). *Computers and learning in the first years of school*. Sydney: Social Sciences Press.
Posner, G., Strike, K., Hewson, P., & Gertzog, W. (1982). Accommodation of a scientific conception: Toward a theory of conceptual change. *Science Education, 66,* 211–227.
Prime Project. (1987). *One year of CAN*. London: SCDC.

Rees, R., & Barr, G. (1984). *Diagnosis and prescription in the classroom: Some common maths problems.* London: Harper & Row.
Reeves, N. (1986). Children writing maths. *Reading Around Series,* No. 3 (August). Melbourne: Australian Reading Association.
Resnick, L. B. (1983). A developmental theory of number understanding. In H. P. Ginsburg (Ed.), *The development of mathematical thinking* (pp. 110–151). New York: Academic Press.
Reyes, L. H. (1984). Affective variables and mathematics education. *Elementary School Journal, 84* (5), 558–581.
Richardson, A. (1969). *Mental imagery.* London: Routledge & Kegan Paul.
Riley, M. S., Greeno, J. G., & Heller, J. I. (1983). Development of children's problem-solving ability in arithmetic. In H. P. Ginsburg (Ed.), *The development of mathematical thinking* (pp. 153–196). New York: Academic Press.
Rogoff, B. (1981). Schooling and the development of cognitive skills. In H. C. Triandis & A. Heron (Eds.), *Handbook of cross-cultural psychology: Developmental psychology* (Vol. 4, pp. 233–294). Boston: Allyn & Bacon.
Rogoff, B., & Lave, J. (Eds.). (1984). *Everyday cognition: Its development in social context.* Cambridge, MA: Harvard University Press.
Romberg, T. A., & Carpenter, T. P. (1986). Research on teaching and learning mathematics: Two disciplines of scientific inquiry. In M. C. Wittrock (Ed.), *Handbook of research on teaching* (3rd ed. pp. 850–873). New York: Macmillan.
Rommetveit, R. (1985). Language acquisition as increasing linguistic structuring of experience and symbolic behavior control. In J. V. Wertsch (Ed.), *Culture, communication, and cognition* (pp. 183–205). Cambridge: Cambridge University Press.
Rondal, J. A. (1983). *L'interaction adulte-enfant et la construction du langage.* Bruxelles: Pierre Mardaga.
Rowlands, S. (1984). *The enquiring classroom.* Lewes, East Sussex: Falmer Press.
Rucker, R. (1987). *Minds tools.* Boston: Houghton Mifflin.
Russell, R. L., & Ginsburg, H. P. (1984). Cognitive analysis of children's mathematics difficulties. *Cognition and Instruction, 1,* 217–244.
Sato, S. (1984). Removing, a sort of subtraction, is easier than addition. Why? In B. Southwell, R. Eyland, M. Cooper, J. Conroy, & K. Collins (Eds.), *Proceedings of the Eighth International Conference for the Psychology of Mathematics Education* (pp. 305–312). Sydney: PME.
Saxe, G. B. (1988). *The interplay between children's learning in formal and informal social contexts.* Paper presented at the conference on the Scientific Practice of Science Education, Berkeley, California.
Scardamalia, M. (1977). Information processing capacity and the problem of horizontal decalage: A demonstration using combinatorial reasoning tasks. *Child Development, 48,* 28–37.
Schoenfeld, A. H. (1985). *Mathematical problem solving.* New York: Academic Press.
Schoenfeld, A. H. (1987). What's all the fuss about metacognition? In A. H. Schoenfeld (Ed.), *Cognitive science and mathematics education* (pp. 189–216). Hillsdale, NJ: Lawrence Erlbaum Associates.
Schutz, A. (1962). *The problem of social reality.* The Hague, Holland: Martinus Nijhoff.
Seagrim, G. N., & Lendon, R. (1976). The settlement child and school: Intellectual assimilation and accommodation. In G. E. Kearney & D. W. McElwain (Eds.), *Aboriginal cognition: Retrospect and prospect* (pp. 222–230). Atlantic Highlands, NJ: Humanities Press.
Searle, J. (1984). *Minds, brains, and science.* Cambridge, MA: Harvard University Press.
Second International Mathematics Study. (1986). *Detailed report of the United States.* Champaign: Stripes Publishing.
Secretaria de Estado de Educação. (1986a). *Profic: Programa de formação integral da criança.* São Paulo: Governo Montoro.
Secretaria de Estado da Educação. (1986b). *Isto se aprende como ciclo básico.* São Paulo: Governo Montoro.

Secretaria de Estado da Educação. (1986c). *Proposta curricular para o ensino de matemática: Primeiro grau.* São Paulo: Governo Montoro.
Shannon, C. E. (1948). The mathematical theory of communication. *Bell Systems Technical Journal, 27,* 379–423, 623–656.
Shulman, L. S. (1986a). Paradigms and research programs in the study of teaching: A contemporary perspective. In M. C. Wittrock (Ed.), *Handbook of research on teaching* (3rd ed., pp. 3–36). New York: Macmillan.
Shulman, L. L. (1986b). Those who understand: Knowledge growth in teaching. *Educational Researcher, 15* (2), 4–14.
Shweder, R. A. (1983). Divergent rationalities. In D. W. Fiske & R. A. Shweder (Eds.), *Metatheory in social science* (pp. 163–196). Chicago: University of Chicago Press.
Siegel, L. S. (1978). The relationship of language and thought in the pre-operational child: A reconsideration of nonverbal alternatives to Piagetian tasks. In L. S. Siegel & C. J. Brainerd (Eds.), *Alternatives to Piaget: Critical essays on the theory* (pp. 43–67). New York: Academic Press.
Siegler, R. S. (1978). The origins of scientific reasoning. In R. Siegler (Ed.), *Children's thinking: What develops?* (pp. 109–149). Hillsdale, NJ: Lawrence Erlbaum Associates.
Siegler, R. S., & Robinson, M. (1982). The development of numerical understanding. In H. W. Reese & L. P. Lipsitt (Eds.), *Advances in child development and behavior* (pp. 242–312). New York: Academic Press.
Sigel, I. E. (1981). Social experience in the development of representational thought: Distancing theory. In I. E. Sigel, D. M. Brodzinsky, & R. M. Golinkoff (Eds.), *New directions in Piagetian theory and practice* (pp. 203–217). Hillsdale, NJ: Lawrence Erlbaum Associates.
Sigel, I. E. (1984a). A constructivist perspective for teaching thinking. *Educational Leadership, 42* (3), 18–21.
Sigel, I. E. (1984b). Reflections on action theory and distancing theory. *Human Development, 27* (3–4), 1988–193.
Silva, J. G. A. (1987). *O ensino da matemática: Da aparência a essência.* Unpublished master's thesis, Universidade Estadual Paulista, Rio Claro.
Silverman, H., McNaughton, S., & Kates, B. (1982). *Le manuel du système Bliss.* Québec: Association de Paralysie Cérébrale du Québec.
Simmel, G. (1895). Ueber eine Beziehung der Selectionslehre zur Erkenntnislehre. *Archiv für systematische Philosophie, 1,* 34–45.
Simon, M., & Schrifter, D. (1988, April). *Evaluation of classroom implementation in constructivist mathematics teacher education programs.* Paper presented at the NCTM/AERA (SIG) Research Presession, Chicago, IL.
Sinclair, A., & Sinclair, H. (1986). Children's mastery of written numerals and the construction of basic number concepts. In J. Hiebert (Ed.), *Procedural and conceptual knowledge: The case of mathematics.* (pp. 59–74). NJ: Lawrence Erlbaum Associates.
Sinclair, H. (1987a). Symbolism and interpersonal interaction. *Cahiers de la Fondation Archives Piaget, 8,* Genève.
Sinclair, H. (1987b). Constructivism and the psychology of mathematics. In J. Bergeron, N. Herscovics, & C. Kieran (Eds.), *Proceedings of the Eleventh International Conference on the Psychology of Mathematics Education,* (Vol. 2, pp. 28–41). Montreal: PME.
Sinclair, H. (1988). Introduction. In L. P. Steffe, P. Cobb, & E. von Glaserfeld. *Construction of arithmetical meanings and strategies* (pp. v–vi). New York: Springer-Verlag.
Skemp, R. (1976). Relational understanding and instrumental understanding. *Mathematics Teacher, 77,* 20–26.
Skemp, R. (1979). *Intelligence, learning, and action.* Chichester: Wiley.
Smith, D. A. (1951). *History of mathematics.* New York: Dover.
Smith, M. I. (1964). *Spatial ability.* London: University of London Press.
Sowder, L. (1986). Strategies children use in solving problems. *Proceedings of the Tenth Interna-*

tional Conference on Psychology of Mathematics Education. In L. Burton & C. Hoyles (Eds.), (pp. 469–474). London: University of London. Institute of Education.
Stambak, M., Barrière, M. Bonica, L., Maisonnet, R., Musatti, T., Rayna, S., & Verba, M. (1983). *Les bébés entre eux*. Paris: Presses Universitaires de France.
Starkey, P., & Gelman, R. (1982). The development of addition and subtraction abilities prior to formal schooling in arithmetic. In T. P. Carpenter, J. M. Moser, & T. A. Romberg (Eds.), *Addition and subtraction: A cognitive perspective* (pp. 99–116). Hillsdale, NJ: Lawrence Erlbaum Associates.
Steen, L. A. (1986). *Forces for change in the mathematics curriculum*. Paper presented at a conference on the The School Mathematics Curriculum: Raising National Expectations, Los Angeles, University of California, Los Angeles.
Steen, L. A. (1988). The science of patterns. *Science, 240*, 611–616.
Steffe, L. P. (1983). Children's algorithms as schemes. *Educational Studies in Mathematics, 14,* 233–249.
Steffe, L. P. (1984a). Children's prenumerical adding schemes. In B. Southwell, R. Eyland, M. Cooper, J. Conroy, & K. Collins (Eds.), *Proceedings of the Eighth International Conference for the Psychology of Mathematics Education* (pp. 190–196). Sydney: PME.
Steffe, L. P. (1984b). Communicating mathematically with children. In A. Bell, B. Low, & J. Kilpatrick (Eds.), *Theory, research, and practice in mathematical education: ICME-5 working group reports and collected papers*. Shell Centre for Mathematical Education: University of Nottingham, U.K.
Steffe, L. P. (1985). *Children's mathematics: A new perspective for mathematics education*. Paper presented at the annual meeting of the National Council of the Teachers of Mathematics, San Antonio, TX.
Steffe, L. P. (1987, March). *Children's mathematics: Its nature, content, and acquisition*. Paper presented at the annual meeting of the National Council of Teachers of Mathematics, Anaheim, CA.
Steffe, L. P., Cobb, P., & von Glasersfeld, E. (1988). *Construction of arithmetical meanings and strategies*. New York: Springer-Verlag.
Steffe, L. P., von Glasersfeld, E., Richards, J., & Cobb, P. (1983). *Children's counting types: Philosophy, theory, and application*. New York: Praeger Scientific.
Steinberg, R. M. (1985). Instruction on derived facts strategies in addition and subtraction. *Journal for Research in Mathematics Education, 16* (5), 337–355.
Steiner, H. G. (1987). A systems approach to mathematics education. *Journal for Research in Mathematics Education, 18,* 46–52.
Stewart, I. (1987). *The problems of mathematics*. Oxford: Oxford University Press.
Struik, D. J. (1948). *A concise history of mathematics*. New York: Dover.
Suydam, M. M., & Osborne, A. (1977). *The status of pre-college science, mathematics and social science education: 1955–1975* (Vol. 2). Columbus, OH: The Information Reference Center for Science, Mathematics, and Environmental Education.
Thom, R. (1973). Modern mathematics: Does it exist? In A. G. Howson (Ed.), *Developments in Mathematics Education. Proceedings of the Second International Congress on Mathematical Education* (pp. 194–209). Cambridge: Cambridge University Press.
Thomas, N. (Ed.). (1985). *Improving schools ILEA*. London: Centre for Learning Resources.
Thompson, A. G. (1985). Teacher's conceptions of mathematics and the teaching of problem solving. In E. A. Silver (Ed.), *Teaching and learning mathematical problem solving: Multiple research perspectives* (pp. 281–294). Hillsdale, NJ: Lawrence Erlbaum Associates.
Thompson, P. (1985). Experience, problem solving, and learning mathematics: Considerations in developing mathematics curricula. In E. A. Silver (Ed.), *Teaching and learning mathematical problem solving: Multiple research perspectives* (pp. 189–235). Hillsdale, NJ: Lawrence Erlbaum Associates.
Tizard, B., & Hughes, M. (1984). *Young children learning*. London: Fontana.

Tizard, J., Schofield, W. N., & Hewson, J. (1982). Collaboration between teachers and parents in assisting children's reading. *British Journal of Educational Psychology, 52,* 1–5.

Tomioka, H. (1961). A study on relative difficulties of addition and subtraction word problems. *Journal of Japan Society of Mathematical Education: Arithmetic Education, 43,* 44–49.

Tough, J. (1977). *The development of meaning.* London: Unwin Education Books.

Treffers, A. (1987). *Three dimensions: A model of goal and theory description in mathematics instruction.* Dordrecht: Reidel.

Turner, K. (1982). *An investigation of the role of spatial performance, learning styles, and kinetic imagery in the learning of calculus.* Unpublished doctoral dissertation, Purdue University.

Tymoczko, T. (Ed.). (1985). *New directions in the philosophy of mathematics: An anthology.* Boston: Birkhauser.

UNESCO-UNICEF (1974). *The development of science and mathematics concepts in young children in African countries.* (Report Regional Seminar). Nairobi: Author.

van den Brink, F. (1984). Numbers in contextual frame works. *Educational Studies in Mathematics, 15,* 239–257.

Vaihinger, H. (1913). *Die Philosophie des Als Ob* (2nd ed.). Berlin: Reuther & Reichard.

Verba, M., Stambak, M., & Sinclair, H. (1982). Physical knowledge and social interaction in children from 18 to 24 months of age. In G. Forman (Ed.), *Action and thought* (pp. 267–296). New York: Academic Press.

Vergnaud, G. (1979). The acquisition of arithmetical concepts. *Educational Studies in Mathematics, 10,* 263–274.

Vergnaud, G. (1987). About constructivism. In J. C. Bergeron, N. Herscovics, & C. Kieran (Eds.), *Proceedings of the Eleventh Conference of the International Group for the Psychology of Mathematics Education* (pp. 42–54). Montreal: PME.

Vico, G. (1710). *De antiquissima Italorum sapientia.* (Translation by F. S. Pomodoro, 1858) Naples: Stamperia dé Classici Latini.

Vinner, S. (1986, July). *True instrumental versus quasi-instrumental performance in mathematics learning.* Paper presented at the University of Warwick, England.

Voegelin, E. (1952). *The new science of politics.* Chicago: University of Chicago Press.

Voigt, J. (1985). Patterns and routines in classroom interaction. *Recherches en Didactique des Mathématiques, 6,* 69–118.

Voigt, J. (in press). Social functions of routines and consequence for subject matter learning. *International Journal of Educational Research.*

von Foerster, H. (1984). On constructing a reality. In P. Watzlawick (Ed.), *The invented reality* (pp. 41–61). New York: Norton.

von Glasersfeld, E. (1983a). Learning as a constructive activity. In N. Herscovics & J. C. Bergeron (Eds.), *Proceedings of the Fifth Annual Meeting of the Psychology of Mathematics Education—North America* (Vol. 1, pp. 41–69). Montreal: Universite de Montreal.

von Glasersfeld, E. (1983b). On the concept of interpretation. *Poetics, 12,* 207–218.

von Glasersfeld, E. (1984). An introduction to radical constructivism. In P. Watzlawick (Ed.), *The invented reality* (pp. 17–40). New York: Norton.

von Glasersfeld, E. (1987). Learning as a constructive activity. In C. Janvier (Ed.), *Problems of representation in the teaching and learning of mathematics* (pp. 3–18). Hillsdale, NJ: Lawrence Erlbaum Associates.

von Glasersfeld, E. (1989). Constructivism in education. In T. Husen & T. N. Postlethwaite (Eds.), *The international encyclopedia of education.* (pp. 162–163). (Suppl. Vol. I). New York: Pergamon Press.

von Glasersfeld, E. & Steffe, L. P. (1987). *Models in educational research.* Unpublished manuscript. University of Georgia, Athens.

von Uexküll, J. (1933). *Streifzügedurch die Umwelten von Tieren and Menschen.* Frankfurt am Main: Fisher.

Vygotsky, L. S. (1934/1956). Learning and mental development at school age. In A. N. Leontiv & A. R. Luria (Eds.), *Selected psychological works* (pp. 438–452). Moscow.
Vygotsky, L. S. (1962). *Thought and language* (E. Hanfman & G. Vakar, Trans.). Cambridge, MA: MIT Press. (Original work published 1934)
Vygotsky, L. S. (1978). Educational implications: Interactions between learning and development (M. Lopez-Morillas, Trans.). In M. Cole, V. John-Steiner, S. Scriber, & E. Souberman (Eds.), *Mind in society: The development of higher psychological processes* (pp. 79–91). Cambridge, MA: Harvard University Press.
Wagner, H., & Zimmerman, B. (1986). Identification and fostering mathematically gifted students. *Educational Studies in Mathematics, 17* (3), 243–259.
Walden, R., & Walkerdine, V. (1985). *Girls and mathematics,* Bedford Way Papers No. 24.
Wales, B. (1984). *A study of children's language use when solving particular problems: Grades two through four.* Unpublished master's thesis, University of Alberta, Edmonton, Canada.
Watts, B. H. (1976). *Access to education: An evaluation of the Aboriginal secondary grants scheme.* Canberra, Western Australia: Australian Curriculum Development Centre.
Watson, H. (1987). Learning to apply numbers to nature. *Educational Studies in Mathematics, 18,* 339–357.
Wavrik J. J. (1980). Mathematics education for the gifted elementary school student. *Gifted Child Quarterly, 24,* 169–173.
Weissglass, J., & Weissglass, T. L. (1987). *Learning, feelings, and educational change.* Santa Barbara: Kimberly Press.
Wells, G. (1985). *Language, learning, and education.* Slough, NFER-Nelson.
Wells, G. (1986). *The meaning makers.* Portsmouth, NH: Heinemann.
Wells, R. (1978). *Noisy Nora.* London: Fontana.
Werner, H. (1973). *Comparative psychology of mental development.* New York: International University Press.
Wertheimer, M. (1959). *Productive thinking.* New York: Harper & Row.
Wheeler, D. (1987). The world of mathematics: Dream, myth, or reality. In J. C. Bergeron, N. Herscovics, & C. Kieran (Eds.), *Proceedings of the Eleventh International Conference on the Psychology of Mathematics Education* (pp. 55–66). Montreal: PME
Wheeler, M. M., & Feghall, I. (1983). Much ado about nothing: Preservice elementary school teachers' concept of zero. *Journal for Research in Mathematics Education, 14* (3), 147–155.
Whitney, H. (1987). Coming alive in school math and beyond. *Educational Studies in Mathematics, 18* (3), 229–242.
Wilker, H. R., & Milbrath, L. W. (1972). Political belief systems and political behavior. In D. Nimmot & C. Bonjean (Eds.), *Political attitudes and public opinion.* New York: David McKay.
Winnicott, D. (1964). *The child, the family and the outside world.* New York: Pelican.
Winograd, T., & Flores, F. (1986). *Understanding computers and cognition: A new foundation for design.* Norwood, NJ: Albex.
Wittgenstein, L. (1956). *Some remarks on logical form.* Oxford: Basil Blackwell.
Wittgenstein, L. (1970). *Zettel.* Berkeley: University of California Press.
Wright, R. J. (1988). The development of the counting scheme of a five year old child. In A. Borbas (Ed.), *Proceedings of the Twelfth International Conference on the Psychology of Mathematics Education* (pp. 649–656). Veszprém, Hungary: PME.
Wright, R. J. (1989). *Numerical development in the kindergarten year: A teaching experiment.* Unpublished doctoral dissertation, University of Georgia, Athens.
Yackel, E., Cobb, P., & Wood, T. (in press). Small group interactions as a source of learning opportunities in second grade mathematics. *Journal for Research in Mathematics Education Monograph.*
Yokochi, K. (1976). For children with courageous spirit/education for children at the age 3–5 (pp. 59–66). Tokyo: Bunka Shuppan.

Yokochi, K. (1978). Perspective geometry and its meaning in mathematics education. *Bulletin for Mathematics Education Study, 19* (1.2), 10–12.
Yokochi, K. (1979). *Teaching of number and figure.* Tokyo: Meiji Tosho.
Yokochi, K. (1983). The child's concept of space, and geometry education for the children at the age from 4 to 6. In M. Zweng, T. Green, J. Kilpatrick, H. Pollock, & M. Suydam (Eds.), *Proceedings of the Fourth International Congress on Mathematical Education* (pp. 175–176). Boston: Birkhaüser.
Yokochi, K. (1984). *The encyclopaedia of kindergarten education.* Tokyo: Meiji Tosho.
Yokochi, K. (1985). Teaching of space and solid for the children at the age from 3 to 7, *Proceedings of ICMI-JSME Regional Conference on Mathematical Education* (p. 269). Tokyo: JSME.
Young, M. (Ed.). (1971). *Knowledge and control: New directions for the sociology of education.* London: Collier-Macmillan.
Zaslavsky, C. (1973). *Africa counts.* Boston: Prindle, Weber & Schmidt.

Author Index

A

Anderson, J. R., 175, 178
Anyon, J., 229
Arnheim, R., 173
Assis, O., 425

B

Bain, J., 157
Baird, J., 385
Balacheff, N., 205, 254
Baldwin, J., 30
Barnes, D., 209, 244, 248, 249
Barr, G., 417
Bartlett, F., 206
Bateson, G., 205, 297
Bauersfeld, H., 200, 205, 209, 212
Baxter, J., 417
Becker, J., 417
Bell, A., 421
Bennett, N., 339
Berger, C., 95
Bergeron, J., 25, 28, 125, 126, 127
Bernstein, B., 191, 193, 229, 298
Bishop, A., 161, 212
Blair, N., 458
Blanchet, A., 23
Bliss, J., 296

Bloor, D., 203, 214
Blumer, H., 207, 211
Bolton, N., 62
Boulton-Lewis, G., 156, 157, 158, 159
Bourke, S., 156
Boyer, C., 182, 183
Brandeis, B., 191
Briars, D., 126
Brissenden, T., 338
Brousseau, G., 205, 308
Brouwer, L., 390
Brown, A., 180
Brown, J., 255, 343
Brown, S., 416
Bruner, J., 165, 191, 193, 200, 204, 210, 212, 245, 298, 412
Buchmann, M., 292
Bulmahn, B., 417
Burton, L., 338, 412
Bush, W., 421
Byers, B., 390

C

Campbell, P., 462
Carpenter, T., 66, 95, 99, 126, 142, 420, 421
Carraher, D., 138, 200, 214, 425, 427
Carraher, T., 138, 200, 214, 425, 427
Case, R., 156, 157

485

486 AUTHOR INDEX

Casey, E., 161
Castiglia, D., 307
Cazden, C., 208, 246, 254, 255
Charney, R., 245
Cherry, C., 34
Christiansen, B., 268
Clements, M., 161, 169, 173, 185, 186
Cobb, P., 7, 28, 45, 73, 92, 127, 159, 200, 204, 205, 209, 235, 236, 237, 238, 239, 242, 243, 244, 245, 288, 290, 293, 326, 327, 393, 394, 420, 463
Cockburn, A., 336
Cohors-Fresenborg, E., 197
Cole, M., 320
Collins, A., 255
Comaroff, J., 211
Comiti, C., 328
Confrey, J., 200, 209
Cooper, R., 92
Corbier, J., 191, 193

D

D'Ambrosio, U., 200, 214, 456, 459
Dantzig, T., 183
Davidson, G., 156
Davis, P., 325
Davydov, V., 92
DeClark, G., 28, 318, 386
De Corte, E., 27, 142, 154
de la Rocha, O., 206
Del Campo, G., 185
Desforges, C., 336
Detlefsen, M., 325
Dewey, J., 184, 291
Dienes, Z., 195
DiSibio, M., 206
Dreyfus, H., 203
Dreyfus, S., 203
Duckworth, E., 316
Duguid, P., 255

E

Easley, J., 217, 219
Edwards, C., 118
Eisenhart, M., 207, 208
English, L., 175, 177
Erickson, F., 208

Eriksson, R., 64, 70, 73
Erlwanger, S., 219
Ernest, P., 84, 85
Eves, H., 183

F

Feghall, I., 419
Fein, G., 462
Feldman, C., 165
Feuerstein, R., 45
Fey, J., 421
Firestone, W., 201
Fischbein, E., 161, 164
Fischer, K., 156
Flegg, G., 182
Floden, R., 292, 421
Flores, F., 205
Forman, G., 118
Fosnot, G., 118
Francis, H., 302
Freeman, D., 421
Freeman, N., 26
Frege, G., 213
French, P., 295
Freudenthal, H., 44, 255, 257, 324, 327, 431
Frye, N., 327
Fuson, K., 126

G

Gadamer, H., 206
Gallistel, C., 126, 136, 420
Gal'perin, P., 95
Garcia, R., 23, 225
Gay, J., 320
Geertz, C., 200
Gelman, R., 92, 126, 136, 177, 420
Georgiev, L., 95
Gergen, K., 109, 210
Gertzog, W., 384
Gillings, R., 183
Ginsburg, H., 64, 126, 136, 159, 174, 420
Glover, R., 419
Godel, K., 203
Goldhaber, J., 118
Goodman, N., 200, 203, 204, 215
Goodnow, J., 296

Gowin, D., 160
Grabiner, J., 214
Greco, P., 126
Greene, M., 290
Greeno, J., 143, 146, 177, 205
Greer, B., 419
Griffiths, H., 389
Guay, R., 161

H

Hadamard, J., 161, 393
Halford, G., 156, 157
Halliday, M., 297
Hamilton, E., 309
Hannon, P., 302
Happs, J., 383
Hardy, G., 202
Harel, G., 419
Harris, P., 184
Harrison, P., 425
Hart, K., 421
Hatano, G., 217
Hatfield, L., 412
Head, J., 384
Heath, S., 302
Heller, J., 143, 146
Henderson, D., 191
Hersch, P., 325
Herscovics, N., 25, 28, 125, 126, 127
Hewson, J., 300
Hewson, P., 384
Hiebert, J., 95, 419
Hodgkin, L., 340
Holt, J., 225
Howson, G., 427
Hughes, M., 295, 302, 460, 462
Hunting, R., 108, 184, 185
Hurford, J., 183

I

Inhelder, B., 23, 24, 93, 113, 114, 118, 164, 166, 169, 173, 180, 184, 194, 296
Ishida, J., 142

J

Jacob, F., 60

Johnson, M., 109
Johnson, W., 177
Johnston, A., 24
Jakobson, R., 194
James, W., 200

K

Kamii, C., 28, 219, 318, 320, 384, 386
Kant, I., 30
Kaper, W., 26
Karmiloff-Smith, A., 113, 114
Kates, B., 197
Kaye, K., 245
Kearins, J., 156
Keranto, T., 43
Kieren, T., 327
Kilpatrick, J., 209
Klahr, D., 178
Klich, L., 156
Kline, M., 42, 257, 258, 340
Kossan, N., 174
Kosslyn, S., 109, 161, 162
Kotou, S., 431
Koyasu, M., 142
Krummheuer, G., 210
Kuhn, T., 232, 421

L

Lakatos, I., 214, 225, 256
Lakoff, G., 165
Lampert, M., 214, 254
Landau, M., 309
Lave, J., 206, 211, 292
Lawler, R., 47, 51, 54, 58, 60
Lean, G., 161, 184, 185, 186
Lendon, R., 156
Lesh, R., 309
Lester, F., 268
Letteri, C., 46
Levina, R., 209, 245
Levi-Strauss, C., 60
Lewis, R., 95, 99
Lin, C., 161
Lindquist, M., 421
Lowenthal, F., 191, 193, 197

M

MacLure, M., 295
Malinowski, B., 208
Mangan, C., 419
Mansfield, H., 383
Martin, G., 419
Marton, F., 64
Mason, J., 412
Maturana, H., 201, 324, 325, 326
Mayberry, M., 157
McCullough, W., 323
McDaniel, E., 161
McGee, M., 165
McKnight, C., 389, 390, 393
McLellan, J., 184
McNaughton, S., 197
Mead, G., 210
Meck, E., 177
Meek, M., 136, 297
Mehan, H., 246
Mellin-Olsen, S., 307
Menninger, K., 184
Merttens, R., 300, 301, 302
Milbrath, L., 201
Miller, K., 93, 95
Minsky, M., 326, 328
Mitchell, I., 385
Morf, A., 126
Moser, J., 66, 126, 142, 158, 420
Mumme, J., 275
Murphy, P., 80, 82
Murtaugh, M., 206
Myrdal, G., 425

N

Nebres, B., 455, 456
Neill, H., 156, 157
Neisser, U., 173
Nesher, P., 260, 419
Neuman, D., 44, 45, 46, 64, 65, 66, 67, 68, 70, 73, 82, 463, 464
Newman, R., 95
Nohda, N., 267, 268
Norton, S., 58
Novak, J., 160

O

Ogborn, J., 296

Ohuche, R., 320
Osborne, A., 421
Otaale, B., 320

P

Paivio, A., 169, 173
Paley, V., 336
Papert, S., 413
Papy, F., 196
Parkin, B., 156
Paul, C., 418
Pea, R., 255
Pereira, R., 460
Perret-Clermont, A., 209, 244
Peterson, P., 420
Piaget, J., 10, 20, 21, 22, 23, 24, 27, 28, 30, 31, 93, 112, 113, 118, 126, 164, 166, 168, 169, 173, 180, 184, 194, 225, 244, 291, 296, 326, 391, 397
Pimm, D., 272
Polanyi, M., 203
Polya, G., 256, 258, 393
Pontecorvo, C., 307
Popkin, R., 31
Porter, A., 421
Porter, R., 462
Posner, G., 384

R

Rees, R., 417
Reeves, N., 234
Resnick, L., 66, 68, 71, 136
Reyes, L., 422
Richards, J., 45, 73, 92, 126, 127, 204, 235, 236, 237, 238, 242, 243, 244, 420, 463
Richardson, A., 173
Riley, M., 143, 146, 177
Robinson, M., 159
Rogoff, B., 188, 292
Romberg, T., 420, 421
Rommetveit, R., 245
Rondal, J., 192
Rowlands, S., 340, 342
Rucker, R., 324
Russell, R., 64

S

Saerens, J., 197

Sato, S., 386
Saxe, G., 214
Scardamalia, M., 176
Schliemann, A., 138, 425, 427
Schmidt, W., 421
Schofield, W., 300
Schoenfeld, A., 200, 207
Schrifter, D., 279
Schutz, A., 200, 202
Schwartz, R., 174
Schwille, 292, 421
Seagrim, G., 156
Searle, J., 205
Shannon, C., 34
Sharpley, C., 108, 184
Shulman, L., 418, 419, 420
Shweder, R., 200
Siegel, L., 193
Siegler, R., 113, 159
Sigel, I., 200, 210, 387, 388
Silva, J., 427
Silverman, H., 197
Simmel, G., 30
Simon, M., 279
Sinclair, A., 23
Sinclair, H., 5, 22, 27, 28, 29, 92, 107, 202
Skemp, R., 86, 419
Smith, D., 182, 183
Smith, M., 161
Sowder, L., 421
Stacey, K., 412
Stambak, M., 22, 28
Stark, R., 58
Starkey, P., 92
Stedmon, J., 25
Steen, L., 325, 398
Steffe, L., 7, 28, 45, 73, 92, 127, 159, 204, 209, 235, 236, 237, 238, 239, 242, 243, 244, 326, 327, 391, 393, 397, 420, 463
Steinberg, R., 420
Steiner, H., 202, 214, 215
Stewart, I., 257, 258, 260
Strike, K., 384
Struik, D., 182, 183
Suydam, M., 421
Swanson, D., 174
Szeminska, A., 93, 126, 184

T

Thom, R., 203, 415

Thomas, N., 300
Thompson, A., 412
Thompson, P., 427
Tirosh, D., 419
Tizard, B., 300, 302
Todd, F., 209, 244, 248, 249
Tomioka, H., 142
Tough, J., 298
Treffers, A., 396
Turner, K., 161, 169
Tymoczco, T., 355

V

Vaihinger, H., 30
Van den Brink, F., 460
Van Lehn, K., 343
Verela, F., 324, 325, 326
Verba, M., 28
Vergnaud, G., 92, 127, 209, 390
Verschaffel, L., 27, 142, 154
Vico, G., 30
Vinner, S., 419
Voegelin, E., 207
Voigt, J., 205
von Foerster, H., 11, 390, 393
von Glasersfeld, E., 3, 7, 22, 28, 45, 73, 123, 127, 159, 204, 206, 209, 210, 235, 236, 237, 238, 242, 243, 244, 266, 326, 327, 393, 397, 420, 463
von Uexkull, J., 33
Vygotsky, L., 236, 242, 244, 255, 307, 392

W

Wagner, H., 415
Walden, R., 302
Walkerdine, V., 302
Walter, M., 416
Walther, G., 268
Watson, H., 461
Watts, B., 156
Wavrik, J., 415
Weissglass, J., 274, 275
Weissglass, T., 274
Wells, G., 295, 297, 298, 299, 302
Wells, R., 439
Werner, H., 69
Wertheimer, M., 393
Wheeler, D., 209, 390

Wheller, M., 419
Whitney, H., 416
Wilker, H., 201
Wilson, B., 427
Winnicott, D., 296, 297
Winograd, T., 205
Wittgenstein, L., 203
Wood, T., 205, 209, 245, 352
Wright, R., 235

Y

Yackel, E., 205, 209, 245, 352

Yokochi, K., 102, 103, 104
Young, D., 417
Young, M., 229

Z

Zaslavsky, C., 320
Zimmerman, B., 415
Zucchermaglio, C., 307
Zwoyer, R., 219

Subject Index

A

Aboriginal Australian children, 156–160, 458
Abstraction, 22, 23, 63–64
  empirical, 22, 24, 319
  reflective, 22, 73, 204, 319, 410
  endogenous processes, 6, 24
Action, 19–22, 31, 164 *see also* Activity
  anticipatory intuitions, 164
  intuition of space, 164
  knowledge in, 203–205
  mathematical, 28
  material, 19–20, 64
  mental, 19–20, 64
  sensory-motor, 204
  schemes of, 5
Action research, 437–438
Activity, 108, 268, *see also* Learning, mathematical
  dialectically constituted, 206
  mathematical, 109
    imagery, 109
  knower-known relationship, 20–22
  result of, 108
    as object, 108
    self-generated action, 108
  visualization, 109
Adaptation, 6, 7, 20–21, 36, 393
  accommodation, 20, 33, 36, 393
  assimilation, 10, 20, 32, 391
  equilibration, 20

Algorithms, 260
  analysis of learning, 260–261
  construction of, 262–264, 365–372
Analyses, 50, 163
  chronometric, 159
  conceptual, 163–164
  logical task, 164
  protocol, 159
Arithmetic, 216, 225
  competence, 51
    count view, 51
    decadal view, 51
    money view, 51
  origin of skills, 63–75
  paper sums, 49–50
  school, 43, 253–265
Assessment, 80

B

Beliefs, 12, 79, 206
  simplicity, 12, 334–337
  enjoyment, 12, 337–340
  reality, in, 12, 340–342
  empty vessel, 12, 342–343
Basic Learning in Primary Schools (BLIPS) project, 436
Boundaries, subject matter, 225, 284
Bricolage, *see* Learning

SUBJECT INDEX

C

Categories of awareness, 327
  complementarities of understanding, 329–330
  development, 331
  mathematical variations and complementarities, 330–331
  multifaceted knowledge, 328–329
  potential for pattern growth, 332–333
Classification, 446–447
Combinations, children's competence, 174–180
  principle of difference, 177–178
  odometer principle, 178–180
Combinatorial laws, 112
Communication, see Learning
  behaviorist approach, 34
  child-directed, 273
  concept of, 34–37
  consensual domain, 212, 245, 394
  cross-cultural studies, 230
  diversity, 8, 216–226
    conceptual, 8, 216–226
    contextual, 8, 216–226
  dyadic, 245
  early childhood, in, 191–199
  exchange of ideas, 232
  experiential, 8, 202
  interactive, 231, 235–243
  interactions, 191
  issues, 284–292
  linguistic, 34
    interpretation, 36
    subjective meaning, 36
  logical structure, 193
  mathematical, 272, 410–411
  mathematics classroom, in the, 228–234, 266–271
    small group, 248–252, 284
    teachers role, 283–293
    whole class, 216–226, 228–234, 254–265, 266–271
  meanings, 7, 34
    intended, 7
    received, 7
  mode of, 192–193
  models of, 230
  multiple perspectives, 200–215
    anthropological, 9, 229, 233
    experiential, 8, 233
    psychological, 9, 223, 229
    sociological, 9, 229
  nonverbal devices, 9, 195–196
  peer dialogues, 216–226
  reasons for, 273
  signals, 7, 34–35
  syntactic component, 193
  system, 193–194
    logical basis, 194
  verbal, 26, 245
Complementarities, 213–215
  empiricism, 213
  information-processing, 213
  Platonism, 213
  radical constructivism, 214
  social empiricism, 213–214
Conceptual splatter, 216–226
Conservation, 23
Constitutionalism, 63
Constraints, see Environment
  historical, 229
Constructivism, 30–31, 78, 279
  assessment, 320–321
  constructivism mechanisms, 28
  independent reality, 37
  in research, 45–46
  meta-theory, 46
  objective existence, 32
  Piagetian, 19
  permanent objects, 31
  radical, 31
    learning, model of, 79
    reconstructing, 283–293
    revolutionary aspect, 3
  social, 226
  task of education, 33–34
Constructivist, 37, 231, 289
  empiricist, 289
  research agenda, 231
  theory of knowing, 137
Context, 108, 200
  anthropological, 207–213
    mathematico-anthropological, 209
    socio-anthropological, 208–209
  cognitive, 204–206
    computer metaphor, 205
    conceptual operation, 204
  definition, 201–202
  experiential, 202–204
    objects of knowledge, 203
    Platonism, 203
    platonist assumptions, 202–203
  the home, 298–299

the school, 299-300
Contextuality of cognition, 200
Contradictions, 110
Cooperative groups, 276
Counting, *see* Schemes
  in preschool, 135
    money, 135
    objects, 135
    one-to-one correspondence, 135
    monitoring activity, 238-239
    pointing acts, 240
    types, 235
Cultural amplifiers, 109
Curriculum, 4, 11
  abstracted, 14, 350, 395
  attained, 318-319, 389
  created, 13, 351, 348
  design features, 390-396
  decisions of teachers, 395
  hidden, 348
  ideal, 389, 390
  implemented, 317-318, 389
  intended, 316-317, 389
  issues, 349-354
    appropriate content, 353
    constructivism, nature of, 349
    framework, constructivist, 350
    professionalism of teachers, 352
  mathematics
    early childhood, 315, 316-319
    teacher education, 319-321
  post hoc, 12-13, 344
  top down approach, 389-390

D

Discourse, 9, 219, 244-252, 284
  classroom, 216-226, 253-265, 309
  collaborative, 244-245, 328-329
  nature of process, 245
  outside schools, 9, 284, 294-299
  pedagogic, 9, 254-256, 284, 299
  social norms, 248-252
  teacher's role, 242-243, 246-248
  teaching experiment, 237-242
Distancing strategies, 387-388

E

Educational Research Group, 304

Empiricism, 209, 213
  social, 213-214
Environment, 10, 30-34, 315, 401-402
  assimilation, *see* adaptation
  concept of, 31-34
  constraints, 33-34, 37
  created, 13
  education, task of, 33-34
  evaluation, 231
  games and puzzles, 320
  iconic representation, 37
  implications for, 327
  mathematical, 10
    actual, 4
    contexts, 10-11, 25, 328-333
    constructive, 407-414
    external reality, 11
    learning, 392, 402, 404
    objective, 32-33
    possible, 4, 10-11, 231
    modifying, 394
    post-hoc activity, 12-13
    subjective, 33
    teacher education, 4, 13
    teacher preparation, 409-414
Equilibrium, 20, 315
  equilibration, 23
Experience, 3, 391, *see also* Adaptation
  consensual domains, 212, 245, 394
  early mathematical, 377-382
  experiential world, 31
  goodness of fit, 31, 266
  human, 31, 62
  informal number, 181
  mathematical, 3-4, 14
  mathematical objects, 125
  numerical, 126
  of the world, 63
  ordering, 200
  past, mathematical, 407-409
    changing world views, 408-409
    crisis in identity, 408-409
  reflection on, 107
  sensory, 31-34

F

Fractions, 110, 181-188, 255-265
  concepts, 110
  children's knowledge, 184-185

494 SUBJECT INDEX

Fractions (cont.)
    mathematical reflections, 185–187
    ratio, 186

G

Games, 84, 91, see also Environment
    checking and justifying, 90
    conjecturing and generalizing, 89
    making predictions, 86–87
    rationale, 84
Geometry, see Knowledge
    learning, 100–105
    solids with clay, 102
        stages, 102
    solids with paper, 104
        stages, 104
    space, direction and relation of things, 103
        stages, 103
Goals, see Learning

H

Handicapped, 283

I

Image construction, 165
    levels, 171–172
    part-whole relations, 169
    re-presented spatial objects, 168
    rotation, 169
    structuring unfilled space, 166
Imaging, 162
Imagery tasks, 111
IMPACT project, 300–302
Information, 156–160
Insight, 53, 393
Instrumentalists, 31
Interpretation, 201

J

Juku, 100–101

K

Knowledge, 4, 19–22, see also Adaptation
    as action, 107

balance, 113–118
combinations, 174–180
constructing, from interactions, 6, 47–61, 63
construction of, 23
constructive activity, 37
constructivist theory, 37
control, 47
endogenously constructed, 326
ethnomathematical, 327
exogenously governed, 326
fraction, 181–188, 254–264
geometrical, 5, 100–105
iconic representation, 37
integrating structures, 49–55
logical, 5
logico-mathematical, 21–22, 319
mathematical, 3, 5, 7, 42
    of young learners, 107–111
meaning in Japan, 101
measurement, 6, 92–99
mental actions, 19–21
microview, 50–55
    channelled description conjecture, 58–60
    integrating diverse, 55–58
number, 21–22
number preconcepts, 125–134
numeration, 135–141
objects of thought, 21–22, 108
    weight, 21–22
personal activity, 107
probability, 118–122
spatial, 161–173
structures, integrating related, 49–55
technical symbolic, 327
test of, 31
thinking strategies, 5, 65–72, 156–160
traditional contention, 31
viability, 22, 33

L

Language, see also Communication, Discourse
    cognitive construction, 37
Learning, 4, 6, 19–29, 78–83, 274, see also Environment
    active mathematical, 393
    adaptation, see Knowledge
    analogy, 83
    bricolage, 6, 60–61
    and cognition, 61

SUBJECT INDEX 495

collaborative 294, 300–302
  through feeling, 297–298
  through language, 297
  through play, 296–297
constructive activity, 209
constructive mechanisms, 24
definition, 6
endogenous, constructive process, 118, 124
experiential, 37
games, 84–91
geometry, 100–105
goals, 8, 31, 33, 38, 60
  development of, 60
  pursuit of, 31
interactions, 24, 47–61
interactive activity, 209
mathematical, 3, 5, 6, 43, 78–83
  beyond activity, 357–376
  instruction, 272
  of young learners, 107–111
meaning in Japan, 101–102
measure, 92–99
phenomenological perspectives, 62–75
play, 296
social interaction, 6, 13, 22–24
  imitation, 22
  society, 22–24
  viability of knowledge, 22
school, process in, 45–46
teaching, 24–29, 394
  communication, 25–26
  comparison and examination, 432–435
  difficulties of mathematics, 27–29
  verbal communication, 26–29
Language development, 193
  and play, 296
  home, 298
  school, 299–300
  structure, 193

M

Mathematics, 3, 12, 272, 324–325, *see also* Knowledge, Learning
  arithmetic, 324
  attitudes, improving, 417–418
  children's, 8, 323
  classical areas, 324
  codified body of knowledge, 107
  conceptions of, 415–417

concepts, principles, and procedures, 107–108
coordinated schemes, 107
early childhood
  agreements, 347
  education, 453–455
  the student, 383–385
  the teacher, 385–388
elementary school, 430–431
experience, 3–4
for children, 323, 413–414
history of, 184
knowledge, improving, 418–419
learning, 19, 41–45
learner's activity, 107
number, 324
numeral systems, stages, 183–184
of children, 109
patterns, building of, 325
relationships and patterns, 107–108, 161
teachers, 8, 409
teaching, 7–8, 25
  nature and forms, 8
the child's, 323
Meanings
  emergent, 210–212
  negotiated, 212
  negotiation of, 109, 245–246
  number words, 241
  shared, 291–292
  societal, 23
  worlds of, 82
Measure, *see* Measurement
Measurement, 5, 92–99
  continuous and discrete, 92
  concept of, 93–94
  length, 380–382
  logo settings, 96–98
  unit of, 92, 94–96
  weight, 379–380
Metacognition, 109–110
Microcomputers, 78
  society, technological, 78
  technology, 5, 11
Misconceptions, 15
Modality, 221
  abstract, 221
  itemization, 221–222
Models, 33
  early number, 205
  mathematical concepts, 127
  physical concepts, 127

Models (cont.)
  possible, mathematics as, 42
  theoretical, number learning, 205, 242
  viability, 33
  working, 243
Modes of thought, 200

N

Necessity, 110, 112–124
Negotiation, see also Communication, 268
Number, 21–22, 64, see also Knowledge
  abstract, 69
  activity, attending to, 359–361
  base ten system, 374–376
  cardinal function, 127
  cardinality, 44
  concept of, 21–22
  conventional formats, 366–372
  exchange process, 365–366
  extending rule, 372–374
  finger, 65–67
  imaginary, 67
  natural, 127
  natural language, 27
  numerals, 26–27
  number, attending to, 361–365
  number bond, perceptual grasp, 81
  object-of-thought, 21
  optical groups, 69
  ordinal function, 127
  ordinality, 44
  preconcepts of, 110, 125–134
  robust knowledge, 82
  subtized, 65, 66
  sentences, 111, 142–155
    canonical, 143
    functions, 142
    noncanonical, 143
    notation, mathematical, 142
    representation, mathematical, 142
  understanding, 358–374
Nsukka study, 321–322
Numeration, see also Knowledge
  knowledge among preschoolers, 135–141
    combining relative values, 136, 138
    generative, 135
    regrouping, 136

O

Open-ended inquiry, 317

P

Pan-African Entebbe Mathematics Project, 317
Patterns, 441–446
  finger, 65–67
  spatial-motor, 237
  subtize, 66, 67
Phenomenology, 62–64
  approach to research, 46, 64–69
  constitutionalism, 63
  phenomenography, 64, 80
Physical concepts, 127
  preliminary, understanding, 127–133
    plurality, 110, 125, 127–130
    position, 110, 125, 127, 130–133
Platonism, 203, 209, 213
  assumptions, 202, 203
Plurality, see Physical concepts
  intuitive understanding, 128
  logico-physical abstraction, 128
  procedural understanding, 128
Possibility, 110, 112–124
Potentialities, 203
Preconceptions, 216
PRIME Project, 344, 406
Primary Mathematics Project, 84–91
Problem solving, 216, 266–271, 438–441
Problematic approaches, 411–412
Problems, 82
  combinatoric, 110
  missing addend, 82
  pedagogical, 261–262
  types of addition and subtraction, 111
  word, 142–155
Progressivism, 293
Project TIME, 274–281
Purpose, see, Phenomenography, intention

Q

Quotity, 126

R

Real World, See Reality

SUBJECT INDEX 497

Reality, 3, 12, 19, 21, 22, 31, 37, 62–64
  Brazilian child, 424–425
  construction of, 31
  fraction knowledge, 187
  knower-known relationship, 20
  mathematical, 202–203
  objects-of-thought, 21
    number, 21–22
    weight, 21–22
  ontological, 3, 37
  physical, 203
  realists, 37
    materialist, 37
    metaphysical, 37
    naive, 37
  sensory objects, 31
  social, 245
  subject and object, 21
  the world, 31, 62
    relativistic view, 391
  unfathomable, 31
Reasoning, see also Knowledge
  analytical, 161
  human, 31
  spatial, 161
  transitive, 111, 157–158
Relations, 69–70
  binary, 156
  human-world, 65, 74
  knower-known, 6, 20
  part-part-whole, 73
  parent/teacher, 301
  personal and social, 6
  quantitative, 69–70
  reciprocal, 11
  subject-object, 20–21, 63
  ternary, 156
  unary operations, 156
Reflective abstraction, see Abstraction
Reflection, 412–413
RAMP Project, 406

S

Schemes, 5, 35, 79, 204
  accommodation, 33
  anticipatory, 241
  conceptual, 35–36
  counting, 5, 44
    double, 70–74, 81
    finger numbers, 65–66

  types, 73
  counting on, 324
  egocentric, 113
  operational, 110–124
  part-part-whole, 324
  presentative, 110–124
  procedural, 110–124
Science Education Programme for Africa, 317
Second International Mathematics Study, 389–390
Sensorimotor system, 57–60
  channelled description conjecture, 59
  sensory modes, 55
Situations, 8
  concrete, 44
  in constructivism, 10–11, 32–34, 37
  interactive, 8
  learning, features, 307–312
  mathematical, 44
  natural, 44
  problematic, 8
  third-world, 13, 317
Social Interaction, 8, 19, 320, see also Learning
  bricolage, 6, 60–61
  complementary roles, 47–49
  deprivation of, 6, 49
  homely binding, 48
  invention, 23
  lonely discovery, 48
  reinvention, 23
  third world situations, 13
Solipsism, 33, 214, 390
Strategies, 65–70, 79, see also Knowledge
  double counting, 70
  finger numbers, 65
  problem solving, 113
  problem posing, 416
  putting biggest first, 68
  scheme, accommodation of, 79
  thinking strategies, 5, 65–72
  using doubles, 67
  what-if-not, 416
Structuring, 113, 119
Subtizing, 65, 69

T

Teacher Education, 11, 13–14
  actions of teacher educators, 402–403
  action research, 437–447

Teacher Education (*cont.*)
  early childhood, 11, 304–305, 319–320
  in Sao Paulo, 427–429
  learning, 274–281, 403–404
  professional development, 405–406
  preparation, 334–338, 409
Teaching experiment, 235
  constructivist, 236–237
Technology, 5
  Logo, 96–98, 462
  society, technological, 78
  microcomputers, 78
  calculators, 78, 463
The new basics, 123
Thinking, 216–217
  children's, 216
  cooperative, 217
Transformation, 23–24

U

Understanding, 110, 127
  prenumber, 110
    formalization, 110, 127
    intuitive, 110, 127, 128
    logico-mathematical, 110, 127
    procedural, 110, 127, 128

Unit Items, 73–74
  abstract, counter of, 73
  figural, 237
Unitize
  figurative items, 326
Units, 92–96, 111
  entities, 93, 94
  number, 96–98
  ranks of, 111
  size, 92
Unity, 64
  of action and object, 64
  Undifferentiated concepts, 378

V

Values, 229
  cultural, 229
Viability, 33

W

Words, meaning of, 266

Z

Zone of proximal development, 24, 236, 392

For Product Safety Concerns and Information please contact our EU
representative GPSR@taylorandfrancis.com
Taylor & Francis Verlag GmbH, Kaufingerstraße 24, 80331 München, Germany

www.ingramcontent.com/pod-product-compliance
Lightning Source LLC
Chambersburg PA
CBHW071618230426
43669CB00012B/1982